Clarkenwell

St Albans

St Johns Gate

Charter Ho.

Turner St.

Cow Cross

Long Lane

St Bartho.

Little Brittaine

Grayes Inn Lane

Ely Place

St Andrews

Holbourne Br.

K

Grey Fryers

New gate Mkt.

Pater nos Row

Old Baily

St Dunstan

Fetter Lane

Shœe Lane

Temple Barr

Fleete Streate

Fleete Br.

St Pauls Church

Water Lane

Black fryer Lane

Bridewell Palace

G

G

G

Fryers

Black fryers

Bayards Castle

I V E R

Bull Bayting

Ex Libris

Veritas
Liberabit
Vos

John Dowland

by the same author

An introduction to lute playing
(*Schott*)

JOHN DOWLAND

Diana Poulton

FABER AND FABER
3 Queen Square
London

*First published in 1972
by Faber and Faber Limited
3 Queen Square London WC1
Printed in Great Britain by
W & J Mackay Limited, Chatham*

ISBN 0 571 08711 6

Acknowledgements

꧁✿꧂

During the course of many years, while the material for this book was being collected, I have received most generous help from a number of friends, and it gives me great pleasure to have this opportunity to express my thanks.

Many facts, which I might never have discovered for myself, have been passed on by people working on closely related subjects, and my thoughts on many of the problems that have arisen in my attempt to present a faithful picture of the life and works of John Dowland have often been cleared by time ungrudgingly given in correspondence and conversation.

I am deeply indebted to Richard Newton who, for many years, not only went to infinite trouble to track down valuable pieces of information but also suggested a number of lines of enquiry for me to work on myself; but for his help and encouragement in the early stages this book might never have materialized.

Edward Doughtie lent me a copy of his thesis 'Poems from the Songbooks of John Dowland' (1963) with full permission to quote any useful information. His careful and thoughtful work supplied me with the names of the authors of several of the lyrics which I had not previously known and also the whereabouts of many of the MS copies of the songs. A copy of his book, *Lyrics from English Ayres 1596–1622* (1970), reached me too late for me to alter all the references, but much of the information I have quoted will be found in this volume. I am most grateful to him for so generously allowing me to use his work.

My thanks are also due to Prof. Benjamin Farrington who translated from the Latin for me, and gave me the origin of several passages; to David Mitchell for his Appendix 'On Fretting and Tuning'; to Basil Lam who read the proofs and made a number of helpful suggestions; to Michael Morrow, Robert Spencer, Ian Harwood, Commander Gordon Dodd, Frau Uta Henning, and John Roberts, all of whom have given me useful information.

The Duke of Portland, the Marquess of Salisbury, Lord de L'Isle and Dudley, the Viscount Downe and the Hon. Robin Neville have all kindly allowed me to use material from their private collections.

I have received valuable help from the British Museum Library; the

Bodleian Library; Cambridge University Library; the Guildhall Library; Westminster Public Library; the Library of Trinity College, Dublin; Edinburgh University Library; Glasgow University Library; the National Library of Scotland; the Fitzwilliam Library, Cambridge; the National Portrait Gallery; the Ministry of Public Buildings and Works; the Public Record Office; the Folger Shakespeare Library, Washington; the Kongelige Bibliotek, København; Fredricksborg Castle, Hilleröd, Denmark; Murhardsche Bibliothek und Landesbibliothek, Kassel; Staatlichen Kunstsammlungen, Kassel; in every case I am grateful to the staff for their help and to the governing bodies for permission to use pictures and documents for which they are responsible.

For permission to use copyright material my thanks are due to Stainer and Bell, Ltd., *The English Lutenist Song Writers*, ed. E. H. Fellowes; the Royal Musical Association, John Dowland, *Ayres for Four Voices*, ed. Dart and Fortune; the Clarendon Press, E. K. Chambers, *Sir Henry Lee: an Elizabethan Portrait*; E. H. Fellowes, *English Madrigal Verse*; and Thomas Whythorne, *Autobiography*, ed. James Osborne; Routledge, Kegan Paul, Ltd., J. Janssen, *History of the German People*; Macmillan and Co. Ltd., A. L. Rowse, *The England of Elizabeth*; the Warburg Institute, Frances Yates, *The French Academies*; Cambridge University Press, *Cambridge History of English Literature*; and E. Welsford, *The Court Masque*; Princeton University Press, Alfred Einstein, *The Italian Madrigal*; Edward Arnold Ltd., J. Huizinger, *The Waning of the Middle Ages*; Chatto and Windus Ltd., and the Author's Literary Estate, Mrs. Disney Leith, *The Boyhood of Algernon Charles Swinburne*; Chatto and Windus and Mrs. Elna Lucas, F. L. Lucas, *The Collected Works of John Webster*; Faber and Faber Ltd., and Norton and Co., O. Strunk, *Source Readings in Music History*; Jonathan Cape, J. E. Neale, *Elizabeth I and her Parliaments*; and Dora Robertson, *Sarum Close*; MacGibbon and Kee, L. Hotson, *The First Night of Twelfth Night*; J. M. Dent and Sons Ltd., Castiglione, *The Book of the Courtier* (Everyman's Library 807); John Stow, *The Survey of London* (Everyman's Library 589); J. W. Cousin, *Biographical Dictionary of English Literature* (Everyman's Library 449); Longman, Green and Co., A. F. Pollard, *History of England*; and J. H. Pollen, *British Catholics in the Reign of Queen Elizabeth*; Ohio State University Press, Ruth Hughey, *The Arundel Harington Manuscript of Tudor Poetry*; A. P. Watt and Son, V. Sackville West, *The Diary of Lady Ann Clifford*; Valentino Bompiani, Milan, Alfredo Obertello, *Madrigali Italiani in Inghilterra*; Oxford University Press, Peter Warlock, *The English Ayre*; and Peter Warlock, *The First Book of Elizabethan Songs*; R. B. McKerrow, *An Introduction to Bibliography*; H. J. C. Grierson, *John Donne. Poems*; The University of Chicago Press,

Charles Read Baskervill, *The Elizabethan Jig* (Copyright by the University of Chicago. All rights reserved 1929); the American Philosophical Society, *The Letters of John Chamberlaine*, ed. N. E. McClure; the Bibliographical Society, McKerrow and Ferguson, *Title-page Borders used in England and Scotland 1484–1640*; Robert Steele, *The Earliest Music Printing*; and Greg and Boswell, *The Record of the Court of the Stationers' Company 1576–1602*; Liverpool University Press, Kenneth Muir, *Sir Thomas Wyatt and his Circle. Unpublished Poems*; and Jean Robertson, *The Poems of Nicholas Breton*; Scholartis Press, G. B. Harrison, Breton's *Melancholike Humours*; Maurice Fridburg Ltd., Wilfrid Mellers, 'John Dowland' in *The Music Masters*, ed. Bacharach; Musical Studies and Documents, C. Palisca, *Girolamo Mei (1519–1594). Letters on Ancient and Modern Music*.

Any mistakes, omissions or misinterpretation of the material are, of course, entirely my own responsibility.

DIANA POULTON

To my daughter Celia

Contents

Contents

Illustrations

Letter from John Dowland to Sir Robert Cecil, dated November 10th, 1595, now in the Library of Hatfield House. *following page* 40

Contemporary portraits by unknown artists of Robert Devereux, second Earl of Essex, and Robert Cecil, first Earl of Salisbury. 40

Florence and Nuremberg. From Braun and Hohenbergius, *Civitates Orbis Terrarum* (1573–1618). 216

Cassel and Elsenor. From Braun and Hohenbergius, *Civitates Orbis Terrarum* (1573–1618). 216

Two views of Westminster; part of Westminster with Parliament House, Westminster Hall and the Abbey; and New Palace Yard, with Westminster Hall and the Clock House. Etchings by Wenceslaus Hollar (1607–1677). 216

Jown Dowland's signature on a receipt dated July 28th, 1600; and 'musical point' in the *Album Amicorum* of Johannes Cellarius. 216

A six-course lute as shown in Adrian Le Roy's *A briefe and easye Instruction* (1568). 344

MS. 1610.1. f.22v. 'Lady Hunsdons Allmande', written in Dowland's own hand. 344

Signatures from MS. 1610.1.; and signature of Dame Ann Bayldon, widow of Sir Francis Bayldon of Kippax, on a document dated February 17th, 1624/5. 344

Christian IV of Denmark, by Peter Isacsh, 1612, in Frederiksborg Castle 344

Maurice, Landgrave of Hesse, engraved by W. Kilian, in the Staatliche Kunstsammlungen, Kassel; and Sir Henry Lee, by A. Mor, 1568. 440

Memorial portrait of Sir Henry Unton by an unknown artist. 440

John Dowland

I

The life of John Dowland

Information about the life of John Dowland is more plentiful than that concerning many other distinguished composers of his time. This is largely due to the fact that he was far from reticent about his own affairs. In the prefatory matter to his books, and in the long letter he wrote to Sir Robert Cecil in 1595, he makes a number of detailed statements about himself, his travels and his opinions. This material is invaluable, but it needs to be treated with caution. To a man as emotional and volatile as Dowland evidently was, events were often coloured by the mood of the moment and, at times, what he says seems self-contradictory, or seems to disagree with information coming from other sources. Nevertheless, a number of facts emerge uncontradicted in his own writings or confirmed by independent evidence, that can be accepted without hesitation. Since what he wrote was, however, spread over some seventeen years and was written with varying purposes in mind, there are tantalizing gaps in the information he left. Some of these can be filled from other documents and records, but much about his life is still obscure and, unless further sources of information come to light, must remain a matter for deduction and speculation only.

His earliest biographers are by no means reliable and some confusion was introduced within a comparatively short time of his death. Thomas Fuller, in *The History of the Worthies of England*,* begins the tangle. In the section on the 'Worthies of Westminster' he gives the following account:

John Douland was, (as I have most cause to believe) born in this City; sure I am he had his *longest life* and best livelyhood therein, being Servant in the Chappel to Queen Elizabeth and King James. He was the *rarest Musician* that his age did behold; having travailed beyond the Seas, and compounded English and Forreign skill in that faculty, it is questionable whether he excelled in *Vocal* or *Instrumental Music*. A cheerful person he was, passing his days in lawful

* Published posthumously by his son John, in 1662, p. 244.

merriment, truly answering the anagram made of him.[1] JOHANNES DOULANDUS ANNOS LUDENDO HAUSI.†

Christian the Fourth, King of Denmark, coming over into England, requested him of King James, who *unwillingly willing* parted with him. Many years he lived (as I am credibly informed) in the Danish court, in great *favour* and *plenty*, generally employed to entertain such English persons of quality as came thither.

I cannot confidently avouch his death at Denmark, but believe it more probable then their assertion who report him returned and dying in England about the year 1615.

[1] By Ralph Sadler Esq of Standen in Hertfordshire who was with him in Copenhagen.*

Anthony à Wood, writing in *Fasti Oxoniensis*,‡ appears to have used Fuller as a source, plus a very superficial examination of *Varietie of Lute-Lessons, A Musicall Banquet* and *A Pilgrimes Solace*. This is his account:

Dom. 1588

An. $\frac{30}{31}$ Elizab.

July 8. JOHN DOWLAND one of the Gent. of Her Majesty's Royal Chappel, was then also with *Tho. Morley* adm. Batch. of Music. He enjoyed the same place also when King James I came to the Crown, being then esteemed a most admirable Lutinist; about which time an Anagram was made on his name (Johannes Doulandus) running thus, *annos ludendi hausi*. He was the rarest Musician that his Age did behold, and therefore admired by Foreign princes, among whom the *King of Denmark* was one, who being infinitely taken with his playing, when he was in England to visit his Sister, the Queen, *an.* 1606, took him with him at his return to *Denmark*; where, as 'tis supposed he died. He hath among other things written *Necessary Observations belonging to Lute-playing*, Lond. 1610, in a thin fol. Bodl. b.5. 12. Art. printed with *Varietie of Lute Lessons*, published by his Son, *Rob. Douland*, a most excellent Lutinist also; who, before (while his Father was absent) had been trained up to the Lute by excellent Masters at the care and charge of Sir Tho. Mounson before-mentioned. The said *Rob. Douland* published also his own Composition *A Musicall Banquet*, Lond. 1610, in a thin fol. and *The Pilgrimes solace for three and four parts, etc.* which was composed by him, as it seems, and not by his Father.

These two curious sets of mis-statements need no special analysis; as the facts emerge they will speak for themselves in correcting the errors.

* The 'old' Sir Ralph Sadler, distinguished statesman and servant to Henry VIII and Elizabeth I, died in 1587. There was no Ralph in the next generation, his sons being named Thomas, Edward and Henry. It is possible that Fuller was thinking of Sir Thomas's son, Ralph, born in 1581. There seems little reason, however, to doubt Henry Peacham's claim to the authorship made first in *Minerva Britanna* (1612), and later in *The Complete Gentleman* (1622). The anagram was printed again in the 1674 edition of Camden's *Remains*, but without any attribution.

† John Dowland, whose Muse I have enjoyed for years.   ‡ 1691, I. col. 760.

It is Dowland himself who gives us the year of his birth, and he mentions it in two separate contexts. In the address 'To the Reader' in *A Pilgrimes Solace* (1612), he says 'being I am now entered into the fiftieth yeare of mine age'. In 'Other Necessary Observations belonging to the Lute' in *Varietie of Lute-Lessons* (1610) he says 'for myself was borne but thirty years after Hans Gerle's book was printed'. This was *Tabulatur auff die Laudten* printed in 1533, so in both cases the year 1563 is indicated. The place of his birth is unknown, although Fuller's claim that he was a citizen of Westminster may possibly be true. Stow, in his *Survey of London* (1598), says that Westminster has 'Parish Churches twain; St. Margaret, a parish church by Westminster. St. Martin in the Field by Charing cross'. In the Registers of St. Margaret's the name Dowland does not occur until 1628, when a Mathew Dowland was buried there on August 13th. Although the Registers of St. Martin-in-the-Fields go back to 1550, no Dowlands are entered there until 1583, when a Susanna Dowland was baptized on October 24th. Unfortunately no details of parentage are given. A large family was established, however, with the marriage of Eduardus Dowland and Winisint Simons on December 15th, 1605. The births, marriages and deaths of their descendants continue to appear in the Registers during the following thirty years. This Eduardus or Edmundus, as his name is alternatively given, is shown, by his will, proved on June 21st, 1647,[*] to have been a tailor. So far no evidence has come to light to connect him with the composer.

The idea that Dowland was born in Dalkey, Co. Dublin, originated in an article by Dr. Grattan Flood printed in *The Gentleman's Magazine* in 1906.[†] Unfortunately this article has been too often accepted without critical examination of the evidence, with the result that these unsubstantiated deductions have been presented by several writers in the form of established facts. So much confusion has arisen in this way that it is worth examining his main points in some detail.

First he states that Dowland was born at Christmas-time in the year 1562 and that his father was John Dowlan, who lived in a cottage at Dalkey—the family name being Dubhlaing. The only documentation for these statements is a reference to *The Calendar of Christ Church Deeds*. No information is given about where these deeds can be seen. I eventually found the calendar, printed

---

[*] Somerset House, P.C.C. Fines Fol. 125.

[†] Vol. 301, pp. 287–91. Dr. Flood made another statement in *Music and Letters*, III (1922), p. 61. In *The English Ayre* (1926), pp. 22–3, Peter Warlock criticized his findings, and Dr. Flood wrote again in *The Musical Times* LXVIII (1927), making several more undocumented claims, the family name now being given as O'Dolan. He was challenged by Gerald Cooper in the same journal of that year, p. 642, and replied on p. 741, with further confusions and inconsistent statements.

in the form of appendices to the reports of the Deputy Keeper of the Public Records in Ireland.* The document upon which Dr. Flood based his assertion is Deed No. 1346 (Report XXIV, app.), which consists of a lease dated June 1st, 1577, by the Dean and Chapter of Holy Trinity, Dublin, to Walter Ball, of various premises, including a cottage place near the east gate of Dalkey, in the occupation of John Dowlinge. There are no other references to any Dowlands in any conceivable spelling, in the Christ Church Deeds, except one to a Johan Dowlyng, wife of a fishmonger called Dungan, living in Fish Street, Dublin, in 1539. The Dowlings, though the name was possibly derived from the same root as Dowland, were, by the sixteenth century, firmly established as a separate family, and many Dowlings are entered in English Parish Registers. That a John Dowlinge was living in Dalkey in 1577 unfortunately proves nothing about the parentage or place of birth of John Dowland. Dr. Flood also attempts to prove that Dowland received part of his musical education at Trinity College, Dublin, in 1597, and that when he refers to himself as 'Bacheler of Musick in both the Vniuersities', he means Oxford and Trinity College and not, as might be expected, Oxford and Cambridge. The evidence he brings forward does not stand up to careful examination. The page on which he bases his argument is printed in Appendix V, on p. 236 of J. P. Mahaffey's *The Particular Book of Trinity College, Dublin* (1904). This shows a list of sums received for 'commons' and 'sisings' and, among other entries are these:

for Sr Dowland† commons 9 weeks	o	16	1½
Sr Dowland and Sr Smiths sisings on			
Sr Usher		7	o

At the bottom of the page the date has been added: 4 May 1605. On the previous page is printed Appendix IV, which shows 'A note of the present state of the College for the year next ensuing from Jan 1 1597 to Jan 1 1598'. Dr. Flood has ignored the date following the list of commons and sizings in Appendix V, has run the two appendices into one and then states 'there are two entries for the year 1597 in which reference is made to John Dowland'. When it becomes clear that the year of these entries is 1605 Dowland's presence in Dublin becomes quite impossible, since, as will be seen later, he had returned by then from leave in England to his post at the Danish Court. Dr. Flood continues, 'so we are not surprised to find that the great lutenist

---

* Reports Nos. XX, XXIII, XXIV and XXVII (index).

† Peter Warlock, in *The English Ayre* (1926), refers to 'the John Dowland who was in commons for nine weeks in 1605 at Trinity College'. In this he is incorrect. There is no christian name in the entry. Geoffrey Pulver, in *A Biographical Dictionary of Old English Music* (1927), makes the same slip.

was recommended by Cecil to Walter Travers, Provost of Trinity College, Dublin'. Unfortunately he gives no indication of how, or where, or on what date this recommendation was made. Nothing of the kind can be identified in the *Calendars of the Salisbury Papers at Hatfield** and the Rev. S. J. Knox has assured me he found no such recommendation in the Muniment Room at Trinity College, while he was working on *Walter Travers: paragon of Elizabethan puritanism* (1962). Furthermore Travers retired in 1598 and Mr. Knox has found no evidence that music was taught as a subject while Travers was Provost.

For the contention put forward by Dr. Flood that the name Dowland was immediately derived from the Irish Dubhlaing, Dowlan, or O'Dolan, it is not difficult to show that the form in which John used it was known in England long before his lifetime. In 1496 a Thomas Dowland, mason, rebuilt the Gild Chapel at Stratford-on-Avon and began building the Gild Tower for Hugh Clopton. He also probably designed the chancel of Stratford-on-Avon Parish Church, *c.* 1480–90.†

In the Stationers' Register‡ there is also, under the year 1556, the entry:

> Roberte Dowlande
> prentes with master smyth the xv Daye
> of octobre....................vj^d.

It is interesting to speculate whether this Robert was in fact the father of John. If this were so, then John's son Robert would have been named not only after his godfather, Sir Robert Sidney, but after his grandfather as well. The elder Robert would have been very young at the time of his marriage— scarcely out of his apprenticeship—but an early marriage was no more impossible in the sixteenth century than it is today. The limited number of christian names in general use at the time, however, makes it dangerous to assume that two men with identical names were necessarily closely related.

A search through London parish documents reveals several entries concerning other Dowlands in the late sixteenth and early seventeenth centuries, but whether any of these were connected with the composer it has been impossible to discover. Henry§ and Adam were buried at St. Michael Paternoster Royal in 1581 and 1582 respectively; a 'ffather' Dowland is assessed for rates in the Poor Rate Book of St. Clements Danes¶ in 1581 and a William

---

* *Reports of the Historical Manuscript Commission*, Ninth Report (1883).
† John Harvey, *An Introduction to Tudor Architecture* (1949).
‡ Edward Arber, *A Transcript of the Registers of the Stationers' Company* (1875), Vol. I, f. 5v.
§ In the Transcript in the Library of the Society of Genealogists Henry's name is queried as possibly Howland. Not so, however, in the case of Adam.
¶ City of Westminster Archives Department, Public Library, Buckingham Palace Road, London, S.W.1.

Dowland in 1585 and, as has been already mentioned, Mathew Dowland was buried at St. Margaret's Westminster in 1628.

The Records of Middlesex Sessions for June 8th and 9th, 1614, have an entry under the heading *St. Clements Danes*, which shows another tailor of the name of Dowland to have been in serious trouble:

Edward Dowland of the same, tailor, charged to have broken the back of John Evans. He promises to him 2/6 every week till the next sessions, and is handed in bail to William Powell, scrivener, and John Westcott, chandler, both of the same.

A family of Dowlands was established in Wiltshire. The marriage of a Gybbes and a Dowland was registered at Mere* in 1575, and other entries are found at Stourton and Dunnet. In Surrey, in 1592, an An Dowland married John Hedger at Nutfield, and Joan Dowland married Nic Martin at Titsey.† The name also occurs in Sussex with a fisherman, Darby Dowland of Rye, whose Will was proved on September 18th, 1581.‡

Dowland also occurs as a place name. The gazetteers give a village of that name in North Devon, five miles north-north-east of Hatherleigh, as well as Dowlands, three and a half miles west-south-west of Lyme Regis. There is a Dowlands Farm in Burstow parish, Surrey, mentioned as Dowlande in the *Valor Eccliasticus* of 1535.§ The name was also known in the north. It is mentioned in a document belonging to the Abbey of Whalley, dated December 16th, 1340, and concerns 'Richard de Radclif seneschal and master fforester of Blackburneschire and of Douland'.¶

The village near Hatherleigh appears in Domesday Book, 1086, as Duuelande, as Duhelanda *c.* 1175, and as Dugheland in 1242.‖ The meaning is regarded probably as 'land frequented by Doves'.

The one piece of evidence that could be read as showing an Irish origin for the family is the dedication of the song 'From Silent Night' in *A Pilgrimes Solace* 'To my louing Country-man *Mr John Forster* the younger,** Merchant of Dublin in Ireland', but this is by no means conclusive. The name Forster is not typical of indigenous Irish surnames, and it must be remembered that there was a large and flourishing family of Forsters in England at the same time. It is not impossible that the Dublin Forsters came from a branch of the

---

* *Wiltshire Parish Registers*, transcribed by T. H. Baker, Vol. 1 (1905).
† Surrey Marriages. Transcripts in the Library of the Society of Genealogists.
‡ Probate Registry, Chichester, Vol. 13, p. 22 (1581).
§ *Place Names in Surrey*, English Place Name Society, Vol. XI (1934), p. 287.
¶ Historical Manuscript Commission, *Calendar of Sir George Wombwell's Papers at Newburgh Priory*, Series 55, Vol. II, p. 12 (1903).
‖ B. O. E. Ekwall, *The Concise Oxford Dictionary of English Place Names* (1936).
** For the identity of John Forster see p. 406.

English family which had been settled in Ireland in the fifteenth, or early years of the sixteenth century. Most of the English settlers continued to think of themselves as English for several generations and if John Forster, though living in Dublin, was descended from English ancestors, then the dedication could as well mean that both he and Dowland were English as that they were both Irish.* That Dowland thought of himself as English is revealed on several occasions. When he wrote to Sir Robert Cecil in 1595 he described himself as having been 'born under her highness'. It is questionable whether an Irishman, born in Ireland at a time when the country was fiercely suffering under English domination, would have spoken of himself in such terms. An inscription is added to each of the part books of the *Lamentatio Henrici Noel* of 1596, in which he writes (with traces of his Italian visit very much in evidence) 'Gio Dolande/infœlice Inglese/ Baccalario in Musica'. In *The First Booke of Songes* (1597), when writing of his desire to perfect himself in the art of music, he speaks of 'sundry times leauing my natiue country, the better to attain so excellent a science', the context making it clear that he is referring to his Continental travels, while 'natiue country' means England. In *A Pilgrimes Solace* (1612), he addresses his public, surely an English one, as 'Worthy Gentlemen, and my louing Countrymen'.

One further indication of an English, rather than an Irish, ancestry is the fact, made clear in his letter to Cecil, that he was brought up a Protestant, and only became a Catholic during the time he spent in France.

Unless the registration of his birth should come to light it is unlikely that this problem can ever be demonstrably and unquestionably settled. Nevertheless, it seems reasonably probable that Dowland came from the English family whose name can be traced back to Domesday Book, and not from the Dowlinges, Dubhlaings, Doolans or O'Dolans in Ireland. That there was a Dowland at Trinity College is certain. There may have been others in Ireland at the same time, as Dr. Flood claims, but that any of these were relations of the composer so far remains unproved.

Where any information can be gathered about the social status of the Dowlands it is noticeable that they belonged to the upper ranks of the artisan class—a mason, a printer, a fisherman and two tailors—and, where wills are extant, the testators have a comfortable amount of personal property to dispose of. A solid enough background, but possibly one which John preferred to keep strictly behind him. By the time he had begun to write about

* It was possibly excess of patriotism that led Miss Purser of Dublin to make herself responsible for the placing of a memorial tablet on the rocks at Dalkey, overlooking the sea. When she wrote to Bernard Shaw for a subscription, he replied 'D . . . Dowland! However, I can't refuse you: though obviously the memorial ought to have been to *me*.' He sent her five guineas.

himself he had already made an entry into a totally different social stratum, where, as will be seen later from the letters of the Landgrave of Hesse and Henry Noel, even allowing for the strict bounds of 'order' and 'degree', he was received with exceptional friendship and cordiality. Was it perhaps a desire that the comparatively humble condition of his family should remain hidden that caused him to maintain such a remarkable reticence about his early years?

Whether or not this was the reason for his silence, the fact remains that, in spite of the freedom with which he writes of the events of his adult life, after indicating the date of his birth, he gives no information whatsoever about his parentage or his childhood's circumstances, and his own account of his life begins in the year 1580, when, at the age of seventeen, he went to Paris as 'servant' to Sir Henry Cobham, Ambassador to the King of France.

In *The First Booke of Songes* Dowland writes of 'the ingenuous profession of Musicke, which from my childhood I haue euer aymed at, sundry times leauing my native country, the better to attain so excellent a science' and it seems not unlikely that he entered the service of Sir Henry Cobham with the express purpose of visiting France in order to add polish to such training as he had already received. If he had by then been drawn towards the lute as his chosen instrument he would have known that some of the most famous teachers in Europe were, at that time, to be found in France.*

He might also have wished to study at first hand the ferment of ideas still occupying the minds of French poets and composers which had been initiated earlier in the century upon an upsurge of Humanist thought, and which manifested itself, at the time of Dowland's visit, in experimental forms such as *musique mesurée à l'antique.*

During his stay in France, according to his own account, he became converted to Catholicism; an event which he later believed was to exert a profoundly unfortunate influence over his worldly career. That he was not brought up a Catholic is clear from the wording of a letter he wrote to Sir Robert Cecil in 1595.

Some confusion exists about the date of his return to England. In this same letter he says: 'Fifteen years since I was in France servant to Sir Henry Cobham, who was Ambassador for the Queen's Majesty, and lay in Paris. . . . Within 2 years after I came into England where I saw men of that faction [Catholics] condemned and executed which I thought was great Injustice taking Religion for the only Cause. . . .' As the sentence stands, the

---

* Adrian Le Roy's *A briefe and easye Instruction*, originally printed in Paris in 1567, made its appearance in England in 1568, translated by John Alford and printed by John Kingston. The contents of the *Instruction* reappeared in several different forms and Le Roy's method formed the basis of English lute teaching until the early years of the seventeenth century.

meaning is ambiguous and the placing of a comma can alter the sense to 'Within 2 years after, I came into England where I saw . . .' or 'Within 2 years after I came into England, where I saw . . .' Peter Warlock★ takes the first to be the meaning intended, but two sets of facts suggest the second is the correct reading. Firstly Dowland is mentioned in a petition of some English merchants condemned to the galleys to Sir Edward Stafford in the year 1584.† Sir Edward Stafford did not become Ambassador until 1583, when Sir Henry Cobham asked to be relieved of his appointment, so the events described in the petition could not have taken place before that date. Secondly, the years 1583 and 1586 were the two in which measures against the English Catholics rose to a high pitch of intensity. In both years this was the result of plots to place Mary Queen of Scots on the throne in place of Elizabeth, by means of a Spanish invasion. In the first Francis Throckmorton was used as a go-between, and in the second, Anthony Babington, in both cases with the full connivance of Mary. The plots were uncovered by Walsingham and a wave of arrests and executions followed. Among others a number of missionary priests, who may or may not have been actively involved, were caught, hanged and quartered. If Dowland had been on leave in England in 1583 he could have seen the executions following the Throck-morton Plot, but this would have been three and not two years after his arrival in France, whereas if he had returned to England for good in 1584, he could have witnessed the executions following the Babington Plot just two years later.

An interesting sidelight on Dowland's life in Paris is the fact that he must have rubbed shoulders with Richard Hakluyt. On going to France in 1583, Sir Edward Stafford appointed Hakluyt as his chaplain‡ and, during this period of service at the Embassy Hakluyt was engaged in writing his famous work, *The Principall Navigations, Voiages, and Discoveries of the English Nation*.

The next event in Dowland's career that can be spoken of with certainty

★ *The English Ayre* (1926), p. 21.

† They have 'binne detayned in prison this vij weekes in most myserable captivitie havinge received ponnyshment by whippynge twyse about the towne of Newehaven [Le Havre] and so conveyed abought the countrye towards the gallyes there to remayne untill the tyme of theyre deth'. They are 'nowe in a most myserable and lothsom prison in parrys, not knowinge what to do nor vnto whome to make theyre mones but vnto your good Lordshepe'. The writer then continues 'And whereas yor good Lo: did send yor favourable charyttie by y^r servant John Dowland he gevynge vs to vnderstand that yor good Lo: yf we herd ony thinge of o^r goinge towards the galleys which newes of o^r going we herd from yor said servante beinge wth vs/ most humbly besechynge yor good Lordshepe to take some order fo^r vs that we may be stayd from going vnto y^t most vylle playse w^cl other wyse we are worse then ded men remaynynge contynually in torments . . . for the reste of his prisonne fellowes 'Wy Wardoure.'

S.P. 78/12/142

‡ *Dictionary of National Biography*.

took place in 1588. This was a year which saw a decisive change in the whole political balance of forces in Europe. The long-meditated plans of Philip II for the subjugation of England were brought to a climax with the sailing of the Armada from Spain in the summer of that year. With the end of the first day's battle on July 21st,* the slow decline of Spanish power began. Just as the final preparations were being made in Lisbon to the Spanish fleet, and the people of England apprehensively awaited its coming, on July 8th Dowland was admitted to his Mus.Bac. from Christ Church, Oxford, together with Thomas Morley. Dr. John Case's mention of Dowland among the most famous musicians of his day in *Apologia Musices*, written in the same year, suggests that Dowland sat for his degree more as seal and confirmation of his status than as a formal termination to his musical education.

The earliest occasion on which we hear of music, almost certainly by Dowland, being performed at a Court ceremony was on November 17th, 1590. Thanksgiving celebrations were held every year on this date to mark the anniversary of the Queen's accession, and one of the usual features of the London commemorations were the jousts held at the tiltyard at Westminster. Here, year by year, the Queen watched members of the nobility, who came from all parts of the country, run at tilt in her honour. On this particular occasion solemn rites were performed to accompany the resignation of Sir Henry Lee from the voluntarily assumed position of Queen's Champion. No ceremony of this kind was complete without its special music, and among the pieces composed for the occasion was a setting of the poem 'His golden locks time hath to silver turned', which, because the Queen 'took some pleasure in his voice', was sung by Robert Hales, one of the Gentlemen of the Privy Chamber.†

Soon after this, John's son, Robert, must have been born. In his Marriage Allegation, made on October 11th, 1626, Robert is described as being 'about xxxv yeares'.‡ No register of his birth has so far come to light, nor is it known whether he was the eldest son. That there were other children is certain, but up till now it has been impossible to identify them among the other Dowlands living at the time.

This evidence about the year of Robert's birth raises the question of the date of John's own marriage, which, in the past, has generally been assumed to have taken place some time before 1586. But even allowing for a later date for the marriage, we are still no nearer penetrating the complete mystery that surrounds the identity of Mrs. Dowland. No record of the marriage has been

---

* Old Style.
† For William Segar's description of the ceremony see p. 237.
‡ The Guildhall Library MS 10,091/11, f. 34. This was first reprinted in full in an article by Cecil Hill in *The Musical Times*, November 1963.

found, but either of two reasons could account for this: the registers of the parish in which it was solemnized, if a church wedding was held, could have disappeared, or, since nothing was done until the Marriage Act of 1754 to control and enforce registration, it could have been a contract entered into by declaration before witnesses. This was a form held to be legal in the sixteenth century, though often leading to subsequent trouble. It is possible to hazard a guess, although this may be doing Dowland an injustice, that she played no great emotional part in his life. She did not accompany him on any of his travels, not even to Denmark when he went to take up what must have been regarded as a permanent position, although this could have been accounted for by the presence of young children and the difficulty of travel at the time. He refers to her several times in the letter to Sir Robert Cecil, but except for the first matter-of-fact statement that the Landgrave of Hesse sent a ring into England for her, valued at £20 sterling, she seems to be part of the rhetorical picture of his miserable state in Italy, rather than a real person whose presence or absence made any great difference to his life. She is heard of once more, in 1601,* and then she vanishes from the scene.

In 1592 an entertainment took place in which, for the first time, there is a definite record of his having played before the Queen. While she was on progress in Gloucestershire she visited Sudeley Castle, the home of Giles Bridges, Lord Chandos. One of the customary entertainments was prepared in her honour and was mounted with the usual lavish expenditure. It was entitled 'Daphne and Apollo' and was presented in the grounds at Sudeley. When the scene was set, two musicians, 'one who sung and one who plaide', were placed on either side of a laurel tree, and the song 'My heart and tongue were twinnes' was performed. Some dialogue follows and then there is a scene between Melibæus, Nisa and Cutter of Cootsholde, in which this remarkable passage occurs:

Nis. . . . You, sirra, that sit as though your wits were a woole-gathering, will you have a question or a commaundement?

Cut. No question of a Queene, for they are hard to be answered; but any commaundement, for that must be obeyed.

Nis. Then sing. And you sir, a question or a commaundement?

Do. A commaundement I; and glad that I am!

Nis. Then play.

Do. I have plaide so long with my fingers, that I have beaten out of play al my good fortune.

The Song.

Hearbes, wordes, and stones, all maladies have cured;
Hearbes, wordes, and stones, I used when I loved;

---

* See p. 244.

Hearbes smels, words, winde, stones hardnes have procured;
   By stones, nor wordes, nor hearbes her minde was moved.
I askt the cause: this was a womans reason,
   Mongst hearbes are weeds, and thereby are refused;
Deceite, as well as truth, speakes wordes in season,
   False stones by foiles have many one abused.
I sight, and then shee saide my fancie smoaked;
   I gaz'd, shee saide my lookes were follies glauncing;
I sounded deade, shee saide my love was choaked;
   I started up, shee saide my thoughts were dauncing.
   O sacred Love! if thou have any Godhead,
   Teach other rules to winne a maidenheade.

Mel.   Well song, and wel plaide; seldome so well among
       shepheards. But call me the Cutter of Cotsholde, that
       looks as though he only knew his leripoope; amorous he
       is, and wise; carying a sheepes eie in a calfs heade.*

Taken in conjunction with the presence of the song 'My heart and tongue were twinnes' there can be no doubt that the contraction 'Do.' stands for Dowland himself. In all probability the second song was set by him too, although no trace of the music has survived. The little scene seems so disconnected with the 'argument' of the entertainment, such as it is, that the possibility can hardly be overlooked that it was introduced to allow Dowland to make a plea before the Queen against the real or imagined neglect which, even at this early date, appears to have become something of a fixed idea in his mind.

During the same year Dowland contributed six harmonizations to Thomas Est's *The Whole Booke of Psalmes*.

Little is heard of him in 1593, except that about this time (certainly after 1592) Thomas Whythorne, the composer, entered the name 'mr Dowland' along with a number of other famous musicians on a slip of paper, known as 'the musical scrap', which was bound into his autobiography.†

In 1594 John Johnson, one of the Queen's musicians for the Lutes, died,‡ and Dowland applied for the vacant post. In his letter to Sir Robert Cecil he tells how, on failing to gain the appointment he decided to spend some time in foreign travel with the intention of an eventual meeting with Luca

---

* John Nichols, *The Progresses of Queen Elizabeth*, Vol. II (1788), p. 9. Second edition, Vol. III (1823), p. 141. I am grateful to Robert Spencer for calling my attention to the two appearances of the character 'Do.' which he noticed while studying the text in order to prepare the music for a *son et lumière* at Sudeley.

† *The Autobiography of Thomas Whythorne*, edited by James Osborne (1961).

‡ The final payment to John Johnson is entered as 'due for ¾ year ending Midsummer 1594'. Audit Office Declared Accounts Bundle 386, No. 32.

Marenzio in Rome, but he planned first to visit the Court of Henry Julius, Duke of Brunswick, to whom he was already known by reputation. He set out forthwith and was received at Wolfenbüttel with marks of great favour. After spending some little time at the Castle, he resumed his journey, travelling towards the Court of Hesse, apparently at the Duke's suggestion, and accompanied by the Duke's own lutenist, Gregorio Howet.

Both the Duke of Brunswick and the Landgrave of Hesse were men with literary pretensions, and were the first princes in Germany to establish permanent theatres at their Courts with English actors as their chief players. Henry Julius made a practice of writing plays for his own theatre, among them the tragedies of *Von der Ehebrecherin* and *Von einem Buhler und einer Buhlerin*. Of his play on the story of Susanna and the Elders it was said:

The conversation of the two old men in Susanna's garden and before the court of justice is here beyond measure obscene and full of the lowest terms of abuse, and yet this piece was performed in the presence of the court.★

Of the religious views held by Henry Julius, Janssen says:

He was brought up a Protestant although during the lifetime of his grandfather, the Catholic Duke Henry, he had been elected Bishop of Halberstadt on condition that he was brought up a Catholic. But when the cathedral chapter invited him to attend the customary Mass to take the episcopal oath, Julius declared that he and his son 'would neither hear nor look on at the Mass, or take any part in such an abomination.'

Furthermore, his father 'caused it to be proclaimed that Henry Julius would not associate himself with the papacy, but would adhere to the Augsburg Confession'.† His strictly Lutheran beliefs did not, however, interfere with Henry Julius's exceptionally heavy drinking nor with his inordinately extravagant mode of living. When his father died he inherited a fortune of nearly a million gulden. When Henry Julius himself died in 1613 he had not only spent his father's entire fortune, but had also contracted debts of 1,200,000 thalers on the princely treasury.‡ He was a great persecutor of witches.

Maurice, Landgrave of Hesse was, in his time, regarded as something of a paragon among princes. Edward Monings, writing to the Countess of Warwick in 1596, gives the following description:

But to speak at length, after a timely observation of this noble Prince, of whose rare giftes and vertues, and discretion in the cariadge of himself, and mannaging of affaires, sufficiently discover him, he is a perfect man (in my opinion) and a most perfect prince.

★ Johann Janssen, *History of the German People* (1925), Vol. XII, p. 25.
† op. cit., Vol. VIII, p. 424.   ‡ op. cit., Vol. XV, pp. 314–15.

First a goodly personage, of stature tall and straight for his proportion, of a good presence and a gallant countenance, manly visaged, with a faire big black eye, deep aburne haire, comlie in behaviour, gratious and persuasive in speech. And his bodie hath a minde suitable unto yt. For his giftes of nature are great, sharpe to apprehend, and sound in judgment, mingling his gravitie with pleasure, his courtesie with taste and honour, love with stoutnes, thereby winning the affection of straungers, and keeping his subjects in a lovely fear, master of his affections, temperat, bounded, not to change, in whom the upper partes commaund the neather.

His education prince-like, generally knowen in all things, and excellent in many, seasoning his grave and more important studies for ability in judgment, with studies of pastime for retiring, as in poetrie, musicke, and the mathematics; and for ornament in discourse in the languages, French, Italian, and English, wherein he is expert, reading much, conferring and writing much. He is a full man, a readie man, an exact man, and so excellent a Prince, that a man may say of him without flatterie, as Tullie did of Pompey, *unus in quo summa sunt omnia*; and for my private opinion I think there are but fewe such men in the world.*

His reputation spread beyond the limits of his own country, and Dowland's friend Henry Peacham wrote of him in 1622:

But above others, who carrieth away the Palme for excellency, not only in Musicke, but in whatsoever is to be wished in a brave Prince, is the yet living *Maurice, Landgrave of Hessen*, of whose owne compositions I have seen eight or ten several sets of Motets and solemne Musicke, set purposely for his owne Chappell; where for the great honour of some Festival, and many times for his recreation onely, he is his owne Organist.†

Some of the occasions of his mingling gravity with pleasure are described by Janssen:

At a display of fireworks got up by the Landgrave Maurice of Hesse in honour of the Christening of his son Otto in 1594, Mount Helicon, together with Pegasus, went off in flames, amid rockets and pillars of fire. In 1596, at the Christening of his daughter Elizabeth, 'there was a grand pyrotechnical display in which 60,000 squibs and firespitting rockets were shot up with fearful and wonderful cracking and noise'.‡

He was a devotee of hunting and

in Hesse, according to a report of the magistrates in 1595, as many as 300 people were called upon to serve at the hare and fox hunts and even to take the place of hounds. All who did not respond to the summons were subjected to severe punishment. In 1591 the Hessian parishes of Allendorf and Verna, because the men did not appear at the right time at the hunt were

---

* J. Nichols, *Progresses of Queen Elizabeth* (1823), Vol. 3, p. 394. Edward Monings was in the train of Lord Hunsdon who was sent as Ambassador to the Court of Hesse in August 1596.
   † *The Compleat Gentleman* (1622), p. 99.   ‡ op. cit., Vol. XV, p. 263.

fined 80 thalers; in 1598, 28 shepherds from the district of Battenburg and Frankenburg lost 110 of their best wethers because they had not sent their dogs to the hunt. A master huntsman of the Landgrave Maurice discharged a load of shot into the body of one peasant who had lingered behind in the chase, struck an ear off another who came up late with his hounds, and slashed in two the head of a third; it was not till he cursed the Landgrave that he was brought to trial.*

Like most of the other German princes of his time, Maurice was a heavy drinker, and on one occasion when he visited the Elector of Brandenburg with a retinue of 3,000 horsemen 'master and servants after a ten day stay went to Spandau in such a mighty state of intoxication that they could scarcely find the gate of the town'.†

In 1604 the Landgrave became a Calvinist, and in the attempt to replace the old Lutheran faith the country was reduced to a state bordering on civil war. Even crucifixes were smashed as 'dumb idols' and the carrying of the cross in funeral processions was prohibited as an 'idolatrous practice'. A number of preachers who refused to conform to the new orders were severely man-handled. The general state of the country is reflected in the Landgrave's complaint in 1601, of the 'idleness and begging that was gaining ground everywhere', and is in pitiful contrast to the strength and magnificence of the five-storey castle at Kassel, described by Monings. A room which particularly impressed him was one which must have been familiar to Dowland:

His Lordshippes owne dining chamber was a very curious roome, made no doubt of purpose to entertaine strange Princes, all of marble, the doores, the flower, the sides, the windowes and roofe . . . the trouble of his rowme is great in winter, when, to keep the stone from cracking and loosening, the stone is continually kept hot.‡

Little indication is given by Dowland of the actual itinerary of the journey, nor of the time he spent in any one place. A few facts can, however, be gathered from other sources, although any attempt at reaching exact dates is complicated by the different calendars then in use in various parts of Europe.

Together with Gregorio Howet, Dowland must have arrived at Kassel sometime before March 21st, 1595,§ since on that day the Landgrave wrote a

---

* op. cit., Vol. XV, p. 212.
† op. cit., Vol. XV, p. 249.
‡ Nichols, op. cit., Vol. 3, p. 385.
§ In his article 'Die Deutchelandreisen John Dowlands' in *Musica*, II, 1951, where the following letter is printed, Eckart Klessmann, together with a number of other mis-statements, says 'On Nov. 5th, 1594, Alessandro Orologio, composer and cornet virtuoso of the Dresden Court Orchestra, reported to the Landgrave, then absent, that "some foreign musicians" had arrived at Cassel on Nov. 1st after having spent some time at Wolfenbuettel'. These 'foreign musicians' were none other than John Dowland and Gregorio Howitt." At my request Dr.

letter to Henry Julio of Brunswick which makes clear that by the date of his writing their visit was ended. According to Klessmann the letter 'accompanied the return of Dowland and Howett, that same day, to Wolfenbüttel'. In translation the letter reads:

Assuring you of our devoted service, and wishing you the best of good fortune, Gracious and High-born Prince, dear loving uncle and cousin, brother-in-law, brother and god-father, we have received and read your Grace's letter with great interest, and deduce from it just what happened there with the lutenists Gregorio Hawitten and Johannes Dulandt. I trust that your Grace has not presumed that the said Johan Dulandt has been engaged by me. He has been staying here voluntarily and availing himself of any chance opportunity to perform. It was exceedingly kind of Your Grace to send us your lutenists and musicians, and we beg you to excuse their belated return, as it was our fault that they tarried here so long. As far as art is concerned, we have heard both lutenists, and although we cannot claim to be experts in this field, we judge them both to be very able performers. Deferring to Your Grace's judgment, we hold the lutenist Gregorius Hawitten to be an experienced and practised performer, and as far as madrigals are concerned, his art is unsurpassed. Dulandt, on the other hand, is a good composer. If, as Your Grace writes, he has belittled your lutenists, and has scorned them in any way, he apologises most humbly and sincerely for it.

Not wishing to presume on Your Grace's patience, we are etc.

Cassel, 21st March, 1595.
Moritz Landgrave Hessen.*

Maria Möller, of the Murhardsche Bibliothek der Stadt Kassel und Landesbibliothek, kindly examined this letter (State Archives, Marburg, 4b, pack 46, No. 2) and she tells me the date is not that given by Klessmann, but is, in fact, November 5th, 1595. The Wolfenbütteler musicians could not then have been Dowland and Howet. The original mis-statement was made by Ernst Zulauf in *Beitraege zur Geschicte der Landgraeflich-Hessischen Hofkapelle* . . . (1903), p. 48.

* Unser freundlich Dienst, undt was wir mehr Liebs und guts vermogenn zuvohr: Ehrwürdig und Hochgebohrner Fürst, freundtlicher Lieber Oheim undt Vetter, Schwager, Bruder undt Gevatter, wir habenn E. L. schreiben empffang u verlesen, undt daras, was sich bey E. L. mit thro Lautenisten Georgio Hawitten undt Johannes Dulandt begeben hat, vernohmenn. Mögen E. L. hinwieder nicht verhaltenn, daß gedachter Lautenist Johan Dulandt in unser bestallung nicht ist, sondernn sich bis daher allein alhier zu vorfallender gelegenheit uffgehaltenn. Das aber E. L. dero Lautenisten undt Musicantenn anhero geschickt, ist unns darann zu angenehmem gefallen geschehen. Undt so wir dieselben uber ihre bestimbte Zeit uffgehaltenn, bittenn wir freundtlich, sie unsernt wegen für entschuldigt zu halten. Was ihr Kunst anlangt, so henn wir auch beyde Lautenistenn gegeneinander gehörtt, undt wiewoll wir Uns uff daß Lauttenschlagen sonderlich nichts verstehenn beduncken sie uns doch beydt gut sein, gebenn E. L. nach, das deroselbenn Lautenist Georgius Hawitten ein erfahrner geübter Lautenist, undt was muteten madrialn zu schlagen anlangt, gar perfect undt wohl Passiert. Hergegen befindenn wir, daß der ander Johannes Dulandt ein guter Componist ist, das er auch, wie E. L. meldenn dero Lautenisten verkleinert undt in einigem wege solte verachtet haben, dessen beschwert undt entschuldigt er sich zum Heftigstenn.

Wolltenn wir E. L. freundtlich nicht verhalten, undt seindt Datum Cassel am 21. Marty anno 1595.   Moritz Lg Hessen.

I do not feel entirely satisfied with Klessmann's deduction from this letter that Dowland returned to Wolfenbüttel. When Maurice speaks of 'your lutenists and musicians' he appears to refer to more than Howet and Dowland only. Possibly Henry Julio sent a small group of players, with whom Dowland travelled to Kassel. It must be remembered that Dowland says in his letter to Sir Robert Cecil that he did not accept the offered employment under the Duke, nor does he speak of having returned to Wolfenbüttel after his visit to Kassel. Dowland and Howet were obviously the star performers of the group, which would account for their names only being mentioned. It appears more likely that Howet and the other musicians returned home carrying the letter to their master, while Dowland proceeded on his journey towards the hoped-for meeting with Luca Marenzio in Rome.

The tone of reserve with which Maurice writes of Dowland suggests he is being politic with his brother-in-law, since it accords very little with Dowland's own account of his reception at Kassel, or with the Landgrave's subsequent attitude towards Dowland. There are two sentences that provide a clue to what may have taken place. Firstly, Maurice says he can deduce 'just what happened there with the lutenists Gregorio Hawitten and Johannes Dulandt', and later 'If, as Your Grace writes he [Dowland] has belittled your lutenists, and has scorned them in any way, he apologises most humbly and sincerely for it.' Does it not appear from this that Dowland said something derogatory about Howet and that the two lutenists had quarrelled and had indulged in some less than diplomatic exchanges? The situation may have been patched up for the journey, and of course, Dowland makes complimentary references to Howet in *The First Booke of Songes*, but this would be natural in the particular context, since he is listing all the famous musicians with whom he has been on friendly terms. If Dowland had left Wolfenbüttel under some such cloud it can be well imagined that Maurice would not wish it to be thought by Henry Julio that he had immediately offered him employment, even though, according to Dowland, he had in fact done so. It is noticeable that Maurice takes good care not to commit himself to a downright opinion as to which is the better player, though leaving it open to Henry Julio to assume that he is in agreement in preferring Howet. Altogether this appears to be a letter written with extreme tact in order to avoid becoming involved in a family dispute on Dowland's behalf, and the general tone, taken in conjunction with the fact that Dowland later returned to Kassel and was employed by Maurice, suggests that on this occasion Dowland's is the more reliable account.

We have no means of knowing how long it took Dowland to travel south and over the Alps into Italy. The journey must inevitably have been slow.

One imagines two lutes at least would have been necessary on such an enterprise, to ensure the availability of one in case of accident. These would have
been carried in heavy wooden or leather cases, possibly metal bound. In
addition, clothes other than those for travelling would be included in the
baggage; some of suitable quality for an appearance in any of the castles or
palaces of the principalities and dukedoms through which he would pass,
where his reputation might gain him an invitation to perform. A pack-horse
would be required; possibly a servant would accompany him. The vulnera-
bility of the instruments, even in their strong cases, would preclude any
attempt at great haste over the treacherous surface of the unmade roads.

The first Italian city he visited was Venice. From there he went on to
Padua, Genoa and Ferrara, meeting with 'favour and estimation' as he went.
Eventually he reached Florence, probably attracted by the high reputation
for appreciation of the arts enjoyed by the Medici Court. As he travelled
through Italy he left traces of his music in the memories of Italian musicians,
especially in the case of the two Garsis, Santino and Donino (father and son or
uncle and nephew) who reproduced his 'Lady Hunson's Puffe' and the 'K.
Dar,' Galliard (see p. 160) under guise of their own composing.*

At Florence he was invited to play before Ferdinando I, Grand Duke of
Tuscany, probably in what is now known as the Pitti Palace which, at the
time, was the Grand Ducal residence. In the Court circle he would undoubtedly have met Giulio Caccini, who was in the Duke's employment.
That Dowland does not mention him in *The First Booke of Songes* together
with his other distinguished musical friends could have been due to the fact
that, as yet, Caccini was hardly known outside Italy and his name would
probably have carried little weight in England.

Dowland does not make clear how long he had been in Florence before he
was approached by the English Catholic exiles living there, but they must
have made contact with him in late May or early June, for at least a month
passed between his first meeting with the English priest John Scudamore and
his receipt of the letter which Scudamore, at Dowland's request, had written
on July 7th, 1595, to Nicholas Fitzherbert in Rome to serve as an introduction
and 'safe conduct'. Here is the letter which, as Dowland tells us, he later sent
home to Sir Robert Cecil for his inspection:

Ryght worshippful
mr ffitzherbert
I know the fame of mr Douland our Countryman for his exquisitenes upon
the lute and his conninge in musick Hath come to yor eares long ago and now

shortely you are like to here hym in person and be the iudge yor self of his musicke wherein he will I assure you geve you content: my request to you is that you according to yor louing nature wold geeve all kynd and courteous entertainment to hym which that you may the safer do, though his coming from England might be some occasion of hynderaunce I do assure in *verbo sacerdotis* that he is no meddler but rather inclined to the good and onli for the fame of *Lucca Emerentiana* and loue of musick hath undertaken this voyage so that I hope there wilbe no occasion to hynder you from doing hym what fauors you can which I pray you againe and againe to shew hym for my sake and I shalbe allwayes bound to you for this and for many other you^r exceading courtesies to me shewn: so praying god to bless you and us all do take leaue (Fiorenza 7° July 1595)

Yrs allwayes at Commaunde,
John Scudamore priest

It could not have been long before he realized he was sailing in deep and dangerous waters. He decided to abandon the plan of visiting Luca Marenzio in Rome and curtail his visit to Italy. He set out on the homeward journey and paused at Nuremberg where, on November 10th, in a state of great perturbation, he wrote the following letter to Sir Robert Cecil:*

To the Right honourable Sir Robert Cecil knight, one of the Queen's Majesty's most honourable Privy Councillors, these

Right honourable: as I have been bound unto your honour so I most humbly desire your honour to pardon my boldness and make my choice of your honour to let you understand my bounden duty and desire of God's preservation of my most dear sovereign Queen and Country: whom I beseech God ever to bless & to confound all their enemies what & whom soever. Fifteen years since I was in France servant to Sir Henry Cobham who was Ambassador for the Queen's Majesty, and lay in Paris, where I fell acquainted with one Smith a priest, and one Morgan sometime of her Majesty's Chapel, one Verstigan who brake out of England being apprehended & one Morris a Welshman that was our porter, who is at Rome; these men thrust many idle toys into my head of religion, saying that the papists' was the truth & ours in England all false, and I being but young their fair words overreached me & I believed with them. Within two years after I came into England where I saw men of that faction condemned & executed which I thought was great injustice taking religion for the only cause, and when my best friends would persuade me I would not believe them. Then in time passing one Mr Johnson died & I became an humble suitor for his place (thinking myself most worthiest) wherein I found many good and honourable friends that spake for me, but I saw that I was like to go without it, and that any may have preferment but I, whereby I began to sound the cause, and guessed that my religion was my hindrance. Whereupon my mind being troubled I desired to get beyond the seas which I

---

* I give a transcription into modern spelling since the frequent contractions and idiosyncratic spelling occasionally obscure the meaning. A facsimile of the letter appears after p. 40.

durst not attempt without licence from some of the Privy Council, for fear of being taken and so have extreme punishment. And according as I desired there came a letter to me out of Germany from the Duke of Brunswick, whereupon I spake to your honour & to my Lord of Essex who willingly gave me both your hands (for which I would be glad if there were any service in me that your honours could command). When I came to the Duke of Brunswick he used me kindly & gave me a rich chain of gold, £23 in money with velvet and satin and gold lace to make me apparel, with promise that if I would serve him he would give me as much as any prince in the world. From thence I went to the Lantgrave of Hessen, who gave me the greatest welcome that might be for one of my quality who sent a ring into England to my wife valued at £20 sterling, and gave me a great standing cup with a cover gilt, full of dollars with many great offers for my service. From thence I had great desire to see Italy & came to Venice & from thence to Florence where I played before the Duke & got great favours, & one evening I was walking upon the piazzo in Florence a gentleman told me that he espied an English priest & that his name was Skidmore & son and heir to Sir John Skidmore of the Court. So I being intended to go to Rome to study with a famous musician named Luca Marenzio: stepped to this Mr Skidmore the priest & asked him if he were an Englishman, & he told me yea: & whose son he was, & I telling him my name he was very glad to see me, so I told him I would go to Rome & desired his help for my safety, for said I, if they should mistake me there my fortune were hard, for I have been thrust off of all good fortune because I am a Catholic at home. For I heard that her Majesty being spoke to for me, said I was a man to serve any prince in the world, but I was an obstinate papist. Whereunto he answered Mr Dowlande if it be not so make her words true. So in further talk we spake of priests, & I told him that I did not think it true that any priests (as we said in England) would kill the Queen or once go about to touch her finger, and said I whatsoever my religion be I will neither meddle nor make with any thing there done, so that they do not anything against the Queen. Whereunto he answered that I spake as a good subject to her Majesty, but said he in Rome you shall hear Englishmen your own countrymen speak most hardly of her and wholly seek to overthrow her & all England. And those be the Jesuits said he who are of the Spanish faction. Moreover said he we have many jars with them & withall wished to God the Queen were a Catholic, & said he, to defend my Country against the Spaniards I would come into England & bear a pike on my shoulders. Among our talk he told me that he had orders to attach divers English gentlemen, & that he had been 3 years [out of?] England, so I brought him to his lodging door, where he told me that there was 9 priests come from Rome to go for England. He came but the day before to Florence, & I think they came altogether, he told me that he would stay there in the town and study in an abbey called *Sancta Maria Novella*, & that he must be in for one month, and that he would write letters of me to Rome, which I should receive very shortly, but I heard not of him in a month after, and then there came two friars to my lodging the one was an

Englishman named Bailey, a Yorkshireman. The next day after my speech with Skidmore I dined with my Lord Gray and divers other gentlemen, whom I told of my speech with Skidmore giving them warning. Whereupon my Lord Gray went to *Sienna*, and the rest dispersed themselves. Moreover I told my Lord Gray howsoever I was for religion, if I did perceive anything in Rome that either touched her Majesty or the state of England I would give notice of it though it were the loss of my life, which he liked well & bade me keep that secret. This friar Bailey before named delivered me a letter which I have here sent your Honour, which letter I brake open before Mr Josias Bodley, & showed what was written in it to him & divers other, after this, this friar Bailey told me he had received letters from Rome to hasten me forward, & told me that my discontentment was known at Rome, & that I should have a large pension of the Pope, & that his Holiness & all the cardinals would make wonderful much of me, thereupon I told him of my wife and children how to get them to me, whereunto he told me that I should have acquaintance with such as should bring them over to me if she had any willingness or else they would lose their lives for there came those into England for such purposes, for quoth he Mr Skidmore brought out of England at his last being there 17 persons both men and women, for which the Bishop weeps when he sees him for joy. After my departure I called to mind our conference & got me by myself & wept heartily, to see my fortune so hard that I should become servant to the greatest enemy of my prince: country: wife: children: and friends: for want, & to make me like themselves. God he knoweth I never loved treason nor treachery nor never knew any, nor never heard any mass in England, which I find is great abuse of the people for on my soule I understand it not. Wherefore I have reformed myself to live according to her Majesty's laws as I was born under her Highness, & that most humbly I do crave pardon, protesting if there were any ability in me, I would be most ready to make amend. At Bologna I met with 2 men the one named Pierce an Irishman, the other named Dracot. They are gone both to Rome. In Venice I heard an Italian say, that he marvelled that King Philip had never a good friend in England that with his dagger would dispatch the Queen's Majesty, but said he, God suffers her, in the end to give her the greater overthrow. Right honourable this have I written that her Majesty may know the villainy of these most wicked priests and Jesuits, & to beware of them. I thank God I have both forsaken them and their religion which tendeth to nothing but destruction. Thus I beseech God night & day to bless and defend the Queen's Majesty, & to confound all her enemies & to preserve your honour & all the rest of her Majesty's most honourable Privy Council. I think that Skidmore & the other priests are all in England for he stayed not at Florence as he said he would to me, & friar Bailey told me that he was gone into France to study the law. At Venice & all along as I came in Germany say that the King of Spain is making great preparation to come for England this next summer, where if it pleased your Honour to advise me by my poor wife I would most willingly lose my life against them. Most humbly beseeching your Honour to pardon my ill writing & worse inditing, & to think that I desire to serve my country & hope to hear of your good opinion of me. From Nurnberg this 10th of November 1595.

Your Honour's most bounden

for ever

*Jo:Doulande**

Like many of his contemporaries, Dowland affected two distinct hand-writings: the secretary hand in which the body of the letter is written, and the italic which he used for the words 'Sancta Maria Nouella', 'Siena' and his signature. All other known inscriptions, titles or signatures are in italic.

Dowland sent Scudamore's letter to Cecil together with his own. On the back of the final page, used as the outer cover, is written the direction to Cecil and, presumably by one of Cecil's secretaries, 'Jo: Dowland to my Mr ffrom Noremberge wth Jo: Scudamore prieste to Nich ffitzherbert.'

There is so much in this letter that is inconsistent and contradictory that speculation about Dowland's motive in writing as he did is inevitably raised. Can it be taken simply as the confused outpourings of a man panic-stricken at finding himself unintentionally involved with dangerous and treasonable activities of a group of exiles, or is there some deeper significance behind what he writes?

To begin with, the elaborate recounting of a number of facts which, clearly, were already known to Cecil, is odd, and his statements about his religion, and particularly about the prejudicial effect he considered it to have had on his chances of securing a post at Court, show themselves, on closer examination, to be difficult to reconcile with historical fact.

Could his Catholicism have been the real reason for his failure to secure the longed-for post? As far as the Queen herself was concerned she was no fanatic. In 1571, after the publication of the Papal Bull of Excommunication, she caused the Lord Keeper to make the following public declaration in the Star Chamber:

Her Majesty would have all her loving subjects to understand that as long as they shall openly continue in the observation of her laws and shall not willingly and manifestly break them by their open acts, her Majesty's meaning is not to have any of them molested by any inquisition or examination of their consciences in causes of religion . . . being very loth to be provoked by the overmuch boldness and wilfulness of her subjects to alter her natural clemency into a princely severity.†

Francis Bacon bears witness that:

Her Majesty, not liking to make windows into men's hearts and secret

---

* This and the letter from Scudamore are Nos. 91 and 94 in Vol. 172 of the Marquess of Salisbury's Papers at Hatfield House.

† J. E. Neale, *Elizabeth I and her Parliaments 1559–1581* (1953), p. 192.

Letter from John Dowland to Sir Robert Cecil, dated November 10th, 1595, now in the Library of Hatfield House. By permission of the Earl of Salisbury.

se my selfe so hardee that I thotee beren sarzant to the gutlest enemye of my prince
Contry: miss: religion: offende: for mane: to make me like them selves, yet
he knoweth I never loved treason no tretchery no never knew of any, no
never heard any mass in england, miss I finde is great alive of the people
so on my parte I understande it not, wherfor I have reformed my self to lyve
according to her matis lawes as I was borne under her highnes: that most
humblye I doe crave perdon, plestinge if her never any abylitie in me, I note
be most to make amende, at Bolona I met in ij men the on named piture an
frenchman, thother named Dvaret, the ar son both to Rome, In prence I hard
an Italyan say that he marveled that king Phillip had never a good
frend in inglande that in his dayes wolde dispatch the quene matis: but say
he god sosserd her in tend to ser her the gretter overthrowe: Right honorable
this have I writtten that her matie may knowe the pristes of the most wicked
prestis & Jesuit & to know of them, I thank god I have bene forsaken them &
their religion miss so selfe to mortimybut supvation or ells I bessege god myght
day to blesse and defend the quene matie & to confonde all her enemies
& to present yor honor & all the rest of her matie most honorabll privie counsell, I think that Stidmore & her cher preste as all in england for he staid not at
florenc as he said he wolde to me & frier Cartin tolde me that he mas son vnto
france to study the lawes of penpe & all along as I com in germany say that
the kinge of spain is making preparation to com for england this next somer,
miss if it please yor honor to advise me of my prote miss I wolde most wislingly
lose my lyfe against them most humbly besechinge yor honor to pdon my ill
writtinge & worse inditinge & to thinke that I desir to serve my Contry &
hope to hear of yor good opinion of me from nomberge this xij of november
1593:

yor honors most bounden

for ever

Jo: Roulande

Contemporary portraits by unknown
artists of (*above*) Robert Devereux
second Earl of Essex, and (*left*) Rober
Cecil, first Earl of Salisbury. By per
mission of the Trustees of the Nationa
Portrait Gallery.

thoughts, except the abundance of them did overflow into overt and express acts or affirmations, tempered her law so as it remaineth only manifest disobedience, in impugning and impeaching advisedly and maliciously her Majesty's supreme power, and maintaining and extolling a foreign jurisdiction.*

As the years passed the increased activities of the English Catholics (largely centred on the person of Mary Queen of Scots), and the influx of seminarists from Douai and Rome, trained to welcome the idea of the martyr's crown, gave cause for growing anxiety and, as it became plain that war with Spain was inevitable, under pressure from her Council, Elizabeth was reluctantly forced to agree to heavy disabilities being placed on those Catholics who refused to conform, but her *personal* attitude remained unchanged:

Parliament met in January, 1581 in some alarm at the success of the missionary priests; and it proceeded to pass an 'act to retain the queen's majesty's subjects in their due obedience' (23 Eliz. C.1). The penalties for recusancy were to be rigidly inforced, and they were enormously increased. Anyone saying mass was to pay 200 marks and suffer a year's imprisonment; anyone hearing it was to pay half that fine, but undergo the same detention; the mere recusant was to forfeit £20 a month; any person or corporation employing a recusant school master was to pay £10 a month . . . Nevertheless, the act did little more than fulfil the usual function of proclamations in frightening the people . . . and the Queen herself was not in earnest. Elizabeth, wrote Leicester, was slow to believe that the great increase of papists was a danger to the realm 'the Lord of his mercy open her eyes'.†

In spite of this repressive legislation the Queen extended her protection to William Byrd from the time he was elected to the Chapel Royal in 1569 until her own death in 1603, although he was a Catholic and was several times prosecuted for recusancy. Her continued favour was shown by the granting to him and Tallis jointly, in 1575, the exclusive licence to print music and music paper. This was never rescinded and eventually Byrd, of his own free will, disposed of the licence to Thomas Morley.

And for Dowland himself, what had he done to qualify for the title of 'obstinate papist'? Unlike the case of Byrd, where the prosecutions for recusancy are fully documented, no trace can be found of any such actions having been brought against him and he himself declares, 'I . . . never heard any mass in England.' (His claim that 'on my soule I understande it not' was surely disingenuous, since on a number of other occasions his knowledge of Latin is conclusively proved.) Furthermore, if he had been known to the

* op. cit., p. 391, quoted from Spedding, *Letters and Life of Francis Bacon*, I, pp. 97–8.

† A. F. Pollard, *The History of England from the Accession of Edward* vi *to the death of Elizabeth* (*1547–1603*), Vol. 6, p. 375, *The Political History of England* (1905), ed. W. Hunt and R. L. Poole.

authorities as a member of the Catholic Church how could he have proceeded to his degree in both universities? Let us look for a minute at the position of Catholics at Oxford:

Although tests were not by statute reimposed, convocation at Oxford, at Leicester's instance, passed decrees, requiring from all undergraduates over 12 years of age, subscription to the articles of 1562, with special stress on the royal supremacy.*

This state of affairs at Oxford is confirmed by J. H. Pollen, S. J. He writes:

The Earl of Leicester, its unworthy chancellor had at first been favourable to Catholics; but after he had gone over to the Calvinists, his vindictiveness towards the ancient faith was signalised, as Anthony à Wood notes, by the increase of Commissioners for Religion, who 'ever and anon, summoned those that smelt of Popery or were Popishly affected, suspending, imprisoning and expelling them'.†

In the very year 1588, when Dowland was admitted Mus.Bac., Anthony à Wood notes:

. . . it was ordered this year 17 January by certain Delegates appointed by Convocation that 1. No scholar should be promoted to the Degree of Bachalaur, nor Bachalaur to Master, unless he can momoriter repeat the Articles of Faith and Religion, and can give a sufficient reason of them . . . before the Vicechancellor for the time being, or Proctors, or Regent Masters.‡

Although J. H. Pollen remarks, 'tests which would seem sufficient to have excluded every single Catholic from the University might occasionally be eluded', it is clear that no Catholic *as a Catholic*, could proceed to a degree at Oxford at this particular time. How was it then that Dowland the 'obstinate papist' was able to elude the tests, unless he kept remarkably quiet about his Romish tendencies?

Within a few years of receiving his degree from Oxford another incident of a puzzling nature took place. At the baptism of Dowland's son Robert, Sir Robert Sidney became the godfather.§ The Sidneys were an unquestionably Protestant family, and Sir Robert would certainly not have assisted at a Catholic baptism which would necessarily have been an illegal and clandestine act. Although Catholics occasionally resorted to Anglican baptism as the only means by which the registration of a birth could be secured, it is hardly likely, even if this course had been adopted, that Sidney would have taken a godfather's vows for the child of parents who were in

---

* *Cambridge History of English Literature*, Vol. 3 (1949), p. 422.
† *English Catholics in the Reign of Queen Elizabeth* (1920), p. 252.
‡ *History and Antiquities of the University of Oxford*, edition of 1796, Vol. 2, Part 1, p. 234.
§ See the Dedication of *A Musicall Banquet*.

the least suspect. It is not known where Dowland was at the time when the christening might be assumed to have taken place, and it could perhaps be argued that he was away and that Mrs. Dowland took the full responsibility. Even so, other incidents followed which throw more doubt on John's devotion to the old faith.

Thomas Est's *Whole Booke of Psalmes,* printed in 1592, was a complete set of four-part harmonizations for the metrical psalter of Sternhold and Hopkins, a book that had become an integral part of Protestant domestic and congregational worship. Nevertheless, in spite of its character, Dowland contributed six items to the collection. Admittedly William Byrd wrote services for the Anglican Church as well as his three Masses, but we find no compensating settings of Catholic liturgy among Dowland's works to offset his apparent conformity in taking part in the production of a work so essentially Protestant in character.

And then later, after his application for a post at Court had been refused, according to his own account, on the grounds of his religion, he tells us 'my mind being troubled, I desired to get beyond the seas'. Instead of seeking asylum in a country where his Catholicism would meet with a sympathetic reception, he proceeds straight to the Court of the Duke of Brunswick, where the Duke himself was of an even more pronounced Protestantism than the sovereign he had left behind. His next host, Maurice, Landgrave of Hesse, was an equally firm adherent of the Protestant cause and eventually became a Calvinist. Yet both these princes welcomed Dowland and treated him with generous hospitality. Had he arrived with the stigma of Catholicism attached to his name it is doubtful whether his welcome would have been so warm.

Furthermore, as he himself remarks, no traveller could legally go abroad without a licence signed by a member of the Privy Council. This control was expressly used to prevent Catholics from passing backwards and forwards between England and the Continent as links between those at home and those abroad who plotted Elizabeth's overthrow. Many slipped through under cover, but many also who tried to travel illegally were apprehended and suffered severely for the attempt. Certainly neither the Earl of Essex nor Sir Robert Cecil would have signed a licence had either suspected Dowland of being a staunch Catholic.

So the odd position is reached where it appears that the Queen gave, as an objection to his suit for a place at Court, a reason that does not seem to agree with her own convictions, a reason, moreover, which is not well founded in the facts of Dowland's life.

Perhaps the answer may be found in Dowland's temperament; as complex and as full of contradictions as the age in which he lived. Immensely self-centred and highly emotional, with a just appreciation of his own powers, but with an almost childishly irritable reaction to criticism; subject from time to time to attacks of melancholy; a man with large ambitions but who, as Peacham said, 'had slipt many opportunities in advancing his fortunes'.* It is more than likely that he had been deeply affected by the colour, the warmth and the emotional appeal of Catholicism—'the idle toys of religion'—during his stay in France; that on his return, when be began to move in the circle of families surrounding Elizabeth, the Cecils, the Sidneys, the Careys and, of course, Essex, he fell in with the generally prevailing Protestant frame of mind and, while moved to horror and indignation by the executions, his Catholicism faded into the background of his mind with the removal of the influences which had first fostered it. Possibly his restlessness was touched into activity by his failure to secure, for whatever reason, the greatly desired post at Court, or again perhaps we may believe him when he says, in the address 'To the Courteous Reader' in *The First Booke of Songes*, that he went abroad to improve his musical qualifications—'the better to attain so excellent a science'—or quite likely both versions are in part true; there would be no inconsistency in that. Whatever the promptings were that sent him abroad on his travels, it must have been an enormous shock when he was brought up against the treasonable activities of the English exiles, so busily plotting the overthrow of Elizabeth. The thought of any rumour of his association with the traitors reaching home must have set him in a fever of anxiety. Most of his patrons would have turned against him on his return to England, even if he escaped imprisonment or worse, and the outlook for his future would indeed have been black. One can imagine the thoughts chasing each other round in his head—the remembered scraps of Court gossip about the reasons for the rejection of his suit; the indiscreet words he may have used in his disappointment—all must have seethed and boiled in his mind, finally exploding into the letter to Cecil in an attempt to justify himself and to reinstate himself by the incriminating details he supplies, should damage have already been done.

An entirely different explanation cannot be entirely ruled out. In the sixteenth century musicians could move about Europe in circumstances exceptionally favourable for carrying on the work of espionage at foreign courts. They could travel on their legitimate business and at the same time pick up scraps of information about the plots and counter-plots with which Europe was seething. Alfonso Ferrabosco the Elder was a notorious spy and Thomas Morley was also involved in the network. It is not impossible that Dowland's departure from England was made easy on the understanding that

* *The Compleat Gentleman* (1622), p. 198.

he kept his eyes and ears open and reported on any suspicious activities that might come to his notice. The sending of Scudamore's letter to Cecil, together with his own, could be taken as support for this interpretation. If Dowland had really been the entirely innocent and guileless character he attempts to present in the letter, would he have sent Scudamore's 'safe conduct' which shows him to have been the very thing that he himself tries to deny? If, however, the gathering of information was a prearranged mission, then Scudamore's letter would be a testimonial to the skill with which the work had been carried out.

The main argument against any more sinister interpretation is, however, the tone of the letter itself, which, with its incoherencies and contradictions, seems to mirror the mind of a man reduced to a state bordering on panic through being entangled in activities that could jeopardize his whole future.

A certain curiosity is provoked as to what became of the lavish payments received from the Duke of Brunswick and the Landgrave of Hesse. Even if he sent part of the money home he must still have run through quite an amount to have been reduced by want to the brink of becoming 'servant to the greatest enemy' of his 'prince, country, wife, children and friends'. Perhaps he was not quite so destitute as he would have had Cecil believe, since he managed to travel as far as Nuremberg before writing his account of the whole unhappy business.

As for the reason behind his failure to secure the post made vacant by John Johnson's death, he may have been the victim of nothing more serious than one of the periodic attempts to reduce expenditure in the Royal Household, for no one was appointed to fill the post until after four years had elapsed. In 1598, on the feast of St. John the Baptist (June 24th), Edward Collard was given the appointment, but no payment was made to him until a Warrant was issued on June 7th, 1599.* After this one entry his name makes no further appearance in the accounts, but whether he died or retired is not known. In the last year of his life, under the heading *Musicians*, Johnson is found in company with Robert Woodward, Augustine Bassano, Mathathias Mason, Robert Hales and Walter Piers.† Except for the one year of Collard's service the five others who served with Johnson continue without any change in their number until 1600,‡ when Robert Woodward vanishes. No one replaces him and the number remains at four until after the Queen's death. Philip Rosseter later takes the place left vacant by the death of Walter Piers, and Robert Johnson replaces Bassano.

* Audit Office Declared Accounts, Bundle 387, No. 37.
† Audit Office Declared Accounts, Bundle 386, No. 32.
‡ Bundle 387, No. 38.

During his absence abroad he was not entirely forgotten by his friends. In 1595 Thomas Campian published a book of Latin verse in which Dowland's fame is celebrated in the following poem:

Ad. Io. Dolandum.

O qui sonora cœlites altos cheli
Mulces, et umbras incolas astræ Stygis,
Quam suave murmur? quale fluctu prominens,
Lygia madentes rore dum siccat comas,
Quam suave murmur flaccidas aures ferit,
Dum lenis oculos leviter invadit sopor?
Ut falce rosa dissecta purpureum caput
Dimittit, undique foliis spargens humum,
Labuntur hei sic debiles somno tori,
Terramque feriunt membra ponderibus suis.
Dolande misero surripis mentem mihi,
Excorsque cordæ pectus impulsæ premunt.
Quis tibi deorum tam potenti numine
Digitos trementes dirigit is inter deos
Magnos oportet principem obtineat locum.
Tu solus offers rebus antiquis fidem,
Nec miror Orpheus confidens Rhodope super
Siquando rupes flexit et agrestes feras.
At O beate siste divinas manus,
Iam iam parumper siste divinas manus,
Liquescit anima, quam cave exugas mihi.*

Whether Dowland returned directly to England from Nuremberg, or whether he thought it more prudent to remain abroad until he could assure himself of a cordial welcome at home, it is impossible to say, but copies of

---

* Thomas Campiani *Poemata* . . . Londini . . . 1595. Sig. Giii, part of 'Epigrammatum liber'. The following translation was made by Professor Benjamin Farrington:

To John Dowland.

O thou, who on the tuneful lyre dost charm the dwellers in high heaven and the shades that inhabit gloomy Styx, how sweet is they strain? How sweet is the strain when Lygia, emerging from the wave, begins to dry her dripping locks and her notes sweetly strike our fainting ears and quiet slumber gently steals over our eyes? As the rose shorn by the knife droops its purple head, shedding its petals on all sides on the ground, even so, alas, my weakening muscles fail and my limbs by their own weight are borne down to the ground. O Doland, unawares thou stealest my poor mind, the strings thou pluckest quite overwhelm my breast. The god who with such divine power directs thy trembling fingers, among the great gods he should hold the leading place. Thou alone hast the power to restore belief in ancient legend. I wonder not that bold Orpheus on Rhodope could move the rocks and the wild creatures. But O thou blest one, stay thy divine hands; now, now, for a moment stay thy divine hands. My soul dissolves, draw it not from me quite.

Lygia, or Lygeia, would mean sweet voiced. She is a nymph in Vergil's *Georgics*. Campian apparently had a mermaid in mind.

The poem was omitted from the *Epigrammatum libri II* of 1619.

letters from Henry Noel and the Landgrave of Hesse make it clear that he returned to the Landgrave's Court some time during 1596 and was still there towards the end of the year.

In August 1596 Lord Hunsdon was sent as Ambassador to the Landgrave and was entertained with great magnificence at his Court. It is possible that Maurice had persuaded Dowland to be present at the time in order to gratify Lord Hunsdon with his playing. There is, however, no proof of this. Edward Monings, in his letter to the Countess of Warwick, makes no mention of Dowland, and it would seem, had he indeed been there, that his presence would have been a matter for remark.

The letter from Henry Noel* is incompletely dated, being subscribed '1 December' only, but that it was written in 1596 can hardly be doubted. It is unlikely to have been written in 1595, since there would scarcely have been time between November 10th when Dowland wrote to Cecil from Nuremberg, and December 1st for him to have returned to Kassel and to have communicated with Noel. By December 1st, 1597, Noel had been dead for the best part of a year.

To Sʳ John Dowland at the Landgraves Courte geve these

John Dowland.
I take well your severall remembrances to me by letters which ere this tyme I wold have answer'd, but for the uncertaintie of your abydinge. Now I understand that you remain in the Landgrave's Courte: a Prince whom I honor for his high renowned vertues, being there desyrous to see him, & have determyned (god willinge) as I passe those partes, with his favor to kisse his hand, if it be not presumption. I wish he knew my desyer to do him service, & where so ere I become, I will with honor and reverence speake and thinke of him. It is reported here of his purpose to see the Queene, I wishe it for the good of eyther, hers to see a Prince without Peere, his to see a Queen without comparison.

You shall not neede to doubt of satisfaction here, for her Maᵗⁱᵉ hath wished divers tymes your return: Ferdinando† hath told me her pleasure twice, which being now certified you, you may therewith answer all objections. Therefore forbeare not longer then other occasions (then your doubts here) do detain you. I have heard of your estimation everywhere, whereof I am

* The MS into which this letter and the one from the Landgrave were copied is now in the Folger Library (MS V.a.321, ff. 52v/53). It contains copies of letters, petitions and other documents dating from about 1580 to 1613. Among them are several letters from Ben Jonson and George Chapman, and it appears to have been written in the early part of the seventeenth century. For a detailed description of the MS, see 'Newly discovered documents of the Elizabethan and Jacobean periods' by Bertram Dobell, in *The Athenæum*, No. 3833, April 13th, 1901. I have to thank Edward Doughtie for showing me this article.

† Possibly Ferdinando Heybourne or Richardson (c. 1559–1618). A pupil of Tallis, and Groom of the Privy Chamber from 1587 to 1611, when he retired with a pension. Eight of his compositions are in the *Fitzwilliam Virginal Book*.

glad, & take that with other parts of your service once to me, for which I will do you all the pleasures I can. I wishe you health & soone return and comytt you to god.

London: 1 December.

Your olde M^r and frend
H. Noel.

On receipt of this letter Dowland must have left the Landgrave and his high hopes as he made his slow journey home can be imagined. But on February 26th, 1596/7, Noel died and with no one to keep his interests alive with the Queen he was once more disappointed. Instead of enjoying the fruits of this friendship he was called upon to provide settings of psalms and canticles for Noel's funeral service in Westminster Abbey.

In addition to supplying the information that Dowland was in the Landgrave's service at this time, Noel's letter helps to fill the gap in our knowledge of the years between his return from France and his second departure from England in 1594. It is clear that some part of this time was spent in Noel's service.

Before these letters had again come to light it had seemed possible that the fine pavan, 'Sir Henry Umpton's Funeral',* had been composed for Unton's burial, and perhaps even that Dowland had taken part in a performance during the ceremonies, but now it appears more likely that Dowland was out of England at the time and that the pavan was a memorial for the dead ambassador and need not necessarily have been in any way connected with the actual interment on July 8th, 1596.

In this same year, 1596, William Barley's *A New Booke of Tabliture* was printed. It contained seven lute solos by Dowland, three in the section for the lute and four in that devoted to music for the orpharion. There can be little doubt that this was the first occasion on which any of his lute music had appeared in print and it is not surprising that his resentment was roused by the inaccuracy of some of the versions used. His protest, in *The First Booke of Songes* (which can hardly refer to any other than Barley's publication), that 'There haue bin diuers Lute-lessons of mine lately printed without my knowledge, falce and vnperfect' is entirely justified. The pity is that he never fulfilled his intention to 'set forth the choicest of all my Lessons in print' thereby correcting some of Barley's errors with authoritative versions.

That he chose the year 1597 in which to publish his first collection probably resulted from the realization that, after the second failure to secure an appointment at Court, his career had reached a critical point, and that some special effort was needed to maintain himself in public favour after his

---

* *Lachrimæ or Seaven Teares* (1604).

absence abroad. The decision to publish songs for this crucial first appearance
may have arisen from the knowledge that he would thereby reach a wider
circle than if he confined himself to solo lute music only. But whether or not
this is a correct interpretation of his motives, he put together twenty-one of
his songs and a galliard 'for two to play vpon one Lute' and published them
in a book which was, musically, to set the fashion for the next twenty-five
years. Although, as Dowland tells us, some of them were already known, the
simultaneous appearance of twenty-one songs of such exceptional beauty
must have made an extraordinary impact and it is little wonder that within
three years another printing was called for, to be followed in 1603, 1606,
1608* and 1613 by further editions.

A few more biographical details may be gathered from the title-page, the
Dedication and the epistle. By this time he had received a degree from Cambridge as well as from Oxford, for he describes himself as 'Lutenist and
Bachelor of musicke in both the Vniuersities'. No information about the
second Mus.Bac. has survived, but there is no reason to doubt his veracity,
since, at that particular time, as we learn from Fuller,† the records were
badly neglected:

$$158\frac{8}{9}$$

Hitherto we have given the List of the yearly Commensers, but now must
break off, let *Thomas Smith* University Register bear the blame, who about
this year entring into his Office, was so negligent, that as one saith, *Cum fuit
Academiæ à memoriâ, omnia tradidit oblivioni*, I can hardly inhold from in-
veighing on his memory, carelessnesse being dishonesty in publick persons so
intrusted.

This state of affairs continued until 1601, when Tabor came into office.

In the epistle 'To the courteous Reader', he repeats many of the facts
about which he had already written privately to Sir Robert Cecil, but here he
gives a totally different reason for his wish to travel, now laying it entirely to
his desire to study and to meet the best musicians of his day, in particular,
Luca Marenzio. Some writers have assumed from the wording of this epistle
that he actually met Marenzio and studied with him, but from the letter to
Cecil it is quite clear that he turned back before he reached Rome, where
Marenzio was living at the time.

The book is dedicated to George Carey, Baron Hunsdon and, amidst the
exaggerated language of conventional flattery, a few sentences of genuine
gratitude towards the Careys are found. He says '. . . your honourable hands

---

* See p. 215.
† *History of the University of Cambridge* (1655), p. 149.

haue vouchsaft to vphold my poore fortunes, which I now wholy recommend to your gratious protection, with these my first endeuors, humbly beseeching you to accept and cherish them with your continued fauors'. Of Lady Hunsdon he says: 'Neither in these your honours may I let passe the dutifull remebrance of your vertuous Lady my honourable mistris, whose singular graces towards me haue added spirit to my vnfortunate labours.' From these phrases it could be deduced that Dowland had been employed by the Hunsdons, or that they had at least given him financial help, possibly during the time he was preparing his songs for publication.

To give a final *cachet* to the book a letter from Luca Marenzio, expressing friendship and admiration for the composer, is quoted in its entirety.

There is no documentary material to show how Dowland was occupied in 1597 after the publication of *The First Booke of Songes*, but on February 9th, 1598, the Landgrave of Hesse, having heard of Henry Noel's death and of Dowland's having again failed to secure the appointment at the English Court, wrote, offering to reinstate him in the post he had left just about a year earlier:

To my loving Frend Mr John Dowland, Bachelor in Musicke:
London.
Mr Dowland, I imagyn'd your departure from me had bene either to serve her Matie, or at least for some other preferment fytt for a man of your worthe: the letter importinge lyttle lesse which cald you home: the which I understand since hath tooke no place, either for want of good frends to prefer you, or by some particular ill hap that many times followes men of vertue, but to the purpose, if you do thinke that the acceptance of my service may any way better your estate, I will assure you that entertainment, that every way you shall hold yourself content; Thus referring you to your best consideration, together with the counsell of your frends; I rest expecting your answere.
                    dated at Zighaine the 9 off February, 1598
                         Maurice the Landgrave of Hessen*

Whether he accepted the invitation from the Landgrave is not known, but the warm and friendly tone of the letter must have afforded Dowland considerable gratification.

Meanwhile his reputation in England was such that during the year he received two literary tributes of some distinction. Firstly Richard Barnfield coupled his name with that of Edmund Spenser in the well-known sonnet:

> If music and sweet poetry agree,
> As they must needs, the sister and the brother,
> Then must the love be great twixt thee and me,
> Because thou lov'st the one, and I the other.

* It is not, of course, known whether this is a translation, but since Maurice had the reputation of being an exceptionally good linguist, probably he wrote in English.

Dowland to thee is dear, whose heavenly touch
Upon the lute doth ravish human sense;
Spenser, to me, whose deep conceit is such
As, passing all conceit, needs no defence . . .
Thou lov'st to hear the sweet melodious sound
That Phoebus' lute, the queen of music, makes:
And I in deep delight am chiefly drowned
When as himself to singing he betakes:
   One god is god of both, as poets feign;
   One knight loves both, and both in thee remain.*

Secondly, his name is included in a list of the most famous English musicians, who are held up as rivals to the Greeks:

As Greece had these excellent Musitians; *Arion, Dorceus, Timotheus Milesius, Chrysognos, Terpander, Lesbius, Simon Magnesius, Philamon, Linus, Strathonicus, Aristonus, Chiron, Achilles, Clinias, Eumonius, Demodochus,* and *Ruffinus*: so Englande hath these; *Maister Cooper, Maister Fairfax, Maister Tallis, Maister Tauerner, Maister Blithman, Maister Bird, Doctor Tie, Doctor Dallis, Doctor Bull, M.Thomas Mud,* sometime fellow of *Pembroke hal* in *Cambridge, M. Edward Iohnson, Maister Blankes, Maister Randall, Maister Philips, Maister Dowland,* and *M. Morley.*†

A few of the reputations have not survived the test of time, but it is, nevertheless, a superb company in which he found himself placed. Furthermore, he had become a figure of sufficient importance in the musical world for fellow musicians to seek his commendation for their works when they presented them to the public, and in this same year he contributed the following somewhat obscure poem to Giles Farnaby's *Canzonets to fowr voyces*:

M. Io. Dowland to the Author.

THOU ONLY SHALT HAVE PHYLLIS,
Only thou fit (without all further gloses)
Crouned to be with euerlasting Roses,
With Roses and with Lillies,
And with Daffadoundillies,
But thy songs sweeter are (saue in their closes)
Then are Lillies and Roses:
Like his that taught the woods sound Amaryllis.
GOLDINGS; you that have too, too dainty NOSES,
Auaunt, go feede you them elswhere on ROSES.

It would seem there must have been a clue that would have made the poem more generally understandable than it appears to be today. There would

---

  * Poems: *In divers humors.* (1598), sig. E.2.
  † *Palladis Tamia*—Wits Treasury. Being the Second part of Wits Commonwealth. By Francis Meres, Master of Arts of both Vniuersities. (1598), p. 288v.

obviously have been no point in printing a verse in commendation of the book and the composer if it were completely unintelligible to the musical public. Even the identification of line 8 with lines 4 and 5 from Vergil's *First Eclogue*:

> tu, Tityre, lentus in umbra
> formosam resonare doces Amaryllida silvas

does not illuminate the meaning of the rest of the poem. There is no meaning of the word 'golding' in the *O.E.D.* or in W. W. Skeat's *Glossary of Tudor and Stuart Words* (1914) that is applicable in this context. A process of somewhat free association suggests the phrase 'go feede you them elsewhere on Roses' may have some allusion to *The Golden Asse* of Lucius Apuleus. William Adlington's translation appeared in 1566 and a knowledge of the adventures that befell Apuleus was widely enough known among the reading public for Nash[*] to write 'such is this golden age wherein we liue, and so replenisht with golden Asses of all sortes . . .' with the certainty that the allusions would be taken by the majority of his readers. Furthermore, one of the 'characters' in *A Wife. Now the Widdow of Sir T. Overburye* (1614), is that of a 'Golden Asse', a young man with more money than brains. Could the meaning of the last couplet then be, that any dainty young man with more money than ability to appreciate Farnaby's canzonets should feed on roses and be changed from the shape of an ass to that of a man?

For Dowland, however, the outstanding event of the year 1598 was his appointment as lutenist at the Court of Christian IV of Denmark, at the exceptionally generous salary of 500 daler a year which, according to A. Hammerich-Elling,[†] was equal to that of an admiral and more than that of a colonel.

Christian was an enthusiastic and discriminating patron of music, and his Court was graced with a number of distinguished musicians although, curiously, there was no indigenous school of lutenist composers of any importance. He was an ardent builder and Copenhagen and other Danish cities were adorned with new palaces built during his reign. But life at the Danish Court, reflecting as it did the personality of the ruler, was very different from that which Dowland knew at home. Although not enjoying a Court appointment, he would have been familiar with the tenor of life in the Royal household, its manners and customs, and with the austerity of certain aspects of Elizabeth's character. Her abstemiousness in eating and drinking were matter for comment, and even those of her circle who drank heavily, in her

---

[*] *Syr P.S. His Astrophel and Stella* (1591) in 'Somewhat to reade for them *that list*'. Sig. 4v.
[†] *Musiken ved Christian den Fjerdes Hof* (1892), p. 22.

presence found it politic to remain sober. In Denmark things were very different. When Shakespeare makes Hamlet speak the following lines he is merely describing conditions that were known to exist at Christian's Court:

> This heavy-headed revel east and west
> Makes us traduced and tax'd of other nations;
> They clepe us drunkards, and with swinish phrase
> Soil our addiction; and indeed it takes
> From our achievement, though performed at height,
> The pith and marrow of our attribute.

In short, His High and Mighty Majesty was frequently dead drunk.

The following letter from Sir John Harington to Mr. Secretary Barlow, written after a banquet at Theobalds given by his brother-in-law James I, during Christian's State visit to England in 1606, describes the kind of social atmosphere that his Danish Majesty apparently created round him. Sir John was obviously making a good story out of the whole disastrous affair, but what he says is amply borne out by other letters and documents of the time. They differ only in displaying less wit than Sir John:

My good Friend,
In compliance with your asking, now shall you accept my poor account of rich doings. I came here a day or two before the Danish King came, and from the day he did come untill this hour, I have been well nigh over-whelmed with carousel and sports of all kinds. The sports began each day in such manner and such sorte, as well nigh persuaded me of Mahomet's paradise. We had women, and indeed wine too, of such plenty as would have astonished each sober beholder. Our feasts were magnificent, and the two Royal guests did most lovingly embrace each other at table; I think the Dane hath strangely wrought on our good English Nobles, for those, whom I never coud get to taste good liquor, now follow the fashion and wallow in beastly delights. The Ladies abandon their sobriety, and are seen to roll about in intoxication. In good sooth, the Parliament did kindly to provide his Majestie so seasonably with money;* for there hath been no lack of good livinge; shews, sights, and banquetings from morn to eve. One day a great feast was held, and after dinner the representation of Solomon his Temple and the coming of the Queen of Sheba was made, or, as I may better say, was meant to have been made, before their Majesties, by device of the Earl of Salisbury and others.—But, alas! as all earthly thinges do fail to poor mortals in enjoyment, so did prove our presentment hereof. The Lady who did play the Queens part did carry most precious gifts to both their Majesties; but, forgetting the steppes arising to the canopy, overset her caskets into his Danish Majesties lap, and fell at his feet, tho I rather think it was in his face. Much was the hurry and confusion; cloths and napkins were at hand to make

---

* The subsidy provided by Parliament to the King after the exposure of the Gun Powder Plot.

all clean. His Majesty then got up and woud dance with the Queen of Sheba;
but he fell down and humbled himself before her, and was carried to an inner
chamber and laid on a bed of state; which was not a little defiled with the
presents of the Queen which had been bestowed on his garments; such as
wine, cream, jelly, beverage, cakes, spices, and other good matters. The
entertainment and shew went forward and most of the presenters went
backward, or fell down, wine did so occupy their upper chambers. Now
did appear in rich dress, Hope, Faith, and Charity: Hope did assay to speak,
but wine rendered her endeavours so feeble that she withdrew, and hoped
the King would excuse her brevity. Faith was then all alone, for I am certain
she was not joyned with good works; and left the Court in a staggering condition. Charity came to the Kings feet, and seemed to cover the multitude
of sins her sisters had committed: In some sorte she made obeysance and
brought giftes, but said she woud return home again, as there was no gift
which Heaven had not already given his Majesty; she then returned to Hope
and Faith, who were both sick and spewing in the lower hall. Next came
Victory, in bright armour, and presented a rich sword to the King, who did
not accept it, but put it by with his hand; and, by a strange medley of versi-
fication, did endeavour to make suit to the King; but Victory did not try-
umph for long, for, after much lamentable utterance, she was led away like a
silly captive, and laid to sleep in the outer steps of the anti-chamber. Now did
Peace make entry, and strive to get foremoste to the King; but I grieve to
tell how great wrath she did discover unto those of her attendants, and, much
contrary to her own semblance, most rudely made war with her olive branch,
and laid on the pates of those who did oppose her coming. I have much
marvelled at these strange pageantries, and they do bring to my remembrance
what passed of this sort in our Queens days; of which I was sometime an
humble presenter and assistant; but I neer did see such lack of good order,
discretion, and sobreity, as I have now done. . . .*

Dowland would have encountered heavy drinking both at Wolfenbüttel
and Kassel as well as at the Danish Court, but he has left no comment on
how this affected him. Squeamishness was not a dominant note in the Elizabethan or Jacobean character and possibly the rough-and-tumble of this kind
of life passed him by, or he may even have found it congenial. It would be
tempting to suggest that perhaps he too fell into the habit of excessive drinking
and that this was one of the contributory causes of the financial difficulties
which he later met with, but there is insufficient evidence for such a theory to
be put forward with any seriousness.

The appointment in Denmark should have been a lucrative one even if it
did not fulfil Dowland's highest ambition. At first all went well, but in 1601
things began to go wrong and from then onwards it is an unhappy tale of
wages drawn in advance, leave overstayed and final dismissal. Brief as are

---

* Sir John Harington, *Nugæ Antiguæ* (1779), pp. 133, 134, 135.

the entries in the palace accounts they tell us much, and so they are given here in full.

RENTEMESTERREGNSKAB (Accounts of the Comptroller)
1/5 1599–1/5 1600

fol. 474. b.   On July 16th His Majesty has most graciously engaged Johann Doulande as lutenist in the service of his Majesty, and his Majesty will pay him 500 Daler a year, of which a copy is made dated Fredericksborg, November 18th, 1598. On August 18th the above-mentioned Johannes Doulanndtt, the lutenist, received 100 Daler of his yearly pay up till November 18th, 1599.

The lack of clarity in the phraseology makes the actual date of his engagement a little uncertain. Possibly the interval between July 16th and November 18th is accounted for by the interchange of letters and the journey, and possibly the contract was not signed until November 18th after his arrival in Denmark. The fact that each year's employment was counted from that date adds to the likelihood of this being the explanation.

Meanwhile another friend in England sought a commendatory poem for his work and the following verse was sent back to Richard Allison for inclusion in *The Psalmes of David in Meter* printed in 1599:

> Iohn Dowland Bacheler of Musicke in commendation of
> *Richard Allison, and this most excellent work*
>
> If Musicks Arte be sacred and Diuine,
> And holy Psalmes a subject more Diuine:
> If the great Prophet did the words compile,
> And our rare Artist did these smooth notes file,
> Then I pronounce in reason and in loue,
> That both combinde, this most Diuine must proue,
> And this dear friend I recommend to thee
> Of thine owne worth a proued veritie:
> Whose high desert doth rather vrge me still
> To shew my weaknes, then to want good-will.

But to return to the Comptroller's Accounts for 1599–1600:

fol. 476 a & b   On November 30th Johannes Doulandt, the lutenist, received his pay of 100 Daler, and according to his Majesty has had all that was due to him from November 18th, 1598 until November 18th, 1599, according to his employment. And on August 18th, 1599 he has already received 100 Daler of his pay from his Majesty's Comptroller. On behalf of his Majesty Harmen Rolsse too, a grocer in Elsinore, has paid Johannes Doulandt 200 Daler of his pay and so he has had his pay for the previous year according to the contract. On February 20th Johannes

Doulannt, the lutenist, received 125 Daler which is his pay for three months from February 18th until May 18th, 1600.

1/5 1600—1/5 1601

fol. 529. b.   On May 30th Mester Johannes Doulandt, his Majesty's lutenist received 125 Daler which is his pay for three months from February 18th until May 18th, 1600.

At about this time Dowland completed his *Second Booke of Songs* and sent the manuscript home to his wife with the dedication dated 'From Helsingnoure in Denmarke the first of June 1600.' Mrs. Dowland sold the manuscript to George Eastland for £20 and half the reward which was expected from Lucy Countess of Bedford for the dedication.★

During this same year *The First Booke of Songes* was reprinted with a certain number of corrections to the text.

On July 28th, 1600, Dowland signed the following receipt for the sum of 600 Daler, paid to him over and above his yearly salary:

I, Master Johannes Dowland, his Royal Majesty's Lutenist, hereby declare that I, from the honest and most honourable man Christopher Walkendorff till Glanup, by order from the Treasurer of the Danish realm and by decree, have received and accepted from the right honest and most honourable men Eenvold till Hiermitzsloffegaard, and Siuert Bech till Føerblouff, his Royal Majesty's treasurers, six hundred old Daler which his Royal Majesty's right honourable treasurers most mercyfully have hereby given to me, and as a receipt have I signed this document with my own hand.

Actum Kiøbenhaffenn. The
28 July anno 1600
Jo: dowlande

It can be seen that it is not precisely stated that this sum was a gift from the King. Had it been, it could be taken as a remarkable act of favour from him, but I think the possibility cannot be discounted that it was a grant mercifully given Dowland to pay off already contracted debts. It seems unlikely that a receipt would have been demanded for an unsolicited gift, whereas if money had been paid over for the specific purpose of relieving him from some financial embarrassment a receipt would certainly have been required. Some support for this interpretation may be found in the words that accompany the entry of the advance made to him on June 6th, 1601, 'which he will have to work for', as if the thought were in the mind of the treasurer 'He won't get it for nothing this time'.

Meanwhile the regular payments at three-monthly intervals continue into the year 1601:

★ For details of the publication of *The Second Booke* and the litigation in which Eastland involved himself, see p. 244.

fol. 530. a. On August 31st Johannes Dowlandt, his Majesty's lutenist, received 125 Daler which is his pay for three months from May 18th until August 18th, 1600.

fol. 532. b. On November 27th Mester Johannes Doulanndt, his Majesty's lutenist received 125 Daler which is his pay for three months from August 18th until November 18th 1600.

On February 24th Mester Johannes Doulanndt, his Majesty's lutenist, received 125 Daler which is his pay for three months from November 18th, 1600 until February 18th, 1601.

Here we must break off from the Comptroller's Accounts to look at another document 'Siellandske Tegnelse' 1596–1604 (XIX), where the following entry is found:

fol. 326. b. The excisemen had a letter saying that they would have back the 300 Daler which they paid Dulandt as he was to buy several instruments in England at his Majesty's command.
Cronneborg 5 Fbris aọ 1601.

The exact date of this journey to England is not known; it must have been a fairly short visit, as there is no significant gap in the regular payments made to Dowland in Denmark.

The Comptroller's Accounts continue from 1/5 1601 to 1/5 1602, and for the first time there are definite signs of trouble:

fol. 711. a. On May 19th Johannes Dowlant, his Majesty's lutenist, received 125 Daler which is his pay for three months from February 18th until May 18th, 1601, which make 500 Daler a year.

On June 6th Johannes Dowlannd, his Majesty's lutenist, received 250 Daler which is his pay for six months from May 18th until November 18th, 1601.

His Majesty most graciously advanced him the money which he will have to work for.

He was still, however in high favour with the King, for it is recorded that he was presented by Christian, at this time, with a 'portrait of his Royal Majesty in crown gold'.★

The Comptroller's Accounts continue the story for the year 1602 to 1603:

fol. 978. b. On June 19th Mester Johannes Duland, his Majesty's lutenist, received 250 Daler which is his pay for six months from November 18th, 1601, until May 18th, 1602.

fol. 979. a. On September 4th Mester Johannes Dowlannd, the royal lutenist, received 125 Daler which is his pay for three months from May 18th until August 18th, 1602.

fol. 982. b. On November 19th Mester Johannes Dowlannd, the royal

---

★ Bildag til Rentemesterregnskaber, 1601–1602. Expenditure Account No. 7.

lutenist, received 125 Daler which is his pay from August 18th until November 18th, 1602. On February 19th Mester Johannes Dowlannd, the royal lutenist received 125 Daler which is his pay for three months from November 18th, 1602, until February 18th, 1603.

As the following entry in 'Siellandske Tegnelse' shows, Dowland was not the only English musician to bedevil the lives of the Danish Court officials:

fol. 379. a.　　Henning Gióe, the knight marshal, had a letter concerning several orders, as follows . . .

Christianus 4

As we want the English lutenist and the dancer dismissed, their contract being up, we ask you to dismiss them and give them the pay which Dulant promised them in England, but you should keep the harp for which we have paid.

As we have learnt that the English musicians who ran away have left an instrument and a viola da gamba at Hermandt Rosse in Elsinore we ask you to appropriate them if they are still there, so that we may have some compensation for the money they ran away with.

Actum den 24 Septembris
a⁰ 1602

Hammerich-Elling* gives the names of the two performers mentioned in the first paragraph as 'Carolus Oralli the harper and Henrik Sandon (Sandam) the dancing master'. The two English musicians who ran away were John Maynard and Daniel Norcombe.† Possibly Dowland was responsible for bringing all four to Denmark.

After the payment made to Dowland on February 19th, 1603, there are no further entries for seventeen months. From the next entry we learn that he had returned to England on leave 'on his own commitments'. One of these commitments was the printing of *The Third and Last Booke of Songs*. This was entered in the *Stationers' Register* on February 21st, and, allowing for the ten days' difference between the Danish and the English calendars, Dowland would have just about had time to make the journey and place the MS with the printer, and for the printer to have obtained the licence to print by the latter date.

Of the songs in this book, two, 'Time stands still with gazing on her face' and 'Say loue if euer thou didst finde', are settings of words that are exag-

---

* op. cit., p. 23.

† See *Grove's Dictionary of Music and Musicians*, 5th edition (1954). Maynard was a singer and composer of *The XII Wonders of the World* (1611). Norcombe was a noted player of the bass viol and composed a number of divisions for that instrument. They fled from Denmark to Venice through Germany and Hungary.

geratedly complimentary to the aged Queen. A third, 'When Phoebus first did Daphne loue', was adapted to convey similar sentiments. Did Dowland, one wonders, hope, by touching Elizabeth's vanity to secure at last the long-sought-after post? If this thought were in his mind, he was again doomed to disappointment, since she died on March 24th, and all hopes of entering her service were for ever ended. If, however, the Queen had lived to see the book, from the point of view of advancing his fortunes Dowland had committed an extraordinary error. As well as the complimentary songs to the Queen, he had also included a setting of 'It was a time when silly bees', the words of which constitute a bitter attack on Court life and, though considerably wrapped up in allegory, on the Queen herself; the poem, most authorities agree, having been written by the Earl of Essex. It is impossible to imagine what impulse betrayed Dowland into such an error of judgement.

There would have been some delay between the date of registration and the publication of the book, and it would be of great interest to know more of the history of this volume. In 1603 London suffered one of the worst visitations of the plague among those of which the figures have been recorded. This epidemic and that of 1625 were only overshadowed in horror by the so-called 'great' plague of 1665. The Court and everyone who could possibly do so left London, even to the less conscientious among the personnel of the administrative and medical services whose charge was the care of the victims. Trade was brought to a standstill and the ceremonies designed for the coronation of James I on July 25th were greatly curtailed, access to Westminster being barred to Londoners both by road and water. The deaths by plague recorded in the Bills of Mortality mounted week by week, culminating in a total of 3,035 for the week from August 25th to September 1st. It is estimated that something like one-sixth of the population of London perished in that single year.*

Perhaps the printing was complete before the beginning of May when the number of deaths from plague began to give cause for alarm. During the summer months, while the pestilence was at its height, there could have been little sale for the book among the remains of the population left in the stricken town. The printer of this volume, Peter Short, himself died during this year, whether from plague or not is not recorded, but that *The Third and Last Booke* was printed before the third edition of *The First Booke*, also dated 1603, is shown by the fact that the title-page of the latter bears the imprint of E. Short, his widow.

And where was Dowland himself during this year? Did he remain in London, or did he remove to comparative safety elsewhere? A hint, but one

* F. P. Wilson, *The Plague in Shakespeare's London* (1927; Oxford Paperbacks, 1963).

on which no great reliance can be placed, may perhaps be drawn from the *Album Amicorum* of Johannes Cellarius of Nuremberg, in which Dowland wrote a musical point★ and signed himself 'Jo: dolandi de Lachrimæ his own hande'. This could not have been written during Dowland's first visit to Nuremberg in 1595, since Cellarius did not begin his volume until 1599.† Dowland, unfortunately, added no date to his contribution, but it does occur in a small group belonging to the year 1603. The drawings, signatures and devices that carry dates run, as a whole, in a fair degree of chronological order, but since there are a few that have been entered out of sequence it is impossible to make an unanswerable case from the position of any one item in the book. It may have been pure chance that led Dowland to place his among others for the year 1603, but the fact that he did so does at least raise the question of whether he returned to the Continent in the spring or early summer of that year and visited Cellarius in Nuremberg or met him in some other city.

That Dowland was back in England by the end of September (if indeed he had been abroad at all at this time) is certain. In *Lachrimæ or Seaven Teares,* which appeared in 1604, he says he 'had access' to the Queen at Winchester. The date of this meeting between Dowland and the sister of his Danish master can be gathered from Nichols, who records:

(1603) . . . The King arrived at Winchester on the 20th September; and with the Queen (who went there two days before him) was received by the Mayor and Corporation with great solemnity . . .
. . . The King continued at Winchester till the 4th of October . . .‡

It seems likely, therefore, that the meeting took place between September 18th and October 4th, the occasion almost certainly being the performance of a masque presented at the Queen's command.

The long gossipy letters of the period are a wonderful source of information about the doings of the Royal family, and it is from one of these, dated 'From Winchester, the 17th of October, 1603' that we hear of the masque having taken place:

. . . the Queen did the Prince the kindnes at his coming hither to entertayne him with a gallant masque. . . .§

Probably Dowland was summoned to Winchester to take part in the music for the masque, possibly even to provide some of the songs, but since no

★ Not a few bars of 'Lachrimæ', as stated by W. Barclay Squire in the *D.N.B.*
† This date is stamped into the leather binding and no entries of an earlier date are found.
‡ *The Progresses etc. of King James I*, Vol. 1 (1828), pp. 274 and 278.
§ From a letter from Sir Thomas Edmonds to the Earl of Shrewsbury, printed in Edmund Lodge, *Illustrations to British History* (1791), Vol. III, p. 202.

details of the subject of the entertainment have survived it is impossible to say whether any of the later published songs were written for the occasion. He may also have seized the opportunity to solicit the Queen for preferment at the English Court.

We hear just one more comment; it appears that censorious tongues were busy with the reputation of the Queen and her ladies:

(1603) . . . now there was much talk of a masque the Queen had had at *Winchester* and how all the ladies about the Court had gotten such ill names that it had grown a scandalous place, and the Queen herself was much fallen from her former greatness and reputation she had in the world.*

That Dowland's name was a household word at this time is shown in the diary and commonplace book of the amateur musician, John Ramsey, in whose opinion Dowland was 'an excellent Musitian', as he says in his list of 'Gentlemen' of 1603.† Ramsey also wrote a set of instructions to his wife on the education of their son in the event of Ramsey's own death. Among other things he says the boy, from seven to ten, should be taught to play on the lute and 'sing to it with the Dytte'.‡ For this purpose he recommends 'Dow-lands bookes',§ three at least of which were in his library.

During the time he spent in England Dowland gave 'their last foile and polishment' to the contents of *Lachrimæ or Seaven Teares*, and the volume was issued with a dedication to the Queen. In the epistle, 'To the Reader', Dow-land says: 'Hauing in forren parts met diuers Lute-lessons of my composition, publisht by strangers without my name or approbation; I thought it much more conuenient, that my labours should passe forth vnder mine owne allow-ance.' Of the Continental lute books that appeared before this date, containing examples of his work, that still survive, are Johannes Rude's *Flores Musicæ* (Heidelberg, 1598), Joachim van den Hove's *Florida* (Ultrajecti, 1601) and J. B. Besard's *Thesaurus Harmonicus* (Cologne, 1603). Besard was a little more scrupulous in acknowledging Dowland's authorship, but this courtesy is offset by the inexactitude of his versions. Antoine Francisque had also appropriated 'Piper's Galliard', with an extremely free setting in *Le Trésor d'Orphée* (Paris, 1600).

In *Lachrimæ or Seaven Teares*, for the first time, the house in Fetter Lane is mentioned, and it seems likely that he acquired it during this visit to England.¶ He attributes the length of his stay in England to 'contrary windes and frost'

* *The Diary of Lady Anne Clifford*, edited V. Sackville West (1923), p. 16.
† Bod. Douce 280, f. 103v.
‡ op. cit., p. 90v.
§ op. cit., p. 120.
¶ Since no Poor Rate Books covering this period have survived for the parish of St. Dunstan-in-the-West, it is impossible to confirm the date of his first occupying the house.

which on two occasions 'forst backe' the boat and prevented his return to Denmark. *Lachrimæ or Seaven Teares* was entered in the Stationers' Register on April 2nd, 1604, and it seems unlikely that he left before then. Possibly his departure was even later since the first payment made to him on his return to Denmark was a year's salary in arrears paid on July 10th. The entry appears in the Comptroller's Accounts, 1/5, 1604–1/5, 1605:

fol. 590. b.   On July 10th m. Johannes Dowlanndt, the Royal lutenist, received 500 Daler which is his pay for 12 months from August 18th 1603 until August 18th 1604, provided that his Majesty most graciously will grant him the money, as he has been in England on his own commitments, and much longer than his Majesty had most graciously allowed him to be, and if his Majesty will not grant him the agreed pay he will have to account for it to his Majesty.

Payment is next made to him on the usual day, when a further three months' salary became due:

fol. 593. a.   On November 19th Johannes Dowlanndt, the lutenist, received 125 Daler which is his pay for three months from August 18th to November 18th, 1604.

After that there is a significant gap of three months when there is no record of his having been paid. Possibly it was withheld against some of the time spent in absence without leave.

fol. 595. a.   On April 30th m. Johannes Dowlandt, the lutenist, received 125 Daler which is his pay for three months from February 18th until May 18th, 1605.

From now onwards the situation becomes desperate; the Accounts from 1/5 1605 to 1/5 1606 show irregularities of all kinds:

fol. 532. b.   On July 9th M. Johannes Dowlandt, his Majesty's lutenist, received 375 Daler which his Majesty most graciously advanced him, and it is his pay for 9 months from May 18th, 1605, until February 18th, 1606.

An entry in another set of accounts* dated October 10th only, shows that the King, possibly with the intention of giving him further financial help, had placed one of the boy singers of the Chapel, Hans Borckratz, in his care to be taught to play the lute. For care and tuition Dowland was to receive an extra 100 Daler a year. That this was in 1605 may be deduced from the final entry in the Comptroller's Accounts where the failure of this arrangement is included among all the other troubles that fell upon the official head:

* *Kancelliets Brevbørger* (1885–1915), Vol. for 1603–1608. Sj.R.15. 65.b.

fol. 535. a.   On November 2nd on behalf on his Majesty Breide Randzow til Ranndzhollen, a governor and an honourable man, has advanced m. Johannes Dowlandt, his Majesty' lutenist, 20 Daler out of his pay for the next year from February 18th and for some time later which will be deducted from his pay.

fol. 536. b.   On March 10th Johannes Dowlandt, his Majesty's lutenist, received 8 Daler and 9½ Skilling which is his present pay for 6 days from February 18th until February 24th 1606, and—he has been discharged—38 Daler, 2 Skilling, 4 Pendinge which he is due to have for lessons and support of the boy whom his Majesty most graciously had given into his charge for four-and-a-half months and two days from October 10th until February 24th which is 100 Daler a year; further 32 Daler and 12 Skilling which he is due to have for lute strings and for the above mentioned boy whom he supported and taught according to the report of Henning Góie, the Knight Marshall. And so he received 20 Daler from Breide Randzow, a governor and an honourable man who paid him on November 2nd on behalf of his Majesty.

According to his own report and the enclosed signed paper, at different times he received 74 Daler, 15 Skilling from Hans Simennssen, a clerk in the same place.

And so he has had his agreed pay which is 500 Daler a year according to the appointment which has now been handed over to his Majesty's Comptroller together with the position which his Majesty most graciously granted him as a teacher of the above mentioned boy.

Nothing is known of what crisis led to this state of affairs; whether it was financial troubles alone that caused his dismissal or whether some other unsatisfactory conduct had exacerbated the situation is not clear. The note of the agreement, drawn up on October 10th, for the care and training of the chorister Hans Borcratz speaks of 100 Daler a year, so presumably the arrangement was visualized as lasting some time, and yet the boy was taken from his care after four and a half months and two days. Could it have been on account of some complaint from the boy of Dowland's treatment of him? This seems unlikely, since the report from Henning Gióe confirms that the support and tuition had been given. Furthermore, it is not entirely clear from whom the dismissal had actually come. Hammerich-Elling[*] says the King was away on a visit to the Duke of Brunswick at the time, but I have been unable to verify the date on which the visit began. When the accounts were made up on March 10th, Dowland had already been given notice to leave, so it remains uncertain whether the action was taken by the King him-

[*] op. cit., p. 23.

self before his departure, or whether the Court officials seized the opportunity
to get rid of a troublesome employee during the absence of their Royal
master.

During Dowland's absence abroad the family continued to occupy the
house in Fetter Lane, since the translation of the *Micrologus* of Ornithoparcus,
printed in 1609, was addressed from there. From the Dedication in *Varietie of
Lute-Lessons* we learn from Robert Dowland that, while his father was away,
he received part of his education in the household of Sir Thomas Monson, a
prominent courtier and a great amateur of music. Sir Thomas prided himself
on his musical establishment, especially on the quality of his singers, and the
training the young Robert received would undoubtedly have been primarily in the art of music.

After Dowland's return from Denmark the earliest source of information
comes in his own prefatory matter to the *Micrologus*. The work is dedicated
to Robert Cecil, by now Earl of Salisbury, in language extravagantly flatter-
ing even for an age in which adulation was a recognized means to the notice
and favour of the powerful. In this dedication he mentions a 'future taske,
more new in subiect' which he will be encouraged to complete should the
present work be favourably received by the Earl of Salisbury. He enlarges on
this in the epistle 'To the Reader' and announces that 'being now returned
home to remain' he intends 'shortly to diuulge a more peculiar worke of
mine owne: namely My *Observations and Directions concerning the Art of Lute-
playing* . . . which is 'already almost ready for Harvest'. That he was being a
little more than optimistic in thus announcing the imminent appearance of
his own book seems clear. Had the *Observations and Directions* been complete
there would have been no reason why the *Necessarie Observations belonging to
the Lute and Lute playing* by Besardus should, a year later, have been included
in *Varietie of Lute-Lessons*, particularly in view of his opinion, stated in the
Micrologus, that 'the true nature of fingering . . . hath as yet by no writer been
rightly expressed'. The conclusion seems unavoidable that his own treatise
had progressed no further than the *Other Necessary Obseruations* that follow
those of Besardus. These consist of no more than four short sections—*For
Chusing Lute-Strings; Of setting the right sizes of Strings vpon the Lute; Of fretting
the Lute;* and *Of tuning the Lute*. Together they might well form the introductory chapter to a full-length study of lute technique.

It seems highly probable that the project of publishing a set of instructions for the lute was identical with his intention, first expressed in 1597, of
setting forth in print the best of his lute lessons. In England all the books of
solo lute music that survive from this period have in fact taken the form of an
instruction followed by 'lessons'—Le Roy with his own instruction; Barley

with an unacknowledged version of Le Roy's instruction; Thomas Robinson with his own instruction; and *Varietie of Lute-Lessons* with the Observations of both Besardus and Dowland—and he may well have intended to adopt a similar make-up for his own book. When provoked by Barley's incorrect versions in 1596, and again in 1604, when he complains of foreign publications that have appropriated his work from poor copies, the natural answer would have been to issue authoritative texts, yet on neither occasion did he do so. The amount of work that he prepared for the press during his life shows that it was not lack of application that prevented the completion of this project, nor was it the lack of ability to express himself easily in words, and it would seem there must have been some deep-seated, perhaps even unconscious, reluctance to 'divulge' in print the best of his solo compositions and the secrets of the technical mastery with which he played them. These composi-tions, growing out of his own performance, perhaps even improvisatory at times, must have been intensely personal to him, probably even more per-sonal than the songs since, as later discussion will suggest, he was no singer, and he may have found it impossible to do more than prepare for publica-tion the nine pieces that were subsequently printed in *Varietie of Lute-Lessons*, and those he included in the song books.

Some authors, writing about Dowland in recent years, have painted a very black picture of his life after his return to England in 1606. For example Wilfrid Mellers★ says: 'The years that followed his return [from Denmark] were not easy ones for him'; 'his material circumstances did not noticeably prosper'; 'he eked out a somewhat obscure existence as lutenist to several noble house-holds'. These opinions are based primarily on the epistle, 'To the Reader', in his fourth book of songs, *A Pilgrimes Solace*, printed in 1612, when he was lutenist to Lord Howard de Walden. To accept all that Dowland says at its face value is to leave out of account certain aspects of his characeter. Let us look at his complaints, compare them with such facts as can be stated with certainty, and see whether the result adds up to the pathetic picture of him-self that he obviously wished to convey.

Firstly he says: 'I have lien long obscured from your sight because I receiued a Kingly entertainment in a forraine climate, which could not attaine to any (though neuer so meane) place at home.' These words are surely written in the sense of an explanation why he accepted an appointment abroad and refer to the old grievance, his failure to secure a post at Elizabeth's Court. As he was actually in the employment of Lord Walden when he wrote this address he could hardly maintain that he was unable to secure employment on his return, although there was certainly some delay before he attained this

★ 'John Dowland' in *The Music Masters* (1948).

post. Employment with the illustrious family of Howard, to most musicians of the time would have been far from contemptible and if to Dowland it failed to present a satisfying prospect for his declining years, the cause of his discontent must be sought in his own constant and unresting ambition that could be appeased only by employment in the Royal household, rather than in any real obscurity or mean condition of his patron.

Theophilus, second Lord Howard de Walden, was the son of Thomas Howard, the Lord Treasurer, created Earl of Suffolk by James I in 1603. On his elevation to the peerage, the Earl thought the old house at Walden insufficiently imposing for the dignity of his state and office and in the same year he commenced to build the impressive mansion of Audley End.* The magnificence of the style of living he felt to be due to him may be judged by the enormous expenditure lavished on this house. Contemporary estimates give the sum as somewhere in the region of £200,000.†

Sir Anthony Weldon, in *Aulicus Cocquinariæ* (1650), has a story that Henry Howard, Earl of Northampton, having built a fine house near Charing Cross, called Northampton House, presented it to his nephew, Lord Howard de Walden, as a New Year's gift. Later it became known as Suffolk House. Weldon omits to give the date on which this magnificent gift was made, but as Northampton died in 1616 it was probably made, if made at all, early enough for Dowland to have spent some part of his time there, during his service with Theophilus. But whether or not Lord Walden lived at Northampton (or Suffolk) House at this time it is clear from contemporary accounts of the prominent part he played in Court activities that his principal residence was in London and not in the country.‡ As lutenist to a courtier who enjoyed a very adequate share of Royal favour Dowland would almost certainly have been known and often heard in Court circles.

If then he was not buried in the country, eating his heart out in obscurity, but was in fact serving a prominent courtier and probably living in close proximity to the Court, is there any evidence to suggest that his dissatisfaction arose from a decline in the popularity of his music among the general public during his absence abroad and in the years immediately following his return? The facts do not seem to support this supposition. Certainly from the

---

* Dr. Fellowes, in the preface to his edition of *A Pilgrimes Solace*, notes that no papers relating to Dowland's employment were found among the records at Audley End. William Addison, in *Audley End* (1953) shows that the house was not completed until 1616, which makes the absence understandable.

† In 1617 the Earl was removed from office and charged with embezzlement. He was imprisoned and the fines which were imposed appreciably reduced the Howard fortune, but these calamities did not overtake the family until after Dowland was safely installed at the Court of James I.

‡ For further information about his life see p. 410.

date of his departure in 1598 he continued to have his works published with considerable regularity, and, although 'obscured from the sight of his country-men' for most of the time during his eight years at the Danish Court, his music continued to sound in their ears with a reassuring persistence. In addition to the works already mentioned that had appeared during his stay in Denmark, the fourth printing of *The First Booke* appeared in 1606, and another almost certainly in 1608; between 1609 and 1612 four major works were published for which he was solely responsible or in the preparation of which he played some major part: *Andrew Ornithoparcus his Micrologus* (1609), *Varietie of Lute-Lessons* and *A Musicall Banquet* in 1610, and *A Pilgrimes Solace* (1612). His solo lute music continued in the repertoire of advanced players, as its presence in the manuscript collections in use during these years testi-fies. His most famous pieces were arranged by Byrd, Morley, Farnaby, Bull, Robinson and other composers, for viols, broken consort, virginals and cittern, while his fellow lutenists such as Bacheler and Cutting wrote their own divi-sions on his strains; early arrangements continued in use and new ones were made. His songs continued to find their way into MS collections until a number of years after his death, and in the year following the appearance of *A Pilgrimes Solace, The First Booke of Songs* was again reprinted.

Both during his stay in Denmark and in the years following his return he was not forgotten by the play-wrights, whose work, whether for private performance at Court or in the public theatres, was always a good sounding-board for public taste. In the anonymous *Second Part of the Return from Parnassus*,★ probably first produced at Christmas 1601–2, the following dialogue occurs in Act V, Sc. 2:

Amoretto's page	Good fayth this pleaseth my sweete mistres admirably: cannot you play *Twitty twitty twatty foole*, or *To be at her, to be at her?*
Sir Raderick's page	Haue you neuer a song of maister *Dowlands* making?

In the following plays lines from his songs are quoted, or reference is made by name to one of his compositions:†
Chapman, Jonson and Marston, *Eastward Hoe* (1605); Anon., *Every Woman in her humour* (1609); Beaumont and Fletcher, *The Knight of the Burning Pestle* (three references). After his appointment to the Court in 1612 the references still continue: Thomas Middleton, *No Wit no Help like a Woman* (1613); John Fletcher, *The Bloody Brother* (1617); Philip Massinger, *The Maid of Honour* (1621); John Webster, *The Devil's Law Case* (1623); Ben Jonson, *Masque of*

★ Ed. J. B. Leishman (1949).
† Further details are given in the discussion of each of the works in question.

Time Vindicated (1622–3); John Fletcher and ? Philip Massinger, *Faire Maide of the Inne* (1626); Philip Massinger, *The Picture* (1629).

Joshua Sylvester, in his translation of *The Divine Weekes and Workes* of Guillaume de Saluste du Bartas, printed in 1605–6, neatly sums up the attitude of a whole generation towards Dowland, in these four lines:

> For, as an old, rude, rotten, tune-less Kit,
> If *famous* Douland *daign to finger* it
> Makes sweeter musick than the choicest Lute
> In the grosse handling of a clownish Brute.

In face of all this evidence it surely cannot be maintained that by 1612 changing fashion had displaced Dowland and his music in the affections of the public.

The only edition of which the actual number printed is known is *The Second Booke*. From the evidence given in Eastland's law suits we find that 1,000 copies, plus some overs, were run off the press. Even if Eastland had somewhat overestimated the market for this volume he must have had some figures to go on from the sales of *The First Booke*, and it is unlikely that there would have been any great disproportion between the numbers printed of *The Second Booke* and the volumes that preceded it and those that came immediately after. Had there been any serious falling-off of sales it is unlikely the printer would have risked another edition of *The First Booke* in 1613.

Unfortunately there is no evidence of what financial reward Dowland received from all these publications, except in the case of *The Second Booke*, for which, as has already been mentioned, £20 was paid to Mrs. Dowland for the MS, plus a promise of half the expected reward for the dedication. The repeated printings of *The First Booke* may have brought him nothing if the printer had bought the work outright in the first place. This need not necessarily have been the case, since all too little is known about the kind of agreement that was entered into between publishers and composers at this time. W. W. Greg and E. Boswell say:

It has often been supposed that the only way in which an author could make money out of a work was by selling the actual manuscript to a publisher outright, and that he could have no interest in subsequent editions. This, however, does not seem to have been always the case.★

They add, in a footnote:

Dr. McKerrow very pertinently observes that much of the obscurity that surrounds the relation of author and publisher may be due to the fact that the records as a rule simply ignore what passed between them as not coming within the jurisdiction of the Court.

★ *The Records of the Court of the Stationers' Company (1576–1602)* (1930), p. lxx.

In the case of *Lachrimæ or Seaven Teares* he acted as his own distributor and would almost certainly have made a satisfactory profit.

The house in Fetter Lane* suggests that the family lived at a reasonably high level of comfort, but it is more than likely that there was never a super-abundance of cash in the household. Possibly Dowland was not earning on the exceptionally high scale of his salary in Denmark, either as a free-lance or in the service of Lord Walden, and the condition of the accounts when he left the Danish Court show that money slipped through his hands with disconcerting ease. But this could have been no new experience. The disappearance of the presents from the Duke of Brunswick and the Landgrave of Hesse bear witness that he was never of a saving nature. Indeed, extravagance and the contracting of enormous debts was such a common feature of the life of a courtier in the reigns of both Elizabeth and James I that it is no matter for wonder that a musician, living within the orbit of such flamboyant characters, should have caught the habit of living beyond his means even if he had not been naturally predisposed to a lack of prudence in money matters. The ability to spend money faster than he made it Dowland shared with many other famous artists and musicians, but shortage of money which had its origin in such a common failing can hardly be laid to the blame of a heedless and forgetful society.

There was, however, good cause for his uneasiness in the new musical fashions that were fast establishing themselves at the Court of James I and his Queen. In 1605, before Dowland's return from Denmark, Ben Jonson and Alfonso Ferrabosco of Greenwich had already staged the first of the series of Court masques which was to make their collaboration famous. The names of Ferrabosco, Robert Johnson, Thomas Campian and Nicholas Lanière are constantly met with as providing music for these entertainments, produced with increasing extravagance, while Dowland's is noticeably absent. It is particularly significant to find in the accounts compiled by Christopher Brook†️ for the 'Masque of the Inner Temple and Lincoln's Inn', given at Whitehall

---

* John Stow, in his *Survey of London* (1598) says: 'Then is Fewter lane, which stretcheth south into Fleet street by the east end of St. Dunstone's church, and is so called of Fewters (or idle people) lying there, as in a way leading to gardens; but the same is now of latter years on both sides built through with many fair houses.' Everyman's Edition, p. 348.

The parish of St. Dunstan-in-the-West, in which the lower part of Fetter Lane lies, appears to have been popular among musicians. Both Campian and Rosseter lived in the district. 'Joane the wife of John Maynard' was buried on June 6th, 1619. This could have been the wife of the John Maynard, author of *The XII Wonders of the World*, who may have been in Denmark for a short time while Dowland was there. On March 7th, 1614/15, 'Margaret Cutting widowe out of ffeuter lane was buried'. Wife, perhaps, of the elusive Francis? A Robert Johnson signed the Church-wardens' Accounts as Auditor in 1609.

† W. P. Baildon, *The Records of the Honourable Society of Lincoln's Inn*, The Black Books, Vol. II (1898), p. 156.

in 1613, that Robert Johnson was paid £45 for 'songs and music' while Dowland was paid £2 10s od as one of the musicians for the lutes. Robert Johnson and Alfonso Ferrabosco had also established themselves in the theatre and were writing music for plays by Beaumont and Fletcher, Middleton, Webster and Ben Jonson.

In *A Musicall Banquet* and *A Pilgrimes Solace* there are one or two songs which appear to have been composed for a special occasion—a masque, entertainment or play, some perhaps for Lord Walden's marriage festivities —but in general, in his later work Dowland shows an increasing preoccupation with religion, and for setting he chooses or writes verses of a serious and introspective character. Such songs as 'In this trembling shadow cast', 'Where sin sore wounding', 'If that a sinners sighes' and 'Thou Mighty God' all appear to come from his final great productive period and they represent the ultimate development of the lute song and ayre, still governed by a fundamentally polyphonic outlook. These qualities, though still fully appreciated in domestic music, were far removed from what was desired in the entertainments devised for the pleasure-loving Court of James I and Queen Anne.

The songs of Ferrabosco, beautiful as many of them are, show, however, an entirely new fashion in song-writing, and it is interesting to find Dr. Burney, though he appears to have an innate antipathy to the lute song, appreciates the complete change from the polyphonic style when, in justification for omitting a transcription of the lute tablature in his version of 'Like Hermit Poore' printed in *A General History of Music*, he says: 'The Lute Accompaniment is mere thorough base which the Chords implied by the figures placed over this Base wholly comprehend.' Robert Johnson and Nicholas Lanière almost completely abandoned the composed accompaniment and the majority of their songs have, in addition to the melody, only the bass line, the filling up of the harmony being left to individual taste, and suitability to whatever instruments were available.

It is surely then, the neglect at Court rather than a failure of popularity in other directions, which rankled so deeply in Dowland's mind and which almost certainly prompted his friend Henry Peacham to write in the year before *A Pilgrimes Solace* was printed:

Erit altera merces
Ad amicum suum Iohannem Doulandum
Musicus ludendo peritissimum.

Iohannes Doulandus.   Anagramma
Annos ludendo hausi.   Authoris.

Heere, *Philomel*, in silence sits alone,
In depth of winter, on the bared brier,

Whereas the Rose, had once her beautie showen;
Which Lordes, and Ladies, did so much desire:
But fruitles now, in winters frost and snow,
It doth despis'd and unregarded grow.

So since (old friend) thy yeares have made thee white,
And thou for others, hast consum'd thy spring,
How few regard thee, whom thou didst delight,
And farre and neere, came once to heere thee sing;
Ingratefull times, and worthles age of ours,
That let's vs pine, when it hath cropt our flowers.★

And what of the rest of his complaints? He goes on to speak with great
bitterness of fellow musicians who have dared to criticize him, and singles out
two groups for special attack: Cantors (he echoes Ornithoparcus in using this
as a derogatory term in contradistinction to the theoretically learned
musician), and young professors of the lute who say he is old-fashioned.
That Dowland met with jealousy and backbiting from members of his own
profession is not altogether surprising. It would be absurd to imagine that
Elizabethan and Jacobean musicians were freer from petty rivalries and un-
charitableness towards each other than musicians of any other age.† That
these things assumed importance in Dowland's eyes is rather evidence of his
special susceptibility to such attacks than that he was the recipient of treatment more unkind and unjust than other musicians have, from time to time,
bestowed upon their fellow artists.

An overelaborate style, though providing a heaven-sent outlet for the
vanity of singers, can have found little sympathy in Dowland's mind, and the
final economy of means by which he expressed his most profound musical
thought leaves no room for exhibitionism on the part of the performer. But
disagreements between composers who wish to express their own ideas and
singers who wish to exploit their voices have provided a kind of tragi-
comedy throughout musical history.

Nor is it clear whom he can have had in mind when he speaks of 'the
young men, professors of the Lute, who vaunt themselues to the disparagement of such as haue been before their time'. It was nearing the end of the
period when the works of Dowland himself, Cutting, Bacheler, Holborne,
Daniel, Thomas Robinson, Francis Pilkington and others of the same school

---

★ *Minerva Britanna* (1612). Entered in the *Stationer's Register*, August 9th, 1611, Arber III,
f. 462.

† See Thomas Morley, *A Plaine and Easie Introduction to Practicall Musicke* (1597). 'Polymathes: (To his Master) whereas you justly complaine of the hate and backbiting amongst the
musicians of our countrey, that I knowe to be most true, and speciallie in these young fellowes'
(p. 150).

were to enjoy unrivalled popularity, but their sun had by no means set in 1612, and even the new masking tunes and the French corantos and voltes that became so popular about this time were far from replacing the older type of composition. The later sources such as *Varietie of Lute-Lessons*, Add. 38,539, Eg. 2046, and even Lord Herbert of Cherbury's MS are still rich in pieces by Dowland and others of the classical school.

Of the composers of any considerable stature writing for the solo lute, this leaves only Robert Johnson and Alfonso Ferrabosco the Younger. As song-writers they had both begun to follow new paths, but in the case of Robert Johnson, in his solo works, it is difficult to detect any startling divergence from the prevailing idiom of the time. There are personal idiosyncrasies in his writing, just as may be traced in the compositions of all the outstanding composers of the period, but these hardly constitute the break with tradition that one would expect to find in any young man who set up to criticize the older school. Johnson, moreover, though twenty years younger than Dowland, was, in 1612, approaching the age of thirty; by no means young according to Jacobean standards. Of Alfonso Ferrabosco as a composer of lute solos it is almost impossible to speak. The identity of names he shared with his father makes certainty of attribution impossible. Among the pieces credited to 'Alfonso' or 'Ferrabosco' a few have the distinguishing words 'of Bologna' added, but of the rest it is only possible to say of some that they must, by reason of their presence in earlier MSS, be by the elder, but his popularity as a composer assured the inclusion of his pieces in collections made during the time when his son could have been writing if, in fact, the younger man did compose for the lute alone. To Ferrabosco of Greenwich the epithet 'young' was even less applicable than to Robert Johnson in this particular context, since he was only junior to Dowland by some eight years.

Of what appears, by the absence of their work in earlier MSS, to be a younger generation working about this time, there remain only a few minor figures such as John Sturt and Robert Kindersley. Their compositions show a shift of interest from the polyphonic to the melodic, particularly in the almains they both wrote, but since they left only a handful of pieces between them it is difficult to be sure that this was the new characteristic of their composing upon which the younger lutenists based the accusation that Dowland was old-fashioned.

Among the exponents of a later, and quite different, style John Wilson was the only English composer for the lute of any considerable stature to reach manhood in, or near, this period of Dowland's life, but, born in 1595, it seems unlikely that he would, by 1612, have been sufficiently mature for attention to be paid to any criticism he might have made. Moreover, if, as has been surmised, he was employed in the theatre as a boy actor and singer, at the age of seventeen his talents would probably have still been fully occupied on the stage.

It seems possible, however, that criticism of the older players might have been made on the grounds of performance.

Any revolutionary change in the technique of a long established art, such as that of lute playing, is likely to have been a gradual process and to have taken an appreciable time to spread into general use. The collecting of evidence on when such changes came to be accepted is made extraordinarily difficult by the wide gaps in time that exist between the printing (or at least between those that survive) of any books that give precise information on the subject. During the period in which we are interested the only two sets of instruction to appear were Thomas Robinson's *Schoole of Musick* in 1603 and the 'Necessary Observations' by Besardus in *Varietie of Lute-Lessons* of 1610, although the latter had already appeared in the *Thesaurus Harmonicus* in the same year in which Robinson's book was printed. In both these the old technique of first finger and thumb for all running passages is advocated, though Besardus modifies this advice for certain passages. In the 'Petit Discours' of the *Secretum Musarum*, printed in 1615, Nicolas Vallet, in explaining the pointing under the tablature letters, makes it clear that he was familiar with the later technique of the first and second finger and that in many instances he preferred it to the old way. Except among the Spanish *vihuelistas*, to whom the technique was known in the mid-sixteenth century, Vallet's is the earliest description of this method of play I have so far found. He does not, however, speak as if its use were in any way exceptional or revolutionary and it may have been generally known on the Continent some years before he actually wrote of it. To any one who does not play the lute the distinction between these two methods may not appear great, but to the lutenist it will be clear that not only is the playing position of the hand greatly altered, but a different kind of sound is produced. If 'the diuers strangers from beyond the seas, which auerre before our faces that we haue no true method of application or fingering the lute' had brought this new technique with them and were spreading its use among the younger players in England, in spite of its many advantages, Dowland's love of the traditional ways could well have been offended.

The use of 'cordes avalées' can be traced in France from about the turn of the century,* but arrangements of intervals which departed from the 'old' tuning were the exception rather than the rule in the first two decades of the

* Antoine Francisque, in *Le Trésor d'Orphée* (1600), and J. B. Besardus, in *Thesaurus Harmonicus* (1603), both make use of lowered strings.

seventeenth century. The first incidence of the use of 'corde avalées' in England is John Danyel's 'Mrs Anne Grene her leaues bee greene' in his *Songs for the Lute Viol and Voice* (1606), but he seems to have set no fashion and the scarcity of lute music in any other than the traditional tuning at the time of the publication of *A Pilgrimes Solace* indicates that up to 1612 at least this innovation had gained no great hold on English lutenists. Slight as they were, however, these intimations of coming change were evidently intensely disquieting to Dowland.

It is possible, too, that his resentment against foreign players may have been roused by the appointment in 1607, of John (Giovanni?) Maria Lugario to the post of Queen's Musician at the exceptionally high salary of £100 a year 'in regaurde of the speciall qualitie and skill he hath in Musycke'.* There had been foreign musicians at Court since long before Dowland's time, and the families of Lupo, Bassano and Lanière had filled, between them, many of the posts. They, however, seem to have received no specially preferential treatment over their English colleagues. The salaries of the English lutenists ranged from about £20 to £40 a year and the discrepancy between these figures and what Lugario received was great enough to provoke hostility. Philip Rosseter, Dowland's neighbour, was one of the lower paid 'lutes' at Court and a sense of grievance may well have been felt among the musicians living in, or near, Fetter Lane.

He raises something of a mystery when he writes 'beleeue me if any of these objections had beene made when those famous men liued which now are thought worthy of no fame, not derogating from these skillfull men present; I dare affirme that these obiections had beene answered to the full, and I make no doubt but that those few of the former time which liue yet, being that some of them are Batchelors of Musicke, and others which assume vnto themselues to be no lesse worthy, wilbe as forward to preserue their reputation'. Of the men whose names are associated with the greatness of English lute music the only ones who were certainly dead were John Johnson, Anthony Holborne, Alfonso Ferrabosco of Bologna (if he can be counted among English lutenists) and Thomas Morley who, though he wrote lute music, was not primarily a composer for that instrument. John Danyel, Francis Pilkington, Philip Rosseter, Robert Johnson and Alfonso Ferrabosco of Greenwich were still alive, and so too, in all probability, were Francis Cutting and Daniel Bacheler. Any one of these would have been well qualified to join issue with the younger men, if, at this time, their reputation had been seriously assailed.

His attack on Tobias Hume is more easily understood. The great increase

* Audit Office Declared Accounts, Bundle 388, No. 44.

in the amount of music for the lyra viol which may be traced from the early years of the seventeenth century suggests that at the time of Dowland's complaints this instrument was beginning to offer itself as a serious rival to the lute among portable solo instruments. The challenge is overt in Tobias Hume's *The First Part of Ayres*, (1605), in which he addresses 'the vnderstanding Reader' in these terms:

> And from henceforth, the statefull instrument
> Gambo Violl, shall with ease yeelde full various and
> as deuicefull Musicks as the Lute.

In 1607* he somewhat modified the statement:

> And from henceforth, the statefull instrument Gambo
> Violl, shall with ease yield full various and
> deuiceful Musicke as any other instrument.

Is it possible, perhaps, that between 1605 and 1607 there had been a passage of arms between Dowland and Hume, so that the Captain withdrew the offensive reference to the lute in his second book? Whether or not this happened, Dowland's anger is still fierce in 1612, even after the interval of seven years, and he quotes the earlier statement. Furthermore, Hume had written songs with accompaniments for a single viol, and in 1609, in *A Musicall Dreame*, Robert Jones had offered, as an alternative to the lute accompaniments to his songs, a set for the viol. In 1615, in his *Sacred Hymns, Consisting of Fifti Select Psalmes*, Robert Tailour reverses the position and gives pride of place to the viol accompaniments and gives those for the lute as an alternative. This changed relationship could be a sign of the encroachment by the viol on the hitherto unchallenged territory of the lute in the accompaniment of the human voice where a single instrument was concerned.

What, then, do all these complaints add up to, and does it really appear that the bitterness and sense of persecution had foundation in fact? Change was in the air, undoubtedly, and in this he perhaps had cause for disquiet, but in 1612 there can be no doubt that he still rode the tide of popularity. The truth seems to be that resentment at his failure to secure a post at the English Court soured all other success, and that reputation at home and abroad as one of the greatest lutenists of his time was robbed of all satisfaction by the one unrealized ambition. It is notoriously difficult to see the justice of the other side in any dispute, and Dowland may not have admitted, even to himself, that his dismissal from the Court of Denmark was something of a disgrace and would constitute a hindrance to an appointment at the Court of Christian's brother-in-law, King James. To a man of Dowland's tempera-

---

* *Captaine Humes Poeticall Musicke*, in the address 'Alwaies to the Reader'.

ment the rankling sense of injustice in being passed over in favour of musicians of lesser capacity than himself could easily become exaggerated into a state bordering on persecution mania, so that molehills become mountains and the jealousies and rivalries of professional life are seen as a monstrous personal attack.

Few men escape the weakness, as age overtakes them, of looking back on the days of their youth as a more propitious and grateful time, and the remembered enthusiasm of earlier days carries the mind back to youthful triumphs and invests them with a savour lacking in the successes of later years. The present, compared with the nostalgic view of the past, is coloured by the loss of vigour and the increase of petty ailments and annoyances, and the discontents of old age transform themselves, often quite unjustly, into a criticism of the current ways of society. Dowland seems to have suffered his full share of this malady, so common among those from whom youth has already fled, and in spite of his own prodigious musical innovations he appears to have nourished a bitter resentment against all forms of change, seeing in them a challenge to his well-established reputation. Moreover, it must be remembered that 'melancholy' was such a common complaint and so grave a problem at this time that it occupied a large part of the attention of both physicians and philosophers, who attempted to find its causes and to prescribe remedies either physical or spiritual. It manifested itself in all sections of society and included under its all-embracing title every kind of psychological disorder from mild fits of depression to acute mania.

The great success of Dr. Timothy Bright's *Treatise of Melancholy*, which went into two editions in 1586 and a third in 1612, shows how general was the interest in this subject, and Robert Burton's great work, *The Anatomy of Melancholy*, though not printed till 1621, was being written precisely during this part of Dowland's life; it is the epitome of this whole mood and the absorbed interest which the mood provoked.

G. B. Harrison, in his edition of Nicholas Breton's *Melancholike Humours*, has an extraordinarily interesting essay on 'Elizabethan Melancholy'. He analyses the political scene in the years following the defeat of the Armada and shows that both at home and abroad there were grave causes for pessimism in the most vital aspects of national policy which induced a general mood of depression, but as an even more immediate and personal cause he follows Dr. Bright in thinking that much of the melancholy was brought on by the shockingly bad diet and the primitive state of dental hygiene. In the following passage he sums up his findings on the strange subject:

Elizabethan melancholy arose from a medley of causes, from the hungry soul unsatisfied, from love betrayed or surfeited; from religion and politics; from the black jaundice of the ill-used liver. Timothy Bright was not far wrong when he regarded indigestion as the main cause of melancholy, but he might have carried his researches further and he would have found another cause in the sensitive mind unable to stomach the squalor, the bawdiness and brutality of the Elizabethan age. Melancholy is only one of its many moods; the melancholics were conscious of the faults of their generation and blind to its many virtues.

Clearly many of the causes of melancholy had been present in earlier ages, but in no period in England before the Elizabethan had the individual been as conscious of the subjective emotions or as articulate in expressing them, and, side by side with the genuine cases of psychological disturbance and justified pessimism, a vogue or fashion for melancholy grew up not only among writers and musicians but among the aristocracy as well. Jacques in *As You Like it* is typical of this mood. He can 'suck melancholy out of a song, as a weasel sucks eggs'. The borderline between the fashionable 'humour' and the genuine state was probably often hard to define; at times the one would almost certainly merge imperceptibly into the other.

If the final years of Elizabeth's reign gave cause for pessimism, the Jacobean age gave cause for despair to many of its most distinguished thinkers. The careful husbanding of economic resources exercised by Elizabeth and her ministers gave way to prodigal spending on lavish entertainments; the relative integrity of the State was replaced by a system of bribery and corruption on a scale hitherto unknown in England; and after the death of Sir Robert Cecil power fell, not into the hands of men such as Cecil and his father, whose lives were devoted to the greatness of England, but into the hands of attractive young men whose physical charms satisfied the perverted eroticism of the King.

That Dowland suffered from periods of intense melancholy is shown throughout his life. Even as early as the Sudeley masque in 1592 he expresses his discontent with fortune, and his 'Melancholy Galliard' and 'Lachrimæ' are among his early compositions; in 1596, following Henry Noel's death, he describes himself as 'Infœlice Inglese'; and the motto he chooses for his first book of songs, *Nec prosunt domino, quae prosunt omnibus artes**—The Arts which help all mankind cannot help their master—comes strangely from a man whose music was beginning to echo round Europe. His preoccupation with tears shows itself from his *First Booke* right through to *A Pilgrimes Solace*, and of the poems he chose for setting many are coloured with a sense of sin and shame. 'Semper Dowland semper dolens', 'Forlorne Hope' and 'Farwell' are all titles that allow a display of intense and brooding emotion.

* Ovid's *Metamorphoses*, I, 525.

Possibly, had he not been subjected to the shock of having his application for a post at Court refused in 1594, the tendency to melancholy might have been appeased by satisfied ambition. As it was, this disappointment, which to a man of more balanced temperament would have been great but not overwhelming, falling on the fertile soil of a mentality already disposed to introspection and depression, appears to have nourished a morbid condition in which the failure took on an altogether exaggerated importance. Only some such state of mind seems to explain the apparently cavalier way in which he treated the post at the Danish Court, or indeed, the writing of such an extraordinary document as the address in *A Pilgrimes Solace*.

There is no doubt that, by the time *A Pilgrimes Solace* appeared, Dowland's creative ability was slowing up and, if he were aware of this process, it would have added to his unease. Difficult as it is to be precise in assigning dates to most of the MSS, it is clear that very little solo music was written after about 1600. In *Lachrimæ or Seaven Teares* (1604) it is noticeable how high a proportion of the contents consists of already existing pieces. The new compositions are of exceptionally high quality; nevertheless the inclusion of nine pieces that had certainly appeared before, and two more that probably had, is a large number out of a total of twenty.

Varietie of Lute-Lessons has no pieces by Dowland that are entirely new, although in some cases the divisions have been rewritten or added to some of the galliards that previously existed only in plain form. Even in *A Pilgrimes Solace* one of the songs may have been written some twenty years earlier, and the lute solo at the end of the book, excellent and ingenious as it is, is not a new creation, but is an adaptation of the already existing 'Lachrimæ Pavan' into triple measure. During the last fourteen years of his life only two compositions and one arrangement are known to have appeared—the two sacred songs in Leighton's *Teares or Lamentacions* (1614), and the new harmonization of Psalm 100 in Ravenscroft's *Whole Booke of Psalmes* (1621).[*]

Whether events were prompted by Peacham's poem it is impossible to say, but on October 28th, 1612, by letters under the Signet, Dowland was, at last, appointed one of the King's Lutes in place of Richard Pyke, at a salary of 20d a day.[†] That some special effort was made to find a post that he could conveniently be offered is suggested by the fact that Pyke died on May 21st, 1568,[‡] and his place had remained unfilled from that date.

He joined the company of Robert Hales and Symon Merson, who were in

---

[*] For discussion of the two compositions in Simpson's *Taffel-Consort* (1621) that cannot be indentified with previously existing pieces, see p. 373.

[†] Audit Office Declared Accounts, Bundle 389, No. 49.

[‡] Bundle 381, No. 8.

receipt of £40 a year each; Robert Johnson, who also received 20d a day; and Philip Rosseter at £20 a year. The Queen's Musician, John Maria Lugario, still enjoyed the salary of £100 a year. I have been unable to discover any evidence to throw light on why Dowland and Robert Johnson were paid on a different basis from their fellow lutenists. It is clear from various other entries in the accounts that there was no question of these two appointments being held as part-time employment with pay according to the number of days worked. The only explanation that seems to account for the discrepancy is that each post had originated in a different way, and probably at a different time, carrying with it its own traditional basis of payment, which conservatively minded officials preferred to maintain, rather than to simplify their work by introducing a standard form of payment.

It is odd that inspiration should have died on the achievement of a lifelong ambition, but as we have seen, the volume of his output had perceptibly lessened during his later years and it seems likely that *A Pilgrimes Solace* was the last magnificent flowering of his genius. The sentence in the epistle, where, in answer to his own question why he did not himself make answer to the criticisms of the foreign lutenists, he says 'I want abilitie, being I am now entered into the fiftieth yeare of mine age' could be understood as a hint that he was beginning to realize that the days of his composing were nearing their end. Nevertheless, only two years before, in *Varietie of Lute-Lessons*, he is described by his son as 'being now gray, and like the Swan, but singing towards his end', which does not suggest that he was infirm or incapable of work, although it is strange to hear death spoken of in connection with a man who had not yet reached the age of fifty and who was, apparently, not suffering from any severe illness. To the inhabitants of Jacobean London, however, death lurked in every street with its foul cargo of stinking refuse, in the vermin-infested houses and the tainted water supply. The constant visitations of the plague and other epidemics made life insecure, and the unhealthy diet lessened resistance to disease, while the case of those who fell into the hands of the doctors was made desperate by the rigours of the fashionable purgings and bleedings. To reach the age of forty-nine under these conditions argued a strong constitution and a fair share of luck. Nevertheless, many people managed to reach a ripe old age and continued to work with energy and application to the end.

Robert Dowland's reference to his father as 'singing towards his end' prompts me to raise the question of whether Dowland was, in fact, a singer, a theory put forward by several writers. For example, J. S. Ragland Phillips in 'Why John Dowland went overseas'* says:

* *Cornhill Magazine*, New Series (1897), Vol. III, pp. 240–57.

Not only was he known to Elizabeth and her advisers as a man of exquisite skill as a player and singer—Fuller records that it was difficult to decide whether he excelled in vocal or instrumental music—but his fame travelled far.

Rosemary Manning in 'Lachrimæ: A study of John Dowland'* writes:

I think it may be assumed that one of the reasons for Dowland's decline in popularity was his failing vocal powers. References of the time indicate that he was admired almost more as a singer and lutenist than as a composer. Certainly it is possible that no one but he could do his songs justice.

As lately as July 12th, 1963, in an article in *The Times*, the question was raised whether he was a male alto or a tenor.

Firstly, I think it is clear that Fuller is speaking of his compositions not his performance when he refers to 'vocal or instrumental music'. Apart from this the only two occasions on which the idea of singing is associated with him are the one by his son, just mentioned, and the one in Henry Peacham's poem in *Minerva Britanna*.† In both cases the word could have been used purely figuratively. In the first, 'singing' could have been employed in its very common literary sense of referring to the work of a poet or musician, and in the second, since Peacham addresses him in the person of Philomel, the nightingale, he has to speak of him as singing.

Against these two pieces of imagery there is a good deal of hard fact to be considered on the other side.

Perhaps the most significant piece of evidence is to be found in the Sudeley masque. Why should a singer have been employed in addition had Dowland been able to fulfil both functions in his own person? Neither character plays an important part in the masque beyond providing the music and this could have been contributed as easily by one with both qualifications as by two separate performers.

The title-pages of his four books of songs make no claim for him as a singer. Dowland was by no means one to hide his light under a bushel and had he possessed the extra qualification it would be most unlike him to have failed to bring it forward as a perfectly justified piece of self-advertisement.

On a number of occasions his playing is commended in verse with no accompanying mention of singing. Thomas Campian's *Ad Io. Dolandum*‡ refers to the strains upon the lyre, the plucking of the strings, and his divine hands, but there is not a word about singing. It is his 'heavenly touch upon the lute' that Richard Barnfield commends;§ and incidentally, the continuation of this poem is a good example of the figurative use of the word 'singing'

* *Music and Letters*, XXV (1944), pp. 45–53.
† See p. 70.   ‡ See p. 46.   § See p. 51.

where there is no intention of conveying the idea of the actual physical act. Clearly Phoebus is singing through Spenser's poetry, or even through poetry in general.

In the Du Bartas lines* it is his fingering of the lute that the poet calls to mind.

In the correspondence between the Landgrave of Hesse and the Duke of Brunswick† when comparisons are made between Dowland and Howet, had Dowland been a singer surely this would have been mentioned, but only his playing and composing are considered.

Neither is there any mention of singing all through the Danish records.

Again, all the way through the record of his employment at the English Court, in the Audit Office Declared Accounts, he is entered as one of the King's Lutes, and there is no mention of him as a singer in this connection either.

In the accounts of the *Masque of the Inner Temple and Lincoln's Inn*‡ it will be seen that he was engaged with others 'for playing of Lutes'; an entirely different entry deals with the singers.

In 1622, Henry Peacham§ speaks of him as 'a rare Lutenist' and as 'one of our greatest Masters of Musicke for composing', but says nothing of him as a singer.

In the Consorte that played during the funeral solemnities of James I,¶ Dowland is listed among the instrumentalists, while Nicholas Lanière is specifically mentioned as the singer.

It should also be noted, though this evidence is perhaps of a more conjectural nature, that when 'His golden locks' was sung before the Queen on November 17th, 1590,‖ it was Robert Hales who performed. If Dowland was the composer it would have been something of an affront to his professional dignity to have been passed over in this way, if he too had been of recognized standing as a singer.

Furthermore, one would hardly expect to find him displaying such a hostile attitude towards singers if he had himself been one of their number.

After taking up his appointment at Court, the next occasion on which we hear of him is the performance of Chapman's *Masque of the Inner Temple and Lincoln's Inn* at Whithall, one of three masques given as part of the marriage celebrations of the Princess Elizabeth and the Count Palatine. The long list of expenses connected with the presentation of the entertainment is preserved in the records of Lincoln's Inn and is of particular interest, as the following

---

* See p. 68.   † See p. 34.
‡ See p. 82.   § See p. 86.
¶ See p. 87.   ‖ See p. 238.

extracts show, for the light it throws on the fees paid to musicians at events of this kind:

Item to Mr Rob^te Johnson for musicke and songes 45^li

    Item to Thomas Cutting, John Dowland and Philip Rosseter for playing Lutes, every one of them   2^li. 10^s

    Item to Mr Thomas Forde for playing of Lute   2^li. 10^s and more for setting songes used at the Maske 5^li, and for Mathias Johnson for singing, 2^li.

    Item to John Sturte, Robert Taylor, Robert Dowland, and Thomas Davies for playing of Lutes, every one of them   2^li.

    Item to Mr Jonas and Mr Mynars,* two of the Musicions for the Maske, 6^li. 13^s. 8^d.

    Item to Thomas Day for (Blank in MS)   3^li. 6^s. 8^d

    Item to 7 singing men, vzt: John Dru, Willm Godball, John Frost, Davies (one of the Queresters), Marke Thwaites, Walter Porter, and Richard Ball, every one of them 2^li., saving Davies, who had about 1^li. 13^s.†

The £45 paid to Robert Johnson for music and songs, and the £2 10s 0d paid to Dowland for playing is significant of the relative favour in which the two composers were held at Court.

Dowland seems to have maintained his taste for writing somewhat obscure verse, and in 1614 he contributed, in addition to two sacred songs, the following commendatory poem to the second edition of Sir William Leighton's *Teares or Lamentacions of a Sorrowfull Soule*:‡

> Vpon this Excellent and Diuine Worke.
> If that be true the Poet doth auerre,
> Who loues not Musicke and the heauenly Muse,
> That man God hates, why may wee not inferre?
> Such as that skill vnto his praise doe vse,
> Are heauenly fauorde, when (as Angels) breath, [breathe?]
> High Mysteries in lowly tunes beneath.
> Such was that sweetest Singer Israels King,
> Whom after his owne heart the Lord did chuse,
> And many moe that did diuinely sing,
> To whom be added thy deuotest Muse,
> Who while she soundes her great Creators prayse,
> Doth her own fame next his high glory raise.
>   I.D.

    The sentence in the second and third lines 'Who loves not Musicke and the heauenly Muse, That man God hates' is an adaptation of a saying in common use among musicians and writers. It is found again in *The Compleat Gentleman*

    * Maynard?

    † W. P. Baildon, *The Records of the Honourable Society of Lincoln's Inn*, The Black Books (1897–1902), Vol. II, pp. 155, 156.

    ‡ The first edition contained no music.

(1622), where Henry Peacham says 'the Italian, having fitted a proverbe to the same effect "Whom God loves not, that man loves not musicke"',' and again Thomas Morley, in his *Madrigals to fiue voyces* (1598), begins the dedication to Sir Gervase Clifton with the following words: 'Good Sir, I euer held this sentence of the Poet, as a Canon of my Creede; That whom GOD loueth not, they loue not Musique.' The idea, of course, stems ultimately from the Greek theory of the Music of the Spheres★ which was generally held among Renaissance musicians and philosophers. Who the Italian poet was to whom Peacham and Morley refer, I have been unable to discover. The same thought is expressed by Shakespeare in *The Merchant of Venice*:

> The man that hath no music in himself,
> Nor is not mov'd with concord of sweet sounds,
> Is fit for treasons, strategems, and spoils;
> The motions of his spirit are dull as night;
> And his affections dark as Erebus;
> Let no such man be trusted.

In the same year, 1614, he contributed a poem to Thomas Ravenscroft's *A Briefe Discourse*. This time the meaning of his verse is quite clear. He takes for his subject the signs used at the beginning of a composition to denote mood and prolation according to fifteenth- and early sixteenth-century practice. By the beginning of the seventeenth century, although musical theoreticians still treated the whole complex system with respect, among practical musicians the tendency was to simplify the code and to allow many of the signs to fall into desuetude. Ravenscroft, to Dowland's evident satisfaction, pays due attention to the subject in his book:

> IOHN DOWLAND *Bachelar* of *Musicke,* and *Lutenist* to
> the *Kings* sacred *Maiestie,* in commendation of this
> *worke.*
>
> *Figurate* Musicke *doth in each* Degree
> *Require it* Notes, *of seuerall* Quantity;
> *By* perfect, *or* Imperfect Measure *chang'd*:
> *And that of* More, *or* Lesse, *whose* Markes *were rang'd*
> *By* Number, Circle, *and* Poynt: *but various vse*
> *Of vnskild* Composers *did induce*
> *Confusion, which made muddy and obscure,*
> *What first* Inuention *fram'd most cleere, and pure.*
> *These (worthy* RAVENSCROFT) *are restrain'd by* Thee
> *To one fixt* Forme: *and that approu'd by* Me

In the following year, among other commendatory letters and poems which prefaced Elias Mertel's great collection *Hortus Musicalis Novus*, the

★ See further on p. 193.

following Latin verse appeared:

> Est ita: naturâ regio quæqunque laborat
>   Artifices celebri laude suos.
> Musica testatum facit hoc: namque Anglia summè
>   Artem Doulandi suspicit, ornat, amat.
> Fert LAURENCINI laudes nimiùm Itala tellus;
>   BOCQUETUS Gallis gloria prima cluet.
> Sed qui Germanis celebres? GREGORIUS ipsis
>   Ante alios metitò & MORNA vehendus ecrit.
> His te, MERTELLI, placet annumerare duobus,
>   Quem Germani, Itali, jureque Gallus ament.
> Dum juvat ingenij fætum dare, & edere scriptis
>   Abdita, quæ studio præmeditatus eras.
> Gratulor ex animo, simul opto, ut fortius instes,
>   Neu labor impediat, suavem adamare chelyn.
> Sic tuus æternum decor iste manebit in ævum,
>   Gloriaque est nullo demoritura die.
>   Gratulabundus exarabat
>   JOHANNES-PHILIPPUS MENDELIUS
>   dictus Jordan. LL.Stud.*

The praise of Dowland in the poem by Mendelius is not surprising, since, at this time and for some years to come, his reputation on the Continent could hardly have stood higher. His music appeared in many printed collections in addition to the *Hortus Musicalis Novus*. Hildebrandt and Fullsack's *Auserlesener Paduanen . . .* (1607), Thomas Simpson's *Opusculum* (1610), Van den Hove's *Delitiæ Musicæ* (1612), Michael Prætorius's *Terpsichore* (1612), Georg Leopold Fuhrmann's *Testudo Gallo-Germanicca* (1615), J. B. Besard's *Novus Partus* (1617), and Thomas Simpson's *Taffel-Consort* (1621) all contained examples of his work in varying degrees of accuracy. Some were attributed to him, many were not. Foreign musicians used his themes for their own compositions, sometimes with credit to Dowland, but often without. MSS written during the same period also continue the evidence of his popularity; 'Lachrimæ', as was to be expected, outdoing all others in its widespread appeal.

---

* Thus it is: every land strives to exalt the renown of its own artists. Music bears witness to this truth. England puts Dowland first, honours and loves him. Italy sings the praises of Laurencini. For France Bocquetus takes the highest place. Whom do the Germans praise? Gregorius and Morna take the palm with them. To these two I add you Mertellius, whom Germans, Italians, and French rightly love; and it is my delight to give proof of your talent by publishing the artful compositions you already have in store. I congratulate you from my heart and pray that the toil may not daunt you but that you will press more boldly on in your devotion to your sweet lyre. Thus your renown will endure for ever and your glory will know no end.

Johannes-Philipus Mendelius called Jordan, student of letters, gratefully penned these verses.

In 1621 his second harmonization of Psalm 100 was contributed to Thomas Ravenscroft's *Whole Booke of Psalmes*, and here, for the first time, he is styled Dr. John Dowland. The degree is confirmed in the Audit Office Accounts, where, from the year 1622* onwards, he is given the title and his name stands first on the list of Lutes. No record appears to exist of where the degree was conferred, possibly it was from some foreign university; but as university records are by no means complete at this period, it is hardly likely that the information will be found.

In 1622 Thomas Tomkins dedicated No. 7 in his *Songs of 3.4.5. and 6. parts* to 'Doctor *Douland*', and it begins:

There can surely be no doubt that Tomkins was quoting from 'Lachrimæ' in the first four notes of the tenor and then, again, much more convincingly, in the first nine notes of the treble. Some of the note values are slightly altered, but the whole melodic curve and the general effect are clearly recognizable. It would be entirely in keeping with Jacobean sentiment if this were intended as a felicitation to Dowland upon his doctorate.†

In this year also, his friend, Henry Peacham, made two mentions of him in *The Compleat Gentleman*. On p. 103 he says:

I willingly, to auoide tediousnesse, forbeare to speake of the worth and excellency of the rest of our English Composers, Master Doctor *Douland, Tho: Morley*, M.*Alfonso*, M. *Wilbie*, M. *Kirbie*, M. *Wilkes*, *Michael East*, M. *Bateson*, M. *Deering*, with sundry others, inferior to none in the world (how much

---

* Bundle 392, No. 61.

† No. 8, 'O let me die for true love', is dedicated to 'Master John Daniell'. The association of Dowland and Danyel in the two halves of what is virtually one madrigal is interesting. Possibly Tomkins knew of Danyel's interest in extreme chromaticism and associated it with Dowland's similar interest.

In his chapter on Danyel in *The English Ayre* (1926), writing about the Dowland-Danyel dedications, Warlock says 'it is just possible that the opening phrase . . .' is a 'deliberate quotation from Dowland's most famous work "Lachrimæ"—although it must be admitted, musical quotations were rarely met with at this time, and the phrase is by no means an uncommon occurrence in the works of composers who knew nothing of Dowland's song'. Did Warlock possibly look at the first two bars of the tenor part only? It is difficult to understand how he could have taken the treble for anything but a quotation. It may be true to say the first four notes are common to other works (though it would be hard to prove that the composers who used them did not know Dowland's tune, if they were anything like contemporary); but it is not true that the first nine notes are 'by no means an uncommon occurrence'. These nine notes alone could justifiably be taken as a 'Lachrimæ' quotation; with the Dowland dedication added there is little room for doubt.

soeuer the Italian attributes to himselfe) for depth of skill and richnesse of conceit.

Again, on p. 198, in the section 'Of reputation and carriage', he writes:

Of my good friend Master Doctor Dowland, in regard he had slipt many opportunities in advancing his fortunes and a rare Lutenist as any of our Nation, beside one of our greatest Masters of Musicke for composing: I gave him an Embleme with this;

IOHANNES DOVLANDVS
Annos ludendo hausi.

In his article on Dowland in *Grove's Dictionary of Music and Musicians* (5th edition, 1954), Dr. Fellowes says that Dowland spent some time at the Court of the Duke of Wolgast in Pomerania, in 1623. In this he was mistaken; it was, in fact, Robert Dowland, as E. K. Chambers shows in *The Elizabethan Stage* (1923), Vol. II, p. 288, where he quotes two petitions in the Stettin archives from some English actors, with whom Robert was travelling, who sought permission, on August 30th, 1923, to leave Wolgast and return to England.

The years that followed seem to have been peaceful enough. The Audit Office Accounts show no irregularities such as those that caused so much worry to the Danish officials. Perhaps if he found contentment and satisfaction in his life at Court he no longer felt the urge towards the extravagances of his earlier years.

In 1624 he is still named among the great ones of the musical profession. William Webbe,* writing a commendatory poem for his friend Francis Pilkington's *Second set of Madrigals*, joins his name with those of Byrd, Bull and Morley:

> To my approued Friend, Master Francis PILKINGTON,
> Bacheler of *Musick*
> A sonnet
> *Those great* Atchieuements *our* Heroicke Spirits
> *Haue done* in Englands *old or later* Victories,
> *Shall we attribute wholly to the Merrits,*
> *Of our* Braue Leaders? And faire Industries
>   *Which their not-named Followers haue exprest*
> Lie hid? *And must the* matchless Excellencies

* *A Short Biographical Dictionary of English Literature* by J. W. Cousin (Everyman edition; reprint of 1946), p. 398, has this to say of him: Webbe, William. (b. 1550).—Critic and translator. Almost nothing is known of him except that he was at Cambridge, and acted as tutor in certain distinguished families, and was a friend of Spenser. He wrote a *Discourse of English Poetrie* (1586), in which he discusses metre, rhyme (the use of which he reprehends), and reviews English poetry up to his own day. He also translated the Eclogues of Virgil in singularly unmelodious hexameters.

Of Bird, Bull, Dowland, Morley *and the rest*
Of our rare Artists (who now dim the lights
Of other lands) be onely in Request?
Thy selfe, (and others) loosing your due Rights
To high Desert? nay, make it(yet)more plaine,
That thou canst hit the Ayres of euery vaine,
Their praise was their Reward, and so 'tis thine:
The Pleasure of thy paines all mens: and mine.★

Only one further incident is recorded in Dowland's life; he was one of the Consort that played during the funeral solemnities of James I on May 5th, 1625:

> 1625. Account for the funeral of James I. List headed 'The Chamber of our late Sovereign Lord King James'.
> This includes:
>
> *The Consorte.*
>
> | | |
> |---|---|
> | Charles Coleman | John Dowland |
> | Francis Cozens | Daniel Farrant |
> | Maurice Webster | Timothy Collins |
> | Philip Squire | John Friende |
> | Robert Johnson | Nicholas Lanier, Singer.† |
> | Robert Major | |

The final entry in the Audit Office Declared Accounts‡ which concerns Dowland runs as follows:

Doctor Dowland for one quarter of a year ending Xmas 1625 & 26 days. Robert Dowland son of the said Doctor Dowland deceased succeeding (by letters under the Signet 26 April 2 Chas. I.)

He was buried at St. Anne, Blackfriars. In the Register of Burials under the year 1625§ the date and name are clearly given: 'Feb.20th. John Dowland Doctor of Musick'.¶

As stated in the Audit Office Accounts, Robert succeeded to the post left vacant by his father's death and the Warrant for his wages and livery was

★ J. C. Bridge's article on Francis Pilkington in *Grove's Dictionary of Music and Musicians* (1927) wrongly attributes this poem to Henry Harpur, who did in fact write a poem for the Pilkington book, but not this particular one. The error is repeated in the 5th edition, 1954.

† Extract from the Lord Chamberlain's Accounts, Vol. 557. Printed in H. C. de Lafontaine *The King's Musick* (1909).

‡ Bundle 392, No. 65.

§ Old Style; 1626 according to our reckoning.

¶ I had the good fortune to discover this in 1962. The church of St. Anne, Blackfriars, was destroyed in the Great Fire of 1666 and was not rebuilt. Two small pieces of the burial ground are still in existence just behind *The Times* building. One piece now forms a rather dismal little garden off Church Entry, the other is a concreted yard off Ireland Row. The tombstones have mostly been removed and there is no trace of Dowland's grave. The Parish Registers are deposited at the Guildhall, London. The Register of Burials is MS 13, 4510/1.

issued on April 26th.* This document will be given in full, as it has, read in conjunction with the final entry in the Declared Accounts, been used as the basis of an argument that Dowland died on the day his employment ended and that his body lay unburied for a month:

Charles R.
Charles by the grace of God King of England Scotland France and Ireland Defender of the faith etc. To our trusty and our wellbeloved servant Sir William Wurdall† Knight Treasurer of our Chamber now being, and to the Treasurer of our Chamber that hereafter for the time shalbe, greeting. Whereas we have appointed Robert Dowland to be one of our Musicians in ordinary for the Consort in the place of his father Doctor Dowland deceased, and are pleased to allow him for his wages Twenty pence by the day, and for his livery sixtene pounds two shillings six pence by ye yere; We doe hereby will and commaunde you out of our treasures from time to time remayning in your custody to pay or cause to be paid to the said Robert Dowland or his assignes ye said wages of twenty pence by the day and sixtene pounds two shillings six pence by the yere for his livery from the day of the death of his said father for and during his naturall life, at the fower usuall feastes or termes of the yere, that is to say at the feaste of the Nativitie of St John Baptiste St Michael tharchangell, ye birth of our lord god and the Annunciacion of the blessed virgin Marie quarterly by even and equall porcions And this our letter shalbe ye sufficient warrant and discharge in his behalf. Given under oure Signett at our Pallace of Westminster ye six and twentieth day of April in the second yere of our Raigne.

The signiture 'Pembroke', that of the Lord Chamberlain of the Household, is added lower on the page.

Under the Warrant is a précis of the contents:

This conteyneth yor Ma^tes warrant under the signett to the treasurer of the Chamber to allow unto Robert Dowland one of the musicians for the Consort in ye place of Dr. Dowland his father deceased twenty pence by the day for his wages, and 16^ll—2^s—6^d for his livery yerely during his life.
By order of the Lord Chamberlain.
ffra: Gălls

Three explanations have been put forward to account for the supposed delay between death and burial:‡ (*a*) that for some reason money was not available for the funeral expenses; (*b*) that there were suspicious circumstances connected with the death, and (*c*) that the weather was too cold for the digging of a grave. Firstly, it must be pointed out that neither the Audit Office

---

* BM. Add. 5750, f. 78.
† Also spelt Vardall in other documents.
‡ Cecil Hill, 'John Dowland: Some New Facts and a Quatercentenary Tribute', *The Musical Times*, No. 1449, Vol. 104, November 1963, pp. 785–7.

Declared Accounts nor the Warrant give an actual date for Robert's appointment. Both documents were written some months after the events and on
April 26th Dowland could be described as 'deceased' on whichever of the
two dates he had actually died, and Robert could still have 'succeeded' to the
post even if the appointment had dated from about the time of the recorded
burial. It could be argued in favour of the later date that the first of the dates
mentioned, on which he is to receive one of the even and equal portions
of his salary, is the Nativity of St. John the Baptist, i.e. June 24th, whereas
had he been appointed as from January 20th or 21st, it might have been
expected that the first payment would have been made on the day of the
Annunciation of the Blessed Virgin, i.e. March 25th. But suppose it were
granted that John died on the earlier date, are any of the reasons for the delay
in burying the corpse really valid?

(a) *There was no money for the funeral expenses.* The Audit Office Accounts
show that Dowland's salary was paid regularly from Michaelmas to
Michaelmas every year, and there is no evidence to suggest that he was
under the same pressure to draw his salary in advance as in the Danish period.

(b) *That some suspicious circumstances were connected with his death.* Clearly lack
of documentation at this period does not finally dispose of a fact, but no post-
mortem inquisition has been found to support such a theory.

(c) *That the weather was cold and the ground too hard for grave digging.* At St.
Anne, Blackfriars, burials took place on January 21st, 22nd and 30th, 1625/6.
In the near-by parish of St. Dunstan-in-the-West the Churchwarden's
Accounts* show entries for 'ground pitt and knell' all through the months of
January and February, and on January 21st an infant was buried 'in the
churchyard without a coffin'.

If the rather unprecise wording of the Warrant and the Audit Office
Declared Accounts is indeed intended to convey the fact that John died on
the 20th or 21st of January, then there is a set of circumstances which easily
explains such an error having been made. In the summer of 1625 the second
of the three devastating outbreaks of plague of the seventeenth century fell
upon London. So severe was the visitation that the Court left Whitehall in
July and did not return until January 7th, 1625/6. During these months, with
a reduced number of courtiers in attendance, the King and Queen visited
Hampton Court, Oatlands, Windsor, Woking, Bisham, Ricott, Woodstock,
Beaulieu, Southampton, Plymouth and Wilton in an attempt to shake off the
disease, which pursued them closely in the unauthorized crowds that followed
in their wake.† In the autumn the death-rate dropped and the runaways who

* Guildhall, London, MS 2968/2.
† See F. P. Wilson, *The Plague in Shakespeare's London* (1927).

had fled to the country began to return to the devastated town. By December the epidemic was over, more than 41,000 persons having perished from the plague in London and the outlying parishes between December 16th, 1624, and December 15th, 1625. In the two parishes of St. Dunstan-in-the-West and St. Anne, Blackfriars, in either or both of which the Dowlands may have been living at the time, 642 plague deaths were recorded in the former and 215 in the latter. There is no evidence to suggest that Dowland was a victim of the plague, but so soon after an epidemic of these proportions burials were hurried forward in the fear, even where the tell-tale symptoms were not observed, that an unsuspected corpse might prove a fresh source of infection.

If John had been taken ill on, or just before, January 20th, it would not have been unnatural that his son should have acted as his deputy. Had it become obvious that his death was not far distant it could well be that Robert's tenure of the post was then made permanent. It can be seen from the Warrant for the payment of Robert's wages that several different people were involved in the process of making out this document and paying out the money. There was the professional scribe who did the actual writing; Sir William Wardall, the Treasurer of the Chamber; the Earl of Pembroke, Chamberlain of the Household; and another whose signature of 'ffra: Găll' is also attached; finally there is the clerk responsible for drawing up the Audit Office Declared Accounts. If it is assumed that the intention was to convey that John died on January 20th or 21st, it is not difficult to imagine one of the officials, having passed through a period of complete confusion and possibly even having been out of London at the time, on hearing that Robert's employment began on January 20th or 21st and that John was dead, thinking that the two events had taken place simultaneously.

After the flight round the palaces and the great houses of the south of England and the return to a city disorganized by the death of such a large proportion of its inhabitants it is perhaps more surprising that the issuing of Warrants and the keeping of accounts were carried on at all, than that a mistake of this kind could be made.

In *The English Madrigal Composers* (1921) Dr. Fellowes says: 'Dowland died in London, and the actual date of his death is given as January 21, 1626, in the papers of the Dublin family of Forster to whom Dowland seems to have been related.' No reference to the whereabouts of this paper is given, and a prolonged search has failed to identify it. Dr. Fellowes accepted Grattan Flood's article in its entirety, without apparently investigating the sources for himself. When the very unreliable nature of these sources is uncovered the existence of such a paper becomes, to say the least of it, problematical, and it seems likely that Dr. Fellowes read something more into Grattan Flood's article than was actually there and omitted to subject the statement to a thorough check. It is somewhat suspicious that he says 'the actual date of his death is given as January 21, 1626'; the *actual* date given would, of course, have been 1625.

In view of the immense debt of gratitude owed to Dr. Fellowes for his publications of Tudor, Elizabethan and Jacobean music, it is sad to have to say that much of the information he gives about Dowland in the various places where he has written of his life, is inaccurate and is not based on a full examination of the original source material.

After John's death little more is known of the family. The marriage allegation of Robert reads:

11th October 1626

This day appeared personally Rob Dowland of ye parish of St. Anne Black-friars, London, a bachelor, aged about XXXV yeares and alledged that he intendeth to marry with Jane Smalley of ye same parish, spinster (ye daughter of John Smalley)* aged about XXV yeares and at her owne disposition, and that he knoweth of noe lawfull lett or impediment by reason of anie pre-contract, consanguinity, affinity or otherwise to hinder this intended marriage & of the truth of the premisses he made fayth and desired licens for them to be married in ye parish church of St. Fayth, London.

Robert Dowland
[sworn before] Arth Ducke

Entries concerning two of Robert and Jane's children, John and Mary, also appear in the Registers of St. Anne, Blackfriars. Their infant son was buried on December 22nd, 1627, and their daughter was baptized on April 24th, 1629.†

Whether more children were born to them is not known, since no other entries are found in these registers, and prolonged search of other registers has revealed no information concerning other children that might have been theirs.

The exact date of Robert's death is uncertain. The final entry in the Audit Office Declared Accounts of his wages having been paid occurs under the heading '1639 to Michaelmas following'. The Accounts for 1640 appear to be missing. The next definite piece of information is found in the Warrant, issued on December 1st, 1641:

---

* The words in brackets have been scored through in the MS, Guildhall Library, 10,091/11, f. 34.

† In his article 'John Dowland: Some New Facts and a Quatercentenary Tribute', *The Musical Times*, Vol. CIV (1963), Cecil Hill appears to believe that he was publishing the facts concerning these two children for the first time. I had already published them in the *Lute Society Journal*, Vol. IV (1962), when I drew attention to the date of Dowland's burial.

for the swearing of Mr John Mercure a musician to his Majesty for the lutes and voices in ordinary, in place of Robert Dowland, deceased.*

The Warrant for '1s. 8d. per diem as wages, and £16. 2s. 6d. per annum as livery' appears in the Lord Chamberlain's Accounts for December 10th of the same year. The Audit Office Declared Accounts† under '1641 to Michaelmas following' show this entry:

John Mercure, in the place of Robert Dowland, (by warrant under the signet, dated 31st‡ Dec 1641,) for a half year ending Lady Day 1642.

This half-year would have run from Michaelmas (September 29th) 1641 to Lady Day (March 25th) 1642 so that, if Mercure had made his first appearance at Court about the time of the earlier date, presumably Robert had made his final appearance some time earlier. There is nothing to show whether death removed him from his post, or whether he retired through illness, but it seems reasonable to suppose that the sequence of events may have been illness, retirement, death and, some months later, the entry in the accounts declaring him to be deceased.

Cecil Hill mentions the coincidence of an entry of burial in the Registers of St. Andrew's, Holborn, under November 1641:

776. Robert DOLING a man sometime servant to the king died in his house in the New Buildings in Chancery Lane the 28th: buried the 29th.

He adds 'no Robert Doling has as yet been identified in the Public Records'. There is only one point that might perhaps be added and that is: with all the variant spellings of the first syllable—Dow, Dou, Do, Du—I know of no instance where the second syllable has been anything but 'land' or in foreign sources 'lant', or 'landt'.

With the death of Robert all trace of the direct line of descent comes to an end, although the possession of the Dowland Lute Book in the eighteenth century by James Dowland of Cuckney, Notts., suggests, if not direct descent, at least descent through a closely connected branch of the family.

Richard Newton, who did some research on this part of the family history, found James Dowland to have been born in 1751, appointed schoolmaster at Kirkby in 1771, and to have been in the Auditor's Office at Welbeck from 1777 to 1794, when he became Agent to Lord Bathurst. His eldest son was named Kaye after the Rev. Sir Richard Kaye, Bart., sometime Rector of Kirkby Clayworth, Notts., and Chaplain to the King in 1766, who had been something of a patron to James in his youth. Richard Newton also told me

---

* Lord Chamberlain's Accounts, Vol. 740, p. 4.
† Bundle 395, No. 77.
‡ A discrepancy with the Lord Chamberlain's Accounts.

that he had once seen, when looking through a bookseller's catalogue, an item comprising a few old Italian drawings with Kaye Dowland's signature on the back.

James Dowland's connection with Welbeck may possibly explain the presence of the 'Lamentatio Henrici Noel' among the Duke of Portland's papers.

The name Dowland recurs with some frequency in parish documents both in London and elsewhere during the seventeenth and eighteenth centuries. An interesting entry, in view of the South Midlands connections of the family, is found in the Marriage Register of St. George's Chapel, Hyde Park Corner, where, on August 1st, 1729, Luke Dowland married Mary Care, both of Beadderwick, Co. Northampton. Unfortunately Parish Registers of this date give so little information that I have been unable to make any connection between the scattered entries.

Occasionally figures appear about whom a little more is known. Foster's *Index Ecclesiasticus* tells us of a John Dowland of Dunnet, Wiltshire, who matriculated from Pembroke College on June 3rd, 1671, aged nineteen, and became Vicar of Wellington, Somerset in 1679.

An early nineteenth-century eccentric, Thomas Dowland, wrote *Divine and spiritual communications through T. Dowland to E. Carpenter for the British Nation . . . declaring what is coming upon this and all nations* (London, 1848). It foretells hideous doom.

The Rev. Edmund Dowland was appointed headmaster of the Chorister's School at Salisbury in 1863.* He was lampooned in a very bad novel, *Tom Pippin's Wedding* (published anonymously, but in fact written by the Rev. W. H. Pullen), under the name of the Rev. Hezekiah Goggs. Miss Robertson goes on to say:

one of his old boys remembers him as a hard man, never seen without a cane in his hand: another, writing in 1931 of the events of seventy years before, remarks: 'Our old master, Rev. E. Dowland, and his wife were of the very best; I always look back with gratitude to them. . . . I still remember the old school and times as they were with affection and gratitude.'

Some members of the family living today, with whom I have corresponded, though willing to help, have been unable to give me enough information upon which to work in order to trace their ancestry back through the centuries.

Thus John Dowland, according to the present state of knowledge, stands as an almost isolated figure, with his own background as dim as the history of his family after the deaths of his son and his infant grandson.

* These details are taken from *Sarum Close* (1938) by Dora Robertson.

II

The solo lute music

❧

Since Dowland's intention of compiling a collection of his best compositions for the lute was never fulfilled, we are dependent, save for the nine pieces in *Varietie of Lute-Lessons* and the four that appear in the song-books, on MS sources.

Unfortunately there is all too little information about most of these MSS, and of necessity many questions remain unanswered. Of some we do not even know the name of the original owner, and to find a MS dated is the exception rather than the rule. In the few cases where a date is given, either at the beginning or at the end of a book, it may be no indication of when a particular piece was written, since, especially with the longer MSS, the process of copying may have extended over a number of years. Careful detective work will, however, sometimes yield scraps of evidence that indicate roughly the years between which certain entries must have been made. This is as far as it is possible to go in assigning dates to many of the lute books.

By far the greatest proportion of Dowland's lute music comes from the group of MSS in the University Library, Cambridge, and the work of Richard Newton,★ David Lumsden† and Ian Harwood‡ on these volumes has elucidated many of the problems concerning their date, origin and contents, but even so, the question of assigning dates to any individual pieces is surrounded with difficulties and the making of an accurate chronological list is an impossibility. Conclusions can, however, sometimes be drawn from such pointers as the date upon which Dowland received his degree and whether this is credited to him in the MS; the marriage date of his patronesses and whether their maiden names are used or those they bore after marriage;

★ 'English Lute Music of the Golden Age', *Proceedings of the Musical Association*, February 23rd, 1939.

† 'The Sources of English Lute Music', unpublished thesis, deposited at the University Library, Cambridge.

‡ 'The Origins of the Cambridge Lute Manuscripts', *Journal of the Lute Society*, Vol. V 1963).

and the dates on which some of his patrons were knighted or succeeded to titles, and whether such titles are mentioned. Tablature for a lute of six courses only can indicate an early date of composition, but does not invariably do so.

Complications are added by the fact that many of the pieces have an early and a late form. It was a common practice with Dowland to resurrect a piece, garnish it with a new set of divisions, name it for a new patron, and present it for some special occasion.

Of more than 200 copies of Dowland's pieces scattered through MS collections, both English and Continental, only three survive in which his own handwriting is discernible; to six others he has added his signature.

The nine compositions in *Varietie of Lute-Lessons* and those in the song-books, since they appear to have been specially prepared or revised for these volumes, give us standard texts, although the *Varietie* pieces are all in late versions with many readings distinct from those of earlier sources; moreover, the misprints in this volume add some special problems of their own. For the rest, only examination of all copies, where more than one exists, and comparison with Dowland's style in the authentic works and with the style of other composers, will suggest which are the correct versions, and indeed which pieces may be accepted as from his pen, since in some instances he may be credited with a work in one MS whereas in another a different attribution may be made. In addition well-known themes by Dowland sometimes appear with divisions so completely foreign to his style that they can confidently be rejected from the canon.

Other variants are undoubtedly erroneous attempts to reproduce the original composition, the faults arising, possibly, from an ill-remembered hearing of a performance. The appearance of identical mistakes in more than one MS suggests that in certain cases an inaccurate copy was in circulation and passed from hand to hand among the compilers of lute books.

A further cause of confusion lies in the fact that the copyist frequently relied on his own memory for composers' names and the titles of the pieces, or used only the most obscure mnemonics to convey essential information. Even in printed books errors and omissions are not infrequent.

An extended list of MSS and printed books containing works by Dowland is given on p. 472; but no attempt will be made to discuss all these in detail. Only those sources will be described that contain the most authoritative versions; that have some direct bearing on the dating of a composition; or which contribute some fragment of knowledge to the mosaic from which so many pieces are still absent. Thus little will be said about most of the foreign books and MSS, since, with one exception only, they contain no works which cannot be found in more reliable sources at home.

Since the printed sources do not appear until comparatively late, the MS lute books will be examined first.

Of the English MSS the most important group is the set of books at the University Library, Cambridge. This consists of four lute books, all in the same handwriting, Dd.2.11.(B), Dd.5.78.(3), and Dd.9.33.(C) and Nn.6.36, (B)., together with books of Consort parts for lute, recorder, cittern and bass viol. Of the books for treble viol and bandora that probably completed the set, there is no trace. In addition there is a book of solo music for cittern.

William Chappell, in his *Popular Music of the Olden Times* (1855–9), states that the four lute books, written in the same hand, had belonged to Dowland. It is true that at some time he must have handled Dd.5.78, since he added the title and his own name at the end of the copy of 'Farwell' on f. 44, but further than that there is no evidence to connect him with the books. A number of writers have put forward various theories concerning the provenance of these books, but the recent researches of Ian Harwood have shown conclusively that the series is written, with occasional additions by other copyists, in the hand of Mathew Holmes, Precentor and Singingman at Christ Church, Oxford, from 1588 to 1597, and Chanter and Singingman at Westminster Abbey from 1597 till his death in 1621.*

Holmes's purpose in compiling these books remains, however, something of a mystery. Altogether they contain some 700 pieces, many of which are duplicated in almost identical form, often within the same volume. Had Holmes been making books for his pupils or as a professional copyist, some agreement in the contents of each might have been expected, but this explanation hardly covers the fact that each book contains a quantity of music not present in the companion volumes or that the re-copying of a piece sometimes occurs within a few folios of its first appearance. Moreover, if Holmes had been making up books of music for sale he would surely have added, to the best of his knowledge, the title and composer's name in each case, whereas, in many instances, where a title or name appears in one context, it is omitted in another. The handwriting which, in the early stages of the work, is bold and clear, gradually deteriorates, a fact which is not surprising when it is remembered that the process of filling the books may have lasted during the passage of some twenty-five years.

He makes no more than the average number of mistakes, the most common fault being, as in all tablature, the placing of a letter on the wrong line. He has, however, at times, an idiosyncratic difficulty in reaching a decision about the presence or absence of an accidental. F or F sharp was his

* 'The Origins of the Cambridge Lute Manuscripts', *Lute Society Journal*, Vol. V (1963).

bugbear, and a curious little symbol, ⟨, is sometimes found, where he has changed a ⟨ on the second line into an *e*, or vice versa.

The musical content of these MSS is of an exceptionally wide range. In time it spans the years with compositions by Taverner, who died in 1545, to pieces which became popular towards the end of the first decade of the seventeenth century. Little toys of an elementary simplicity are there, so are compositions demanding a virtuosity found only among the greatest players. All the most notable English lutenist composers are represented and there are a few pieces by some of the great Continental masters. Reductions for the lute of vocal music by Orlando di Lasso and Archadelt also appear. The collection is, in fact, a complete cross-section of the repertoire of lute music in common use in England between about 1580 and 1615.

Dd.2.11 is certainly the earliest of the group, though possibly it was not started before 1588 since in one instance Dowland is given his Mus.Bac., and Edward Pierce is described as 'Regie Capellæ'. Nevertheless Dowland's name, either in full or reduced to initials occurs without the degree no less than eighteen times. Moreover the 'Mus.Bac.' is attached to a piece that has been used as a fill-up at the bottom of a page, and could have been copied in after the rest of the MS was finished. Richard Newton believes the likely year of its completion to have been 1595, but a substantial part was, in all probability, written before 1591. Katherine Darcy married Gervase Clifton in that year and all her pieces in this volume carry her maiden name. It is virtually certain, in any case, to have been completed by 1600, the year in which Edward Pierce, described on f. 56v as 'Regie Capellæ', left the Chapel Royal to go to St. Paul's. This is a large, closely written book, and contains about 310 pieces, fifty-four of which are for bandora.

Dd.5.78 appears to be the next in chronological order although it is possible that the process of copying was partly contemporaneous with Dd.2.11. The main evidence lies in the fact that the handwriting and the system of time marks still closely resemble those of the earlier MS and do not show the weakening of the letters and modification of the time marks which, with Holmes's increasing age and ill health, begin to appear in Dd.9.33. It is curious that in this MS the titles are almost invariably omitted even where Holmes has inserted them in Dd.2.11, and composers' names are generally reduced to initials. There are about 150 pieces, all English with only a few possible exceptions. On f. 44 Dowland has added his signature and the title of the fancy, 'Farwell'. The modern binder has displaced a number of folios and a few are missing.

In Dd.9.33 Holmes's handwriting shows a marked deterioration and on f. 23v he begins to change his manner of writing time marks and introduces a system nearer that of many of the printed books. Although he does not entirely abandon the early 'gridiron' form, in which every note is accounted for, in a number of cases he uses the later 'flag' method, by which a sign is placed only at a change of note values. Having discovered the advantages to the copyist of this abbreviated method, Holmes carried his shorthand some steps further and in the later form the absence of a sign over a note can be understood either as indicating that the same value continues, or that it represents the value ♪. Thus the following indication [musical notation] *a a a a a a* would, in Holmes's late tablature, have the meaning [musical notation]. Furthermore, in passages of dotted rhythm, he sometimes omits all time marks save for a dot placed over the note in question.

Some clues to the period during which Holmes was copying the contents are revealed in the volume. Katherine Darcy's married name is used on f. 28 in 'Mrs Cliftons Allmaine' and, as will be remembered she became the wife of Gervase Clifton in 1591. The copy of this piece, therefore, could not have been made before that year. Some time could have elapsed before Holmes wrote it in his book, although it is likely to have been before 1597 since by then Clifton had received a knighthood. Another clue is at the back of the book where Holmes has entered a memorandum of two prayers, the first of which is dated February 28th, 1600/1, and is on behalf of 'on[e] Davie were dwelling in theving lane★ being prentice to Robert Wilson, who hath bene a very long time sicke', the other, undated, is for William Hoper, also in 'grievous sicknesse'. Presumably they were given to Holmes that they might be said in the Abbey, and he jotted them down in the lute book upon which he was working at the time. Finally, Cutting gives Sir Fooke [Fulke] Greville his title when he names a pavan for him on f. 18 and Greville became a Knight of the Bath on July 25th, 1603.† The copying, therefore, could not have been completed before that date. Almost all the 150 pieces are English, only a ballet and a few corantos and voltas being of French origin.

Nn.6.36. is the latest in the series; in it Holmes employs three types of time marks—the early 'gridiron', the later 'shorthand', and the signs used in ordinary mensural notation, i.e. semi-breves, minims, crotchets, etc., all three types being interspersed throughout the folios. No examples of the third type of marking are found in Dd.9.33, although the association of the symbols of

★ Of 'theving Lane' John Stow says: 'And now to pass to the famous monastery of Westminster: at the very entrance of the close thereof, is a lane that leadeth towards the west, called Theiving lane, for that theives were led that way to the gate-house, while the sanctuary continued in force.' *The Survey of London* (1958). Everyman's Library, No. 589 (Revised edition 1956), p. 405.

† William Shaw, *The Knights of England* (1906).

mensural notation with tablature began to occur in England just about the time that Holmes was making the final entries in this book. The fact that he employs these symbols for the first time in Nn.6.36 strongly suggests that he began to make his final collection after the completion of Dd. 9.33 in 1603 or 4. The presence of a pavan and galliard in one of the French tunings at the end of the MS makes 1610 to 15 a likely time for the writing of the latest entries. The contents are notable for the number of compositions by Daniel Bachelar although it is less interesting to the student of Dowland as it contains only three of the authentic pieces. A few of the tablatures are unmistakably written for the viol; one of them bears the name of James Shirley. Born in 1596,* Shirley could hardly have begun his active life as a composer much before 1615—one further proof of the late date of completion of the MS.

Cambridge University Library has three other lute MSS, Dd.4.22 (E), Add. 3056 (D), and Add.2764 (C), all of which contain some works by Dowland. Dd.4.22 is a small collection, covering only twelve folios. A few pages are blank. All three types of time marks are used, although in this case the 'short-hand' type follows the style of most of the English printed books. From beginning to end there is little noticeable change in the handwriting, and probably the copying of so short a MS was accomplished without much delay. Some idea of the date is given by the inclusion of an anonymous composition called 'the noble menes mask tune'.† This, in all probability, is part of the music from Cyril Tourneur's lost tragi-comedy, *The Nobleman*, which was played at Court in 1612/13, and is known to have contained a masque.

The second of these books, Add. 3056, was presented to Cambridge in 1891, by Francis Jenkinson, Librarian, who bought it from Cosens the antiquary. At the beginning of the volume some folios are missing, and those that remain are marked 2 to 83. Of these some pages are blank. The neat writing and time marks in the 'gridiron' style are uniform throughout, and show no marked change from folio to folio. The MS is of interest on account of the independence of mind of the writer. He appears to have been a musician who, in a number of cases, preferred not to accept the already composed divisions on some well-known pieces, but to make his own arrangements. Some of these, including an arrangement of 'Lachrimæ' are marked with the initials 'C.K.', as also are some compositions which appear to to be his own. His identity still remains hidden. Seventeen pieces of Italian origin occur in the middle of the book, but for the rest, the music is English. On ff. 60–61v the compiler has written out 'Mrs Anne Grene her leaues be greene' from

---

* David Lumsden, 'The Sources of English Lute Music'.

† Also in Add, 38,539, where it is called "the Noble Man", and without title in Add. 10,444.

John Danyel's *Songs to the Lute, Viol and Voice* of 1606. He has given no title or ascription, but his copy of this piece, in a *cordes avallées* tuning, is exceptionally exact and it seems evident it was made direct from the printed book. This gives 1606 as the earliest possible date for completion of the MS.

The last of these, Add. 2764 (C), until recently consisted of a few fragments removed from the binding of another book in the Library. More fragments have now been recovered from the bindings of other books in the same series. It reveals no unknown pieces by Dowland but gives a complete copy of a 'Lachrimæ' setting in A, without divisions, analogous to the copy in the Hirsch MS, and adds the title 'Capit[ain] Candishe his Galy[ard]' to a version of No. 21. Fragments of other pieces are listed under their appropriate numbers, according to the provisional foliation given by Robert Spencer, who kindly allowed me to study his photographs. Written for a six-course lute, the tablature is neat with 'gridiron' time marks and shows a fair number of ornament signs. The scantiness of the material makes it difficult to assign a date to the folios but their general appearance and the absence of diapasons suggest they come from a lute-book which was probably among the earliest to contain pieces by Dowland.

Archbishop Marsh's Library, Dublin, has a lute-book, MS Z. 3. 2. 13, of which a large part was written at the very beginning of the 'golden age' while some of the compositions date from even earlier. Of the 150 pieces, or thereabouts, the majority have no composers' names, but John Johnson (*d.* 1594) is mentioned several times and pieces by Weston ('Westones pauion', Giles Lodge, f. 20) and Parsons★ also occur. An anonymous galliard, named for Lord Hereford (Walter Devereux, created Viscount Hereford in 1550) would probably have been written before 1572 when he was created Earl of Essex, but in any case it would have been before 1576 when the title became extinct with the death of the second Viscount. An anonymous, untitled fragment of 'Lady Rich's Galliard', makes 1581† the earliest possible date for the completion of this part of the MS, although the probability remains that this galliard was not written until after Dowland's return from France in 1584. On the evidence it seems safe to assume that this particular copyist finished his work within two or three years of that date. The ten pieces in a slightly later hand, from p. 380 onwards, include two by Dowland—'my ladie Richis galliard'

★ A 'Master Weston', page to Henry VIII and lutenist, was in the charge of Philip van Wilder in the 1530s (Stevens, *Music and Poetry at the Early Tudor Court*, 1961, p. 381). Account Books at Belvoir Castle, Historical MSS Commission, 4, p. 381, show that a Weston was engaged there as lutenist in 1557/8. Whether this Weston was identical with Henry VIII's page, or whether either was the composer of this piece it is impossible to say. Robert Parsons was drowned in the River Trent at Newark, on January 25th, 1569/70. See Edward Rimbault, *The Old Cheque Book of the Chapel Royal* (1872), p. 2.

† The year in which Penelope Devereux married Lord Rich.

and 'An almayne Douland' (Sir John Smith's)—and arrangements of two songs that later appeared in *A Musicall Banquet*—Richard Martin's 'Change thy mind' and the anonymous 'O dear life' to Philip Sidney's words from *Astrophel and Stella*. A probable time for the copying of these pieces could be somewhere between about 1591 and 1595. The original hand continues at p. 397. Both copyists have written for a six-course lute.

Another MS in Dublin is William Ballet's book, in the Library of Trinity College. As a source-book for Dowland this MS is a borderline case. By giving the title of Dowland's 'Fortune' as 'fortune my foe to the consort', it does, however, provide an explanation of the incomplete character of this piece. Contrary to statements made by some earlier writers this book is un-dated, but the presence of works by Holborne and Daniel Bacheler points to the latter end of the sixteenth century, while the inclusion of 'Robinson's toye', No. 15 from *The Schoole of Musicke* (1603), might suggest the very early years of the seventeenth. A section in the middle, in a different hand, is devoted to music for the Lyra viol and contains a setting of 'Lachrimæ'. These pages could not have been completed before 1609 since they include an arrangement of the 'Witches Dance' from Ben Jonson's *Masque of Queens*, first played in that year.

The beautiful book, now known as the Wickhambrook MS, is of early origin. It is written in an exquisitely neat and precise hand and is in excellent preservation. It came up for sale in the 1930s and was bought by Miss Dulcie Lawrence-Smith of Wickhambrook in Suffolk. From her it passed into the hands of Eric Marshall Johnson, who sold it to the University of Yale. Formerly it had belonged to Mr. O. G. Knapp, who gave the following information about how it came into his family:

The MS came into my possession on the break-up of my mother's old home, the Mansion House, Bengeworth, Evesham, in 1906, and the writing on the paper cover is that of my grandfather, Thomas Beale Cooper, who succeeded his uncle, the Rev. Thomas Beale at the Mansion House in 1805, and died in 1854. I think therefore that in the course of that half century he must have picked it up at some sale in the neighbourhood—he had rather an eye for curiosities of that sort—but when and where I have no idea.*

The first nine folios are missing and the collection extends only as far as f. 17v, but small as it is, it is of very high quality. There is little change in the handwriting from start to finish and the whole appears to have been compiled within a short time, probably about the year 1590.

To the student of Dowland a MS of exceptional interest is the one now in

---

* I am grateful to Richard Newton for allowing me to quote these details which were given in a letter to him.

the Folger Shakespeare Library, Washington, D.C. This book was entirely unknown to musicologists until 1926 when it was brought to Sotheby's for sale by a Mrs Dowland, the widow of a descendant of the composer himself, it having been in the possession of the family since it was first compiled. Four distinct hands have copied the music: No. 1, that of Anne Bayldon, whose rather untidy tablature fills the first six folios; No. 2, which takes over in the middle of 'The Queenes Treble' and continues to f. 22; No. 3, in which four corantos are written on ff. 24v/25; and finally, Dowland's own, in which he has written 'my Lady Hunsdons Allmande' on f. 22v, at least some part of an untitled copy of 'What if a day' on f. 23 and, also without title, the first strain of 'Lady Clifton's Almain' on f. 23v. He has also added his signature to five other compositions. A further fragment of his writing occurs on some pages following f. 25, which, except for a few random jottings, are otherwise blank. The upper line, in the bass clef, appears to be a bar or two of an instrumental bass and below is a line of tablature for a lute in the tuning D—d. The same notes are shown in the tablature but it is not an identical transcription of the line above, some of the values of the notes in the upper line being divided in half and repeated in the tablature; other notes sometimes being shown in a different octave. Possibly it is the tail end of a composition for which Dowland was working on a part for a bass lute and had jotted down the bass line in tablature before filling in the harmony. Or possibly it was a part for a Lyra viol.

The fly-leaves of this MS are, in their way, no less interesting than the musical contents. There are scraps of pious sentiments such as 'The Lord of hostis', 'I lyft myne hart to ye'; in fact, the kind of phrases often used as writing exercises. There are some lines of Latin verse including the opening of Book I of Vergil's *Aeneid*:

> Arma uirumque cano, Troiæ qui primus ab oris
> Italam fato profugus Lauinaque uenit
> litora, multum. . . .

Several owners of the book have, from time to time, added signatures. Among these is that of Anne Bayldon,* who copied the pieces in the first

* The extensive history of the family, *Baildon and the Baildons* (1912), by F. J. Baildon, shows Anne to have been a name in very common use among the Baildons of the late sixteenth and early seventeenth centuries. Moreover, some members of the family with the name Agnes were also known as Anne. I attempted to trace the history of several of these Annes in the hope that I might find one whose life at some point touched that of Dowland or the lives of some of his other patrons and friends. One appeared whose circumstances seemed to show several links with some of the families among whom Dowland is known to have moved. This was Anne, widow of Francis Colby, who, it is said, became the wife of Sir Francis Baildon or Bayldon at Kippax, Yorkshire, on May 2nd, 1604, although the registration of the marriage has not been traced. As well as his estates in Yorkshire, this Sir Francis owned land

part of the MS. Lower on the page is a single name in a totally different style, somewhat Germanic in appearance. It has been suggested that this could be interpreted as the name Dulandt or Dulants, but this explanation is not entirely satisfactory. The inscription 'James Dowland Cuckney Notts.' is in a beautifully clear, eighteenth-century hand.

Opposite the last page of tablature, on the first blank page, with the book held upside down, another signature has been written in a late sixteenth- or early seventeenth-century hand. The quill was overfull of ink and some letters have filled up. The first name, Thomas, is clear enough, but the second is very illusive. With so little of the script for comparison there is nothing by which to check the form of the letters and the first three offer several alternatives. What appears to be written is 'B--thby', but the name Boothby, which immediately comes to mind, does not quite fit, and the presence of a dot over the third letter suggests it might be an 'i'.

In addition to the problems left by the uncertainty in identifying Anne Bayldon and some of the other names, other puzzling questions remain unanswered. Whose were the handwritings that follow that of Anne, and why should Dowland have added his name to some of his compositions and not to others? In the case of 'Lacrame', as will be seen later, the explanation could possibly be that he considered it a bad version, alternatively, his name is already given and he may have felt it unnecessary to add a signature. This too, might apply in the case of 'The Battell gallyard' and 'Doulands rounde battell galyard', where the authorship is also indicated, but why did he allow 'winter jomps' to remain anonymous? It is one of the pieces attributed to him

---

in Lincolnshire, and his signature appears together with that of Sir Gervase Clifton, Knight and Baronet, on a Commission, dated August 14th, 1616, in which they are directed to hold an inquest on September 3rd of that year at Lincoln Castle, on the death of one George St. Paule. It will be remembered that Katherine Darcy, for whom Dowland wrote four pieces, married Gervase Clifton in 1591. Also in the year 1616, Sir Francis was involved in a syndicate to buy the Manor of Wensleydale in Yorkshire, from Ludovic Duke of Lennox for the sum of £10,000. Two other members of the syndicate were Sir Thomas Smith of Bidborough, Kent, and Sir William Smith, of Hammersmith. Since Smith is such a common name it is impossible to say whether these were the Thomas who, six years earlier, had contributed a commendatory poem to *Varietie of Lute-Lessons*, or the William who married Brigide Fleetwood, but it seems something of a coincidence that the names should be associated in this way. I traced the existence of a signature of this Anne Bayldon on a document in the possession of Lord Downe, and with his help and the help of Mr. C. K. C. Andrew, the County Archivist at Northallerton, Yorkshire, I obtained a photograph of the deed, dated February 17th, 1624/5. Unfortunately the signature is very different from the one in the lute MS. Certainly in twenty years, changing fashions in handwriting could have brought about modifications of the earlier script, and the lack of agreement does not completely rule out the possibility that both were written by the same woman. Nevertheless, the 1624/5 signature cannot, with honesty, be said to support the other facts which point to Dame Anne as the possible owner of the book. In *Baildon and the Baildons* an extract from her Will is quoted, but its whereabouts is not mentioned, and so far I have been unable to trace it.

by Barley which, though he criticized as inaccurate, he did not disown. These many uncertainties make any attempt to date this MS extremely difficult. One fairly reliable fact, however, seems to emerge: 'Johnsons gallyard' on f. 22, in script No. 2, is, in Nn.6.36, f. 11, attributed to Robert Johnson; if this attribution is correct it would exclude the possibility of the MS having been written much before the end of the sixteenth century, since Robert would have been no more than about seventeen in the year 1600. If the Anne Bayldon of this MS were indeed the same person as the wife of Sir Francis Bayldon (but, of course, her identity is by no means proved) then her signature could not have been written on the final page before 1604, although clearly she could have copied the tablature before that date. With the absence of more precise data it would be unsafe to make a more definite estimate than that the MS was probably written in the early years of the seventeenth century.

The British Museum has five English MSS containing lute music by Dowland. Add. 31,392 is a fine volume in a good state of preservation. It has a set of pavans and galliards for virginals by William Byrd and some pieces for bandora in addition to the lute music. The tablature, which begins on f. 13, is in two different handwritings, both of which are beautifully clear. The first uses the 'flag' type of time mark and ornament signs are entirely absent. The second begins at f. 22v and uses 'gridiron' time marks, but in this case the double-cross ornament sign is employed with great freedom. At f. 26 the original hand returns and continues to the end. Compositions by Dowland, Cutting and Pilkington form the greater part of the repertoire and the collection can hardly have been written out before 1595 as Pilkington is given his Mus.Bac. by both copyists. Indeed the section in hand No. 2 could not have been completed until after 1600, since Mrs. Marie Oldfield, for whom Pilkington wrote a galliard (ff. 22v/23), was not married until that date, when as Mary Somerford she became the wife of Phillipe Oldfield of Somerford.* Hirsch MS 1353 contains fifty-four pieces, but only two by Allison and one by Holborne have the composers' names. So far it has been possible to identify four by Dowland, five by Cutting, four by Holborne, and two each by Allison, Byrd, Ferrabosco and Strogers. All the pieces are for a six-course lute except two, which have a seventh course tuned at F. It is probably among the earlier MSS, possibly contemporary with Dd.2.11.

Add. 6402 is a single folio containing only four pieces, two of them being by Dowland. The words 'Baliol Coll: Statutes' have been added in a later hand, and the Hughes-Hughes Catalogue gives the date as 1610.

---

* *Visitation of Cheshire, 1613*, Harleian Society, Vol. 59 (1909).

Add. 38,539 is often spoken of as the John Sturt MS. The original binding, however, is stamped with the Letters 'M.L', which are said, in the Catalogue, to stand for Matthew Locke. If the MS was indeed ever in his possession then the letters were a later addition since the book itself dates from a period somewhat earlier than Locke's. The letters are more likely to stand for the Margaret Mary whose surname has been torn away with part of the fly-leaf. The number of masque tunes among the contents makes about 1615 a very probable date for the collection, and the presence of a piece called 'The Noble Man' suggests it could not have been started much before 1612–13. The only fact known about its later history is that it was purchased by the Museum from Captain Granville, through Messrs. Sotheby on June 8th, 1912. The MS is noticeable for the exceptional care with which the performing directions are written into the text. Almost every note has its fingering point for the right hand; hold marks are drawn for the upper voice as well as in the bass; and two ornament signs, the single cross and the double cross, are used with great profusion. Many of the pieces are written for a ten-course lute.

The tablature and captions of Eg. 2046 are written in the same hand as that of the inscription on the fly leaf: 'Jane Pickeringe owe this Booke 1616'. Clearly it is her own personal collection of music and not one acquired from a professional copyist. The contents include examples of the most highly developed virtuoso music of the time and the owner must have been a performer of considerable ability. The absence of masqueing tunes or voltas and corantos in the French taste such as those in Add. 38,539, indicates a somewhat conservative taste in 1616, but there is nothing to indicate whether Jane added her signature early or late in the process of forming her collection. At the end of the book later hands have added some pieces by John Lawrence and Gautier, all in various forms of the French tuning. According to the Hughes-Hughes *Catalogue of Manuscript Music in the British Museum*, Vol. III (1908), p. 66, Jane Pickering was probably the daughter of Sir Thomas Puckering, created a baronet in 1612, and niece to the Dorothy Puckering who married Sir Adam Newton, tutor to Prince Henry. Sir Thomas had three daughters by his wife Elizabeth, Frances, Jane and Cecilia, but Jane was the only one to survive. The details of this family are confirmed in the *Dictionary of National Biography* under the heading Puckering, Sir John (1544–96), of whom Sir Thomas was the third son, but some further information is given. It appears that Sir Thomas married Elizabeth, only daughter of Sir John Morley of Halnaker in Sussex in 1616, and even allowing for the remarkable speed with which women provided themselves with large families in the seventeenth century, Jane could hardly have been born and acquired her beautiful handwriting within the same year as her mother's marriage. There were in fact, several large families flourishing in the first half of the seventeenth century who spelt the name precisely as Jane spelt hers, and possibly future research will reveal the real Jane who was such an accomplished lutenist.

One of the more recent MSS to be rediscovered is the Euing Lute Book, in the Library of Glasgow University. It is a well-written oblong folio in excellent condition. Its contents are closely related to the Cambridge books even, occasionally, to the reproduction of identical mistakes made by Holmes in his copies. Of its seventy-one pieces only three have titles or composers' names. The first part appears to be contemporaneous with all but the latest of the Cambridge books, but another hand, probably of the mid-seventeenth century, has added an extremely interesting set of instructions for the realization of figured bass on the theorbo.

The Weld Lute Book, which, in 1893, was referred to by Professor Wooldridge in his edition of Chappell's *Popular Music of the Olden Times*, was, at that time, known to be in the possession of Lord Forester. For many years it was lost sight of and the only traces that remained were copies of a few pieces which Professor Wooldridge had handed to Arnold Dolmetsch who, in turn had passed on some of them to the present writer. In September, 1960, Robert Spencer, with Lord Forester's permission, searched the library and eventually discovered the MS in the strong-room where it had lain unnoticed, probably from the time when Professor Wooldridge had examined it. The book appears to have belonged to John Weld of Willey (Lord Forester's name being Weld-Forester), who was born in 1581 and was admitted to the Middle Temple on August 2nd, 1600. In 1613 he became Town Clerk of London, which office he held, except during the years of the Commonwealth, until his death in 1666, shortly after the destruction of his town house during the Fire of London.

The writing of the clear and accurate tablature and the rubrics in the body of the book bears no resemblance to the hand in which John Weld's signature is written and was probably that of a professional copyist from whom Weld may have bought the book. The composers represented include John Dowland, John and Robert Johnson, Anthony Holborne, Daniel Bacheler, Alfonso Ferrabosco, Edward Collard and Mathias Mason.*

The MS in the possession of Mr. W. S. Gwynn Williams of Llangollan is of extraordinary interest historically, quite apart from its musical value. When Richard Newton first examined the book he noticed a Coronet stamped into

---

* For a full account of this MS and its history, with a list of contents and concordances, see 'The Weld Lute Book' by Robert Spencer in the *Lute Society Journal*, Vol. I (1959).

the original leather binding, surmounted with the Badge of the Garter. At the top of the Coronet are two small letters ^R_E. On the verso of the final fly leaf is a letter written in a good hand, but with several alterations and small interlineations. Here is Richard Newton's transcription into modern spelling of what is written:

From a mind delighting in sorrow, from spirits wasted with travail, care, and grief; from a heart torn in pieces with passion from a man that hateth himself and all things that keepeth him alive, what service can your Majesty reap? Since my service past deserves no more than banishment and proscription into the most cursed of all countries, with what expectation or to what end should I live longer? No, no, your rebels' pride and success must give me means to ransom myself (my soul, I mean) out of the hateful prison of my body: and if it should happen so,* your Majesty may believe that you shall have no cause to mislike the fashion of my death: though the course of my life may not please you.

Ardbrackane, 30th August 1599
Your Majesty's exiled servant
Essex.†

The Tollemache Lute MS, formerly in the possession of Lord Tollemache of Helmingham Hall, Suffolk (owner of the well-known Orpharion by John Rose),‡ came up for sale at Sotheby's on June 14th, 1965, and was bought by Robert Spencer. It dates from approximately 1610 and consists of twenty-six pieces for a seven-course lute, of which nine are duet parts. It is important for the fact that among these are several which supply the second part of duets hitherto incomplete. The versions of the Dowland pieces are interesting in that they all show an individual treatment, slightly at variance with the more generally accepted forms. Of the two copies of 'Mrs White's Choice', that on f. 7 has the rubric 'per Henricum Sampson scriptorem libri' and possibly he is responsible for those arrangements that are copied in his hand. A second hand also appears, up till now unidentified, which has also contributed to C.U.L. Dd.4.22, Dd.9.33, and B.M. Add. 15117.§

Lord Herbert of Cherbury's Lute Book at the Fitzwilliam Museum, Cambridge, is the latest English MS containing lute music by Dowland, and for the purpose of this book, that is its most interesting feature. It appears to

---

* Defect in the MS.

† A fair copy was sent to the Queen and is reproduced in W. B. Devereux, *Lives and Letters of the Devereux Earls of Essex* (1853), Vol. 2, pp. 120–1, quoted from the Hulton MSS.

‡ For a description of this instrument see Donald Gill, 'An Orpharion by John Rose', *Lute Society Journal*, Vol. II (1960), pp. 33–40.

§ See Robert Spencer, 'The Tollemache Lute Manuscript', *Lute Society Journal*, Vol. VII (1965), pp. 38–9.

be a fair copy made from loose papers, collected over a number of years, the two final compositions, both by Lord Herbert himself, being dated 1640 and 1639 respectively. It includes works by a number of the leading masters of the English classical school, a few by Italians, and a quantity by leading French composers from about 1600 to 1640. Part of the volume is written in the hand of Cuthbert Hely, who also contributed some of his own compositions to the collection.*

The only foreign MS that contains unique copies of works by Dowland is Leipzig, Staatbibliothek II, 6.15; a large collection, dated 1619, of extra-ordinarily varied contents. As a source it is far from satisfactory. Where it is possible to collate any of the items with reliable copies, the versions included here are often found to be faulty. The MS is in German tablature and the handwriting is clear. Many of the page numbers have disappeared, probably by cutting. The two pieces, 'Pauana Dulandi 24' and 'Galiarda Dulandi 8', are discussed on p. 180.

Apart from his own song-books and *A Musicall Banquet*, there are two English printed sources for Dowland's lute music: William Barley's *New Booke of Tabliture* (1696) and *Varietie of Lute-Lessons* (1610). Barley's little book is beautifully printed and is charming to look at. It is of great interest as being the earliest English book devoted entirely to the works of native composers. Fourteen of the pieces are declared to be for the orpharion, although there is no particular difference of treatment to distinguish these from the lute music. Six others are for the bandora and there are, in addition, four songs with bandora accompaniment, although, unfortunately, the words of two have been omitted altogether. The composers represented besides Dowland are Francis Cutting, Philip Rosseter, Edward Johnson and Anthony Holborne. Although Barley's erroneous versions make its musical value somewhat limited for our purpose, its historical value is considerable in proving that the seven works by Dowland included in its contents had been composed prior to the date of its publication.

Varietie of Lute-Lessons is the last and most important of the English printed books for the lute in the old tuning. It is a collection of the very highest order and includes works by some of the finest lutenist composers of the time, both English and continental. The title-page border is the same as that used for *The Second Booke of Songs*† with the difference that the oval at the top is filled with a wood-cut of a viol and bow lying together with a lute and a sheet of music. Round this, on a band, is written:

---

* For a complete description of the MS and its contents, see Thurston Dart, 'Lord Herbert of Cherbury's Lute-Book', *Music and Letters*, Vol. XXXIII, April 1957.

† For a description see p. 247.

COR: MVSICA LÆTIFICAT

The inscription in the centre panel runs as follows:

VARIETIE
OF
LUTE—lessons
Viz.
Fantasies, Pauins, Galliards, Almaines, Corantoes,
and Volts: Selected out of the best approued
AVTHORS, as well beyond the Seas as
of our owne Country.
By *Robert Douland.*
Whereunto is annexed certaine Ob-
seruations belonging to LVTE-playing:
By *Iohn Baptisto Besardo* of Visonti.
Also a short Treatise thereunto appertayning:
By *Iohn Douland* Batcheler of
MUSICKE

The imprint, in the lowest panel, reads:

LONDON
Printed for *Thomas Adams*
1610.

The book is dedicated in the following manner:

TO THE RIGHT WORSHIP-/FVLL, WORTHY, AND VER-
TVOVS/ Knight, Sir *Thomas Mounson.*

SYR, the gratefull remembrance of your bountie/ to me, in part of my
Education, whilst my Father / was absent from *England*, hath embouldned
me/ to present these my first Labours to your worthi-/nes, assuring my selfe
that they being *Musicall*/ will be acceptable to the Patron of *Musicke*,/ and
being onely out of duety Dedicated, you will daine to receiue/them as a poore
Testimonie of his gratitude, who acknowledgeth/ himselfe for euer vnable by
his vttermost seruice to merit your/ Fauours. All that I can is to pray to
Almighty God for the health/ and prosperitie of You and Yours, which I
will neuer cease to doe./ Your Worships in all duety,/ *Robert Douland*

And here is the epistle:

To the Readers whosoeuer.

Gentlemen: I am bold to present you with the first fruits of my Skill,/ which
albeit it may seeme hereditarie vnto mee, my Father being a Lutenist, and/
well knowne amongst you here in England, as in most parts of Christen-
dome/ beside. I am sure you are not ignorant of that old saying, *Labore Deum
omnia*/*vendere*: And how perfection in any skill cannot be attained vnto without the/ waste of many yeeres, much cost, and excessiue labour and industrie,

which/ though I cannot attribute to my selfe, being but young in yeeres, I haue ad-/uentured like a desperate Souldier to thrust my selfe into the Vant-gard, and/ to passe the Pikes of the sharpest Censures, but I trust without daunger, because we finde it true in/ Nature that those who haue loued the Father, will seldome hate the Sonne. And not vnlike in reason/ that I should distaste all, since my meanes and helpes of attaining what I haue, haue been extraor-/ dinary. Touching this I haue done, they are Collections gathered together with much labour out/ of the most excellent Authors, as well of those beyond the Seas, as out of the workes of our owne/ Countrimen. The Treatise of fingering I thought no scorne to borrow of *Iohn Baptisto Besardo/* of Visonti, being a man generally knowne and honoured for his excellencie in this kinde. But what-/soeuer I haue here done (vntill my Father hath finished his greater Worke, touching the Art of/ Lute-playing,) I referre it to your iudicious censures, hoping that that loue which you all generally/ haue borne vnto him in times past, being now gray, and like the Swan, but singing towards his/end, you would continue the same to me his Sonne, who in the meane time will consecrate my best/ indeuours at the shrine of your fauours, and shall euer remaine obliged vnto you for curtesies/ to the vttermost of my power.

Robert Douland.

The following commendatory poem completes the prefatory matter:

> *Thomas Smith Gent:*
> *In Praise of the Worke.*
> Where *Merit* far surmounts the pitch of Praise,
> The *Good-worke* there, transcends the reach of *Words*:
> This *Worke* is such: then good-words cannot raise
> Their waight so high as these *Heau'n*-scaling *Cordes*:
> Then let their vertue their owne glory raise,
> Least it be said a *Smith* hath forg'd their praise.

The translation of the 'Necessarie Observations' of Besardus is given pride of place and appears first in the book, with the following heading:

NECESSARIE OBSERVATIONS BELONG-/ING TO THE LUTE, AND LVTE / playing, by *John Baptisto Besardo* of Visonti: with/ choice varietie of LVTE-lessons, partly Inuented, and partly Col-/lected out of the best AVTHORS, by *Robert Douland,/*and *Iohn Douland* Batcheler of *MUSICKE.*

Immediately following those of Besardus come Dowland's 'Other Necessary Obseruations' which deal with stringing, fretting and tuning.

The volume consists of forty-two compositions, seven under the heading of each form announced on the title-page. A slight liberty is taken in the section devoted to Almains with the inclusion of 'The Witches daunce in the Queenes Maske' which is in $\frac{6}{8}$ rhythm. Presumably the intention was to present this together with the other pieces from the same masque irrespective of its rhythmic structure. John contributed ten pieces to the collection and two are ascribed to Robert, although one of these, 'The Right Honorable the Lady Cliftons Spirit', is undoubtedly by his father. Other composers whose work is represented include Diomedes of Venice, Jacobus Reis, Laurencini and/or The Knight of the Lute,★ Alfonso Ferrabosco of Bologna, Gregorio Huet or Howet of Antwerp, Maurice Landgrave of Hesse, Anthony Holborne, Thomas Morley, Daniel Bachelar, Perrichon and Saman.

Fine as the collection is musically, it must, however, be said that the printing is full of inaccuracies. These vary in importance from the simple placing of a letter on the wrong line to serious confusions which are difficult to correct unless comparison can be made with a more accurate copy.

None of the foreign printed lute books contain unique copies of works by Dowland, but the list on p. 475 shows how frequently he is represented in the great Continental collections. The compilers of these books served him with differing degrees of exactitude. Besardus (or more probably his printer) omitted the top note of the first chord in 'Lachrimæ', thereby destroying the famous descending phrase; van den Hove in *Delitiæ Musicæ* printed seven of the lute parts from *Lachrimæ or Seaven Teares* as solo works, a great disservice since five of these lack the melody which, in the complete version, is taken by the treble viol or violin; G. L. Fuhrmann, in *Testudo Gallo-Germanicca*, gives a badly mangled version of 'Bonny Sweet Robin' and attributes the 'Battle Galliard' to Robert Dowland, but among four other pieces by Dowland, described as of uncertain authorship, is a version of 'Mrs vaux galliard' and we can be grateful to Fuhrmann for supplying a correct reading of the penultimate bar which, in the only other known copy, in Dd.9.33, has gone badly astray. The beautifully printed *Hortus Musicalis* (1615) of Elias Mertel has copies of 'Forlorne Hope' and Fantasia No. 6, the former, though containing some errors, provides more accurate readings for several bars unsatisfactorily copied by Holmes in Dd.9.33. The 355 preludes and fantasias in this book are distinguished only by numbers and no list of contents has been included. This omission is not merely the chance mis-binding of the British Museum copy, the one in the Mazarine Collection, Bibliothèque Nationale, Paris, being similarly incomplete.

FANTASIES AND OTHER CONTRAPUNTAL COMPOSITIONS

Of the seven solo pieces of this type to which Dowland's name is attached, five are composed on diatonic themes while the remaining two are wholly

---

★ 'Laurencini of Rome' may have adopted the style 'Equis Romanus' after having had the Order of the Golden Spur conferred on him by the Pope.

chromatic in character. Of those using diatonic material the most widely
known was the one which appears as Fantasie No. 7 in *Varietie of Lute-Lessons*
(No. 1). Seven copies of this still exist.

The 'point' was not entirely Dowland's own composition, and was used,
with some slight variants, by other composers as well, a notable example
being the unknown writer of No. 83 in Elias Mertel's *Hortus Musicalis*. It
appears to be founded on the opening phrase of an Italian *lauda*, which, in
Matteo Coferati's *Corona di Sacre Canzoni* (1675), is called 'Alla Madonna':

SI, ch'io ti vuo' lo - da - re

Most of the *laude spirituali* came into existence at a period considerably
earlier than the date of publication of Coferati's book, and he was undoubtedly
the collector rather than the composer of the contents of his volume. Although
the author has so far been unable to trace an earlier copy of this *lauda* it seems
not unreasonable to suppose that it was in use in Italy at the time of Dowland's
visit and that the melody remained in his mind and served for the opening
bars of this Fantasie.

The piece evolved into two distinct versions; the earlier is found in all the
MS sources and in the *Thesaurus Harmonicus* of Besardus; the later, in *Varietie
of Lute-Lessons*. There are a number of different readings among the MSS
which probably represent the small changes which inevitably creep in when
a piece passes from hand to hand and is written out by one copyist after
another. In *Varietie of Lute-Lessons* many small points, where the MSS seem
to have strayed, are cleared up, and two major alterations are introduced. At
the beginning of bar 29 two beats are dropped and from then onwards the
bar lines are placed two beats earlier; and seven bars are eliminated after bar
44. Altogether this version is musically more satisfying and represents
Dowland's mature revision of the work, although its appearance in Add.
38,539 (probably written after 1615) suggests that the earlier version continued in use after the printing of *Varietie of Lute-Lessons*. It is noticeable that
the piece is not found in any of the really early source books for Dowland's
work and it is likely that it was among the later compositions of his great
creative period. It opens with the lovely serene passage:

After this theme has been worked through a complex contrapuntal section a series of short phrases follows, each one with its echo at the octave:

Here Dowland makes great play with the device of resolving the leading note an octave or two octaves below. He follows with a swiftly running section, and the Fantasie ends with a display of virtuosity for the player:

In many ways the two chromatic fantasias, No. 2, 'Forlorne Hope Fancye',
and No. 3, 'Farwell', are among the most remarkable of all Dowland's solo
works for the lute. Both are built on the plan which takes for its subject a six-
note fragment of the chromatic scale, descending in 'Forlorne Hope' and
ascending in 'Farwell'. In the former the chromatic phrase is used seventeen
times and in the latter, fourteen. The ascending and descending forms never
occur in the same piece and Dowland confines himself strictly to the chromatic degrees lying between G and the D below, and those between D and A
below, except in 'Forlorne Hope' where the phrase twice starts on A, descending to E. Nothing could better express the title of this piece than the heavy
foreboding of the opening phrase:

Another quotation from the same piece shows how in one place the alto
starts the phrase before the bass has completed it; it is followed by the treble
which enters on the third note of the theme in the alto voice:

The last two appearances of the chromatic hexachord, in the bass, are joined
by making the last note of the first phrase serve as the first of the next; thus a
continuous chromatic scale of eleven notes is formed:

When Mathew Holmes copied 'Forlorne Hope' into his lute-book he became confused at this point and made several errors in the bass. The passage is given correctly in No. 70 of Mertel's *Hortus Musicalis*.

The rising chromatic phrase of 'Farwell', though equally emotional, expresses a totally different anguish and has none of the brooding disquiet of 'Forlorne Hope':

Both fantasies are developed with the same complexity of detail and both demand a superb technique for their performance.

It is something of a mystery why Dowland should have chosen 'Farwell' out of the twenty-two of his compositions contained in Dd.5.78 to which to add his own name and degree.

No. 4, 'Farwell', though having the same title as No. 3, is an entirely different piece, and is, in fact, an In Nomine, with the Gloria Tibi Trinitas theme in the Cantus voice:

At bar 40* the rhythm changes to $\frac{12}{8}$ and continues in the same measure until the end.

No. 5 is a comparatively short fantasie of thirty-five bars. The first theme consists of an ascending and descending scale passage:

* In the MS the second group of three quavers is omitted and the In Nomine theme is thrown out of balance. Richard Newton pointed this out to me and sent me a copy with his conjectured reconstruction of the bar.

and fragments of the scale combined in decorative patterns reappear all through this fantasia.

No. 6, a fantasie in G minor, opens as follows. Here the altus voice enters at the interval of a fifth below the cantus, unlike the other two fantasies of this type, Nos. 1 and 5, in which the second voice enters at the octave:

After No. 1, this appears to have been the next most popular of the fantasies, with four known copies still existing. Mertel included it as No. 69 in his *Hortus Musicalis* (1615).

No. 7 is an extremely long piece—the longest of all the fantasies. Technically it is elaborate although musically it is not as complex as No. 1 or any of the chromatic fantasies. The opening is almost entirely in two parts and an imitation of the first bar of the bass soon appears in the upper voice:

The greater part consists of decorative melodic patterns either above a simple bass line, or below held notes in the upper voice. At bar 61 the measure changes to $\frac{12}{8}$ and five bars are introduced in which the figuration closely resembles that of the final section of Fantasie No. 1:

At this point a third voice enters, moving, for three bars, in a rapid passage of parallel sixths with the upper voice, over a bass of minim beats. The piece ends with a typical 'trumpet' flourish, leaping up and down the top string in intervals of fifths and thirds.

PAVANS

Of No. 8, 'Piper's Pavan', eight copies of the lute solo are still extant, six being in English, the other two in Continental sources. Three of the versions, that of Barley's *New Booke of Tabliture* and the two Continental ones, are however, very poor and should not be regarded as basic texts. Apart from Barley, Add. 3056 is the only source to give a division on the third strain, but the writer of this MS appears frequently to compose his own divisions and since the whole text shows a number of variants it is probable that the final division is his work and not Dowland's. Seven arrangements for other solo instruments, consort or voice are also found, the total number suggesting that, among the pavans, it stood next in popularity to 'Lachrimæ'. Though this pavan and its galliard are not composed on precisely the same melodic structure as are the Lachrimæ pair, nevertheless, comparison will show how the first three bars of the galliard are derived from the melody of the pavan:

After the first indebtedness, however, the galliard develops along completely individual lines.

The title of No. 9 is given completely and correctly only in *Lachrimæ or Seaven Teares* where it appears as 'Semper Dowland Semper Dolens'. In Jane Pickering's MS it becomes 'Dowlandes Lamentation Semp dolent' and in the Weld MS 'Semper dolens'. In the third source for the solo piece, the Euing MS, it is anonymous and has no title. In its complete form the phrase is interesting for the clue it appears to provide to the sixteenth-century pronunciation of the composer's name. Since his re-emergence as a figure of importance in the musical world his name is generally pronounced with the first syllable rhyming with 'now', and indeed, this pronunciation is used by the surviving members of the family today, but the title seems to have point only if the diphthong 'ow' and the vowel 'o' have the same sound. In the Cellarius album he writes 'Dolandi' and the inscription in the 'Lamentatio Henrici Noel', presumably copied from his own hand, gives 'Gio. Dolande'; apart from these, all other known signatures give the name as 'Doulande' with the 'u' sometimes approaching the form of a 'w', while 'Doland' or 'Dolande' are frequent variants of the spelling found in MS sources. The identity of sound between the diphthongs 'ou' and 'ow' with the vowel 'o' is heard in many other words, for example, 'soul', 'mould', 'poultry' and indeed, the present author's own surname; and 'to throw', 'to show' and 'to tie a bow'. The similarity of pronunciation called for in the jingle of the title 'Semper Dowland semper dolens' seems to suggest that Dowland himself would have expected to hear his name rhymed with 'Poland'.

The odd title gives rise to a certain curiosity as to the nature of the impetus that set Dowland's mind playing round the words 'Dowland' and '*dolens*', turning them this way and that, savouring their similarity, and finally perhaps, hearing them fall into place in the form of a punning sentence. Possibly the following passage from *The Diary of John Manningham, 1602–1603** may supply the clue:

Dec. 7, 1602.

Out of a little book intitled *Buccina Capelli in laudem Juris*:† Lawe hath God for the author, and was from the beginning . . . Doleo quia semper dolens dolere nescio. Quo modo nisi per dolores sanabitur, qui per delectationes infirmatur? Doce me salutarem dolorem?

The idea that Dowland may have seen this book and retained the passage in his mind, is prompted not only by the words 'semper dolens' but by the repetition—doleo . . . dolens . . . dolere . . .; from that to 'semper

---

* Camden Society Publication, Vol. 99 (1868), p. 99.

† The editor's footnote says: We have not found any other trace of this 'little book'. It was probably a work of one of the celebrated French Protestants of the name of Cappel. (*La France Protestante*, iii, 198.)

Dowland semper dolens' is a very short step, especially in an age when it was habitual for the mind to play with words in just this particular way. The sense of the passage too, is likely to have found an immediate response in Dowland, and might almost have come from his own pen, 'I sorrow, because ever sorrowing, I know not how to sorrow. He that is made sick through delights, how shall he be healed, save by sorrows? Teach me a salutary sorrow'.*

True to its name, all the way through, this pavan expresses a profound melancholy. The third strain, with its broken and repeated falling phrases, as shown in these four bars, is a particularly moving expression of a poignant and deeply felt emotion:

The solo version of the piece is quite distinct from the lute part in *Lachrimæ or Seaven Teares*, the copy in the Weld MS, in particular, showing a number of variants in the reading. All MS sources agree, however, in giving this ending for the solo:

while *Lachrimæ or Seaven Teares* gives this very remarkable final bar:

There is no question of a note having been omitted at the end since all the viol parts have the rests clearly marked, and the treble viol agrees exactly with the lute.†

* I have to thank Richard Newton for calling my attention to this passage in Manningham.
† Van den Hove reprints the consort part as a lute solo in *Delitiæ Musicæ* and when Dr. Hans Dagobert Bruger transcribed this in his *John Dowland's Solostücke für die Laute* (1923), the end was too much for him, and he resolved it comfortably on an undefined chord of D, having transposed the whole piece down a fourth.

The titles of Nos. 10 and 11, 'Solus cum sola' and 'Mrs Brigide Fleetwoods pauen als Solus sine sola', suggest the two pieces are in some way connected, although musically they have nothing in common except that both are in pavan form. 'Solus cum sola' is lively and tuneful, though not particularly distinguished, while 'Solus sine sola' is in serious mood. Both appear to be early compositions and are written for a six-course lute, though Barley adds a seventh course to 'Solus cum sola' and includes it among the pieces for orpharion. He prints the three strains only, although the three MS copies all have divisions to the repeats. The copies in Add. 31,392 and the Euing MS agree very closely, but the earliest copy, that of Dd.2.11, differs considerably in the treatment of the repeat of the first strain.

The sole remaining copy of 'Solus sine sola' was written at a time when ill health had already interfered with the clarity of Holmes's handwriting and several passages are difficult to transcribe, but these few uncertainties are not serious enough to obscure the grave beauty of the piece. Brigide Fleetwood's marriage in 1589 sets that year as the latest possible date for its composition.

A clue to the mystery of the titles may be found in a monkish Latin proverb which runs:

Solus cum sola non cogitabuntur orare pater noster.

This might be translated freely as 'A man and a woman, alone together, will not think of saying their Pater Noster', meaning perhaps, 'A man and woman, alone together, can hardly be expected to spend their time in prayer'.* I suspect the whole thing may be an esoteric joke connected with some incident in the life of the Fleetwood family, the meaning of the two phrases, 'the male with the female' and 'the male without the female' being quite plain to anyone in the know.

There can be little doubt that No. 12, 'Dr Cases Pauen' was written for the John Case, author of *Apologia Musices* (1588), in which Dowland is, for the first time, mentioned among the great composers of his age, and for whom Byrd wrote a six-part madrigal on Thomas Watson's poem 'A Gratification unto Master John Case'. He qualified as a Doctor of Medicine in 1589, thus fixing the earliest date at which the pavan could have been written. The final bars closely resemble the last section of the song 'Farewell unkind, farewell',

---

* Robert Spencer has shown me some correspondence he had with Mr. John Creswell about the phrase 'Solus cum solo'. Mr. Creswell says 'The phrase was first used by Plotinus (A.D. 205–c. 270), the great pagan mystic of Alexandria. According to the whim of the translator the passage reads: "a flight of the *alone to the Alone*" or "escape in *solitude to the Solitary*", the Latin solus meaning alone, only, single, one.' The feminine ending 'sola' in Dowland's title, however, excludes, in this case, the direct application of Plotinus's mystical phrase. Basil Lam has told me of an early motet by Josquin Depres, 'Illi bata dei virgo nutrix', which contains an illusion to this phrase in the words 'salve tu sola cum sola amica'.

No. 14 in *The Third and Last Booke of Songs*. Since this book was not printed until 1603, and Dowland speaks of the contents as being 'newly composed' (although perhaps this is not to be taken too literally; it could be 'sales talk'), it seems probable that the idea first germinated in the pavan and was later adapted to the song with some alterations to the middle and lower voices. Here are the relevant bars from the pavan:

*This note is an octave higher in the M.S.

and here, the last section of the song:

'then fare - well,   then fare - well,   O   fare-well,   wel – come my loue

wel – come my ioy   for   e – – uer.   – uer.

There is no other similarity between the two works.

No. 13 exists in two forms. In Nn.6.36 there is a version with no ascription.

It has divisions to the first and second strain. In this MS it is called 'resolucŏn', though what significance this title has it is now impossible to say. In *The Second Booke of Songs* it is called 'Dowland's adew for Master Oliuer Cromwell' and a Bassus part is added which doubles the bass line of the lute. There are no divisions. The solemn character of this pavan, together with the use of the word 'adew', might suggest it was written to commemorate the death of an Oliver Cromwell, but the identity of a member of the family with that name who died at the appropriate time has eluded the search of several writers who have been interested in the question. Mark Noble, in his very thorough and detailed history of the Cromwells,* records no such person, and it can only be assumed that the pavan was dedicated to the Protector's uncle, Oliver Cromwell (created a Knight of the Bath by James I on July 25th, 1603)† for some occasion less tragic than death but which, nevertheless, called for an 'Adew'.

No. 14, 'Sir John Langton his Pauin', as it appears in *Varietie of Lute-Lessons*, is a fine open-hearted piece in D major, with exceedingly elaborate divisions to the repeats. Another version of the solo, anonymous and without title, occurs in Dd.5.78, while in *Lachrimæ or Seaven Teares* it appears in F major and is called 'M: John Langtons Pauan'. The earlier solo version of Dd.5.78 and that of *Lachrimæ or Seaven Teares* have much in common, especially in strain B, which in these two cases has seven bars while in *Varietie of Lute-Lessons* it has eight. In addition, in *Varietie* an extra beat has been created in bar 2 of this strain which changes the position of the bar lines, the strong beats of the earlier version becoming the weak beats of the later:

Dd.5.78

* *Memoirs of the Protectoral-House of Cromwell* (1787).
† William A. Shaw, *The Knights of England* (1906).

Varietie of Lute-Lessons

Mr. John Langton was knighted in June 1603, and clearly the news had not reached Dowland by the time *Lachrimæ or Seaven Teares* went to press, possibly he had lost touch during the years in Denmark. The title is correctly given in *Varietie of Lute-Lessons* in 1610.

The pavan, 'Lachrimæ', No. 15, was one of those exceptional compositions which, from time to time, appear, and achieve an altogether extraordinary popularity. In its original form as a lute solo it found its way into almost all the important English MS collections of the period and it appears in numerous Continental lute-books, both MS and printed. Many of the copies, though purporting to be by Dowland, are very inaccurate and have divisions entirely different from Dowland's own. Some have divisions frankly acknowledged as being by other composers. A number of lutenists, especially abroad, honoured Dowland by using the Lachrimæ theme as a basis for their own compositions. Besardus, Van den Hove and Valentine Strobelius are notable among those who wrote independent and interesting works which make no pretence of following Dowland's own setting. Its popularity was so great that, subsequently, arrangements were made for almost every domestic instrument then in use. In addition to Dowland's own arrangement for five viols and lute, William Byrd, Thomas Morley, Giles Farnaby, Benjamin Cosyns, 'Mr Randell', Melchior Schildt, Jan Sweelinck, H. Scheidemann and others made settings for keyboard; it appeared in Morley's *First Booke of Consort Lessons*; Johann Schopp made a setting for strings and continuo; and versions are found for cittern, bandora, lyra viol and recorder.

As a song it had an exceptionally long life. In England and Scotland it was known from its first appearance in 1600 until the 1682 edition of John Forbes's *Songs and Fancies*. In the Netherlands it was printed in a very inaccurate form in the *Nederlandsche Gedenck-Clanck* (1626) of Adrianus Valerius, with a set of Dutch words. In all six editions, from 1647 to 1690, of Dirck Rafaelzoon

Camphuyzen's *Stichtelycke Rymen* a version appears with another set of Dutch words. In the early editions it is called 'Lachrimæ à 4 Duodecimi Toni', but later the Cantus part only was printed.

As well as the composers who took the whole, or at least the greater part, of the tune and used it with acknowledgement of the title or the composer, a number of others took the four notes of the opening phrase:

and in a purely allusive manner, wove it into the texture of a composition. One of the earliest instances of the adoption of this phrase appears in Anthony Holborne's 'Pauana Plorauit' (printed in 1599), though Holborne, in his title, shows he is conscious of what he is doing. When Maurice, Landgrave of Hesse made his pavan in honour of Dowland, to point the compliment with elegance and finesse, he used the famous phrase four times in the first strain:

Other composers to use this device were William Brade, Johann Schopp, Leonhard Lechner and William Lawes, one of whose pavans* begins:

With Dowland, whose imagination was so often stimulated by the memory of an already existing *motif*, it is tempting to look among his predecessors for some similar arrangement of notes. Otto Mies† suggests it was the opening phrase of the Superius of Thomas Créquillon's 'Cessez mes yeulx',‡ which, in this case, provided Dowland with his material:

(time values halved)

The increased pathos when the semitone is shifted to lie between the third and fourth notes instead of between the second and third is consistent with Dowland's constant search for the exact expression of sadness and melancholy,

* Bodleian MS Mus. Sch. B.2., see 'A Pavan by W. Lawes'. Anon. *The Musical Antiquary.* Vol. I (1909), p. 108.
† 'Dowland's Lachrimæ Tune', *Musica Disciplina*, Vol. IV (1950), pp. 59–64.
‡ Phalèse, *Premier Liure des Chansons à Quatre Parties* (1553).

and this might well have been accepted as the source of his inspiration were it not that the sequence of notes, requiring no additional accidentals, is found in the Superius of Cauleray's *chanson* 'En esperant':*

le faire ———— puis - - - - - - - - - - - - sance—

Occurring as it does, in this case, within a longer melodic line, it is less obvious than in the case of 'Cessez mes yeulx', but here, in addition to the intervals being identical with Dowland's, so also is the rhythm.

Of Dowland's own three versions of the piece the order of their appearance seems to be: (1) The Lachrimæ Pavan for solo lute; (2) 'Flow my teares' for voice and lute with a sung bass; and (3) the arrangement for viols and lute in *Lachrimæ or Seaven Teares*, in which it was given the name 'Lachrimæ Antiquæ'. The problem of the date of composition of the original Lachrimæ Pavan is bound up with the chronology of the Cambridge lute MSS, the dating of which has already been discussed. If the evidence is accepted which points to the year 1595 as a likely date for the completion of Dd.2.11, the earliest volume in the series, then we can at least say that the lute solo was in existence by that date as two copies of the piece, one in G minor and one in A minor, are found in this MS.

That it had already appeared by the year 1596 is shown by its inclusion in *A New Booke of Tabliture* and Dowland's expostulation about the 'false and unperfect' version presented by Barley.

In *The Second Booke of Songs* (1600) the vocal setting appears in the Table of Contents as 'Flow my teares fall from your springs'. In the body of the book it is, like all the other songs, headed with a number, but above the Cantus part and again above the Bassus, the word 'Lacrime' is printed. This is the only occasion throughout Dowland's song-books where a title other than the opening words of the poem is used. Surely the intention is clear'—Here is a song to my already famous tune Lacrime'. Had the song arrangement been made at an appreciably earlier date it is difficult to find any adequate reason for his having refrained from including it in *The First Booke of Songes* since he obviously regarded it as his greatest composition and, in 1597, no version of which he approved had appeared in print. The use of the title 'Lachrimæ Antiquæ' in 1604 clearly sets this version for five viols and lute as a later arrangement.

Since Dowland himself left no authorized copy of the Lachrimæ Pavan it is only by comparison of the numerous copies in English sources that an opinion may be reached as to what constitutes a standard text. Firstly, it can

* Phalèse, *Quatriesme Liure des Chansons à Quatre Parties* (1555).

be said with complete confidence that the solo version was originally written in the key of G minor, that is, to the extent it can be considered to lie within either a major or a minor scale. This conclusion is based both on the number of copies extant in this key and on the technical facility it affords the player. The higher key of A gives, however, a more comfortable range for the voices and viols although for the lute it considerably increases the difficulty of performance. In both the song and the consort version, the lute, as the accompanying instrument, is not called upon to execute elaborate divisions and the key is, therefore, not so vitally important to the player. The second point that can be stated with certainty is that the original version was written for a six-course lute. On f. 81 of Dd.2.11 which, in my opinion, is the earliest extant 'good' version, it is interesting to find that in a few places a diapason at D has been added either in another hand, or in the hand of Mathew Holmes at a later date. Where these have been added, the higher octave, c on 5, has not been removed. In later copies such as those in Add. 38,539 and Lord Herbert of Cherbury's Lute Book, the diapason D is consistently used and the note in the higher octave is then omitted.

In the list, on p. 481, of the copies of Lachrimæ which, up till now, I have been able to find, the first eight show a sufficient agreement both in the main structure and the treatment of the divisions, and in their conformity with Dowland's style, to make it safe to conclude that they represent his original intention. Even among these, however, a great number of minor variants are found; these include such differences as the addition or omission of un-essential notes in chords, or the dotting of the rhythm in one version where it is written plain in another.

For the more extreme variants it may be of interest to give the first strain from Dd. 5.78 with the division from the same source, and then, for comparison, the very individual treatment of the same division from Add. 3056:

Add. 3056

If the copy in Dd. 5.78 is accepted as one of the group which may fairly be considered to represent Dowland's intention, then the following eight bars, which comprise Barley's version of the repeat of strain 1, will show to what extent Dowland was justified in claiming them to be 'false and un-perfect':

(1) This chord and the following note printed 1 line too high

The same eight bars from the Folger-Dowland Lute Book also show a different treatment in a number of passages, and it is significant that Dowland did not put his signature to this version in spite of the fact that he added his name to six other pieces in the MS.

Two more versions in English sources should be mentioned for the fact that they are in A minor. The one in the Hirsch MS, f. 15v, is without decorated repeats and that of Dd.2.11, ff. 75v/76, is notable for the elaboration of the repeat of the second strain:

Neither of these versions agree in detail with the lute part of 'Lachrimæ Antiquæ'.

Of the copies which found their way into foreign lute-books, both MS and printed, few are worth much consideration. Of the version which Besardus includes in *Thesaurus Harmonicus*, two oddities may be noticed—he calls it 'Fantasia Ioannis Dooland Angli *Lachrimæ*' while it is, of course, in true pavan form, and his printer omitted a on 1 in the tablature, the first note of the melody, although he has given it correctly at the beginning of the repeat. When, however, Besardus came to make a version for three lutes for the *Novus Partus* of 1617, he was singularly unsuccessful. He chose to arrange it for Nova Testudo, Testudo Minor, Testudo Maior, with a Superius and Bassus, presumably for viols. The Nova Testudo as he explains has the first and second courses tuned an octave lower. Unfortunately he appears to have been unable to remember from time to time which tuning he is writing in, and without some drastic editing the piece is unplayable.

Johannes Rude in his *Flores Musicæ* of 1600 has a setting called 'Pavan à 5 voc. Dulandi Angli'. It is a 'short' version in G minor, and is clearly the reduction of a five part setting which must have pre-dated that of *Lachrimæ or Seaven Teares*. Though lacking decorated repeats, the melody itself is considerably decorated in the strains themselves. Musically the piece is of no great value.

That the popularity of 'Lachrimæ' spread far outside purely musical circles, either professional or amateur, is shown by the number of references to the piece which occur in the dramatic literature of the time. Clearly the way in which the name is repeatedly used shows the writers were confident that at least the majority of the theatre-going public would pick up the meaning of the allusion with ease. As the following examples will show the references continue to appear until well after Dowland's death:

Citizen: . . . You musicians, play *Baloo*!
Wife: No, good George, let's ha' *Lachrymæ*.
          Beaumont and Fletcher, *The Knight of the Burning Pestle* (1611)

Now thou playest Dowland's *Lachrymæ* to thy master.
          Thomas Middleton, *No Wit, no Help like a Woman* (1613)

Arion, like a dolphin, playing *Lachrimæ*
          John Fletcher, *The Bloody Brother* (c. 1617)

Or with the hilts, thunder about your ears
Such music as will make your worship dance
To the doleful tune of *Lachrymæ*.
          Philip Massinger, *The Maid of Honour* (1621)

You'll be made to dance *Lachrymæ*, I fear, at the cart's tail.
          John Webster, *The Devil's Law Case* (1623)

Eyes. No, the man
In the moon dance a coranto, his bush
At's back a-fire; and his dog piping *Lachrymæ*.
          Ben Jonson, *Masque of Time Vindicated* (1622/23)

In brief he is a rogue of six reprieves,
Four pardons o'course, thrice pilloried, twice sung Lachrimæ
To the virginals of a carts taile.
          John Fletcher and ?Philip Massinger, *Faire Maide of the Inne*
          (1626)

                          Is your theorbo
Turn'd to a distaff, Signior? and your voice
With which you chanted *Room for a lusty Gallant*
Tun'd to the note of *Lachrimæ*?
          Philip Massinger, *The Picture* (1629)

I would have all lovers begin and end their pricksong
with *Lachrimæ*, till they have wept themselves as dry
as I have.
          Thomas Nabbes, *Microcosmus* (1637)

   The name of the song appears again in a very different context in William
Prynne's *Histrio-mastix* (1633):*

Alas there are but few that finde that narrow way . . . and those few what
are they? Not dancers, but mourners: not laughers but weepers; whose tune
is Lachrimæ, whose musicke, sighes for sinne; who know no other Cinqua-

   * Prynne's attack on the popular amusements of the day was punished with inhuman
severity. He was brought before the Star Chamber, fined £5,000, pilloried, and had both his
ears cut off.

pace but this to Heaven, to goe mourning all the day long for their iniquities; to mourne in secret like Doves, to chatter like cranes for their own and others sinnes.

Although I have found no ballads written to the tune of Lachrimæ, the name itself is mentioned in the Second Part of 'Wit's never good till 'tis bought' (To the tune of Basses Careere):*

> And I oft like a bird have bin caught
> In the prison to stay
> Where I sung Lachrima:
> Thus true wit's never good till 'tis bought.

The name is also quoted in *Sir Thomas Ouerbury His Wife. With additions of New Newes, and diuers more Characters. The tenth impression augmented* 1618 :†

Does any man desire to learne musique? euery man heere sings *Lachrimæ* at first sight, and is hardly out, hee runnes diuisions vpon euery note . . . From the 'character' *A Prison*.

And finally, a quotation from an undated MS poem 'A Pastorall Elegie on ye untimely death of ye watchfull and painfull Pastor's Mr Lawrence Howlet':‡

> Shepherds, leaue your frollicke Layes
> Gleeful Hymes & Roundelayes,
> Sorrow now requires their bee
> No songe heard but Lachrimæ

No. 16, an untitled pavan from Dd.5.78, ff. 47v/48, begins with the Lachrimæ phrase, but even though the first few bars show some slight similarities with 'Lachrimæ Antiquæ Novæ', the likeness is not maintained and it does not appear to be a solo version of any other pavan in *Lachrimæ or Seaven Teares*.

No. 17, 'The Lady Russell's Pavan' is a dignified piece, with elaborate repeats; very suitable for the somewhat formidable lady for whom it was probably written. Holmes's two copies agree closely with the one in the Euing MS, but that of Add. 3056 has a number of very obvious errors.

No. 18 is a pavan of which the opening theme is closely allied to that of

---

* *Roxburghe Ballads*, edited W. Chappell, Vol. III (1875), p. 68.

† This curious book, called in the first edition *A Wife now the Widdow of Sir T. Overburye. Being a most exquisite and singular Poem of the choice of a Wife* (1614), was printed after Overbury's murder in 1613, with 'characters' added to the original poem both by Overbury and others. Possibly the sensational nature of the murder and subsequent trials played some part in the extraordinary popularity it enjoyed. It was again 'augmented' in the ninth and tenth impressions. In all some seventeen editions appeared in London, with others printed in Dublin, the seventeenth impression appearing in 1664. Subsequently the original poem 'The Wife' appeared in a number of collections during the eighteenth century.

‡ The Library of St. John's College, Cambridge. U.26., f. 161v.

'The Lady Russells Pauen', No. 18 being in the minor while the latter is in the major:

No. 18   'Lady Russell'

GALLIARDS

The galliard was Dowland's favourite form among those available to composers of the time. No less than thirty can be attributed to him with certainty and several others, though lacking his name in any source, bear strong traces of his personality. Many of the authenticated pieces exist in four distinct media: lute solo, solo song with lute accompaniment, four-part ayre and for five viols and lute. Within the bounds of this strict form he achieved an immensely varied emotional content ranging over the martial 'Battle Galliard', the elegiac 'Digorie Piper', the tender beauty of 'Lady Rich' and the forthrightness of 'Ferdinando Earl of Derby'.

Except that it can be said with confidence that the versions in *Lachrimæ or Seaven Teares* are later arrangements, it is exceptionally difficult to be sure in which of the media these pieces in dance form were originally conceived. The majority of the sung galliards appear in *The First Booke of Songes*, but the first printing of 1597 is no guide to the date of composition since Dowland himself, in the epistle, 'To the courteous Reader', says of the songs, 'the greater part of them might haue been ripe inough by their age'. Each case has, therefore, to be examined separately for what evidence can be found in the musical text, in the words, or in the background of social and historical circumstances.

Of all the galliards, the one written for Digorie Piper (No. 19) is perhaps the most beautiful, in whichever form it appears. It would seem likely that it was written during the lifetime of the young pirate who died in 1590, and its inclusion in Dd.2.11 would bear out the probability of an early date of composition. However, the naming of a galliard for a patron or friend was on occasion, as will be seen later, a posthumous tribute, and so in this case the use of Piper's name is no absolute proof of composition prior to 1590. How long the vocal versions had been in existence before their appearance in the printed book it is impossible to say, and indeed, Dowland may have meant only that the tunes themselves had been in existence for some time, not necessarily in song form, just as his comment, in *Lachrimæ or Seaven Teares*, that he has 'mixed new songs with olde' clearly does not mean that the familiar pieces in this collection had previously existed in consort form. Nevertheless, in spite of all the uncertainties, two details point to the lute solo as the earlier form. Firstly, in bar 5 in both the vocal and consort versions, beat 3 has the note C in the melody which is absent in all copies of the solo galliard. There is no technical difficulty in playing this note on the lute and, indeed, it is found in the lute part in *Lachrimæ or Seaven Teares*. Its presence so greatly strengthens the melody that it seems certain it was a later improvement, added when the song was made, rather than that it was omitted in a reduction of the song as a lute solo. Secondly, the underlay of the words in several instances in the Altus and Tenor voices is very awkward and destroys the natural verbal rhythms to an extent that suggests the four-part ayre was something of an afterthought.

All four versions are in the same key, and comparison of the respective eight bars of the first strain of each arrangement will show how, in general, Dowland remained faithful to the harmony and structure of the original composition, no matter for what medium of performance it was subsequently set:

Lute solo

Lute song

If my com – plaints could pas – si – ons move

Or make love see where – in I suf – fer wrong.

Four–part ayre

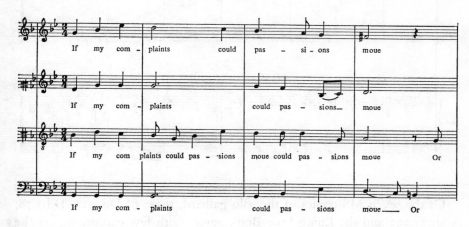

If my com – plaints could pas – si – ons moue

If my com – plaints could pas – sions moue

If my com – plaints could pas – sions moue could pas – si,ons moue Or

If my com – plaints could pas – sions moue Or

Or make loue see where- in I suf – 'fer wrong:

Or make loue see where – in I suf – fer wrong:

make loue see where – in I suf – fer wrong:

make loue. see ——— where- in I suf – fer wrong:

'*Captaine Digorie Piper his Galiard*' *from* '*Lachrimæ or Seaven Teares*'

Of the seven MS copies of the solo galliard, those of Dd.2.11, Dd.5.78, Add. 31,392 and the Euing Lute Book agree, with few exceptions, on the main details of the treatment; they do, however, fail in unanimity on the false relation between F and F sharp in bar 5. Holmes's two copies in this group follow the arrangement given above, while Add. 31,392, the Euing Lute Book and a version without decorated repeats in the Hirsch MS follow the Altus part of the consort version with an F natural. This note is omitted from both vocal arrangements.

Two copies, those of Add. 3056 and Dd.9.33 share some passages in common which stand outside the more generally accepted treatment. In the repeat of the second strain the following figure is introduced at bars 29, 30 and 31, written thus in the tablature:

which may be transcribed as:

The full name and style is only given to Piper in *Lachrimæ or Seaven Teares*, where the piece is called 'Captaine Digorie Piper his Galliard'.

No. 20, 'Dowlands Galliard', No. 33, 'Mr Langtons Galliard' and No. 40, 'The Battle Galliard', also known as 'The King of Denmarke, his Galliard', are closely related, all being derived from material that had its origin in two compositions that swept into popularity throughout Europe in the first half of the sixteenth century. These were 'La Guerre' or 'La Bataille' by Jannequin, written to commemorate the Battle of Marignano in 1515, first printed in 1529, and 'Die Schlacht vor Pavia' or 'La Battaglia Taliana' by Matthias Werrecore, first printed in 1544.* Both were written for four voices and the composers attempt, by onomatopoeic sounds and words, to convey the raging of a battle, with trumpet calls, the noise of kettle drums and scraps of battle songs incorporated into the musical fabric.† Almost immediately both pieces began to appear in a diversity of instrumental arrangements varying considerably in the closeness with which they followed the original material. As time passed the arrangements diverged further and further from the parent compositions until eventually it becomes difficult to tell from which one some of the later battle pieces are derived; only certain distinguishing phrases remain to mark a common line of descent.

This is not the place to give a detailed history of this *genre* of compositions, nor to list the number of composers who made use of the material; it is enough to say here that battle pieces, incorporating traditional phrases, continued to appear well into the second half of the seventeenth century. It is of interest, however, to trace some of these phrases in the works of English composers where they show similarities with *motifs* used by Dowland in these three galliards.

In William Byrd's 'The Battle',‡ the section called 'The marche of horsemen' has the following bars:

---

* In Wolfgang Schmeltzel, *Guter Seltzamer*.

† Werrecore claims to have been an eyewitness of the Battle of Pavia in 1525, but Alfred Einstein, in *The Italian Madrigal* (1949), Vol. II, p. 744, suggests the battle was more probably that of Bicocca (1522), since it was there that Duke Francesco Sforza gained the victory over the French, celebrated in the song.

‡ *My Ladye Nevells Booke*; finished September 11th, 1591, ed. Hilda Andrews (1926), p. 22.

'A Battle and no Battle', ascribed to Bull,★ gives a similar passage:

Compare these bars with the first strain of 'Dowlands Galliard' from Dd.2.11:

The same passage in 'A Galliard by Dowla' from the Tollemache MS, though the piece is still in the minor key, has the first three chords in the major.

When we come to the 'King of Denmarke his Galliard' we find the whole strain in the major key, with a variant introduced in the previously descending phrase of bar 2:

In 'Mr Langtons Galliard', the phrase is lifted a fourth higher and is not introduced until bar 34:

★ Paris Conservatoire MS 18548, Piece No. 84.

The same four bars, in the form in which Dowland used them, appear again in the anonymous Battle of the Folger-Dowland MS (ff. 19v–21v), this time at bar 49:

This long and incredibly boring piece has 318 bars, most of which consist of repetitive pattern making on the chord of F major. Two versions, those of Dd.2.11 (ff. 29v–31, anonymous and without title), and Jane Pickering's Lute Book (an anonymous arrangement for two lutes, ff. 52v/53 and 53v/54), have the sixth course lowered to F. This *scordatura*, so necessary in the absence of a seventh course, suggests an early date of composition, although its presence in the Pickering MS and in Add. 38,539 shows it to have continued in the English lutenist repertoire into the second decade of the seventeenth century.

It is from this battle also that Dowland took his material for the second strain of the 'King of Denmarke'. In bars 93–100 of the Folger-Dowland copy we have the following monotonous phrases:

By Dowland's lively imagination these were transmuted into the following vivid and shapely passage:

Bars 33–6 of Byrd's 'The marche of horsmen':

also appear to have a common origin with bars 17–20 of the 'King of Denmarke':

Of the three known copies of No. 20 those of Dd.2.11 and the Thysius MS agree except for minor details, but that of the Tollemache MS has some major divergencies, particularly in bars 5–8:

Dd.2.11, f. 7v

Tollemache MS, f. 6v

No. 33, 'Mr Langtons galliard', is in a most unusual form: AA' B, with rather more than half of B repeated.

Eight copies of the solo form of No. 40 have come down to us; in five of these it is called 'The Battle Galliard' with various vagaries of spelling; in Dd.9.33 it is called 'Mr Mildmays Galliard'; in the Tollemache MS it is attributed to 'Johnson', and in the *Testudo Gallo-Germanicca* it is attributed to

Robert Dowland. In *Varietie of Lute-Lessons* it appears with the title 'the most high and mightie Christianus the fourth King of Denmarke, his Galliard', the piece having first been named for Dowland's Danish master in *Lachrimæ or Seaven Teares*.

Each strain is of four bars with a division to the repeat but, a characteristic it shares with the majority of battle pieces, it is of exceptional length for a galliard, the complete twenty-four bars being repeated four times over. Every repetition is a different variant on the first statement but it is, in fact, something of a hybrid, since a few alterations are made in the bass towards the latter end of the piece, though hardly enough to put it into the true variation form.

In the eight copies the various sections are somewhat differently disposed, but in *Varietie of Lute-Lessons* Dowland gave it its definitive shape. He also added an entirely new arrangement of the final repetition of strain 3 and its repeat.

I think it may be said, without injustice to other composers, that Dowland was the only one to handle this intractable material, based largely on the imitation of non-musical sounds, in such a way as to mould it into coherent and shapely musical form.

No. 21 has no title in either Dd.2.11 or the Hirsch MS, but in the Mynshall MS it is called 'John Dowlands Galliard' and in Add. 2764 'Capit[ain] Candishe his Galy[ard]'. This last has a variant, and almost certainly incorrect, reading of bar 1. It is a neat and charming little piece, in two strains, with no divisions to the repeats in any of the copies.

No. 22, another 'Dowlands Galliarde', occurs in Dd.2.11, f. 95. An arrangement of this piece in the Cambridge Consort Books and another in the Cittern book, Dd.4.23, give it the title 'Dowlands first galliarde'. Whether indeed it was the first he wrote it is impossible to say, but from the character of the piece it is safe to conclude that it must be one of his earliest.

No. 23. Of the six versions for solo lute of the 'Frog Galliard' it is possible to be certain of Dowland's authorship in only one case, and that is the version that bears his autograph in the Folger-Dowland MS. The others could be arrangements by fellow composers. The extreme popularity that this galliard achieved brought it into the category of tunes that became almost common property. Dowland himself used it again for the song 'Now, O now I needs must part', and Thomas Morley arranged it for *The First Booke of Consort Lessons* (1599 and 1611), where it is included without Dowland's name.* The

---

* Morley was not entirely scrupulous in attributing compositions to their composers. This may have caused some offence since Rosseter remarks in the epistle *To the Reader* in his *Lessons for Consort* (1609): 'The Authors name I haue/ seuerally prefixt, that euery man might obtaine his right.'

tune passed into common usage in ballad literature⋆ and arrangements were made for virginals, cittern and other instruments. That it became known in the Netherlands is shown by its presence in 'Het Luitboek van Thysius', The *Nederlandtsche Gedenck-Clanck* (1626), and Camphuysen's *Stichtelyke Rymen* (editions of 1647, 1652 and 1654–5), where it is used once as a song and once for a version of Psalm XXIII.

The copy that bears Dowland's autograph in the Folger-Dowland Lute Book has an attractive arrangement of triplets in the repeat of the last eight bars of the first strain; a device found in no other version:

Edward Doughtie† puts forward the interesting suggestion that Dowland was influenced in the composition of this piece by the following song from Le Roy's *Second Livre de Guiterre* (1555), with which Dowland may well have become acquainted during the years in France:

Quand j'en-tens le per-du temps De plus-ieurs qui sont à moi

The trochaic rhythm is unusual in English galliards and is unique among those by Dowland.

⋆ Euing Collection, p. 217a, 'The Shepheards Delight. To the Tune of Frog Galliard' (Entered December 14th, 1624), and p. 356, 'The True Loves Knot Untied. To the Tune of, Frogs Galliard' (Entered March 1st, 1675).

† Unpublished thesis *Poems from the Songbooks of John Dowland*, presented to Harvard University, 1963.

There is no evidence to explain the name 'Frog Galliard', but it is a well-known fact that Queen Elizabeth often referred to the Duc d'Alençon (later Duc d'Anjou) as 'her frog', and it could be that the tune, whether originally written by Dowland or not, was named after the last and most persistent of her suitors. The music is in no way related to that of the French 'Ballet des Grenouilles'.*

For whether the song 'Now, O now I needs must part' or the lute solo came first from Dowland's pen, evidence is almost completely lacking. Although the two anonymous versions in Dd.2.11., f. 40v and f. 93, differ in many points of detail, there is enough agreement between them and the Folger-Dowland setting to allow of the possibility of Dowland as composer, nevertheless, complete certainty cannot be claimed. To the uncertainty of authorship in this early source must be added the uncertainty of date of many of the songs in *The First Booke*. The slight differences in the tune between the sung version and the instrumental form offer no help in any attempt to decide on precedence.

The title of No. 24, as written in Dd.2.11., presents something of a problem. What appears to be written is 'fr: Dac: Galliard'. After long consideration of what this contraction could stand for, both by the author and Richard Newton, the suggestion was eventually put forward by Mr. Newton that it was an erroneous contraction of the name Katherine Darcy. This is supported by the fact that immediately preceding it on the same page is 'K. Darcies Spirite', and 'K. Darcyes Galliard' appears on the other side of the folio. Katherine Darcy married Sir Gervase Clifton in 1591 which sets this year as the latest date for the composition of the galliards dedicated to her under her maiden name. Later Dowland named the pieces he wrote for her with the title she acquired on her marriage.

The galliard is interesting in itself as being an early form of the song 'Awake sweet love', but in this case the second note of the melody is the old modal seventh of the scale. When Dowland re-wrote it later he changed this note to the sharp seventh of the modern major scale. The slight awkwardness in the Cantus part where the unaccented syllable of the word 'awake' falls on the accented first beat of the bar is easily understood when it is realized that

---

* Collection Philidor, II p. 61, 'Ballet des Paysans et des Grenouilles, 1606, 1 re Entrée'; M. Praetorius, *Terpsichore* (1612) p. 141, 'Ballet de Grenoville, CCLII, à 5. M.P.C.'; and Robert Ballard, *Premier Livre* (1611), p. 34, 'Ballet des Manans'. This is probably the dance mentioned by Jean Héroard in *Journal sur l'enfance et la jeunesse de Louis XIII (1601–1628)*, edited by E. Soulié et E. de Barthelemy (1868), p. 195.

Le 28 juin, mercredi, a Saint-Germain 1606.

. . . Après souper il se joue en sa chambre, joue du violon en concert avec le luth, et chante *En m'en retournant*, etc., puis danse le ballet des grenouilles, la morisque, fort joliment et en cadence, sans avoir été instruit.

the melody existed first as a galliard and that the words were fitted to it at a later date.

The Dd.2.11. copy and that of Add. 3056, where it is called 'Galliard J.D.', are both without decorated repeats. In the earlier MS six courses only are employed, while in the later Add. 3056 in certain cases a diapason D is substituted for the D in the higher octave. A third version comes in Dd.5.78. where it is called 'A galliarde fr. Cuttinge'. This has decorated repeats which show unmistakable characteristics of Cutting's style, and is evidently an example of the quite extensive category of pieces in which one composer writes a set of complimentary divisions on the work of an admired colleague.

A slightly less direct compliment is found among the works of Santino Garsi quoted by Helmuth Osthoff in *Der Lautenist Santino Garsi de Padua* (1926),* where a piece called 'Gagliarda' has a second strain almost identical with the first strain of 'Awake sweet loue', while the first strain has four bars like enough to bars from the second strain of Dowland's ayre to make the derivation almost certain.

Of No. 25 it is difficult to see why Dowland should have singled it out for the title 'Melancoly Galliard' from among the many others that have an underlying vein of sadness throughout. It is in the unusual key of F minor and has some poignantly used suspensions in the first strain. A descending phrase of four notes recurs throughout the piece. The eight bars of the third strain are particularly fine:

As a lute solo No. 26 has no title, although the initials 'J.D.' are added in the single source, Dd.5.78. It can, however, be identified with 'My thoughts are wingd with hopes', No. III in *The First Booke of Songes* and 'Sir John Souch his Galiard' in *Lachrimæ or Seaven Teares*. The copy in Holmes's hand is not entirely satisfactory and has some passages that suggest it may have been arranged from the vocal setting. The apt word painting in the song, discussed on p. 222, also supports the probability that the words inspired the melody rather than that the verses were composed to fit an already existing tune. There is, however, one circumstance that implies an early date for its having become an instrumental galliard and that is Anthony Munday's use of the

* See Brian Richardson, 'New Light on Dowland's Continental Movements', *Monthly Musical Record*, XC (1960), pp. 3–9.

tune for his Ditty No. 17 in *A Banquet of Daintie Conceits,* 'Entered to T. Hackett' on July 6th, 1584.★ The instruction says only 'To Dowlands Galliard', but there is no other that will accommodate the rhythmic structure of the ditty:

1. It chanc-ed on a time, that a lewde theefe Did en-ter in a man's house—
2. The good man of the house lay in his bedde, And heard how fast his goods—

— for some re-leefe, Where seek-ing bu-si-lie what he might finde;
— a broad were spread, He thought to let the theefe take his own pleasure,

At length he found such things as pleasde his minde; Sort-ing them ear-nest-ly, what
And for to fill his bagge at his own leysure: And when he sud-dain-ly should

he did— lacke, At last, of all the best he made a— packe.
packe a— way, Then would he man-ful-lie cause him to— stay.

The years 1581–7, given by Walter Oakeshott† as the probable period in which Ralegh's poem was written, would not exclude the possibility of the instrumental version having been made from the song by the time at which *A Banquet of Daintie Conceits* was printed. In making 1588 the latest date at which this galliard could have been composed, the piece is established as the earliest about which there is any chronological evidence.

No. 27, an untitled galliard, is a fine sombre piece in 'short' form. The strains are of unequal and unconventional length, the first having twelve bars, the second eight, and the third fourteen.

No. 28. In Add. 38,539 this piece is subscribed 'A gallyard upon the gallyard before' and it is immediately preceded by 'A gallyard by Mr Dan: Bacheler' made upon the first four bars of Bacheler's own song 'To plead my faith' (*Musical Banquet*, No. VI). Dowland, in fact, takes little from Bacheler but the first five notes of the tune, and after that treats the work in a highly original manner. The repeat of the second strain is of exceptional interest in being, in the treatment of bars 33 and 34 (i.e. the repeat of bars 24 and 25), not a division at all, but a free variation, since at this point he completely destroys the original harmonic framework:

★ The B.M. copy is dated 1588.
† *The Queen and the Poet* (1960), p. 157.

In the *Thesaurus Harmonicus* Besardus has confused the two pieces and
prints, under Dowland's name, a simplified version of the Bacheler galliard
without the elaborate divisions of Add. 38,539. A curious feature of three
copies (Add. 38,539, Dd.5.78, and Lord Herbert of Cherbury's MS) is the
presence of an extra bar at the end of the first strain. In other copies either
the extra bar or the one preceding it is used to end the strain but in these
three cases what appear to be alternative bars have both been included as if
they were intended to follow on, one after the other.

The sole copy of No. 29, as a lute solo, comes in Dd.5.78, ff. 16v/17, without title. The galliard is in conventional eight-bar strains, with elaborate
divisions to the repeats with many passages written in high *barré* positions,
calling for considerable technical accomplishment in performance. Later it

was arranged for *Lachrimæ or Seaven Teares* with the title 'M. Giles Hobies Galiard'. The lute part of this version appears in Lord Herbert of Cherbury's MS, f. 10, called 'Gagliarda J: Doulande'. There is no indication to show whether Lord Herbert knew this was not a solo piece but was, in fact, the lute part from the consort version; one of the few in which the melody is completely absent.

No. 30 is a 'long' galliard in G minor with three strains of eight bars each. The division to the third strain is very attractive with its unusual arrangement of repeated notes:

No. 31. Dowland uses the Walsingham tune for the first strain of this exceptionally beautiful 'short' galliard. The melody, however, is sometimes concealed in an inner voice. I give an example from bar 2, 'tailed' in a rather unnatural way, to make the device clear:

The second and third strains depart from the traditional melody but develop with complete logic from the first strain. The piece is compact and written with great economy and can be counted among the most successful of his smaller compositions.

'Mrs Vaux Galliarde', No. 32, is a 'short' galliard constructed on an unusual pattern. The first strain has eight bars, the second seven, and the third thirteen. Luckily the anonymous copy in the *Testudo Gallo-Germanicca* supplies a correct version of the penultimate bar, of which Holmes, in Dd.9.33, gives a very confused account.

For No. 33, 'Mr Langtons Galliard', see pp. 137–139.

The title of No. 34 is given once as 'Mignarde' and once as 'Mignarda', and appears to derive ultimately from the French word *mignarde*—'delicate, pretty, mincing'. *Mignardise*—'delicateness, delicacy, mincing, fondling, cockering, cuddling' are also given* and it is interesting to find Nicolas Vallet in his *Regia Pietas* (1620), in the 'Advertisement aus Amateurs de ce Present Livre' speaks of 'l'embellissement & mignardise du Luth'. The special relationship of the word to a galliard is given, however, by Thoinot Arbeau in *Orchésographie* (1588), f. 57v. He says:

Vous ferez les pas mignardez, quand extendrez les cinq minimes blanches en dix minimes noires, & qu'en lieu de faire vn pas en mesme instāt, auec son petit sault, vous en ferez deux morceaux, anticipant vn peu ledit petit sault sur la première minime noire, & incontinent aprés faisant le pas sur la deuxième minime noire: Et telles façons de pas mignardez ne sont à la verité que les cinq pas, mais ils ont meilleurs grace & sont moins lourds, car en lieu de tumber le corps a plōb d'vn coup, on l'assiet en traisnant.

That Dowland, in giving this name to his galliard, had in mind its particular meaning as applied to a manner of performing the 'cinq-pas' or basic step of the dance, explains the apparent contradiction between the usual meaning of the word *mignarde* and the forthright, masculine character of the composition.

There are two 'short' versions and one, in Dd.9.33, with decorated repeats. These divisions are not entirely consistent with Dowland's style and may not be from his hand. They are, however, interesting as an example of the way in which a contemporary player would treat his music. All three copies are in the Cambridge lute-books and Holmes may have adapted the piece from a version in staff notation since in each he had considerable difficulty with the accidentals. He appears to have been particularly worried in making the decision between ♮D and ♯D. In *Lachrimæ or Seaven Teares* it has the title 'M. Henry Noell his Galiard' and in *A Pilgrimes Solace* it appears as the song 'Shall I striue with wordes to moue'.

No. 35, a piece without title in the familiar galliard form of three strains of eight bars each, has repeats to the first and second strains, while the third has none. In the repeat of the first strain the divisions on the upper voice are exceptionally free, but the bass line follows strictly that of the plain statement.

'Mr Knights Galliard', No. 36, is in short form with the conventional eight bars in each strain. A diapason at D is used very freely, not as an occasional octave but as part of the bass line, with the notes D, E, and F occurring frequently throughout the piece. The opening phrase:

* Cassell's *French-English Dictionary*.

used as a point of imitation, is almost certainly not of Dowland's composing since identical, or almost identical, phrases are used by several other composers: Anthony Holborne, 'Mr. D. Bonds Galliard' (Euing MS, f. 30, and Dd.5.78, f. 5v.), and *Pauans, Galliards, Almains . . .* No. 44, 'Nec Invideo'; William Brade, *Newe auselesener Paduanen/Galliarden/ Canzonen/ Allmand und Coranten* (1609)* and Praetorius, *Terpsichore* (1612),† 'Galliarde. CCCVII, à 4. Incerti'.

At the end of *The First Booke of Songes* Dowland has included a most ingenious piece called 'My Lord Chamberlaine his Galliard' (No. 37), an 'inuention', as he calls it, for two to play upon one lute. The players sit side-by-side and use both hands. Cantus plays high on the fingerboard and is confined to the first and second courses of the lute. Bassus plays on the lower frets and the lower courses. At one point, in bars which echo each other, they change position, Cantus playing low while Bassus plays high. Quite apart from the curiosity of the mechanics this is a most excellent galliard, full of vitality and with a brave, swinging tune. A number of corrections to the text were made in the various printings between 1597 and 1613, and, it must be admitted, some fresh errors were introduced. There can be little doubt that it was this piece that prompted Tobias Hume when he wrote his 'A Lesson for two to play upon one Viole'.‡

In the Table of Contents of *A Musicall Banquet*, No. 38 is called 'Syr Robert Sidney his Galliard' while on the actual page it has the title 'The Right Honourable the Lord Viscount Lisle, Lord Chamberlaine to the Queenes most excellent Maiestie, his Galliard'. Both titles refer, of course, to the same man, so there is no discrepancy except in words. In Dd.2.11. a 'short' version has the title 'Susanna Galliard'. This is interesting in view of the fact that the first five notes agree exactly with the first five notes of the *chanson* 'Suzanne un jour'§ as set by Orlando di Lassus, and the next seven notes follow the outline of the original very closely:

'The Lord Viscount Lisle':

'Suzanne un jour' (Cantus):

---

* Engelke's edition, p. 271.
† Oberst's edition, p. 181.
‡ *The First Part of Ayres* (1605), p. 111.
§ For an excellent history of 'Suzanne un jour' see Kenneth Jay Levy in *Annales Musicologique*, Tome I, 1953 (Société de Musique d'autrefois, Paris).

Without the use of the name 'Susanna' it might have been just possible to accept the opening phrase as a coincidence, but as it stands there can be little doubt that Dowland had the sixteenth-century *chanson* in mind when he wrote his galliard. When the whole volume was dedicated to Sir Robert Sidney he evidently dressed up 'Susanna' with a very fine set of new divisions and included it in the contents to reinforce the compliment. The figuration is exceptionally florid, but he never loses sight of the original design and the whole piece has a sombre magnificence. 'Susanna' was adapted for five viols and lute in *Lachrimæ or Seaven Teares* and was given the title of 'M. Bucton his Galiard'.

'Doulands rounde battell galyarde', No. 39, may have been played as a solo, and indeed it sounds quite well that way. On the other hand it fits very convincingly with the remaining parts in the Cambridge Consort Books. If, in fact, it is a consort part, then it is almost certainly incomplete, since the lute very seldom carries the melody in this particular group of arrangements. Nevertheless, in my opinion, it stands quite satisfactorily in its own right as an uncomplicated little piece. There appears to be no use of battle material unless it be in the 'trumpet' flourish on the tonic, third and fifth in the third bar of the final strain, or the very slight resemblance in the outline of bars 11 and 12 to a figure sometimes found in the 'Schlacht vor Pavia' derivatives, as for example, in the Mercurius setting in Fuhrmann's *Testudo Gallo-Germanicca*, p. 185.

'rounde Battell galyarde':

'Schlacht vor Pavia':

For No. 40 see pp. 137–140.

No. 41 exists in two versions, the early one in Dd.2.11 being called 'K. Darcyes Galliard' and the later, in *Varieties of Lute-Lessons*, 'The most sacred Queene *Elizabeth*, her Galliard'. The changes in the later copy are only slight and are confined mostly to the decorated repeats. It is impossible even to guess at Dowland's motive in changing the name of this piece in 1610. The Queen was already dead so there was no question of a reward, and had he seriously intended to honour her memory it would have been more appropriate to write a really fine new galliard rather than to serve up again what must have been one of his quite early compositions.

Comparison of this galliard with the Cambridge Consort Books establishes the identity of a piece labelled with one of the most puzzling orthographical problems of the collection. There must have been some illegibility in the originals from which Holmes made his copies and the interpretation of what he found added further confusion. The title, as given in the three surviving parts, reads as follows:

Cittern, Dd.14.24, f. 20, 'Do. Re. Ha. Galliard'

Recorder, Dd.5.21, f. 5v, 'Dowl. Reads H Galliard'

Bass viol, Dd.5.20, f. 5v, 'Dowl R. H. Galliard'

In spite of all this it is undoubtedly 'K. Darcyes Galliard'. A possible explanation could be the misreading of the original title, which, carelessly written, could have looked something like this:

which would, of course, read as Dowl: Ka: Da: Galliard, but could, just possibly, be misread as Dowl: Re: Ha: Galliard. There are many pieces by Read in these books and it might be imagined that Holmes made a wild shot and jumped to the conclusion that what he took to be 'Re' was, in fact, a contraction standing for the name Richard Read.

Certainly an early work, No. 42 appears twice in Dd.2.11. without title, and again in Barley's *New Booke of Tabliture* (1596) called simply 'A Galliard'. It then became known as 'Can she excuse' after the song in *The First Booke*, whose identity it shares. In *Lachrimæ or Seaven Teares* it was given the name of the Earl of Essex,★ and the late version in *Varietie of Lute-Lessons* keeps this name. It is impossible to be certain, but for reasons that will be shown later, it seems likely that in this case the song form preceded the solo galliard.

The rhythm of this piece shows many examples of the swing from $\frac{3}{4}$ to $\frac{6}{8}$, so typical of the galliard of this period. In the best hands the device lends an enchanting grace to a form which, with less skilful writing, can be somewhat monotonous in its beat:

★ For discussion of the change of title see p. 225.

The development of the solo form can be traced from the simple statement of the early copies, through the moderately elaborate decoration of the
repeats of 'Can she excuse' in the Folger–Dowland MS (to which Dowland
added his autograph), to the magnificent *panache* of 'The Right Honourable
Robert Earle of Essex, high Marshall of England, his Galliard' in *Varietie of
Lute-Lessons* of 1610. In all these and in the arrangement for five viols and
lute in *Lachrimæ or Seaven Teares* the main structure remains constant. The
melody, with the exception of the first and second bars, the bass, and the
introduction of part of the tune 'The Woods so wilde'★ in the third strain,
agree in all versions, with slight differences according to the medium of
performance.

In the Giles Lodge MS an early version of 'The Woods so wilde' is called
'Will ye go walke the woode so wilde', and in *My Lady Nevells Booke*† the
set of variations by Byrd has the title 'Will yow walke the woods so wylde'.
These two titles suggest the many instrumental settings were derived from a
ballad or popular song, which may be identical with the *fremens* song 'As I
walked the wode so wylde' said to have been sung by Sir Peter Carew and
Henry VIII,‡ but no words exactly fitting the tune have so far come to light.

The poem by Sir Thomas Wyatt, which begins with the stanza:

> I muste go walke the woodes so wyld,
> And wander here and there
> In dred and Dedly fere;
> For wher I trust, I am begilyd,
> And all for your Loue, my dere§

★ The settings by Byrd and Orlando Gibbons both have this title in the *Fitzwilliam
Virginal Book*, and traces of 'the wo so wi' can be seen in the Ballet MS, p. 84.
† Edited Hilda Andrews, 1926.
‡ John Stevens, *Music and Poetry in the Early Tudor Court* (1961), p. 44.
§ Kenneth Muir, *Sir Thomas Wyatt and his circle. Unpublished Poems* (1961), p. 26.

may have been the rewriting of an earlier ballad, but his five-line stanza does not fit the melody as given by Byrd:

The resemblance of the first line of Wyatt's poem to the extended title seems too close to be pure coincidence, but if Wyatt did write to a pre-existing ballad tune it can hardly have been this one since, from its earliest known appearance in the Giles Lodge MS* to the late version in *The English Dancing Master* (1650), where it is called 'Greenwood', although some variants appear in the melody, there is no alteration in the total length.

When Dowland introduces the tune he begins at the second bar, and here is how he uses it in the solo galliard 'Can she excuse':

It is interesting to compare this with the second variation in Byrd's setting which reveals, even though Byrd uses the entire tune, considerable similarity of treatment, especially in the held notes of the upper voice, and in the outline of the bass:

* The name Cha: Jackson is written below the last line of tablature of this piece. The time marks are exceedingly erratic and many alterations have to be made before the piece can be brought into recognizable form.

A similar, but not identical, tune is introduced in 'Dr. Bull's Juell', No. CXXXVIII of the *Fitzwilliam Virginal Book.*

As will be seen later, the Cantus line of the vocal setting, 'Can she excuse my wrongs', differs from the lute solo in the first two bars, appearing in all known editions of *The First Booke of Song* as:

The absence of the B flat in the second bar is discussed on p. 223.

The popularity of this piece outside England is shown by the number of Continental sources in which copies may be found: Fuhrmann's *Testudo Gallo-Germanicca* (1615) has a very simple version followed by a set of variations by Strobelius; Nicolas Vallet gives a long and elaborate setting, 'Gaillarde du comte essex', in *Le Secret des Muses. Premier Livre* (1615); the Thysius MS has a copy, 'Can she excuse', though of extreme inaccuracy; the Nauclerus MS contains two anonymous and untitled copies on ff. 30, and 126v; and Nürnberg MS 33748 has four on ff. 6v, 7, 7v and f. 65v, all miscalled 'Galliard Pipers No. 1', 'Galliard Pipers No. 2', 'Galliard Pipers No. 3' and 'Galiarta Pipers'. A fifth, on f. 66 is headed 'Aliter'. No. 1 has the further confusion of beginning with the opening phrase of the galliard ultimately derived from Bacheler's song 'To plead my faith'.* Camphuyzen included a song to the tune in all editions of his *Stichtelycke Rymen* between 1624 and 1690.

Kurt Fischer, in an article 'Gabriel Voigtländer',† discusses the influence of this tune on Continental composers. He remarks on its frequent incidence in German and Dutch MSS and printed books and, in addition to quoting the well-known sources for the complete piece, he gives some interesting examples (including a song by his own composer) in which, either consciously or unconsciously, the distinctive intervals of the opening phrase of the melody have been reproduced. His examples demonstrate the persistence of the theme well into the eighteenth century:

H. L. Hassler, *Lustgarten Newer teutscher Gesang . . .* (1605)

Johann Rist, *Galathe* (1642), f. 7v. Daphnis Lobgedicht auff eine Tugendreiche Schäfferin

* See p. 145.
† *Sammelbände der Internationalen Musik-Gesellschaft* (Leipzig, 1910–11), pp. 17–93. I am grateful to Basil Lam for showing me this article.

Gabriel Voigtländer, *Erster Theil Allerhand Oden vnnd Lieder* . . . (1642)

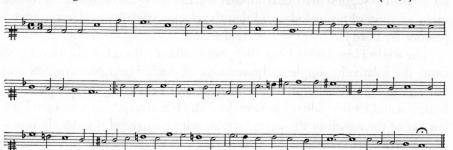

With Voigtländer the plagiarism can hardly have been unconscious since, as can be seen, he also adopts the 'Shall I go walk the woods so wild?' *motif* for his final section.

Georg Heinrich Weber, *Sing- u. Spiel-Arien* (1665). Musik von J. Frch. Zuber

Adam Kreiger, *Newe Arien* (1676), III, 5

Ballard, *La clef des chansonniers* . . . (1717)

It would seem that all but one of these Continental arrangements, both the direct settings for lute, or the allusive appearance of the melody in the vocal music, stem, in fact, from the song and not from the lute solo, since, with the exception of the Thysius copy, it is from the three-note version of bar 1 that the melodies are derived; furthermore, as will be seen in the list on p. 224, the majority show the characteristic semitone interval between the first and second notes of bar 2.

Incidentally, in writing of the versions in the Nürnberg MS called 'Galliard Pipers', Fischer adds the explanation (Pipers= für Pfifer, Bläser), presumably having not seen any versions of the pavan or galliard where the words 'Captain' or 'Digorie' are used.

Lord Herbert of Cherbury's MS contains an interesting setting of this

galliard by Daniel Bacheler.★ A notable feature being the fourfold repetition
of strain three. It follows immediately after Dowland's setting of Bacheler's
galliard on the opening phrase of 'To plead my faith'. It is perhaps not too
far-fetched to suggest that one composer was returning the compliment for the
other's setting of his melody, and that the placing of the two pieces in juxta-
position by Lord Herbert was not accidental.

'The Right Honourable Lady Rich, her Galliard', No. 43, is also developed
from the relatively simple early versions of Archbishop Marsh's MS and
Dd.9.33 to the full elaboration of *Varietie of Lute-Lessons*. It is an exceptionally
beautiful and tender galliard in G major. The F is always sharpened until the
last bar of the repeat of the second strain, where a natural is suddenly introduced with startling effect. At first hearing it is tempting to reject this as an
error, but with familiarity a liking for it grows, and in my opinion it is
intentional:

'The Right Honourable Ferdinando Earle of Darby, his Galliard', No. 44,
is also in G major, but is entirely different in character from that of 'Lady
Rich'. Like the 'Mellancoly Galliard' it begins on the second quaver of the
second beat of the bar; an unusual opening for Dowland, and, in fact, found
only in these two pieces. The character is grave but bold and the repeat of the
second strain is particularly interesting for its use of the ornamental shake
written in as an integral part of the division:

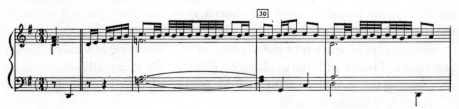

★ 'Gall: Mr D:B:', f. 55.

In the first two bars of the third strain there is a very effective change from the modal to the sharp seventh:

In common with most of the other galliards in *Varietie of Lute-Lessons*, 'The Earle of Darby' underwent considerable revision before appearing in print, but in the process, either an imperfect copy was handed to the printer, or the printer himself committed the error of omitting the penultimate bar, so that the third strain has twelve bars and its repeat only eleven, the division on bar 47 (present in Nn.6.36, f. 2) having fallen by the wayside. During the course of binding the lower part of the folio has been cut in the British Museum copy and some notes are missing from the final bars of the bass line, the Bodleian Library copy is, however, still perfect.

'The Right Honourable the Lady *Cliftons* Spirit' is attributed to Robert Dowland in *Varietie of Lute-Lessons,* but the identity of the strains with the 'short' 'K. Darcies Spirite' of Dd.2.11., which must have been written before 1591, and the characteristic style of the divisions, make it certain that this is an error and that the piece is by John. It is another of the galliards with many changes from $\frac{3}{4}$ to $\frac{6}{8}$ and back again, and is indeed full of 'spirit' and charm.

'Galliard to Lachrimæ' (No. 46) is a most ingenious transmutation of the theme into triple time:

The divisions in each of the two forms have an entirely distinct character; those of the pavan running up and down the lute like scarcely breathed sighs, while those of the galliard accentuate and point the rhythm of the dance.

ALMAINS

'Sir *John Smith* his Almain' (No. 47) is one of the curious cases in *Varietie of Lute-Lessons* where the composer's name has been omitted although clearly it was known to the editors since John added his own name to the copy in the Folger–Dowland MS. The anomalous form of this piece is very odd. It is based on a theme of two eight-bar strains. In the first thirty-two bars each strain is stated and is then followed by its division. The arrangement can be shown thus:

Strain	A	A′	B	B′
Bars	1–8	9–16	17–24	25–32

This double statement then becomes the theme for a further set of divisions, and may be shown thus:

Strain	A2	A2′	B2	B2′
Bars	33–40	41–8	49–56	57–64

but on examination of strain B′ it appears there is no division on the first two bars of strain B (bars 17–18) and that the third and fourth bars (19–20) are varied twice over (25–6 and 27–8). Strain B2′ is arranged in the same way. There is no division on bars 17–18, but bars 19–20 are again varied twice (57–8 and 59–60). This irregular form might be dismissed as a series of mistakes were it not that it is given authenticity by Dowland's signature in the Folger-Dowland MS and is also confirmed in other sources.

Another version, No. 47a, called 'Smythes Allmayne' is found in Add. 38,539, and here B′ is a straight division on B. No composer's name is given and there is no proof that this setting is by Dowland. The divisions consist of a single line of melody only, and it could be argued that this arrangement was by another hand were it not that Dowland signed his name to another almain (No. 48a) in which the divisions are treated in a similar manner.

No. 48 is another almain with two distinct versions. The copies in Dd.2.11, the Wickhambrook MS and the Weld MS all agree quite closely and have the strains, without divisions, arranged in the following order: A B C D E D. The Mynshall MS gives another arrangement: AA' BB' D E D, with C omitted altogether, but the copy is full of confusion and should not be treated as a source. Various forms of this version appear in Continental books and MSS, and Dutch words were fitted to a garbled attempt at the tune in Camphuysen's *Stichtelycke Rymen*, where it is called 'Doulants Almande'. The melody of the first strain bears a striking resemblance to the first strain of the version, believed to be its earliest appearance in print, given by Adrianus Valerius in *Nederlanstsche Gedenck-Clanck* (1626), of the Dutch National Anthem, 'Wilhelmus van Nassouwe':

'Dowland's Almain'

Possibly both stem from some now-forgotten popular tune, known in England and the Netherlands in the early sixteenth century.

No. 48a. With the title 'the Lady Laitones Almone', Dowland has added his signature to a different version of the piece in the Folger-Dowland MS. Here, as in 'Smythes Allmayne', the repeats are an elaboration of the melody only, with no bass line. The arrangement of the sections is AA' BB' CC' D E (which approximates to a division on E of the previous version) and D'. Besardus prints a copy of this alternative form in the *Thesaurus Harmonicus* with the title 'Chorea Anglicana Doolandi', but he omits section E and arranges the remaining strains in the more conventional order of AA' BB' CC' DD'. At first sight this setting and that of 'Smythes Allmayne' suggest they might be consort parts, single parts of duets, or arrangements to play with a bass viol, but comparison with the bass of each strain will show that the divisions do not fit over an exact repetition without involving serious grammatical errors.

No. 49, a piece without title, is an almain in 'short' form, consisting of eight bars in the first strain and four each in the second and third. It is an agreeable little composition, but not particularly distinguished in any way.

'Mistris Whittes thinge', No. 50, on the other hand, is entirely charming. It is neat, compact and wittily written. The above title is only given in full in the Wickhambrook MS. A short version in Dd.2.11 has the odd mnemonic

'W Thinge'. In Add. 38,539, transposed from G to F, it is called 'Mrs Whites Choyce', and in the Tollemache MS, where there is a copy in each key, it also has this name. An arrangement in five parts appears in Valentin Haussmann's *Rest von Polnischen und andern Tänzen* (Nürnberg, 1603), No. LXXXIX, with the title 'Mein Hertz mit schmertz ist überall verwundet &c'.

The loose construction and somewhat unsatisfactory harmony at several points in No. 51, a piece without title, suggest that either the copyist was at fault or that the composition is not by Dowland. There is no other copy by which to check that of Dd.5.78; an unfortunate fact as the piece is attractive in many ways. It is written for a seven-course lute with the diapason tuned to D. This is used with considerable freedom and effect.

No. 52 seems to have existed as a lute solo, with no special title until the publication of *Lachrimæ or Seaven Teares*, when the consort arrangement received the name of 'Mrs Nichols Almand'. The rather four-square little tune is relieved, towards the end of the second strain, by some ingenious syncopation. See also p. 368.

'Mrs Cliftons Allmaine', No. 53, must have been written between the years 1591, when Katherine Darcy became Mrs. Clifton, and 1597, by which date her husband had received a knighthood. The incomplete copy in Dowland's own hand in the Folger-Dowland MS has many points of difference from those of Dd.9.33 and the Euing MS.

No. 54, 'my Lady Hunsdons Allmande', or 'puffe' as it is called in Add. 6402, is a most attractive piece, with a charmingly fresh melody. The construction is shapely and elegant. There is considerable difference in the arrangement of the strains between the copies in the various sources. The version in Dowland's own hand in the Folger-Dowland MS has AA' B C D C, while Dd.5.78 and Add. 6402 both have AA' B C D. Dd.9.33 gives A B C D only.

Brian Richardson★ calls attention to an appearance of this almain with the curious rubric 'Balletto di me Donino Garsi fatto per il S. Duca di Mantua', reproduced in Helmuth Osthoff's *Der Lautenist Santino Garsi da Parma* (1926), p. 171. This piece, from the Dusiacki MS† which Osthoff dates at about 1620, is almost identical with 'Pezzo italiano' from a MS transcribed by Oscar Chilesotti.‡ Donino Garsi would probably have been too young in 1595 to have learnt the piece directly from Dowland, but Richardson suggests that Santino Garsi, father or uncle of Donino, who, as the Farnese archives show, was in Padua at the time of Dowland's passing through on his way to Flor-

---

★ 'New Light on Dowland's Continental Movements', *Monthly Musical Record*, XC (1960), pp. 3–9.
   † Destroyed during the Second World War.
   ‡ *Da un Codice Lauten-buch del Cinquecento* (1890), p. 78. The whereabouts of this MS, in the possession of Chilesotti at the time of his writing, is no longer known.

ence, may have heard Dowland play and have stored the piece in his memory, later passing it on to Donino who claimed the arrangement as his own. The fact that Santino wrote a galliard highly reminiscent of 'Awake sweet love'* lends force to the argument in favour of a connection between Dowland and the elder Garsi. Nevertheless, the existence of a third Italian version of the almain, this time a keyboard arrangement,† shows it to have achieved some popularity in Italy and the piece may have passed into the flow of Italian music by other means than through the agency of Santino Garsi, or of the Duke of Mantua himself who is suggested by Richardson as a possible alternative sponsor of Donino's arrangement.

A Villanella by the Polish lutenist Alberti Dlugorai, in Besardus's *Thesaurus Harmonicus* (1603), f. 48, though the rhythm is changed to that of a Polonaise, has an opening phrase almost identical with that of Donino Garsi's 'Balletto'.

JIGS, CORANTOS AND OTHER PIECES IN $\frac{6}{8}$ RHYTHM

'Mistris Winters Jumpe', No. 55, is one of Dowland's happiest short pieces. In the key of C major, it has no trace of underlying melancholy. In the Folger-Dowland MS it was copied by Anne Bayldon, whose signature occurs on one of the flyleaves of the book. The title, rather oddly, becomes 'winters jompe', but her tablature is more reliable than her spelling and the version in her hand has very attractive little decorations in the repeat of the first strain. The rhythm and construction suggest it should be classed as a coranto and this is the category into which it is placed by Prætorius in *Terpsichore*, where it appears as No. CLVII à 4. Incerti. Many pieces of this type served, however, both for the coranto and for the volta and, since there is no particularly noticeable jump in the coranto, possibly the word 'jump' in the title refers to the moment in the volta when the female partner leaps into the air, assisted by the male partner's knee under her bottom; the moment caught in the painting, at Penshurst Place, of Queen Elizabeth dancing with the Earl of Leicester. On the other hand, Prætorius gives another copy of the piece under the title 'Gaillard', No. CLXXXV à 4. Incerti'. The Italian dance, the *saltarello* (literally 'little jump') is a close relation of the galliard and some such association of thought could have suggested the name, but it seems a little far-fetched and the more usual use of the $\frac{6}{8}$ bar in English sources tends to exclude this possibility. 'Mrs Whites Nothing', No. 56, appears to be a companion piece to 'Mrs Whites thinge' although musically they have nothing in common. The

---

* Osthoff, p. 142, from Staatsbibl. Berlin, Mus. ms. 40032 and Brussels, Bibl. Roy. MS II. 275.

† Florence, Bibli. naz. MS Magd. XIX. 115. ff. 5/5v. I have to thank Michael Morrow for finding this and kindly giving me a copy.

'Nothing' is full of vitality, but, to modern ears, its minor key produces an effect curiously lacking in cheerfulness.

'Mrs Vauxes Gigge', No. 57, is a really fine piece. The four-bar strains all begin on the up beat and are generally linked to the repeats by semiquaver runs. This device gives a great feeling of fluidity instead of the rigid form of the more strictly defined strain and repeat more often found in dance forms at this period. The key of C minor gives an almost sombre character to this jig in spite of the fact that the movement is rapid throughout.

When Dowland wrote 'The Shomakers Wife A Toy', No. 58, he was only one among many writers and musicians who joined in a curious kind of *mystique* concerning the shoemakers' trade. Thomas Deloney,* in his three-in-one novel, *The Gentle Craft*, gathers much of this scattered lore into a connected form. In his first two stories, which concern the lives of St. Hugh and St. Crispin, the patron saints of shoemakers, he makes use of material from medieval legends. In the third he pins his story on an historical character, Sir Simon Eyre, Lord Mayor of London in 1436, who died in 1459. In each case, however, he cleverly manipulates the tales to show 'the worthy deeds and great Hospitality' of shoemakers in the past. He also tells how the cordwainer's kit of tools became known as St. Hugh's bones, and declares the cause why the trade came to be called The Gentle Craft, and also how the proverb first grew—A shoemaker's son is a prince born. This novel was entered in the Stationers' Register in 1597 and continued in print until 1760. The third story gave Thomas Dekker the plot for his famous comedy *The Shoemakers' Holiday,* played before the Queen on January 1st, 1600. In about 1608 William Rowley followed with a far less successful drama *A Shoemaker a Gentleman,* based on the first two. The novel and the plays, together with ballads and songs in plenty, representing the shoemaker as gentle, jovial, bold and brave, and not least important, earning a good living, all helped to cast a kind of glamour over the trade, and it is interesting to find this picture reflected in the document

The Gentlecraft's Complaint; or, the jolly Shoemakers humble petition to the Queen and Parliament; with their great hopes of the advancement of each leather trade. 1710.†

Much of this lore, particular to shoemakers, remained alive within the craft until relatively modern times, and a weekly journal devoted to the interest of boot- and shoemakers, which flourished from 1869 to 1878, was

* 1543–1600. He was one of the most prolific ballad writers of his day. His novels, in addition to *The Gentle Craft*, include *Thomas of Reading* and *Jack of Newbury*. They all deal with the lives of simple citizens and tradespeople.

† Rox. III, 662.

called, after their patron saint, *St. Crispin*. From Deloney's time onwards, in addition to Dowland's piece, a number of other instrumental works were given names having some association with the trade, such as 'The Cobbler' (Folger-Dowland MS), 'The Cobler's Jig' (*The English Dancing Master*, 1651), 'The Shoe-maker, a Scotch Tune' (*Apollo's Banquet*, 1691) and 'The Souters o' Selkirk', from a Scottish traditional song, in the same book.

It might easily be assumed that Dowland's toy 'The Shomakers Wife' was inspired either by the Dame of the Master Shoemaker of Feversham who befriended Crispin and Crispianus in Deloney's second tale, or Mistress Margery Eyre in *The Shoemakers' Holiday,* but if any evidence exists to show that this is so, it still remains to be traced.

The piece itself, quite apart from any association it may have, is altogether delightful. Lively and witty, in $\frac{6}{8}$ rhythm, it consists of three short sections of four bars each with decorated repeats.

'Tarletones Riserrectione', No. 59, is one of Dowland's small-scale masterpieces. Consisting of no more than a line-and-a-half of tablature, its grace of design and beauty of execution place it in excellence beside the miniatures of Hilliard. Extraordinary distinction is given to the melody in the opening phrase by the use of a B flat closely followed by a B natural:

It is almost certainly an early piece since it would have been written to commemorate the death, in 1588, of the famous comic actor Richard Tarleton.

SONG ARRANGEMENT

No. 60, 'Come away', as it is called in Nn.6.36, where it appears anonymously, is based on the same melody as that of 'Come againe: sweet loue doth now enuite', No. 17 in *The First Booke of Songes*. The piece does not fall very conveniently into any of the recognized dance forms, although in **K10** it is called 'Paduana'. It also appears twice in the Leipzig MS, II, 6. 15, with the curious title 'Commia gūinæ Dulandi'.

SETTINGS OF BALLADS AND OTHER
POPULAR TUNES

It is difficult to be sure whether Dowland is the composer of 'Orlando Sleepeth', No. 61, or whether he is the arranger of an already existing tune. The particular form of the title, only found on the one copy in Dd.2.11, suggests that he may have had some specific dramatic situation in mind, and a very appropriate moment occurs in Robert Greene's play *Orlando Furioso*. There is a scene in which Melissa charms Orlando asleep and, according to the stage directions of the 1594 edition, 'satyres enter with music and plaie about him, which done they staie, he awaketh and speakes'.

In support of Dowland as composer is the fact that the earliest version so far known has his initials attached. On the other hand the seven other, later versions that have been examined 'Orlando' in William Ballet's MS, 'Orlando furiosoe' in the Mynshall MS, 'Orlando' (second half only) in the Thysius MS, 'Orlandus Furiosus' in *Testudo Gallo-Germanicca*, 'Orlando Furioso' in Kassel 108, 'Orlando-Chanson Englesæ' in the Prague University MS 485 XIII F. 174—are all anonymous.

The possibility cannot be altogether discounted that the piece has some connection with the original poem of Lodovico Ariosto. This was published in 1516 and between that date and 1623 more than 250 vocal settings of stanzas from the poem were made;* the 'Orlando' tune, as known to Dowland, could perhaps have devolved from a reduction into tablature of one of the earlier of these vocal compositions. Against this possibility, however, must be set the fact that the titles in three of the Continental sources suggest an English origin.

The main justification for its being classed as a ballad tune is the dialogue, in *Shirburn Ballads,* between a soldier departing for the wars and the girl he leaves behind, 'My dear Adieu! My sweet love, farewell' (No. LVIII), to 'Orlandoes Musique'. A somewhat corrupt version of the tune is given, with Cantus and Bassus parts.† The ballad appears to have escaped being entered in the Stationers' Register and the date of its printing is unknown.

That the piece was generally connected with the madness of Orlando, is suggested in Webster's *The Devil's Law Case* (1623):

. . . and my onely ambition is to have my Ship furnisht with a rare consort of Musicke; & when I am pleased to be mad, they shall play me Orlando . . .‡

Dowland's setting of 'Fortune my foe', No. 62, was certainly played as a solo, but there is little doubt that it originated as the lute part of a consort version. This accounts for the fact that, unlike his other settings of ballad

---

* See Albert Einstein's 'Orlando Furioso and La Gerusalemme Liberata as set to Music during the sixteenth and seventeenth Centuries' in *Notes*, September 1951.

† The Editor, Andrew Clark, misunderstood the directions for the music and attributed it to Orlando Gibbons. C. R. Baskervill, in *The Elizabethan Jig* (1931), was also mistaken in accepting the attribution.

‡ *Works*. Edited by F. L. Lucas (1927), Vol. II, p. 319.

tunes, the melody is never stated. It is very possible that William Barley launched this piece on its mistaken career as a lute solo since no copy of an earlier date than his has so far come to light.

The tune was very popular and many settings besides Dowland's are found in the lute MSS and other music books of the time. The ballad seems to have originated with 'The Lover's complaint for the Loss of his Love'* of which the first stanza goes as follows:

Fortune, my Foe, why dost thou frown on me?
And will thy favours never better be?
Wilt thou, I say, for ever breed my pain?
And wilt thou not restore my joys again?

The eleven stanzas of the young man's complaint are followed by 'The Ladies Comfortable and Pleasant Answer'.

In common with many other ballad tunes it changed its name during the course of its history. At one time it became known as 'Aim not too high' or 'Aim not so high' from the first line of a widely sung moralization described as 'An excellent Song, wherein you shall finde Great Consolation for a troubled minde'.† Among the many ditties written for this tune are a number of Lamentations—ballads purporting to be the last words of notorious criminals—specially produced for sale at the public executions. Many of these are entirely worthless in their poetic or dramatic content and were turned out by hack writers with no claim to distinction, but among the pages of doggerel lie hidden a few that have all the stature of high tragedy. One of these is 'The Lamentation of George Strangwidge, who for consenting to the death of Mr. Page of Plimoth suffered death at Barnstable'.‡ An account of the trial and execution may be read in the report of the Assizes held before the Lord Chief Justice, Sir Edmund Anderson, at Barnstaple, in March 1589/90.§

A short piece called 'Complaint', No. 63, closely resembles 'Fortune my Foe', but the second half of the tune begins at a minor third above the tonic instead of at the interval of a fifth as appears in the more generally accepted version of the melody.

In his setting of 'Go from my Window', No. 64, Dowland gives a simple statement of the tune and follows with seven variations. In using the variation form for extended and elaborately worked out settings of ballad and popular tunes, Dowland was conforming to a convention which held good with the

* *Bagford Ballads*, edited J. W. Ebsworth (1878–80), p. 961.
† *Roxburghe Ballads*, edited J. B. Ebsworth (1871).
‡ *Shirburn Ballads*, edited Andrew Clark (1907).
§ J. B. Gribble, *Memorials of Barnstaple* (1830).

majority of composers in the treatment of this particular type of music. In all
dance forms, where the pieces have divisions to the repeats of the strains, it is
unusual for the bass to differ in the repeat from the form in which it is stated
in the strain. Even in a piece as long and complex as 'The Battle Galliard',
where the whole galliard is repeated four times in its entirety, only a few
divergencies from the original statement of the bass are found. In the settings
of ballad tunes, however, the bass itself is often subjected to considerable
variation as the repeats of the subject follow each other. Comparison of the
opening eight bars of Dowland's 'Go from my Window' with the third
variation shows a typical treatment of this kind:

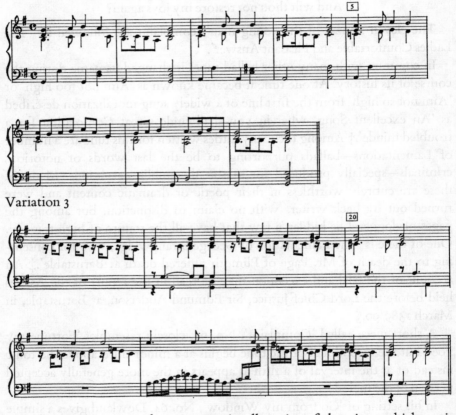

Variation 3

In bar 68 a curious phrase occurs in all copies of the piece which, as it
stands, involves, in the transcription, the use of an F double sharp:

If the pattern of the sequence is examined it will be seen that this note is an error, and that the upper voice of bar 68 should read as:

I strongly suspect that William Barley's careless printing introduced this fault, and that it was perpetuated by scribes who subsequently copied it without paying due attention to the musical meaning of what they were writing.

Historically the use of an F double sharp is not precluded. Newsidler made occasional use of the note as early as 1536,[*] but in these instances it fits logically into Newsidler's musical phrase whereas, in this case, it does violence to the pattern of Dowland's sequence and is out of character with the rest of the composition.

Several other mistakes also seem to stem from Barley's copy, but these are of less interest since they raise no questions of historical possibility.

Although this tune was widely used by composers and many different settings exist, it is not among those most frequently chosen by ballad writers to accommodate fresh sets of words. It is, however, one of the four tunes listed for the acts of 'Mr Attowell's Jigge', one of the best-known productions of its kind. On March 4th, 1587/8, John Wolfe was granted a licence to print a ballad called 'Goe from the window'. No copies are known to have survived and the words have vanished unless those sung by Merrythought in *The Knight of the Burning Pestle* are quoted from the original:

> Go from my window love, go.
> Go from my window my dear.
> The wind and the rain
> Will drive you back again,
> Thou canst not be lodged here.

'Lord Strangs March', No. 65, was also known as 'The Earl of Oxford's March' and 'My Lord of Oxenfords Maske'. It was set by a number of composers none of whom made much of the rather dull little tune, except Thomas

* C. van den Borren, in *The Sources of Keyboard Music in England* (1913), trans. J. E. Matthew (1914), p. 323n., points out that lutenists were able, at this early date, to use these exceptional modifications, since they were not bound by the restrictive rules of vocal music and of traditional notation, nor were they hampered by the limits of the unequal temperament of keyboard instruments.

Morley whose lively descant part for the lute in *The First Booke of Consort Lessons*, gives a vitality none of the other settings possess. Anthony Munday, in *A Banquet of Daintie Conceits* (1588), calls it 'a very gallant note', and sets his fourth ditty, 'Adieu! my former pleasure', to it. The name probably refers to Lord Strange, the title borne by Ferdinando Stanley until, upon the death of his father in 1593, he became the Earl of Derby.

Dowland has two settings of No. 66, the tune which came to be known by the name of Lord Willoughby. The first of these appears in four different sources as an extremely simple statement of the melody without any artifice whatsoever. The second, in the Folger-Dowland MS, is more elaborate and repeats the entire sequence A B B' twice over. In this case, however, in the second time through, the bass remains constant to the first statement, and the elaboration is introduced in the form of divisions.

The Tollemache MS has a piece with the rubric 'Lo: Wilobies welcom hom by Jo: Dowland'. On examination this proves to be a part for a second lute which fits exactly with the Folger-Dowland arrangement. For a lute duet the arrangement is unusual since the bass is doubled by the two instruments all the way through while the top line of the second lute amounts to an elaborate altus part, sometimes lying below the main melody, sometimes soaring above it. Attractive as the whole piece is when both parts are combined, I think there can be no doubt that the Tollemache half is a later addition to an already existing solo, whether by Dowland himself or not, it is hard to say.

The history of this tune and the ballads written to it is of exceptional interest. It often appears with the name 'Rowland' attached to it as, for example, in William Byrd's setting, No. CLX in the *Fitzwilliam Virginals Book*, and Charles Read Baskervill shows, in *The Elizabethan Jig*, that this was derived from the association of the melody with a series of comedy jigs of that name, for two characters, almost certainly written by Will Kemp, the famous clown. One of these, 'the Seconde parte of the gigge between Rowland and the Sexton', was entered to Thomas Gosson on December 16th, 1591, but the entry would have been made only at the time of the jig's having been printed and the wording suggests it had probably been played for some years previously. No copies of the English texts of this or any other of the Rowland jigs have been discovered, but some of them were taken to the Continent, possibly by Kemp himself when he was with the Earl of Leicester in the Low Countries in 1585 and in Denmark in 1586, and one at least, and possibly two, have survived in German translations. In his book Baskervill includes the text of one of these songs, printed in 1599 with the title 'Rolandgenandt. Ein Fewr new Lied/ der Engellendisch Tantz genandt/

zugebrauchen auff allerley Instrumenten/ &c. Gar kurtz weilig zusingen und zu Dantzen: In siner eignen Melodey'. It begins

[Roland:]   O Nachbar Robert/
                mein hertz ist voller Pein:
Robert: O Nachbar Roland/
                warumb soll das so sein?
Roland: Johan Küster liebt mein Greten/
                und das bringt mir ein Schmertz.

The story of the jig is the old favourite from *The Decameron* of the man who, in order to test the fidelity of his wife, plans his own mock death and funeral, and the disillusionment he suffers in consequence. Many imitations of the ballad followed with occasional variants on the names of the two protagonists. In England the original name was used again in 'Now Welcome Neighbour *Rowland*'.* The metre is the same as that of the Rowland ballads, but the tune given is 'Twenty pound a yeere'. As nothing is known of this melody it may well be another name for the same tune. One of the ballads gathered together in the Euing Collection† has a reference to what appears to be another manifestation of the same tune under a still further disguise:

> A wonderful Example of God's Justice,
> shewed upon one Jasper Conningham . . . .
> To the Tune of O Neighbour Robert.

It begins:

> It was a Scotch-man
> a Scotch-man lewd of life.

As can be seen, it is possible to fit this to the rhythm of the first strain of the 'Rowland' tune:

It was   a Scotch+man a — Scotch man lewd of life,

Baskervill is of the opinion that the names 'Lord Willoughby's Tune' and 'Lord Willoughby's Welcome Home' only became associated with the melody after the return, in 1589, of Peregrine Bertie, Lord Willoughby de Eresby, from his Command of the English forces in the Low Countries, and the appearance of the ballad 'The fifteenth day of July'‡ which celebrated his exploits there. Certainly none of the lute settings could be proved to have been in existence before that date, and among the widely distributed Continental versions, it goes by the following names: Leipzig II. 6. 15, p. 371

* *Pepys Ballads*, I, 210.
† p. 399.
‡ *Roxburghe Ballads*.

'Der Rolandt'; Fabritius MS, p. 9, 'Rolandt'; Nicolao Schmall's MS, f. 21v, 'Roland'; Thysius MS, f. 389, 'Soet, Soet Robertgen'; Valerius, *Nederlandtsche Gedenck-Clanck*, f. 83, 'Soet Robertgen'; and Besardus, *Thesaurus Harmonicus*, p. 134, 'Allemande'.

Dowland's second setting of the Walsingham tune, No. 67, is far less satisfactory than the one in galliard form. Unfortunately the copy in Dd.9.33 is unique and there is no way of knowing whether this is Dowland below his normal form, or whether Holmes had it from a bad source. Support for the latter case lies in the fact that, at times, Holmes himself seems uncertain of what the notes should really be, and in some variations the music, as written, is demonstrably incorrect. The beautiful balance of the original eight-bar melody has been destroyed by the addition of four extra bars, and this elongated twelve-bar theme is carried through in all six variations. Holmes appears to have been worried by the extra bars as he places a double bar two-thirds of the way through the second variation and is then left with four bars on his hands. Any satisfactory reconstruction of this piece is greatly hindered by the poor condition of the MS itself which, in places, has suffered destruction from damp.

Before the dissolution of the monasteries in the reign of Henry VIII, the image of the Virgin Mary at Walsingham in Norfolk was famous all over Europe as a place of pilgrimage. In 1538, this image, together with one from Ipswich, was taken to Chelsea and burned. Bishop Percy, in his *Reliques of Ancient Poetry* (1765),* says:

The pilgrimages undertaken on pretence of religion, were often productive of affairs of gallantry, and led the votaries to no other shrine than that of Venus.

The exact text of the Walsingham ballad is uncertain, but the large measure of agreement between the versions as rewritten by Sir Walter Ralegh and that printed by Thomas Deloney in *The Garden of Goodwill* (c. 1650) shows that both must be closely derived from a common ancestor. The melody is the first of those given for the performance of 'Mr. Attowell's Jigge', of which Act I opens with a parody of the Walsingham verses. Although not frequently found in use for other ballads it was among the most popular of those chosen for instrumental settings. In J. Phillips's 1687 translation of *Don Quixote* a charming passage shows it to have remained in favour through the later years of the seventeenth century. He speaks of

. . . An infinite number of little birds, with painted wings of various colours, hopping from branch to branch, all naturally singing 'Walsingham' and 'John come kiss me now'. . .†

* Everyman Edition, Vol. I, p. 345.   † p. 278.

In 1728 a version in common time was incorporated into John Gay's *The Beggar's Opera*.

Walsingham is, of course, one of the ballads quoted by Ophelia in her madness.★

No. 68. The recently discovered Trumbull Add. MSS 6 in the Berkshire County Record Office† provides a clue to this set of variations on a hitherto unidentified eight-bar theme. In this unfoliated MS, at the end of the copy, the word 'Alo' is written and in the margin another hand has written the letter 'e'. This presumably identifies the theme as being the tune of the ballad 'The George Aloe'. Quiller-Couch, in *The Oxford Book of Ballads* (1910), p. 697, gives a version, of which the first line goes as follows:

> The *George Aloe*, and the *Sweepstake*, too,

Unfortunately these stanzas are not of a construction that can be fitted to this particular tune. However, in Act III, Sc. 5 of *The Two Noble Kinsmen*‡ the Gaoler's Daughter enters, and sings two verses of a different ballad about the same ship, of which this is the first:

> The George alow came from the south
> From the coast of Barbary-a;
> And there he met with brave gallants of war,
> By one, by two, by three-a.

These words can, in fact, be fitted to the tune, with no more contrivance than is often necessary in cases where a ballad tune is known only from an instrumental version. Neither of these ballads mentions Digorie Piper so it would appear that, if the incidents related have any historical basis, they occurred when the *Sweepstake* sailed under a different captain.

The three copies, in Dd.5.78, where it is followed by the initials 'J.D.'; the Euing MS, where it is anonymous; and the Trumbull copy; all agree with exceptional closeness of detail.

'Loth to departe', No. 69, is the longest and, in some ways the most advanced of Dowland's compositions in this *genre*. It consists of a sixteen-bar theme and six variations. After the first statement, as the successive repeats are developed, the principle of variation by division of the original notes is abandoned altogether and the melody is subjected to a series of modifications with only a hint here and there to recall the theme as first stated. This type of treatment can be seen clearly by comparison of the first sixteen bars with variation No. 2:

★ See also F. W. Sternfeld, 'Ophelia's Version of the Walsingham Song'. *Music and Letters*, Vol. 45, No. 2, April 1964, pp. 108–13.
† I am grateful to Ian Harwood for showing me his set of prints.
‡ *The Works of Shakespeare*, ed. Alexander Dyce (1895), Vol. 9, p. 166.

Variation No. 2

Several settings of 'Loth to depart' were made by other composers; apart from Dowland's the most notable being that of Giles Farnaby in the *Fitzwilliam Virginals Book*, No. CCXXX. Nothing is known, however, of the original ballad although a particular class of broadside seems to have come into circulation known as a 'Loth to depart', made on the departure of some well-known character, a typical example being 'London's Loathe to departe', made for the Earl of Essex on the occasion of his leaving England to take command of the English forces in Ireland in 1599. Whether the same tune was always employed or whether it was the occasion that gave rise to the use of the title, is not clear.

Dowland's setting of 'Robin', No. 70, is both extended and elaborate, although he never travels as far from his statement of the original theme as he does in his setting of 'Loth to departe'. The strains and their repeats consist of A (four bars) A', B (eight bars) B'. This sequence is then varied twice over in its entirety. He follows the more usual pattern of the melody in bars 4 and 5, ending the phrase with the descent of a fourth, unlike the version of Add. 31,392 which ends with the descent of a semi-tone:

Dowland.
Dd.9.33,
ff. 29v/30

Anon.
Add. 31,392
f. 25

This was one of the most popular of all ballad tunes and was set in a number of different versions for lute, virginals, viols, bandora and combinations of various instruments. The name appears as 'Robin', 'Sweet Robin', 'Jolly Robin', 'Bonny sweet Robin', 'My Robin is to the greenwood gone', 'Robin Hood is to the greenwood gone' and in Kassel Mus. MS 108, I, as 'Schön wehr ich gern etc'. Ballads to the tune are found in the *Roxburghe Ballads* and in *The Crown Garland of Golden Roses* (3rd edition, 1659). It survived into the eighteenth century and appears in A. Stuart's *Music for the Tea Table Miscellany* (1725) with stanzas fitted to it beginning 'There Nancy's to the greenwood gone'. The original text is no longer extant but it is probably from this lost ballad that Ophelia quotes (*Hamlet*, Act IV Sc. 5) 'For bonny sweet Robin is all my joy'.★

References to the piece occur in a number of literary sources of the period and the name slipped easily off the pen of the Elizabethan courtier. Sir Walter Ralegh, writing to the Earl of Leicester on March 29th, 1586, says:

The queen is in very good tearms with yow, and thanks be to God, well pacified, and yow are agayne her 'Sweet Robyn'.†

Its great popularity suggests this may have been the tune that William Webbe‡ had in mind when he wrote:

★ For discussion of the possible survival of words from the early ballad in Robert Jones's 'In Sherwood lived stout Robin Hood' see F. W. Sternfeld, *Music in Shakespearean Tragedy* (1963), p. 71. A list of all known musical settings of the 'Robin' tune is also given.

† John Bruce, *Correspondence of Robert Dudley, Earl of Leycester, during his Government of the Low Countries, in the years 1585 and 1586* (1844).

‡ *A Discourse of English Poetrie* (1586), edited Edward Arber (1870), p. 36.

Nor though many such can frame an Alehouse song of fiue or sixe score verses, hobbling vpon some tune of a Northern Jygge, or Robyn hoode or La lubber etc. . . .

PIECES OF UNCERTAIN ASCRIPTION

a. *Anonymous, but probably by Dowland*

No. 71, 'A Fantasia', from Jane Pickering's MS (Eg. 2046), f. 24, is a chromatic fancy that shows all the characteristics of Dowland's style in this type of composition. It is based on a descending chromatic hexachord which during the course of the piece is repeated twenty-seven times. It opens with a closely knit contrapuntal section with each voice entering in strict imitation, the second voice at the fifth below the first; the third at the octave; and the fourth at the fifth below the third voice. This is followed by two sections for two voices only, with the chromatic theme repeated six times in the upper voice. During the last three of these repetitions the rhythm changes to $\frac{6}{8}$ and the lower part moves in a pattern of repeated notes extremely reminiscent of No. 1, the fancy from *Varietie of Lute-Lessons*:

In the following bar the rhythm returns to common-time and the chromatic theme passes to the lower voice, in this case moving down the whole chromatic scale from g to G, with rapid figuration in the upper part. The twelve note passage is then repeated in the higher voice moving downwards from d' to d. The last section is mainly in three-part counterpoint with the theme passing from voice to voice and making its last appearance in the highest part, descending through the chromatic notes from g' to g.

No. 72, a chromatic fancy of which a unique copy is found, anonymously and without title, on ff. 42v/43 of the Euing MS, allows a little more room for doubt concerning the authorship than does No. 71. A number of points suggest its having come from Dowland's hand, but at the same time, compared with the other authentic chromatic fancies, certain features appear as uncharacteristic. To take first the points in favour of Dowland as composer: In the MS it is placed immediately after a copy of 'Farwell' (No. 3) which also lacks any indication of title or composers name, and both pieces occur in a series of twenty-three compositions by Dowland all of which suffer the same lack of identification but which can be verified from other sources. This group extends from f. 16 to f. 44, but it is not entirely unbroken as one gap occurs from f. 38 to f. 41, immediately preceding 'Farwell', and another, on f. 43v, follows the fancy now under discussion. Both are filled with works by other composers. With these facts in mind it can be seen that its position in the MS is strongly indicative of Dowland as composer although it does not present 100 per cent proof.

In the opening bars the writing is very typical of the style set by Dowland in his other chromatic fancies:

The second half of bar 7 and the first half of bar 8, it will be noticed, bear a strong resemblance to phrases in 'In Darkness let me dwell'. From bar 10 to 14 Dowland's very characteristic wide spacing between the subject and the upper parts is found, the chromatic phrase, in this appearance, lying between A and E in the bass. After the sixth repetition which again lies in the bass, at bar 23 the descending phrase is inverted and appears rising from A to D in the bass. Later another subject is introduced:

This is interspersed with the plain ascending hexachord until bar 62. From here to the end at bar 74 none of the subjects appears in anything but fragmentary form.

If Dowland's practice in his other chromatic fancies is accepted as a norm, then clearly there are radical departures from this in the writing of the present piece. In 'Forlorne Hope Fancye', 'Farwell' and the Jane Pickering 'Fantasia' one subject only is used in each case and the ascending and descending forms of the chromatic hexachord never appear together in the same composition. In this particular fancy, when it departs from the original subject the monumental sense of unity of the other pieces somewhat disappears, and, in the opinion of the author, the latter half does not live up to the promise of the earlier part. Is the piece then an experiment by Dowland which was not altogether successful? Is it by another composer writing in imitation of Dowland, or is the first half by Dowland and the rest from another hand? Unless some further evidence comes to light it seems unlikely that the attribution can ever be more than a question of opinion.

The initial theme of No. 73, an anonymous fancy without title from Dd.9.33, ff. 44v/45/45v, bears a strong resemblance to the popular tune 'All in a garden green'.* Several of Dowland's favourite devices are employed, notably the use of little upward scales with the first note repeated and the use of many times alternated tonic and dominant chords in approaching the final cadence.† In the MS it is immediately preceded by No. 6, also anonymous and without title.

No. 74, from Add. 31,392, f. 24, is a short anonymous fancy, without title, opening with the same subject as that of No. 1. The use of this theme suggests Dowland might be the composer, although it is by no means certain proof that he is. Other musicians also used the theme, notably the unknown writer of Fantasia No. 83 in Elias Mertel's *Hortus Musicalis Novus* (1615). The very skilful construction is typical of Dowland, so also is the change to the minor key at bar 26, which only moves back to the major for the final chord.

The style of No. 75 is again suggestive of Dowland; so also is its position in Dd.2.11 where, on f. 48, it immediately precedes No. 48, here subscribed 'Allmaine', and under this is written 'J. Dowland'. The end of No. 75 is written right up to the edge of the page leaving no room for any kind of inscription, and the title, 'A Dream', is crowded in on the lowest line of the

---

* See *Fitzwilliam Virginals Book*, No. CIV, by William Byrd, and the anonymous setting for Lyra viol in William Ballet's MS.
† cf. No. 2 and No. 9.

tablature stave in the final bar. As the two pieces lie together on the page the whole layout could easily bear the interpretation that the attribution following the second was intended to refer to both. It will be remembered that a version of No. 48, in the Folger-Dowland MS has the title 'Lady Laitons Almone', and this name provides a further link with No. 75. In Dd.14.24 a consort part for cittern fits exactly with the piece under discussion. The very unusual form of the three strains—seven bars, seven bars and ten bars—makes a random coincidence impossible and it is clear that this is the remaining part of a consort version of the same piece. In the cittern book the title is given as 'Lady Leightons Pauen', and the association of both compositions with the same patron strengthens the likelihood that Dowland wrote the pavan as well as the almain. On the other hand it must be said that in the Hirsch MS the pavan occurs with neither title nor ascription, in a part of the book where no authentic Dowland pieces are found.

The opening phrase of No. 76, called 'Galliard' in Dd.9.33, f. 42, is the same as that of No. 19, 'Pipers Galliard' and many of Dowland's characteristics of composition are present in the piece. In addition to the stylistic indications its position in the Euing MS, between No. 3 ('Farwell') and No. 72, might also point to Dowland as the composer. Following the word 'Galliard' is a contraction or mnemonic which appears to be 'W th'. No other composer is known whose name could be represented by these letters, although this does not necessarily rule out the possibility that one existed, since there are a few cases where a musician is represented by a single work only. It will be remembered, however, that one of Dowland's almains was called 'Mistris Whittes Thinge', and that in Dd.2.11 the title is abbreviated to 'W Thinge'. A possible explanation is that Holmes, forgetting the earlier piece, was confused, and attached this title to the galliard in error, reminding himself of the name by which he thought it was known by the mnemonic 'W th'.

In the case of No. 77, 'Mistris Norrishis Delight' (Archbishop Marsh's MS, f. 382), there is no evidence beyond the character of the piece to support a claim to Dowland as the composer, but its rather unusual and spirited tune suggests it might be his. It is, however, all too easy for an author to lay claim to most of the attractive anonymous pieces for his, or her, particular composer!

The position of No. 78, a jig-like piece on f. 26 of the Euing MS, strongly indicates Dowland as the composer. It occurs in a group which contains some of his best known works; six precede it and three more follow, all without title or composer's name. The general character, with its underlying melancholy, recalls other pieces of his of similar rhythmic structure.

No. 79. There can, I think, be no doubt that this untitled and anonymous setting of 'What if a day' is by Dowland. As far as bar 18 the piece is written in his hand; from there onwards there is an element of doubt. In the first chord of bar 19, the highest note of the three is still in his hand, but on the lower two the quill has either been re-cut or changed, and from there onwards the tablature has a somewhat different appearance. Careful examination of the MS, greatly magnified, shows similarity of penstrokes in the formation of most of the characters, and the slight dissimilarity of the total appearance could be accounted for by the latter part having been added at another time or with a quill cut in a different manner. If the hand is not Dowland's own, then it belongs to someone who was making a close imitation. No other item in the Folger-Dowland MS (on f. 26 of which this piece is found), except those known to be written by Dowland, shows agreement with this particular hand. Apart from any question of authorship, the piece itself is a delightful setting of a very beautiful tune. The treatment of the last strain which, in the usual very simple versions of the piece, appears as:

is particularly characteristic of Dowland when it takes on the following decorations:

No. 80, 'A Coye Toye', bears a strong resemblance to No. 57, 'Mrs vauxes Gigge'. It is possibly an early version. As with most of the other pieces in the Mynshall MS its time marks are extremely erratic.

No. 81. In Dd.2.11, on f. 52, an anonymous piece, without title, has been identified by Richard Newton as being a solo version of 'Tarleton's Jigge' in the Cambridge Consort Books. An arrangement of the same piece for cittern in Dd.4.23 is called 'Tarletons Willy'. The style is extremely reminiscent of

Dowland's other jigs and the title of No. 59 suggests he had some connection with the famous clown, Richard Tarlton. On the title-page of *News out of Purgatory* (c. 1590) ascribed to Tarlton and containing many of his jests, though indeed not by Tarlton at all, the contents are described as 'onely such a Jest as his Jigge, fit for Gentlemen to laugh at an hour'. Although printed after his death in 1588, the interval before the appearance of *News out of Purgatory* was so short that the reference to the jig is fairly reliable evidence of its existence, though nothing is known of it now. Possibly these three settings represent the tune to which it was sung and danced.

b. Pieces ascribed to Dowland, probably incorrectly

No. 82. The names Dowland and F Cutting are both inscribed under this galliard which begins on f. 22 of Dd.9.33. Although it could be by either composer, the style seems more consistent with Cutting's work than with that of Dowland.

In the Mynshall MS No. 83 goes by the title of 'Dowlands Galliard', but in the Folger-Dowland MS and Add. 38,539 it is attributed to Johnson; and in Nn.6.36 specifically to Robert Johnson. In the Welde MS no composer's name is given and it is called 'My Lady Mildmays delighte'. Of these sources the Folger-Dowland and Welde MSS both date from about 1600 when Robert Johnson would have been some seventeen years old, since he was probably born in 1583. Young for a composer by today's standards, but not to the Elizabethans who matured early. It is significant that in the Folger-Dowland MS, where Dowland added his signature to six pieces, he did not lay claim to this galliard. This, however, is not incontrovertible proof that he did not write the piece since for some reason he also left the copy of 'Mrs Winter's Jump' without his signature. The use of the name Mildmay might be taken as support for Dowland's claim, as some connection with the family is suggested by the title of 'Mr Mildmays Galliard' for the 'Battle Galliard' in Dd.9.33. The weight of evidence is, however, in Johnson's favour rather than in Dowland's.

On f. 17 of Dd.9.33, No. 84 is subscribed 'Hasellwoods Galliard Jo Dowland'. It is, in fact, No. 12 of Anthony Holborne's *Pavans, Galliards, Almains,* etc. (1599). There is no reason to doubt that Holborne is the original composer of the galliard and if Dowland is in any way connected with it it can only be as having made the arrangement for the lute. In this setting, however, the original composition is treated with little respect and the harmony is altered with no apparent reason. Another version, anonymous and without title, in the Hirsch MS, is very inaccurate; the divisions are undistinguished and the bass of these is frequently inconsistent with the bass of the strains. In all, the evidence suggests, unless these two versions happen to be exceedingly poor copies, that Dowland was not responsible for either, and that Holmes was mistaken in crediting the piece to him.

No. 85. Under the title of 'Galliarda Dulandi 39' Leipzig, Mus. MS II, 6. 15 gives a rather poor version of a piece which in other MS sources is attributed to different composers. Dd.2.11 and Add. 31,392 both ascribe it to Cutting; Archbishop Marsh's MS calls it 'Galliard Alfonsus'; and the Thysius MS has it as 'Maister Hayls Galliard'. The latter could mean, of course, either 'Maister Hayls' as composer or as dedicatee. The style, however, is very typical of Francis Cutting and the galliard is almost certainly by him.

c. Possibly by Dowland, but which exist only in bad versions

No. 86, 'Pauana Dulandi 24', and No. 88, 'Galliarda Dulandi 8', both from Leipzig II, 6.15, are in such poor shape that it is difficult to reach any conclusion about the quality or authorship of either. In the pavan a trace of Dowland may be felt here and there in a typical suspension, but the crudity of the harmony throughout most of the three strains suggests that if he was the original composer then the version given here must have come to the compiler in a very corrupt form. The so-called 'Galliarda Dulandi 8' is not a galliard at all; possibly it is the setting of a chorale or psalm tune, but it is not recognizable as any of those that Dowland is known to have written or arranged. The final six bars hardly seem to belong to the earlier sections of the piece.

See also Appendix I.

III

The song-books

Dr. Fellowes remarks: 'The English School of lutenist song-writers stands by itself as something that had no parallel in contemporary Europe'.* It is true that the English lute-song derived certain special characteristics from its own native background that differentiate it from those of Italy, France and Germany, but it is misleading, particularly to the non-specialist, to suggest that in England the composers in this particular form existed as an isolated phenomenon outside the general European tradition.

Owing to the absence of written music for the lute before the first decade of the sixteenth century it is impossible to say with exactitude the date at which the lute-song first made its appearance in Europe, but evidence suggests that as early as 1480 the method of performance with solo voice and lute was already in favour. About the year 1484 Johannes Tinctoris speaks of lute players who are able to sustain three, and even four, parts on their instruments, and clearly by that date technique was sufficiently advanced to allow of adequate performance of the usual two parts of the early lute accompaniments. An Italian MS† of the first years of the sixteenth century supports this early date with the presence of lute accompaniments to the two French *chansons*, 'Amors, Amors' by Hayne van Ghizeghem and 'Ge ne fay plus' by Antoine de Busnois (or alternatively by Gilles Mureau) both of which were composed before 1480. Comparison of the lute accompaniments (which consist of a reduction into tablature of the two lower voices) with the original version in three parts, shows a decorative figuration of the tenor in a style consistent with the accompaniments having been made at the same period as that in which the *chansons* were composed.

* General Preface to *The English School of Lutenist Song Writers*. Dr. Fellowes was, of course, writing in the early days of research in this field, but since the Preface has been retained in the Revised Edition of 1960, without modification or note, some comment seems called for.

† In the library of G. Thibault. See 'Un Manuscrit Italien pour Luth des Premières Années du XVIe Siècle', in *Le Luth et sa Musique* (1958).

The poet Serafino del'Aquilar (1466–1500) is said to have sung his own verses and those of other poets to his own accompaniment on the lute. Paolo Cortese,* writing soon after his death, likens him to Petrarch, who, he says, was thought to have been the first poet to sing his 'lofty songs' to the lute. Serafino del'Aquilar, he says, was, however, pre-eminent in restoring the tradition in recent years.

The first printed books to contain songs with lute accompaniment were the *Tenori e contrabassi intabulati col sopran in canto figurato per cantar e sonar col lauto, Libro Primo* and *Libro secondo* of Francisco Bossinensis, printed by Petrucci in 1509 and 1511. These were followed by *Frottole de Misser Bartolomio Tromboncino et de Misser Marcheto Cara con Tenori e bassi tabulati con soprani in canto figurato per cantar e sonar col lauto. c.* 1521. Meanwhile Arnolt Schlick's *Tabulaturen etlicher lobgesang und lidlein* was printed at Mainz in 1512. Next came Pierre Attaignant's *Tres brève et familière Introduction,* at Paris in 1529.

Baldassare Castiglione, writing in 1528, tells us some of the reasons why this type of performance appealed so strongly to Renaissance taste:

Pricksong is a faire musicke, so it be done upon the booke surely and after a goode sorte. But to sing to the lute is much better, because all the sweetnes consisteth in one alone, and a man is much more heedful and understandeth better the feat manner, and the aire or veyne of it, when eares are not busied in hearing more than one voice: and beside every little errour is soon perceived which happeneth not in singing in company, for one beareth out another.

But singing to the lute with the dittie (me thinke) is more pleasant than the rest, for it addeth to the wordes such a grace and strength, that it is a great wonder.†

Judging by the extant music from the period, the songs Castiglione speaks of were not primarily composed as solo songs, but were of the type of arrangement included in the collections already mentioned. In Spain, however, in 1536, Luis Milan, in his *Libro de Musica de Vihuela de Mano intitulado El Maestro,* included a number of *villancicos* and *romances* in which he broke away from the strict contrapuntal adaptation and developed his accompaniments in a highly individual instrumental style. In the same year *Madrigali di Verdelotto da cantare et sonare nel lauto, intavolati per Messer Adriano* appeared in Venice, but this again, as the title makes clear, was a collection of arrange-

---

* *De Cardinal, cit.* Bruce Pattison, *Music and Poetry of the English Renaissance* (1948), p. 119, quoted from Tiraboschi, *Storia della Letteratura Italiana,* Bk. VI, pt. III, p. 1244. See also John Stevens, *Music and Poetry in the Early Tudor Court* (1961), p. 281.

† *The Booke of the Courtier.* English translation by Sir Thomas Hoby, 1561. Everyman edition, p. 101. Hoby's use of the word lute is a mistranslation of Castiglione's 'viola'. Nevertheless the argument is valid whichever instrument is named.

ments for solo voice with intabulation of the lower voices for the lute. A reprint of this book appeared in 1540. With the appearance of the second part of the Phalèse *Hortus Musarum* at Louvain in 1553, in which some twenty-four items of vocal music are arranged in this form, the lute-song may be said to have firmly established itself on the Continent.

In England its history is far more difficult to trace owing to the complete absence of any examples of tablature from before about 1540. Nothing but the written word remains to provide information about the use of the lute as an accompaniment to the solo voice until many years after the Italian, German and French printers had issued their first collections.

Geoffrey Chaucer (1340?–1400), in *The Canterbury Tales*, is witness to the lute's presence in England in the fourteenth century, as for example, in the following lines from 'The Pardoner's Tale':

> Whereas with harpes, lutes and giternes,
> They dance and plaie at dis bothe day and night.

Canon Galpin★ cites some further documentary evidence from the fourteenth century and also some visual representations from the fifteenth, while Stevens quotes a list of music owned by a musician from the latter century, written on the back of an Irish ecclesiastical document, in which the writer notes, among other items, 'all the songes for the leute'† that he has.

At the Court of Henry VIII the lute was highly prized, there being no less than twenty-six in the royal collection,‡ while the luters, Maister Giles, and Philip and Peter van Wilder were paid handsome salaries ranging from thirty shillings to sixty-six shillings and eight pence a month.§ Henry himself was a performer and the three royal children were all instructed. Edward‖ continued to play during his short life and took some pride in his performance, as he shows in his *Journal*, when he sets down the details of a visit paid him by the Mareschal St. André in 1550:

He dined with me, herd me play on the lute, ride (read?), came to me in my study, supped with me, and so departed to Richmond.¶
The pleasure that Henry VIII took in a brilliant performance was described

★ *Old English Instruments of Music* (1910), Third Edition, pp. 41–2.
† op. cit., p. 279, from B.M. Add. MS 38163, 'Song' could mean any piece of music. cf. Dowland's use of the word for the compositions in *Lachrimæ or Seaven Teares*.
‡ F. W. Galpin, *Old English Instruments of Music,* pp. 292–300. The Inventory is given in full from B.M. Harl. MS 1419.
§ *Musical Antiquary*, Vol. 4 (1913), pp. 55 and 178.
‖ J. G. Nichols, *Literary Remains of Edward VI* (1857), Letter No. 21, Edward thanks his father for sending his servant Philip 'who is both excellent in music and a gentleman', to instruct him in playing the lute.
¶ op. cit., p. 332.

by Nicolo Sagudino, a secretary of the Italian Ambassador, Giustiniano, in a letter to Alviso Foscari, dated May 19th, 1517.* He gives an account of how he, with the Ambassador, visited the Court at Richmond, where they heard 'the King sing and play'. Then he says:

Monsignor Dionisio Memo† was there, and at his request the King made them listen to a lad who played upon the lute, better than ever was heard, to the amazement of his Majesty, who never wearies of him, and since the coming of the lad, Zuan Piero‡ is not in such favour as before, and complains, and is quite determined on returning to Italy *sane bene peculiatus*, and he does wisely.

To the lute as an accompanying instrument references are, however, rare. The Viscount Chateaubriant in his memoirs§ says of Anne Boleyn:

Besides singing like a syren, accompanying herself on the lute, she harped better than King David and handled cleverly both flute and rebec.

A generation later Mary Queen of Scots excelled in the same accomplishment:

Elle avoit (says Brantôme) la voix tres douce et tres bonne, car elle chantois tres bien, accordant sa voix avec le luth, qu'elle touchoit bien solidement de cette belle main blanche et de ces beaux doigts si bien faconnés.||

It is an interesting point that both these ladies spent their formative years in France, Anne from 1514 to 1522 and Mary from 1548 to 1561, where they probably acquired their skill in this type of performance.

Thomas Whythorne (1528–after 1590), who was taught to play the lute by John Heywood, in his *Autobiography*¶ makes a number of references to singing to his own accompaniment on the lute, particularly during his wooing of a 'yoong mayden', but unhappily he included no songs of this type in his *Songes of three fower and fiue Voyces* (1571) or in his collection of 1590.

Christopher Tye writes on the title-page of his *Actes of the Apostles* (1553) that they are 'supplied with notes to eche chapter, to synge and also to play upon the lute', and in the nineteenth verse of the dedicatory poem to Edward VI he adds:

---

* *Four Years at the Court of Henry VIII*. Letters of S. Giustiniano, trs. Rawdon Lubbock Brown, Vol. II, 1854, p. 75. A summary of this letter is given.
† The King's Italian organist.
‡ Carmeliano.
§ A. Strickland, *Lives of the Queens of England*, Vol. IV (1840), p. 168.
|| W. Dauney, *Ancient Scottish Melodies* (1838), p. 107.
¶ Edited by James M. Osborn (1961).

That such good thi[n]ges, your grace might moue,
Your lute when ye assaye:
In stede of songes of wanton loue
These stories then to play.

While it is quite possible that a singer might arrange the additional voices as a lute accompaniment, it is doubtful whether these sentences add much evidence one way or the other since purely instrumental performance of the psalms was certainly not unknown. Tallis, in Archbishop Parker's *The Whole Psalter* (1567), although he does not mention the lute, offers a similar alternative of singing or playing:

The Tenor of these partes be for the people when they will sing alone, the othere parts put for greater queers, or to such as will sing or play them alone.

In this connection it is perhaps not irrelevant to mention Adrian Le Roy's *Tiers Livre* of 1552 which contains twenty-one psalms set for the lute. They have no vocal part and the decoration of the melodic line and the relatively complex structure of the music are entirely consistent with the intention of solo performance. Eight somewhat similar settings are included in the 1574 English edition of the *Instruction*.

Owing to the scarcity of texts both MS and printed, the character and extent of the repertoire of early songs with lute accompaniment remain uncertain. In the earliest extant MSS there are a limited number of pieces that bear the titles of songs, for example, 'Pastyme' in Royal Appendix 58:* 'If care do cause men cry' among the pieces 'written by one Raphe Bowle to learne to playe on his Lutte in anno 1558'; 'Blame not my lute,'† 'Will ye go walke the woode so wilde', 'Of loue to learne to skyll', 'Robin Hood' and 'All of grene willowe' from the Giles Lodge MS;‡ and 'the tender love that dredethe losse', 'I sayde not soe', 'Care who so wyll' and again 'If care doo cause men crie' from the Braye MS.§ Of these 'The tender love that dredethe losse' is particularly interesting, since the melody is written in staff notation above the tablature, showing the top line of the lute to be doubling with the

* B.M., copied before 1540.
† It has frequently been said that this piece is written on the *folía* bass. Michael Morrow has pointed out to me that it is, in fact, a composition called 'La Gamba' or 'La Cara Cossa', in which the bass, though similar, is not identical with that of the *folía*. This piece, one of the four most popular Italian dance tunes of the sixteenth century, appears in numerous Italian, Spanish, Netherlandish and German sources over a period of about 100 years.
‡ Folger Library, MS 448, copied between 1559 and 1571, according to Reese, *Music in the Renaissance* (1954), p. 842. The list of 'money owning to Giles Lodge 1591' on f. 1v was undoubtedly added after the rest of the MS was completed.
§ Yale, Box 22, No. 10, in the possession of James Marshall Osborn. I am grateful to Robert Spencer for allowing me to study his set of prints after I had been refused the courtesy of a microfilm by the owner.

voice in the first two stanzas. The remainder of the pieces mentioned here
have no separate voice part and could be solos or consort parts although the
presence of the tune on the lute does not necessarily preclude their having
been used as accompaniments, since Le Roy, for example, doubled the vocal
line on the lute as a matter of normal practice in his arrangements of *airs de
cour*. A few items are indisputably accompaniments, as for example, on f.
54v in Royal Appendix 58, where a piece can be identified as the lower voices
of 'Ough war der mount', No. 42 of Henry VIII's MS.★

The contents of Royal Appendix 58 and Raphe Bowl's MS, and the pieces
in the first handwriting in Giles Lodge's MS are not of a high level of development, and the tablature is far from accurate; many of the time marks are
incorrect or are absent altogether. The second handwriting in Giles Lodge is
very similar to, though not identical with, that of the Braye MS, and in both
these cases the tablature is more accurate and the music is of a higher order.
The Braye MS shows a cosmopolitan influence, with two fantasias by Francesco da Milano (Nos. 6 and 7 from *Intabolatura de Lauto. Segondo Libro.*
(1546); a pavan and galliard on 'La Traditora', another of the four most popular Italian dance tunes of the time; an untitled piece that can be identified as
'Je file' (Add. 4900, f. 62, and Brogyntyn MS f. 13v.) and 'Philips song'
identified by John Stevens as being by Philip van Wilder. This MS appears
to be of approximately the same date as the Lodge MS, although, in a few
pieces a relatively developed technique can be seen, with the use of high
barré positions.

Although these early tablatures throw some light on the music in current
use in the second and third quarters of the sixteenth century, the very naïve
character of much of it and the inadequacy of the tablature suggests they were
the property and playing books of amateurs rather than of professionals.
Only the later folios of the Giles Lodge MS and the Braye MS contain music
that might be rated at professional level or show any real mastery of the
system of notation. The amateur character of the Braye MS is confirmed,
however, by the fact that the music is copied into a commonplace book which
also contains medicinal prescriptions and a number of poems, among them
the complete text of Benedick's song in *Much Ado about Nothing*, 'The God of
love that sits above'.

One MS only, B.M. Add. 4900, introduces us to songs arranged for lute
and voice, of a rather different level of development. Said by the Hughes-
Hughes *Catalogue of Manuscript Music* to have been copied *c.* 1600, the contents represent a repertoire of some forty years earlier. Here are settings of
vocal pieces such as 'What harte can thincke' by John Heywood, 'Alleluya'

★ B.M. Add. 31922. See Stevens, *Music and Poetry in the Early Tudor Court*, p. 279.

by Taverner, 'Benedicam Domino' by Johnson and the anonymous 'I lothe that I did loue' and 'My lytell prety one' written out for solo voice with lute accompaniment. The lute parts show some advance in accomplishment, and it is greatly to be regretted that the MS yields no certain evidence of the date at which the settings were made.

The late appearance of lute tablature as a notational system, and the fact that no music for this instrument is known to have been recorded in any form prior to its invention is fairly reliable evidence that the medieval lutenist relied entirely on his ear and his memory. A large part of the professional repertoire probably consisted of improvisations on already existing melodies and basses. Even after the invention of tablature it is likely that this tradition persisted for some time, and indeed, at first, the composer-performer, far from feeling that the publication of his compositions was desirable, may well have felt uneasiness at the idea of making public on a wide scale the secrets of his own personal art. That these secrets were jealously guarded by Spanish vihuelistas is commented on by Fray Juan Bermudo:*

What shall I say of those players . . . who, in playing, do not like the position of their hands to be seen lest someone steal from them? That which some masters could say completely in one month they reserve for the day of judgment. . . . What a pity it is (and those who have christian understanding must weep for it) that great secrets of music die in a moment and are finished with the person of the musician, for the lack of having communicated them to others. Grief it is, and no small one, to lose at one stroke that which has cost thirty or forty years of continuous work.†

Though Bermudo was distressed that it should be so, the fact that professional musicians adopted this esoteric attitude towards their work is very understandable and it is hardly likely that it was confined to Spain alone. To a man brought up in the earlier tradition it must have taken some foresight and independence of mind to see the advantages that would eventually follow the publication of his music.

There were probably only a few exceptional amateurs sufficiently gifted

---

* *Declaración de Instrumentos musicales* (1555), Prologo primero para el piadoso lector. My thanks are due to John Roberts who first brought this passage to my notice. The two valuable prologues to this work are omitted in the facsimile edition published by Bärenreiter-Verlag (1957).

† 'Que dire de aquellos tañedores, que tañendo . . . no quieren que los vean la postura de las manos: porque no se la hurten? Lo que algunos maestros podia dezir complidamente en un mes: lo reserven para el dia de juyzio . . . Lastima es (y los que tienen entendimiento christiano, lo avian de llorar) que mueron grandes secretos de musica en un momento, y se acaben junctamente con la persona del musico: por no cõmunicarlos: Dolor y no pequeño es perderse en un punto: lo que costo treynta o quarenta años de continuo trabajo.'

These criticisms are repeated almost word for word in Martin de Tapia, *Vergel de Musica* (1559) in the Exortacion Al discreto y curioso lector.

to compose or improvise a repertoire for themselves and it is likely that the majority of amateurs were dependent on their teachers to provide 'lessons' that could be committed to memory. It could well have been the impulse of the Italian Renaissance towards the highly cultivated personality of the Humanist ideal, in which a knowledge of music and the command of an instrument were considered to be one of the prime necessities, that led to the publication of the first books of lute tablature, since a wider market would be provided by the courtiers and in the commercial urban communities where wealth made it possible to follow courtly fashion, than would have been the case had sales been limited to purely professional circles.

In England, in the early years of the sixteenth century, when Petrucci was beginning to publish his lute-books in Venice, it would have been hard to find a market to absorb an edition of an economically rewarding size.

That the enjoyment of music, apart from its purely ceremonial use, played so important a part in Court life was largely due to Henry VIII himself. Outside the Court and the courtly amateurs who surrounded the King, the cultivation of music for domestic enjoyment was far from common. Professional musicians, perhaps a few lutenists among them, might be engaged in the houses of some of the nobility and gentry, and in a few of these families amateur musicians might be found, but musical literacy appears to have been rare.

Although the population began to show an upward trend by about 1485, early Tudor society numbered only two to three million in all, mainly dispersed in isolated rural communities, the only large town, London, having no more than 75,000 inhabitants at the beginning of the sixteenth century.* Only a fraction of the urban population had by then acquired the wealth, position and inclination to develop any sophisticated musical skill.

As the century advanced so the population continued to increase, and by 1558 it had reached some four and a half million, the upward curve continuing till some five million was reached in 1603.†

By 1600 London contained 300,000 inhabitants in its teeming parishes, becoming with that number the largest town in Europe. Hand-in-hand with the numerical growth important changes in the composition of society came about during the course of the century, and the gentry emerged, as A. L. Rowse says, 'as the most dynamic class in Tudor society'. He continues:

. . . the rise of the gentry was the dominant feature of Elizabethan society. One may fairly say that most of the leading spirits of the age, those who gave it its character and did its work, were of this class.‡

* S. T. Bindoff, *Tudor England*, Penguin edition (1950), pp. 24 and 41.
† A. L. Rowse, *The England of Elizabeth* (1951), p. 218.   ‡ op. cit., p. 255.

Furthermore, in the growing towns, in London in particular, a large urban monied class was developing, enriched by trade and land speculation after the Dissolution of the monastries. The new rich, both among the gentry and the city bourgeoisie, were bent on demonstrating their newly gained wealth, and houses were built with lavish decoration and furnishings, *objects d'art* were bought, libraries instituted, and the cultivation of the arts assumed a place of major importance in domestic life.

When, in 1568, there appeared in London a translation of Adrian Le Roy's *Instruction pour apprendre la tablature du luth et la manière de toucher cet instrument* (1567),* under the title *A Briefe and easye instru[c]tion to learne the tableture to conducte and dispose thy hande unto the Lute englished by J. Alford Londenor*, the time was evidently ripe for such a book, since a second edition, *A Briefe and Plaine Instruction*, was printed in 1574, with a different collection of lessons consisting of lute arrangements of a number of *chanson*, and eight psalm tunes.

The Stationers' Register for the years July 22nd, 1565 to July 22nd, 1566, and 1566 to 1567 shows two earlier entries of books connected with lute playing. In the first, John Alde received a licence 'for pryntinge of a boke intituled *the Sequence of of lutynge*' and in the latter, Edward Sutton paid six pence 'for his lycense for the pryntinge of a boke intituled an *exortation to all kynde of men how they shulde lerne to playe of the lute* by Roberte Ballarde',† but no copies of either have survived.

A number of blank years followed as far as the printing of tablature was concerned. The responsibility for this may be partly due to the obstructive attitude of Thomas Tallis who, together with William Byrd, was granted the monopoly of music printing in 1575. In the same year their *Cantiones Sacræ* was printed and proved a financial failure. Tallis thereupon refused to print any more music during the rest of his life, and all other printers, by the terms of the licence, were prevented from issuing any music books with the exception of psalters. Byrd subsequently arranged that Thomas Este should become his assigné, and in 1587 printing recommenced. No books of lute music were, however, included in the volumes that appeared in the next nine years. Possibly the tablature fount used in the printing of the Le Roy books had been destroyed in the interim and no one had thought it worth while to cut or import new characters. Whether or not this was the reason, the fact remains that it was not until 1596 that the printing of tablature was resumed with William Barley's *New Booke of Tabliture*; the first publication to include English songs

---

* No copy from this edition has survived.

† Edward Arber, *A Transcript of the Registers of the Stationers' Company* (1875), Vol. I, pp. 133b and 156.

with a plucked-string accompaniment. The four songs (of which the words of only two are given) are, oddly enough, to sing to the bandora, an instrument, to judge by its surviving literature, not frequently used as an accompaniment to the voice.

In the following year *The First Booke of Songs or Ayres* by John Dowland was printed by Peter Short and the fashion was set that was to last, in England, for the next twenty-five years.

With Dowland's visit to France at the age of seventeen it would not be surprising to find traces of French influence in his song writing and indeed, in the early songs this influence is certainly there to some extent, but in my opinion his deep roots in English traditional song cannot be overlooked. When he first left England the lute-song was already established, though possibly in a somewhat undeveloped form and songs for solo voice and viols—consort songs as they have been called*—had since the 1570s become an accepted, and in the theatrical performances of the choir-boy companies, a frequently used form. There are, of course, distinguishing features between the two species; five parts are more general in the consort song as against four in the ayre, and the singing voice, although it may be, is not necessarily the highest of the group. But whether or not the solo voice lies at the top, the 'first singing part' as Byrd calls it, is generally given a predominancy over the other parts which resembles the homophonic character of the lute-song and four part ayre. In the consort song, although the combination of voice and viols naturally lends itself to contrapuntal writing, the string accompaniments vary between an independent polyphonic texture as, for example, in Richard Nicholson's 'In a Merry May Morn'† and Nathanael Pattrick's 'Send Forth Thy Sighes'‡ and the almost completely chordal structure of, for example, the anonymous 'Sweet was the Song the Virgin Sung'§ where most of the time the viols are moving note for note with the voice, and, where any separate movement occurs, it is confined to a single viol at a time. Similarly the lute-song and four part ayre show the same diversity between such songs as John Dowland's 'In this trembling shadow' and 'If that a Sinners sighes' in which, though the Cantus voice predominates, the feeling is largely contrapuntal, and others such as 'Fine knacks for Ladies', 'Daphne was not so chaste' and 'Sleepe wayward thoughts' in which, except for an occasional divergence into a contrapuntal device of some kind, the

* Philip Brett, *The English Consort Song, 1570-1625*, Proceedings of the Royal Musical Association, 88th Session, 1961-2, pp. 73-88.
† Peter Warlock, *The first Book of Elizabethan Songs* (1926), No. 1, and *The Third Book of Elizabethan Songs* (1926), Nos. 2 and 3.
‡ ibid.
§ ibid.

accompaniment is almost entirely chordal. In the treatment of words there is
perhaps, slightly more repetition in the consort song than in the ayre, but even
this can be matched in, for example, Dowland's 'Sorrow sorrow stay'. As
with the Cantus voice of the ayre, the word setting is simple; not entirely
note for syllable, but largely so, with occasional melismatic phrases used for
illustrative word painting. Compare bars 22, 23 and 24 of the anonymous
'This mery pleasant spring':*

night - in - gale de - li _____ vers.

with bars 48, 49 and 50 of John Danyel's 'Like as the Lute':†

pleas - ing rel - ish here _____ I _____ use.

The affinity between the two forms is shown by the fact that no incon-
gruity is felt in the setting for voice and lute of 'Pandolpho'‡ originally
composed for voice and viols by Robert Parsons (d.1570), or conversely, in
the two settings for voice and viols of Dowland's 'Sorrow sorrow stay', one
by William Wigthorp in BM. Add. 17786–91, and the other an anonymous
setting in BM. Add. 37402–6.

It has been suggested that Dowland's use of dance forms for a number of
his songs was derived from his association with French musicians, and the
voix de ville or *chanson à danser* has been cited as his probable model, particularly those in the forms of pavanne, galliarde, bransle gay and bransle de
Poitou set for solo voice and guitar in Adrian Le Roy's *Second Livre de Guiterre* (1555). In fact Dowland can hardly have escaped a knowledge of the
practice of setting words to pre-existing dance tunes if he had any acquaintance with the English musical scene, as he surely must have had, before leaving for France. As Baskervill§ remarks 'throughout the sixteenth century the
combination of song with dance remained a living and creative force'. Sir
Thomas Elyot, in *The Boke of the Governour* (1531), speaks of the names of
dances that are taken from 'the first wordes of the dittie';‖ George Gascoigne
devotes a verse of 'The Fourthe Songe'¶ to the subject and John Northbrooke

* Peter Warlock, *The First Book of Elizabethan Songs* (1926), No. 2.
† *Songs for the Lute, Viol and Voice* (1606). Ed. E. H. Fellowes, The English School of
Lutenist Song Writers, Second Series.
‡ King's College, Cambridge, Rowe MS 2, No. 5.
§ *The Elizabethan Jig* (1929), p. 9.
‖ Everyman Edition, p. 93.
¶ *Works*, edited John W. Cunliffe (1910), Vol. 2, p. 553.

describes how people 'daunce with disordinate gestures, and with monstrous thumping of the feete, to pleasant soundes, to wanton songes, to dishonest verses'.* William Webbe, in his *Discourse of English Poetrie* (1586), writes on p. 61:

neither is there anie tune or stroke which may be sung or plaide on instruments, which hath not some poetical ditties framed according to the numbers thereof, some to Rogero, some to Trenchmore, to downe right Squire, to Galliardes, to Pauines, to Iygges, to Brawls, to all manner of tunes which euerie Fidler knows better then myself.

For examples of ditties set to dance tunes it is unnecessary to look further than to *A Handfull of Pleasant Delites* (1584)† by Clement Robinson and others, where verses are supplied for singing to the following dance tunes: 'Quarter Braules' (1566), 'Cecilia Pauin' (1566), 'the Blacke Almaine' (1570?), 'the new Almaine' (?), and 'the Downright Squire' (*c.* 1566). The dates in brackets represent the years in which Rollins believes the ballads first appeared.

While it is true that the ditties that make up this collection had originally appeared as broadside ballads and were therefore not primarily, like the contents of *England's Helicon*, addressed to a sophisticated audience, nevertheless when issued in book form, the printers must have expected to sell to a somewhat higher income group than that in which broadsides were generally bought, and the constant quoting of ballads in the dramatic literature of the time, by characters whose 'degree' is far above the social standing of the 'vulgar', to whom the ballads were originally addressed, is clear indication of how widely they were known.

Among the many volumes of ballads and ditties framed to existing tunes that appeared in the late sixteenth, and early seventeenth, centuries, Anthony Munday's *Banquet of Daintie Conceits* (1588)‡ is of special interest, since Munday used one of Dowland's galliards.§ Of the twenty-two items there are only four where the titles of the tunes do not give clear indication of their having been drawn from the prevailing dance repertoire. Among those that Munday gives are such prime favourites as 'Monsieures Allemaigne', 'the flatte Pauin', 'the Quadrant Pauin', 'the Quadrant Galliard', 'the Spanish Pauin', 'the Countess of Ormonds Galliard', 'La vecchia Pauin' and 'Wigmores Galliard', all of which may be found in settings by the most distinguished composers of the day.

Thomas Morely, in 'The Third Part of the Introduction to Music. Treating

* *A Treatise wherein Dicing, Daucing . . . are reprooued* (1579), f. 66v.
† *A Handful of Pleasant Delights.* Edited Hyder E. Rollins (1924). Rollins believes there was an earlier edition of the *Handful* in 1566.
‡ See note p. 145.
§ See p. 145.

of Composing or Setting of Songs',* also speaks of 'light music (in contra-distinction to Motets) as Madrigals, Canzonets, Pavanes and Galliards'.

When Edward Doughtie† points to the similarity between the songs 'Now O now' ('The Frog Galliard') and 'Quand j'entens le perdu temps', and suggests Le Roy's book was the most likely source for Dowland's knowledge of the *voix de ville,* he is very probably correct, but I doubt whether this is proof that it was in France that Dowland received his first introduction to the custom of writing songs to already existing dance forms. Furthermore, the fact that the trochaic rhythm is unique among his galliards suggests to me that his fancy was captured by this particular song, if indeed, the tune is of his composing, rather than that the *voix de ville* exerted any general influence on his work.

What Dowland can hardly have escaped becoming familiar with in France was the ferment of ideas which, on the Continent, surrounded the application of Humanist thought to the whole conception of the function of music in society.

Broadly speaking, the theoreticians of music of the middle ages followed the general philosophical ideas of the time which were compounded mainly from the works of Plato and Aristotle and from Genesis. In this scheme of thought the universe was seen as an elaborately worked out system of cosmic order. Celestial order, harmony and concord were mirrored in the world of man with 'order' and 'degree'. In the words of Clement of Alexandria 'man the microcosm is the reflection of the macrocosm'. In the heavens, under God, the angels had their hierarchy of three main orders, and in earthly kingdoms every subject had his appointed rank under Royal supremacy. In the animal and vegetable kingdoms the same idea was maintained and an order of rank was formulated. 'Cosmic' disturbances such as violent storms and falling stars were thought to be closely linked with disturbances in the body politic, and disastrous events, such as rebellion or the murder of a king, carried with them an aura of temerity as of an assault on the order of the universe, decreed and established by God.

Within this formalized scheme, music, so the philosophers thought, held its place in an interdependence with celestial harmony, and, while the planets moved in a cosmic dance to the music of the spheres, terrestrial music, to the extent in which it reflected celestial concord, worked as a rectifying agent in the nature of man. Thus music came to be regarded as being the symbol of supra-human qualities and many theoreticians involved themselves in pre-

* *A Plain and Easy Introduction to Practical Music* (1597), edited R. Alec Harman (1952), p. 228.
    † op. cit.

occupations of a purely non-aesthetic character such as, for example, the nature of the number three and the perfect circle by which it was represented, both of which were considered to have an altogether special significance. Even as late as 1613 the Spaniard Pedro Cerrone,* basing himself mainly on the writings of St. Augustine and of Pythagoras, gives a long disquisition on the six reasons for the perfection of the Ternary Number. To show the kind of reasoning that still persisted here are a few passages:

. . . The numbers are infinite because count as many as you like, there are still more to come . . . Count one, two, three, up to ten; and return to one, saying eleven; and to two saying twelve, and thus of all up to twenty: in this way you may proceed to infinity. Do you not see the excellence and perfection that the Unity has, in that after all the tens you return to the repetition?

The Ternary number is composed of three Unities, which have the above mentioned perfection; then the whole (which is the Ternary number) will be perfect.

. . . All beginnings . . . cannot be the said beginning except in comparison with something else: and the end cannot be the said end, except in relation to something else: and we cannot go from the beginning to the end except by means of the middle. What number will have the beginning, the middle and the end made up of the Unity, which has the said perfection, but the Ternary number? Because this number is composed of three Unities (as has been said) and the Unity has the pre-eminence and perfection that we repeat it after every ten, and because the said Ternary has beginning, middle and end, it must be perfect . . .

Each one of these three things (by this must be understood the beginning, the middle and the end) is one, because the Ternary number is a Unity; they are also three because three times one is three. No other number has this perfection: because if you take four, or any other number, it can well have a beginning, a middle and an end, but it will be very different to the Ternary number. Let us take it that the Unity will be the beginning of this Quartern number, that the middle will consist of two, and that the end will be another Unity. Do you not see then, that the parts are dissimilar, that beginning, middle and end are three, but in this Quartern number they are four? To support this reasoning of Saint Augustine, we can say with the Philosopher, that ALL and PERFECT are one and the same thing. Whatever thing is all, for the same reason we can say it is perfect.

Cerrone continues at great length along these lines of thought to show the superiority of the number Three over all others, and that it must follow that Triple time in music is Perfect, while all other rhythms are necessarily imperfect.

Furthermore, complicated mathematical calculations concerning 'proportion' were considered to be of great importance. That the more abstruse

* *El Melopea y Maestro*, p. 941.

of these ideas were not always carried into practical effect by composers can be seen in the very human quality of much of the secular music of the late Middle Ages, nevertheless, in theory the ideal was that music should symbolize celestial proportion and harmony and should thereby bring men's souls closer to the divine and the good. The intention that music should play upon the emotions of the hearer and move him to laughter or tears was an aim entirely outside the musical aesthetic of the time, and indeed, the stirring of emotion by music was gravely distrusted as leading to lewd and lascivious thoughts.

Although many aspects of the same philosophical outlook continued to be very generally accepted in England until the early seventeenth century,* on the Continent the revival of interest in classical learning, with the rediscovery of forgotten texts and the re-reading of others, with which the Renaissance opened, led to a questioning of many statements of dogma which had, for generations, been held as true, on the basis of scholastic authority. In musical thought this re-awakened interest in Antiquity among Humanist scholars was to bring about a profound and far-reaching change. In reading the legends of Orpheus, of Arion and of Timotheus, they pondered on the miraculous powers which the music of the Greeks was said to have possessed, and it seemed to them, as in all periods of vital change, when the truths and beauties of the preceding age are violently misjudged, that the music of their own time no longer acted as a moral force, or brought about the miraculous effects of which they had read.

In all the more important centres of thought where these problems were considered, one point above all was isolated for condemnation and that was the general failure of musicians to treat words in such a way that they were intelligible to the listener, and elaborate polyphonic music became the main object of criticism. With a certain amount of justification it was argued that when several voices sang together in counterpoint, with each voice pronouncing the words at a different time, often with meaningless repetition and with unimportant syllables prolonged in extensive melismata, the text itself, no matter how significant, could make no emotional impact upon the hearer.

As Huizinger points out, one of the distinguishing features of the art of the late Middle Ages was an extreme preoccupation with minute details of exact realism:

the perspective of the cell of Jerome, a ray of light falling through a fissure, drops of sweat on the body of a woman in a bath, an image reflected in a

* See E. M. Tillyard, *The Elizabethan World Picture* (1943). Peregrine Books (1963).

mirror, a burning lamp, a landscape with mountains, woods, villages, castles, human figures, the distant horizon, and once again, the mirror . . .

and he quotes Michelangelo as saying:

In short, this art is without power and without distinction; it aims at rendering minutely many things at the same time, of which a single one would have sufficed to call forth a man's whole application.*

Similarly in music an extreme overindulgence in realistic pictorialism in the treatment of individual words, without due regard to its appropriateness to the total structure of the composition was seen as detracting from what the Humanists judged to be the all-important aim of music: the production of 'effects' upon the listener.

In France the study of Humanism as applied to music found its first main support in Pierre de Ronsard and the other poets of the Pléiade, most of whom were born in the twenties and early thirties of the sixteenth century. They gave careful study to what they could discover about ancient music and sought to restore to it its miraculous powers, mainly through a return to classical poetic forms and the exact marriage of words and music. They found that the Greeks had chanted their odes to the sound of the lyre, and that even choral singing had been entirely monodic. They equated the lyre to the lute of their own time, and in a manifesto, *La Deffense et Illustration de la langue Francoise* (1549), Joachim du Bellay exhorted the poets of France to study the Greek and Roman pattern, to write their odes and to sing them to the lute's accompaniment:

> Ly, donques, & rely premierement ô Poete futur,
> feuillete de main nocturne & journelle, les exemplaires
> Grecque & Latins . . .
>
> Chante moy ces Odes, incognues encor' de la Muse
> Francoise, d'un Luc bien accordé au son de la Lyre
> Greque & Romaine . . .†

The four poetic forms that Ronsard chose for writing verses destined for musical setting were the *ode*, the *chanson*, the *sonnet* and the *hymne*, and during the earlier years of his poetic life his main interest was in producing verse for music. Later, from about 1557, his attitude changed considerably and he wrote a quantity of poems with no intention of their being allied to music.‡

Although the Pléiade and their followers were not unanimously in favour

---

* *The Waning of the Middle Ages* (1919), English Translation, F. Hopman (1924), pp. 243, 244.

† From the edition of 1561, f. 21v.

‡ See Raymond Lebègue, 'Ronsard et la Musique' in *Music et Poésie au XVI siècle* (1954), pp. 105–19.

of the solo voice, and were willing to accept vocal part writing provided it was homophonic in character and treated the words with respect for their meaning, Pontus de Tyard, the main philosopher of the group, was a firm believer in its greater efficacy, and was strongly opposed to vocal music in parts:

vù que la Musique figurée le plus souvent ne rapporte aux oreilles autre chose qu'un grand bruit, duquel vous ne sentez aucune vive efficace: Mais la simple & unique voix, coulée doucement, & continuée selon le devoir de sa Mode choisie pour le merite des vers, vous ravit la part qu'elle veut. Aussi consistoit en ce seul moyen la plus ravissante energie des anciens Poëtes lyriques, qui mariant la Musique à la Poësie (comme ils estoient nez à l'une & à l'autre) chantoient leurs vers, & rencontroient souvent l'effect de leur desir: tant la simplicité bien observée aux Modes de chanter est doüée d'une secrette & admirable puissance.*

In 1570, Jean Antoine de Baïf, a member of the Pléiade, together with Joachim Thibaut de Courville, formed the *Académie de Poésie et de Musique*, and royal recognition was given to the moral and aesthetic aims of the founders. In the Letters Patent by which the King of France officially confirmed the opening of the *Académie*, it is stated:

It is of great importance for the morals of the citizens of a town that the music current in the country should be retained under certain laws . . . for where music is disordered, there morals are also depraved, and where it is well ordered, there men are well tutored.†

Inspired by the idea of a return to classical purity, the poets associated with de Baïf and Thibaut de Courville set to work to reconstruct the basis of French prosody on the lines of quantitative metre, and when music was used in conjunction with measured verse it was made to follow the longs and shorts of the syllables as faithfully as possible; the result was known as *musique mesurée à l'antique*. In its full application the vogue for this particular aspect of the Humanist movement was short lived, but in the increased awareness among musicians of the importance of the just setting of long and short syllables, it left its mark upon the later French *air de cour*.

From about 1530 there had developed, side-by-side with the more elaborate and artificial polyphonic setting of literary texts such as *rondeaux, dizains, epigrammes, elégies* and the earliest sonnets, a type of song with a long tradition going back to the Middle Ages, which possessed many of the characteristics later to be included among the *desiderata* of the Pléiade. Known as

---

* *Les Discours Philosophique de Pontus de Tyard* (1587), f. 114.
† Translation from Frances Yates, *The French Academies of the Sixteenth Century* (1947), p. 36.

voix de ville, vau de ville or *chanson à danser*, these strophic songs were written with the highest voice predominating and in such a form as to give particular emphasis to the syllabic structure of the verse. The use of this form of song was encouraged by the Pléiade, and Arcadelt's first collection of *chanson* in the form of *voix de ville*, printed in Paris by Pierre Attaignant in 1547, inaugurated a flow of similar publications which continued to appear until the later years of the century. In 1551, Le Roy, in his *Second Livre de Guiterre*, printed a number of these *voix de ville* arranged for solo voice and guitar.

Beginning with the *Chanson de P. de Ronsard, Ph. Desportes et autres* by Nicholas de la Grotte in 1569, an altogether looser rhythmic structure came into favour, and new poetic forms such as the *plainte*, the *ode* and the *complainte* were chosen for musical setting. The name *chanson* gave place to *air*, and then, in 1571, in Le Roy's collection of settings for solo voice and lute, the *Livre d'Airs de Cour*, in which many of the La Grotte *chanson* were included, for the first time the term *air de cour* was adopted.

Following Le Roy's collection no further books of *airs de cour* for solo voice and lute appeared in France until Gabriel Bataille commenced his great collection with the *Premier Livre* of his *Airs de Différents Autheurs* in 1608, although the Frenchman, Jean-Baptiste Besard included a number in his *Thesaurus Harmonicus* (Cologne, 1603). By 1643 no less than twenty-three volumes of *airs de cour*, set for voice and lute, had been printed in France, together with reprints of Bataille's first three books.

Perhaps the main characteristic of the seventeenth-century *air de cour* is the exceptional freedom of the rhythmic structure. Bar lines to mark a rhythmic beat are dispensed with altogether, and those that are used are generally placed only at the end of a complete musical phrase; in some cases one double bar only is placed at the end of the first line to mark a repeat, and from then on the song is unbarred until the end, the accentuation of the music being dictated entirely by the rhythm of each verbal phrase. The result is a captivating fluidity which resembles the spoken word, allied to a supremely elegant melodic line.

In Italy too, musicians had been searching for the key that would unlock the secrets of Greek music and its miraculous effects, but lack of a mind trained in the exacting discipline necessary for the elucidation of the relevant texts had, as elsewhere, led to many misunderstandings and many wrong paths being followed. It was not until the last quarter of the sixteenth century that any significant advance was made. When it came it was mainly due to the historian and philologist, Girolamo Mei, and the discussions, arising from his work, that took place at Florence in the literary and musical circle surrounding Count Giovanni Bardi. This group, known as the *camerata*, counted among its members Vincenzo Galilei, theoretician, composer and lutenist, and Giulio Caccini, composer and singer. Mei, a man of great learning, though, he confesses, unable to play, sing or dance, had the immense advantage of being a trained philologist and historian, and it was this training that enabled him to become the first Renaissance scholar with an accurate understanding of the principles of the Greek musical system. He expounded the results of his researches in a series of letters to Galilei and Bardi, which began on May 8th, 1572.* His two great contributions were first, his insistence that Greek music, choral as well as solo was monodic, and secondly that 'the essential characteristic of Greek tonal practice was the use of transposition of the whole system up and down'.† He believed the effects described by ancient writers could only have been brought about by a single musical line, since it was the pitch of the voice, either high, low or medium, each having its special characteristics, which produced the desired effect upon the hearer. In polyphony, he maintained, with the mixing together of notes of different pitch, high counterbalancing low, the precise emotive effect of each register of the voice was totally lost. Mei also showed the established ecclesiastical modes, with which Greek names and properties were associated, bore little resemblance to the ancient system. Although Mei, in his letters from Rome, put his knowledge at the disposal of the *camerata*, he had no interest in the musical reforms that occupied the attention of its members. It was in the discussions arising from the correspondence that the idea of a 'new music' was evolved; Bardi, Galilei and Caccini becoming the chief disseminators of its theory and practice.

Bardi has left an account of how these reformers regarded the involved contrapuntal style of contemporary madrigal writing:

For in truth it would seem a sin to the contrapuntists of today (may they be pardoned these mixtures of several melodies and several modes!)—it would seem, I say, a mortal sin if all the parts were heard to beat at the same time with the same notes, with the same syllables of the verse, and with the same longs and shorts; the more they make the parts move, the more artful they think they are. This, in my opinion, is the concern of the stringed instruments, for, there being no voice in these, it is fitting that the player, in playing airs not suited to singing or dancing—it is fitting, I say, that the player should make the parts move and that he should contrive canons, double counterpoints, and other novelties to avoid wearying his hearers. And I judge this to be the species of music so much condemned by the philosophers, especially by Aristotle in the Eighth Book of his *Politics*, where he calls it artificial and

* Claude Palisca, *Girolamo Mei (1519–1594). Letters on Ancient and Modern Music to Vincenzo Galilei and Giovanni Bardi* (1960).

† op. cit., p. 46.

wholly useless . . . lacking the power to move a man's mind to this or that moral quality . . .*

Bardi goes on to counsel Caccini on the prime importance of the words in composing vocal music, and how they may be treated in a manner more nearly approaching the Greek ideal:

In composing, then, you will make it your chief aim to arrange the verse well and to declaim the words as intelligibly as you can, not letting yourself be led astray by the counterpoint like a bad swimmer, who lets himself be carried out of his course by the current and comes to shore beyond the mark he had set, for you will consider it self-evident that, just as the soul is nobler than the body, so the words are nobler than the counterpoint.†

Galilei selects for special ridicule the composer of his day who isolated particular words from the text and subjected these to illustrative painting without regard to the context or the mood of the entire poem:

At another time they will say they are imitating the words when among the conceptions of these there are any meaning 'to flee' or 'to fly'; these they will declaim with the greatest rapidity and the least grace imaginable. In connection with words meaning 'to disappear', 'to swoon', 'to die', or actually 'to be extinct' they have made the parts break off so abruptly, that instead of inducing the passion corresponding to any of these, they have aroused laughter and at other times contempt in the listeners, who felt that they were being ridiculed. Then with words meaning 'alone', or 'two', or 'together' they have caused one lone part, or two, or all the parts together to sing with unheard-of elegance. Others, in singing of this particular line from one of the sestinas of Petrarch:

And with the lame ox he will be pursuing Laura,

have declaimed it to staggering, wavering, syncopated notes as though they had the hiccups. . . . Finding words denoting diversity of color such as 'dark' or 'light' hair and similar expressions, they have put black or white notes beneath them to express this sort of conception craftily and gracefully. . . . At another time, finding the line:

He descended into hell, into the lap of Pluto,

they have made one part of the composition descend in such a way that the singer has sounded more like someone groaning to frighten children and terrify them than like someone singing sense. In the opposite way, finding this one:

This one aspires to the stars,

* Giovanni de'Bardi, *Discourse on Ancient Music and Good Singing*. Addressed to Giulio Caccini, called Romano. *c.* 1580. From Oliver Strunk, *Source Readings in Music History* (1952), p. 294.

† op. cit., p. 295.

in declaiming it they have ascended to a height that no one shrieking from excessive pain, internal or external, has ever reached. And coming, as sometimes happens, to words meaning 'weep', 'laugh', 'sing', 'shout', 'shriek', or 'false deceits', 'harsh chains', 'hard bonds', 'rugged mount', 'unyielding rock', 'cruel woman' and the like, to say nothing of their sighs, unusual forms and so on, they have declaimed them, to color their absurd and vain designs, in manners more outlandish than those of any far-off barbarian.*

To this he contrasts the practice of the Greeks:

When the ancient musician sang any poem whatever, he first considered very diligently the character of the person speaking: his age, his sex, with whom he was speaking, and the effect he sought to produce by this means; and these conceptions, previously clothed by the poet in chosen words suited to such a need, the musician then expressed in the tone and with the accents and gestures, the quantity and quality of sound, and the rhythm appropriate to that action and to such a person.†

What came about from the quickening effects of these discussions was not a return to the past, but the emergence of the monodic recitative style, which, the *camerata* believed, represented the pure 'antique form'. Of this type of music the poet Grillo wrote to Giulio Caccini, in a letter dated 1600:

We are indebted to you for the invention of a new species of Music; for *singing without air*, or rather for a melodious kind of speech, called *recitative*, which is noble and elevated, neither mangling, torturing, nor destroying the life and sense of the words, but rather enforcing their energy and spirit. This most beautiful manner of singing is your own, and perhaps a lucky recovery of the ancient and long lost method of singing used by the Greeks and Romans; an idea in which I am the more confirmed, by hearing the beautiful pastoral of Rinuccini sung to your Music; which all those who complain of the absurdity of *always singing in chorus*, even in dramatic poetry and representation, agree to admire. In short, this new Music is now universally adopted by all persons of good ears and taste; from the courts of Italian princes it has passed to those of Spain, France and other parts of Europe, as I am assured from undoubted authority.‡

Indeed, as Palisca says, what Mei's work had achieved was to devalue 'the role of mathematics, cosmology and ethics' and 'restore music to its natural sisters, poetry and oratory'.§

Sir Thomas Moore was the first writer in England to express the Humanist attitude towards music, in his *Utopia* (1516). In his ideal country he sees music as producing effects in the listener in a manner exactly similar to that described by the ancients:

* Strunk, op. cit., pp. 316–17. 'Dialogo della musica antica e della moderna.'
† op. cit., p. 308.
‡ Charles Burney, *A General History of Music* (1776–89), Vol. 4, p. 134.
§ Palisca, op. cit., p. 45.

But in one thynge dowteles they goo exceedinge farre beyond us.

For all theire musicke, both that they playe upon instruments, and that they singe with mans voyse, doth so resemble and expresses naturall affections; the sound and tune is so applied and made agreeable to the thynge; that whether it be a prayer, or els a dytty of gladnes, of patience, of trouble, of mournynge, or of anger, the fassion of the melodye dothe so represent the meaning of the thing, that it doth wonderfully moue, stire, pearce and enflame the hearers myndes.*

Among those writers who were concerned with education, however, an attitude of more restrained enthusiasm was shown and a warning was given, particularly to those whose function in the state was to govern, lest an over-indulgence in its practice should interfere with a devotion to duty and the public weal. Sir Thomas Elyot wrote:

The most noble and valiant princis of Grece often tymes, to recreate theyr spirites, and in augmentynge their courage, embraced instrumentes musicall . . . But in this commendation of musycke, I wolde not be thought to allure noble men to have too moche delectation therein, that in playinge and syngynge onely, they shuld put theyr hole study and felicitie: As dyd the emperour Nero . . . It were therefore better, that no music were taught to a noble man, than by exacte knowledge therof, he shuld have therin in-ordinate delyte: and by that be illicted to wantonnes, abandonynge grauitie and the necessary cure and office in the publike weale to him committed . . . Yet notwithstanding, he shall commende the perfecte understandynge of musyke, declarynge how necessary it is for the better attaining the knowlege of a publike weal, which as I before sayd, is made of an order of estates and degrees, and by reason thereof conteyneth in it a perfect harmony: which he shall afterward more perfectly understand, when he shall happen to rede the bokes of Plato and Aristo. of publike weales: wherein be written dyvers examples of musyke and geometry. In this fourme may a wise and cyrcum-specte tutor, adapte the pleasant science of musicke to a necessary and laud-able purpose.†

Roger Ascham, Greek scholar, master of languages to the Princess Elizabeth and Latin Secretary to Edward VI, Mary and then to Elizabeth, was particu-larly fearful of the demoralizing effects upon the character of overindulgence in what he considered to be this enervating art:

Muche Musicke marreth mennes maners, sayth Galen, although some men wil saye that it dothe not so but rather recreateth and maketh quycke a mannes mynde, yet me thincke by reason it doth as hony doth to a mannes stomache, whiche at first receyveth it well, but afterwarde it maketh it unfit to abyde any good stronge nourishynge meate, or els anye holsome sharpe and quicke drincke. And euen so in a maner these Instrumentes make a

---

* Ralph Robynson's translation (1551). Sig. R.V.v.
† *The Boke of the Governour* (1531), ff. 21–3.

mannes wit so softe and smoothe so tender and quaisie, that they be lesse able to brooke stronge and toughe studie. Wittes be not sharpened, but rather dulled and made blunte wyth suche sweete softnesse, euen as good edges be blunter, which menne whette upon soft chalke stones.*

Singing he excepts from these strictures, not upon any aesthetic or moral considerations, but purely on the utilitarian function it can perform in helping to build a healthy physique.

The writers of this period, however, who gave thought to the question, were thinking *about* Humanism and the Humanist attitude towards music, and were not themselves directly involved in the search for appropriate art forms based on antiquity, in which this attitude could find fitting expression. It was in the work of the poets, Sir Thomas Wyatt and the Earl of Surrey, that the influence of antiquity, or rather the Italian vision of antiquity, first made itself manifest in actual creative activity. It has been argued that Wyatt wrote with the express intention of uniting his words with music,† but John Stevens puts forward a convincing argument to show that, in spite of the frequent mention of the lute in his poems, this theory is not necessarily true.‡ What is clear, however, is that though Wyatt was preoccupied with the Petrarchan sonnet and other verse forms of the Italian Renaissance, the music of the Court of Henry VIII was still governed by medieval ideas concerning the *expression* of emotion while ignoring the Humanist attitude towards its *effect* on the hearer.

Of the musicians of the mid-century, Thomas Whythorne was the one who, in his *Autobiography*, left the most detailed account of the musical life of his time. He was a man of considerable education with a knowledge of the classics as well as of the literature of his own period. He often quotes from the works of Plato and he knows Plato's high opinion of the art of music:

Plato in his first book of his laws, saith that Music doth contain all kind of learning, and that music cannot be worthily intreated of without all kinds of knowledge.§

He mentions some of the famous musicians of antiquity and is familiar with the legendary properties of the Greek modes. He also quotes the authorities that recognize the therapeutic power of music in mental disorders:

* *Toxophilus, The schole of shootinge* (1545), f. 10.

† E. K. Chambers, *Sir Thomas Wyatt, and some collected Studies* (1933); A. K. Foxwell, *A Study of Sir Thomas Wyatt's Poems* (1911); Kenneth Muir, 'Unpublished Poems in the Devonshire MS', *Proceedings of Leeds Philosophical Society*, VI, 1947; Bruce Pattison, *Music and Poetry of the English Renaissance* (1948); and others.

‡ *Music and Poetry in the Early Tudor Court* (1961).

§ *Autobiography*. Edited James Osborn (1961), p. 236.

Gallenus and Fucsius do say that music doth appease the dolours of the mind. Likewise Sir Thomas Elyot in his *Castle of Health* doth allow of it for that purpose although in his *Governor* he doth inveigh against them that do not use it as they ought to do.*

But to Whythorne these are calm statements of fact, containing none of the excitement and proselytizing zeal of, for example, Du Bellay, nor does he leave any indication whether he thought the practice of the ancients should have any bearing on the form of his own musical composition.

The growth of Humanism in England in the early years of the century did not long continue without challenge. Hardly had its influence been clearly shown in literature than its ideas were crossed with, and in some aspects, opposed by, those of the religious Reformation. Both movements, though impelled by motives entirely distinct from each other, curiously enough, where the setting of words was concerned, coincided closely in their ideals, and achieved some similar results.

In all the various manifestations of religious thought within the general framework of the English Reformation, one point was agreed upon by all, namely the necessity of making available to everyone the word of God in clear and simple language. One part of this endeavour was a renewed attempt to overcome the complexity and obscurantism that still enveloped much church music.

Both Luther and Calvin, from whom the two main streams of reformed thought in England were derived, were fully aware of music's power to stir the emotions, and both gave careful consideration how best to use it in the service of God:

. . . if we wish to honor well the holy decrees of our Lord, as used in the Church, the main thing is to know what they contain, what they mean, and to what end they tend, in order that their observance may be useful and salutary and in consequence rightly ruled. . . And in truth we know by experience that song has great force and vigour to move and inflame the hearts of men to invoke and praise God with a more vehement and ardent zeal. It must always be looked to that the song be not light and frivolous but have weight and majesty, as Saint Augustine says, and there is likewise a great difference between the music one makes to entertain men at table and in their homes, and the psalms which are sung in the Church in the presence of God and His angels . . . Now among other things proper to recreate man and give him pleasure, music is either the first or one of the principal, and we must think that it is a gift of God deputed to that purpose . . .†

* op. cit., p. 239. Spelling modernized in both quotations.
† Jean Calvin, The Geneva Psalter (1543), from O. Strunk, *Source Readings in Music History*, pp. 346–7.

On the treatment of music for use in the Churches of the two reformers, there were, however, considerable differences of opinion. Calvin confined its use to the congregational singing of psalms, and that in a single melodic line only, while Luther approved of a far more generous outlook, and allowed that harmony could possess a virtue of its own:

. . . These, further, are set for four voices for no other reason than that I wished that the young (who, apart from this, should and must be trained in music and in other proper arts) might have something to rid them of their love ditties and wanton songs and might, instead of these, learn wholesome things and thus yield willingly, as becomes them, to the good; also because I am not of the opinion that all the arts shall be crushed to earth and perish through the Gospel, as some bigoted persons pretend, but would willingly see them all, and especially music, servants of Him who gave and created them . . .*

The Anglican Church tended to follow the less stringent policy, and music appeared, not only in the singing of psalms, but also in anthems and in the actual celebration of the Service itself. It was, however, in the psalm tunes that Church music reached outward and exercised its greatest influence on secular song.

In both the Lutheran and Calvinist Church, one of the most strongly held principles was that of complete participation of the congregation in the act of worship. There were to be no passive onlookers. In order that all present should be able to join in singing the psalms it was essential that the melodies should possess certain definite characteristics. Firstly they had to be plain, so that the word of God should be immediately intelligible. Thomas Cranmer speaks of this necessity in a letter to Henry VIII, written in 1544:

. . . But in my opinion the song that should be made thereunto would not be full of notes, but as near as may be, for every syllable a note, so that it may be sung distinctly and devoutly . . .†

Furthermore, since in most cases the psalms were not to be performed by a fully trained choir, but were left to the singing of a congregation most of whom would have little mastery of the art, the melodies had to consist of easily sung intervals in an uncomplicated rhythm. Above all, the tunes had to be memorable. Calvin understood this need and stated it clearly:

. . . Now the peculiar gift of man is to sing knowing what he is saying. After the intelligence must follow the heart and the affection, which cannot be unless we have the hymn imprinted on our memory in order never to cease singing.‡

* Martin Luther, Foreword to the Wittenberg Gesangbuch (1524). Strunk, op. cit., p. 342.
† Strunk, op. cit., p. 351.
‡ op. cit., p. 348.

One of the most obvious means of giving the tunes for the newly translated metrical psalms the widest possible appeal was to fit them to already existing popular melodies or, when new ones were composed, to model them on popular idiom. Martin Luther was aware of this and so was Louis Bourgeois, the musical director of Calvin's first psalter, who was expert in harnessing the special qualities of popular music to the service of the Reformed Church. Because it was the psalter prepared by the English divines exiled in Geneva during the reign of Mary Tudor that was eventually adopted into the English Church, it is the influence of Bourgeois that is mainly felt in the English book. Not only were a number of the tunes lifted without change from the French-Genevan psalter, but when others were added they followed along similar lines. So exactly were these melodies fitted to their purpose and so eagerly were they accepted for domestic as well as public worship that, by the time Dowland began to compose, they had been assimilated into the national consciousness and in their turn played a part in the development of English secular song.

When in England, following Luther's example, four-part settings were made, harmonic clarity and simplicity were required for the same reasons that these qualities were required of the melodies, and all obscurities of elaborate counterpoint were banished. In those settings where the church-tune is carried by the Cantus instead of, according to the earlier *cantus firmus* tradition, by the Tenor, a type of composition emerged with which the four-part ayre stands in close kinship. The similarity of musical outlook is emphasized in Richard Allison's *The Psalmes of Dauid in Meter* (1599), in which the layout, with Cantus and lute on one page, and the three other voices disposed on the opposite page, is identical with that of the secular lutenist song-books.

The French Huguenot psalter, though it found its way into many households, even of Catholics, failed to gain quite the same standing since it received no official acceptance in the Catholic Church, although the popularity of many of the psalms was widely spread through the settings of such composers as Morlaye and Le Roy. The affinity with the *air de cour* is also shown in those psalms (mostly with the translations of Desportes) arranged with lute accompaniment and included by Gabriel Bataille in his volumes of *Airs de Differents Autheurs* (1608–15).

Although it is known that Italian madrigals had been in circulation in England from 1564 onwards,[*] when Dowland first left for France in 1580, native composers had hardly begun to graft the new Italian manner on to the earlier style of English part-song. By the time of his return the invasion was steadily growing and with the publication of Nicholas Yonge's *Musica*

* E. H. Fellowes, *The English Madrigal Composers* (1921), p. 38.

Transalpina in 1588, the full impact began to be felt. Although a number of compositions by William Byrd from his *Psalmes, Sonets and songs* of 1588, are known, through a set of MS part books, to have been in existence from the year 1581,[*] it is from the date of this first collection that the English madrigal school is generally considered to have become established. It was not until the 1590s, however, that the collections began to appear in any quantity. By this time, the Italian school, though composers such as Marenzio, Croce and Gesualdo were still working, had almost reached the end of its life. Before the English school had even become firmly established, Bardi, Galilei and their circle in Florence were already preparing the way for the New Music which would soon supplant the older forms.

In the England of the final decade of the century the new ideas from Florence appear to have been hardly known at all. Dowland's visit, in 1595, put him in an exceptional position, but in general there is no evidence of any conscious reaction to, or implementation of, the Florentine theories among English musicians until some years later.

Thomas Morley, who, in *A Plaine and Easie Introduction to Practicall Musicke* (1597), gives one of the most reliable pictures of musical theory in his time, in 'Annotations' to the First Part, discusses the construction of the Greek scale, but he gives no indication that he is aware of any controversy concerning the nature of Greek music and its effects upon the listener, or that it has lessons to offer the musician of his day. Indeed, he devotes the whole of the Third Part, *Treating of Composing of Songs*, to the writing of sound polyphony, without a glance sideways at the possibility of monodic structure. Nevertheless, within the style of which he treats, he is scrupulous in the advice he gives on the setting of words. This passage is so much in accord with Dowland's own musical outlook that it is, though long, worth quoting in full:

It followeth to shew you how to dispose your musicke according to the nature of the words which you are therein to expresse, as whatsoeuer matter it be which you haue in hand, such a kind of musicke must you frame to it. You must therefore if you haue a graue matter, applie a graue kinde of musicke to it: if a merrie subiect you must make your musicke also merrie. For it will be a great absurditie to vse a sad harmonie to a merrie matter, or a merrie harmonie to a sad lamentable or tragicall dittie. You must then when you would expresse any word signifying hardnesse, crueltie, bitternesse, and other such like, make the harmonie like vnto it, that is somewhat harsh and hard but yet so y^t it offend not. Likewise, when any of your words shal expresse complaint, dolor, repentance, sighs, teares, and such like, let your harmonie be sad and dolefull, so that if you would haue your musicke signifie hardnes, cruelty or other such affects, you must cause the partes proceede

[*] op. cit., p. 39.

in their motions without the halfe note, that is, you must cause them proceed by whole notes, sharpe thirdes, sharpe sixes and such like (when I speake of sharpe or flat thirdes, and sixes, you must vnderstand that they ought to bee so to the base) you may also vse Cadences bound with the fourth or seuenth, which being in long notes will exasperat the harmonie: but when you woulde expresse a lamentable passion, then must you vse motions proceeding by halfe notes. Flat thirdes and flat sixes, which of their nature are sweet, speciallie being taken in the true tune and naturall aire with discretion and iudgement, but those cordes so taken as I haue saide before are not the sole and onely cause of expressing those passions, but also the motions which the parts make in singinng do greatly helpe, which motions are either naturall or accidental. The naturall motions are those which are naturallie made betwixt the keyes without the mixture of any accidentall signe or corde, be it either flat or sharpe, and these motions be more masculine causing in the song more virilitie then those accidentall cordes which are marked with these signes #, ♭, which be in deede accidental, and make the song as it were more effeminate & languishing then the other motions which make the song rude and sounding: so that these naturall motions may serue to expresse those effects of crueltie, tyrannie, bitternesse and such others, and those accidentall motions may fitlie expresse the passions of griefe, weeping, sighes, sorrowes, sobbes, and such like.

Also, if the subiect be light, you must cause your musicke to go in motions, which carrie with them a celeritie or quicknesse of time, as minimes, crotchets and quauers: if it be lamentable, the note must goe in slow and heauie motions, as semibreues, breues and such like, and of all this you shall finde examples euerie where in the workes of the good musicians. Moreouer, you must haue a care that when your matter signifieth ascending, high heauen, and such like, you make your musicke ascend: and by the contrarie where your dittie speaketh of descending lowenes, depth, hell, and other such, you must make your musicke descend, for as it will be thought a great absurditie to talke of heauen and point downwarde to the earth: so will it be counted great incongruitie if a musician vpon the worde's hee ascended into heauen shoulde cause his musicke to descend, or by the contrarie vpon the descension should cause his musicke to ascend. We must also haue a care so to applie the notes to the wordes, as in singing there be no barbarisme committed: that is, that we cause no sillable which is by nature short be expressed by manie notes or one long note, nor no long sillable bee expressed with a short note, but in this fault do the practitioners erre more grosselie, then in any other, for you shall find few songes wherein the penult sillables of these words, *Dominus*, *Angelus*, *filius*, *miraculum*, *gloria*, and such like are not expressed with a long note, yea many times with a whole dossen of notes, and though one should speak of fortie he should not say much amisse, which is a grosse barbarisme, & yet might be easelie amended. We must also take heed of seperating any part of a word from another by a rest, as som dunces haue not slackt to do, yea one whose name is *Iohannes Dunstaple* (an ancient English Author) hath not onlie deuided the sentence, but in the verie middle of a word hath made two long rests, thus, in a song of foure parts vpon these words, *Nesciens virgo mater virum.*

lp – sum   re – gem   an – ge – lo   rum

so   la   vir   go   lac – ta   bat.

For these be his owne notes and wordes, which is one of the greatest absurdities which I haue seene committed in the dittying of musicke, but to shewe you in a worde the vse of the rests in the dittie, you may set a crotchet or a minime rest aboue a coma or colon, but a longer rest then that of a minime you may not make till the sentence be perfect, and then at a full point you may set what number of rests you will. Also when you would expresse sighes, you may vse the crotchet or minime rest at the most, but a longer then a minime rest you may not vse, because it will rather seeme a breth taking then a sigh, an example whereof you may see in a very good song of *Stephano venturi* to fiue voices vpon this dittie *quell'aura che spirando a Laura★ mia?* for coming to the word *sospiri* (that is sighes) he giueth it such a natural grace by breaking a minime into a crotchet rest and a crotchet, that the excellency of his iudgment in expressing and gracing his dittie doth therein manifestlie appeare. Lastlie, you must not make a close (especiallie a full close) till the full sence of the words be perfect: so that keeping these rules you shall haue a perfect agreement, and as it were a harmonicall concent betwixt the matter and the musicke, and likewise you shall bee perfectly vnderstoode of the auditor what you sing, which is one of the highest degrees of praise which a musicion in dittying can attaine vnto or wish for. Many other pettie obseruations there be which of force must be left out in this place, and remitted to the discretion and good iudgement of the skilful composer.†

As these diverse but interacting influences were brought to bear on Dowland's genius, is it possible to trace their effect on his musical thought or to see a pattern of development as travel added knowledge of new styles and experience of life deepened his emotional understanding? I think a clear picture emerges, covering the span of his life, of a mind ready and able to assimilate such new experiences as came its way, with the ability to mould them to its use, without ever losing its very personal, but deeply traditional, English outlook.

That his vocal compositions were mainly cast in the form of the lute-song and the four-part ayre may have been due to French influence, both direct and indirect. Direct, from his encounter with the more fully developed *air de cour* during his stay in France; indirect, in the sense that English music had

★ Morley gives *Paura.*
† pp. 177–8.

already received transfusions from across the Channel before Dowland began to compose. His mastery of the lute would also predispose him towards this type of composition.

From his native background he inherited the tradition of the older polyphonic part-song, while the particular attitude towards the setting of words, made manifest in the English metrical psalms, would have fostered the capacity for the simple and direct type of word treatment shown in his early songs. Perhaps the influence of the *air de cour* encouraged the development of his feeling for verbal rhythms, though he never experimented with *musique mesurée à l'antique*, as was done by Thomas Campian, for example, some years later. The fact that he was one of the few among the foremost English composers who did not fall under the spell of the madrigal may also have been due to the formative years in France, where his taste may have been predisposed against this type of composition. Certainly the early songs conform to certain aspects of French style, with their simple strophic pattern and their almost complete freedom from chromaticism. There is plenty of evidence that chromaticism and harmonic innovation were already in the air in England at the time of the publication of *The First Booke of Songes*. It is unnecessary to look further than Thomas Weelkes's *Madrigals to 3.4.5.* and *6 Voyces*, printed in the same year, and Giles Farnaby's *Canzonets to Fowre Voyces* in the next, for confirmation of this fact, and yet the songs in this book are only occasionally touched by it. In Italy* he cannot have failed to come in contact with the experiments in extreme chromaticism being carried out there, particularly by composers attached to the Court at Ferrara. He could even have heard some of Gesualdo's madrigals since Gesualdo was living in that city at the time of Dowland's visit.† Possibly it was just such experiences as these that were needed to set his mind, which had not been greatly stirred by the work of his English contemporaries, working along new lines. At the same time the Florentine influence can hardly be disregarded, and in, for example, 'Sorrow stay', the Cantus line shows the beginning of an affinity with the monodic recitative style. From *The Second Booke* onwards these two forces make themselves increasingly felt. Strophic verse is used less often; chromaticism is harnessed to the expression of grief; conventional forms such as the pavan and galliard are abandoned in favour of a free following of the verbal rhythms; and every phrase is lovingly allied to its most eloquent musical expression. Nevertheless, in spite of the influence of the French *air*

---

* A footnote in Burney, *A General History of Music*, edition of 1789, Vol. III, p. 204, mentions of Marenzio's madrigal 'Solo e pensoso', that has a chromatic scale extending from G to the A a ninth above, and then returning to D. The whole passage is also quoted in Gray and Heseltine, *Carlo Gesualdo, Prince of Venosa* (1926), p. 115.

† *The English Ayre* (1926), p. 31.

de cour and of the Florentine monodic style, in both of which word-painting was frowned upon, Dowland apparently never lost his conviction that this device was serviceable and had its justifiable uses.

Contrary to the practice in France, where the four-part *chanson* or *air de cour* seems to be the primary form, with the solo voice and lute as a secondary arrangement, Dowland's songs, with few exceptions, give the impression of being composed in the opposite order. Possibly it was the English love of part-singing that led to the alternative versions being provided, and the reasons Thomas Campian gives, though he was writing sixteen years later, may have been equally cogent in Dowland's case:

> . . . These Ayres were for the most part framed at first for one voyce with the Lute, or Violl, but upon occasion, they have since beene filled with more parts, which whoso please may use, who like not may leaue. Yet do we daily obserue, that when any shall sing a Treble to an Instrument, the standers by will be offring at an inward part out of their owne nature; and true or false, out it must, though to the peruerting of the whole harmony.*

In recent years the authorship of a number of the poems used by Dowland has been traced, but many remain where, so far, no identification has been made. Some of these may possibly have been provided by his distinguished patrons. In addition to the few really fine poets in the Queen's immediate circle, many of the courtiers were capable of writing respectable verse, although convention demanded anonymity except among the author's closest friends. This dislike of publicity among the nobility and gentry concerning their poetic works is responsible for much of the unclaimed verse of the period not only in the lutenist song-books, but in the madrigal collections as well. The same type of author may also have produced the translations from Italian lyrics occasionally used by composers of the time.

The suggestion has sometimes been put forward that Dowland himself wrote some of the poems he set to music. Although there is no definite evidence to prove his authorship of any stanzas in the song-books he certainly showed he could write verse by the commendatory poems he contributed to his friends' publications. These, however, mostly fall far below the level attained by many of the lyrics he made use of. What is certain is that he had a keen and sensitive ear for poetry and a quick appreciation of such verses as were suitable for his purpose.

Dowland's *First Booke of Songes* established a format that was followed by all the English composers in the same medium for the next twenty-five years. Each of the books contains about twenty-one items. Some have precisely this number, others have twenty or twenty-two. It has been suggested that some

* *The First Booke of Ayres* (c. 1613).

special significance was attached to the number twenty-one, and had it been exact in every case this conjecture might have been sustained on the grounds of its being the multiplication of the mystic numbers three and seven, but any such significance is lost when the number is either twenty or twenty-two. It seems more probable that it was some more mundane reason, possibly connected with the economics of publishing, that dictated this particular size. The music is disposed with the Cantus and lute tablature together on one page, visually coinciding with each other, not absolutely exactly, but within the limit of the bar. Where other voices are added, they are unbarred, and are placed on the opposite page, facing outwards from the centre, so that all taking part may sit round a table and read from the same book. As far as the technique of contemporary printing allows, the underlay of the words is treated with care.

A word or two should be said about the printer's part in the production of these books. There seems, at the time, to have been no adequate system of proof reading and errors are frequent both in the music and in the words. The musical misprints are, as a rule, not difficult to set right, but the words, where printer's errors are coupled with the vagaries of Elizabethan spelling, sometimes give rise to formidable difficulties. The greatest skill and understanding is demanded from the editor who sets out to render the words in modern spelling, and many are the pits that have been fallen into.

Of the actual manipulation of the type and of the faces used for printing English tablature, Robert Steele gives the following account:

Music in tablature was printed by means of a longitudinally compressed alphabet made to fit between the bars of a sort of gridiron. The letters of the alphabet indicated the fret on which the player's finger must rest while the corresponding string is plucked. The form of the letters indicates that Kingston in 1574 copies the French typefounder, Le Bé's lute type of 1544 – 1545. Short and East, who printed at the revival of lute music in 1597, use a new type, as does Barley, the dexterity of whose printing from the point of view of type setting is marvellous. Short uses separate grill types for the lute music, into which the letters are inserted before printing, while Barley uses the old gridiron.*

Each of the Dowland song-books has an elaborate title-page border. These borders were part of the stock-in-trade of the printer and were used many times over with little regard for their suitability to the book in question, and often with little respect for the borders themselves which were, at times, grossly mutilated in order to fit them to the size of various volumes. A central panel was left vacant into which the title of the book and the com-

---

* *The Earliest Music Printing*, Bibliographical Society (1903), p. 7.

poser's name was inserted. A smaller panel, low on the page, was reserved for the names of the licensee and printer together with the date and, sometimes, the instruction as to where the volume might be bought. Occasionally composers or authors had a motto or some personal device, such as a line of music, added somewhere on the page.

In writing of the songs and their words it is inevitable that constant reference is made to Dr. Fellowes's edition of the song-books in The English Lutenist Song Writers series, and also to his *English Madrigal Verse*. The importance of his work in making this *corpus* of music easily available cannot be overestimated, nor can his contribution to the understanding of the verbal texts be passed over. The notes in *English Madrigal Verse* give much useful information concerning the origins of the poems and the meaning of obsolete words. Suggestions are also made for the clarification of obscure passages. Nevertheless, it must be admitted that at times he was less than perceptive about the meaning of Elizabethan forms of construction, and occasionally his alterations are far from justified. Unhappily he has not noted his changes in the song-books and many quite erroneous versions of the words have become firmly established. Furthermore, the proof reading has been inadequate, and even in the revised edition of 1960, many mistakes, particularly in the tablature, are present.

Where I have disagreed with Dr. Fellowes I have tried to give the reasons on which my opinion is based. Where I agree with him I have generally made no comment. This may belie my very real admiration for his work, and may suggest my attitude is only critical. This is not so. My reason for not duplicating many of the notes in *English Madrigal Verse*, especially those concerning the meaning of obsolete words and the replacing of missing syllables, is purely a question of space. Already this book has assumed a larger size than I ever intended, and the addition of the extra material would increase it beyond all bounds. I therefore refer the reader who wishes for more detailed information of this kind to *English Madrigal Verse* in the edition recently revised by F. W. Sternfeld and David Greer.

THE FIRST BOOKE OF SONGES

The entry in the Registers of the Stationers' Company,* under the year 1597 reads as follows:

Ultimo octobris
Peter Short Entred for his copie vnder the hand of master
Man warden/ a booke called *the ffirst booke of*

* Arber, op. cit., Vol. III, f. 25ᵇ.

Songes or Aires made of ffowre partes with Tablature
for the Lute by JOHN DOWLAND *Bacheler of Musicke.*

The text of the title-page is enclosed in an elaborate border. It reads:

THE FIRST BOOKE/ of Songes or Ayres/ of fowre partes with Ta-/
bleture for the Lute:
So made that all the partes/ together, or either of them seue/ rally may be
song to the Lute,/ Orpherian★ or Viol de gambo. Composed by *Iohn Dow-*
land Lute-/nist and Bacheler of musicke in/ both the Vniuersities./ Also an
inuention by the sayd/ Author for two to playe vpon one Lute.

The lower panel contains a Latin motto and the imprint:

Nec prosunt domino, quæ prosunt omnibus, artes.†
Printed by Peter Short, dwelling on / Bredstreet hill at the sign of the
Starre. 1597.

The decorative woodcut that encloses the text is described by McKerrow
and Ferguson in their book on title-page borders:

An elaborate compartment with, at top, Time bringing Truth and Antiquity
to light. Figures of Tolomeus, Marinus, etc. At foot, Mercurius as a bearded
man (possibly intended as a portrait of John Day).
Signed I B. F, or possibly I B & F. If the former is the correct reading the
initials may possibly stand for *Iohannes Bettes fecit.* John Bettes is mainly
known as a miniaturist, but he is said to have had some connection either as
designer or engraver with the pedigree compartment in Edward Halle's
Chronicle. . .‡

Below the figures of Time, Truth and Antiquity there is a globe supported
on a scroll which bears the words 'Virescit VVlnere Veritas' which seems to

---

★ A flat-backed, wire-strung instrument of the lute family. Since the tuning and the
method of playing were similar, music for the lute and orpherian were generally interchangeable.
† Ovid's *Metamorphoses,* I, 525. Apollo is pursuing Daphne. He urges all his accomplishments, among them that he is the god of healing. 'But alas love resists all medicinal herbs, and
the arts which help all mankind cannot help their master.' I am grateful to Professor Benjamin
Farrington for the identification of this passage, and the translation.
Robert Burton in *The Anatomy of Melancholy* (1621), Part III, Sect. II, Memb. IV, Subsect. I,
also uses the same quotation:
'Bid me not love, bid a deaf man hear, a blind man see, a dumb speak, lame run, counsel can
do no good, a sick man cannot relish, no Physick can ease me Non prosunt domino quæ
prosunt omnibus artes, as *Apollo,* confessed, and *Jupiter* himself could not be cured.'
‡ *Title-page Borders.* Bibliographical Society (1932). The border was first used for William
Cunningham's *Cosmographical Glasse* (1559). A list of books in which this border was used
contains, among others, the following:
1597. T. Morley, *A Plaine and Easie Introduction to practicall Musicke.*
1601. P. Rosseter, *A booke of ayres.*
1605. Sir Philip Sidney, *The Countess of Pembroke's Arcadia.*
1605. Sternhold and Hopkins, *The whole booke of psalmes.*

be an adaptation of 'Virescit vulnere virtus', a quotation from Furius in the *Noctes Atticae* (18, 11) of Aulus Gellius (*c.* A.D. 117–80).

The symbolical figures of the design have no connection with Dowland, although appropriately enough the little figure of Musica in the lower right-hand corner, is playing a lute. The same border was used for all printings of *The First Booke of Songes* and also for *The Third and Last Booke of Songs* in 1603.

After the 1597 printing further editions appeared in 1600, 1603, 1606, 1608 and 1613. Copies of all except the 1608 printing are still extant, but so far I have been unable to trace an exemplar of this date. At least one copy was known in the nineteenth century. W. C. Hazlitt, in his *Hand-Book to the Popular, Poetical and Dramatic Literature of Great Britain* (1867), p. 163, includes this date in his list of reprints. Since he also mentions the edition of 1603 there can be no question of a confusion between these two dates. In 1870 A. B. Grosart spoke of 'Dr. Rimbault after examination of Dowland in no fewer than three editions 1597, 1600 and 1608 . . .',* and in *Grove's Dictionary of Music and Musicians*, 1st edition (1879), William H. Husk, writing on Dowland, also mentions it. Husk might possibly have accepted Hazlitt on trust and taken his information from that source, but even so, that would still leave two independent witnesses to its existence, and Rimbault appears to have actually handled it. What can have happened to the book since is a complete mystery.

The edition of 1600 was also printed by Peter Short, but the 1603 edition has the colophon 'Printed at London by E. Short, and are to be sold/by Thomas Adams, at the signe of the white/Lyon in Paules Church-yard. 1603'. E. (Emma) Short was the widow of Peter Short who died in that year. A few books appeared with her imprint before she married Humphrey Lownes† in 1604. On her marriage most of the Short titles passed to Lownes, and it is under his imprint that the 1606 and 1613 editions appeared. Presumably he was also the printer of the 1608 issue.

The type was distributed after each printing and was reset when a new edition was needed, each one being described, as it appeared, as 'Newly corrected and amended'.

The second and third editions show only minor changes; a word here and there has been emended and occasional corrections have been made to the additional voices. In the printing of 1606, however, some of the lute accompaniments have, in places, been substantially rewritten, although it is notice-

---

* *The Works in Verse and Prose Complete of the Right Honourable Fulke Greville, Lord Brooke* (1870), Vol. 2, p. 133.

† R. B. McKerrow, *A Dictionary of Printers and Booksellers 1557–1640* (1910).

able that the more widely known of the songs, for example 'If my complaints' and 'Can she excuse', have been subjected to little or no alteration.

There can be no doubt, in my opinion, that the alterations were made by Dowland himself, the extensive rewriting in 1606 representing the considered re-appraisal of certain passages after the elapse of nine years or more.

All too little is at present known of the exact relationship of author or composer to the publisher or printer to whom he sold the copyright of a work, but authorities appear to be agreed on the fact that it was incumbent upon the owner of the copyright to produce, to the best of his knowledge and ability, an accurate version of the author's MS. R. B. McKerrow says:

It is probable that in the event of any gross infringement, actual or proposed, of an author's rights, an appeal to the authorities would have resulted in pressure being brought to bear on the delinquent, which, even if not in strict accordance with legal forms, would have been difficult to resist.

Furthermore he says:

When an author complains of publication without his consent, the chief point of his grievance seems generally to have been that his work was printed from a faulty manuscript.*

Although Thomas Adams may have had some financial share in the 1603 edition, there can be no doubt that the title was the property of the Short-Lownes family, and in it they obviously possessed a 'best seller'. Humphrey Lownes can have had no possible interest in incurring the extra expense of employing another musician to tamper with Dowland's texts, nor is he likely to have wished to find himself in the position where Dowland would have had a legitimate cause of complaint. On two other occasions Dowland made unfavourable comments on the unauthorized printing of his works, and it seems inconceivable that he should have made no objection in this case, between the printing of the editions of 1606 and 1613, had the alterations been made by any other hand but his own.

The discrepancies in the vocal parts have been carefully noted in the *Ayres for Four Voices*,† but the editors have not dealt so faithfully with the words. Many of the variants have been missed and several errors have been introduced.

E. H. Fellowes used the 1597 printing for his edition of *The First Book of Songs* (Winthrop Rogers, 1920, Stainer and Bell, 1924); the revised edition by Thurston Dart (1965) follows the text of the 1613 printing.

In addition to the textual changes made by Dowland himself there are a

* *An Introduction to Bibliography* (1927, reissued 1951), pp. 143–4.
† Edited Thurston Dart and Nigel Fortune, *Musica Britannica*, Vol. 6 (1955).

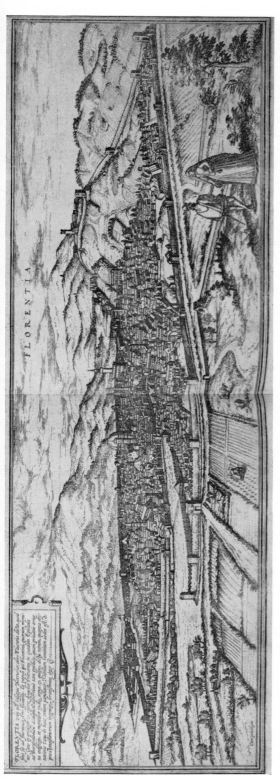

Above, Florence; *below*, Nuremberg. From Braun and Hohenbergius, *Civitates Orbis Terrarum* (1573–1618). By permission of the Trustees of the British Museum.

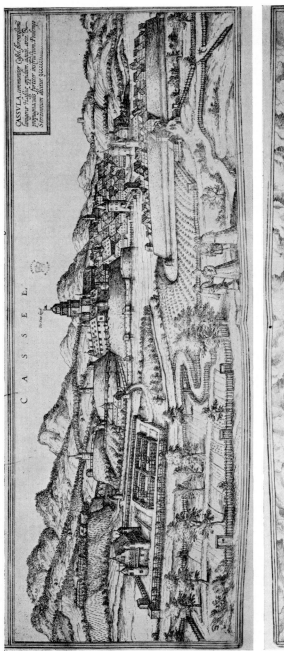

Above, Cassel; *below,* Elsenor. From Braun and Hohenbergius, *Civitates Orbis Terrarum* (1573–1618). By permission of the Trustees of the British Museum.

Two views of Westminster; *above*, part of Westminster with Parliament House, Westminster Hall and the Abbey; *below*, New Palace Yard, with Westminster Hall and the Clock House. Etchings by Wenceslaus Hollar (1607–1677). By permission of the Trustees of the British Museum.

Above, John Dowland's signature on a receipt dated July 28th, 1600, from the Treasury Accounts, the Royal Library, Copenhagen; *left*, John Dowland's signature and 'musical point' in the *Album Amicorum* of Johannes Cellarius.
By permission of the Trustees of the British Museum.

number of features in the extremely divergent spelling and typography that appear to be idiosyncrasies of the individual printer. Collation of the available editions shows some marked differences between Short and Lownes, although neither is uniformly consistent with himself and each may show as many as four variants in the spelling of one word. Nevertheless, each has some marked preference for certain forms. Thus Short usually prints proper names in italics while Lownes keeps them uniform with the rest of the type. In words such as 'unkindness', 'sickness', 'peerless' the first three editions are mostly uniform in ending with 'es'; the fourth and last generally give 'esse'. Short more often gives 'eies' and 'ioies' while Lownes favours 'eyes' and 'ioyes'. Both printers also vary in their use of apostrophes, hyphens, ampersands, and punctuation in general, though here it is less easy to trace any pattern of characteristic usage and neither seems to follow any set rules.

The arms of Lord Hunsdon are printed on the verso of the title-page of the 1597 and 1600 printings; subsequently they were omitted. The usual preliminaries—dedication, epistle to the reader, complimentary poem, and table of contents follow:

TO THE RIGHT HONOVRABLE SIR GEORGE CAREY, OF THE MOST HONORABLE ORDER OF THE GARTER KNIGHT.

Baron of Hunsdon, Captaine of her Maiesties gentlemen Pensioners, Gouernor of the Isle of Wight, Lieutenant of the countie of Southt. *Lord Chamberlaine of her Maiesties most Royall house, and of* her Highnes most honourable priuie Counsell.

That harmony (Right honorable) which is skilfullie exprest by Instruments, albeit, by reason of the variety of number & proportion of it selfe, it easilie stirs vp the minds of the hearers to admiration & delight, yet for higher authoritie and power hath been euer worthily attributed to that kinde of Musicke, which to the sweetnes of instrument applies the liuely voice of man, expressing some worthy sentence or excellent Poeme. Hence (as al antiquitie can witnesse) first grew the heauenly Art of musicke: for Linus Orpheus and the rest, according to the number and time of their Poemes, first framed the numbers and times of musick: So that Plato defines melody to consist of harmony, number & wordes; harmony naked of it selfe: words the ornament of harmony, number the common friend & vniter of them both. This small booke containing the consent of speaking harmony, ioyned with the most musicall instrument the Lute, being my first labour, I haue presumed to dedicate to your Lordship, who for your vertue and nobility are best able to protect it, and for your honorable fauors towards me, best deseruing my duety and seruice. Besides your noble inclination and loue to all good Artes, and namely the deuine science of musicke, doth challenge the patronage of all learning, then which no greater titles can bee added to

Nobility. Neither in these your honours may I let passe the dutifull remembrance of your vertuous Lady my honourable mistris, whose singular graces towards me haue added spirit to my vnfortunate labours. What time and diligence I haue bestowed in the search of Musicke, what trauel in forren countries, what successe and estimation euen among strangers I haue found, I leaue to the report of others. Yet all this in vaine were it not that your honourable hands haue vouchsaft to vphold my poore fortunes, which I now wholy recommend to your gratious protection, with these my first endeuors, humbly beseeching you to accept and cherish thē with your continued fauors.

Your Lordships most humble seruant,
Iohn Dowland.

To the courteous Reader

HOW hard an enterprise it is in this skilfull and curious age to commit our priuate labours to the publike view, mine owne disabilitie, and others hard successe doe too well assure me: and were it not for that loue I beare to the true louers of musicke, I had concealde these my first fruits, which how they will thriue with your taste I know not, howsoeuer the greater part of them might haue been ripe inough by their age. The Courtly iudgement I hope will not be seuere against them, being it selfe a party, and those sweet springs of humanity (I meane our two famous Vniuersities) will entertain them for his sake, whome they haue already grac't, and as it were enfranchisd in the ingenuous profession of Musicke, which from my childhoode I haue euer aymed at, sundry times leauing my natiue countrey, the better to attain so excellent a science. About sixteene yeeres past, I trauelled the chiefest parts of France, a nation furnisht with great variety of Musicke: But lately, being of a more confirmed iudgement, I bent my course toward the famous prouinces of Germany, where I founde both excellent masters, and most honorable Patrons of Musicke: Namely, those two miracles of this age for vertue and magnificence, *Henry Iulio* Duke of *Brunswick,* and learned *Maritius Lantzgraue* of *Hessen,* of whose princely vertues and fauors towards me I can neuer speake sufficientlie. Neither can I forget the kindnes of *Alexandro Horologio,* a right learned master of Musicke, seruant to the royal Prince the *Lantzgraue* of *Hessen,* & *Gregorio Howet* Lutenist to the magnificent Duke of *Brunswick,* both whome I name as well for their loue to me, as also for their excellency in their faculties. Thus hauing spent some moneths in *Germany,* to my great admiration of that worthy country, I past ouer the Alpes into *Italy,* where I founde the Cities furnisht with all good Artes, but especiallie Musicke. What fauour and estimation I had in *Venice, Padua, Genoa, Ferrara, Florence,* & diuers other places I willingly suppresse, least I should any way seeme partiall in mine owne endeuours. Yet can I not dissemble the great content I found in the proferd amity of the most famous *Luca Marenzio,* whose sundry letters I receiued from Rome, and one of them, because it is but short, I haue thought good to set it downe, not thinking it any disgrace to be proud of the iudgement of so excellent a man.

Multo Magnifico Signior mio osseruandissimo.
PEr una lettera del Signior *Alberigo Maluezi* ho inteso quanto con cortese affetto si mostri desideroso di essermi congionto d'amicitia, doue infinitamamente la ringratio di questo suo buon' animo, offerendomegli all' incontro se in alcuna cosa la posso seruire, poi che gli meriti delle sue infinite uirtù, & qualità meritano che ogni uno & me l'ammirino & osseruino, & per fine di questo le bascio le mani. *Di Roma a' 13. di Luglio.* 1595.

D.V.S. Affettionatissimo seruitore,
Luca Marenzio

Not to stand too long vpon my trauels, I will onley name that worthy maister *Giouanni Crochio* Vicemaster of the chapel of S. Marks in *Venice*, with whome I had familiar conference. And thus what experience I could gather abroad, I am now ready to practise at home, if *I* may but find encouragement in my first assaies. There haue bin diuers Lute lessons of mine lately printed without my knowledge, falce and vnperfect, but *I* purpose shortly my selfe to set forth the choisest of all my Lessons in print, and also an introduction for fingering, with other books of Songs, whereof this is the first: and as this findes fauor with you, so shall *I* be affected to labor in the rest. *Farewell.*★

Iohn Dowland.

Tho. Campiani Epigramma de
instituto Authoris.
Famam, posteritas quam dedıt Orpheo,
Dolandi melius Musica dat sıbi,
Fugaces reprimens archetypis sonos;
Quas & delitias præbuit auribus,
Ipsis conspicuas luminibus facit.†

★ Notes on the various characters mentioned by Dowland are included in Chapter VII.
† An Epigram of Tho. Campian on the innovation of the Author.

The renown which posterity gave to Orpheus the
music of Dowland better gives to hersel. By arresting
the fleeting notes in the printed signs she
makes plain to our very eyes the delights she
afforded to our ears.

Campian is presumably referring to the fact that Dowland's was the first book of its kind to be printed in England.

A Galliard for two to plaie vpon one Lute at the end of the booke.

The words of four of the songs from this book are included in *England's Helicon* (1600), as Nos. 119–22:

Burst foorth my teares.
Come away, come sweet Loue.
Away with these selfe-louing-Lads.
My thoughts are wingde with hopes.

These are followed by a note (in which 'three' is obviously a mistake for 'four'):

These three ditties were taken out of Maister Iohn Dowlands booke of tableture for the Lute, the Authours names not there set downe, & therefore left to their owners.

'Unquiet thoughts' (No. 1), although charming and melodious has no particular distinction except for a pleasant little piece of illustrative writing. In the first stanza the poet enlaces the minting of coin and the coining of words in a nice conceit, and Dowland, in the last line, to the verbal content adds the beating of the coiner's hammer in repeated notes:

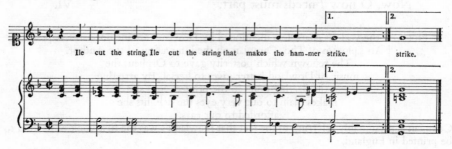

Ile cut the string, Ile cut the string that makes the ham-mer strike.   strike.

The main alterations in the 1606 edition occur in bar 4, where, on beat 2, a chord of the augmented fifth has been eliminated and some other, minor changes have been made. The bar itself has been divided into two:

The difference in the tablature letters e and d makes the change from F sharp to F natural unmistakable.

'Who euer thinks or hopes of loue for loue' (No. 2) is a setting of Sonnet V of Fulke Greville's 'Cælica'. The verses were printed in *Certaine Learned and Elegant Workes of the Right Honourable Fulke Lord Brooke* (1633) and show some discrepancies with the text used by Dowland, particularly in the first line where the 1633 reading gives 'Who trusts for trust or hopes of loue for loue'. Geoffrey Bullough★ considers the poem used by Dowland to have been an early version. Martin Peerson has a setting for five voices in *Mottects Or Grave Chamber Musique* (1630), beginning 'Who trusts for trust or hopes of loue for loue', but in other respects the lines are much altered.

This accompaniment is among those that have been subjected to the most numerous changes. Some of the most interesting of these are found in bars 3 and 4, where decorative figures have been added to the upper voice in the lute part. In the second half of bar 3, the earlier form followed the Altus of the four-part setting, while the later version has a figure based on the Tenor. In bar 6 the decoration is quite independent:

★ *Poems and Dramas of Fulke Greville First Lord Brooke* (1938), Vol. I, p. 232.

'My thoughts are wingd with hopes' (No. 3) is a superb melody in galliard
form. Dowland used the same theme as a lute solo and as 'Sir John Souch his
Galliard' in *Lachrimæ or Seaven Teares.** That the song came first and that the
instrumental pieces were derived from it seems certain. The upward leap of a
sixth in the Cantus on the word 'mount' and again of a fourth on the word
'moon' are characteristic examples of word painting which appear to be a
direct response to the poetic image. The poem has been assigned to various
authors by a number of different editors. R. Warwick Bond includes it among
the Doubtful Poems of John Lyly. He notes that it is attributed, in Francis
Davison's MS list of the contents of *England's Helicon*,† to the 'Earle of
Cumberland', and it is to this author that Norman Ault ascribes it in
Elizabethan Lyrics (1925). J. Payne Collier says: 'The stanzas are subscribed
W.S. in an English Common-place book in the City Library of Hamburgh,
and have by some been considered as the authorship of Shakespeare.'‡
Rollins, in his notes on the poem, says W.S. may stand for William Smith,§
but he gives no indication of what his evidence is, or who this William Smith
may be. Possibly he is referring to the author of *Chloris, or the Complaint of the
passionate, despised Shepherd* (1596). A. B. Grosart includes it as No. IV of
Fulke Greville's Minor Poems,‖ but in a note on the poems in this section he
says: 'No. IV is assigned to him [Fulke Greville] by Mr. J. Payne Collier (Bib.
Catal. s.n.) on the authority of Dowland's "First Book of Songs": but this is
a mistake . . . Dr. Rimbault after examination of Dowland in no fewer than
three editions (1597, 1600 and 1608) informs me that in none is there the
slightest allusion to authorship. In Malone's copy of the Helicon (1600) he has
assigned the four to Brooke: but Nos. III and IV in his MS Index are placed
within brackets, as if doubtful.'¶ The most convincing case so far made is by
Walter Oakeshott in *The Queen and the Poet* (1960), who places it among the

---

* See pp. 144 and 358.
† B.M. MS Harl. 280, f. 99.
‡ *Lyrical poems selected from the musical publications between the years 1589 and 1600* (1844).
§ *England's Helicon* (1600), edited E. Hyder Rollins (1935).
‖ *The Works in verse and prose* (1870), Vol. 2, p. 139.
¶ op. cit., Vol. 2, p. 133.

'Cynthia'* poems of Walter Ralegh and suggests it was written between 1581 and 1587. Munday's use of Dowland's tune† would support these dates. W. J. Linton, in *Rare Poems* (1883), also suggests Ralegh as the author.

'If my complaints could passions moue' (No. 4) is discussed together with the instrumental versions on p. 133.

Since many copies of the Fellowes edition of 1920 are still in use it may perhaps be worth drawing attention to a passage where inconsistency of spelling in the last four lines of the second stanza has led to complete nonsense in the transcription. The original gives:

> Die shall my hopes, but not my faith,
> That you that of my fall may hearers be
> May here despaire, which truely saith,
> I was more true to loue than loue to me.

At the very point where modern spelling can make the sense clear, Fellowes left it as it was instead of altering it to:

> May hear Despair, which truly saith
> I was more true to love than love to me.

The correct spelling is given in the *Ayres for Four Voices* (1955).

'Can she excuse my wrongs' (No. 5). When Fellowes produced his edition of 1920, he added a flat to the B in bar 2, in the Cantus part which, in all the original editions, carries no accidental:

He had some justification for this in the presence of the B flat in the accompaniment and also in the use of this interval in the lute solo and the version in *Lachrimæ or Seaven Teares*. Thurston Dart, in the revised edition of 1965, based on the 1613 edition, restores the note to its position without the flat, and calls attention to the later re-writing of the accompaniment which, at this point, is brought into exact conformity with the Altus part:

* p. 158.
† See p. 144.

Can she ex - cuse my wrongs

Although the elimination of the flat may come as a shock to many people familiar with the Fellowes edition, there are a number of instances to show contemporary acceptance of this arrangement of the intervals, several cases being in tablature where there can be no question of an accidentally omitted flat sign. Such an arrangement is found in the following sources:

Thomas Morley, *The First Booke of Consort Lessons* (1599 and 1611). Sidney Beck, in his edition of 1959, has added an editorial flat in the Treble viol part. This has necessitated the addition of flats in the Flute and Bandora parts. The tablature from Nn.6.36, f. 37, which Beck believes to be the missing lute part, suggests the presence of a flat, but there is no proof that this was Morley's original, and the part may have belonged to an arrangement based on the solo version. See p. 152.

Vallet, **SdM** pp. 36/37/38. (Lute).

Fuhrmann, **TGG**, p. 121. The first interval is wrongly given as a third, but the rest of the melody is correct. (Lute)

Camphuysen, **SR** Numerous editions. (Vocal line only).

B f. 30; f. 124. Rather inaccurate copies, but each shows the semitone interval. (Lute).

Nür f. 7, 'Galliard Pipers No. 2'; f. 65v, 'Galliarta Pipers'. There is more confusion than in the name only, but the semitone interval is there. (Lute).

Bod Mus. MS f. 7–10. (Four vocal part books).

Of the composers who made use of the opening bars of the tune, the following conform to this pattern:

H. L. Hassler
Gabriel Voigtlander
Georg Heinrich Weber

The sources that give the interval of a tone at this point are:

Add. 24,665 (Cantus and Bassus)
Rowe 2 (Voice and lute; transposed up a fourth from the original, with greatly altered accompaniment)

The composers to use the theme in this form are:

Johann Rist
Adam Kreiger
Christoph Ballard

In every case the three-note version of bar 1 is used.

The writer of the version in the John Bull Virginal Book,★ ff. 78v/80, though he adheres to the three-note pattern is finely impartial where the accidental is concerned. He uses a natural in the statement of the theme and a flat in the division.

Conradus Hagius, in *Newe Kunstliche Musicalische Intraden* (Nurnberg, 1616), f. 46, has a version called 'Pypers Galliard', à 5. The bass is undoubtedly that of 'Can she excuse', but unfortunately the whereabouts of the Cantus book is unknown.

A satisfactory explanation of this curious situation is hard to suggest, but in my opinion it seems more possible that there was an error in the tablature of the early editions than that the omission of the flat sign should have escaped correction through each successive printing from beginning to end, particularly when it is remembered that the type was re-set for each occasion. If it is accepted that a distinction between the vocal and instrumental versions was originally intended, it is not particularly difficult to accept also that on occasions they might be confused one with the other.

The stanzas of this song, though they have no author's name in the songbook, reveal some evidence of belonging to a group of ayres which, in my opinion, were written by Robert Devereux, Earl of Essex, to play their part in the tortured and tragic relationship that existed between him and Queen Elizabeth I. One song in this group, by Daniel Bachelor, has the superscription 'The Right Honourable Robert, Earle of Essex: Earle Marshall of England. To Plead my faith where faith hath no reward',† and this is important, since it is this poem, known to be by Essex, to which 'Can she excuse' shows a noticeable similarity of ideas and poetic construction.

The history of Essex, from his first appearance at Court in 1584 until his execution in 1601, has as its central theme the struggle between Essex's soaring ambition and the combination of the strange emotional nature and political acumen of the Queen. With these conflicting interests and nervous tensions it is not surprising that the years were marked with fierce quarrels and uneasy reconciliations. Without going into a detailed history of these clashes of temperament and ambition it may be said that it was something of a habit with Essex, after a quarrel with the Queen, to absent himself from Court, either to sulk until the Queen's affection overcame her anger and she commanded his return or, on the other hand, should she prove adamant, to set himself to work, by every means in his power, to regain her favour. He wrote

★ Fitzwilliam Museum, Cambridge.
† *A Musicall Banquet*, No. 6.

indignant letters and humble and loving ones, and his ability as a poet was also brought into play in his efforts to reinstate himself in the powerful position he enjoyed by virtue of his hold on her affections. Some of the verses he wrote under this urge appear, on the surface, to be no more than the normal courtly love poems written by the lover who thinks himself rejected by his mistress, but woven into the fabric are references that had a particular meaning as applied to Elizabeth and himself. On one occasion at least we know he used one of his poems to foil the attempt of intriguers to introduce a rival in his place. Sir Henry Wotton, his onetime confidential secretary, gives the following account:

There was another time long after, when Sir *Fulke Grevill* (late Lord Brooke) a man in appearance intrinsecall* with him, or at the least admitted to his Melancholy houres, eyther belike espying some wearinesse in the Queene, or perhaps with little change of the word though more in the danger some wariness towards him, and working upon the present matter (as he was dexterous and close) had almost super-induced into favour the Earle of *Southampton*; which yet being timely discovered, my Lord of Essex chose to evaporate his thoughts in a Sonnet (being his common way) to be sung before the Queene, (as it was) by one Hales,† in whose voyce she took some pleasure; whereof the complot, me thinkes, had as much of the Hermit as of the Poet:

> And if thou shouldst by Her be now forsaken,
> She made thy Heart too strong for to be shaken.

As if he had beene casting one eye back at the least to his retirednesse. But all this likewise quickly vanished, and there was a good while after faire weather over-head. Yet still, I know not how like a gathering of Clouds, till towards his latter time, when his humours grew Tart, as being now in the Lees of favour, it brake forth into certain suddain recesses; sometimes from the Court to *Wansteed,* otherwhiles unto *Greenwich,* often to his own Chamber; Doors shut, Visits forbidden . . .‡

Let us return to the song 'To plead my faith' and consider the words:

> To plead my faith where faith hath no reward,
> To moue remorse where fauour is not borne:
> To heape complaints wher she doth not regard,
> Were fruitlesse, bootelesse, vaine and yeeld but scorne.
> I loued her whom all the world admir'de.
> I was refus'de of her that can loue none:

---

* = intimate. *O.E.D.*

† Presumably the Robert Hales who contributed song No. 3 in *A Musicall Banquet* (1610), and who sang before the Queen on November 17th, 1590, at the Tiltyard at Westminster. See p. 238.

‡ 'A Parallell betweene Robert late Earle of Essex, and George *late* Duke of Buckingham.' Written by *Sir Henry Wotton* . . . London, 1641. *Reliquæ Wottoniæ*, 2nd edition, 1654, pp. 9–10.

> And my vaine hopes which far too high asspir'de
>> Is dead and buri'd and for euer gone.
> Forget my name since you haue scornde my Loue,
>> And woman-like doe not too late lament:
> Since for your sake I doe all mischiefe★ proue,
>> I none accuse not nothin doe repent.
> I was as fond as euer she was faire,
>> Yet lou'd I not more then I now despaire.

In general it can be seen that the sonnet fits the Essex–Elizabeth situation perfectly well, but there are two lines that would have a special meaning in the context: 'I loued her whom all the world admir'de'—whom did all the world admire more than Elizabeth?—and 'I was refused of her that can loue none'—did not Ben Jonson tell Drummond of Hawthornden that Elizabeth 'had a membrana on her which made her uncapable of man'?† Though the anatomical reason for Elizabeth's much-vaunted virginity is dismissed, probably quite rightly, by Lytton Strachey‡ as mere gossip of the time, nevertheless, gossip of this sort there was, and the line would have coincided with an opinion held by many. 'I was as fond as euer she was faire, yet loued I not more then I now despaire' is, in sentiment, very like a passage from a letter written by Essex to the Queen during one of his periods of retirement at Wanstead: 'I do carry the same heart I was wont, though now overcome with unkindness, as before I was conquered by beauty.'§ Surely there is a case here for believing this poem was the result of another occasion when Essex let off steam or 'evaporated his thoughts in a sonnet' it 'being his common way', after some particular moment of crisis in his relationship with the Queen. The words of the song 'Can she excuse' not only show an extreme coincidence of emotional content but have a striking similarity of construction in their opening lines. Notice how each line is divided in two with some antithesis of the thought in the first half being expressed in the second:

To plead my faith	where faith hath no reward,
To moue remorse	where favour is not borne.
To heap complaints	where she doth not regard,

Compare this with:

Can shee excuse my wrongs	with vertues cloake:
Shall I call her good	when she proues vnkind.
Are those cleere fiers	which vanish into smoake:
Must I praise the leaues	where no fruit I find.

★ *O.E.D.* = Evil plight or condition, misfortune, trouble, distress.
† Ben Jonson, *Discoveries, 1614. Conversations with William Drummond of Hawthornden, 1619.* Edited G. B. Harrison (1923).
‡ *Elizabeth and Essex* (1928), p. 23.
§ Quoted by Lytton Strachey, p. 149.

Two lines that occur later in the poem would have a very particular meaning: 'Was I so base that I might not aspire Vnto those high ioies which she houlds from me.' Essex was not only an Earl but his mother was a first cousin of the Queen, and the family was descended, through Thomas of Woodstock, from Edward III. Obviously in his own mind he answers the question in the negative and, had the poem been intended to reach the Queen's ears in some way, perhaps already with Dowland's music, she would have been fully alive to the meaning of the lines. Then again he says: 'Better a thousand times to die Then for to liue thus still tormented.' On one occasion, as far back as 1587, after a violent quarrel with Elizabeth on account of her defence of Ralegh, when he was about to ride to Margate, determined to cross the Channel and take part in the Dutch wars, had he not written to his friend Edward Dier, 'If I return, I will be welcomed home; if not, *una bella morire*, is better than a disquiet life'?* Added to the internal evidence of the poem is the fact that in 1604, when the tragedy was ended and Elizabeth herself was dead too, Dowland called the piece 'The Earl of Essex Galiard' in *Lachrimæ or Seaven Teares*. Previously the lute versions had appeared either without a title or as 'Can she excuse', and when he gave the name of Essex to the arrangement for strings and lute he may have wished to give recognition to the fact that the tune had originally been inspired by the verses of the ill-fated Earl. If these various points constitute a strong enough case for it to be assumed that the words are by Essex, then it would be fairly safe to conclude that it was in vocal form that the piece was first written. It will be remembered that Dowland himself makes it clear that many of the songs in this volume had been in existence for some time before he decided on publication; the fact that the piece appeared as a lute solo in William Barley's *New Booke of Tabliture* in 1596 provides no evidence one way or the other, since the song could have been composed some years earlier and could have been arranged as a solo by the time Barley went into print. That the poem had appeared by 1596 is shown by a very corrupt copy found by John Payne Collier among the papers of Edward Alleyn, the actor, at Dulwich College, of which he was the founder. I give the stanzas as printed by Collier, together with his comment:

LOVE VERSES

(It is evident that what follows is a copy of love-verses, much corrupted in the transcription by some ignorant hand, who sadly mangled most of the lines. We do not recollect any printed work in which they are found, and they

---

* Walter Bourchier Devereux, *Lives and Letters of the Devereux Earls of Essex* (1853), Vol. I, p. 188.

were perhaps incorrectly copied from some original manuscript by an author of that day.)

> Can she excuse my wronges with vertuous cloke?
>> Shall I call her good, when she proves so unkinde?
> Shall those cleare fires vanish into smoke?
>> Shall I praise the leafes wher no frut I find?
> No, no: wher shadowes do for bodyes stande,
>> Thou mayest be deseved yf thy lite be dime.
> Could love is like to words written in sand,
>> Or to bubbels which upon the water swime.
> Wilt thou be thus deluded still,
>> Seinge that she will right thee never?
> Yf thou canst not overcom her will,
>> Thy love will be but frutles ever.
>
> Was I so base that I might not aspire
>> Unto those high joyes which she holds so from me?
> As they are hy, so hy is my desire.
>> Yf she this deny, what may graunted be?
> Or yf that she will graunt to that which reson is,
>> It is resons will that trewe love should be just.
> Deare, make me happi, then, by graunting this,
>> Or cut off my days, yf so be dy I must.
> Better a thousand times to dy, then for to live thus still tormented.
>> Deare, but remember it was I that for thy love did dy contented.
>> FINIS. 1596.*

'Now, O now I needs must part' (No. 6) is set to the tune of the 'Frog Galliard', see p. 141.

The sixth line of the first stanza appears to have troubled modern editors, although it is clearly printed in the original, and all editions agree in giving:

> Loue liues not when hope is gone.

Dr. Fellowes, however, in the 1920 edition of the song-book† altered it to:

> Loue dies not when hope is gone.

and the editors of Dowland's *Ayres for Four voices*‡ give the line as:

> Love lies not when hope is gone.

The popularity of this galliard has already been mentioned, and the use of the tune for ballads. The following quotation from the anonymous play *Euerie Woman in her Humor* (1609)§ shows the song to have been sufficiently widely

---

* *The Alleyn Papers* (1843), p. 21.
† The English School of Lutenist Song Writers.
‡ *Musica Britannica*, Vol. 6 (1953).
§ *A Collection of Old English Plays*. Edited A. H. Bullen. Vol. IV (1885), p. 313.

known for a line from the first stanza to have been expected to get across to the audience:

Philautus: . . . All hayle to my belooued; then
for your departure, sad dispaire doth
driue me hence: for all must be to effect.

'Deare if you change Ile neuer chuse againe' (No. 7).

The 'Earth, heauen, fire, aire' of the penultimate line of the second stanza would, to the Elizabethan mind, have held overtones of reference to the current philosophical ideas of the properties and motions of the four elements, Earth, Air, Fire and Water.★

The setting of the final line of the stanza, with the simple device of the misplaced accent, is at the same time a most ingenious treatment of the words and musically satisfying in its effect:

and on   my   faith,   my   faith   shall   ne – – uer breake.

'Burst forth my teares' (No. 8). In *England's Helicon* the copy of the poem is headed 'To his Flocks'. In the 1920 edition Fellowes altered the penultimate line of the second stanza:

And beauty hope in her faire bosome yokes,

to:

And Beauty Hope in her fair bosom locks,

the intention being, presumably, to give an exact rhyme with 'rocks', the final word of the last line. The meaning of the original seems quite clear, however, and near rhyme such as this is by no means rare in other poems in the song-books.

Only two very small changes were made to the accompaniment in the later editions.

In 'Go christall teares' (No. 9), although the means are exceedingly simple, Dowland never achieved a more enchanting passage than the opening phrase. The descending sequence of the altus part seems to imitate the crystalline splash of the falling tears:

★ See E. M. W. Tillyard, *The Elizabethan World Picture* (Peregrine Books, 1963). The Elements, p. 77.

Go chris-tall teares, like to the morn — — ing showers,

The first edition of 1597 gives the first line of the second stanza as 'Hast haplesse sighs'. This was altered in the printing of 1600* to 'Hast restlesse sighs'. It continued in this form (with variant spellings) in all subsequent printings. In his edition of 1920 Fellowes changed the reading of the second line from:

> & sweetly weepe in to thy Ladies breast

to:

> And sweetly weep into my lady's breast.

The change from 'thy' to 'my' seems quite unnecessary.

Obertello suggests the words are an adaptation of Petrarch's sonnet *Ite caldi sospiri*. An early setting of the Italian words, probably the first, was made by Giovanni Brocco.† Robert Jones, almost a hundred years later, set the sonnet again in *A Musicall Dreame* (1609). In the poem as set by Dowland the rhyme 'heart' and 'desert' between the second and fourth lines of the second stanza, falls rather flat in modern spelling, but 'desarte', as in the original (which represents the pronunciation of the period) completes the rhyme perfectly.

In the later editions there is a particularly interesting alteration to the accompaniment in the last two bars where the bass has been lowered an octave. This change suggests that the solo form of the song to the lute alone may have been the one more generally used in performance. If this had become apparent to Dowland, the strengthening of the bass by its being placed an octave lower would be an obvious improvement.

'Thinkst thou then by thy fayning' (No. 10). The not very profound little poem of this song is given an odd and brittle character by Dowland's setting.

I should not have thought it necessary to comment on the meaning of the line:

> When louely sleepe is armlesse,

* Not 1612 as stated in Thurston Dart's revised edition of 1965.
† Alberto Obertello, *Madrigali italiani in Inghilterra* (1949).

were it not that on one occasion I was asked by a singer, who shall be nameless, why sleep had no arms. The meaning is, of course, nothing to do with the physical members, but refers to the unarmed, or harmless condition of the poet's Love, when asleep.

'Come away, come sweet loue' (No. 11) is one of the most serene and lyrical of all Dowland's songs. Neither bitterness nor melancholy touches it. In *England's Helicon* the verses are headed with the title 'To his Loue'. In the 1920 edition Fellowes suggests altering the word 'Rosie' in the sixth line of the original arrangement of the stanza, to 'roseate', presumably in order to create the semblance of an internal rhyme with 'And sweet roseate lips to kiss' so that it may match the internal rhyme in the second stanza, 'Playing, staying in the groue'. There is, however, no matching rhyme in the third stanza and, in a sense, Fellowes has created the need for one by his elaborate layout of the lines.

'Rest a while you cruel cares' (No. 12) has no particularly outstanding characteristics. A conventional piece of word painting occurs in the setting of the final couplet, with the upward movement of the voice on the word 'heauenly'. Only minimal changes were made in the accompaniment in the later editions. One of these, on the third minim of bar 26, where a C has been added in the bass to make it agree with the Bassus part, is probably no more than the correction of an omission on the printer's part.

'Sleepe wayward thoughts' (No. 3) is one of the most outstandingly beautiful of all Dowland's songs, its success being achieved by the simplest possible means. The melody is smooth and flowing and the words are set note for syllable. The accompaniment is almost entirely chordal with the addition of a few decorative figures on the lute where the Cantus has a long note. This is one of the less common examples among the strophic songs where the words and music are equally happily married in the succeeding stanzas as they are in the first.

The number of copies that found their way into MSS of the time shows how justly popular it became, and this popularity is confirmed by quotations in theatrical productions of the early seventeenth century. *Eastward Hoe* (1605) by George Chapman gives us the following lines:

Girtred . . . off with this gowne for shames sakes, off with this gowne: let not my Knight take me in the Citty cut in any hand: tear't, pax ont (does he come) tear't of. *Thus whilst shee sleepes I sorrow, for her sake, etc.*[*]

Again in *Euerie Woman in her Humor* (1609), in the same scene between

---

[*] *Eastward Hoe. As it was played in the Black-friers. By the Children of her Maiesties Reuels. Made by Geo: Chapman. Ben: Jonson. Ioh: Marston* (1605). I am grateful to Richard Newton for this reference.

Philautus and a boy, where there was a quotation from 'Now O now', we find:

Phil: Boy, sleepe wayward thoughts?*

Unlike the majority of Elizabethan songs, 'Sleepe wayward thoughts' survived the change of fashion and persisted until after the Restoration. It was printed, with the attribution to Dowland, in John Playford's *A brief introduction to the skill of musick* . . . (third edition, 1660), p. 41, and was reprinted in the unnumbered edition of 1662. It travelled to Scotland and there, curiously, the tune became associated with the words 'If fluds of teares could clense my follies past', No. 11 of *The Second Booke of Songs*. John Forbes included it in this form, as well as with the original words, as No. 13 of his *Songs and Fancies* in all three editions (1660, 1662 and 1680). In the Skene MS† it appears as an instrumental solo with the title 'Floodis of teares'. John Squyer's MS‡ (dated 1696–1701) shows it to have been still known, in its original form, until the turn of the century.

In the first two strains the only difference between the early and late editions lies in the addition of an A in the middle voice of the lute part on beat 5 of bars 6 and 13 to bring them into conformity with the penultimate bar of the song. The original omission may have been purely accidental since the lute player will find himself almost automatically supplying the missing note. In bars 23 and 24, however, important changes were made:

'All ye whom loue or fortune hath betraide' (No. 14) is a complete contrast to the preceding song. Polyphonic in structure, with the melody broken into shorter phrases and with repetition introduced on such words as 'whose sighes' and 'who sings my sorrowes' to point the emotion. For the first time, too, Dowland uses chromaticism for the expression of grief:

* A. H. Bullen, op. cit., p. 312.
† National Library of Scotland.
‡ Edinburgh University Library, MS La., III, 490, p. 71.

R. Warwick Bond,* without any supporting evidence, claims the poem for John Lyly. Apart from this it has been ascribed to no other author. The final couplet of the first stanza:

> Lend eares and teares to me most haples man,
> That sings my sorrowes like the dying Swanne.

is an expression of the commonly held belief, having its origin in classical legend, that the swan sings once only, on the approach of death. The idea occurs again in 'Me me and none but me', No. 5 of *The Third and Last Booke*, and, of course, as referring to Dowland himself, in *Varietie of Lute-Lessons*. Shakespeare alludes to the story five times† and Tilley lists it among the proverbs of the time, 'Like a swan, he sings before his death'.‡ Orazio Vecchi's 'Il bianc'e dolce cigno' became known in England as 'The white delightful Swanne' in Nicholas Yonge's *Musica Transalpina. The Second Booke of Madrigalles* (1597). Orlando Gibbons, too, used a stanza on the same subject for his madrigal 'The Silver Swan'.§ The source for the story best known to the Elizabethans would probably have been Ovid's *Heroides* in George Turbervile's translation, *The Heroycall Epistles*, first printed in 1567. Epistle VII, 'From Dido to Æneas', begins with these lines:

> Euen so when fates doo call,
>   ystretcht in moysted spring,
> Vpon Meanders winding bankes
>   The snowish Swanne doth sing.

In the first part of the song one chord only is filled out with an additional note in the later editions, but bar 13, as given in the preceding example, was changed to a form in which the higher voice on the lute conformed more closely to the Altus part of the four-part ayre:

---

* John Lyly, *Complete Works* (1902), Vol. 3, p. 492.
† A. L. Rowse, *William Shakespeare, A Biography* (1963), p. 37.
‡ M. P. Tilley, *A Dictionary of the Proverbs in England in the 16th and 17th Centuries* (1950), S1028.
§ *Madrigals and Mottets of 5 Parts* (1612).

'Wilt thou unkind thus reaue me of my heart' (No. 15) has a melancholy charm. The words are aptly set, and the means used to express sadness, as for example, the sudden sharpening of the leading note on the word 'part', though conventional, are none the less effective:

Beaumont and Fletcher show its popularity by giving a garbled version of the refrain to Old Merrythought in *The Knight of the Burning Pestle* (1613).* He sings:

> But yet, or ere you part (Oh, cruel!)
> Kiss me, kiss me, sweeting, mine own dear jewel!

In the early part of the song the accompaniment has been slightly filled out in the later editions, but in the final bar an important change has been made where the chord of A has been replaced by a chord of C thereby bringing the lute into line with the voices of the four-part ayre.

'Would my conceit that first enforced my woe' (No. 16). In this song the words express similar sentiments of frustrated hopes and 'inward paine' as those of No. 14. They may well have been chosen by Dowland as a vehicle for his grief at the shattering of his own hopes when his application for a post at Court was refused.

Most of the notes added to the accompaniment in the later editions are of such a character that they may well have been accidentally omitted in previous printings. One interesting change, however, is made in bar 6, where the final note, a G, has been lowered an octave to bring it to the same pitch as the Tenor voice.

* Edited R. F. Patterson (1944), Act I, Scene 4, p. 19.

'Come againe: sweet loue doth now enuite' (No. 17). In his notes to the
1920 edition Fellowes remarks that the last line of each of the first two stanzas
contains two syllables more than the corresponding line in each of the following stanzas. He suggests the composer interpolated a word for musical purposes to match the metre of the previous line and that he had not anticipated
more than two stanzas being sung. A curious fact is that in the song-book,
after stanza 2, the numbering starts again at 1 and continues to 4. Edward
Doughtie★ suggests the possibility of these stanzas having belonged to an
entirely different poem. Bruce Pattison† points to the similarity of the metre
with that of a poem by Thomas Lodge in *The Phoenix Nest* (1593 ed., p. 49),
but Doughtie shows it is only the last four stanzas that resemble Lodge's
'Strive no more'. Thomas Oliphant included the first two stanzas as No. 162 in
La Musa Madrigalesca (1837) with the comment 'There are four stanzas more,
but much inferior to these'. Giles Earle,‡ in his MS copy of the song, seems
to have found difficulty in accommodating the final stanza to the music, and
in the last line 'Did tempt while she for triumphs laughs' he adds the word
'mightie' before 'triumphs'.

There appears to be no good reason why the later stanzas should have been
added if Dowland did not intend them for use and the absence of the extra
syllable makes them by no means unsingable. It needs only careful choice of
words for repetition in the fifth line (according to the layout of the poem in
the song-book) and any of them will fit the music, although it is only in the
first two that the complete aptness of the setting is fully realized. The fourth
line (fifth in the Fellowes edition):

with the crescendo of excitement in the first stanza and the decline into despair
of the second, is, in each case, perfectly matched with its music and, as one
follows the other they make a complete antithesis. The corresponding lines of
the later stanzas, though not unacceptable when broken with the rests, lack
the intensity which this device gives to the lines illustrated above. Un-

★ op. cit., p. 319.
† *Music and Poetry in the English Renaissance* (1948), p. 154.
‡ B.M. Add. 24665 (1615–25), ff. 26v–27.

fortunately modern singers often ignore the last rest of the series under the delusion they know better than Dowland, and that the meaning is made clearer by carrying the word 'die' over the rest and joining it to 'with thee againe . . .' Dowland obviously knew what he was doing, and when he reaches the climax of the sequence of disjointed phrases 'To see—to heare—to touch—to kisse—to die' (and surely here the words 'to die' are used in the figurative sense, meaning to reach the final transports of physical love) the contemplation of his happiness is too much for him, and he catches his breath before he adds 'with thee againe in sweetest simpathy'. An extremely corrupt version of this song appears in Landesbibliothek Kassel MS Mus. 108.1, f. 32v, with Italian words:

> In me non é piu vita
>   che per se giuř amor é gia finita
> E púr mi sento gran martire
>   Che non si puo soffrire.

For the lute solo based on the same melody see p. 163.

'His golden locks time hath to siluer turnde' (No. 18). An account of the occasion upon which these stanzas were originally sung is given by Sir William Segar* in *Honor, Military and Civill* (1602).

CHAP. 54

The Original occasions of the yeerely Triumphs in ENGLAND.

Here will we remember also (and I hope without enuie so may) that these annuall exercises in Armes, solemnized the 17. day of Nouember, were first begun and occasioned by the vertuous and honourable Sir *Henry Lea*, Master of her Highnesse Armorie, and now deseruingly Knight of the most noble Order, who of his great zeale, and earnest desire to eternize the glory of her Maiesties Court, in the beginning of her happy reigne, voluntarily vowed (unlesse infirmity, age, or other accident, did impeach him) during his life, to present himselfe at the Tilt armed, the day aforesayd yeerely, there to performe, in honor of her sacred Maiestie the promise he formerly made. Whereupon the Lords and Gentleman of the sayd Court, incited by so worthy an example determined to continue that custome, and not vnlike to the antient Knighthood *della Banda* in *Spaine*, haue euer since yerely assembled in Armes accordingly: though true it is, that the Author of that custome, (being now by age ouertaken) in the 33 yeere of her Maiesties reigne resigned and recommended that office vnto the right noble *George* Earle of *Cumberland*. The ceremonies of which assignation were publiquely performed in presence of her Maiestie, her Ladies and Nobilitie, also an infinite number of people beholding the same, as followeth:

On the 17 day of Nouember, *Anno 1590.* this honourable Gentleman,

---

* Principal King at Arms. He contributed a commendatory poem to Peacham's *Minerva Britanna*.

together with the Earle of *Cumberland*, hauing first performed their seruice in Armes, presented themselues vnto her Highnesse, at the foot of the staires under her Gallery window, in the Tilt yard at *Westminster,* where at that time her Maiestie did sit, accompanied with the *Viscount Turyn* Ambassador of *France,* many Ladies and the chiefest Nobilitie.

Her Maiesty beholding these armed Knights comming toward her, did suddenly heare a musicke so sweete and secret, as euery one thereat greatly marueiled. And hearkening to that excellent melodie, the earth as it were opening there appeared a Pauilion, made of white Taffata, containing eight score elles, being in proportion, like vnto the sacred Temple of the Virgins Vestall. This Temple seemed to consist vpon pillars of Pourferry, arched like vnto a Chruch, within it were many Lampes burning. Also, on the one side there stood an Altar couered with a cloth of gold, and thereupon two waxe candles burning in rich candlesticks, vpon the Altar also were layd certaine Princely presents, which after by three Virgins were presented vnto her Maiestie.

Before the doore of this Temple stood a crowned Pillar, embraced by an Eglantine tree. . . .

The musicke aforesayd was accompanied with these verses, pronounced and sung by M. *Hales,*[*] her Maiesties seruant, a Gentleman in that Arte excellent, and for his voice both commendable and admirable.

> My golden locks time hath to siluer turnd,
> (Oh time too swift, and swiftnes neuer ceasing)
> My youth gainst age, and age at youth hath spurnd.
> But spurnd in vaine, youth waineth by encreasing.
> Beauty, strength, and youth, flowers fading beene,
> Duety, faith and loue, are rootes and euergreene.
>
> My Helmet now shall make an hiue for Bees,
> And louers songs shall turne to holy Psalmes:
> A man at Armes must now sit on his knees,
> And feed on pray'rs, that are old ages almes.
> And so from Court to Cottage I depart,
> My Saint is sure of mine unspotted hart.
>
> And when I sadly sit in homely Cell,
> I'le teach my Swaines this Carrol for a song,
> Blest be the hearts that thinke my Souereigne well,
> Curs'd be the soules that thinke to doe her wrong.
> Goddesse, vouchsafe this aged man his right,
> To be your Beadman now, that was your Knight.

The gifts which the Vestall maydens presented vnto her Maiesty, were these: A vaile of white exceeding rich and curiously wrought: a cloke and

---

[*] The same who sang the Earl of Essex's Sonnet on another occasion. See p. 226.

safegard set with buttons of gold, and on them were grauen Emprezes of excellent deuise: in the loope of euery button was a noblemans badge, fixed to a pillar richly embrodered. . . .

But to return to the purpose, These presents and prayer being with great reuerence deliuered into her Maiesties owne hands, and he himselfe disarmed, offered vp his armour at the foot of her Maiesties crowned pillar; and kneeling vpon his knees, presented the Earl of Cumberland, humbly beseeching she would be pleased to accept him for Knight, to continue the yeerely exercises aforesaid. Her Maiesty gratiously accepting of that offer, this aged Knight armed the Earle, and mounted him vpon his horse. That being done, he put vpon his owne person a side coat of blacke Veluet pointed vnder the arme, and couered his head (in lieu of an helmet) with a buttoned cap of the countrey fashion.

Dr. Fellowes* suggests that Robert Hales may have been the composer of the music sung at the Tiltyard, but it appears far more likely that Dowland's setting was the one used. It is hardly probable that he would have chosen to reset a poem so closely linked with its own special occasion, an occasion moreover, which at the time of the printing of *The First Booke of Songes* in 1597, would not yet have faded from people's memories. The likelihood that Sir Henry Lee himself (or someone closely associated with him) was the author of the stanzas, and that Dowland set other poems from the same hand, further strengthens the probability. Of the poem itself, Fellowes accepts George Peele as the author, on the grounds of a copy, entitled 'Sonet', having been bound in the back of Peele's *Polyhymnia* (1590),† an account in verse of the Tiltyard ceremony. David W. Horne, one of Peele's latest editors, has investigated the problem with considerable care and finds the attribution unsatisfactory.‡ He concludes that Lee may have been the author of the three related poems set by Dowland, namely 'His golden locks', the trilogy of *The Second Booke*, Nos. 6, 7, and 8, and 'Farre from triumphing Court', No. 8 of *A Musicall Banquet*. He suggests, however, that Richard Edes, who wrote the verses for the Ditchley entertainment§ given by Sir Henry Lee for Queen Elizabeth in 1592, may have collaborated in writing the poems. In my opinion, except that they share the common form of the six-line stanza, there is little resemblance between Edes's work and the verses under consideration. Lee's claim as author is strengthened by the fact that his name is printed above the song in *A Musicall Banquet*, in which the stanzas both echo phrases and

---

* *English Madrigal Verse.*

† Only two extant copies of the printed work are known; one at the Huntington Library, the other at the Library of Edinburgh University. A MS transcript at St. John's College, Oxford, does not include the poem.

‡ *The Life and Minor Works of George Peele* (1952), pp. 165–73.

§ See E. K. Chambers, *Sir Henry Lee, An Elizabethan Portrait* (1936), Appendix E, p. 276, where the complete text is given.

ideas from the earlier poem, and refer, with particularly personal expressions of emotion, to the visit paid him, at his home, by Queen Anne in 1608. Evidence of contemporary MSS into which 'His golden locks' was copied with Lee's name attached, suggests he was generally accepted as its author at the time. R. Warwick Bond★ attempts to claim the poem for John Lyly on the grounds of similar phrases and imagery occurring elsewhere in Lyly's work, but the claim is in no other way substantiated.

In the later editions the tendency has been to add a note here and there to strengthen the accompaniment, but in bar 3 a definite change has been made:

'Awake sweet loue' (No. 19). The relation of this song to the lute solo is discussed on p. 143.

Several passages in this accompaniment have been largely re-written in the later editions. A particularly interesting example occurs in bars 1 and 2, where the revision brings the lute part much closer to the solo version:

(Time values halved.)

Fellowes, in his edition of 1920, substituted the note G for the A at the top of the second chord, without mentioning that he had done so. He thus introduced

★ op. cit., Vol. I, p. 410.

a misprint which had appeared in the editions of 1600 and 1603. The harmony
of the emended edition of 1606 shows the repeated A, as printed in 1597, to
have been correct.

In bar 7 the G and F which had formed an inner voice have been raised an
octave higher, and in the first part of bar 8 the notes in the bass, which appear
to have been misplaced in the early editions, have been corrected:

In bar 23 the rather irritating quavers have been removed from beat 2:

In the penultimate bar, on beat 2, C in the bass has been removed to bring
the lute and voice into agreement.

'Come heauy sleepe' (No. 20). This most beautiful and expressive song is
another masterpiece of absolute simplicity, and here Dowland makes use of
his knowledge of the special sonorities of the lute with moving effect, particularly at the junction of the fourth and fifth lines. The last words of line four
'sorrows sigh swoln cries' end on a full close with a chord of G major; a chord
which on the lute is mainly composed of notes on the open strings, giving a
clear ringing quality. This will support a considerable volume of tone from the
singer. The next line begins on a B major chord which, by the position of the
notes on the strings of the instrument, has a somewhat more muted tone
colour. If the singer drops his voice to match the natural change of quality in
the accompaniment the repeated notes of the invocation to sleep then take on a
kind of hushed urgency, exceptionally expressive of the emotionally charged
sentence:

sor - rows sigh swoln cries: Com & po - sses my tir ed

thoughts, worne _____ soule,

In the original print the last couplet of the first stanza (part of which is given above) has the following reading:

> Com & posses my tired thoughts, worne soule,
> That liuing dies, till thou on me bestoule.

This form appears in all four voice parts of all the editions I have been able to check. In the 1920 edition of the song-book Dr. Fellowes has altered the lines as follows:

> Come and possess my tired thought-worn soul,
> That living dies till thou on me be stole.

In the notes on the *First Book of Songs* in *English Madrigal Verse* (1929) he writes:

It would seem that the composer, or whoever made the transcription for him, misunderstood the meaning of the line and taking *worn soul* for the vocative, added the *s* to *thought*. There can be little doubt as to the true construction of the line.*

The explanation may be, however, that 'worne soule' is not a vocative, but is 'in apposition' with 'tired thoughts', the word 'and' being omitted. If the line as it stands is spoken aloud with that idea in mind, it sounds perfectly intelligible, and both the adjectives 'tired' and 'worn' will be slightly stressed, which agrees completely with the musical setting. Dr. Fellowes's conjecture has, nevertheless, been to a certain extent justified in recent years by the discovery of a setting by Robert Johnson† of the first stanza of the same poem,

* p. 615.
† New York Public Library, Drexel MS No. 4041, No. 39. Printed in English Lute Songs, Second Series, No. 17, edited by Ian Spink.

where the words 'thought worne' are in fact, used:

> Com heavie slepe thou image of true deth
> and close up these my weared weping eyes
> whose springes of teares doe stopp my vitall breath
> and tyers my harte wth saurowes sighes swolen cries
> com and pooses my tyred thought worne soule
> y^t living dies till thow one me bee stolen

Since Dowland made no correction and the same reading was carried through to the edition of 1613, though other texts were emended, it would seem that he was satisfied with the words as they stand and had no wish to change them. Thomas Oliphant in *La Musa Madrigalesca* (1837) includes a copy of the words from the song-book, and to them attaches the following note:

In this invocation to Sleep the hand of a scholar is easily to be traced. Its consanguinity with night, and relationship to death—*the image of true death* (Mortis imago), or as Shakespeare terms it, *Death's counterfeit,* all emanate from the Pierian spring of heathen mythology.★

In the fifth line he prints 'my tired care-worn soul' without any note of the alteration, and in the sixth line he gives 'till thou on me bestole'. He explains the last word as 'Cover me, like a mantle' but the *O.E.D.* has no such definition and cites Dowland's use of the word 'bestoule', giving 'besteal' as the present tense with the meaning: to move stealthily upon someone. In the second stanza Dr. Fellowes alters 'child to this black fast† night' to 'child to the black faced night'. A small point but the original reading seems preferable and fits the accent of the music better. The verbal patterns are, however, very different in the second stanza and the words can hardly be fitted to the music without some distortion of the natural rhythm.

In the later editions a number of small alterations have been made in the accompaniment:

Bar 4, beat 4

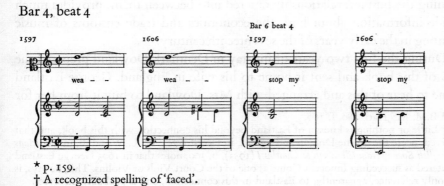

★ p. 159.
† A recognized spelling of 'faced'.

'Away with these selfe louing lads' (No. 21). This is a straightforward, lively little song; another of the rare examples of Dowland in an entirely untroubled mood. The note for syllable writing is unvaried throughout and the general structure is reminiscent of an almain. Although anonymous in the song-book, Fulke Greville's authorship of the words is undisputed. The poem was printed as No. LI of the Cælica cycle in *Certaine Learned and Elegant Workes of the Right Honorable Fulke Lord Brooke* (1633). It is also ascribed to 'F Greuill' in Francis Davison's MS list of the contents of *England's Helicon*.*

On four occasions a B natural has been removed from a G major chord in the later editions. Some slight added elegance is thereby given to the accompaniment.

On the penultimate note of bar 1 a G has been added in the bass, and on the last note of bar 3 a D in the bass and an A above it have been added. These notes could possibly have been accidentally omitted from the earlier printings.

In bar 7 the B flat has been removed from the final chord, and the note G has been substituted.

THE SECOND BOOKE OF SONGS

Considerable interest, of a purely non-musical character, surrounds the publication of this volume. The series of lawsuits brought, one against the other, by George Eastland,† the publisher, and Thomas Este, the printer, concerning the business relationship entered into between them, provides much inside information about both the economics and trade customs of music printing in the early years of the seventeenth century.

During the first two years of his stay in Denmark Dowland prepared the MS of this book and sent it home to his wife in England. George Eastland came to hear of this and arranged with Mrs. Dowland to buy it from her for

---

* B.M. MS Harl. 280, f. 100.

† Little or nothing is known of Eastland beyond his connection with this book, and that he lived 'neere the greene Dragon and Sword, in Fleetstreete'. W. L. Woodfill, in *Musicians in English Society from Elizabeth to Charles I* (1953), p. 300, notes that in 1603 George Eastland is entered as succeeding Innocent Come as one of the Court Viols or Violins. This, he says, is the only reference, apparently, to Eastland in this connection, and is probably incorrect.

£20 and half the reward expected from Lucie, Countess of Bedford for the dedication. He approached Thomas Este with the proposal that he should print the book since it was known that Este 'had the name for the true imprinting of musicke'. The matter was arranged with Thomas Morley and his associate, Christopher Heybourne, who held the patent for music printing at that time, and with Este, who by an indenture of May 29th, 1600, had become their assign for a period of three years. After some difficulties a draft agreement was eventually reached between Eastland and Este, stipulating that 1,000 copies of the book should be printed with twenty-five extras for proofs and complimentary copies, which, by custom, were given to Morley, to Heybourne and to 'such as did worke in the printing of the same'. No sooner had the book left the press than trouble started. Eastland became suspicious that more copies had been printed than were legitimately allowed by the agreement; on the other hand Este also had a grievance. Eastland had paid the £10 due to Este for actual printing before the 1,000 copies were delivered to him, but he had omitted to complete the payments due to Morley and Heybourne as the patentees. He had paid 40s in advance, without which the printing could not begin, but a further charge of 6s per ream of paper printed, amounting to £7 10s od had not been settled. Within a short time Eastland caused Este to be arrested, charging him with having printed more copies than the agreement allowed, with intent to sell them for profit. This proved the first of several occasions on which Eastland invoked the aid of the law against Este in this matter, but in the end he failed to obtain any compensation, in spite of the fact that two of Este's apprentices confessed they had printed thirty-three copies without their master's knowledge or consent. Meanwhile Este had sued Eastland for his debt of £7 10s od in the Court of King's Bench. This claim was upheld, plus 20s.

During the course of the hearing of the complaint made by Eastland in the Court of Requests on May 4th, 1601, he estimated the expenses incurred over the publication had amounted to about £100. Este said this was absurd and countered with his own detailed estimate of what Eastland had spent:

	£	s	d
To Mrs Dowland for the MS	20	0	0
To Morley and Heybourne	9	10	0
To Este	10	0	0
To Este's servants		2	0
For paper	7	16	0
For waste paper		1	0
To Este and his servants		2	0
	£47	11	0

Eastland subsequently reduced his estimate to £66 6s 8d. Este's charges, as can be seen, appear to cover nothing more than the actual printing—twenty-five reams at 8s per ream—and the evidence tells us nothing about the condition of the books when delivered. Although Mrs. Este, Este's brother Alexander and the apprentices took part in counting the sheets and damping the paper for printing, nothing is said about gathering and folding, after the printing was done. The Playford catalogues* show that books in the middle and late seventeenth century, and presumably, earlier, were ordinarily sold unbound (where they were stitched or bound the prices were higher), but even so, the work of gathering and folding must have been carried out at some point before the books were offered for sale to the public, and possibly the cost of these processes explains Eastland's higher figure.

There is considerable variation in the price at which the copies were eventually sold. Eastland is reported to have asked 4s 6d per copy; this, Este said, was an exorbitant price. Este's two apprentices got rid of twenty-five of their illicit copies to one William Cotton, apprentice to a stationer, for 40s, and Matthew Selman, another stationer, bought nine for 18s. Matthew Selman also bought one of Cotton's copies for 4s. If Eastland succeeded in selling his entire print of 1,000 copies at his own price he must have made an exceedingly handsome profit. In view of the great success of *The First Booke of Songes* his risks were small and his attitude towards money, revealed in these proceedings, appears somewhat out of tune with the altruistic sentiments expressed in his address 'To the courteous Reader'.†

The reports of this litigation‡ yield a few further details of musical interest.

John Wilbye, the madrigalist, and Edward Johnson, both in the employment of Sir Thomas Kitson of Hengrave Hall, appeared as witnesses, having been entrusted with the proof reading. Philip Rosseter was also called upon to testify. All three left their signatures on the documents.

The Second Booke of Songs was registered in Este's name at Stationers' Hall, July 15th, 1600, in the following words:

master East   Entred for his copie vnder the handes of the wardens A booke called *The second booke of songes or Ayres of Twoo, ffowre, and ffyve, partes with tablatures for the Lute or orpherian, with the viol de gambo* Composed by JOHN DOWLAND bachelour of

---

* B.M. Harl 5936, illustrated and quoted in C. Humphries and W. C. Smith, *Music Publishing in the British Isles* (1954).

† For a fuller account of these proceedings see 'The Printing of John Dowland's Second Booke of Ayres' by Margaret Dowling, read before the Bibliographical Society on November 16th, 1931. Printed in *The Library*, Fourth Series, Vol. XII, No. 4, March 1932.

‡ P.R.O. Court of Requests 2/203/4 and 2/202/63.

musick and lutenist vnto the most famous: CHRISTIAN, the iiij by the grace of GOD kinge of Denmark, Norway &c
vj^d ★

The main panel of the title-page has this inscription:

THE/ SECOND BOOKE/ of Songs or Ayres,/ of 2. 4. and 5. parts:/ With Tableture for the Lute or/ Orpherian,† with the Violl/ *de Gamba.*/ Composed by IOHN DOWLAND Batcheler / of Musick, and Lutenist to the King of Den-/mark: Also an excelent lesson for the Lute/ and Base Viol, called/ *Dowlands adew.*/
Published by George Eastland, and are/ to be sould at his house neere the greene Dragon/ and Sword, in Fleetstreete.

The smaller panel has the imprint:

LONDON:/ Printed by Thomas Este,/ the assigne of Thomas/ Morley. 1600.

The title-page border is described by McKerrow and Ferguson:‡

132. (269 × 178 mm. enclosing 108 × 97 mm.)

An elaborate compartment with two cherubs holding cornucopias at top, termini at sides; David and Samson in small panels below.

A close copy of a compartment used by Christopher Plantin at Antwerp, (see no. 2 in the Appendix), but the figures in the two panels at foot have been altered to David and Samson, and the block has been shortened by the omission of the six small panels with a Medusa head in the centre, above the termini. The original appears in Thomas a Veiga, *Commentarii in Claudii Galeni Libros sex de Locis affectis,* Antwerpiae ex officina Christophori Plantini, 1566.

At the top of the border, in an oval between the two cherubs, are two staves of music, a round on Psalm 150, to the words 'Praise God vpon the Lute and Violl':

Psal. 150

PraiseGOD'v‑pon the Lute and Vi — — — oll.

Set out in three parts, it goes as follows:

★ Edward Arber, op. cit., Vol. III, f. 62.
† A flat-backed, wire-strung instrument of the lute family. Since the tuning and method of playing were similar, music for the lute and orpherian was generally interchangeable.
‡ op. cit., p. 114.

The canon was probably written by Dowland himself since an entirely different one, '4. parts in 1.' is enclosed, in the same oval when the border appears again in Francis Pilkington's *First Booke of Songs* (1605), and in John Danyel's *Songs for the lute, viol and voyce* (1606) the oval contains a printer's ornament.

The title-page is followed by the prefatory matter, with, in this case, the somewhat unusual insertion of a poem and epistle, 'To the curteous Reader', from the publisher. First comes Dowland's dedication:

TO THE RIGHT/ Honorable the Lady Lucie/ Comptesse of BED-FORD./ EXcellent Ladie: I send vnto your La: from the Court of a forreine Prince, this volume of my second labours: as to the worthiest Patronesse, of Musicke: which is the Noblest of all Sciences: for the whole frame of Nature, is nothing but Harmonie, as wel in soules, as bodies: And because I am now remoued from your sight, I will speake boldly, that your La: shall be vn-thankfull to Nature hirselfe, if you doe not loue, & defend that Art, by which, she hath giuen you so well tuned a minde.

Your Ladiship hath in your selfe, an excellent agreement of many vertues, of which: though I admire all, Yet I am bound by my profession, to giue especiall honor, to your knowledge of Musicke: which in the iudgement of ancient times, was so proper an excelencie in Wœmen, that the Muses tooke their name from it, and yet so rare, that the world durst imagin but nine of them.

I most humbly beseech your La: to receiue this worke, into your fauour: and the rather, because it commeth far to beg it, of you.

From Helsingnoure in Denmarke the first of Iune.   1600

Your Ladiships
in all humble deuotion:
Iohn Dowland.

Eastland followed this with an ingenious poem and his own epistle:

To the right Noble and Vertuous/Ladie, Lucie Comptesse of/ BEDFORD.

G. Eastland. To I. Dowlands Lute.
L Vte arise and charme the aire,
V utill a thousand formes shee beare,
C oniure them all that they repaire,

I nto the circles of hir eare,
E uer to dwell in concord there,

B y this thy tunes may haue accesse,
E uen to hir spirit whose floweing treasure,
D oth sweetest Harmonie expresse,
F illing all eares and hearts with pleasure
O n earth, obseruing heauenly measure,
R ight well can shee Iudge and defend them,
D oubt not of that for shee can mend them.

To the curteous Reader.

Gentlemen, if the consideration of mine owne estate, or the true worth of mony, had preuailed with me, aboue the desire of pleasuring you, and shewing my loue to my friend, this second labours of Maister Dowland, (whose very name is a large preface of commendacions to the booke,) had for euer laine hid in darknesse, or at least frozen in a colde and forreine country. I assure you that both my charge and paines in publishing it, hath exceeded ordinary, yet thus much I haue to assure mee of requitall, that neither the work is ordinary, nor are your iudgements ordinary to whom I present it, so that I haue no reason but to hope for good increase in my labours, especially of your good fauours toward mee, which of all things I most esteeme. Which if I finde in this, I meane shortly (God willing) to set at liberty for your seruice, a prisoner taken at *Cales,* who if hee discouers not something (in matter of Musicke) worthy your knowledge, let the reputation of my iudgement in Musicke aunswere it. In the meane time, I commend my absent friend to your remembrance, and my selfe to your fauorable conceits.

George Eastland.
From my house neere the greene Dragon
and sword in Fleetstreet.

Before leaving Eastland to the obscurity that surrounds his subsequent activities, there is one point in his epistle that deserves notice—his reference to the 'prisoner taken at *Cales*'. Cales was, of course, the old name for Cadiz. Could then a prisoner of musical interest have been taken there during the famous raid of 1596?

Peter Warlock says: 'The identity of "the prisoner taken at Cadiz" to whom Eastland refers is unknown.'[*] Surely the words should not be taken literally. It is unlikely that Eastland, as a private citizen, could obtain possession of the person of a Spanish prisoner of war, and even if he had, how could the prisoner be 'set at liberty' for the 'service' of purchasers of Eastland's publications? Is not the more likely answer, and one which is entirely consistent with the Elizabethan love of word-play, that the prisoner was not a Spaniard captured during the raid, but a book from the famous library seized

---

[*] *The English Ayre,* p. 35.

at Faro, on July 14th, on the return journey? The volumes were brought back to England, some by Walter Ralegh, some by Edward Doughtie, chaplain to the expedition, but most were brought by the Earl of Essex, a large proportion of whose spoils, as a result of the Earl's gift in 1600, still rest in dusty serenity on the shelves in Duke Humfrey's Library, in the very positions assigned to them by Bodley's first Librarian, Dr. Thomas James. There are many contemporary accounts of this famous incident, probably the best-known being that by Admiral Sir William Monson★ (brother of Dowland's patron), but he seems to have been unfortunately responsible for the generally accepted idea that the library at Faro belonged to Bishop Hieronimus Osorio. In an article 'A Grand Inquisitor and his Library',† K.M.P. shows that this is not so, that Osorius had been dead for sixteen years, and that the spoils were, in reality, filched from Ferdinand Martins Mascarenhas, bishop of Faro from 1594 to 1618, and later Grand Inquisitor of Portugal.

Doughtie, who was dean of Hereford (and a shameless pluralist) from 1607 to 1616, left his share of the loot to Hereford Cathedral‡ (one volume was later found at the Bodleian) and the volumes are there to this day, still bearing the inscriptions of the original owners together with Doughtie's signature as witness to his part in the affair. Doughtie apparently confined his attention to theological works, and those at the Bodleian that can be identified§ are also for the most part sixteenth-century treatises on theology, scholastic philosophy and canon law, such as might have been expected from an episcopal library. Neither collection contains anything that could have been of musical interest to Eastland's patrons. However, others on the expedition also seem to have done a little private looting on their own account. In the library at Christ Church, Oxford, is a fine, beautifully bound copy of Victoria, *Motecta Festorum Totius Anni* (Rome, 1585), which bears the inscription 'Liber Rob: Westhawe ex domo Episcopali Faronensi, 1596'‖ (Robert Westhawe's book, from the episcopal house at Faro, 1596). If this volume of music was in the Bishop's library, may there not also have been others? Is it not within the bounds of possibility that Essex, noticing a book on music kept this back among others that interested him, while the bulk of the library, consisting mainly of theological works, was handed on to Bodley? What follows now

---

★ 'Naval Tracts' in *A collection of voyages and travels*, Vol. III (1704), p. 187.

† *Bodleian Quarterly Record* (1922), Vol. III, No. 34, pp. 239–41.

‡ P. S. Allen, 'Books brought from Spain in 1596' in *The English Historical Review* (1916), Vol. 31, pp. 606–10.

§ A list of the titles appears under the year 1600 in the *Registrum Benefactorum*.

‖ Walter G. Hiscock, *A Christ Church Miscellany* (1947). The following entry from Cooper, *Athenæ Cantabrigienses* (1927) II, p. 179, seems to relate to the same Robert Westhawe:

WESTHAWE, Robt. Matric. from Trinity, Easter, 1577; B.A. 1580–1. Author, Almanacke for 1595.

is nothing but speculation and there is no shred of evidence to support the suggestion, but is it not possible that this book was the *Musice Active Micrologus* of Andreas Ornithopacus (Leipzig, 1517) that Dowland eventually published in translation in 1609?

We know that Dowland had some connection with Essex; that he may even have been in Essex's confidence in the matter of setting the Earl's verses to music. Is it so very unlikely that Essex, finding a copy of *Musice Active Micrologus* among his valuable prizes, should have handed it to Dowland, possibly even with the suggestion that he might translate it?

Eastland speaks of Dowland as his friend, and unless he were already known to the Dowland family his appearance in connection with *The Second Booke* is somewhat unaccountable; he may even have made some arrangement with Dowland for the publication of the two books before his departure for Denmark. That the *Micrologus* remained unpublished until six years after Eastland's announcement is not altogether surprising. The work is quite large, amounting to some ninety-one pages in translation, and is full of technical detail; a taxing undertaking under the best of conditions. Dowland tells us, however, that the work was done during the course of his travels when time for private and sedentary work would have been limited and conditions far from perfect.

After the trials experienced by Eastland in publishing *The Second Booke*, he may well have withdrawn from any further commitments in this direction, leaving the book on Dowland's hands.*

But to return to *The Second Booke of Songs* and the final page of the preliminaries. The contents are set out as follows:

A TABLE OF ALL/

the Songs contained in this/

Booke.

Songs to two voices.

I saw my Lady weepe:	I
Flow my teares fall from your springs:	II
Sorow sorow stay, lend true repentant teares:	III
Dye not before thy day:	IIII
Mourne, mourne, day is with darknesse fled:	V
Tymes eldest sonne, old age the heire of ease: First part.	VI
Then sit thee downe, and say thy *Nunc demittis*: Second part.	VII
When others sings *Venite exultemus*: Third part.	VIII

* I am grateful to Richard Newton who traced the sources of information on the Grand Inquisitor's library, and generously gave me the results of his search.

FINIS.

The songs for two voices are not duets in the strict sense that the second voice sings an independent and indispensable part. In the first eight songs in the book a sung bass line is provided, which, in all important essentials, doubles the bass of the lute. Just why Dowland should have adopted this form of writing is impossible to say, particularly as it often results in serious distortion of the words in the second vocal line.

'I saw my Lady weepe' (No. 1). The Basso part to this song is wrongly marked Canto. It has above it the words 'To the most famous Anthony Holborne'. A work of extraordinary beauty, it is, in the freedom of its construction, different from any of the songs that went before. There are no repeated sections and indeed, after the second line of the stanza the melody is carried through on the flow of thought almost unhampered by the formal division of the lines. In the Cantus voice treatment of the words has assumed paramount importance and the attention to the musical counterpart of verbal rhythm goes beyond anything that Dowland had previously done:

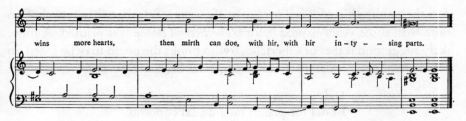

wins   more hearts,   then mirth can doe, with hir, with hir   in - ty - - sing parts.

Alfonso Ferrabosco of Bologna used a text for a madrigal which was included in Nicholas Yonge's *Musica Transalpina* (1588) with the following
translation:

> I saw my Lady weeping, & loue did languish,
> & of their plaint ensued so rare consenting,
> that neuer yet was heard more sweet lamenting,
> made all of tender pittie & mournfull anguish,
> the flouds forsaking their delightfull swelling,
> stayd to attend their plaint, the windes enraged,
> still & content to quiet calme asswaged,
> their wonted storming, & euery blast rebelling.
>
> Like as from heuen the dew full softly showring
> doeth fall, & so refresh both fields and closes,
> filling the parched flowers with sappe & sauour?
> so while she bath'd the violets & the roses,
> vpon hir louely cheekes so freshly flowring,
> the spring reneued his force with hir sweete fauour.

The first line only has any direct connection with the poem set by Dowland,
but it could well have been these words that, maturing in the poet's mind,
gave rise to the verses used by Dowland. Thomas Morley, in *The First Booke
of Ayres or Little Short Songs* (1600)* set the first stanza of the same poem as
No. V, 'I saw my Ladie weeping'. In addition to the word 'weeping' in the
first line, Morley's version of the stanza has two other variants: at the end of
the third line he gives 'kept' instead of 'keepe', and in the fifth line he gives
'as winnes mennes heartes', an obvious misprint since it makes nonsense when
followed by the last line 'then myrth can doo with her entising partes', R.
Warwick Bond† attributes the poem to Lyly and suggests it is the missing song
of the shepherds in his *Woman in the Moone* (1597). In respect of the words, Bond
may be right, although he was addicted to claiming poems for Lyly on little
or no evidence, but I have the strongest doubts that Dowland had composed
the music by 1597. It appears to me to represent his genius in its development

---

* English Lutenist Song Writers, Vol. 16 (1932), edited E. H. Fellowes, pp. 21–3.
† op. cit., Vol. 3, pp. 248 and 471.

after the publication of *The First Booke of Songes*, even though a period of no more than three years elapsed before *The Second Booke* was printed. A more likely suggestion is that of Obertello,★ who thinks the poem may be based on an Italian sonnet by Alessandro Lionardi, in his *Secondo Libro de le Rime* (1550):

> Vidi pianger Madonna, & seco Amore
> Et del lor pianto farsi un tal concento
> Che non fu mai il piu dolce lamento
> Formato di pietate, o di dolore.
> Lasciando i fiumi'l lor soaue errore
> Stauan' ad ascoltar & ciascun uento,
> Et parea mitigato insieme et spento
> L'usato orgoglio, & uinto il duro core.
> Come da ciel seren rugiada suole
> Cader, & hor quel fior, hora quest' herba
> Rinfrescando nudrir al tempo estiuo;
> Cosi bagnar le rose & le uiole
> Che fiorian nel bel uiso, onde superba
> N'andaua primauera & ogni riuo.

'Flow my teares' (No. 2). The origin of the music of this song in the instrumental pavan 'Lachrimæ' has already been discussed (p. 123), but the words and their setting remain to be considered. If it is agreed that the lute solo was composed before the song, then it seems certain that the words were written specially to fit the music, a practice in common use at the time, especially in the case of dance music. It would be an extreme coincidence to find a poem, written independently of the music, that would fuse with it in such an exact unity. Here are the words as they appear in the song-book:

> Flow my teares fall from your springs,
>   Exilde for euer: Let mee morne
> where nights black bird hir sad infamy sings,
>   there let mee liue forlorne.
>
> Downe vaine lights shine you no more,
>   No nights are dark enough for those
> that in dispaire their last fortuns deplore,
>   light doth but shame disclose.
>
> Neuer may my woes be relieued,
>   since pittie is fled,
> and teares, and sighes, and grones my wearie dayes,
>   of all ioyes haue depriued.

★ op. cit., pp. 440–1, see note p. 231 ante.

Frō the highest spire of contentment,
   my fortune is throwne,
and feare, and griefe, and paine for my deserts,
   are my hopes since hope is gone.

Harke you shadowes that in darcknesse dwell,
   learne to contemne light,
Happie, happie they that in hell
   feele not the worlds despite.

The lyrics of two other songs, 'Mourne, mourne, day is with darknesse fled' (*The Second Booke*, No. 5), and 'In darknesse let me dwell' (*Musicall Banquet*, No. 10), show a remarkable similarity of ideas and images to the above stanzas, so much so indeed, that the possibility arises of their having been written by a single author. Consider, for example, the following parallels:

you shadowes that in darcknesse dwell	(II, 2)
in darkenesse learne to dwell	(II, 5)
In darknesse let mee dwell	(*M.B.* 10)

also:

learne to contemne light	(II, 2)
Mourne mourne, looke now for no more day	
nor night	(II, 5)

and again:

Neuer may my woes be relieued	(II, 2)
Thus wedded to my woes	(*M.B.* 10)

The idea of hell, not so much as a place of fire and torment, as of blackness and perpetual night, is present in all three poems and the consciousness of this particular hell is frequently reiterated:

Happie, happie they that in hell	(II, 2)
o none, but hell in heauens stead	(II, 5)
no more day	
nor night, but that from hell,	(II, 5)
hellish jarring soundes	(*M.B.* 10)

These ideas agree very closely with what Dowland appears to have believed about his own life and circumstances, and moreover, by 1600 the composition, under its name 'Lachrimæ', had already reached considerable fame and had become to Dowland a kind of 'signature tune' (did he not sign himself Jo: dolandi de Lachrimæ?). All these indications seem to point in one direction—to the composer himself as author of the three poems. There is, however, one fact which appears to offer a serious objection: Giovanni Coperario

(John Cooper) had, in 1606, included a setting of 'In darkness let me dwell' with a second stanza, where Dowland only sets one, in his *Funeral Teares* on the death of the Earl of Devonshire. The additional stanza★ shares none of the distinguishing characteristics of the other poems. The date of the *Funeral Teares*, four years before the appearance of *A Pilgrimes Solace*, would appear to rule out the likelihood of Coperario's having seen Dowland's stanza, set it, and found someone to supply the additional lines. Uncertainty then remains. The poems may not be from the same hand; the similarities may be nothing more than the coincidence of commonplace poetic images; and the stanzas of 'Flow my teares' may not be by Dowland at all. But whether by Dowland or some other author the words are fitted to the melody with an exquisitely sensitive ear for the rhythm and the rise and fall of the spoken word. Note, for example, the lift of the voice on the word 'infamy' which mirrors exactly the pattern of speech:

hir   sad in - fa - my sings,

After the extreme skill with which the words and music are matched in the Canto part it is surely suggestive, if any further evidence were needed to support the claim that the song was a secondary development from the solo pavan, that the words have to be subjected to considerable distortion before they can be made to fit the bass line. Some syllables have to be jettisoned, even at the expense of the meaning, in order to accommodate the words to the existing notes. The first sentence, for example, becomes:

> Flow teares from your springs,

and in the repeat:

> Down lights shine no more,

Later we have:

> my wearie dayes
> all ioyes haue depriued.

If Dowland had been setting pre-existing words it is hard to believe he would not have written a bass that would have distorted them less.

The copy of this song in Giles Earle's MS song-book† has several important variants, particularly in the words of the repeat of the first strain:

> Downe vaine delightes, shine yee noe more,
> noe nightes are darcke inough for those

★ See p. 317.
† B.M. Add. 24665 (1615–26), ff. 11v/12.

> that in dispaire their loste fortunes deplore,
> light doth but sinne disclose

Fellowes, I think mistakenly, in his edition of 1920, adopted the readings 'delights' and 'lost fortunes' from Giles Earle. Surely it is the vain 'lights' that are required to shine no more, and is not the word 'last' used in exactly the same sense as in *The Third and Last Booke of Songs*, that is, the latest book, and their latest or present fortunes that are to be deplored?

John Forbes, in the 1666 edition of *Songs and Fancies* (I have not seen the other two), has a very curious change in the last two lines. He gives:

> they that in heaven
> feele not the worldes despite.

'Sorrow sorrow stay' (No. 3). This fine song is a remarkable instance of how Dowland could absorb foreign influences and make use of them at will without ever being overwhelmed by them or being diverted from his own completely personal outlook. In their declamatory style many passages show the effect of Florentine influence, particularly the words 'pitty, pitty, pitty', which, mounting a tone higher on the repetition, form an anguished recitative. Later 'Alas I am contempned euer' has exactly the quality of the 'melodious kind of speech' spoken of by Grillo. 'No hope, no help' appear as broken exclamations on descending thirds, while the end of the sentence 'ther doth remaine' falls through a third to the key note of G. This is followed by one of the most magnificent pieces of colouring that Dowland ever wrote, confounding all Galilei's precepts:

An arrangement in five parts for voice and viols by William Wigthorp called, in the Superius book, 'Dowlands Sorrow', has a slight variant in the reading of the first line with 'Sorrow, sorrow come', while six extra lines are provided, either as a repeat, or possibly as an alternative ending, to give a religious cast to the poem:

> Pity sweet Jesu, help now and ever,
> marke me not to endlesse paine.
> Alas that I have synd,
> I hope I hope help doth remaine
> Though that downe, downe, downe, downe I fall
> Yet I shall rise and never fall.★

These words appear to admit a ray of hope totally absent in the stanza used by Dowland, but as verse they are not very satisfactory. That Beaumont and Fletcher made Merrythought sing a travesty of the concluding lines:

> Down, down, down they fall.
> Down and arise they never shall†

is a good indication that the song had, in spite of its complexity, become one of the 'song hits' of the day.

'Dye not before they day' (No. 4) consists of a single stanza only. The Canto line is simple with the interest often depending on the more elaborate and faster-moving lute part. Typical repetitions of words and phrases are used where special emphasis is required by the text, the accompaniment being varied to avoid dullness. For example:

The last eight bars consist of an unusual passage in triple measure:

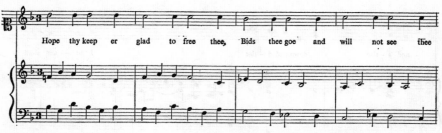

★ B.M. MS Add. 17786–91. † *The Knight of the Burning Pestle* (1613).

'Mourne, mourne, day is with darknesse fled' (No. 5) is a long stanza of ten lines, set to a slow beat alternating between common and triple measure. The structure of the lines would have allowed the second four to have been sung to a repeat of the melody of the first four, and the repetition of the words 'Mourne, mourne' might have suggested such a treatment, but Dowland preferred to through-compose the entire piece. At the repetition of the words he does, in fact, use the same downward leap of a fourth, but with the difference here of a minor chord on the lute instead of the major chord of the first bar—a most beautiful effect. From this point the setting moves forward in a completely different pattern. Again, the lute has an independent and fully contrapuntal part.

'Times eldest sonne, old age the heyre of ease' (No. 6), 'Then sit thee downe and say thy *Nunc Demittis*' (No. 7), and 'When others sings *Venite exultemus*' (No. 8). The three stanzas of this song are treated as a through-composed sequence. It is clear from the Table of contents where they are marked First, Second and Third part, that they form a single whole, although in the body of the book they are given separate numbers. Great rhythmic freedom is used in setting the words and, though a certain gravity of mood covers the whole, each stanza is well contrasted with the other two. The structure of the first is almost entirely chordal, but a more contrapuntal texture is introduced in the second and third.

If Sir Henry Lee wrote the words of 'His golden locks' there can be little doubt that he is also the author of these stanzas. The similarity of form, and of the phrases and images used is too close to be a mere coincidence. Compare, for example, the grouping of nouns in the last two lines of the first stanzas of each poem:

Bk.I, No.18.   Beauty, strength, youth are flowers but fading seene, Duty, Faith, Loue are roots and euer greene.
Bk.II, No.6.   But thinks sighes, teares, vowes, praiers and sacrifices, As good as showes, maskes, iusts, or tilt deuises.

In both cases the word 'saint' is used for Elizabeth:

Bk.I, No.18. But though from court to cotage he departe
His saint is sure of his vnspotted heart.
Bk.II, No.7. O that thy Saint would take it worth thy hart,
thou canst not please hir with a better part.

And finally, in the last stanza:

Bk.I, No.18. And when he saddest sits in homely Cell,
Hele teach his swaines this Caroll for a song,
Bk.II, No.8. and teach those swaines that liues about thy cell,
to say *Amen* when thou dost pray so well.

Oliphant* remarks on the similarity of the poems, and commends the aptness of the words:

This is exceedingly clever, and from the style of composition, as well as from the references to Queen Elizabeth, I should say was from the pen of the same author as No.CLXIII [i.e. 'His golden locks']. The application of the different heads of the Romish service in contradistinction to each other, is very happy.

The introduction of the words *Nunc Demittis*, the beginning of the *Canticum Simeonis*, 'Lord, now lettest thou thy servant depart in peace', in the second stanza, is particularly appropriate to Lee's own situation at the time of the Westminster ceremonies, and suggests this poem also had its origin in the events of November 17th, 1590. Moreover, the idea in the final couplet of the old man, fit only to pray for the Queen, is echoed in a letter from Lee to Sir Thomas Heneage, dated September 18th, 1591:†

. . . I followed Her Majesty until my man returned and told me he could get neither fit lodging for me nor room for my horse. All these things considered hath made me return, with my more ease, to my poor home, where I am much more fit to pray for Her Majesty than now to wrestle with the humours of Court. . . .

At this point Dowland returns to the solo song with alternative presentation in the form of the four-part ayre.

'Praise blindnesse eies' (No. 9). Although Dowland has set this as three four-line stanzas, followed by the final couplet in an 'envoy', the poem appears to be a sonnet. Lines five to twelve are set out, below the Cantus and lute parts, without any division into stanzas, as if Dowland himself were indeed aware of the form but had deliberately chosen to disregard it. R. Warwick Bond ascribes the poem to John Lyly‡ on the grounds of the similarity of line 9:

* *La Musa Madrigalesca* (1837), p. 163.
† E. K. Chambers, op. cit., p. 163, from *Calendar of the MSS of the Marquess of Salisbury at Hatfield House*, IV, 136.
‡ op. cit., Vol. 3, p. 484.

Now none is bald except they see his braines

with a line in *Euphues and his England* (1580), but M. P. Tilley★ gives no less than ten other occasions for the use of this line in the most varied contexts, before the mid-eighteenth century.

'O sweet woods, the delight of solitarinesse' (No. 10). The couplet that forms the refrain of this song:

> O sweet woods the delight of solitarinesse,
> O how much doe I loue your solitarinesse,

is almost identical with a couplet that appears at the beginning of a poem in a dramatic interlude by Sir Philip Sidney, printed at the end of the 1598 edition of *The Countess of Pembrokes Arcadia*:

> O sweete woods, the delight of solitarinesse!
> O how well I doe like your solitarinesse!

The rest of the poem, however, bears no resemblance to the one set by Dowland, Sidney's being one of quiet contemplation, having none of the bitter resentment of the other. Obertello† points to the similarity of Sidney's lines with the poem of Pietro Bembo, 'Lieta e chiusa contrada ov'io m'involo', but Mona Wilson‡ suggests Giovanni della Casa's 'O dolce selva solitaria, amica' for comparison. Possibly both couplets originally stem from one or other of the poems. The name Wanstead in the last stanza sets the locality of the woods, and points to the possibility of one or other of two authors: Sidney himself, who is known to have stayed at Wanstead House on several occasions when it was in the possession of his uncle, the Earl of Leicester, or Robert Devereux, Earl of Essex, who had the use of it later. G. B. Harrison§ records two occasions, one in 1597 and one in 1598, when Essex is known to have retired to Wanstead in a self-imposed exile while out of favour with the Queen.‖ Although in 1580 Sidney went through a period of disillusion with Court life and retired to the country home of his sister, the Countess of Pembroke, at Wilton, the sentiments of the poem are not entirely consistent

---

★ *A Dictionery of the Proverbs in England in the Sixteenth and Seventeenth Centuries* (1950). B.597.
† *Madrigali Italiani in Inghilterra* (1949), p. 136.
‡ *Sir Philip Sidney* (1931), p. 314.
§ *The Life and Death of Robert Devereux, Earl of Essex* (1937), pp. 171, 174, 206 and 208.
‖ John Chamberlain wrote to Dudley Carleton on August 30th, 1598,
. . . the erle of Essex . . . retired to Wansted where they say he means to settle, seing he cannot be receved in court, though he hath relented much and sought by divers means to recover his hold: but the Quene sayes he hath playde long enough upon her, and that she means to play a while upon him, and to stand as much upon her greatnes as he he hath done upon stomacke.
N. McClure, op. cit., Vol. 1, p. 41.

with his particular circumstances. He stood in no special relationship to the Queen, who is surely the 'mistress' of the poem, and he suffered no spectacular 'fall'. Even on the the occasion of his writing the well-known letter of expostulation to Elizabeth on her proposed marriage to the Duc d'Anjou she seems to have borne him no special grudge. But in the case of Essex many points in the poem fit very noticeably with the events of his life, his own particular characteristics, and his position in relation to Elizabeth. 'Love is disdained when it doth look at kings'; was not Elizabeth a veritable king among kings, and did not Essex, even up to the last, continue to protest his 'love' for her? Were there not many occasions when he considered himself 'doomed' by her displeasure? The same wish for the life of a hermit is expressed in other poems and letters, particularly:

> Happy were he could finish forth his fate
> In some unhaunted desert, most obscure
> From all society, from loue and hate
> Of worldly folkes, there might he sleep secure.*

In fact the whole poem fits exactly with what may be called Essex's 'Wanstead mood'. The fourth stanza runs as follows:

> You woods in you the fairest Nimphs haue walked,
> Nimphes at whose sight all harts did yeeld to Loue,
> You woods in whom deere louers oft have talked,
> How doe you now a place of mourning proue,
> Wansted my Mistres saith this is the doome,
> Thou art loues Childbed, Nursery and Tombe.

Surely 'the fairest Nimphs' were Elizabeth and her ladies when she visited Wanstead during the progress of 1578. For her visit the Earl of Leicester gave an elaborate entertainment written by Philip Sidney, called *The May Lady*. Nichols† reprints the following account of Elizabeth's meeting with some of the characters of the interlude:

From Theobald's, the residence of the Lord Treasurer, the Queen, after visiting Mr Bache's at Stanstead Abbas, proceeded to Barrett's at Bell-house, a fine old mansion, in the way to Wanstead, in Waltham Forest, which was the Earle of Leicester's seat, where she was entertained by the following dramatic inter-lude, written on the occasion by Sir Philip Sidney, and printed at the end of his 'Arcadia'; the subject of which was a contention between a Forester and a Shepherd for the May-Lady. Her most Excellent Majesty walking in Wanstead Garden, as she passed down into the Grove, there came suddenly among the train one apparalled like an Honest Man's Wife of the Country;

* *The Poems of Robert Devereux, Earl of Essex.* Ed. A. E. Grosart (1872–6). Fuller's Worthies Library, Vol. 4.
† *The Progresses of Queen Elizabeth*, Vol. II, p. 94.

where crying out for justice, and desiring all the Lords and Gentlemen to speak a good word for her, she was brought to the Presence of Her Majesty, to whom upon her knees she offered a supplication. . . .*

The second stanza has given rise to a number of variant readings from editors who have transcribed it into modern spelling. Here is the original:

> Experience which repentance onely brings,
> Doth bid mee now my hart from loue estrange,
> Loue is disdained when it doth looke at Kings,
> And loue loe placed base and apt to change:
> Ther power doth take from him his liberty,
> Hir want of worth makes him in cradell die.

The earliest editor to lift the poem from the song-book was Thomas Oliphant. For the final couplet he gives:

> Their power doth take from him his liberty,
> Her want of worth makes him in cradle die.†

John Payne Collier compromises between old and new spelling with:

> Their power doth take from him his liberty,
> Hir want of worth makes him in cradell die.‡

Dr. Fellowes has another version:

> There power doth take from us his liberty;
> Her want of worth makes him in cradle die.§

The editors of *John Dowland Ayres for Four Voices*‖ give a reading all their own:

> Their power doth take from him his liberty;
> Her want of worth makes him in cradle lie.

There is, of course, no problem about the last line. 'Hir' is the normal Elizabethan spelling of 'her' and there is no single deviation from this usage throughout *The Second Booke*, where some thirty-nine instances are found. The last word is undoubtedly 'die'. 'There', in the penultimate line, allows more room for uncertainty. As meaning 'there' it occurs five times in this volume; as 'their', never. Statistically, then, Dr. Fellowes is justified in his reading, and the meaning could be 'At Court power doth take from Love his

* Dr. Fellowes, in *English Madrigal Verse*, observes that this entertainment was given on the occasion of the Queen's visit to Chancellor Rich in 1561. Philip Sidney was born in 1554. Even in those days of precocious scholarship he would hardly have been writing interludes at the age of seven. It was, of course, as Nichols makes clear, for the entertainment of 1578 that Sidney's *May-Lady* was written.

† *La Musa Madrigalesca* (1837).

‡ *Lyrical Poems, selected from musical publications between the years 1589 and 1600* (1844).

§ *The English School of Lutenist Song Writers* (1920).

‖ *Musica Britannica*, Vol. 6 (1955).

liberty' (there is no possible excuse for the use of 'us'), but I think the majority opinion must be accepted on the strength of its meaning, and that 'ther' is not the usual abbreviation for 'there', but is a misprint for 'their'. The meaning then becomes 'The power of Kings doth take from Love his liberty'.

'If fluds of teares could cleanse my follies past' (No. 11). The first three lines of the six-line stanza are set with conventional harmony, and in what, with note values halved, may conveniently be expressed as $\frac{3}{2}$ in a bar, but on the fourth line the rhythm changes to $\frac{2}{2}$ and the words 'error pardon win' are set with a series of suspensions, the phrase finally resolving, when pardon is won, upon the chord of A major:

The two stanzas were first printed, without name, initial or any other distinguishing rubric, as the final poem of those that were added, possibly by the printer Thomas Newman, at the end of the surreptitious edition of Sir Philip Sidney's *Astrophel and Stella* which appeared in 1591, with a prefatory epistle by Thomas Nashe. Dowland has only three variants from Newman's text, of which the most important is 'breede' instead of 'breath' in stanza two, line four. This is closer agreement than exists with any of the other several versions of the words, and it is likely he used this volume, or a subsequent printing, for his source. John Payne Collier, in his Introduction to *Pierce Penilesse his supplication to the deuill* (1592),[*] ascribes the stanzas to Nashe, and points out that their existence 'has never been hinted at by any of the biographers of Nash, nor by a single bibliographical antiquary'. Grosart makes no mention of them in his *Complete Works of Thomas Nashe* (1883–5), but R. B. McKerrow[†] includes them among the 'Doubtful Works' (Vol. III [1905], p. 396), although he expresses the opinion that they are probably not by him (Vol. V, 1910, pp. 139–40). Bond[‡] ascribes them to Lyly, but produces no convincing evidence to support the claim. As already noted on p. 233, these stanzas were printed in all three editions of John Forbes's *Songs and Fancies* to the tune of 'Sleep wayward thoughts', and in this form the song

[*] The Shakespeare Society, 1842, pp. xxi–xxii.
[†] *Complete Works of Thomas Nashe*.
[‡] op. cit., Vol. III, p. 484.

continued to be known in Scotland until the late years of the seventeenth century. Forbes adds the following stanza to the two given by Dowland:

> Since man is nothing but a mass of clay,
> Our days not else but shadows on the wall:
> Trust in the Lord who lives and lasts for ay;
> Whose favor found will neither fade nor fail.
> My God to thee I resign my mouth and mind:
> No trust in youth, in youth, nor faith in age I find.

Thomas Bateson also set the first stanza for solo voice and three viols in his *Second Set of Madrigales to 3. 4. 5. and 6. Parts: Apt for Viols and Voyces* (1618), and William Corkine set a similar poem, 'If streames of teares Could lessen extreame griefe', in his *Ayres to Sing and Play to the Lute and Basse Violl* (1610). Edward Doughtie★ speaks of a closely related poem (Elegie III) from Giles Fletcher's *Licia* (n.d. 1593) and suggests all three may have been based on a foreign original. Another setting, different from either Dowland's or Bateson's, and with two additional stanzas, is found in Tenbury MS 1019.

The close similarity of the opening bars of Bateson's tenor part with Dowland's Canto part can hardly be coincidence. Either Bateson knew Dowland's setting, or both were drawn from an already existing melody:

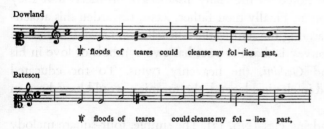

'Fine knacks for ladies' (No. 12) is another song in strophic form with a lively and charming melody. The rhythmic fidelity of words and music is perfectly worked out in the first stanza; the second and third only fall slightly short of the same excellence. The main interest lies in the Canto part, the accompaniment being largely chordal in structure with only occasional independent movement from the lower voices. This song inevitably calls to mind the pedlar's songs that Shakespeare gave to Autolycus in *The Winter's Tale*, 'Lawn as white as driven snow' and 'Will you buy any tape', but these lack the wise saws wrapped up in the light-hearted lines of Dowland's song; saws which, in many different guises, proclaim that virtue may be hidden in a plain exterior and that a loving heart may be concealed under a beggar's rags. In this respect 'Fine knacks' comes nearer to Thomas Whythorne's 'Buy

★ op. cit.

new Broome★ in which proverbial sayings are also brought into the text, in this case 'The new broom sweepeth clean'; 'The hot love is soon cold'; and 'The temp'rate fire doth make the sweet'st malt'. In the fourth line of the second stanza Dr. Fellowes has altered the word 'orienst' to read 'Orient's'. This is quite unnecessary. Orienst is a good Elizabethan word, the superlative of orient, meaning of superlative value or brilliance, as pearls from the Orient were considered to be.† A more difficult problem of interpretation lies in lines three and four of the third stanza and up till now I have seen no satisfactory explanation:

> But [in] my heart where duety serues and loues,
> Turtels & twins, courts brood, a heauenly paier,

'Turtels' is, of course, the old name for turtle-doves, which according to the *O.E.D.*, are noted for soft cooing and affection for mate and young. Brood, also according to the *O.E.D.*, has the specific meaning of a hatch of young birds or other egg-produced animals: 'courts brood, a heauenly paier' stands then for the *Dioscuri*,‡ Castor and Pollux, the royal twins who, together with their sister Helen, were hatched from a single egg, laid by their mother, Leda Queen of Lacedæmon, after she had been ravished by Zeus. During their lives these twins became noted for the many instances of brotherly love they showed towards each other. Finally their father, Zeus, rewarded this attachment by placing them among the stars as the constellation *Gemini*. What the lines are intended to convey is that the poet has two symbols of love in his heart, turtle-doves and *Gemini*, the heavenly twins. To the educated Elizabethan, well versed in classical legend, the meaning would have been in no way obscure.

'Now cease my wandring eies' (No. 13). The simple, four-square melody in common time, consisting of two short repeated sections, agrees with all the main characteristics of an almain and may be grouped with Dowland's other songs in dance form.

'Come yee heauy states of night' (No. 14) is more declamatory in style with a very free rhythmic structure. The first three lines of the Canto part are worked on an ingenious pattern. The first word, 'Come' is sung on a rising major third:

Come ──

★ *Songes of three, fower, and five Voyces* (1571), included in *The Second Book of Elizabethan Songs* (1926), edited by Peter Warlock.
† *O.E.D.*
‡ See *A Smaller Classical Dictionary*, Everyman Edition, edited E. H. Blakeney (1910), p. 197.

The next two lines begin with an ascending third in similar rhythm, each from the degree of the scale below the preceding one. Thus the ascending and descending interval are associated as the melody unfolds. The exact repetition of the first three notes is effectively used on the word 'sorrow' in the first bar of the refrain. The stanzas, in which a young woman laments the death of her father, suggest the song must have found its context in a play or masque. In a copy of the Canto and Basso parts in the library of Christ Church,★ MS 439, p. 47, the word 'states' in the first line has been replaced by 'Stars'.

'White as Lillies was her face' (No. 15) is another example that shows Dowland's mastery of his art, clothed in complete simplicity. The setting of the Canto part, except in one instance, is note for syllable all through, with very little change in the note values. The musical material is simple in the extreme, consisting largely of a few short phrases repeated and combined in different order. The first bar is repeated for the beginning of the second line, while the descending interval of a third in the second bar is balanced by an ascending third in the fourth bar:

(Note values halved)

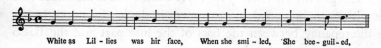

White as Lil‐lies was hir face, When she smi‐led, She bee‐guil‐ed,

The refrain begins on the word 'Quitting'† with the pattern of the first bar placed a fifth higher, followed by the notes of the second bar; the next two bars consist of the repeated Gs of the beginning linked with the notes of the second and third bars; then by the rise of a tone the voice is connected to the rising phrase of the fourth bar and finally falls note by note to the tonic:

Quitt‐ing faith with foule dis‐grace, Ver‐tue ser‐uice thus neg‐lect‐ed,

Heart with sor‐rowes hath in‐fect‐ed.

In the song-book the final line of the last stanza is missing. Dr. Fellowes was able to fill the gap from a copy of *The Second Booke* in the library of St. Michael's College, Tenbury, where a contemporary hand has completed the poem by adding the line indicated here by square brackets:

★ I am indebted to Edward Doughtie for this information.
† The repeat mark is omitted by Dr. Fellowes.

8 For my hart though set at nought,
      Since you will it,
      Spoile and kill it,
I will neuer change my thoughts,
But grieue that beautie ere was borne.
[And so I'll live as one forlorn.]

John Forbes, however, has a different ending in *Songs and Fancies*:

But grieve that Beauty e're was born,
To banish love with froward scorn.

This has a more authentic sound and in the case of Forbes there is at least the possibility that he had seen Morley's setting of the same poem. He included 'With my love my life was nested', No. 4 of Morley's *First Booke of Ayres* (1600), as No. 43 of his own collection and was therefore, it may be presumed, familiar with this publication. Unhappily the only existing copy lacks the last nine numbers including 'White as Lillies' so there is no possibility of comparing the two versions. The word 'Quitting' in the first stanza, 'Quiting' as Forbes gives it, according to the *O.E.D.* means repaying or requiting.

'Wofull hart with griefe oppressed' (No. 16) is treated in a somewhat more elaborate style with some independent movement in the lower voices. In bar one there is a discrepancy between the bass of the lute part and the Basso voice on the opposite page. The lute has:

while the bass voice has:

I suspect that the tablature is incorrect since it is unlikely that the true bass would be left to the voice. If the song were to be performed with Cantus and lute only the C major chord would be intolerably jovial in connection with the words 'wofull hart'. In performance on the lute, however, if the A is added it becomes difficult to hold the suspension, but this would hardly be an adequate reason for omitting it. All the lower voices have a repeat mark at the beginning of the refrain at the words 'those sweet eyes'. This is omitted in the Canto and lute parts, probably accidentally. The second stanza is written as follows:

> Fly my breast, leaue mee forsaken,
> Wherein Griefe his seate hath taken,
>   All his arrowes through mee darting,
> Thou maist liue by hir Sunne-shining,
> I shall suffer no more pining,
>   By thy losse, then by hir parting.

Dr. Fellowes has altered 'thy' in the last line to 'her'; and the editors of the *Ayres for Four Voices*★ have substituted 'my'; surely no change is needed. The poet is apostrophizing his woeful heart when he says 'Fly my breast, leaue mee forsaken' and in the last two lines he means he will suffer no more grief, even in the loss of his own heart (perhaps he means by death) than he will suffer in parting from his love.

'A Shepheard in a shade' (No. 17) is one of Dowland's rare settings of pastoral verse. The loves of shepherds and their nymphs, so popular among the madrigalists, seem to have held only occasional attraction for him. The words are charmingly and neatly set, but no great emotion is expended on them. The change from major to minor adds poignancy to the refrain, particularly to the repeated cry 'Fye on this loue, fye on this loue, it is a foolish thing'.

'Faction that euer dwells' (No. 18). These stanzas appear as No. XXVIII of Fulke Greville's 'Cælica' sonnets, printed in *Certaine Learned and Elegant Workes of the Right Honorable Fulke Lord Brooke* (1633). Fellowes† notes that Dowland changed the name 'Myra' as used by Greville, to 'Joan', in the fourth stanza. It was not Dowland, however, who made the change, since the poem had already appeared with the name 'Ione' in 1591 (in company with 'If fluds of teares') among the 'rare sonnets of divers Noblemen and Gentlemen' in Sir Philip Sidney's *Astrophel and Stella*. In this volume it has the title 'Megliora Spero' and is subscribed 'Finis E.O.'‡ Nevertheless, it seems unlikely that this was Dowland's source, as, in addition to a number of smaller variant readings, an extra stanza appears between stanzas one and two of the song-book:

> *Cupid* which doth aspire, to be God of Desire,
>   Swears he giues lawes:
> That where his arrowes hit, some ioy, some sorrow it,
>   *Fortune* no cause

★ *Musica Britannica*, Vol. 6 (1953).   † *English Madrigal Verse*.
‡ On the strength of these initials A. B. Grosart includes the poem in *The Works of Edward de Vere, Earl of Oxford* (1872–76).

Possibly Dowland was supplied with a copy of the poem in which the second stanza was already omitted. John Payne Collier* makes a curious mistake in transcribing lines one and two of the second stanza. He gives:

> Fortune swears weakest harts,
> The booke of Cupid's darts,

and adds the comment, 'Should we not read *butt* for "booke" in this line? The old broad pronunciation of *butt*, perhaps, caused the error; the printer having composed from his ear.' Since the line is clearly printed 'The booke of *Cupids* arts' in the song-book, his ingenious emendation is beside the point.

'Shall I sue, shall I seeke for grace' (No. 19) is in strophic form and is set in Dowland's simple manner. It is a song of great beauty and subtlety but has at the same time an immediate appeal. The melody is first based on a descending minor third; it then appears in notes of double the original time value; it is later inverted and leads into an ascending scale passage to the note F on the words 'Shall I strive to a heauenly Ioy'. This is followed immediately by a descending phrase on the words 'with an earthly loue?' These are, of course, purely conventional pieces of word painting, but so great is Dowland's art that such devices never obtrude, and in this song they appear to grow inevitably from the organisation of the preceding phrases and to be the exact and only possible means of expressing the words. The two last lines are treated in a similar way, but here, on the words 'the clouds', the Canto part leaps the interval of a fourth to the note G and then falls to the F before descending to the close on the identical phrase previously used for the words for 'an earthly love'. Syllabically and rhythmically the following three stanzas fit the music well, but it was obviously the first that provided the inspiration.

'Tosse not my soule' (No. 20). In the table of contents No. 20 is listed as 'Finding in fields my Siluia all alone', but beside the song stands the rubric 'for Finding in fields: ye shall finde a better dittie'. As the change was presumably made after the printing of the Table, it must have been very much of a last minute decision. Edward Doughtie† raises the interesting point as to whether it was in fact Eastland who made the change, since Dowland was in Denmark and could not have been on the spot to make the substitution himself. In my opinion, however, this is unlikely. Dowland dates the Dedication 'From Helsingnoure in Denmarke the first of Iune. 1600', and the book was entered on July 15th. Even if printing commenced almost immediately after this date it would still have allowed time for

---

* *Lyrical poems, selected from musical publications between the years 1589 and 1600* (1844).
† Unpublished thesis, already quoted.

Dowland's second thoughts to have been dispatched to Eastland or to Mrs.
Dowland by letter. We have no evidence that Eastland had any skill in this
direction and, in spite of his protestations in the 'Epistle to the curteous
Reader', the impression emerges from reading the law suit that his interest in
the venture was primarily financial. On the other hand the poem itself is very
much in Dowland's taste. The poet beseeches Love to give him assurance one
way or the other. Much as he craves happiness, he feels that even to know the
worst is preferable to his state of uncertainty. The setting is contrapuntal and
makes much use of a descending scale passage and its inversion.

At this point, following No. 20, there is a note at the side of the page saying
'The end of the foure parts'.

'Cleare or Cloudie sweet as *Aprill* showring' (No. 21) has an alternative
setting of the first part for four voices, but a fifth voice joins them at the
refrain. The part is headed 'For a treble violl' on the left hand side, and on
the right, 'Quinto'. Words are printed under the music and, presumably, the
intention was that the part should be used by a fifth voice when the song was
performed as an ayre, but should be played an octave higher on the treble
viol when treated as a solo with lute accompaniment. The part is given here
at its original pitch:

Dr. Fellowes omits any mention of the instrumental part in his edition of 1920. It is, however, included, as a fifth voice, in the *Ayres for Four Voices*. Obertello★ compares this poem with Thomas Morley's 'Aprill is in my Mistris face':†

> Aprill is in my Mistris face,
> And Iuly in hir eyes hath place,
> With in hir bosome is September,
> But in hir heart, a could December.

According to Obertello this is the translation of the first stanza of a poem by Livio Celiano, 'Porta nel viso Aprile', from *Rime di diversi celebri poeti* (1587). A translation of the same stanza is also found among the works of Robert Greene:‡

> Faire is my loue for Aprill in her face,
> Hir louely brests September claimes his part,
> And Lordly Iuly in her eyes takes place,
> But colde December dwelleth in her heart.
> Blest be the months, that sets my thoughts on fire,
> Accurst that Month that hindreth my desire.

'Humor say what mak'st thou heere' (No. 22) has the caption 'A Dialogue'. The second voice follows the bass of the lute, and, the layout of the parts suggests, doubles with a bass viol, since the first two lines sung by the treble voice, have no words to the bass. The Altus and Tenore parts are instrumental as far as the chorus and then words are added. The Quintus part, marked 'For a treble Violl' is entirely instrumental, with only the word 'Princes' to cue in the player at the point where the bass voice enters. This complex structure is not mentioned by Dr. Fellowes. There can be little doubt that the song was written for a masque. The words themselves have little merit, but within its dramatic context the piece was probably very effective. A MS copy in the British Museum§ gives a different version of the words:

> Saye fonde love what seekes thowe heere,
> in the sylence of the night,
> heere I seeke those Ioyes my deere,
> that in silent (sic.) most delight,
> nightes heavy humor Calls to sleepe
> But loves humor watch doth keepe
> let never humor hapie prove,
> but that wch onelye pleasethe love.

★ op. cit., pp. 514–16.
† *Madrigalls to Fovre Voyces. The First Booke* (1594), No. 1.
‡ *Plays & Poems*, edited J. C. Collins (1905), Vol. 2, p. 247.
§ Add. 15117, f. 12.

The additional voices and instruments are omitted, and several variants have been introduced into the music. The accompaniment has been greatly simplified and wherever possible the D major chord is written 𝄞 instead of in the more difficult form 𝄞.

THE THIRD AND LAST BOOKE OF SONGS

This volume was entered at Stationers' Hall on February 21st, 1602/3, in the following words:

Thomas Adams Entred for his Copie vnder th[e h]andes of the
wardens A booke called *the Third booke of songes
or ayres newlie Composed to singe to the lute,
Orpharion, or violes, and a Dialough for a bass
and meane Lute with v voices to singe thereto.*
By John Dowland Bacheler in musicke, and Luteniste
to the most highe and mightie Christian, the
FOURTH by the grace of GOD kinge of Denmarke and
Norwaye &c.   vjd*

The title-page border is the same as that used for *The First Booke of Songes*. The full title of the book, contained, as before, in the centre panel, is as follows:

THE THIRD AND / LAST BOOKE / OF SONGS OR / AIRES./ Newly composed to sing to the/ *Lute, Orpharion, or viols, and a dia-* / logue for a base and meane/Lute with fiue voices to/ sing thereto. *By* IOHN DOWLAND, *Bacheler* / *in Musicke, and Lutenist to the most*/ *high and mightie* CHRISTIAN/*the fourth by the grace of God*/*king of Denmark and Norwey, &c.*

In the lower panel are the motto and the imprint:

Bona quò communiora eò meliora.
Printed at London by P.S. [Peter Short] for Thomas Adams,/ *and are to be sold at the signe of the white Lion in* / Paules Churchyard, by the assignement of a Pa-/ tent granted to Thomas Morley. 1603.

On the verso of the title-page are printed the arms of Sir John Souch (or Zouch)† with eight quarterings. Dowland, however, still refers to him as "Iohn Souch Esquire" in the dedication, which goes as follows:

TO MY HONORABLE GOOD FRIEND
Iohn Souch Esquire, for many curtesies for which I imbol-*den my selfe,*

* Arber, op. cit., Vol. III, f. 92b.
† Knighted April 23rd, 1603.

presuming of his good fauour, to present this simple worke, as a token of my thankefulnes.

The estimation and kindnes which I haue euer bountifully receiued from your fauour, haue mooued me to present this nouelty of musick to you, who of al others are fittest to iudge of it, and worthiest out of your loue to protect it. If I gaue life to these, you gaue spirit to me; for it is alwaies the worthy respect of others that makes arte prosper in it selfe. That I may therefore professe, and make manifest to the world both your singular affection to me, and my gratefull minde in my weake ability to you, I haue here prefixt your honourable name, as a bulwark of safetie, and a title of grace, thinking my selfe no way able to deserue your fauours more, then by farther engaging my selfe to you for this your noble presumed patronage. He that hath acknowledged a fauour, they say, hath halfe repaide it: and if such payment may passe for currant, I shal be euer readie to grow the one halfe out of your debt, though how that should be I knowe not, since I owe my selfe (and more, if it were possible) vnto you. Accept me wholy then I beseech you, in what tearmes you please, being euer in my vttermost service

Deuoted to your Honours kindnesse,

IOHN DOWLAND.

The Epistle to the Reader.

THE applause of them that iudge, is the incouragement of those that write: My first two bookes of aires speed so well that they haue produced a third, which they haue fetcht far from home, and brought euen through the most perilous seas, where hauing escapt so many sharpe rocks, I hope they shall not be wrackt on land by curious and biting censures. As in a hiue of bees al labour alike to lay vp honny opposing them selves against none but fruitles drones; so in the house of learning and fame, all good indeuourers should striue to ad somewhat that is good, not malicing one an other, but altogether bandying against the idle and malicious ignorant. My labours for my part I freely offer to euerie mans iudgement, presuming, that fauour once attayned, is more easily encreased then lost.

IOHN DOWLAND.

A Table of all the Songs contained in/*this Booke*

XI.   Lend your eares to my sorrow good people.
XII.   By a fountaine where I lay.
XIII.   Oh what hath ouerwrought my all amazed thought.
XIIII. Farewell vnkind farewell.
XV.   Weepe you no more sad fountaines.
XVI.   Fie on this faining, is loue without desire.
XVII.   I must complaine, yet doe enioy.
XVIII. It was a time when silly Bees could speake.
XIX.   The lowest trees haue tops.
XX.   What poore Astronomers are they.
XXI.   Come when I call, or tarrie till I come.

'Farewell too faire' (No. 1). The most noticeable feature of this song is the sudden change, when, from the key of the first part which vacillates between A major and minor, with the words 'This is proud beauties true anatomie', the refrain begins in the key of G major.

'Time stands still with gazing on her face' (No. 2). The setting of the last three lines of the stanza is a most beautiful piece of writing on a recurring note pattern:

In the second stanza, it must be admitted, words and music fit together exceedingly badly, moreover the sense is extremely involved and obscure. Thomas Oliphant includes a garbled version of the first stanza in *La Musa Madrigalesca* (1837) with the waspish comment: 'These lines must surely have been addressed to Queen Elizabeth. The flattery is too gross for any body but her to have swallowed.'

'Behold a wonder here' (No. 3). Oliphant notes: 'Very much in the same style as the preceding song: probably by the same author, and with a similar intention.' Dowland may even have intended to underline the similarity when he used precisely the same note pattern (though rhythmically different) for the last phrase, as he used for the end of 'Time stands still':

Edward Doughtie suggests this song may have had a place in 'A deuice made by the Earle of Essex for the entertainment of the Queene'. The suggestion is based on the similarity of the idea expressed in the poem to the 'argument' of the entertainment, and, in particular, with the similarity of the lines 'Behold a wonder here Loue hath receiu'd his sight' and a phrase in the text.* In the device a blind Indian prince is presented to the Queen, while his guide explains that he has come on the advice of an oracle, in order that Elizabeth may cure his blindness. The cure is, apparently, brought about, and the boy is then revealed to be Cupid. It is at this point that Doughtie thinks the song may have been sung, although, as he points out, there is no such indication in the text. The guide then begs Elizabeth to admit Cupid to her Court for 'now that loue hath gotten possession of his sight, there can be no error in policie or dignity to receiue him'.

If this song did in fact have a place in the device then possibly 'Time stands still' was also included since the speaking of such an entertainment would almost certainly have been interspersed with both vocal and instrumental music.

Doughtie adds a note that Essex's authorship is doubtful and refers to James Spedding, *The Letters and Life of Francis Bacon*, Vol. I (1861), 374–392, where the relationship of this device and another entertainment given by Essex, but known to have been written by Bacon, is discussed.

'Daphne was not so chaste as she was changing' (No. 4). This very bitter pair of stanzas is most beautifully set. The last line paints the words 'false light' with a remarkable cross rhythm:

* Public Record Office. S.P. 12/254, No. 67. Calendared under the year 1595.

still the false light the false light of thy trait-er - ous fires.

'Me me and none but me' (No. 5). The extraordinary beauty of this song lies in a deeply felt grief expressed in terms of complete simplicity. Even where the Cantus line makes the conventional upward movement on the words 'fly to heauen aboue' the voice seems impelled in its flight by the intensity of the emotion. In the lower voices too, the words are treated carefully, without cuts or meaningless repetition. There is no trace of the melancholic vogue, and the stanzas appear to have evoked a response in Dowland which perhaps reflected some personal sorrow in his own life.

'When Phœbus first did Daphne loue' (No. 6) is a light-heartedly raffish little song, rather unusual in its character among the graver stanzas generally chosen by Dowland. The words are printed in *Poems, Written by the Right Honorable William Earl of Pembroke Lord Steward of his Majesties Household. Whereof Many of which are answered by way of Repartee By Sᵣ Benjamin Ruddier, Knight* (1660). The presence of the poem in this volume is not, however, conclusive evidence that either Pembroke or Sir Benjamin Ruddier (or Rudyard) was the author. The collection was made by John Donne the younger and in the epistle 'To the Reader' he explains how the poems came into his hands:

In the collecting of these Poemes, (which were chiefly preserved by the greatest Masters of Musick, all the Sonnets being set by them) I was fain first to send to Mr Henry Laws, who furnishing me with some, directed me for the rest, to send into Germany to Mr Laneere,* who by his great skill gave a life and harmony to all that he set; so that if by their wandring some be surreptitiously got into their company; or, if (the Author leaving no other issue but these of his brain) some of these Nymphs seem a little more wanton than the rest, of which there are but two or three Copies can be suspected, they desire that they may not make their retreat, untill the next Impression; and then you will find many more ready to supply their room, which were not come unto my hands when I published these.

From this it is clear that Donne himself was not entirely certain about the

---

* Nicholas Lanier or Laniere (1588–1666). Painter, singer and composer. Appointed Master of the King's Music in 1626. Lived in the Netherlands during the Commonwealth, but returned to his post at Court at the Restoration.

ascription of some of the poems, and Sir S. Egerton Brydges* says 'there are among them, unnoticed, poems of Sir Walter Raleigh, Carew and others'. In this collection the poem is called 'Apollo's Oath', and has a third stanza:

> Yet silly they, when all is done,
> Complain our wits their hearts have won;
> When 'tis for fear that they should bee
> Like *Daphne*, turn'd into a Tree:
> And who herself would so abuse,
> To be a tree, if she could chuse.

Edward Doughtie lists five other sources for the poem, all in MSS, which show a number of variant readings. One of these, Bod. Add. B.97 (after 1609), f. 18ʳ, has a copy headed 'A songe' and subscribed 'Ch:Riues', 'who' Doughtie says 'probably is the author of the added fourth stanza':

> By this they gett sweet mothers name,
> And are not barren wᶜʰ were blame,
> Besides by this procure they can,
> The world a child, the prince a man.
> Now *Stoick* tell me yf in this,
> That any thing be done amisse.

Another Bodleian MS, CCC 328 (*c.* 1650), f. 74ʳᵛ, headed 'Apollo's oath A sonnet' has a note in the margin, added later, 'Pemb. p. 115'. Fellowes† suggests the words 'but one' were interpolated by the composer, in the last line of the first stanza. Doughtie confirms that all the copies of the poem, except that of the song-book, have 'None should live a maid'. It was probably in compliment to the elderly virgin on the throne that the change was made. The story of Daphne and Apollo is told by Ovid in the *Metamorphoses*. The translation most widely used at the time was that of Arthur Golding, in ballad metre, first printed in 1567.

'Say loue if euer thou didst find' (No. 7) is a fast moving, wittily constructed song almost entirely chordal in character. The compass of the cantus part is confined to a sixth, and, with the exception of one quaver, crotchets only are used with a minim to end each line. Yet from these deliberately limited means a most memorable tune is evolved with some particularly attractive features, such as the answering notes between the Cantus and lute (or Cantus and three voices) on the repeated short syllables of the penultimate line in each verse:

---

* *Poems of William Herbert Third Earl of Pembroke, K.G., and Sir Benjamin Rudyard* (1817). p. xii.
† *English Madrigal Verse* (1929).

Oliphant* says of this song: 'These very fantastic lines evidently apply to the Maiden Queen, who albeit she was in love with every proper man about the court, yet forsooth must compare herself to the icicle on Dian's temple.' Fellowes† calls attention to the line 'There is no queene of loue but she', and notes that it also occurs in George Mason and John Earsden's *Ayres that were sung and played at Brougham Castle* (1618), No. 6, 'Robin is a louely lad'.

'Flow not so fast yee fountaines' (No. 8). Moved as always by the poetic image of tears, Dowland produces in this song another deeply felt masterpiece. The dropping of the salt tears is exquisitely illustrated by the gradually falling line of the Cantus part, after the leap of an octave, and the repeated pattern of dotted notes on the word 'dropping':

'What if I neuer speede' (No. 9). This fast-moving setting of a half ironic poem has all the appearance of having been primarily composed for four

* op. cit., p. 171.
† *English Madrigal Verse*, p. 616.

voices and only subsequently having been given a lute accompaniment. The tune is first rate and easily memorable. Rhythmically it fits the words admirably but emotionally it is somewhat detached, and would be equally satisfactory on instruments.

'Loue stood amaz'd at sweet beauties paine' (No. 10) is a complete contrast to the preceding song, being highly dramatic, with the music, as the following passage will show, unmistakably inspired by the meaning of the words:

'Lend your eares to my sorrow good people' (No. 11) is a beautiful song full of quiet melancholy. The first line is set to an elaborate cross rhythm, while the beginning of the last line of the stanza 'in sad despaire can find no ease of tormenting' suddenly changes to trochaic metre, reminiscent of the treatment of the words 'sad dispaire' in 'Now O now I needs must part' (*First Booke*, No. 6). Dr. Fellowes★ points to the phrase 'rude like to my rhyming' and shows how it is illustrated by the poet by the express avoidance of rhyme in the last three lines of the stanza although the two following stanzas are treated regularly.

'By a fountaine where I lay' (No. 12) is in a key which, as far as it may be said to be a key at all, is G minor, but the frequent change of E flat to E natural gives the song a modal flavour blended with melancholy, as if the pastoral pleasures and the welcome to the shepherds' Queen were touched by the sadness of fleeting youth and ever-present death. Oliphant,† completely in-

★ *English Madrigal Verse* (1929).
† op. cit., p. 173.

sensitive to the charm of this song, says 'Another dish of flattery somewhat in the Oriana style . . .' An obsolete word and a technical term perhaps need explanation: 'cheere', according to the *O.E.D.*, means face or expression, and 'ground', in this case short for 'ground bass', means a melodic figure used as a bass in a composition, constantly repeated without change except by way of transposition, while the upper structure of the music is developed freely at the composer's will.

'Oh what hath ouerwrought my all amazed thought' (No. 13) is con-structed on an unusual pattern. The three stanzas consist of two of six lines and one of five. Dowland has set the first two to the same music and the third differently. This, I feel, is one of Dowland's less distinguished works. There is little or no rhythmic or harmonic subtlety and the repetitions become some-what boring. The poem suggests, however, that the song may have been written for a masque, and possibly in its context it was effective, particularly if it were designed to accompany a dance.

'Farewell vnkind farewell' (No. 14). Although this song appears to have been written to fit a particular situation in a play, the words are set with such distinction that the composition stands on its own merit. The sentiments expressed are, apparently, those of a young girl eloping from the home of her rich father, taking with her his fortune. Were it not that there is no record of any such occasion it would be tempting to suggest the song could have been interpolated into a performance of *The Merchant of Venice*, at the point where Jessica runs off with Lorenzo, carrying with her Shylock's ducats. The situation is parallel even down to the lines 'Loue, not in the bloud (i.e. her Jewish blood), but in the spirit doth lie'. The objection to the idea of the song's having been connected with a play was raised by Cecil Hill★ on the grounds that the title-page of this volume describes the contents as being 'Newly composed', and that Dowland was, at this period, in Denmark, and would therefore not have been in a position to contribute the setting to a play. Dowland's unbroken residence in Denmark from the time of the publi-cation of *The Second Booke* till his arrival in London in February 1603 is far from certain. In view of the fact that he may have visited London in late 1600 or early 1601 (see p. 57), Mr. Hill's point is hardly proved. This song has the most deceptive appearance of ingenuousness, perhaps to correspond with the outward character of the young woman, but the cross-rhythm on the words 'Since my heart holds my loue most deare' and the repeated descending note pattern on the words 'then farewell', with the imitations in the lower voices, are Dowland at his most artificial, in the truly Elizabethan sense of the word. In the first stanza:

★ *The Musical Times*, Vol. 105, No. 1453, p. 199.

Farewell vnkind farewell, to mee no more a father,
   since my heart holdes my loue most deare:
The wealth which thou doest reape, anothers hand must gather,
Though thy heart still lies buried there,
   Then farewell, O farewell,
Welcome my loue, welcome my ioy for euer.

Dr. Fellowes alters the word 'thy' in the fourth line, to 'my'. This change distorts the meaning. The girl is addressing her father and what she says is: her own heart holds her love most dear, but her father's heart ('thy' heart) is buried in his money bags, even though someone else will enjoy the benefit of his wealth. The other change, in the second line of the second stanza, 'Makes my mind to liue, though my meanes do die' into 'though my meanes to die' seems unnecessary. See also p. 121.

'Weepe you no more sad fountaines' (No. 15) is among the most beautiful of all Dowland's songs. Here he has freed himself from all conventions of word-painting, and relies on the purely musical perfection of each phrase to express the words. Even on 'but my sunnes heauenly eyes', although the voice rises, as might have been expected, it does so more to balance the preceding descending phrase than in deference to convention. The last section, initiated by the lute or Altus voice, with the Cantus entering in imitation a fourth higher and gradually falling till it rests on the major third of the final chord, is extraordinarily expressive. The rhythmic structure is entirely dictated by the flow of the words, and bar lines are reduced to a minimum so that no preconceived idea of accentuation shall interfere with the verbal rhythm:

The printer was in some uncertainty about the word 'lie' or 'lies' in the last line. As can be seen in the above example he gives it once each way in the Cantus part. In the Altus he gives 'ly' twice and 'lies' once; the Tenor has 'ly' three times; and the Bassus, 'lies' twice. Of the alternatives Dr. Fellowes has chosen 'lies'. I find the reading 'lie' preferable. It is, after all, the 'sunnes heauenly eyes' that 'now lie sleeping', and even though Elizabethan syntax appears to have allowed disagreement between subject and verb, where there is agreement in some of the voices it seems more likely the form 'lie' was intended in all. Perhaps it was confusion with the second stanza, where, clearly, 'lies' is correct, that gave rise to the discrepancies.

'Fie on this faining' (No. 16) is an uncomplicated melody, resembling an almain in construction. The bitterness of the words, however, is illustrated with discords—augmented and diminished fifths.

'I must complaine, yet doe enioy my loue' (No. 17). The words of this song are by Thomas Campian, and it is interesting to compare the poet's own setting* with that of Dowland. Within the limits set by musical style in the early seventeenth century the two versions could hardly be more different. Campian's tune is graceful, evenly flowing, set in common time throughout, with chordal accompaniment in unadventurous harmony. Words or phrases within the lines are never repeated, and the setting, with one exception, is note for syllable. The third and fourth lines are sung to the repeated twelve bars of the first and second; the fifth and sixth lines are set in a further twelve bars, which are then repeated, making a formal and symmetrical whole. Dowland, on the other hand, through-composes the stanza from beginning to end; his rhythm is free, and he repeats words and phrases for emphasis, such as 'enioy, enioy my loue', the last three words being set to a cross-rhythm. 'Thence is my griefe' is drawn out in an extended cry:

On the words 'she had no leisure' and the repeat of the phrase the music goes into a triple measure, then for a final repeat of 'no leisure' and the completion of the sentence there is a return to common time:

* *The Third and Fourth Booke of Ayres* (1617?), *The Fourth Booke*, No. 17.

She has no lei-sure she has no lei-sure   no lei-sure left   to   make   her true,

As can be seen from these two excerpts, Dowland makes effective play with both contrapuntal and chordal treatment. With the first four lines of the stanza the voices move independently, then, at the beginning of the last couplet, all move together simultaneously till their ways part again in the last two bars.

'It was a time when silly Bees could speake' (No. 18). Edward Doughtie[*] notes twenty-two other sixteenth- and seventeenth-century sources for this poem, eleven of which attribute it to Robert Devereux, second Earl of Essex. Others, while not actually bearing Essex's name, are found among papers connected with him. Three MSS assign it to Henry Cuff, alternatively described as 'Chaplaine 'or 'Secretary' to Essex. On the strength of one source only,[†] R. Warwick Bond claims the poem for John Lyly.[‡] In spite of some interesting stylistic and biographical material produced in support of the ascription, the evidence is overwhelmingly in favour of Essex. The Rawlinson MS is interesting, however, in that the poem was copied into the MS immediately preceding one dated 1598. This year and the one before would both correspond with periods when Essex retired to Wanstead,[§] sick with a distempered spirit at his failure to impose his ambitions on the ageing, but still imperious, Queen. His self-imposed exile from the Court would have inspired just such sentiments as the poem expresses. The poem also reflects precisely the image—fortune's victim—that Dowland was coming to associate with himself, and in setting the lines:

> And in that time I was a sillie Bee,
>> who fed on Time until my heart gan break,
> yet neuer found the time would fauour mee.
>> of all the swarme I onely did not thrive,
> yet brought I waxe and honey to the hiue,

he must have experienced the bitterness of his own exiled condition in that of

---

[*] op. cit., pp. 448–54.
[†] Bod. Rawl. MS Poet. 148, ff. 87–8.
[‡] *The Complete Works* (1902), Vol. 3, pp. 445–7.
[§] See p. 261.

Essex. But if he still had ambitions in the direction of the English Court, surely this was a most injudicious moment to bring this song into the light of day. At the time *The Third Booke* was entered Essex had been dead for two years, and the Queen, still broken by the shock of his treason and execution, was within a few weeks of her own end. Dowland was not to know that she would not recover from her illness and hear of the publication of the song. It could hardly be expected that his selection for setting to music of Essex's undisguised and bitter complaint would endear him to the Queen or predispose her to grant him a post at Court.

'The lowest trees haue tops' (No. 19). Whether treated as a solo song or as a four-part ayre, the setting of these stanzas has a curiously angular quality, largely the result of the many leaps of a fourth, a fifth, a sixth and an octave, used to express the antithetic ideas of the poem. The first bar is typical, with the downward and upward leaps of a fifth in the Cantus part, to express 'low' and 'tops':

The low-est trees haue tops

Though very ingenious, this, in my opinion, is one of Dowland's less satisfactory compositions, the word painting having got somewhat out of hand. The stanzas were first printed, with the subscription *Incerto*, in Francis Davison's *A Poetical Rhapsody* (1602). H. E. Rollins, in the notes to his edition of 1931, gives the opinion that this volume was Dowland's source. Davison included the title in his MS 'Catalog of all the Poems in Rhyme & measured Verse by A. W.',[*] which initials, both Rollins and W. J. Linton[†] believe, stand for Anonymous Writer. The stanzas are, however, ascribed to Sir Edward Dyer in Bod. MS Rawl. Poet. 148, f. 103. Of the copy in Bod. MS Tanner 169, f. 192^v, Ruth Hughey says: 'an entry in the commonplace book of Sir Stephen Powle, with an introductory comment dated September 7, 1618. "Verses given as I suppose by Mr Lea to Laut; intimating that secret Loue speakes little but sithence I did vnderstand that they were Sr W. Rawleighs verses to Queen Elizabeth: in the beginning of his fauours" (the latter portion apparently written later).'[‡] She gives eleven sources for the

[*] Included in *A Poetical Rhapsody*, Vol. II (1932), pp. 54–62.
[†] *Rare Poems of the Sixteenth and Seventeenth Centuries* (1882), p. 260.
[‡] *The Arundel Harington Manuscript* (1960), Vol. II, p. 306.

poem, of which three, Tanner 169, Bod. MS Malone 19, f. 50ᵛ, and Folger MS 452, 4, f. 37, follow stanza one with these lines:

> The Ermin hath the fairest skin on earth
> Yett doth she chuse the wezell for her peere
> The Panther hath a sweet perfumed breath
> Yett doth she suffer apes to draw her neere
> Noe flower more fresh, then is the damaske rose
> Yett next her side the nettle often growes.*

There are many variant readings between the different sources all of which are fully listed by Hughey.

'What poore Astronomers are they' (No. 20). This is light and charming, and the words are dextrously set, but the song as a whole has no particular distinction. It is mainly chordal in structure, but in the last couplet the texture is more fluid with quaver figures in the bass. A. B. Grosart† ascribes the stanzas to Nicholas Breton on the strength of the lines in *Wits Priuate Wealth* (1611), p. 7/2, 1.21, 'Hee that makes beauty a starre, studies a false Astronomy, and he that is soundly in love, needs no further purgatory'. These words he compares with:

> What poore Astronomers are they,
> take wome[n]s eies for stars

and adds, 'I have little or no hesitation in claiming the anonymous lyric for Breton.' Since the song-book antedated *Wits Priuate Wealth* by eight years the argument is not altogether convincing. Breton could, consciously or unconsciously, have picked up the phrase from the song, or some such commonplace may have been current at the time, and have found its way into both the poem and Breton's work entirely independently.

'Come when I call, or tarrie till I come. A Dialogue' (No. 21). This song is scored for two solo voices, a lute in G; a bass lute a fourth below; Quintus, Tenor and Bassus parts for viols with voices added to each of these parts at the chorus. The setting of the words is based largely on patterns of repeated notes. This characteristic becomes more accentuated at the chorus, with a point of imitation which passes from voice to voice.

A PILGRIMES SOLACE

Dowland's fourth book of songs was entered in the Stationers' Register on October 28th, 1611:

---

* Quoted by Hughey from Folger MS 452, 4.
† *Nicholas Breton, Works in Verse and Prose* (1879), Vol. I, Gleanings No. 9.

Matthue Lownes	Entred for their Copy by/ assignmente from William
John Browne	Barley/ and with the consent of master/ [H] umfrey
Thomas Snodham	Lownes warden vnder/ his hand *A booke of Ayres made/ and sett forth bothe for the/ Lute and basse vyoll with voyces/ to singe to*, by *John Dowland* vjd*

McKerrow and Ferguson† give the following description of the title-page border:

249.　(246 × 175 mm., enclosing 176 × 108 mm.) A compartment of white interlaced strap work on a black criblé ground.

　　Apparently copied from a compartment used in 1544
　　at Paris by Simon de Colines (Orontii Finaei In sex
　　priores libros Geometricordum clementorum Euclides
　　demonstrationes) or from a very similar one used
　　also at Paris by Michel de Vascosan in 1555 (Le
　　Féron, Catalogue des illustres Mareschaulx de France),
　　see A. F. Johnson, *One Hundred Title-Pages*, p. 49.

The full text of the title-page is as follows:

A Pilgrimes Solace.

Wherein is contained Musicall/ Harmonie of 3. 4. and 5 parts, to be / sung and plaid with the Lute/ and Viols. By *John Douland*, Batchelor of Musicke in/ both the Vniursities: and Lutenist to the/ Right Honourable the/ Lord Walden.

1612
LONDON.

Printed for *M.L. J.B.* and *T.S.*‡ by the Assignment of/ *William Barley.*

The preliminary matter is as follows, the dedication being to the patron in whose service he was at the time:

TO THE RIGHT HOnorable/ *THEOPHILUS*, LORD WALDEN, SONNE/ AND HEIRE TO THE MOST NOBLE, *THOMAS*, BARON/ OF WALDEN, EARLE OF SUFFOLKE, LORD CHAMBERLAINE/ OF HIS MAIESTIES HOUSEHOLD, KNIGHT OF THE MOST/ Noble Order of the Garter, and one of his Maiesties most Honourable/ *Priuie Counsell.*

Most Honoured Lord:

As to excell in any qualitie is very rare, so is it a hard thing to finde out those that fauour Vertue and Learning; but such being found, men of Iudgment are drawne (I know not by what Sympathie) to loue and Honor them, as the Saints and Soueraignes of their affections and deuices: wherefore (most Worthy Lord) your Honor being of all men noted (as natural borne heire of your most Renowned father and mother) to be the onely and alone Supporter of goodnes and excellencie, knowne to none better (vnles I should be the

---

* Arber, op. cit., Vol. III, f. 212b.
† op. cit.　　‡ Matthew Lownes, John Brown and Thomas Snodham.

most vngratefull of all others) then my selfe, who am held vp onely by your
gratious hand; for which I can shew no other meanes of thankfulnes then these
simple fruits of my poore endeauors which I most humbly present as a publike
pledge from a true and deuoted heart, hoping hereafter to performe something, wherein I shall shew my selfe more worthy of your Honorable
seruice. In the meane time you shall haue a poore mans praiers for your
Lordships continuall health and dayly increase of Honor.

Your Honours/ humble seruant

IOHN DOWLAND.

TO THE READER.

Worthy Gentlemen, and my louing Country men; mooued by your many
and fore-tasted courtesies, I am constrained to appeare againe vnto you. True
it is, I haue lien long obscured from your sight, because I receiued a Kingly
entertainment in a forraine climate, which could not attaine to any (though
neuer so meane) place at home, yet haue I held vp my head within this
Horizon, and not altogether beene vnaffected elsewhere. Since some part of
my poore labours haue found fauour in the greatest part of Europes, and
beene printed in eight most famous Cities beyond the Seas. *viz*: *Paris,
Antwerpe, Collien, Nurenburge, Franckfort, Leipzig, Amsterdam,* and *Hamburge*:*
(yea and some of them also authorized vnder the Emperours royall
priuiledge,) yet I must tell you, as I haue beene a stranger; so haue I againe
found strange entertainment since my returne; especially by the opposition
of two sorts of people that shroude themselues vnder the title of Musitians.
The first are some simple Cantors, or vocall singers, who though they seeme
excellent in their blinde Diuision-making, are meerely ignorant, euen in the
first elements of Musicke, and also in the true order of the mutation of the
Hexachord† in the *Systeme*, (which hath ben approued by all the learned and

---

* He must surely mean that works of his have been included in collections printed in those
cities, not that complete books of his compositions have appeared. If this is so, the following
publications could fulfil the conditions of time and place:
Paris. Antoine Francisque, *Le Trésor d'Orphée* (1600). The piece included here, 'Gaillarde', f.
13, is however, only an arrangement by Francisque of 'Piper's Gallard', and is not attributed
to Dowland.
Cologne. J. B. Besardus, *Thesaurus Harmonicus* (1603).
Nuremburg. Valentin Haussman, *Rest von Polnischen und andern Tänzen* (1603).
Frankfort, T. Simpson, *Opusculum* (1610).
Hamburg, Zacharias Füllsack, *Auselesener Paduanen und Galliarden* (1607).
I have been unable to find books published in Antwerp, Amsterdam and Leipzig before 1612,
that contain compositions by Dowland.
† A system of dividing the musical scale into groups of six notes, which Guido d'Arezzo
in the eleventh century called Ut, Re, Mi, Fa, Sol and La from the initial syllables of the lines
of a medieval hymn to John the Baptist:

Ut queant laxis
Re-sonare fibris
Mi-ra gestorum
Fa-muli tuorum
Sol-ve polluti
La-bii reatum
Sancte Iohannes.

skilfull men of Christendome, this 800 yeeres,) yet doe these fellowes giue their verdict of me behinde my backe, and say, what I doe is after the old manner: but I will speake openly to them, and would haue them know that the proudest Cantor of them, dares not oppose himselfe face to face against me. The second are young-men, professors of the Lute, who vaunt them-selues, to the disparagement of such as haue beene before their time, (wherein I my selfe am a party) that there neuer was the like of them. To these men I say little, because of my loue and hope to see some deedes ensue their braue wordes, and also being that here vnder their owne noses hath beene published a Booke* in defence of the Viol de Gamba, wherein not onely all other the best and principall Instruments haue beene abased, but especially the Lute by name, the words, to satisfie thee Reader I haue here thought good to insert, and are as followeth: *From hencefoorth, the statefull Instrument Gambo Violl, shall with ease yeeld full various, and deuicefull Musicke as the Lute: for here I protest the Trinitie of Musicke, Parts, Passion, and Deuision, to be gracefully united in the Gambo viol, as in the most receiued Instrument that is &c.* Which Imputation, me thinkes, the learneder sort of Musitians ought not to let passe vnanswered. Moreouer that here are and daily doth come into our most famous kingdome, diuers strangers from beyond the seas, which auerre before our owne faces, that we haue no true methode of application or fingering of the Lute. Now if these gallant yong Lutenists be such as they would haue the world beleeue, and of which I make no doubt, let them remember that their skill lyeth not in their fingers endes: *Cucullus non facit Monachum.* I wish for the Honor therfore and generall benefit of our Countrie, that they vndertake the defence of their Lute profession, seeing that some of them aboue other, haue most large meanes, conuenient time, and such encouragement as I neuer knew any haue, beleeue me if any of these obiections had beene made when those famous men liued which now are thought worthy of no fame, not derogating from these skillfull men present; I dare affirme that these obiections had beene answered to the full, and I make no doubt but that those few of the former time which liue yet, being that some of them are Batchelors of Musicke, and others which assume vnto themselues to be no lesse worthy, wilbe as forward to preserue their reputation. Perhaps you will aske me, why I that haue trauailed many countries, and ought to haue some experience, doth not vnder goe this busines my selfe? I answere that I want abilitie, being I am now entered

---

Thomas Morley, in his *Plaine and Easie Introduction* (1597) gives a very clear diagram, which he calls 'The Gam', showing how the system works. Each hexachord could begin on one of three notes; the lowest starting on the G on the bottom line of the bass clef, the next on the C above; the next after that on the F above; these were repeated four times starting on G, C and F, counting upwards. In a diagramatic presentation of the system the letters of the octave from the Greek letter *gamma* to the G above, were placed beside the groups of hexachords, hence the names often found on sixteenth- and seventeenth-century compositions such as *Preludium in C fa ut.* The 'mutation' was the change of mode brought about when the basic note series was moved from one hexachord to another. In this system the syllables Mi-Fa had to be on a semitone interval. In the hexachord beginning on F therefore, the B had to be flattened. Thus the first accidental was introduced.

* Tobias Hume, *The First Part of Ayres, French, Pollish and others* (1605). "To the vnder-standing Reader".

into the fiftieth yeare of mine age: secondly because I want both meanes, leasure, and encouragement. But (Gentle Reader to conclude, although abruptly) this worke of mine, which I here haue published, containeth such things as I my selfe haue thought well of, as being in mine opinion furnished with varietie of matter both of Iudgement and delight, which willingly I referre to the friendly censure, and approbation of the skilful: hoping it will be no lesse delightfull to all in generall, then it was pleasing to me in the composition. *Farewell.*

Your friend
Iohn Douland.

THE TABLE

FINIS

The first seven songs have alternative versions for four voices. 'Disdaine me still' (No. 1) is more ornate in character than any of the songs in *The Third and Last Booke*, as this quotation from the Cantus line will show:

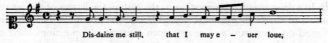

Dis-daine me still, that I may e — uer loue;

The rising scale passage through a fifth, which appears first at the end of bar one, is used as a unifying motif, and returns twice more, once from the dominant and once from the submediant. The last line has a fine cross-rhythm with the repeated phrase, both verbal and musical, on 'And still Ile loue':

As Dr. Fellowes notes in *English Madrigal Verse*, the words of this song are included in *Poems, Written by the Right Honorable William Earl of Pembroke* . . . [and] *S*[r] *Benjamin Ruddier* (1660). The reasons why this evidence of authorship must be considered inconclusive apply in this case as they did with 'When Phœbus first did Daphne loue'. See p. 277.

'Sweete stay awhile, why will you?' (No. 2). Dedicated 'To my worthy friend Mr. *William Iewel* of Exceter Colledge in Oxford'.*

This frankly erotic poem drew, in response from Dowland, a supple and extraordinarily expressive setting. The verbal rhythm is followed with great exactitude, beginning in triple measure and then changing to common time. The first two lines are treated simply, on a chordal basis; more movement is introduced in the lute, or lower voices, on the words 'The day breakes not, it is my heart, To thinke that you and I must part'; and then, in the fourth line, with a series of repetitions in a cross rhythm, the Cantus part rises to the point of climax and gradually descends through an octave to the word 'die':

* Written E sharp in original

★ See p. 412.

The last line is set without repetition of words, but with a decorative figure in the Tenor voice (or lute) supporting the upper voice towards the final close. The first stanza of this song has often been attributed to John Donne, but more modern editors exclude it from among the authentic works. E. K. Chambers* notes that it appeared first in the 1669 edition of Donne's poems 'not as a separate poem, but as a first stanza to the following which had begun in previous editions with "'Tis true, 'tis day, what though it be". The two are, however, obviously of different metrical structures . . . Probably the initials J. D. led to its being ascribed to Donne.' H. J. C. Grierson, in his edition of 1912, follows Chambers in his opinion and says it is 'Probably by John Dowlands'. In the edition of 1669 and Stowe MS 961, as quoted by Grierson, the poem is as follows:

> Stay, O sweet, and do not rise,
> The light that shines comes from thine eyes,
> The day breaks not, it is my heart,
> Because that you and I must part.
> Stay, or else my joys will die,
> And perish in their infancie.

> Breake of day.

> 'Tis true, 'tis day; what though it be?
> O wilt thou therefore rise from me?
> Why should we rise, because 'tis light?
> Did we lie downe, because 'twas night?
> Love which in spight of darknesse brought us hether,
> Should in despight of light keepe us together.

> Light hath no tongue, but is all eye;
> If it could speak as well as spie,
> This were the worst that it could say,
> That being well, I faine would stay,
> And that I lov'd my heart and honor so,
> That I would not from him, that had them, goe.

> Must businesse thee from hence remove?
> Oh, that's the worst disease of love,
> The poore, the foule, the false, love can
> Admit, but not the busied man.
> He which hath businesse, and makes love, doth doe
> Such wrong, as when a married man doth woe.†

* *The Poems of John Donne* (1896), Vol. I, p. 224.

† The stanzas beginning "Tis true, 'tis day' are set by William Corkine for voice and bass viol in his *Second Booke of Ayres* (1612).

As Dowland set it, the poem goes as follows:

> Sweet stay awhile, why will you rise?
> The light you see comes from your eyes:
> The day breakes not, it is my heart,
> To thinke that you and I must part.
> O stay, or else my ioyes must dye,
> And perish in their infancie.
>
> Deare let me dye in this faire breast,
> Farre sweeter then the Phœnix nest.
> Loue raise desire by his sweete charmes
> Within this circle of thine armes:
> And let thy blissefull kisses cherish
> Mine infant ioyes, that else must perish.

Other MS versions give the first line as 'Lye still my Deare', and in this form it was set anonymously in B.M. Add. 10337* (c. 1630).

Doughtie also notes a different setting in B.M. Add. 29481 (c. 1630). Altogether Grierson lists some twenty-odd sources for the poem, in one or other of its forms.

'To aske for all thy loue' (No. 3). Although bar lines are placed at regular intervals of eight crotchets the extreme fidelity with which verbal rhythm and accent have been expressed in the music takes all meaning from them except that of a convenient indication of togetherness of lute and voice. Every nuance of the spoken word is preserved, and even the rise and fall of the melody is the rise and fall of natural speech translated into music. In the last line Dowland employs, with immense effect, the quaver rest of the indrawn sigh, before the final words 'but sadness'. Dr. Fellowes, in *English Madrigal Verse*, says these stanzas are by John Donne. It is true that Grierson includes a copy in *Poems of John Donne* (1912), under the title 'Love's Exchange', and with the word 'sue' in the first line instead of 'aske', from the O'Flaherty MS (Harvard Eng. 966.5), but he denies its authenticity and says: 'The poem "Love's Exchange" is obviously an imitation of Donne's "Lovers infinitenesse".' The two poems bear a remarkable resemblance to each other in the use of certain phrases, and it seems a rather remote likelihood that they should have come into being entirely independently of each other. Here are the two for comparison. First the stanzas used by Dowland:

> To aske for all thy loue, and thy whole heart t'were madnesse,
>   I doe not sue,
>   nor can admit
>   (fairest) from you to haue all,

* Arnold Dolmetsch, *Select English Songs and Dialogues* (1912), Book II, No. 9.

yet who giveth all
hath nothing to impart but sadnesse.

He that receiueth all, can haue no more then seeing.
  My Loue by length
  of euery houre,
  Gathers new strength,
  new growth, new flower.
You must haue daily new rewards in store still being.

You cannot euery day giue me your heart for merit:
  Yet if you will,
  when yours doth goe,
  You shall haue still
  one to bestow:
For you shall mine when yours doth part inherit.

Yet if you please, Ile finde a better way, then change them:
  For so alone
  dearest we shall
  Be one and one,
  anothers all.
Let vs so ioyne our hearts that nothing may estrange them.

Here is 'Lovers infinitenesse':

  If yet I have not all thy love,
  Deare, I shall never have it all,
  I cannot breath one other sigh, to move,
  Nor can intreat one other teare to fall,
  And all my treasure, which should purchase thee,
  Sighs, teares, and oathes, and letters I have spent.
  Yet no more can be due to mee,
  Then at the bargaine made was ment,
  If then thy gift of love were partiall,
  That some to mee, some should to others fall,
    Deare, I shall never have Thee All.

  Or if then thou gavest mee all,
  All was but All, which thou hadst then;
  But if in thy heart, since, there be or shall,
  New love created bee, by other men,
  Which have their stocks intire, and can in teares,
  In sighs, in oathes, and letters outbid mee,
  This new love may beget new feares,
  For, this love was not vowed by thee.
  And yet it was, thy gift being generall,
  The ground, thy heart is mine, what ever shall
    Grow there, deare, I should have it all.

Yet I would not have all yet,
Hee that hath all can have no more,
And since my love doth every day admit
New growth, thou shouldst have new rewards in store;
Thou canst not every day give me thy heart,
If thou canst give it, then thou never gavest it:
Loves riddles are, that though thy heart depart,
It stayes at home, and thou with losing savest it:
But wee will have a way more liberall,
Then changing hearts, to joyne them, so wee shall
    Be one, and one anothers All.★

There is, however, no proof that Dowland wrote either 'Sweet stay awhile'
or 'To aske for all thy loue'. Neither poem bears any stylistic resemblance to
those few known to be by him, and indeed, 'To aske for all thy loue' is more
polished than any other verses written by him. But it is a curious fact that
these two poems, both to a certain extent associated with Donne, should have
been placed next to each other in the song-book. Is it possible that Dowland
believed them to be by him, although they are rejected by modern scholarship?

'Loue those beames that breede' (No. 4). This is an altogether delightful
song, equally satisfying in either version. Though the words are gracefully
fitted to the pattern of the music, and no fault can be found with their setting,
it is not, I feel, one of the songs where the poem has served for more than the
initial impetus to write an enchanting tune. Only in one place, at the beginning of the second couplet, on the words 'But alas teares coole this fire in
vaine' does the use of E natural in the key which, up to that point, has been
G minor, introduce a sudden chill. On the whole, however, although the
poet is suffering the pangs of unrequited love, the song wears its melancholy
very lightly.

'Shall I striue with words to moue' (No. 5) appears also as the lute solo
'Mignarde' (No. 34)† and as 'M. Henry Noel his Galliard' in *Lachrimæ or
seaven teares* (Galliard No. 4). Both these versions antedate the printing of
A Pilgrimes Solace and it is possible that Dowland reverted to the earlier practice of setting words to pre-existing dance measures; I think it more likely,
however, that both this and No. 6 were composed sometime before they
actually appeared in print. Compared with *The First Booke* the following
two volumes had shown a steady movement towards a less constricted form
of setting with the rhythm and meaning of the words playing the dominant

★ *The Poems of John Donne*. Edited by H. J. C. Grierson (1912), p. 16.
† See p. 147.

part in determining the structure of the melodic line, while the three songs in *A Musicall Banquet* had gone far beyond any such formal limitations. Beautiful as the ayres in dance form are, nevertheless at this period a return to the earlier type of song seems out of line with the main direction of Dowland's development. Dr. Fellowes* says it may be doubted whether the poem originally followed the order of the lines as given in the song-book. He suggests a rearrangement, but there seems no good reason for this. Moreover in his edition of *A Pilgrimes Solace* he has destroyed the form of the galliard with its conventional repeats by lifting the underlaid words on the repeat of each strain and treating them as a second stanza. This is contrary to Dowland's normal practice in which words to the repeats are underlaid but subsequent stanzas are printed below. Possibly Dr. Fellowes was misled by the absence of dots at the double bar, but these are also absent in other songs in this volume where there is no question but that certain lines are repeated. The editors have restored the correct form in the *Ayres for Four Voices*.

'Were euery thought an eye' (No. 6). This stanza is most wittily set to a coranto rhythm. In the original printing black minimes are used; a method which M. Prætorius commends as being the most reasonable way, common to the English, of writing this particular measure. Again Dr. Fellowes has falsified the structure by treating the repeats as a second stanza. He also makes the curious mistake of imputing to the printer a non-existent error.† He states that in line 20 (according to his layout of the poem) the original has 'but none knows how'. On the contrary, it is correctly written as 'but how none knowes'.

'Stay time awhile thy flying' (No. 7) is another song, which, though apparently simple, is full of the utmost subtlety of setting. The last two lines, with the descending figure in the inner voices, and the cross-rhythm, are among the most polished examples of Dowland's art:

Come, come close mine eyes, bet — — ter to dye bless-ed,

* *English Madrigal Verse*, p. 618.
† *English Madrigal Verse*, p. 618.

* A crochet in the original

'Tell me true Loue' (No. 8). The influence of the declamatory style of the contemporary Italian secular monodists is particularly noticeable in this song, although, like all Dowland's work, it is coloured with his own very distinctive and personal style. It is full of subtle rhythmic changes following the complexities of the verbal pattern, and even quite considerable fluctuation in *tempo* seems called for in performance, so freely is the music written to express and point the words. The accumulated tension, released in the bravura passage at the end, is highly reminiscent of the treatment of the final bars of Giulio Caccini's 'Dovrio dunque morire' and 'Amarilli mia bella'.* In the opening phrase Dowland returns to almost the exact note pattern, but with some changes of rhythm, that he used for 'Come ye heauy states of night':

Curiously, both these bear a strong resemblance to Caccini's 'Dovrio dunque morire', though here the harmonization is different:

In the preface to his edition of *A Pilgrimes Solace,* Dr. Fellowes says this song 'is for solo voice with four voices entering in chorus at the words "Thou

* First printed in *Nuove musiche* (1602). Included in *A Musicall Banquet* (1612) with Caccini's thorough-bass realized for the lute, probably by Dowland himself.

canst not die"'", but he does not print the three extra voice parts, and in his transcription the song appears as if it were for a solo voice all through. In the song-book the Cantus sings through to the end with accompaniment of lute and bass viol. It is then made quite clear by the word 'Repetition' printed over the Altus and Tenor voices, by the addition of the words to the Bassus part, and by the correct number of rests, that the three extra voices join at the repeat of the refrain, from the words 'Thou canst not die'. It is a great pity the full scoring has been omitted from the most widely used edition since the effect is particularly beautiful:

(bar lines have been added at the half bars).

The next three compositions, 'Goe nightly cares', 'From silent night' and 'Lasso vita mia', are something entirely new in song-writing of the period. The solo voice is accompanied by the lute; the gamba, with a few exceptions, doubling the lute bass; and, in all three songs, an entirely independent obbligato for treble viol. Possibly Dowland was here borrowing an effect from the viol-consort song, but if so, his borrowing was done with genius. He had already made tentative advances in this direction in, for example, 'Humor say what mak'st thou heere' (*Second Booke*, No. 22), by adding, over the second voice of the dialogue, a treble viol, which doubled the upper part of the lute, but the addition of these soaring descants lifts these three great songs onto a completely new plane. The parts for the treble viol are, in each song, labelled 'Cantus', and no instrument is actually mentioned, but that the treble viol is intended is clear from the title-page.

'Goe nightly cares' (No. 9). The solo voice in this song is headed Altus. The first section is written in long uneven bars and begins with the instruments alone in a smoothly flowing measure. The voice enters on the second minim of the second bar with the exclamatory interjection 'Goe nightly cares'. These bars are repeated; the composition then moves forward, the next three lines being extended with repetitions and achieving a continually mounting intensity till the words 'of life bereaved quite' are reached. This is followed by a remarkable section in triple time, where the voice drops into a low monotone, while the instruments move above and below in a complex texture (see p. 300).

The return to the first tempo suddenly relaxes the tension and the repeated phrases 'Welcome sweete death' have a quiet tranquillity. This is suddenly shattered with the three broken cries 'Oh life', 'no life', 'A hell'. The voice

*C2 in original

again sinks on to a monotone of despair, till, on the final word 'farewell' it falls gently through the interval of a fourth while the instruments come to rest on the tonic chord with the usual Tierce de Picardie. In all, a most deeply moving and beautiful work.

'From silent night' (No. 10). The singing part is here marked Cantus. This is another song of unrelieved despair. The voice moves on its measured course against the instrumental ensemble which, at times, breaks into agitated movement. Much use is made of the sighing quaver rest, both before the actual word 'sighes' and in a descending chromatic passage on the repeated words 'her woe'. The passage is then inverted for the next line:

of   sad   dis-pair,   And

An ascending chromatic passage is used once more, starting from B natural. The voice then takes the line 'Sounding nought else but sorrow, griefe and care', repeating and pointing the words 'nought else but sorrow' throughout the best part of eight bars. At the cadence the instruments have a linking passage which leads back to the repeat beginning on the second appearance of the words 'And to the world brings tunes of sad despayre'. Edward Doughtie traced the origin of the words of this song, and I can do no better than quote what he says: 'I have found this song is made up of stanzas 1, 2, and 11 of a much longer poem of 63 stanzas, which was first printed in 1601 with the title *The Passion of a Discontented Minde*. The poem was reprinted in 1602 and 1621; all editions were anonymous. Dowland's source was probably the 1601 or 1602 edition; all three editions have only one variant from the song, reading "wel-springs" for "well-spring" in line 15.'

A copy of the 1602 edition is bound up with several pieces by Nicholas Breton in a volume called 'N. Breton's Works' which is now in the Bodleian (Tanner 221). Thomas Corser, *Collectanea Anglo-Poetica* (1867), Part III, p. 42, attributed the poem to Breton, since it 'has all the marks of Breton's style, and is usually attributed to his pen by competent bibliographers'. John Payne Collier reprinted the 1602 edition in his *Illustrations of Old English Literature* (1866), I, No. 6, but doubted Breton's authorship (pp. i–ii) because the poem was not printed by a stationer Breton usually employed. Collier conjectured that Robert Southwell was the author. A. B. Grosart did not include the poem in his edition of Breton's *Works in Verse and Prose* (1879) because the copy he mentions, the 1601 edition, 'has neither his name nor initials nor the mint-mark words of the period, whereby the Breton authorship should have been betrayed' (I, p. lxxiii). But Mrs. Jean Robertson, Breton's latest editor, points out that the printers of the *Passion* printed other acknowledged Breton pieces; that Grosart accepted other anonymous works of Bretons'; and that the *Passion* does indeed contain characteristic phrases which Grosart called 'mint-mark words'. She compares numerous passages of several of Breton's poems with the *Passion,* and concludes: 'I have no hesitation, in the absence of any evidence to the contrary, in assigning *The Passion of a Discontented Minde* to Nicholas Breton, on the strength of the close resemblance in style and subject-matter to his recognised works' (*Poems by Nicholas Breton* [1952], pp. xcii–xcviii).

Mrs. Robertson's evidence is as good as that sort of evidence can be, and Breton may very well have written the poem. Nevertheless, there is some evidence against Breton's authorship. In an early seventeenth-century collection of speeches and accounts of the trial and execution of the Earl of Essex (B.M. MS Sloane 1779, f. 208ᵛ) there is a copy of the poem with the partly obliterated heading, 'Es [sex] made . . . the Tower.' Tanner must have seen a similar manuscript, for in one of his miscellanies (Bod. MS Tanner 76, ff. 114ʳ–116ᵛ) he copied part of the poem along with this note:

A Penetential wᶜʰ I found with other Papers concerning the Earl of Essex's Crimes, and Arraignmᵗ in a MS. of that time. Whether mad by him, (or for him) in the time of his C_ofinemᵗ to the Ld Keeper's House, from Octobʳ 1599, to April 1600; Or . . . in the time of his Retiremᵗ into the Country between the hearing of his Cause by the Queen's Delegates June 5th 1600, and his breaking out into open Rebellion: In both wᶜʰ Intervalls of time he gave himself wholly to Devotion and divine Meditation, as Mʳ Cambden expressly witnesseth, pp. 187 & 215.

'Although Tanner does not mention the period of Essex's imprisonment, parts of the poem, if they concern Essex at all, seem to be appropriate to his stay in the Tower. The ministrations of his chaplain, Mr. Ashton, had reduced Essex to a state of mind very like that described in the poem; for example, the outburst against bad company in stanzas 43–9 may be related to Essex's accusations of his friends in his confession . . . (See J. E. Neale, *Queen Elizabeth I,* [1934], p. 375.) Yet it seems unlikely that Essex, in the short period before his execution, would compose three hundred and seventy-eight lines of facile verse, even though he had been known to 'evaporate his thoughts in a Sonnet' (see p. 225 above). It is possible that some hack, such as Breton, took advantage of the sensation by writing a poem which was just close enough to actual events to profit from current interest in them.'. . . .

Copies of the poem are found in BM MS Sloane 1779, f. 208ᵛ, and in BM MS Egerton 2403, f. 38ʳ. Tanner's MS lacks the first few stanzas.* Doughtie lists the variants, but they are not particularly relevant to the present book.

'*Lasso vita mia, mi fa morire*' (No. 11). The solo voice is marked Altus. It is, of course, a commonplace that artificial conceits, musical riddles and puns

---

* Doughtie, op. cit., pp. 494–6.

were greatly appreciated in the sixteenth and seventeenth centuries, and that such devices were often used by composers, even in serious works, as a form of exercise in technical ingenuity. This must be borne in mind together with the fact that in Dowland's time singing was still taught by means of the Solmization system, based on the syllables Ut, Re, Mi, Fa, Sol, La of the hexachord. All singers were drilled in this method and were as much at home with it as the singer of today is at home with the system based on the octave.*

It is sufficient to emphasize here that the only syllables that could be fitted to a semitone were Mi–Fa; they were vitally important since they defined the mode or scale of any given piece. It is perhaps not altogether surprising then, to find that Dowland, in setting '*Lasso vita mia, mi fa morire*', was careful to fit the Italian words *mi fa* to the Solmization syllables Mi and Fa. In addition, Dowland sets the first syllable of the opening word *Lasso* to the Solmization syllable La (the hexachord here starting on the note C), and the final syllable of *morire* to Re. Further, the final syllable of *Lasso* is only Sol without its l, and to Sol it is duely set:

A little later he again sets the words *mi fa* to the semitone interval, first of the hexachord beginning on G, followed immediately by that of the hexachord beginning on F:

Dowland was not the first to use this conceit. He may well have known the madrigal '*O fere stelle homai datemi pace*' by his admired Marenzio, first printed in 1587. This ends with the words:

> Ch' io non son forte a sostener la guerra
> Ch'Amor mi fa co'l suo spietato laccio.†

The *mi fa* of the last line being sung to the notes E and F. Einstein also prints a madrigal by Willaert, '*Amor mi fa morire*'.‡ This begins:

---

* The importance, and the difficulty of learning Solmization in Elizabethan times is illustrated by a quotation given in Strachey's *Elizabeth and Essex*, p. 60. Anthony Standen, it appears, thought Essex lacked tenacity of purpose, and that 'he must be continually pulled by the ear, as a boy that learneth *ut, re, mi, fa*'.

† Alfred Einstein, *The Italian Madrigal* (1949), Vol. III, p. 255. The poem is by Jacopo Sannazaro.

‡ op. cit., Vol. III, p. 59. Words by Bonifazio Dragonetto.

It will be seen that the voices are here treated in pairs, cantus-altus and tenor-bassus, the upper voice of each pair having the words *mi fa* on the semitone interval. In particular the phrase given to the tenor for the words *mi fa morire* should be compared with Dowland's setting of the same words in the first line, in the example already given. Edward Doughtie, when working on his thesis, made an extensive search in the hope of discovering the provenance of the stanza used by Dowland. He was unable to trace it and concludes it was probably formed from a number of *clichés* from Italian madrigalian verse strung together for the occasion. Certainly the verse alone has no great significance, but as a peg upon which to hang the lovely lamenting music it has considerable merit, and, adopting the Italian declamatory manner, Dowland uses the disjointed phrases, with frequent repetitions, to produce a cumulative effect of mounting grief.

The next five songs, Nos. 12–17, fall into a special category of their own; filled with a deeply religious spirit they are still secular compositions in the sense that the texts are not taken from recognized scriptural sources. The words are mostly penitential in feeling, but express a profound belief in the redeeming power of God's forgiveness. No songs of precisely this character had appeared in any of Dowland's previous song-books, and, judging from what had appeared in print, he had written no religious works since the *Lamentatio Henrici Noel* of 1596. It seems fairly safe to conclude, then, that these songs were composed in the years immediately preceding the publication of *A Pilgrimes Solace* in 1612. Although the arrangement of the lower voices lies entirely convincingly on the lute, nevertheless the feeling of vocal polyphony is so strong throughout, it can hardly be doubted that it was in this form that these songs first took shape in Dowland's mind. Every artifice is employed to heighten the expressiveness of the words. There is great rhythmic freedom, and beautifully worked out harmonic contrasts are used to differentiate between, on the one hand, grief and pain, and on the other, serenity and hope.

'In this trembling shadow cast' (No. 12). The sense of brooding unease of the 'trembling shadow' is immediately set in the opening bars when the movement of the two voices suddenly strikes an augmented fifth. The first section is almost entirely contrapuntal with suspensions maintaining the feeling of strain. Suddenly, on the words 'Songs to the Lord will I make', the structure changes and block chords support the voice in a serene succession of root positions and first inversions. The counterpoint is resumed in the highly emotional passage 'Darknesse from my minde then take' and continues to the end, although the tension is relaxed and the last line 'Till they feele thy light within' has a quiet assurance. The song appears to be composed entirely on the first stanza, the emotional content of the lines being far less appropriately fitted to the music in the second and third. An odd discrepancy is found in line two. The Cantus has 'From those boughes which thy wings shake', while the three other voices have 'thy windes shake'. Poetically either is acceptable, but weight of numbers is in favour of 'windes'.

'If that a sinners sighes' (No. 13). Here again Dowland makes much illustrative use of discord. The three lower voices have the first two and a half bars alone, and the mood is set with a diminished fourth anticipating the word 'sinners', and in the line 'Or that repentant teares be Angels wine', the wine is well salted with an augmented fifth. The words used here are part of a longer poem set by William Byrd in *Psalmes, Sonets & Songs of Sadnes and Pietie* of 1588 (No. 30). Possibly Dowland drew on this source for his text. Dr. Fellowes★ says John Milton the Elder set the same stanza in Sir William Leighton's *Teares or Lamentacions of a Sorrowful Soule* (1614). Although the first sentence is identical, the poem used by the poet's father continues entirely differently.

Nos. 14 to 16 form an extended trilogy, consisting of 'Thou mightie God', 'When Davids life' and 'When the poore Criple'. Edward Doughtie† finds the text of this group of songs to be 'based on a sonnet by Nicholas Breton in his *Soules Harmony* (1602), sigs. C3ᵛ–C4ʳ. The first two lines of the poem, however, are not Breton's at all, but were adapted by Dowland from the first two lines of stanza 9 of the 'Bee' (the first two stanzas of which Dowland had already set to music in III, 18). These lines originally read (from B.M. MS Harl. 6974 f. 230ᵛ):

> Greate kinge of Bees, that rightest every wronge
> Listen to Patience in her dyinge songe.

See also Bond's *Lyly*, III, 496'. In Dowland's hands the lines become:

> Thou mightie God, that rightest euery wrong,
> Listen to patience in a dying song.

For the first part of the trilogy he takes this couplet and adds four lines from Breton. The whole text then becomes a kind of meditation on the afflictions of Job. Appropriately enough, the phrase 'Listen to patience' is given great

★ *English Madrigal Verse*, p. 618.   † op. cit., p. 508.

prominence, being repeated several times by each voice in an intricate counterpoint. Later again, in the line, 'Patience asswaged his excessiue paine', repetitions of the word 'patience' pass from voice to voice, dwelling on Job's so much admired ability to accept the trials to which he was subjected by the Hebrew God.

The second part, 'When Davids life' (No. 15), takes the next four lines from Breton, which reflect upon patience in another context: that of David under the persecution of Saul. The section opens with the voices in canon:

Suspensions and chromatic changes are used to heighten David's grief, and the tension is maintained until it is relaxed in the final bar.

The third part, 'When the poore Criple' (No. 16), consists of six lines from Breton, in which the misery of the cripple is described with the miracle of his cure by the sight of Christ. The poet then compares himself with Job, David and the cripple, and calls upon Christ to give him equal patience. The poignancy with which the trilogy is set suggests that Dowland may have been identifying himself with the tragic implications of the poet's thought.

In bar 1 there is a discrepancy between the lute and the Tenor voice of the four-part ayre on beats 4 and 3, the lute having the note D (c on 5 in tablature) while the Tenor has E natural. Although the phrase as given to the lute is possible in the solo version, it is clearly unacceptable with the four voices. In my opinion it is not unlikely that the two tablature signs c are a printer's or copyist's error, the confusion between c and e being a common mistake. It is probable that the lute part should read as:

In the *Ayres for Four Voices*** the adjustment has been made. Then the passage reads as follows:

'Where Sinne sore wounding' (No. 17). The subject of this poem is the grace of God's forgiveness and Dowland's response to the words is a compo-

---

* *Musica Britannica*, Vol. 6, p. 105.

sition of great beauty. It opens with the Tenor voice, the three others joining in a contrapuntal structure in which the imitations are similar only in the
first four notes. In spite of the appearance of such words as 'sin', 'wounding',
'torment' and 'death' the harmony is, for Dowland, surprisingly free from dissonance. Melodically, however, in the Cantus the words are set with extreme
sensitivity both to the meaning and to the inherent rhythm and accent. This
is particularly noticeable in the second and third lines, with the sense of exalta-
tion in the rising melody which reaches its climax on the repeat of the words
'grace abounding':

There Grace a - bound-ing, Grace a - bounding   free - ly,

free - ly   doth, re - dresse___ mee:

'My heart and tongue were twinnes' (No. 18). In his notes to *A Pilgrimes
Solace*★ Dr. Fellowes remarks that the poem of this song is 'printed in *England's
Helicon* with some variation of text'. The main difference lies in the final
couplet, and from the description of the entertainment in which the song was
originally included, it would seem that it was probably Dowland who made
the alteration, possibly to give the piece a less particular meaning, when he
gave his song to the public in 1612. An account of the performance, given
before the Queen at Sudeley in 1592, is preserved in *Speeches delivered to her*
MAJESTIE *this last Progresse, at the Right Honourable the Lady* RUSSEL'S
*at Bissam; the Right Honourable the Lorde CHANDOS' at Sudeley; and the
Right Honourable the Lord NORRIS'S at Ricorte.*† First the text of a laudatory
speech is given, and then, the description says:

This Speech ended, her Maiesty sawe Apollo with the tree, having on the one
side one that sung, on the other one that plaide:

> Sing you, plaie you, but sing and play my truth;
> This tree my lute, these sighes my notes of ruth:
> The Lawrell leefe for ever shall bee greene,
> And Chastety shal be Apolloes Queene.
> If gods may dye, here shall my tombe be plaste,
> And this engraven, 'Fonde Phoebus, Daphne chaste'.

After the Verses, the Song:

★ *English Madrigal Verse*, p. 618.
† Reprinted in Nichols, *Progresses of Queen Elizabeth*, Vol. III (1823), pp. 138, 139.

My heart and tongue were twinnes, at once conceaved;
　The eldest was my heart, borne dumbe by destinie;
　The last my tongue, of all sweete thoughts bereaved,
　Yet strung and tunde to play hearts harmonie.
Both knit in one, and yet asunder placed,
　What heart would speake, the tongue doeth still discover;
What tongue doth speake, is of the heart embraced,
　And both are one to make a new found lover:
New founde, and onely founde in Gods and Kings,
　Whose wordes are deedes, but deedes not words regarded:
Chaste thoughts doe mount, and she with swiftest wings,
　My love with paine, my paine with losse rewarded:
Engrave upon this tree, Daphnes perfection,
'That neither men nor gods, can force affection'.

In 1600 the poem was reprinted in *England's Helicon*[*] with the following
note, 'This Dittie was sung before her Maiestie, at the right honourable Lord
Chandos, at Sudley Castell, at her last being there in prograce. The author
thereof vnknowne.' R. Warwick Bond ascribes the text of the whole entertainment to John Lyly.[†] Although no other author has ever been suggested
and Bond may be right, nevertheless his claims for Lyly are notoriously unreliable, and in this case he produces no convincing evidence. Dowland has
treated the poem as three four-line stanzas, followed by a Conclusion consisting of the final couplet, which now appears as:

> Then this be sure, since it is true perfection,
> That neyther men nor Gods can force affection.

There can be little doubt that this is the setting used at the Sudeley masque
in 1592. Since Dowland's connection with the event seems clear from the
evidence[‡] it is highly unlikely that any other composer would have been
involved, moreover the style is consistent with its having been an early composition and it shows none of the characteristics of his later work.

'Up merry mates' (No. 19). This song must certainly have been written for
a masque or entertainment, probably for some occasion when a ship-car was
part of the spectacle. Enid Welsford[§] finds the inclusion of ships was common
in ritual and folk mummery from very early times and, she continues 'Certainly in the Middle Ages ship processions were held as spring celebrations
in England, Germany and the South of Europe, sometimes a plough taking

---

[*] Edited Rollins (1935), Vol. I, p. 122.
[†] *The Complete Works* (1902), Vol. I, pp. 477–90.
[‡] See p. 29.
[§] *The Court Masque* (1927).

the place of the ship' (p. 13). She also speaks of Tudor disguisings and quotes a passage from Edward Hall's *Henry VIII*:*

on their return from the woods the King and his company were met by a ship called *Fame*, which had for its cargo Renown, and which sailed before them to the tilt-yard.

Elaborate sea-cars were used in the festivities which celebrated the marriage of Cosimo II, Grand Duke of Tuscany in 1608, and drawings of these cars appeared in a pamphlet or pamphlets which gave a full description of the proceedings. According to Enid Welsford,† Inigo Jones must have possessed copies of these, so the latest thing in Continental design would have been available for the construction of such machines. The song itself is described as a dialogue, although the second voice, the Bassus, has only two short solo phrases in each stanza, where he answers the principal voice, whose part, in the song-book, is headed Tenor. These two voices are accompanied by the lute alone, and are joined by Cantus and Altus at the Chorus. Both these parts lie within the male alto range, and it would seem that an all-male quartet was originally intended. In the first stanza 'seas are smooth, sailes full, and all things please'; in the second, 'seas are rough, sailes rent, and each thing lowres'. The Conclusion, sung after the two stanzas, each with its Chorus, praises the 'constant spirit' that remains faithful to the 'golden meane' in all extremities. The writing is descriptive; the word 'high' mounting to F, the highest note in the song; the 'wat'rie Nymphs' are accompanied by a quaver figuration on the lute, which anticipates the pattern of notes for the word 'dance'; and the Conclusion, expressive of the 'golden meane', is cast in a flowing triple measure. The whole piece must have made a most spirited episode in its original presentation.

The words, though not of a very high poetic order, appear to be one of several instances among the lyrics of the song-books in which the Aristotelian admiration for the moderate or the Golden Mean is expressed. Other references to this teaching which immediately come to mind are, for example, Philip Rosseter's 'Though far from Joy'.‡ This has, for the second stanza:

> The higher trees, the more stormes they endure,
> Shrubs be troden downe,
> But the meane, the golden meane,
> Doth onely all our fortunes crowne,
> Like to a streame that sweetly slideth,
> Through the flourie banks, and still in the midst his course guideth.

* With an introduction by Charles Whibley (1904). *The Lives of the Kings*, Vol. I, p. 15. Text from the 1550 folio edition.
† op. cit., p. 187.   ‡ *A Booke of Ayres* (1601), No. 11.

Thomas Morley, in 'Loue wing'd my hopes',* also has the lines:

> For true pleasure liues in measure which if men forsake,
> Blinded they into follie runne, And griefe for pleasure take.

Earlier, in Spain, Enriquez de Valderrabano† expresses the same idea in a *villancico*:

> De donde venis amore?
> Bien se yo de donde.
> Caballero de mesura,
> Caballero de mesura.

Doubtless a systematic search would reveal many more illustrations of the same underlying thought.

'Welcome black night' (No. 20) is a most beautiful epithalamium. The Cantus secundus sings a highly decorative line accompanied, on the lute, by an almost equally elaborate part. They are joined, at the Chorus, by four other voices which begin with this lovely passage:

*Printed D

Edward Doughtie‡ suggests this song, the next one, and possibly the preceding, were written for the wedding celebrations of Lord Howard de Walden (in whose employment, it will be remembered, Dowland was at the time of

---

* *The First Booke of Ayres* (1600), No. 10.
† *Silva de Sirenas* (1547).
‡ op. cit.

the publication of *A Pilgrimes Solace*) on his marriage to the Lady Elizabeth Home, daughter of the Earl of Dunbar. According to G. E. Cockayne,* the marriage contract, dated November 17th, 1606, stipulated that the marriage should take place 'within three months after the said Lady Elizabeth should accomplish the age of twelve years'.† The ceremony was, however, delayed by the death of the Earl on January 29th, 1610/11,‡ who was, as Calderwood says 'by death pulled down even when he was about to solemnise magnificently his daughter's marriage with the Lord Walden'. The marriage was again delayed by disputes about the Lady Elizabeth's portion and was not solemnized until March 1612.§ On November 3rd, 1612, John Chamberlain wrote to Sir Ralph Winwood‖ 'the Lord Walden that hath ben now a goode while wedded to the Lord of Dunbars daughter, was not bedded with her till the last weeke, and that by speciall commaundment'. Possibly the marriage in March was no more than a formal ratification of the contract and there may have been no special festivities organized for the event. If this were so it may be the songs were never performed in the surroundings for which they were originally written. It seems hardly likely that Lord Walden would have agreed to their inclusion in a volume entered as early as October 1611, had he intended they should later be heard on the occasion of his marriage.

'Cease these false sports' (No. 21) is written in the same form as the preceding song, with the solo part given to the Cantus secundus, while four other voices join at the Chorus. It is very much a companion piece to 'Welcome black night'. Here too, the solo voice has a decorative line, but the lute part is, on the whole, a more thickly chordal texture. The last line before the chorus has a beautiful sequence on the repetition of the words 'rise to the sun':

As in 'Welcome black night', the Chorus begins with the words 'Hymen, O Hymen', although it continues differently.

The volume ends with 'Galliard to Lachrimæ'. (See p. 157.)

* *Complete Peerage*, XII, Part 1, edited G. F. White (1953), p. 467.
† Richard Griffin, Baron Braybrooke, *History of Audley End* (1836), pp. 42–3.
‡ Reg. P. C. S., Vol. IX, p. 128.
§ *Dictionary of National Biography*.
‖ *Letters of John Chamberlaine*, edited N. E. McClure (1939), Vol. I, p. 385.

A MUSICALL BANQUET

As John Dowland certainly had some part in the preparation of this volume, even though it was put out under Robert's name, it seems appropriate to include some general account of it here, although only Dowland's three songs will be treated in detail.

The title-page is the same as that used by Thomas Este for *The Second Booke of Songs*, but, as in *Varietie of Lute-Lessons*, the oval at the top contains a viol and bow, a lute and a sheet of music. It is surrounded with a band on which are printed the words COR: MUSICA LÆTIFICAT. The full title is as follows:

A/MVSICALL/BANQUET/
Furnished with varietie of delicious
Ayres, Collected out of the best Authors in
English, French, Spanish and Italian.

By *Roberte Douland*
LONDON
Printed for Thomas Adams.
1610

The dedication and epistle are as follows:

TO THE RIGHT HO/NORABLE SYR ROBERT/*SYDNEY*, KNIGHT: Lord Gouernour of Vlissingen, and the Castle of Ramekins, Lord *Sydney* of Penshurst,/ Viscount *Lisle*, and Lord Chamberlaine to the Queenes/ Most excellent Maiestie.

Right Honourable Lord: Since my best abilitie is not able in the least manner to counteruaile that dutie I owe vnto your Lordship, for two great respects; the one in regard (your Lordship vndertaking for mee) I was made a member of the Church of Christ, and withall receiued from you my name: the other the loue that you beare to all excellency & good learning, (which seemeth hæreditarie aboue others to the Noble Familie of the *Sydneys*,) and especially to this excellent Science of Musicke, a skill from all antiquity entertayned with the most Noble & generous dispositions. May it please your Honour therefore to accept these few, and my first labours, as a poore pledge of that zeale and dutie which I shall euer owe vnto your Honour, vntill time shall enable me to effect something more worthy of your Lordships view, hauing no other thing saue these few sheetes of Paper to present the same withall.

To your Honour
in all dutie most deuoted,
Robert Douland

To the Reader.

Gentlemen: Finding myselfe not deceiued in the hope I had of your kinde entertayning my collected Lute-lessons which I lately set foorth, I am further encouraged to publish vnto your censures these AYRES, being collected and gathered out of the labours of the rarest and most iudicious Maisters of Musick that either now are or haue lately liued in Christendome, whereof some I haue purposely sorted to the capacitie of young practitioners, the rest by degrees are of greater depth and skill, so that like a careful Confectionary, as neere as might be I haue fitted my Banquet for all tastes; if happily I shall be distasted by any, let them know what is brought vnto them is drest after the English, French, Spanish and Italian manner; the assay is taken before, they shall not need to feare poysoning. You Gentlemen and friends that come in good-will, and not as Promooters into a country Market, to call our viands into question, what soeuer here is, much good may it doe you, I would it were better for you: for the rest I wish their lips such Lettuce as *Silenus* Asse,* or their owne harts would desire.

Thine,
Robert Douland.

The epistle is followed by a Latin poem of Commendation by Henry Peacham.

The Table of Contents, at the back of the volume, is headed by Dowland's galliard for Sir Robert Sidney;† this is followed by ten English ayres, three French, three Spanish and four Italian. Beside Dowland himself the composers represented include Anthony Holborne, Richard Martin, Robert Hales, Daniel Bacheler, Guillaume Tessier, Domenico Maria Megli and Giulio Caccini. Nine songs are anonymous. *A Musicall Banquet* is exceptional among the song-books in that in many cases the names of the authors of the poems are given. These include George Clifford, Earl of Cumberland; Sir Philip Sidney; Robert Devereux, Earl of Essex; and Sir Henry Lee.

All the songs have a bass part, but none are arranged as four-part ayres. With few exceptions the words are written in full under the Bassus as well as under the Cantus, which suggests the bass was intended for singing, as with the first eight numbers of *The Second Booke*. This is borne out by the fact that No. 8, where no words are written to the bass, is described as 'For one Voice only to sing'.

'Farre from triumphine Court' (No. 8). The name 'Sir Henry Lea' is printed at the top left-hand side of the Cantus part. The song is described as 'For one voice only to sing', the Bassus being intended for a bass viol. Dowland's

---

* Silenus, one of the Satyri, a constant companion of Dionysius. He is described in William Smith's *A Smaller Classical Dictionary* as a jovial old man, with a bald head, a puck nose, fat and round like his wine-bag, which he always carries with him. He is generally intoxicated. As he could not trust his own legs, he is generally represented riding on an ass. The proverb 'Like lips, like lettuce' was derived from a saying of M. Crassus, when he saw an ass eating thistles: *Similem habent labra lactucam.* Thomas Morley uses a similar phrase, 'Such lips, such lettuce, such authority, such imitation'. See *A Plaine and Easy Introduction to Practical Music,* edited R. Alec Harman (1952), p. 217.

† See p. 149.

rhetorical setting is very suitable to the courtly sentiments of the aged knight. In the first stanza Lee laments the death of Queen Elizabeth, but in the second and third he records his joy at a visit paid to him and his mistress, Mrs. Anne Vavasour, by Queen Anne. In the final stanza he reverts to phrases from the earliest of the three related poems, and cries out against Time that has turned his golden locks to silver, and old age that prevents his offering meet service to the new Queen. The event that called forth the poem is described in a letter from John Chamberlaine to Dudley Carleton, dated from Ascott, September 27, 1608:

The Quene, before her going out of this countrie dined with Sir Henry Lea at his little Rest, and gave great countenance and had longe and large discourse with Mistris Vavassor: and within a day or two after sent a very fayre jewell valued above an hundred pound. Which favor hath put such new life into the old man to see his sweet hart so graced, that he will have one more fling to the court before he die, though he thought he had taken his leave this sommer when he went to present the Prince with an armour that stoode him in 200[11] . . .*

Possibly the 'starre fixed to his head' of stanza two, line five, is the 'very fayre jewell' referred to by Chamberlaine, although his letter seems to suggest the gift was made to Mrs. Vavasour rather than to Lee himself. This could, of course, be the inaccuracy of information passed from person to person by letter or by word of mouth. The exceedingly personal quality of this poem, both in the ideas themselves and in the manner of their expression, makes it, to my mind, unlikely that the stanzas were ghosted for Lee, or were the product of any hand but his own. If this is so, there can be little doubt that he also wrote the other two. *A Musicall Banquet* is unlike Dowland's own four books in having a number of the poems assigned to their authors, and the fact that the general rule of anonymity was here abandoned would account for Lee's authorship being given in this case, when it was suppressed in the earlier volumes. The other attributions appear to be trustworthy and there seems no good reason to doubt that the Dowlands knew what they were doing when they attached Lee's name to the stanzas.

'Lady if you so spight me' (No. 9). The Bassus part, unlike that of 'Farre from triumphing Court', has underlaid words. For the only time in his accompaniments Dowland uses a ninth course tuned at C. Rhythmically this song is exceedingly free, the original bars consisting of eight, twelve, fourteen, and sixteen crotchet beats. There is no musical word painting, but the words themselves are played with in a kind of fantasia, and repetition, both of single

---

* *Letters of John Chamberlaine*, edited N. E. McClure (1939), Vol. I, p. 263. SP. Dom. Jac. I, XXXVI. 40.

words and whole phrases, is present more than in any other song. In an otherwise mostly syllabic setting, attention is called to words of prime importance such as 'spight' and 'and die' by the introduction of groups of rapid ornamental notes on a single syllable.

The single stanza is a translation from Cesare Rinaldi, *Madrigali* (1588):*

> Donna se voi m'odiate
> A'che si dolci poi baci mi date?
> Forse accio l'Alma per estrema gioia
> Di dolcezza ne moia?
> Se per questo lo fate
> Baciate pur baciate;
> Che contento mi fia
> Finir, baciando voi, la vita mia.

According to Obertello† the poem was set by Antonio Orlandini in his *Madrigali* (1598), by Horatio Vecchi in *Convito Musicale* (1597), and by Benedetto Palavicino *Madrigali* (1604).‡ It became known in England through a setting by Alfonso Ferrabosco in Nicholas Yonge's *Musica Transalpina* (1588), there the words are translated into English. It is likely that this was Dowland's source. An instrumental arrangement à 4 appears as No. XIX, 'Aria', 'J. Douland', in Thomas Simpson's *Taffel-Consort* (1621).

'In darknesse let me dwell' (No. 10). This astonishingly lovely song stands among the greatest ever written in the English language. From the opening bars, where the lute and bass viol set the sombre mood, to the final repetition of the words 'in darknesse let me dwell', when the voice drops the last despairing note into the silence, Dowland's consummate mastery shows itself in every phrase. Leaving the strophic form of the earlier songs far behind, the words, the melody and the harmonic structure are woven together into the most poignant expression of anguished grief. The subtlety of the rhythmic flow transcends the bounds of conventional bar lines, yet the monumental shape of the whole piece never loses its clarity. As may be expected with Dowland, the words 'sorrow' and 'woes' call forth biting discords; on the repetition of the first, a major seventh, and on the second, a chord of the augmented fifth. A descending chromatic phrase accompanies the words 'Hellish, jarring sounds'. 'O let me liuing die' is declaimed somewhat after the Italian manner, and is reminiscent of the treatment of 'pity, help now or neuer' in 'Sorrow, sorrow, stay'. The emotion mounts to a climax with the words 'Till death do come', the voice rising to the highest note of the whole

---

* Edward Doughtie, op. cit.
† op. cit., 242, 448.
‡ Printed earlier in *Il Quinto libro de' Madrigali* (Venice, 1593).

composition. With the return of the opening words and the unresolved ending, the feeling of deep and endless grief is far removed from conventional melancholy. The hearer is left with the conviction that this is the expression of a profoundly tragic experience. The Bassus part, at one or two points, moves independently of the lute, and should, therefore, not be omitted in performance. The words and their close resemblance of phrase and imagery to 'Flow my teares' and 'Mourne, mourne, day is with darknesse fled' have already been discussed on p. 255. Assuming that Coperario set the poem in its original form, then Dowland changed line 6 which, in 1606, appeared as:

> O let me dying liue till death doth come.

to

> O let me liuing die till death doe come.

Here is the second stanza from the *Funeral Teares*:

> My dainties griefe shall be, and teares my poisned wine,
> My sighes the aire, throgh which my panting hart shall pine:
> My robes my mind shall sute exceeding blackest night,
> My study shall be tragicke thoughtes sad fancy to delight.
> Pale Ghosts and frightful shades shal my acquaintance be:
> O thus my haples ioy I haste to thee.

The last line suggests the stanzas may have been originally written as a death song in a now forgotten play.

Apart from the poor quality of these lines, after the tragic finality of Dowland's ending, the addition of another stanza is unthinkable.

To quote any part of this great work in isolation from the whole can only produce less than the full effect of its being heard within the context, nevertheless the ending, where the final entry of the voice, preceded by the instruments alone, on a repeat of the opening phrase, is so remarkable, that there may be justification in quoting it as a fitting conclusion to this chapter on the song-books.

mee———————dwell.

IV

Psalms and spiritual songs

Of the thirteen psalms, canticles and prayers harmonized by Dowland, all the verses and ten of the tunes belong to the English metrical psalter that is generally known by the name of 'Sternhold and Hopkins', after its first two contributors.

Ever since the Reformation first shook England, versions of the psalms in English verse had appeared from the pens of poets and scholars, and several psalters were printed comprising varying numbers of psalms with tunes to which they could be sung. None of these, however, attained the same degree of popularity as the one that had its beginnings in nineteen metrical versions made by Thomas Sternhold, Groom of the King's Robes to Edward VI. In 1547 or 1548 these psalms were printed in a small book that could easily be carried in the pocket of a gown and used for private meditation. According to Anthony à Wood:*

Being a most zealous reformer, and a very strict liver he became scandaliz'd at the amorous and obscene songs used in the court, that he forsooth turn'd into English metre 51 of David's Psalms, and caused musical notes to be set to them, thinking thereby that the courtiers would sing them instead of their sonnets, but did not, only some excepted.

Wood is mistaken in thinking he wrote fifty-one paraphrases. His total output numbered thirty-seven in all. He died in 1549 and shortly after his death another volume appeared in which eighteen more of his translations were added to the original nineteen, together with seven by John Hopkins. This volume went under the title:

All suche Psal/mes of Dauid, as Thomas Sternholde,/ late Grome of the Kin/ges Maiesties Rob/es, did in his/ life tyme/ drawe/ into/ Englishe/ metre.

It was reprinted in 1550, 1551 and 1553. When Mary came to the throne in 1553 all such publications were, for the time being, brought to an end, and

* _Athenæ Oxoniensis_ (1691, Bliss edition, 1815), Vol. I, p. 183.

many of the leading protestant figures of Edward's reign fled to Germany and Switzerland. The presence of Calvin in Geneva attracted a large group of exiles and a congregation of some two hundred English protestants attached itself to Calvin's church. The need for a psalter for use in the reformed church service was soon felt and the volume of metrical versions by Sternhold and Hopkins was chosen as the basis on which to work. Although he held strict views about the character of music used in the church service and discouraged overelaboration in any form, Calvin fully appreciated the value of music in heightening religious experience. Under his guidance the English psalter not only grew in size but tunes were composed and others were borrowed and adapted until fifty-one metrical versions were complete, each supplied with a melody suitable for congregational singing. This collection was printed in Geneva in 1556.

In 1558 another Anglo-Genevan psalter was published, and then in the early part of 1559, Elizabeth having succeeded to the throne in November of the preceding year, most of the exiles returned home. The first English psalter, based on the Genevan model, was printed in 1560, and in 1561 an enlarged collection was printed in England and another in Geneva, by the few exiles who had remained behind to complete the new translation of the bible.

At last, in 1562, the work begun by Sternhold in 1548, was completed and the whole one hundred and fifty Psalms of David were printed by John Day. This is a fine handsome book, printed in blackletter type with the following rubric on the title-page:

THE WHOLE BOOKE/ of Psalmes, collected in Eng=/lysh metre by T. Starnhold I. Hopkins/ & others: conferred with the Ebrue,/ with apt Notes to synge thē with/ al, Faithfully perused and alow=/ ed according to thordre appo-/inted in the Quenes maie-/sties Iniunctions.

In this first edition of the complete Sternhold and Hopkins psalter sixty-five tunes are included: some are used as common to a number of different psalms while several are proper to one only. The melodies themselves are greatly influenced by the Huguenot Psalter of Clément Marot and Théodore de Bèze, of which Louis Bourgeois was musical director; in fact, several of the French tunes, including the one now known as the Old Hundredth, were included without alteration.

After the original forty-four metrical versions of Thomas Sternhold and John Hopkins, the remaining one hundred and six psalms, verses for the Lord's Prayer, the Te Deum, the Ten Commandments, other prayers, evangelical hymns and spiritual songs which preceded and followed the psalms in the 1562 book, were provided by John Hopkins, William Kethe, William Whittingham, Thomas Norton, John Pulleyn or Pullen, Robert

Pont, John Craig and John Marckant. Their work varies greatly in quality. Some of the verses have simple and very moving dignity, others, to modern ears, seem trite almost beyond belief; yet this book so exactly fulfilled a need in the majority of English and Scottish protestant congregations that it became standard usage for the next one hundred and fifty years, while some of the verses and tunes have remained in use to the present day.

As edition followed edition, slight changes were made in the contents with substitutions and additions both in the verses and the melodies,* nevertheless, the sixty-five tunes of the *Whole Booke of Psalmes* of 1562 continued to form the major part of the group of 'church tunes' upon which numbers of composers wrote their harmonizations in succeeding years. The first of these harmonizations appeared in 1563, printed in four separate part-books. Each of these has its description on the title-page, for example:

Tenor

of the whole psalmes in foure partes, whiche/ may be song to al musicall instruments, set forth for/ the increase of vertue: and abolischyng of other/ vayne and triflyng ballades./

> Imprinted at London by John Day,/ dwelling ouer Aldersgate, beneath/ Saynt Martyns/
> Cum gratia et priuilegio Regiae Maiestatis./ per Septennium/ 1563.

Following the traditional use of plain-song melodies, the church tunes, with few exceptions, appear in the tenor voice.

The Scottish Psalter, which appeared in 1564, took a somewhat independent path and a greater number of changes were made in the contents than in that of the English book. Many editions followed the first and reprinting continued until the later years of the seventeenth century.

In England, *The Whole Booke of Psalmes* with the single line of melody was printed again and again in many different formats, the licence passing from printer to printer. John Day, Richard Day, John Wolfe, John Windet, Thomas Est and William Barley all had a hand in the numerous issues. Finally the licence passed into the keeping of the Stationers' Company.

Among the harmonizations that appeared, of considerable interest were three sets by William Damon or Daman. The set of 1579 has the church tunes in the tenor and so also does the first of the two sets of 1591. The second set of this same year is exceptional in having the church tunes in the Cantus voice.

In 1592 *The Whole Booke of Psalmes* was reissued in an entirely new format

---

* For a complete history of the 'Old version' Psalter, with the additions, alterations and substitutions among the tunes, see Maurice Frost, *English and Scottish Psalm Tunes* (1953).

and with the harmonizations brought up to date by ten distinguished composers of the time. Instead of four separate part-books, for the first time a single book is used with the vocal parts so disposed on the page that all four singers can read from the same psalter. The complete wording of the title-page is as follows:

The/WHOLE BOOKE OF/ PSALMES:/ WITH THEIR WON-/ted Tunes, as they are song/ *in Churches, composed* into *foure partes*:/ All which are so placed that four may sing/ ech one a seueral part in this booke. Wherein the Church/ tunes are carefully corrected, and thereunto added other/ short tunes vsually song in London, and other places of/ this Realme. With a Table in the end of the/ booke, of such tunes as are newly added/ with the number of ech Psalme pla-/ced to the said Tunes./ COMPILED BY SONDRY AVTHORS,/ who haue so laboured heerein, that the vnskilfull/ with small practice may attaine to sing/ their part, which is fittest/ for their voice./ IMPRINTED AT LON-/DON by Thomas Est, the assigné of William Byrd: dwelling in Aldersgate/ streete at the signe of the black Horse/ and are there to be sold./ 1592.

The sundry authors are John Farmer, George Kirbye, Richard Allison, Giles Farnaby, Edward Blancks, William Cobbold, Edmund Hooper, Edward Johnson, Michael Cavendish and John Dowland. The church tunes are in the Tenor throughout and, in general, the harmonizations conform to the pattern of extreme simplicity handed on from the Calvinist compilers of the Anglo-Genevan psalters. With few exceptions the music runs note for syllable, the harmony moves in chordal structure and vocalizations are entirely absent. Est's *Whole Booke* was reprinted in 1594, 1604 and 1611.

About 1599 (the year is not certain) a volume appeared under William Barley's imprint which has some rather curious features. It is virtually a reprint of Est's book and, except for the colophon, the title-page is almost identical. A few changes have been made in the numbers to which the tunes have been allocated and several are given with the Tenor and Bassus only. The pages are small, and the book is so excessively fat that complete opening of the pages is difficult. The pages themselves are badly laid out, and, although the title-page declares the settings to be 'composed in foure parts', it is seldom possible to read the four voices from the same page. The alterations which are in fact the reverse of improvements on Est's book, were presumably introduced to protect Barley from the penalties for infringement of Est's licence. Dowland's six harmonizations from Est's *Whole Booke* are included in Barley's volume.

Dowland's contribution to Est's book consisted of the following six works:

Psalm 38: 'Put me not to rebuke, O Lord'.

Words by John Hopkins; first printed in *The Whole Booke of Psalmes* of 1562. The tune first appeared in the Scottish Psalter of 1564/5 where it is used for Psalm 108.

Est uses this setting as common to the following psalms: 47, 51, 53, 56, 60, 64, 71, 75, 80, 85, 95, 98, 101, 106, 109, 114, 118, 142 and 'A Thanksgiving'.

In the reprints of 1594 and 1604 and again in that of 1611, issued under the imprint of the Stationers' Company, the following psalms were added: 2, 10, 13, 17, 20, 26, 28, 32 and 35.

Barley gives the Tenor and Bassus only for every occasion on which he employs this tune. He adds psalms 26, 28, 32 and 35 to Est's original list.

Ravenscroft in his *Whole Booke of Psalms* (1621) discards Dowland's setting and substitutes one by Thomas Morley on a different Tenor. By this time the Tenor upon which Dowland had worked had acquired the name 'Oxford Tune'.

In 1643, William Slatyer in his *Psalmes of David in 4 languages and 4 Parts* uses for Psalm 5 'I. Douland his setting of 38'.

Psalm 100: 'All people that on earth do dwell'.

Words by William Kethe, first printed in the English and Anglo-Genevan psalters of 1561. The tune, probably composed by Louis Bourgeois, was first printed in the French-Genevan psalter of 1551. Here is the version given in *Octanteneuf Pseaumes de David, mis en Rime Francoise par Clement Marot & Théodore de Besze* (1556):

Pseaume CXXXIV

In 1561 the tune in its French form was set to the English words of Psalm 100 and William Whittingham's metrical version of the Lord's Prayer without alteration, but on its next appearance, in John Day's volume of 1563, notes 26 and 27 have had their value changed from semibreves to minims. When Dowland used the tune in 1592 further alterations in the note values were introduced:

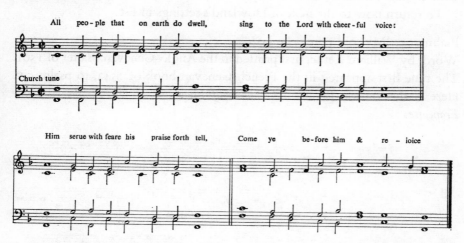

Barley reprints Dowland's complete setting for Psalm 100, but when he uses the Church Tune for 'A Psalme before morning prayer' and 'A Psalme before evening prayer' he adds only the Bassus.

Here, it is perhaps of interest to leave the strict sequence of the setting in Est's *Whole Booke* and look, for comparison, at the later setting that Dowland made for Thomas Ravenscroft's *Whole Booke* of 1621. In this the rhythmic structure of the Tenor is much nearer that of the French original:

This setting is used again by Ravenscroft for 'A Psalm before Evening Prayer'.

The tune which, on the introduction of the revised psalter of Nahum Tate and Nicholas Brady in 1696, became known as the Old Hundredth, continued to be included in collections of psalms and hymns in Dowland's two settings and in settings by other composers, both in England and the United States, until the present day.

To return now to the next of Dowland's settings in Est:

Psalm 104: 'My soul praise the Lord'.
Words by William Kethe, first printed in the Anglo-Genevan Psalter of 1561. The tune first appeared in the French-Genevan book of 1542, to psalm civ. Here is the version given in *Octanteneuf Pseaumes de David, mis en Rime Francoise:*

Most of the early English settings retain the rhythm of the French original, but in Dowland's setting considerable alteration appears:

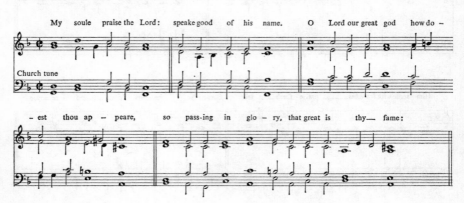

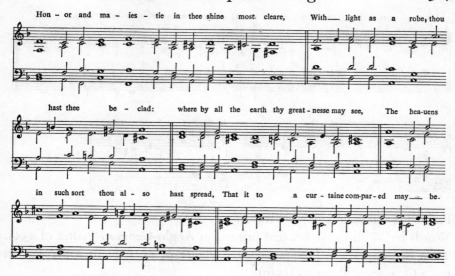

Barley reproduces Dowland's setting complete.

Psalm 130: 'Lord to thee I make my moan'.
Words by William Whittingham, first printed in the Anglo-Genevan Psalter
of 1556. The tune first appeared in *Aulcuns Pseaulmes et Cantiques* (1539):*

In Goudimel's version of the tune, given for Pseaume cxxx in *Octanteneuf
Pseaumes de David, mis en Rime Francoise* (1556), the reading of the second line
has been altered. It is this version that is followed in English texts. Here is
Dowland's setting:

* *Calvin's First Psalter 1539*, edited R. R. Terry (1932) (facsimile).

Psalm 134: 'Behold and have regard'.

Words by William Kethe, first printed in Anglo-Genevan Psalter of 1558. Tune first appears in French-Genevan Psalter of 1551. Here is the version from *Octanteneuf Pseaumes* (1556):

The tune needed considerable adaptation to take Kethe's verses, and here is how it appeared in the Anglo-Genevan Psalter of 1561:

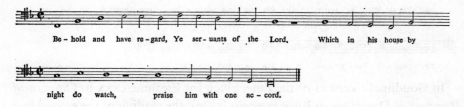

The English words are a translation of the French Psalm cxxxiv; the psalm originally associated with the tune that became the English Old Hundredth.

Further alterations were made in Dowland's setting:

Barley gives the Tenor and Bassus only of Dowland's version.

'A Prayer for the Queens most excellent Maiestie.'
The author of the words is unknown. The verses appeared for the first time in Est's *Whole Booke*. The tune also makes its first appearance in this volume and is listed among those newly added. When set to Psalm 146 by John Farmer it is called 'Chesshire Tune'. Richard Allison, in *The Psalmes of Dauid in Meter* (1599), prints the first line in his Table of tunes as proper to Psalm 146, but it is not included in the body of the book. Barley uses the Tenor and the same words, but the harmonization is by John Bennet. Thomas Ravenscroft calls it 'Cheshire' and uses it for Psalms 31, 80, 129 and 146. It is included among the common tunes in the Scottish books of 1634 and 1635, and William Slatyer uses a variant for Psalm 14 in his *Psalmes of David in foure languages and foure Parts* (1643). Here is Dowland's setting:

The 'Lamentatio Henrici Noel' consists of seven compositions in four separate part books, bound in black. Inside each is inscribed 'Mr./ Henry Noell his / funerall psalmes./ Composed by Jo: Doulande./Bacheler of musick./' After No. 1, at the foot of the page, is written 'Gio.Dolande/ infœlice Inglese/ Bacalario in Musica'. All four books are beautifully and clearly written; not in Dowland's hand, but probably in that of a professional copyist.

This collection presents a marked contrast to the earlier settings. Here Dowland was not writing for 'the unskilfull' as he was in Est's book. With performance by the professional choir at Westminster Abbey in mind, he was able to write without the need to avoid technical difficulties and, although not necessarily more beautiful, these psalms are on an entirely different level of complexity.

All through the set the Church tunes are in the Cantus voice.

No. 1: 'The Lamentation of a sinner'.

Above this is inscribed 'Lamentatio Henrici Noel'. Strictly speaking 'The Lamentation of a sinner' is not a psalm but is one of the canticles that had a fixed place in the church service. The words are by John Marckant and both verses and tune were first printed in the English Psalter of 1561:

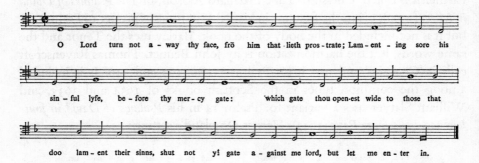

It continued in use through the first half of the seventeenth century and the tune survived the revisions of Tate and Brady, appearing in John Playford's *Psalms and Hymns* of 1671 for Psalm 77, and in his *The Whole Book of Psalms* of 1677, for Psalms 77 and 141.

Here is Dowland's setting:

No.2: Psalm 6, 'Domine ne in furore'.
Words by Thomas Sternhold, first printed in *All suche Psalmes* (1549).
Source of tune unknown.

No. 3. Psalm 51, 'Miserere mei Deus'.
Words by William Whittingham. Both tune and words first printed in the
Anglo-Genevan Psalter of 1556. Here is the Tenor as it appears in the English
Psalter of 1561:

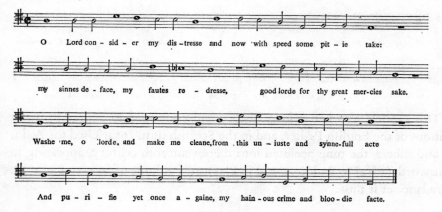

And Dowland's setting:

No. 4: 'The humble sute of the sinner'.

Words by John Marckant. Both words and tune appeared for the first time
in the English Psalter of 1562. The tune was also used for Psalm 35.

This canticle also had a long history and continued to appear in many
editions of the English Psalter, and in the Scottish until 1634. Used for Psalm
35 and others, the tune persisted into the seventeenth century, appearing in
Ainsworth (1612) to Psalm 59, and in Playford's volume of 1677 to Psalm 38.
Dowland set it thus:

No. 5: 'The humble complaint of a sinner'.

The anonymous words of this canticle were first printed in the English Psalter of 1562, where the tune also appears for the first time:

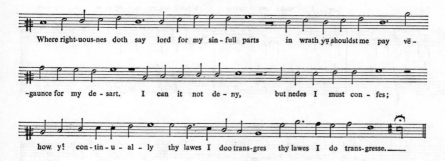

The tune underwent some modifications before it reached Dowland. A few accidentals were added, and William Damon, in *The Former Booke of the Musicke* (1591), changed the last line to the form in which it subsequently appears. In Est's *Whole Booke* the tune, in the Tenor, already has all the characteristics of Dowland's melody:

No. 6: Psalm 130, 'De profundis'.
Words by William Whittingham, first printed in the Anglo-Genevan Psalter of 1556. Origin of tune unknown.

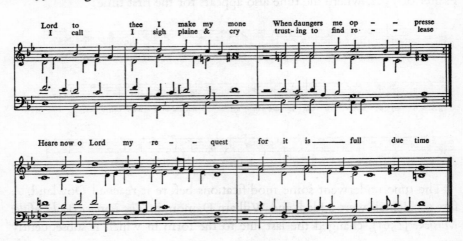

No. 7: Psalm 143, 'Domine exaudi'.
Words by Thomas Norton, first printed in the English Psalter of 1562.
Origin of tune unknown.

The three tunes for which, after the most patient and diligent search, no origin has been found, may have been composed by Dowland himself, although it is difficult to make any suggestion as to his reason for having done so. The fact that they did not, apparently, pass into the accepted repertoire of English and Scottish Church tunes tends to support the probability of their having been entirely personal to Dowland.

In a nineteenth century MS collection at St. Michael's College, Tenbury,* are two four-part settings of psalms ascribed to John Dowland. The first is a setting of Psalm 33, 'Ye righteous in the Lord', but neither of the customary Church tunes is used either in the Cantus or in the Tenor. The second is a setting of Psalm 100, with the 'Old Hundredth' tune in the Cantus. The harmonization does not agree with either of Dowland's settings. There is no earlier documentary support for these attributions, nor is the style particularly reminiscent of Dowland's work.

Sir William Leighton's *Teares or Lamentations of a Sorrowfull Soule* was first written as a set of spiritual meditations and the first edition appeared with the words only, a licence being issued by the Stationers' Company on January 27th, 1612/13, to the printer Ralphe Blore.† By the time the book had

* Tenbury MS 711, ff. 34v/35.
† Arber, Vol. III, f. 234*b*.

reached the press Leighton had already conceived the idea of having the verses set to music, for he announces that he intends '(God willing) likewise to divulge very speadely in print some sweete Musicall Ayres and Tunable accents'. In the Dedication 'To the Most High and Mighty Prince Charles, Sonne to our Soueraigne Lord the King' he again speaks of the 'Melodious Musicke' that will shortly appear. He must have worked quickly and persuasively, since he prevailed on some of the most celebrated musicians of the time to set the poems, and the book was printed, by William Stansby, the following year.

His contributors included Bull, Byrd, Coperario, Dowland, Ford, Orlando Gibbons, Robert Johnson, Robert Jones, Thomas Lupo, John Milton (father of the poet), Peerson, Pilkington, John Ward, Weelkes and Wilbye, as well as lesser figures such as Leighton himself, Giles, Hooper and Robert Kindersley. Dowland contributed a commendatory poem,★ a consort song for four voices, 'An heart thats broken and contrite', and a five-part setting of 'I shame at my unworthiness'. The style of these two compositions is completely distinct, each setting being appropriately called forth by the particular medium.

'An heart that broken and contrite' is one of Dowland's noblest and most beautiful works. Written in the four-part psalm tradition the voices have no very elaborate counterpoint and, at times, move in block harmony. The repetition of words in the madrigalian style is avoided entirely. Twice, however, words are repeated, as in the lute songs, for the sake of added emphasis. In the first stanza the words chosen are 'sweet' and 'far more'. Again, as often happens in the lute songs, this device does not fit so appropriately in the later stanzas. The accompaniment adds a great richness of sound to the *ensemble*, each instrument contributing its own particular tone quality and, in the case of the plucked instruments, distinct and individual phrases. Since this work is so little known I give it in its entirety:

★ See p. 82.

*Bb in original

'I shame at mine unworthines' is fully contrapuntal all through. By
continual repetition of the words the short four-line stanza:

> I shame at mine vnworthines,
>> Yet faine would be at one with thee
> Thou art a ioy in heauines,
>> A succour in necessity,

is elongated into a work of sixty-six bars. The first and second Altus open in
canon, and the first line of the stanza presents an opportunity for typical
word-painting. The note A appears in the second bar sounding against a G
and chords of the augmented fifth add bitterness to the shame:

The tension is maintained until bar 21, when, with the establishment of the
second line, the harmony becomes less tortured. The words 'Thou art a ioy'
take the Cantus on a soaring flight, but with 'heaviness' discordant sounds
return and, if the printer is to be believed, bar 39 has two F naturals and an F
sharp sounding simultaneously:

J. Stafford Smith and E. T. Warren Horne accepted this without comment in their late eighteenth-century transcript,* but Sir Frederick Bridge omitted the composition from his edition of 1922,† although he included 'An heart thats broken and contrite'. Perhaps, like Charles Burney, he found the dissonances not 'very grateful to nice ears'.

From here to the end there are a few passing discords, but nothing to equal the clash of sound at this point.

* B. M. Add. 31,418. (All instrumental parts are omitted.)

† *Sacred Motets and Anthems for four and five voices by William Byrd and his Contemporaries.* (All instrumental parts omitted.)

V

Lachrimæ or Seaven Teares *and other consort music*

❦

With the publication of *Lachrimæ or Seaven Teares* in 1604, Dowland again presented English music-lovers with something quite new. Music specifically written for five viols, or violins, and lute had never before appeared in England. Moreover the make-up of the book was an innovation, since the only consort music previously printed had appeared in sets of separate part-books while *Lachrimæ or Seaven Tears* had all the parts in the same volume, disposed on the open folio, after the pattern of the four-part ayres in the song-books, so that each player had his part clearly visible as the group sat round a table with the book placed in the centre.

The entry for the volume in the Stationers' Register runs as follows:

2 aprilis [1604]
Thomas Adams Entred for his copy vnder the hand of master Byshop our
Master A book called *Seven Teares of* JOHN DOWLAND *figured in seven passionate pavans &c sett forth for the Lute &c in ffyve partes* vjᵈ★

The title-page, unlike those of the song-books, has no elaborate border although decorative panels appear across the top of both the recto and verso of the first two folios. The text of the title-page reads:

LACHRIMÆ,
OR SEAVEN TEARES
FIGVRED IN SEAVEN PASSIO-
nate Pauans, with diuers other Pauans, Gali-
ards, and Almands, set forth for the Lute, Viols, or
Violons, in fiue parts:
By Iohn Dowland Bacheler of Musicke, and Lute-
nist to the most Royall and Magnificent, *Christian* the fourth, King of

★ Arber, Vol. 3, f. 107b.

Denmarke, Norway, Vandales, and Gothes, Duke
of Sleswicke, Holsten, Stormaria, and Ditmarsh:
Earle of Oldenburge and
Delmenhorst.
Aut Furit, aut Lachrimat, quem non Fortuna beauit.*

Under this is a decorative tablet bearing the rubric 'For thou shalt Labor'
with, in the centre, a small figure surrounded by scrolls upon which are
written the words 'Peace and Plenty' and 'For thou shalt labour'.

The Imprint at the bottom says:

LONDON
Printed by Iohn Windet, dwelling at
the Signe of the Crosse Keyes at Powles Wharfe,
and are to be solde at the Authors house in Fetter-Lane
neare Fleet-streete.†

On the verso of the title-page the following pair of Elegiac couplets appear:

ANNÆ REGINÆ
Sacrum.
Ter fælix te Regina Scotus-Anglus-Hybernus:
Tu soror, & coniux Regis, itemq parens.
Iuncta tenes tria Regna, tenes tria numina in uno,
Iuno *opibus, sensu* Pallas, & ore Venus.‡

The Dedication is placed immediately opposite:

TO THE MOST GRACIOVS
and Sacred Princesse Anna Queene of England, Scotland, France and Ireland.§

Since I had accesse to your Highnesse at Winchester, (most gracious Queene)
I haue beene twice vnder sayle for Denmarke, hastning my returne to my
most royall King and Master, your deare and worthiest Brother; but by contrary windes and frost, I was forst backe againe and of necessitie compeld to
winter here in your most happie Kingdome. In which time I haue endeuoured
by my poore labour and study to manifest my humblenesse and dutie to your
highnesse, being my selfe one of your most affectionate Subiects, and also
seruant to your most Princely Brother, the only Patron and Sun-shine of my

* Whom Fortune has not blessed, he either rages or weeps.
† In the B.M. copy, after the words 'Fleet-streete', the date 1605 has been added in what
appears to be a seventeenth-century hand. In the copy at Manchester Public Library the date
has been added in a modern hand. Peter Warlock accepted this as the year of publication.
‡ Dedicated to Queen Anne.
With thee as queen thrice blessed are the Scots, the English and the Irish. Thou art the sister,
wife, and mother of a king. Three realms thou holdest joined, three divinities in one,—a Juno
in power, a Pallas in wisdom, and a Venus in beauty.
§ The words ' & wife of James the first' have been interlined in handwriting in the B.M.
copy.

else vnhappie Fortunes. For which respects I haue presumed to Dedicate this worke of Musicke to your sacred hands, that was begun where you were borne, and ended where you raigne. And though the title doth promise teares, vnfit guests in these ioyfull times, yet no doubt pleasant are the teares which Musicke weepes, neither are teares shed alwayes in sorrowe, but sometime in ioy and gladnesse. Vouchsafe then (worthy Goddesse) your Gracious protection to these showers of Harmonie, least if you frowne on them, they bee Metamorphosed into true teares.

Your Maiesties
in all humilitie deuoted
IOHN DOWLAND.

The address 'To the Reader' follows:

Hauing in forren parts met diuers Lute-lessons of my composition, publisht by strangers without my name or approbation; I thought it much more conuenient, that my labours should passe forth vnder mine owne allowance, receiuing from me their last foile and polishment; for which consideration I haue vndergone this long and troublesome worke, wherein I haue mixed new songs with olde, graue with light, that euery eare may receiue his seuerall content. And as I had in these an earnest desire to satisfie all, I do likewise hope that the peruser will as gratefully entertaine my endeauours, as they were friendly meant.

This onely obseruation I must set downe in the playing of my Lute-lessons for tuning of the Lute, which is, that the 7. 8. 9. string open, do answere in the eight the base string aboue, what letter soeuer it be that carries the base: As for example:

Yours
IOHN DOWLAND

On the next page, headed with the same decorative band as that of the title-page, the twenty-one items of the contents are listed:

THE TABLE OF ALL THE
Songs contained in this Booke.

Lachrimæ Antiquæ.
Lachrimæ Antiquæ Nouæ.
Lachrimæ Gementes.
Lachrimæ Tristes.
Lachrimæ Coactæ.
Lachrimæ Amantis.
Lachrimæ Veræ.

* As far as I am aware, this is the earliest documentation for the use of a nine-course lute in England.

Semper Dowland semper Dolens.
Sir Henry Vmptons Funerall.
M. Iohn Langtons Pauan.
The King of Denmarks Galiard.
The Earle of Essex Galiard.
Sir Iohn Souch his Galiard.
M. Henry Noell his Galiard.
M. Giles Hoby his Galiard.
M. Nicho. Gryffith his Galiard.
M. Thomas Collier his Galiard with two trebles.
Captaine Piper his Galiard.
M. Bucton his Galiard.
Mʳˢ Nichols Almand.
M. George Whitehead his Almand.

The clefs used throughout are   Cantus   or   Altus

Tenor   or   Quintus   Bassus   or

In the quotations from *Lachrimæ or Seaven Teares* I have used modern clefs and, unless otherwise stated, I have halved the time values. In certain passages I have followed Warlock, in clarifying the rhythm, by the use of ties instead of dotted notes. At times my transcription of the lute tablature differs from his in points of detail.

All twenty-one pieces are written for five viols, or violins, and lute, but the slight ambiguity in the description of the contents, on the title-page, as being 'set forth for the Lute, Viols, or Violons, in fiue parts', has opened the way for a theory, held by some groups of viol players, that if the five bowed instruments are present the lute is unnecessary. In support of this idea the fact is put forward that the lute doubles at least four of the parts throughout the majority of the pieces and, in particular, the doubling of the Cantus by the lute is cited as being both unnecessary and objectionable. I am convinced this whole argument is incorrect and that the lute is essential to a satisfactory performance.

Careful examination of the score shows an infinite variety of devices are used in the lute part, each of which makes its individual contribution to the texture. While it is true that the melody is doubled in many of the pieces, in some the tune is entirely absent from the lute, the upper voice being doubled with the Altus, or even with the Tenor or Quintus. On other occasions one of the inner voices is inverted with the Cantus so that the melody is doubled at the octave. At times an entirely independent voice occurs on the lute which does not coincide with that of any of the bowed instruments. Furthermore

AN INSTRVCTION TO THE LVTE.

The first Rule.

Vnderstand this that the Lute is ordinarilie strung with sixe stringes, and although that these six stringes be double except the Treble, and make a leauen in number, yet they must be vnderstood to bee but sixe in all, as thou maiest see them here marked on this Lute figured.

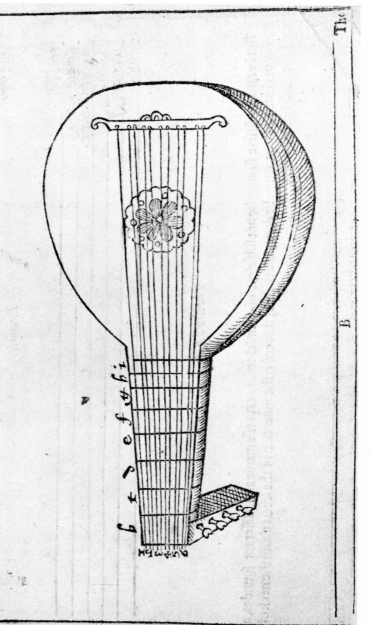

B

A six-course lute as shown in Adrian Le Roy's *A briefe and easye Instruction* (1568)

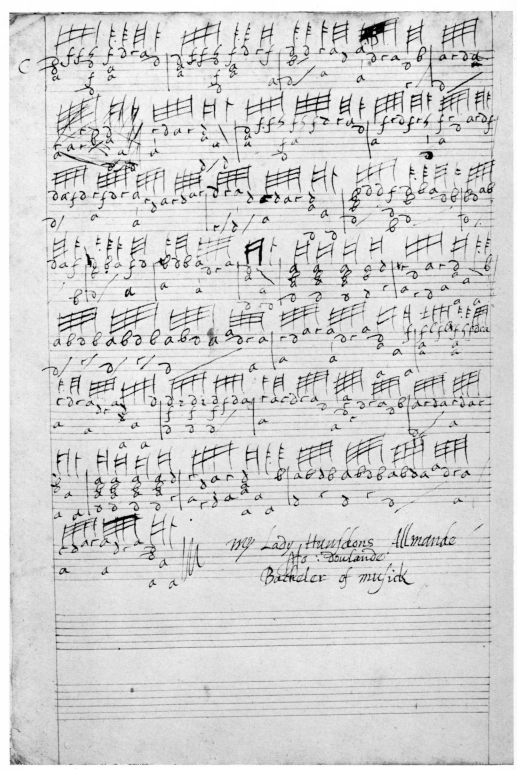

MS. 1610.1. f.22v. 'Lady Hunsdons Allmande', written in Dowland's own hand. By permission of the Folger Shakespeare Library, Washington.

Signatures from MS. 1610. 1. By permission of
the Folger Shakespeare Library, Washington.

Signature of Dame Ann Bayldon, widow of Sir Francis Bayldon of Kippax, on
a document dated 17 February 1624/5. ZDS.g.5 in North Riding Record Office,
Northallerton. By permission of the Rt. Hon. The Viscount Downe.

Christian IV of Denmark, by Peter Isacsh, 1612, in Frederiksborg Castle, Hilleröd, Denmark.

decorative figures are used to embellish the line both of the melody and the bass as well as of one or other of the inner parts.

For the doubling of the Cantus part on the lute, where this occurs, precedents can be shown from earlier composers both of vocal and instrumental music. Adrian Le Roy does precisely this in his reductions of *chansons* for solo voice and lute in his *Livre d'Airs de Cour* (1571), and Emanuel Adriansen includes in the *Nouum Pratum Musicum* (1592) intabulations of madrigals and five galliards to which, although the lute part is complete in itself, he adds a Cantus and Bassus instrumental line. On several occasions in his writings Dowland shows a familiarity with Continental lute music, and a book of the importance of Adriansen's would hardly have escaped his notice especially as Besardus mentions him in the 'Necessarie Observations'; it is possible that the idea of a series of compositions for lute and viols, or violins, sprang from Adriansen's 'elegant field'.

Of the seven pavans that go to make up the Lachrimæ set, each of the six that follows 'Lachrimæ Antiquæ' begins with the four notes of the famous theme in one of the five voices. In addition, a phrase from bars 9 and 10 of the original composition appears as a recurring motif:

Five decorative closes on the lute that serve to fill the final bars of the strains otherwise occupied only by held notes on the bowed instruments, by their reappearance throughout the series (even though some are stock phrases found elsewhere), help to establish a sense of unity. The first of these is taken over from the end of strain 1 of the Lachrimæ Pavan:

The other four are all decorations on the alto part:

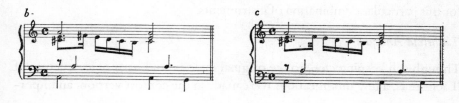

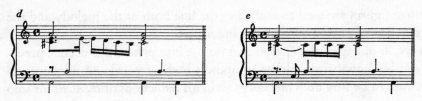

These are a series of variants on the half close from the Lachrimæ Pavan:

In composing for the viols, or violins, Dowland evolved a style completely personal to himself. Not only does he occasionally use progressions and melodic intervals not generally met with in viol music of the period, but he weaves a fabric of which one of the main characteristics is the exploitation of continual momentary dissonance. Suspensions, false relations, and the clash of parts moving against each other at temporarily discordant intervals are combined in a musical texture expressive of extraordinary emotional intensity. Even in the arrangement of some passages of pre-existing lute solos which had previously been entirely concordant, discords of this type are purposefully introduced.

The first part of the book, made up of the 'seaven teares', constitutes a prolonged expression of deeply-felt tragic emotion, only equalled in intensity among the secular compositions of the period by the very greatest examples of madrigalian art.

A performance of the seven pieces lasts some twenty-seven minutes and yet, in spite of the lack of variety in the structure of the pavan, the persistence of the same basic key, and the limited dynamic range of the instruments involved, so perfect is Dowland's art that their extraordinary beauty engages the listener's delighted response from start to finish.

Of the remaining compositions in the volume only four, 'Sir Henry Vmptons Funeral', 'M. Nicholas Gryffith his Galiard', 'M. Thomas Collier his Galiard' and 'M. George Whitehead his Almand', so far remain unaccounted for in an earlier form and appear to have been originally composed for this particular combination of instruments.

'Lachrimæ Antiquæ'

Though still keeping close to the original melodic and harmonic structure of 'Lachrimæ', a few modifications were made in the consort version, an important change being the introduction of a suspended seventh at the beginning of bar 2:

An extremely effective false relation is also achieved at bar 23 by the entry of the Altus being brought forward on to the second quaver of beat 1, instead of a clean break being made between the two chords, as in 'Flow my teares':

Full use is made of the three diapasons at F, E and D.

In the second strain the repetition of the short phrases in each of the five parts creates a texture of great richness:

'*Lachrimæ Antiquæ Nouæ*'

The melody of the first strain is typical of the ingenuity with which Dowland enlaces the old material with the new. Starting with the four notes he immediately develops the tune along fresh lines, but with reminiscent phrases at bars 4 and 7 and 8:

The eighth bar is filled with closed on the lute.

As in 'Lachrimæ' the second strain opens with a chord on the mediant, and for a short while a feeling of C major persists:

* Written a on 7.

Within two bars the reminiscent phrase

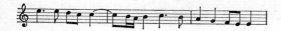

is brought back in the Cantus, and the section ends in the original key on the half close. The third strain owes less to the earlier piece, but, to preserve the feeling of unity, at the end, the decorative close a comes back on the lute.

As can be seen from bar 9, the second of the alternative bass tunings given by Dowland in the address 'To the Reader' is used in this case.

Of the six pavans that follow 'Lachrimæ Antiquæ' this is the only one so far traced in a Continental publication. It appears in Thomas Simpson's *Opusculum* (1610) as No. III à 5 called 'Pauan', and the attribution 'Iohan. Douland' is given. Simpson, reprehensibly, omits the lute part, but both in this book and the *Taffel-Consort* (1621) the works that can be compared with their original sources show him to have taken considerable liberties in the arrangements he made.

'Lachrimæ Gementes'

This is the third of the pieces to open with the four-note theme in the Cantus part. Here it is closely followed by an allusion, in the Tenor, to the often quoted phrase from bars 9 and 10 of 'Lachrimæ':

From the last bar of strain 1, the bass makes a sudden and surprising leap of a seventh to the first beat of strain 2, with a chord of G major, while the Cantus leads into a quotation in bar 2 from precisely the same bar in 'Lach-rimæ Antiquæ', but a semiquaver rest follows the third note, so that the fourth note becomes, with a misplaced accent, the first note of a new phrase:

The third strain is one of the most meltingly beautiful of the whole group of pieces:

'Lachrimæ Tristes'

Here the four-note theme is given to the Altus, while the Cantus enters at a third above. From beat 3 of the first bar until the end of the third bar the lute part has almost the exact Cantus inverted with the Altus, so that the Cantus and the second voice on the lute, with only slight divergences, double at the octave:

The series of suspensions in this strain intensifies the emotional expression of the sad tears of the title.

The first three bars of strain 2, with the rising melody and the introduction of the chord of B flat, are of exceptional beauty:

* A in original

'*Lachrimæ Coactæ*'

The four-note theme returns to the Cantus for the fifth pavan; almost immediately the Altus makes an allusion to the bar 10 phrase, echoed one bar later in the bass. In bar 1 the lute doubles the four notes of the Cantus, but on

the last quaver the higher voice is omitted and the top line of the lute follows
the Altus part until the second half of bar 3, where it again takes up the
Cantus line. From here to the end, following the more usual practice, the lute
joins the Cantus in the melody. Strain 2 is notable for some bold harmonies, a
chromatic passage in the bass in bars 12 and 13, and particularly for its
rhythmic fluidity:

Strain 3 has two more allusions to the bar 10 phrase and ends with the decorative close a.

'Lachrimæ Amantis'

This pavan is distinguished from its fellows by having the four-note theme, here announced in the Tenor, begin on the dominant instead of on the tonic.

The same four notes are imitated by the Cantus in bars 2 and 3, but except for the cadences at the ends of strains 1 and 2 and decorative closes a and b, there are less allusive passages than in the preceding four 'tears'.

A chord of C sharp minor in bar 10, and the rising chromatic notes of bars 11 and 12, are particularly poignant:

'Lachrimæ Veræ'

The four notes are here given to the Bassus and begin on the tonic. The
Cantus, one crotchet later, has the four notes beginning on the dominant,
but continues down the scale to G sharp.

The lute again has some bars in which the upper voice is used independently
as in bar 3, for example, where a suspended fourth adds a discordant bite.
Once more in bar 4 a chord of B flat is suddenly introduced with great effect:

In strain 2 Dowland has gone outside the Lachrimæ material and uses a
self-quotation from another source; significantly enough from a work again
inspired by tears. Compare bars 11 and 12 (the lute part here provides a short
score):

with bars 13 and 14 of 'I saw my Lady weepe':

But such a woe (be-leeue me) as

The addition of the flat makes the third chord of bar 11 so much more woeful that the question arises whether a flat was omitted in the printing of *The Second Booke* where the B natural introduces a sudden and unwanted sense of cheerfulness and confidence.

In the final strain the busy movement of internal part writing is brought to a more tranquil mood, and the last five bars are written with great simplicity. The series is rounded off with the return of the familiar cadence and the decorative close e:

'*Semper Dowland semper Dolens*'

This beautiful composition is as satisfying in this setting as it is as a lute solo. The changed ending in the consort version has already been discussed on p. 119. In his edition of 1926 Peter Warlock says, in a note to bar 5:

'Occasional discrepancies between the lute and viol parts suggest that the lute was not used when the five viols were present.'

The two chords in bar 5, however, which prompted this note, are, I am convinced, wrongly placed as the result of a copyist's or printer's error. If the position of these chords is transposed in the tablature the text then agrees with the viol parts and, moreover, it agrees exactly with the solo version. The only other discrepancy of importance is in bar 9 and lies between the Altus and the second voice on the lute where suspensions involve the interval of a minor second between the two parts, but the clash of these momentary discords is an essential feature of Dowland's writing in these pieces and other examples may be quoted, such as the simultaneous sounding of G Sharp and G natural in bar 23 of 'Lachrimæ Antiquæ' where the discord has been deliberately introduced into a previously concordant passage.

'*Sir Henry Vmptons Funerall*'

This pavan in G minor is subdued and sombre in character, well fitting the mournful occasion it commemorates. The form is asymmetrical, having eight bars in strains 1 and 2, and ten in strain 3. Strain 1, is itself unusual in being divided into two sections with a half close and a pause at the end of the third bar. In these opening bars the Cantus and Bassus parts maintain slow notes while the inner voices move in such a way as to provide a series of momentary discords:

The upper voice of the lute mostly coincides with the Cantus, but a number of decorative passages are added of which those of the last four bars are typical:

'M. John Langtons Pauan'

The F major of this piece comes as a marked contrast to the minor keys of the nine preceding pavans. Its shape is irregular, there being eight bars in strain 1, seven in strain 2, and nine in strain 3. The difference between the early and late forms has already been discussed on p. 122.

For this arrangement Dowland uses his second tuning of the diapasons and, at the end of the first strain he puts the lute bass an octave below the Bassus, thereby adding great richness to the sound:

A very slight and rather curious alteration to the melody in the consort arrangement in bars 2 and 3 of the third strain has resulted in a phrase highly reminiscent of bars 13 and 14 of the song 'Awake sweete loue':

'*Sir Iohn Langton his Pauin*' *from* '*Varietie of Lute Lessons*' (1610)

'*M. Iohn Langtons Pauan*' *from* '*Lachrimæ or Seaven Teares*' (1604)

'*Awake sweete loue*' *from* '*The First Booke of Songes*' (1597)

Seem — ed   faire: she on - ly   I   could loue,

It is all too easy (and dangerous) to be fanciful about an occurrence such as this but, nevertheless, it is tempting to speculate whether the phrase 'she only I could love' was running in Dowland's head to any special purpose when he re-wrote the passage.

Thomas Simpson included this piece in his *Opusculum* (1610) under the title 'Pauan', No. XXI à 5, with Dowland's name attached. Although transposed a tone higher it is virtually the *Lachrimæ or Seaven Teares* text.

'*The King of Denmarks Galiard*'

Apart from the thickening of the texture by the additional parts nothing of fresh significance has been introduced into this version.

'*The Earle of Essex Galiard*'

This galliard has already been discussed at some length on pp. 151–156 and pp. 223–229. Little more can be said here but to repeat the fact of its great popularity and to mention again the lateness of the date to which a memory of the tune persisted.

'*Sir Iohn Souch his Galiard*'

This is a particularly successful arrangement of a previously existing song to the present medium. Though the main outline of the melody is maintained and the harmonic structure generally remains unchanged, Dowland has adopted a somewhat different manner of treatment from that of the four-part ayre 'My thoughts are wingde with hopes', giving far more fluidity of movement to the inner voices, as comparison of the first strain of each will show:

'*Sir Iohn Souch his Galiard*'

Furthermore he adds some decorative elaborations to the Cantus part as, for example, in bars 9 and 10:

And say as she doth in the hea – uens mooue

A charmingly light-hearted treatment is given to the Cantus line in the opening bars of strain 3 which, in the song, by the demands of the words, is kept at a more sober level:

And whis – per this but soft – ly in her.__ eares.

'M. Henry Noel his Galiard'

For discussion of the lute solo 'Mignarda' and the song 'Shall I striue with words to moue' see pp. 147–148 and pp. 395–396.

In all three settings of this galliard it has the unusual form of eight bars in strain 1, sixteen in strain 2, and eight in strain 3.

The key has been lifted a third higher in this arrangement and, curiously, the interval at the end of the second phrase of the melody (bar 4) which, in the lute solo and song appears as that of fifth:

is here changed to a tone:

Apart from this the general outline of the melody remains the same, although occasionally it is treated in a more decorative manner than in the song. The inner voices in this piece are also written with a similar fluidity to those of 'Sir Iohn Souch his Galiard'. In several bars the lute omits the tune and leaves it to the Cantus alone.

'M. Giles Hobies Galiard'

This is a symmetrical galliard of eight bars to each of the three strains. It has here been transposed a tone higher from the key of the original lute solo but in other ways it has been very little altered. The addition of the inner voices, however, gives an extra richness and interest to the whole.

In this and the next two galliards Dowland omits the melody wholly or almost entirely from the lute. Unfortunately Joachim Van den Hove failed to appreciate this point and collected from some unreliable source copies of this lute part and those of 'Nicholas Gryffith his Galiard', 'Thomas Collier his Galiard' and the two almands at the end of the book, which are also incomplete, and printed them in *Delitiæ Musicæ* (1612) as lute solos. Dr. Hans Dagobert Bruger fell into the same trap. Putting his trust in Van den Hove he lifted 'Giles Hoby', 'Thomas Collier' and the two almands straight into his book of guitar transcriptions, *John Dowland's Solostücke für die Laute* (1923).

'M. Nicholas Gryffith his Galiard'

In this galliard of eight, twelve and eight bars to the three strains, the main interest lies in the somewhat different treatment given to the lute. Here in the upper line it very seldom coincides with the Cantus, nor does it consistently follow the Altus. At times, as, for example, in bar 1, it doubles with the Quintus:

At others, as in bar 6, it has an independent inner voice that only partly coincides with the Quintus:

Again at bar 12 it acts somewhat independently, inverting a phrase similar to but not identical with, the Cantus, with a similar, but not identical, phrase from the Quintus:

In bars 18 and 19 there is an inversion of the Quintus with parts of the Tenor and parts of the Cantus so that the top line of the lute is playing most of the notes of the Quintus an octave higher:

In the third strain the upper voice on the lute doubles mainly with the Altus for the first few bars and then mainly with the Tenor; the Cantus line appearing for the notes of the final cadence.

'M. Thomas Collier his Galiard with two trebles'

The use of two trebles in this galliard of eight bars to each strain, allows Dowland to write two Cantus parts of equal importance that exchange and imitate the same musical phrases. This interchange is well shown in the last strain:

The lute generally, though not invariably, follows the second Treble. In bar 11 there is an interesting passage where Dowland has used a figuration in the bass simultaneously with a phrase of similar rhythmic pattern and almost identical notes in the second Treble:

As can be seen in the first quotation, in bar 19 the lute has a somewhat similar figuration, but this time only rather distantly related to a phrase in the Tenor.

'Captaine Digorie Piper his Galiard'

This galliard has been discussed previously on pp. 133–137 and p. 223. In this setting Dowland returns to the earlier manner of doubling the Cantus and the upper voice on the lute. Almost the only independent movement from the lute comes at the end of each strain, where it has the function of filling the bars to held notes on the viols.

'M. Buctons Galiard'

See also under 'The Right Honourable the Lord Viscount Lisle, his Galliard' and 'Susanna galliard', p. 149.

In arranging this piece for viols, or violins, and lute, Dowland has treated the first strain in a far more polyphonic manner than he has in either of the solo versions. Both in the earlier 'Susanna galliard' and in the later 'Lord Viscount Lisle' the structure is almost entirely chordal, but here the 'Suzanne un jour' notes are used as the basis for a series of imitations, the phrase, after the first announcement in the Cantus, being taken up first by the Quintus and then by the Tenor:

The second strain has even more differences, since it diverges both harmonically and melodically from the solo versions:

'*The Lord Viscount Lisle, his Galliard*'

'*M. Buctons Galiard*'

In the third strain, although the melody is almost identical, the bass shows a number of discrepancies between the solo and consort versions:

'*The Lord Viscount Lisle, his Galliard*'

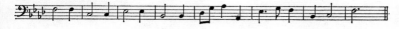

'*M. Buctons Galiard*'

Hildebrant and Füllsack included an arrangement of this composition in *Auselesener Paduanen und Galliarden* (Hamburg, 1607) as 'Galliarda à 5' by 'Ihon Douland'★, but it appears to be closer to the original 'Suzanna galliard' than to the consort version of *Lachrimæ or Seaven Tears*:

★ Quoted from C. R. B. Engelke, *Musik und Musiker am Gottorfer Hofe. Veröffentlichungen der Schleswig-Holsteinischen Universitätsgesellschaft*, No. 15, I (1930–).

'Mistresse Nichols Almand'

This cheerful little piece first existed as a very simple lute solo. In this arrangement it becomes far more sophisticated. The melody of the first strain is identical in both versions, but in the second strain of the Cantus part some slight revisions have made it more elegant:

Dd.2.11, f. 100v.

Lachrimæ or Seaven Teares

* (time values as in original)

In his edition of 1926 Peter Warlock gives the following reading at bars 7, 8 and 9:

In point of fact, the chord marked SIC is, in the original, not as he gives it, nor do the redundant quavers occur at the spot where the asterisk is placed. For the sake of clarity, here are bars 7, 8 and 9 of the tablature exactly as they stand:

(The dotted lines indicate Warlock's barring.)

In my opinion more has gone wrong with this passage than simply the inclusion of the redundant quavers. I would suggest that on beat 1 of bar 8 the lute bass is correct, agreeing as it does with the Bassus part, and that the inner voice, beginning at beat 4 of bar 7, should follow the Tenor, giving the following reading:

It is something of a mystery how the extra beats came to be included since they certainly do not belong to any known solo version.

Three other arrangements of this almain are found in varying number of parts. Add. 10,444 has a version called 'An Almain' (No. 26), on f. 9 of the Cantus book, and f. 64 of the Bassus book. Valentin Haussmann gives a version à 5 in his *Rest von Polnischen und andern Tänzen* (Nürnberg 1603) as No. LXXI, without title or acknowledgement,★ and Thomas Simpson has a setting à 4, No. IIX of the *Taffel-Consort* (Hamburg, 1612), called 'Aria' and attributed to 'Johan:Douland'.

All these have differences of reading one from another, but all appear to be derived from the solo version rather than from Dowland's own consort setting. For example, all have the three minims in the melody in the second half of bar 5 and of bar 6, which Dowland himself broke down for his Cantus part. A curious distortion of the tune appears in the second bar of both Add. 10,444 and Haussmann's setting, where the quavers of beat 2 are written a third lower. Haussmann also elongates the second strain to 13 bars, but he adds his extra beats in bars 10 and 11; his arrangement, therefore, throws no light on the extra beats of the *Lachrimæ or Seaven Teares* lute part. In none of these three arrangements does the bass agree with Dowland's, nor are they in agreement with each other.

★ A modern edition of this is found in Haussmann's instrumental works, Vol. 16 of the *Dankmaler Deutscher Tonkunst.*

'M. George Whitehead his Almand'

This is another exceedingly good-humoured piece with a rhythm very apt for dancing. The mood seems lighter than is suggested by Morley's description of the almand as being a 'more heauie daunce then this [the galliard] (fitlie representing the nature of the people, whose name it carrieth) so that no extraordinarie motions are vsed in dancing of it.'★

Can it be pure coincidence that there is such a striking resemblance between the first four bars of strain 2 and the opening of the old tune for the Athanasian Creed given among the Proper Tunes in an early seventeenth-century MS?

★ (Time values as in original; bar length halved).

Christ Church, Oxford, MS 48†

Perhaps Dowland heard the tune on some occasion, stored it in his memory and brought it to light again in this form.

★ Thomas Morley, *A Plaine and Easie Introduction to Practical Musicke* (1597), p. 181.
† These bars are quoted in the Library Catalogue, p. 22.

Other consort music

Four more pieces exist in consort form that have not been identified with any known compositions by Dowland. Of these one appears in Add. 10,444, the others in Thomas Simpson's two volumes, *Opusculum* (Frankfurt, 1610), and *Taffel-Consort* (Hamburg, 1621).

Add. 10,444, No. 16, 'Doulands Allmaine', f. 6v for Cantus, f. 61v for Bassus (modern numbering of folios).

This MS consists of three sections bound into one volume. Two of these comprise Cantus and Bassus part-books in which the majority of the pieces are connected with masques performed between the years 1603 and 1622, while the third contains Fantasias by Matthew Locke. The Hughes-Hughes Catalogue gives the date as 'after 1635, see f. 36ᵇ'. This was accepted by W. J. Lawrence[*] and several other writers, but J. P. Cutts shows it to be incorrect when applied to the Cantus and Bassus part-books.[†] In describing the group 8–26 he says: 'Item (16) may refer either to John or his son Robert. Items (21) and 25 are obviously complementary and probably belong as all the Almans here, to particular masques as part of the revels.' The Hughes-Hughes Catalogue also suggests (with a query) Robert as the composer. What none of the writers on this MS seem to have realized is that Item 26, though anonymous and called simply 'An Almaine', is in fact Dowland's early lute solo, later known as 'Mrs Nichols Almand' (see p. 160). The late, but incorrect, date accepted by Hughes-Hughes makes the suggestion of Robert as composer of No. 16 reasonable, but with the earlier dating of Cutts the unqualified name 'Douland' would undoubtedly still have referred to John and not to Robert. Furthermore, the presence of one authentic piece by John adds to the likelihood of the other being from his hand also. 'Mrs Nichols Almand' may have been inserted into a masque, but it was certainly not written expressly for any of those mentioned by Cutts since its presence can be traced to MSS that pre-date the earliest masque quoted in his article. Moreover, the divergence of the bass line from that of several versions whose authenticity is undisputed, and the incorrect placing of the two quavers in bar 2, show this to be a derivative and not the original composition. It is surprising that Cutts missed the fact of its presence since this in itself is a supporting factor for his argument in favour of the writing of the MS having been carried out at a date anterior to 1635. It also, of course, raises the question of whether the other pieces, including No. 16, whose titles give no further information than, for

[*] 'Notes on a collection of Masque Music', *Music and Letters*, January 1922, Vol. III, pp. 49–58.
[†] *Music and Letters*, July 1954, Vol. XXXV, pp. 185–200.

example, the word almain, were in fact written for masques, or whether they were not, like No. 26, arrangements of already existing compositions. Add. 10,444, No. 16:

(Time values unchanged; bars and double bars added).

Thomas Simpson, *Opusculum*, has three compositions attributed to Dowland, of which No. XI, à 5, 'Pauan', 'Iohann Douland', appears nowhere else. Here is the Cantus of strain 1:

(Time values unaltered; bar lines added).

Thomas Simpson, *Taffel-Consort*. No. V, à 4, has the title 'Paduan' with the attribution 'Iohan Douland'. The Cantus of strain I goes as follows:

(Time values unaltered; bar lines added).

The two upper voices are of equal importance, with considerable inter-change of figuration. Both lines lie high, and the music appears more suitable for violins than for viols. The style is not particularly reminiscent of Dowland's other pavans in consort form and, without the attribution, I doubt whether his name would have come to mind as that of the composer. Simpson's arrangement may be responsible for obscuring its individuality, but in my opinion the possibility exists that the piece is not by Dowland.

A transcription of this pavan has been included in *Jacobean Consort Music*,★ edited by Thurston Dart and William Coates.

No. XXXIX à 4, 'Volta', 'Ioh. Douland' is tuneful and spirited but has little to distinguish it from numbers of other pieces in the same form written between about 1610 and 1620. The Cantus part of strain 1 goes as follows:

(Time values halved and bar lines added).

The piece appears in a selection from Simpson's *Taffel-Consort*,† edited by Helmut Mönkemeyer in the series 'Consortium'.

Simpson provided all the pieces in his later collection with a figured bass.

Of the eight pieces attributed to Dowland in *Opusculum* and *Taffel-Consort* only one, 'Lachrimæ Antiquæ Novæ' in the former, can be established as having originally been composed by Dowland in consort form; four of the remaining seven had existed previously either as songs or as lute solos (the version of 'Mrs Nichols Almand' in *Taffel-Consort* is not Dowland's arrange-ment from *Lachrimæ or Seaven Teares*) and were cast into their four- or five-part form by Simpson. Of the three unidentified pieces the *Opusculum* pavan seems

★ Musica Britannica, Vol. 9. (1955), p. 192.
† Undated, but published in the early 1960s.

nearest to Dowland's style though none of them reveals the unmistakable signature of his genius.

Little or nothing can be offered in the way of proof, but in my opinion it is unlikely that they are late productions, specially composed for Simpson. In the circumstances I think it more probable that they are either the sole remains of dances that had originated as lute solos, or that they are not by Dowland at all.

Early seventeenth-century collectors and arrangers often show themselves to be in a state of confusion about which pieces may properly be attributed to Dowland, and while many of his genuine compositions were going about with no attribution, others such as the Tobias Kün 'Respondens Lachrimæ' and the Besardus version of Bacheler's galliard on the 'To plead my faith' theme were wrongly given his name. I for one should not be altogether surprised if it were ever shown that any one of the three had come from the hand of another composer.

VI

Dowland's translations

❧❧❧

'THE MICROLOGUS' OF ORNITHOPARCUS

Andreas Vogelsang, or Ornithoparcus as he preferred to be called, was born at Meiningen *c.* 1485 and died at Munster *c.* 1536. Little is known of him except that he was M.A. of Tübingen and, during the year 1516 had some connection with the University of Wittenberg. His *Musice Active Micrologus* was printed at Leipzig in 1517.

Dowland, as he tells us himself, made the translation during his travels, perhaps occupying himself during the enforced hours of waiting in inns when darkness or storms made progress on the roads impossible. He may have added the finishing touches after his return from Denmark, since the licence to print was not entered to Thomas Adams until January 20th, 1608/9.*

The translation agrees in all major respects with the original. Dowland appears to have added nothing to the text, and to have omitted only a few extraneous paragraphs from the end, which occur after Ornithoparcus's 'Peroratio ac libri conclusio'. The illustrative figures are the same, although in the recutting of the blocks some small differences in the appearance have crept in. It may be partly due to the charm of Dowland's translation but Ornithoparcus comes through as a rather endearing character in his enthusiasm for his subject, his genuine anxiety to reach the truth and to pass on his knowledge, especially to young people. His matter is excellent and constitutes a clear and concise exposition of the philosophical ideas governing musical practice in the fifteenth and early sixteenth centuries, and of theoretical questions such as musical notation, the intervals, the hexachords, keys, modes, time and time signatures. He also deals with purely practical subjects such as the correct accenting of the words in singing the psalms and the gospels. The Table of Contents gives an idea of the scope of the volume:

* Arber, Vol. III, f. 178ᵇ.

Wherefore Rests are put in the Counterpoint, Chap. 7.
Of the diuers fashions of Singing, Chap. 8.

The wording of Dowland's title-page is as follows:

ANDREAS
ORNITHOPARCUS
HIS *MICROLOGVS*
OR
Introduction:
Containing the Art of
Singing.
Digested into Foure Bookes.
Not only profitable, BVT
also necessary for all that are studious
of Musicke
ALSO THE DIMENSIONS AND PER-
fect Vse of the Monochord, *according to*
Guido Aretinus.
By Iohn DOVLAND LUTENIST,
Lute-player, and Bachelor of *Musicke* in both
the *Uniuersities*
1609
LONDON.
Printed for *Thomas Adams*, dwelling in *Paules*
Church-yard, at the Signe of the
White Lion.

The whole is enclosed in a border of printers' ornaments.

The prefatory material consists of the customary dedication and epistle:

TO THE RIGHT HONO-/RABLE *ROBERT* EARLE OF SALIS-
BURY, Viscount *Cranborne*, Baron of *Essingdon*, / Lord High *Treasurer of
England*, Principall *Secretarie* to the Kings most/ excellent Maiestie, Maister of
the Courts of Wards and Liueries,/ *Chancellor of the most famous Vniuersitie
of* Cambridge, *Knight*/ *of the most Noble order of the Garter, and one of his
Maiesties*/ most honourable Priuie Counsell.

Your high Place, your princely Honours and Vertues, the heriditary
vigilance and wisedome, wherewith Hercules-like, you assist the protection
of the whole State: Though these (most honoured Lord) are powerfull
encitements to draw all sorts to the desire of your most Noble protection.
Yet besides all these (in more particular by your Lordships speciall Fauors
and Graces) am I emboldened to present this Father of Musicke Ornithoparcus to your worthyest Patronage, whose approoued Workes in my
trauails (for the common good of our Musicians) I haue reduced into our
English Language. Beseeching your Lordship (as a chiefe Author of all
our good) graciously to receiue this poore presentment, whereby your
Lordship shall encourage me to a future taske, more new in subiect, and

as memorable in worth. Euery Plant brings forth his like, and of Musitians, Musicke is the fruit. Moreouer such is your diuine Disposition that both you excellently understand, and royally entertaine the Exercise of Musicke, which mind-tempering Art, the graue Luther was not affraid to place in the next seat to Diuinity. My daily prayers (which are a poore mans best wealth) shall humbly sollicite the Author of all Harmonie for a continuall encrease of your Honors present happinesse with long life, and a successiue blessing to your generous posteritie.

Your Lordships humbly deuoted
Iohn Douland.

To the Reader:

Excellent men haue at all times in all Arts deliuered to Posteritie their obseruations, thereby bringing Arts to a cartaintie and perfection. Among which there is no Writer more worthy in the Art of Musicke than this Author *Ornithoparcus*, whose *Worke*, as I haue made it familiar to all that speake our Language, so I could wish that the rest in this kinde were by the like meanes drawne into our knowledge, since (I am assured) that there is nothing can more aduance the apprehension of *Musicke,* than the reading of such Writers as haue both skilfully and diligently set downe the precepts thereof. My industry and on-set herein if you friendly accept (being now re-turned home to remaine) shall encourage me shortly to diuulge a more pecu-liar worke of mine owne: namely, *My Obseruations and Directions concerning the Art of Lute-playing:* which Instrument as of all that are portable, is, and euer hath been most in request, so it is the hardest to mannage with cunning and order, with the true nature of fingering; which skill hath as yet by no Writer been rightly expressed: what by my endeauors may therein be attained, I leaue to your future Iudgement, when time shall produce that which is already almost ready for Haruest.

Vale, From my house in Fetter-lane this tenth Aprill, 1609.

Your Friend
Iohn Douland.

The dedication of the original book, as given by Dowland, is:

TO THE RIGHT HONORABLE, WORTHY AND WISE/ GOVERNOVRS OF THE STATE OF LVNENBVRG,/ *ANDREAS ORNITHOPARCUS* OF *MEYNING*, MAISTER OF THE LIBERAL SCIENCES.

With little more ado Ornithoparcus is soon launched upon his exposition of the nature of music and its governing philosophy; an exposition fundamental to the position of the writer with claims to be judged a 'speculative musician':

... For Socrates, and Plato, and the Pythagoreans did generally enact, that young men and maides should be trayned up in Musicke, not to the end their mindes might be incited to wantonnesse by those bawbles, which make Art to be so vilely reputed of: but that the motions of the minde might be ruled and gouerned by law and reason. For seeing the nature of young men is unquiet, and in all things desiring delights, & therefore refuseth seuerer arts, it is by the honest delights of Musick brought to those recreations, which may also solace honest old age.

Among those things wherwith the mind of man is wont to be delighted, I can finde nothing that is more great, more healthfull, more honest, than Musicke: The power whereof is so great, that it refuseth neither any sexe, nor any age, and (as Macrobius, a man of most hidden & profound learning saith) there is no brest so sauage and cruell, which is not moued with the touch of this delight. For it doth driue away cares, perswade men to gentlenesse, represseth and stirreth anger, nourisheth arts, encreaseth concord, inflameth heroicall minds to gallant attempts, curbeth vice, breedeth vertues, and nurseth them when they are borne, composeth men to good fashion. For among all those things which doe admit sence, that onely worketh upon manners of men, which toucheth his eares, as Aristotle in his musicall problemes doth more at large discourse. Hence was it that Agememnon being to goe Generall for the Troian warres, as Philelphus reports, left a Musitian at his house, who by singing the prayses of womens vertues might incite Clytemnestra to a chaste and honest life, wherein he did so farre preuaile, that they say she could not be ouercome by Egistus his unchaste attempts, till the ungodly wretch had made away with the Musitian, who onely hindered him from his wicked purpose. . . .

In *The generall Description of Musicke* he says:

Musicke (as *Franchinus Gafforus* in the third Chapter of the first booke of *Theoric* writeth) is a knowledge of *Tuning*, which consists in *sound* and *Song*. In *sound* (I say) because of the musicke which the motion of the cœlestial Orbes doth make. In *Song,* least that melody which ourselues practise, should be secluded out of our definition.

and *Of the Musicke of the World*:

When God (whom *Plutarch* proues to haue made all things to a certaine harmonie) had deuised to make this world mouable, it was necessary that he should gouerne it by some actiue and moouing power, for no bodies but those which haue a soule, can moue themselues, as *Franchinus* in the first Chapter of his *Theoric* saith. Now that motion (because it is the swiftest of all other, and most regular) is not without sound: for it must needs be that a sound is made of the very wheeling of the Orbes. . . . The like sayd *Boêtius*, how can this quick-mouing frame of the world whirle about with a dumb and silent motion? From this turning of the heauen, there cannot be remoued a certain order of Harmonie. And nature will . . . that extremities must needs sound deepe on the one side, & sharp on the other. So then the worlds Musicke is an Harmonie, caused by the motion of the starres, and violence of the Spheares. . . . Now the cause wee cannot heare this sound according to *Pliny* is, because the greatnesse of the sound doth exceede the sence of our eares. But whether wee admit this Harmonicall sound of the

Heauens, or no, it skils not much; sith certaine it is, that the Grand Work-
maister of the *Mundane Fabricke*, made all things in number, weight, and
measure, wherein principally, *Mundane Musicke* doth consist. (pp. o/1.)

Of Humane Musicke he tells us:

Hvmane Musicke, is the Concordance of diuers elements in one compound, by
which the spirituall nature is ioyned with the body, and the reasonable part is
coupled in concord with the vnreasonable, which proceeds from the vniting
of the body and the soule. For that amitie, by which the body is ioyned vnto
the soule, is not tyed with bodily bands, but vertuall, caused by the proportion of humors. For what (saith *Cælius*) makes the powers of the soule so
sundry and disagreeing to conspire oftentimes each with other? who recon-
ciles the Elements of the body? what other power doth soder and glue that
spirituall strength, which is indued with an intellect to a mortall and earthly
frame, than that Musicke which euery man that descends into himselfe finds
in himselfe? For euery like is preserued by his like, and by his dislike is
disturbed. Hence it is, that we loath and abhorre dischords, and are delighted
when we heare harmonicall concords, because we know there is in our
selues the like concord. (p. 1.)

How did Dowland, who loved discords as a cat loves cream, reconcile
himself to the final paragraph, one wonders.

Ornithoparcus continues with a description of Organicall Musicke,
Harmonicall Musicke, Inspectiue Musicke, Actiue Musicke, Mensurall
Musicke and Plaine Musicke.

On the medieval doctrine concerning the relative positions of the musical
theoretician and the practical musician, Dowland would have found himself
entirely in agreement with Ornithoparcus. His 'simple Cantors, or vocall
singers, who though they seeme excellent in their blinde Diuision-making,
are merely ignorant, euen in the first elements of Musicke' might have come
direct from the pages of the *Micrologus*. Ornithoparcus is at pains to make the
position clear and it seems worth while quoting him in full on a point which
was held to be of cardinal importance:

Of the differences betwixt a Musitian, and a Singer.

Of them that professe the Art of *Harmony*, there be three kindes; (saith
Franchinus in the first Book the 4. chap. of his *Theoric*) one is that which deal-
eth with Instruments; the other maketh Verses; the third doth iudge the
workes both of the instruments, and of the verses. Now the first, which deal-
eth with Instruments, doth herein spend all his worke; as *Harpers* and
Organists, & all others which approue their skil by Instruments. For thy are
remoued from the intellectuall part of Musicke, being but as seruants, and
vsing no reason: voide of all speculation, and following their sence onely.
Now though they seeme to doe many things learnedly and skilfully, yet is it

plaine that they haue not knowledge, because they comprehend not the thing they professe, in the purenesse of their vnderstanding; and therefore doe we deny them to haue Musicke, which is the Science of making melodie. For there is knowledge without practise, and most an end greater, than in them that are excellent Practitioners. For we attribute the nimblenesse of fingering not to Science, which is onely residing in the soule, but to practise, for if it were otherwise, euery man the more skilfull he were in the Art, the more swift he would be in his fingering. Yet doe we not deny the know-ledge of Musicke to all that play on Instruments; for the Organist, and he that sings to the Harpe, may haue the knowledge of Musick, which if it be, we account such the best Artists.

The second kind is of *Poets*, who are led to the making of a verse, rather by a naturall instinct, than by speculation. These *Boêtius* secludes from the specu-lation of Musicke, but *Austin* doth not.

The third kind of Musitians, be they which doe assume vnto them the cunning to iudge and discerne good *Ayres* from bad: which kind (sith it is wholy placed in speculation and reason) it doth properly belong to the Art of *Musicke*. (pp. 3/4).

Who is truely to be called a Musitian

Therefore he is truely to be called a *Musitian,* who hath the faculty of speculation and reason, not he that hath onely practicke fashion of singing: for so saith *Boêtius lih.* 1. *cap.* 35. He is called a Musitian, which taketh vpon him the knowledge of Singing by weighing it with reason, not with the seruile exercise of practise, but the commanding power of speculation, and wanteth neither speculation nor practise. Wherfore that practise is fit for a learned man: *Plutarch in* his Musicke sets downe (being forced vnto it by *Homers* authoritie) and proues it thus: *Speculation breedeth onely knowledge, but practise bringeth the same to worke.* (p. 4.)

Who be called Singers

The *Practitioner* of this facultie is called a *Cantor*, who doth pronounce and sing those things, which the Musitian by a rule of reason doth set downe. So that the *Harmony* is nothing worth, if the *Cantor* seeke to vtter it without the Rules of reason, and vnlesse he comprehend that which he pronounceth in the puritie of his vnderstanding. Therefore well saith *Ioun Papa* 22. *cap.*2. To whom shall I compare a *Cantor* better than to a *Drunkard* (which indeed goeth home,) but by which path he cannot tell. A *Musitian* to a *Cantor* is as a *Prætor* to a *Cryer*. . . . (p. 4).

Thomas Morley, in *A Plaine and Easie Introduction to Practicall Musicke* (1597), shows a very different attitude in this matter of speculative and practical music. The very title is a bold break with tradition, and his treatment of the subject is, in its way, revolutionary. Instead of beginning with an exposition of the current musical philosophy, he plunges straight into practical teaching, in the form of a conversation between three characters:

Polymathes, Philomathes and Master. Before they have gone far, the following exchange takes place:

MA. . . . But haue you learned nothing at all in Musick before?
PHI. Nothing. Therefore I pray begin at the verie beginning, and teach mee as though I were a childe.
MA. I will do so, and therefore behold, here is the Scale of Musicke which wee tearme the *Gam*. (p. 2.)

Then he is off immediately on a clear exposition of all that concerns the art of reading and understanding music according to the practice of his time. It is not until he comes to the end of the book, and adds a section called 'Annotations' that the question of Speculative and Practical music is raised. He abandons the conversational form and speaks in his own person, quoting authorities on the nature of the division. He sums up by saying:

As for the diuision, Musicke is either *speculatiue* or practicall. *Speculatiue is that kind of musicke* which by Mathematicall helpes, seeketh out the causes, properties, and natures of soundes by themselues, and compared with others, proceeding no further, but content with the onlie contemplation of the Art. *Practicall* is that which teacheth al that may be knowne in songs, eyther for the vnderstanding of other mens, or making of ones owne. . . .

Though he has a short paragraph on the doctrine of the Music of the Spheres, makes formal obeisance, and quotes Authority on the subject, clearly it is not in such questions that his main interest lies. His attention is devoted in much more detail to problems concerning the physical make up of the notes, the relationship between the degrees of the scale, the exact nature of Mood, Time and Prolation, and what may be termed the scientific aspect of speculative music, rather than the metaphysical. In this respect Morley, in 1597, belonged to the future, while Ornithoparcus, in 1609, belonged to the past.

In accordance with the prevailing musical theories of his day, Ornithoparcus believed the ecclesiastical tonal system to have descended directly from, and to be identical with, the Greek system of the *tonoi*. He also accepted that, in addition to bearing the Greek names, every tone, or mode, still retained the characteristic powers which ancient writers held to be inherent in the Greek tones. In the fourth chapter he describes both 'The Authentic and the Plagall' and then he sets forth the names:

Now these Eight *Tones* (as *Franc. lib.* 5. *Theor.* and last Chapter, and *lib.* 1. *pract.* 7. *cap.* saith) are by the Authors thus named, The first *Dorian*; the second, *Hypodorian*; the third, *Phrygian*; (which *Porphyrio* cals barbarous;) the fourth, *Hypophrygian*; the fift, *Lydian*; the sixt, *Hypolydian*; the seuenth,

Myxolydian; the eight, some call *Hypomyxolydian*; others say it hath no proper name. (pp. 10/11).

In the thirteenth chapter he continues with his information about the tones, or modes, and says:

That diuers men are delighted with diuers Moodes
Euery mans palate is not delighted with the same meate (as *Pon.* writes in the 16. ch. of his Musick.) but some delight in sharp, some in sweet meates: neither are all mens eares delighted with the same sounds: for some are delighted with the crabbed & courtly wandring of the first *Tone.* Others do affect the hoarse grauitie of the second: others take pleasure in the seuere, & as it were disdainful stalking of the third: others are drawn with the flatring sound of the fourth: others are moued with the modest wantonnes of the fift: others are led with the lamenting voyce of the sixt: others do willingly heare the warlike leapings of the seuenth: others do loue the decent, & as it were, matronall carriage of the eight. . . .
The Darian *Moode* is the bestower of wisdome, and causer of chastity. The *Phrygian* causeth wars, and enflameth fury. The *Eolian* doth appease the tempests of the minde, and when it hath appeased them, luls them asleepe. The *Lydian* doth sharpen the wit of the dull, & doth make them that are burdened with earthly desires, to desire heauenly things, an excellent worker of good things. Yet doth *Plato lib.* 3. *de Rep.* much reprehend the *Lydian,* both because it is mournful, and also because it is womanish. But he alloweth of the *Dorian,* both because it is manly, & also doth delight valiant men, & is a discourser of warlike matters. . . . (p. 36.)

By the time Dowland made the work of Ornithoparcus 'familiar to all that speake our language', Mei and the *camerata* in Italy, and the theoreticians of the Académie de Poésie et de Musique in France, though still accepting the miraculous powers of Greek music to achieve these 'effects', had already shown the error of identifying the Church modes with the Greek tonal system. In England, though no similar searchings of musical antiquity had occupied the theorists, the new ideas were, in certain directions at least, being tacitly accepted. It is noticeable that Thomas Morley, though giving a very thorough analysis of the construction of the modes, confines himself to a scientific discussion of the musical intervals of which the modes are composed and attributes to them no extra-musical properties. He gives the 'eight tunes' their Greek names but of any further attributes he says no more than of the Dorian 'the ancient Dorius, so famous and recommended in the writings of the philosophers'.* That he realizes they are not the true Greek *tonoi* is shown when he says:

. . . And these be (although not the true substance) yet some shadow of the ancient *modi* whereof *Boethius* and Glareanus have written so much.* (p. 147.)

* *Annotations. Upon the third part.*

Another subject on which the writings of Ornithoparcus were inapplicable to the time and place appears in the Third Booke, where he treats of Accent in the singing of gospels, epistles and psalms. His rules apply exclusively to Latin texts which were, of course, no longer in use in the Jacobean Church.

Dowland can hardly have failed to realize the changes that had come about since Ornithoparcus's time, nor is it likely he was unaware of the publication of Morley's *A Plaine and Easie Introduction to Practicall Musicke*. Without in any way belittling the quality of the *Micrologus*, or underestimating its importance as a historical document, it may be said with truth that some sections were obsolete in relation to the English musical scene in 1609, and that the contents of the still relevant chapters had been carefully and expertly handled by Morley. Yet Dowland nowhere suggests that his motive in publishing is to make available a work important mainly as a historical record of ideas and practises either just passed into, or rapidly on their way towards, desuetude. Possibly he found an identity of outlook with Ornithoparcus on certain questions (singers for one, undoubtedly!), which blinded him to its shortcomings as a textbook for 1609, or possibly once launched upon the work he was reluctant to abandon the results of such an extensive labour. It would be interesting to know the reaction of the musical public, and whether the sales justified the cost of publication. Perhaps the sub-title, *Introduction: Containing the Art of Singing*, and the chapters devoted entirely to this subject, carried enough interest to insure an adequate market.

A lighter side to the *Micrologus* is provided by the remarks about Cantors that appear throughout the volume. They suggest that the standard of singing in cathedrals and churches, at least in the towns and cities Ornithoparcus knew, was far from satisfactory. On p. 75 he tells us how he has travelled in order to hear many different choirs:

. . . And (if I may speake without vain-glory) for that cause haue I seene many parts of the world, and in them diuers Churches both *Metropolitane* and *Cathedrall,* not without great impeachment of my state that thereby I might profit those that shall liue after mee. In which trauell of mine I have seen the fiue Kingdomes of *Pannonia, Sarmatia, Boemia, Denmarke,* and of both the *Germanies* 63. Dioceses, Cities 340, infinit fashions of diuers people, besides sayled ouer the two seas, to wit, the *Balticke,* and the great *Ocean,* not to heape riches, but to increase my knowledge. All which I would haue thus taken, that the Readers may know this booke is more out of my experience, than any precepts.

On p. 88, out of his experience, he tells us *Of the diuers fashions of Singing.*

. . . the English doe carroll; the French sing; the Spaniards weepe; the Italians, which dwell about the Coasts of *Ianua* caper with their Voyces; the others barke; but the Germanes (which I am ashamed to vtter) doe howle like Wolues.

He ends his treatise with a chapter entitled *Of the Ten Precepts necessary for euery singer*, and says:

Being that diuers men doe diuersly abuse themselues in Gods praise; some by mouing their body vndecently; some by gaping vnseemely; some by chang-ing the vowels, I thought good to teach all Cantors certaine precepts, by which they may erre lesse.

The following are a few points from his list:

3. Let euery Singer conforme his voyce to the words, that as much as he can he maketh the *Concent* sad when the words are sad; & merry when they are merry . . .
4. Aboue all things keepe the equalitie of measure. For to sing without law and measure, is an offence to God himselfe, who hath made all things well, in number, weight and measure. . . .
7. Let a Singer take heed, least he begin too loud braying like an Asse, or when he hath begun with an vneuen height, disgrace the Song. For God is not pleased with loud cryes, but with louely sounds: it is not (saith our *Eras-mus*) the noyse of the lips, but the ardent desire of the Art, which like the lowdest voice doth pierce Gods eares. . . . But why the Saxons, and those that dwell vpon the Balticke coast, should so delight in such clamouring, there is no reason, but either because they haue a deafe God, or because they thinke he is gone to the South-side of heauen, and therefore cannot so easily heare both the Easterlings, and the Southerlings.
9. The vncomely gaping of the mouth, and vngracefull motion of the body, is a signe of a bad Singer.
10. Aboue all things, let the Singer study to please God, and not men; (saith *Guido*) there are foolish Singers, who contemne the deuotion they should seeke after: and affect the wantonnesse which they should shun: because they intend their singing to men, and not to God: seeking for a little worldly fame, that so they may loose the eternall glory; pleasing men that thereby they may displease God: imparting to others that deuotion, which themselues want: seeking the fauour of the creature, contemning the loue of the Creatour: to whom is due all honour, and reuerence, and seruice. To whom I doe deuote my selfe, and all that is mine, to him will I sing as long as I haue being: for he hath raised me (poore Wretch) from the earth, and from the meanest basenesse. Therefore blessed be his Name world without end. *Amen.**

The end of the Worke

But this was not quite the end, for Ornithoparcus added a *Peroratio ac libri Conclusio*, of which, in Dowland's translation, the final words are:

* pp. 89–90.

... Wherefore let those courteous Readers (that be delighted with Ornithoparcus his paines taken) be contented with these few things, for as soone as I can but take breath, they shall see matters of greater worth.

THE 'NECESSARIE OBSERVATIONS' OF BESARDUS

There is no absolute certainty as to whether this translation in *Varietie of Lute-Lessons* is by John or Robert.* There seems to have been a determined effort to make the volume appear as the sole work of Robert, and John's name is not given on the title-page. Nevertheless, the caption at the beginning of the instructions reads as follows:

NECESSARIE/ OBSERVATIONS BELONG-/ING TO THE *LUTE*, AND LVTE/ playing, by *John Baptisto Besardo* of Visonti: with/ choise varietie of LVTE-lessons, partly Inuented, and partly Col-/lected out of the best AVTHORS, by *Robert Douland*, and *Iohn Douland* Batcheler of/ *MUSICKE*.

If John's responsibility is acknowledged here, why does his name not appear elsewhere, unless he himself was making an attempt to push forward a not-so-brilliant son? The above caption was, presumably, written on the manuscript when it went to the printers, but when the title-page was made up with Robert's name only, possibly the presence of the tell-tale name of John was forgotten and was not removed.

It is true that in lines 14, 15 and 16 of the address 'To the Reader whosoeuer' Robert says:

The Treatise of fingering I thought no scorne to borrow of *Iohn Baptisto Besardo* of Visonti, being a man generally knowne and honoured for his excellencie in this kinde. But whatsoeuer I haue here done (vntill my Father hath finished his greater Worke, touching the Art of Lute-playing,) I referre it to your iudicious censures. . . .

In line 12, however, he says, claiming the credit for the whole collection:

Touching this I haue done, they are Collections gathered together with much labour out of the most excellent Authors . . .

This, even though John's part is acknowledged on the opposite page.

If lines 14, 15 and 16 are carefully examined it will be seen that, in fact, Robert makes no specific claim to the translation and what he says could apply to nothing more than the decision to include the 'Observations' in the volume.

Unfortunately so little is known of the shadowy figure of Robert that we

* Julia Sutton, in 'The Lute Instructions of Jean-Baptiste Besard', *The Musical Quarterly*, Vol. LI, pp. 345–62, accepts it as the work of Robert, without question.

are not in a position to say for certain whether he possessed the necessary qualifications and ability to have carried through the translation. My own opinion is that John was probably the moving spirit behind the publication of both *Varietie of Lute-Lessons* and *A Musicall Banquet* and that he may well have made the translation himself, and even written the prefatory matter, with the express intention of pushing Robert forward into the public eye. If Robert had possessed the required ability to prepare these two volumes unaided how is it, one wonders, that no further editorial work was ever undertaken by him?

We know from his translation of the *Micrologus* that Dowland had an excellent knowledge of Latin, and all his writings show a most persuasive English style. Both of these, I believe, at this point, he turned to the advancement of his son.

Jean-Baptiste Besard (*c.* 1567–*c.* 1625) was the son of a merchant of Besancon.* He lived successively in Rome, where he became the pupil of Laurencini; at Cologne, where his *Thesaurus Harmonicus* was printed in 1603, and his collection of historical documents, *Mercurii Gallobelgici* in 1604; in Augsburg, where his *Novus partus, siue concertationes musicae,* his *Antrum philosophicum,* a book of medical information, and *Isagoge in artem testudinariam,* all appeared in 1617. He is described by Castan as:

> . . . ce célèbre amateur, licencié et docteur en droit, compilateur de gros livres historique, philosophiques et medicaus, qui s'intitulait lui-même 'adepte des arts liberaux, et très habile musicien'.†

The 'Observations' included in *Varietie of Lute-Lessons* are a translation of the *De modo in testudine libellus* appended to the *Thesaurus Harmonicus* with, as Julia Sutton says, 'minor changes'. In the *Novus partus,* published in September, 1617, Besardus appended a revised and enlarged set of instructions with the title '*Ad artem Testudinis breui*'. Just prior to this, in June of the same year, his *Isogoge* appeared, being a translation into German of the '*Ad Artem Testudinis breui*' by 'I.N.', with some emendations, and some comments by the translator.‡

As printed in *Varietie of Lute-Lessons,* the 'Observations' consist of some general remarks, and then, with side headings, the following sections:

To chuse a LVTE.
What lesson to begin withall.
For vsing of both hands together.
For Griping of stops in B.

* Auguste Castan, 'Notes sur J. B. Besard', *Mémoirs de la Sociétié d'emulation du Doubs,* 5ᵉ serie, Tome I, Besancon, 1876, p. 25.

† op. cit., p. 40.

‡ For some of this information I am indebted to Julia Sutton's article.

Of Holding.
For the vse of the right hand.
To know how to strike single strings, being found among stops.
Wherefore the numbers before the letters serueth.
Of playing with the two fingers.
A good Note.

Among other pieces of general advice he makes the sensible suggestion that the student will make better progress

if hee stint himslefe in his learning with such labour and exercise that is moderate, and continuall, nor such vnreasonable pains as many doe weary themselues with:

He also advises practice at such times as the student feels willingness:

For there is a certaine naturall disposition, for learning the ARTS naturally infused into vs, and shewing it in vs rather at one time then another, which if one will prouoke by immoderate labour, he shall fight against Nature. Therefore when thou shalt finde thyselfe aptlie disposed, and hast time and opportunitie, spare no paynes, yet keepe this course.

On choosing a lute he says:

First and formost chuse a LVTE neither great nor small, but a midling one, such as shall fit thine hand in thine owne iudgement. Yet I had rather thou didst practise at first on a LVTE that were somewhat greater and harder, vnlesse thy hand be very short: because that is good to stretch the sinewes, which are in no sort to be slackned.*

He is wise in his time in suggesting the beginner should start with an easy lesson, it being apparently, the custom to begin on pieces that overtaxed the student's capacity. He also tells the student he should get one piece 'reasonably perfect', not 'straggling from one to another'. He recommends that pieces should be memorized, the fingering of each hand having first been carefully marked and noted.

In the section on left-hand fingering he gives all the usual rules, but emphasizes the fact that different circumstances demand the use of different fingers.

He stresses the necessity of understanding the counterpoint and of keeping the component voices alive:

. . . nothing is more sweete, then when those parts (the mothers of *Harmonie*) are rightly combined, which cannot be if the fingers be sodainly taken from the strings: for that voyce perisheth sodainly, when the stopping thereof is ended. . . . Therefore keepe your fingers in what strings soeuer you strike

---

* This advice needs to be treated with care. In my teaching experience I have found a too large instrument can be exceedingly discouraging to the student.

(especially when you strike the Base) whilst the other fingers are stopping other stops, and remoue them not till another Note come, which doth immediately fall vpon another Base, or some other part.

It is, however, in the instructions for the right hand that, in my opinion, the 'Observations' are of most interest, since they represent a transitional stage between the early technique and that which was finally to supersede it.

Since the appearance of Thomas Robinson's *Schoole of Musicke* in 1603, no other instructions for the lute had been printed in England, and Robinson, while advocating the thumb for running passages in the bass, still taught, without modification, the use of the thumb and first finger for all such passages on the upper strings. Besardus, however, recommends the use of the second and first fingers in all passages where the upper voice is accompanied by notes in the bass, thus avoiding the excessive movement of the hand if the thumb is to play a note in the bass and then move rapidly over to take its place on one of the upper strings. Nevertheless, he still maintains the importance of the thumb and first finger for all passages without bass notes.

By the time that Mace's *Musick's Monument* appeared in 1676 the thumb and first finger technique had almost entirely disappeared, although Mary Burwell's tutor (*c.* 1668–1671) still recommends its use for fast running passages from the bass to the treble.★

On the subject of ornamentation he avoids the problem altogether by saying:

You should haue some rules for the sweet relishes and shakes if they could be expressed here, as they are on the LVTE: but seeing they cannot by speach or writing be expressed, thou wert best to imitate some cunning player, or get them by thine owne practise, onely take heed, least in making too many shakes thou hinder the perfection of the Notes. In somme, if you affect biting sounds, as some men call them, which may very well be vsed, yet vse them not in your running, and vse them not at all but when you iudge them decent.

He ends with this injunction to the student:

Therefore take in good part this one Methode of practising on the LVTE howsoeuer it be: composed in such sort as an ingenious man, and one that professeth another Art could attayne vnto: receiue it I say with as kinde a heart as I offer it with, and so shall I be ready hereafter to furnish thee with some other worke of mine owne more serious. *Farewell.*

★ Thurston Dart, 'Mary Burwell's Instruction Book for the Lute'. *Galpin Society Journal*, No. XI, May, 1958, pp. 3–62.

VII

Patrons and friends

꧁ ❦ ꧂

In an age when England had no more than about five million inhabitants, and when marriage among the aristocracy, the gentry and the 'new rich' was an important means of consolidating estates and families and of securing political alignments, it is not surprising that many of the families in the Court circle, from which a large proportion of Dowland's patrons was drawn, were, in fact, related to each other. There is no need to look to the remote ramifications of the various families to find these connections. Within the generations of Dowland's own time the singularly close integration of this society can be seen.

The fact that death so often removed one or other partner within a few years of marriage, and that a closely ensuing remarriage was the normal practice, often meant that a man or woman had successively two, three or even four, wives or husbands, the family connections spreading wider and wider with each new marriage. One group only from among Dowland's patrons and friends gives a typical picture of these family relationships among the upper classes in sixteenth-century England. Thus Lady Russell was, through her sisters, the aunt of both Sir Robert Cecil and Sir Francis Bacon (who, though not a direct patron of Dowland's, must, by reason of his close association with the Earl of Essex, have been at least acquainted with him); Giles Hoby was her first husband's half-brother; and she was, of course, the aunt by marriage of Lucie Countess of Bedford. Sir Robert Cecil was the uncle of Elizabeth 'the young Lady Derby', sister-in-law of Ferdinando Earl of Derby, whose wife Alice was the sister of Elizabeth Carey, Lady Hunsdon. Cecil's wife, Elizabethan Brooke was the niece of Sir Henry Cobham. Lord Hunsdon's sister Margaret Carey, married Sir Edward Hoby, the son of Lady Russell by her first husband; and so the Cecils, Russells, Hobys, Stanleys, Spencers, Careys and Brookes were all linked together in various degrees of kinship.

The custom of dedicating books of music to an influential patron was general, not only in England but on the Continent as well, composers vying with each other in the use of strange and exaggerated compliments. No flattery seems to have been too gross to be acceptable and Dowland was merely following the fashion in his use of extravagant adulation.

There appears to have been a slight difference of motive behind the choice of a patron for a book and for the naming of an individual piece. In the case of Dowland's printed books it is noticeable that people of position and influence are always chosen: Sir George Carey (*The First Booke of Songes*); Lucie Countess of Bedford (*The Second Booke of Songs*); Sir John Souch (*The Third and Laste Booke of Songs*); Lord Howard de Walden (*A Pilgrimes Solace*); Anne, Queen of England (*Lachrimæ or Seaven Teares*); and the Earl of Salisbury (*The Micrologus*); and it is clear that expediency, the hope of financial reward or favours to come lay behind the choice. With the individual pieces a less calculating attitude is apparent. Certainly some may have been commissioned, others certainly were not. For example Henry Noel's Galliard, the Earl of Essex's Galliard, and Queen Elizabeth's Galliard were not so named until after the death of the three dedicatees when further favours of any kind could no longer be expected. These can only have been acts of disinterested homage. The altogether obscure Thomas Collier and the not very distinguished M.P. for Carnarvon, Nicholas Griffith, may have bought themselves immortality by commissioning galliards, but did the expressions of friendship for John Forster, William Jewel and Anthony Holborne also have their price or were they purely the result of a generous impulse?

Perhaps the most puzzling of all the dedications are those of the pavan and galliard to the young Cornish pirate Digory Piper. Was Piper a lover of music and did he commission the two pieces or was he a friend for whom Dowland was prepared to make a defiant gesture? Had Piper been engaged in the gentlemanly occupation of harrying the Spaniard, association with him would have been in no way likely to tarnish Dowland's reputation, but he was preying on shipping of countries with whom Elizabeth had no quarrel, he was in trouble with the authorities and, though not hanged for piracy, must have been perilously near it; and he died in poverty with creditors administering the estate. Altogether a questionable character for the musician aspiring to royal favour to associate with on terms of friendship. Moreover, when, in 1604, in *Lachrimæ or Seaven Teares*, Dowland renamed an older piece 'The King of Denmark's Galliard' the intention was, undoubtedly to gratify his royal master. It would have been more tactful, to say the least, to have omitted from the volume the name of the pirate who had caused so much trouble to Christian's father. Other pieces in the book were renamed for the occasion, then why not the galliard named after Digorie Piper, or if it was too well known under that name, why not omit it altogether? It can only be supposed, I think, that Piper was a friend, and that in naming the two pieces for him and including the galliard in the *Lachrimæ* volume he was following the dictates of a character which, on the one hand, was possessed with an ambition to secure the highest employment music could offer and, on the other, was prepared to set no limits on freedom of action, even when such action could be detrimental to the realization of that ambition.

In addition to those of the dedicatees, biographical notes are given of a number of other characters who played some part in Dowland's life: members of the nobility under whom he served; musicians and others with whom he came into contact; and poets and writers with whom he worked.

Of the historically famous men and women like Queen Elizabeth, James I, the Earl of Essex and the Earl of Salisbury, detailed biographies are not given and only a few dates are mentioned to set them in the period in relation to Dowland's life and work. Where, however, it has been possible to trace any special musical interest or association these have been thought relevant to the subject and have been included, so also, from time to time, have odd anecdotes from contemporary sources which throw a little beam of light upon a distant figure, enliven it and bring it close in an immediately perceived humanity.

For ease of reference the notes are arranged alphabetically.

Anne, wife of James I, sister of Christian IV of Denmark, Queen of England from 1603 till her death in 1619. She is chiefly remembered for the masques and entertainments in which she, the Courtiers and the ladies of her Court frequently played the leading parts. The enormous sums of money spent on these productions caused grave concern among the more responsible sections of society, while accounts of the costumes and the bearing of the Queen and her ladies during the performances often scandalized the more puritanical families among the aristocracy and the middle class. Nevertheless, extravagant and foolish as she often was, the writers, designers and musicians that were brought together to work for her, were all among the finest in their various professions, and from such evidence as can be pieced together from the scripts, designs and music that have survived, some of these entertainments must have achieved a high standard of distinction.

Bertie, Peregrine, eleventh Baron Willoughby de Eresby was the son of Katherine, Duchess of Suffolk, third wife of Charles Brandon, Duke of Suffolk. After his death she married an obscure gentleman Richard Bertie. Of firm Protestant belief they were compelled to fly the country during the

Marian persecution.* Peregrine is reported to have been born in a church porch during a violent storm, while his father was seeking help at a farm near Wesel.† Eventually, through the intervention of a friend, the King of Poland interested himself in their case and they were granted an estate in Poland on which they lived until Elizabeth's accession, when they returned to England.

In 1586 he went to the Low Countries with the Earl of Leicester's army, and when, in the following year, the Earl was recalled, Lord Willoughby was made General of the English forces in the United Provinces in his place. In March 1588/9, finding himself with his health undermined and, through the failure of the English Government to pay back the large sums laid out in necessary payments to the troops, in financial difficulties, he asked to be allowed to give up his command and return home. The request was granted and soon after he spent some months travelling on the Continent, visiting, among other places, Venice and Vienna. In 1589 he was sent to France to command a small and badly equipped force of about four thousand men to help Henry of Navarre. Although he was one of the most able and conscientious soldiers of his day he failed to rise again to any of the more spectacular military commands and Robert Naunton says of him:

. . . I have heard it spoken, that had he not slighted the court, but had applied himself to the queene, he might have enjoyed a plentiful portion of her grace; And it was his saying, (and it did him no good), that he was not one of the *Reptilia*: intimating, that he could not creepe on the ground, and that the court was not his element . . .‡

He was made Governor of Berwick in February 1597/8, and died in 1601.

His exploits in the Low Countries were celebrated in the ballad 'The fifteenth day of July', although, as with many other ballads of the period, the facts as reported are not, historically speaking, strictly true.

Bodley, Sir Josias (1550?–1618), was the son of John Bodley of Exeter, being the younger brother of Sir Thomas Bodley, founder of the Bodleian Library, Oxford. He spent much of his youth abroad with his family at Wesel and Geneva. It is possible that he studied for a short time at Merton College, Oxford, but if so, he left without proceeding to a degree. He appears to have travelled considerably, having visited Poland and then having served with the English army in the Netherlands. Subsequently he was engaged in military service in Ireland, where he was knighted by Lord Mountjoy on March 25th, 1604. He died in Ireland in 1618.

* Their adventures are told in a ballad, 'The Duchess of Suffolkes Calamitie', in Deloney's *Strange Histories* (1602).
† As a matter of historical fact the picturesque story is frowned on.
‡ *Fragmenta Regalia* (1653), edited Arber (1870), p. 37.

I have been unable to discover the reason for his having been in Italy in 1595.

Brunswick, Henry Julio, Duke of (1564–1613), *see* p. 31.

Bucton, Mr. In *The Visitation of Yorkshire, 1563 and 1564*★ some details are given of the family of Sir Pyers Bucton of Bucton in Yorkshire. No dates are included, however, so even a guess at the identity of Dowland's Mr. Bucton is impossible. I have been unable to discover any further information about this family.

Carey, George, second Baron Hunsdon (1547–1603). Soldier, diplomat and courtier. His father Henry, first Baron Hunsdon, was the son of Mary Boleyn and Harry Carey, and was thus the first cousin of Queen Elizabeth. The younger Carey took part in the fighting against the Scots in the campaign of 1573–4, when an army was sent under the Earl of Sussex to carry out reprisals after the assassination of the Regent Moray. The following story is told of his exploits outside Dunbarton Castle:

Lord Fleming, who held Dumbarton Castle for the Queen of Scots, had demanded a parley with Sir William Drury; during which he treacherously caused him to be fired upon; happily without effect. Sir George Carey, burning to avenge the injury offered to his commander, sent immediately a letter of defiance to Lord Fleming, challenging him to meet him in single combat on this quarrel, when, where and how he dared; concluding thus; 'otherwise I will baffle your good name, sound with trumpet your dishonour, and *paint your picture with the heels upwards, and bear it in despite of yourself*'.

He took an active part in the suppression of Roman Catholicism and was member of a commission empowered to 'examine in the Tower, Harte, Bosgrave and Pascall, arrested within the realme coming from Rome and other places beyond the seas with intent to pervert and seduce the queen's subjects', December 24th, 1580. He was Governor of the Isle of Wight from 1586 to 1587 when the threat of invasion from Spain was imminent. He succeeded to the title on the death of his father in 1596 and in March 1596/7 he was appointed Lord Chamberlain of the Household. His name is on the General Commission for the Suppression of Schism, issued on November 24th, 1599. He was the patron of the company of actors known as the Lord Chamberlain's Men of which Shakespeare was a member. His house, in the precinct of Blackfriars, was part of the old friary building, not far from the

---

★ *Harleian Society Publications*, Vol. XVI, p. 41.

room given over to the use of the Blackfriars Theatre.* Thomas Morley's
1597 volume of *Canzonets* was dedicated to him. His youngest sister, Margaret Carey, married Sir Edward Hoby, elder son of Lady Russell by her
first marriage to Sir Thomas Hoby.

Carey, Lady Elizabeth, wife of the above and second daughter of Sir John
Spencer of Althorp, Northamptonshire. Edmund Spenser was among her
relations and he dedicated his *Musiopotmos* to her. He also wrote of her in an
introductory poem in the *Faery Queen*. Nash also dedicated *Christs Tears over
Jerusalem* to her. The possibility of Dowland's having served in the Carey
family is discussed on p. 50. Lady Carey's elder sister Alice married, as her
first husband, Ferdinando Earl of Derby.

Case, Dr. John, born at Woodstock, he became a chorister at New College
and Christ Church, Oxford. In 1564 he was elected to a scholarship at St.
John's. He became M.A. in 1572 and was made a Fellow of his college.
Anthony à Wood says of him that he was 'popishly affected, and left his
fellowship and married'.† He became a private tutor, reading philosophy and
logic with a number of young men, many of whom were said to be Catholics.
He took his degree as Doctor of Medicine in 1589 and built up a successful
practice. On his death on January 23rd, 1599/1600. he left sums of money to
St. John's College, New College, and the poor of Woodstock. He was buried
in the Chapel of St. John's and his portrait hangs in the Bodleian Library.

His works chiefly consist of books on various aspects of Aristotle's writings,
but he also wrote *Apologia Musices, tam vocalis quam instrumentalis, et mixtæ*
(1588) in which, on p. 44, he mentions Dowland:

... & quæ causa nunc est cur hos superstites adhuc viros Birdum, Mundanum,
Bullum, Morleum, Doulandum, Ionsonum, aliosque hodie permultos instrumentorum peritissimos iustis suis laudibus non persequamur? ...‡

The book is dedicated to Sir Henry Unton and Sir William Hatton.

The Praise of Musicke (1586)§ is also ascribed to him on the evidence of a
poem by Thomas Watson, the poet and translator of *The first sett of Italian
Madrigalls Englished* (1590), who wrote *A Gratification unto Master John Case*

---

* Irwin Smith, *Shakespeare's Blackfriars Playhouse* (1964), First British Commonwealth
Edition 1966, pp. 95, 106.

† *Athenæ Oxoniensis* (1691), edited Bliss (1815), col. 685.

‡ Which may be translated '. . . and what cause is there now, why we should not mention, with their just praise, these still surviving men, Bird, Munday, Bull, Morley, Douland,
Johnson and others (today very many) highly skilled upon instruments? . . .'

§ Dedicated to Sir Walter Raleigh by the printer Barnes, who calls it 'an orphan of one of
Lady Musick's children'.

for his learned booke made lately in the praise of Musicke. His verse has a certain charm:

> Let others praise what seems them best,
> I like his lines aboue the rest
> Whose pen hath painted Musickes prayse
> He soundly blames the senceles foole
> And barbarous Scithyan of our dayes,
> He writes of sweetly turning Spheres,
> How Byrds and Beasts & Worms rejoyce,
> How Dolphyns lou'd Arions voyce
> He makes a frame for Midas eares.

The words were set as a six-part madrigal by William Byrd.

Case contributed a poem (not listed among his works in the *Dictionary of National Biography*) to the collection *Funebria nobilissimi præstantissimi equitis, D. Henrici Untoni* . . (1596), made on the death of Sir Henry Unton (or Umpton) by a number of Oxford dignitaries in Latin, Greek, Hebrew and Italian.

He appears to have been well known to Ferdinando Earl of Derby, who, when seized by his fatal illness, 'sent to Chester for one Dr. Case'; though why Dr. Case should have been in Chester is not known. That the reference is to the same man seems almost certainly proved by Case's own will* in which he requires of his wife 'that she never sell the basin and ewre wch I had of the most honorable Ferdinando Erle of Derbye, nor the greate goblet wth cover wch he sent unto her:'. Later in the testament he speaks of 'my chaine of gold wch was giuen me by the said most honorable Ferdinando of Derbye'.

Cecil, Sir Robert (*c*. 1563–1612), son of William Cecil, Lord Burleigh, by Mildred, daughter of Sir Anthony Cooke. He was knighted in 1591 and sworn of the Privy Council in the same year, but it was not until 1596 that he was appointed Secretary of State. He continued in this appointment under James I, and was created Earl of Salisbury in 1605. He was a small man with a slight curvature of the spine (Elizabeth called him her 'little elf' and James called him his 'little beagle'), but in spite of this he seems to have been something of a ladies' man. Lady Anne Clifford, in 1603, writes in her Diary:†

. . . The next day we went to Mr *Griffin* of *Dingley*'s which was the first time I ever saw the Queen and Prince *Henry*, when she kissed us all and used us kindly; thither came also my Lady of *Suffolk*, my young Lady *Derby* and my Lady *Walsingham*, which three ladies were the great favourites of Sir *Robert Cecil* . . .

* Bodleian Library. Univ. Arch. Reg. G. G.
† *The Diary of Lady Anne Clifford*, edited by V. Sackville-West (1923), p. 8.

In the previous year William Browne had written to the Earl of Shrewsbury telling him of a very strange incident that had involved Sir Robert Cecil and the same 'young' Lady Derby. The letter is dated 18th September, 1602, and the Queen referred to is, of course, Elizabeth:

. . . I send your Lo. here inclosed some verses compounded by Mr Secretary, who got Hales to frame a ditty unto itt. The occasion was as I hear, yt the young Lady Darby wearing about her neck, in her bosom, a picture wch was in a dainty tablet, the Queen, espying itt, asked what fyne jewell that was: The Lady Darby was curious to excuse the shewing of itt, butt the Queen wold have itt, and opening itt, and fynding itt to be Mr Secretarye's, snacht itt away, and tyed itt upon her shoe, and walked long with itt there; then she tooke itt thence, and pinned itt on her elbow, and wore it some tyme there also; wch Mr Secretary being told of, made these verses, and had Hales to sing them in his chamber. Itt was told her Ma^{ty} yt Mr Secretary had rare musick and songs; She wold needes hear them; and so this ditty was soung wch you see first written. More verses there be lykewyse, whereof som, or all, were lykewyse soung. I do boldly send these things to your Lo: wch I wold not do to any els, for I hear they are very secrett. Some of the verses argew that he repynes not thoghe her Ma^{ty} please to grace others, and contents hemself wth the favour he hath.*

The 'young' Lady Derby was Elizabeth, the wife of William Stanley, sixth Earl of Derby, who succeeded his elder brother Ferdinando to the title. She was, in fact, Robert Cecil's niece, being the daughter of Edward de Vere, seventeenth Earl of Oxford, and Ann, elder daughter of William Cecil, Lord Burleigh.

Robert Cecil married Elizabeth, daughter of William Brooke, seventh Lord Cobham, niece of Sir Henry Cobham.

Holding, as he did, a position of considerable power, it is not surprising to find writers and musicians offering dedications to the Earl of Salisbury. Among these are Thomas Morley's *First Booke of Ballets* (1595); Robert Jone's *First set of Madrigals* (1609); and Dowland's translation of the *Micrologus* of Ornithoparcus. In *Parthenia, or the Maydenhead of the first musicke that euer was printed for the Virginals* (c. 1615), No. VI, 'Pauana The Earle of Salisbury' by William Byrd, and No. XVIII, 'The Lord of Salisbury's Pauin' by Orlando Gibbons may have been written to commemorate his death which occurred on May 24th, 1612. He left debts, it is estimated, of some £38,000.

* Talbot Papers at the College of Arms, Vol. M, f. 36. Unfortunately neither verses nor ditty are with the letter. It has been suggested that the verses beginning 'Though your strangeness frets my heart', set by both Thomas Campian and Robert Jones, are the ones referred to here. Although some of the lines could be understood as comment on the incident, the meaning of the complete poem hardly fits the circumstances.

Cellarius, Johannes (1580–1619) was born at Nürnberg, studied law, and afterwards became steward to the Baron von Egg, with whom, in 1610, he visited Holland, France, England and Italy. After his return he became Syndic of the City of Nürnberg. He died in Venice. The *Album Amicorum*,* in which Dowland wrote, follows the form common at the time, being a classical text bound for the owner with plain interleaving. The title-page reads:

Cato: sive/ Speculum morale;/ Privatum vitae genvs/ concernens: quod in locos suos redactum,/ et tam Planudis Graeca, quam rhythmo-/rum vernacula versione explolitum,/ instar ALBI Amico-/RVM se habet. etc. Francofurdi, Apud Iohannem Welchelum MDLXXXV

The inscription 'J.C.N.1599' is stamped on the leather binding and the first entries were made during that year. It contains a number of autographs of scholars and nobles of the time, most of them dated from Altdorf, Jena, Brunswick and Nürnberg. Dowland's entry occurs among a group dated 1603. The latest date in the Album is 1606.

Christian IV, King of Denmark. Reigned from 1588 to 1648. He invited a number of foreign musicians to his Court, several Englishmen among them. William Brade was in Denmark from 1594 to 1596 and again from 1599 to 1606; part of this time, therefore, was spent in company with Dowland. After Dowland's dismissal from his post Queen Anne wrote to Lady Arbella Stuart asking her to allow her lutenist Thomas Cutting to go to the Danish Court in his place.† He reached Denmark about March 1607 and remained there for about four years at a salary of 300 daler a year.‡ Possibly the liking for English lutenists began with Thomas Robinson, who says, in the dedication of *The Schoole of Musicke* (1603) to James I, 'And yet I can say for myselfe, that once I was thought (in *Denmarke* at *Elsanure*) the fittest to instruct your Maiesties Queene, our most gracious Ladie and Mistres'.

It has already been mentioned that Christian paid James I a state visit in 1606, arriving in England on July 17th. James had been granted a subsidy by Parliament after the discovery of the Gunpowder Plot and most of this was expended in entertaining his brother-in-law. It was estimated that about £43,000 were spent on two royal visits, that of Christian and of the Prince de Vaudemont shortly after. The exceptionally heavy drinking of the Danes was adversely commented on at the time, and the visit was regarded as a political disaster.

As a military leader Christian was singularly unsuccessful and Denmark suffered several severe defeats in the Thirty Years War.

---

* B.M. Add. 27,579.   † BM Harl. MS 6986.
‡ Hammerich-Elling, op. cit., p. 40.

Clifton, Lady, *see* Darcy, Katherine.

Cobham, Sir Henry (1538–1605?). The fifth son of George Brooke, sixth Lord Cobham, but he always subscribed himself Henry Cobham. During the reign of Elizabeth he was employed on a number of ambassadorial visits to many European Courts, visiting Madrid, Vienna and Antwerp in the course of his duties. He was knighted at Kenilworth in the summer of 1575. In 1579 he succeeded Sir Amyas Paulet as resident Ambassador in Paris, where he remained until 1583, when he was recalled, his place being taken by Sir Edward Stafford. He represented Kent in the Parliaments of 1586 and 1589. He was living in 1604, but probably died soon after that date.

He married Anne, daughter of Sir Henry Sutton of Nottinghamshire, widow of Walter Haddon, Master of Requests.

Croce, Giovanni (*c.* 1557–1609), was a pupil of Zarlino and was known in his day both as a singer and a composer of sacred and secular music. He became *vice-maestro di capella* of St. Mark's at Venice and, on the death of Donato in 1603, he was elected *maestro di capella*. Thomas Morley,★ in discussing the composition of madrigals, places Croce among the best of the Italians in this field, and says:

. . . I would appoint you these for guides: *Alfonso Ferrabosco* for deepe skill, *Luca Marenzio* for good ayre and fine inuention, *Horatto Vecchi, Stephano Venturi, Ruggiero Giouanelli,* and *Iohn Croce,* with diuers others who are verie good, but not so generallie good as these.

Morley does not, however, fail to note 'yea, *Croce* himselfe hath let fiue fiftes together slip in one of his songs'.† Henry Peacham enlarges upon his many gifts:‡

Then that great Master, and Master not long since of S. *Markes* Chappel in *Venice*; second to none, for a full, loftie, and sprightly veine, following none saue his owne humour: who while he liued, was one of the most free and braue companions of the world. His Pœnetentiall Psalmes are excellently composed, and for pietie are his best.

Croce became known in England through the madrigals printed in the second book of *Musica Transalpina* (1597) and those included in Morley's *Canzonets. Or Little Short Songs to Foure Voyces* issued in the same year. He was the only foreign composer to be represented in *The Triumphes of Oriana* (1601). His *Septem Psalmi poenitentiales* was printed by Est in 1608, with English words, under the title *Musica Sacra*.

★ *A Plaine and Easie Introduction to Practicall Musicke* (1597), p. 180.
† op. cit., p. 150.   ‡ *The Compleat Gentleman* (1622), p. 102.

Cromwell, Sir Oliver (1563–1655), represented his own county of Huntingdon in the Parliaments of 1589, 1593 and 1601, and became Sheriff of the Counties of Huntingdon and Cambridge in 1598. In April 1603, when James I was on his way to London to be crowned, he was entertained by Master Oliver Cromwell at Hinchingbrooke

where there was such plenty and variety of meats, such diveristy of wines, and these not riff raff, but ever the best of the kind; and the cellars open at any man's pleasure: and who at his Majesty's remove, distributed 50^l among his Majesty's officers.★

Thomas Fuller† was also impressed with the stories of the lavish hospitality of this occasion, and says:

All the *pipes* about the house expressed themselves in no other language than the severall sorts of the choicest *wines*.

King James was so gratified with his entertainment that he is reported to have remarked in his broad Scots, 'Morry mon, thou hast treated me better than anyone since I left Edinburgh.'

He was created a Knight of the Bath on July 25th, 1603.‡ His spendthrift ways could not be supported by his income and he was forced to sell a great part of his estate to satisfy his creditors. He was the uncle of the Protector.

Darcy or Darcie, Katherine, was the daughter and heiress of Sir Henry Darcy by his second wife Katherine, daughter of Sir John Fermor, and widow of Michael Pulteney. On June 25th, 1591, she married Gervase Clifton, son of Sir John Clifton of Barrington Court, Somerset, by Anne his wife, daughter of Thomas Stanley, Lord Mounteagle.§ Gervase Clifton was knighted some time before 1597, represented the County of Huntingdon in several Parliaments and was created a peer in 1608. In the four pieces that Dowland wrote for Katherine it is possible to trace her progress to the peerage by the changing name and style of address. Brigide Fleetwood was related to her by marriage, Brigide's elder brother Sir William (who became Recorder of London) having married Joan (or Jane) Clifton, the sister of Gervase. Katherine was also distantly related to the Kitsons of Hengrave Hall, Lord Darcy of Chich having married Mary, the daughter of the second Sir Thomas Kitson in 1583.

On her marriage Katherine brought her husband the house of Leighton

---

★ Much information concerning this member of the Cromwell family is in Mark Noble, *Memoires of the Protectoral House of Cromwell* (1787). He is incorrect, however, in giving the date of Master Oliver's knighthood as 1598.

† *The History of the University of Cambridge* (1655), p. 157.

‡ W. A. Shaw, *The Knights of England* (1906).

§ William Byrd wrote a 'Lord Mounteagle's Pavan' for virginals.

Bromswold in Huntingdonshire, which, about two years before his death, Gervase Clifton began to rebuild. He only finished the great gate-house, however, which is now, or was until fairly recently, used as the vicarage.

Gervase Clifton was himself a patron of music and it is to him that Thomas Morley dedicated his *Madrigals to fiue voyces* (1589). This little group of families, the Darcys, the Cliftons and the Fleetwoods, is brought before our eyes, a vivid picture in their music-making, when we see that the British Museum copies of all five part books of this set of madrigals, bear on the title-page the signature of Conyers D'arcy, the eldest son of Sir Henry Darcy's brother, and therefore, Katherine's cousin.

John Manningham tells the following story of Gervase Clifton:
Febr. 1601 Sr Jaruis Clifton beinge at a bare baytinge in Nottinghamshire: when the beare brake loose and followed his sonne vp a stayres towards a gallery where he himself was, he opposed himself with his rapier against the fury of the beast, to saue his sonne. This same his beloued sonne not long after dyed, and his death was opened vnto him very discreetely by a gent. that fayned sorrowe as the case had bin his owne, till Sr Jaruis gave him wordes of comfort, which after he applyed to Sr Jaruis himselfe.
(*My cosen*)*

William Dugdale† says that he came from the ancient family of Clifton of Nottinghamshire, and after speaking of the title that was conferred on him says:

. . . but of him I have not seen anything further memorable, than his commitment to the Tower 30th Dec. 15 Jac. by reason he expressed, that he was sorry he had not stabed Sir Francis Bacon Knight, when Lord Keeper of the Great Seal, for decreeing a case in Chancery against him; and that in October An. 1618 (16 Jac.) he murthered himself: leaving issue by Catherine his wife, sole daughter and heir to Sir Henry Darcy of Brimham, in com Ebor. Knight . . .

All writers who mention him are agreed that he committed suicide in 1618; a fit of melancholia generally being given as the reason.

Derby, the Earl of, *see* under Stanley, Ferdinando.

Devereux, Penelope, Lady Rich (1562 or 3–1607), the elder daughter of Walter Devereux, first Earl of Essex and sister of Robert Devereux. As her father lay dying he expressed a wish that she and Philip Sidney should eventually marry. This wish was never fulfilled. In 1581 she was married by her

---

* *Diary of John Manningham, 1602–1608.* Edited J. Bruce. Camden Society, Vol. XCIX (1868), p. 22.
† *The Baronage of England* (1676), Vol. 2, p. 424.

guardians, against her will and in spite of her protestations of a previous engagement to Charles Blount, to Lord Rich. Later she left Lord Rich and joined Charles Blount, Lord Mountjoy. In 1606 Lord Rich divorced her and she married Lord Mountjoy, who was, by that time, the Earl of Devonshire.

Philip Sidney seems to have fallen in love with her after her first marriage and the series of songs and sonnets, *Astrophel and Stella*, which was inspired by this passion was, after private circulation, surreptitiously printed in 1591.

John Florio describes her in hyperbolic terms in a sonnet and the Arundel-Harington MS has a series (Nos. 201–21) entitled 'Mr. Henry Constables sonets to the Lady Ritche. 1589'. Guillaume Tessier dedicated his 1597 book of ayres★ to her.

She incurred Elizabeth's extreme displeasure by her open support of her brother's cause in the events leading up to the rebellion of 1601. She died in 1607.

Devereux, Robert, second Earl of Essex (1567–1601), son of Walter Devereux, first Earl of Essex and of Lettice Knollys his wife. The history of the Earl, his rise to power, his rebellion, disgrace and execution in 1601 are too well known to call for repetition here. Dowland must have been personally known to Essex, since he signed the permit which allowed Dowland to travel on the Continent. Writers upon a great variety of subjects dedicated works to Essex; among the musical offerings were Thomas Watson's *The first sett of Italian madrigalls Englished* (1590) and John Mundy's *Songs and Psalms* (1594). The popularity of Essex, particularly with the citizens of London, gave rise to several ballads. On his departure for Ireland a ballad was entered in the Stationers' Register:

March 31. 1599.
"Londons Loathe to departe" to the noble Erle of Essex. Erle marshall of England and Lord generall of her maisties forces agaynst the Tyronish Irishe Rebelles. vj^d†

His execution produced a number of lamentations the best known being 'A Lamentable DITTY made on the Death of *ROBERT DEVERUX*, Earl of *ESSEX*, who was beheaded in the *Tower of London*, on *Ashwednesday*, 1603 (sic.) The Tune is, *Welladay*.' It begins:

> Sweet England's pride is gone,
> welladay, welladay,

★ *Le l. liv. des chansons et airs de cour tant en francois qu'en italien et gascon*, à 4 et 5 p. Londres 1597.
† Arber, op. cit., Vol. 3 (1876), f. 49.

Which made her sigh and groan,
        evermore still;
He did her fame advance,
In Ireland, Spain and France,
And by a sad mischance
        is from us tane.

Dracot, ?. According to Barclay Squire* he 'seems to have been a member of an old Shropshire or Staffordshire family, whose name occurs in connection with Babington's conspiracy'.

Elizabeth I (1533–1603) came to the throne in 1558. Of Queen Elizabeth's ability as a musician several stories are told. Sir James Melville,† Ambassador from the Scottish Court, gives an account of how he heard her play the virginals:

The same day, after dinner, My Lord of Huntsdean drew me up to a quiet gallery, that I might hear some music (but he said he durst not avow it), where I might hear the Queen play upon the virginals. After I had hearkened a while, I took by the tapestry that hung before the door and entered within the chamber, and stood a pretty space, hearing her play excellently well, but she left off immediately so soon as she turned herself about, and came forward, seeming to strike me with her hand, alledging she was not used to play before men, but when she was solitary to shun melancholy . . .

John Playford‡ said of her:

Queen Elizabeth was not only a lover of this Art, but a good proficient therein, and I have been informed by an ancient Musician and her Servant, that she did often recreate her Self on an excellent instrument called the Poliphant [Orpharian?], not much unlike a lute, but strung with wire: Nor did she delight only in Civil, but took especial care for the Divine use thereof in the Worship and Service of God . . .

There were occasions, however, when the use of music in the worship and service of God afforded her less than complete delight. Anthony à Wood§ relates:

Dr. Tye was a peevish and humoursome man, especially in his latter days; and sometimes playing on the organ in the Chapel of Queen Elizabeth, which contained much music, but little delight to the ear, she would send the verger to tell him that he played out of tune: whereupon he sent word that her ears were out of tune.

* *The Musical Times*, February 1897.
† *Memoirs*, printed 1752. p. 50.
‡ *A briefe Introduction to the Skill of Musick* (1666), in the chapter 'Its Divine and Civil Uses'.
§ Quoted by Nichols, *The Progresses of Queen Elizabeth* (1823), Vol. I, p. 293.

On December 22nd, 1589, John Stanhope wrote to Lord Talbot:*

My Lo. the Q. is so well as I assure yow VI or VII gallyards in a mornynge, besydes musycke & syngynge, is her ordynary exercyse.

An account of the Queen's pleasure in music is given by Nichols in the description he prints† of the entertainment given by the Earl of Hertford at Elvetham House in Hampshire. The Queen's visit began on Monday, September 20th, 1591 and in the evening:

... after supper was ended, her Majestie graciously admitted into her presence a notable consort of six Musitions, which the Earl of Hertford had provided to entertaine her Majestie withall, at her will and pleasure, and when it should seem good to her Highnesse. Their musicke so highly pleased her, that in grace and favour thereof, she gave a newe name unto one of their Pavans, made long since by Master Thomas Morley, then organist at St. Paul's Church.

On the fourth day she enjoyed a different kind of entertainment but apparently the same consort of musicians was used:

After this speech, the Fairy Queen and her maides daunced about the garden, singing a Song of six parts, with the musick of an exquisite consort; wherein was the lute, bandora, base-violl, citterne, treble-viol and flute.‡

And this was the Fairies Song:

> Eliza is the fairest Quene,
> That ever trod upon this greene,
> Elisaes eyes are blessed starres,
> Inducing peace, subduing warres.
> Elisaes hand is chrystal bright,
> Her words are balme, her lookes are light.
> Elisaes brest is that fair hill,
> Where vertue dwels, and sacred skill,
> O blessed bee each day and houre,
> Where sweet Eliza builds her bowre

This spectacle and musicke so delighted her Majestie, that she commanded it to be sung and danced three times over, and called for divers Lords and Ladies to behold it: and then dismist the Actors with thankes, and with gracious larges, which of her exceeding goodnesse she bestowed on them.

Settings of 'Eliza is the fairest Queen' for treble voice and instruments, and 'Com agayne' (not the same stanzas as those that Dowland set), from the same

* Edmund Lodge, *Illustrations of British History* (1791), Vol. II, p. 411. From Talbot Papers, Vol. K, f. 67.

† *The Progresses of Queen Elizabeth* (1823), Vol. III, p. 119.

‡ The composition of the consort of instruments is exactly that for which Thomas Morley wrote his *First Booke of Consort Lessons* (1599).

entertainment, for two treble voices and instruments, by Edward Johnson are found in B.M. Add. 30,480–4. Whether these are the settings upon which the arrangement for the consort of instruments was based is not known.

In France it was even believed that she died to the sound of music:

On trouve dans les Memoires de M.*l'Abbé Vitorio Siry*, que la Reine Elizabeth d'Angleterre étant au lit de la mort, & se souvenant des effets de la Musique, fit venir toute la sienne dans sa chambre; afin, disoit-elle, de pouvoir mourir aussi gayement qu'elle avoit vécu; & pour dissiper les horreurs de la mort, elle écouta cette symphonie fort tranquillement jusqu' au dernier soupir.*

In his *Journal* André Hurault, Sieur de Maisse, who came as Ambassador to her Court in 1597, tells many anecdotes, too numerous to mention here, concerning her love of music and her proficiency in the art. He also speaks of her 'having learnt in the Italian manner to dance high'.†

It is odd that Dowland, who must have known of her love of music, should not have dedicated any of his compositions to Elizabeth during her lifetime. When, after her death, he eventually did so, instead of writing a new piece worthy of her personality and the greatness of her reign, he furbished up what must have been one of his earliest works, and renamed it.

Essex, Robert Earl of, *see* Devereux.

Fitzherbert, Nicholas, came from a family whose members had suffered greatly on account of their religion. The father of Nicholas died in prison after twenty-six years' incarceration. He was educated at Douai and was a member of the household of Cardinal Allen, of whom he wrote a biography. He was also in receipt of a pension from the Pope.

Fleetwood, Brigide, the daughter of Thomas Fleetwood, Esq., of the Vache, Chalfont St. Giles,‡ Master of the Mint and Sheriff of the County of Buckinghamshire in 1564. He was married twice and one pedigree says he had twenty-six children, but it seems more likely that the number was eighteen. The Bridget for whom Dowland wrote was one of the younger daughters of his second wife, Bridget, daughter of Sir John Spring, Kt. On the last Tuesday

---

* Pierre Bonnet, *Histoire de la Musique* (1715), p. 72.

† André Hurault, Sieur de Maisse, *A Journal*. Translated by G. B. Harrison (1931), p. 95.

‡ The Vache, an old manor house, about a mile north-east of Chalfont St. Giles, also has literary associations. E. S. Roscoe, in *Penn's Country* (1914) says (he has been talking about Milton and his visits to the Bulstrodes and Hedgerley): 'and he went further to Chalfont St. Peter and on up the Misbourne valley to Chalfont St. Giles thirteen miles away, where the Vache, the large house above the village, was the home of George Fleetwood, whose brother, Charles, was his intimate friend.'

in December 1589* Bridget Fleetwood married Sir William Smith, nephew and heir to the famous Sir Thomas Smith, Principal Secretary of State to Edward VI and Queen Elizabeth. The favourite seat of the distinguished statesman was Mount Haut or Hill Hall† at Theydon Mount in Essex, and this was the house that became Bridget's home after her marriage. Until the age of thirty her husband followed the wars in Ireland and became a colonel, but on succeeding to the estate of his uncle he retired from military life and was made Deputy Lieutenant of the Shire. He died on December 12th, 1626, aged 76, and was buried in the church at Theydon Mount, where a handsome monument may still be seen bearing the following inscription from his wife:

TO THE PIOVS MEMORIE OF HER LOVED AND LOVING HVSBAND S^R WILLIAM SMITH OF HILL HALL IN THE COVNTY OF ESSEX KNIGHT WHO TILL HE WAS XXX YEARES OLD FOLLOWED THE WARRES IN IRELAND WITH SVCH APPROBATION THAT HE WAS CHOSEN ONE OF THE COLONELS OF THE ARMY, BVT HIS UNCLE S^R THOM. SMYTH CHANCELLOVR OF THE GARTER & PRINCIPALL SECRETARY OF STATE TO TWO PRINCES KING EDWARD THE SIXT & THE LATE QVEENE ELIZABETH OF FAMOUS MEMORIE DYING HE RETVRNED TO A FAIRE & FVLL INHÆRITANCE, AND SO BENT HIMSELF TO THE AFAIRES OF THE CONTREY THAT HE GREWE ALIKE FAMOVS IN THE ARTES OF PEACE AS WARRE ALL OFFICES THAT SORTED WITH A MAN OF HIS QVALITY HE RIGHT WORSHIPFULLY PERFORMED AND DIED ONE OF THE DEPUTY LIEVTENANTS OF THE SHIRE A PLACE OF NO SMALL TRVST AND CREDIT.
BRIDGET (HIS VNFORTUNATE WIDOW WHO DVRING THE SPACE OF XXXVII YEARES BARE HIM III SONNES AND IIII DAVGHTERS) DAVGHTER OF THOMAS FLEETWOOD OF THE VACHE IN THE COVNTY OF BVCKINGHAM ESQ AND SOMETIME M^R OF THE MINT TO ALLAY HER LANGVOR AND LONGING AFTER SO DEARE A COMPANION OF HER LIFE RATHER TO EXPRESSE HER AFFECTION THAN HIS MERIT THIS MONVMENT ERECTED DESTINATING THE SAME TO HERSELF THEIRE CHILDREN AND POSTERITIE HE LIVED YEARES LXXVI DYED THE XII DAY OF DECEMBER 1626.

Her brother, Sir William Fleetwood, married Jane, the sister of Sir Gervase Clifton, and thus Bridget became a connection by marriage of Katherine Darcy, Lady Clifton.

Florence, the Duke of, *see* Medici, Ferdinando.

Forster, John 'the younger'. Grattan Flood‡ says: 'This John Forster the Younger was a grand-nephew and heir to John Forster, Alderman of the City

---

* Edmund Lodge, *Illustrations of British History* (1791), Vol. II, p. 382, in a letter from William Fleetwood to the Earl of Derby.
† Now an 'open' prison for women.
‡ *The Gentleman's Magazine*, Vol. 301 (1906), pp. 287–91.

of Dublin, whose will is dated August 22nd, 1613, and was proved on October 5th of the same year. Dowland's "loving countryman" was of a wealthy Dublin family, whose name may be traced all through the sixteenth century and previously, and he was Mayor of Dublin in 1594. His uncle Christopher was knighted.' As a footnote he adds: 'The elder John Forster's brother, Thomas, had a son Richard, who received a State Pardon on March 10, 1547–8 (Fiants of Edward VI). Richard, who in 1547 was living at Santry, had two sons, John and Thomas (Prerogative Will of John Forster in the Record Office). This John Forster the Younger, was Dowland's friend. In 1593 he was living in Trinity Lane as a tenant of Christ Church Cathedral (Rental of Ch. Ch. 1592–1593).' A few more details of the family may be added from other sources. A John Forster was Sheriff of Dublin in 1578–9, and Mayor in 1589; he may be identified as the John Forster who was admitted, as the son of a freeman, to the franchise in 1592.* It is probably the elder John who, in 1573, figures in the *Records of the Dublin Gild of Merchants*,† when:

certain members of the Gild, namely . . . John Forster . . . were appointed to peruse and correct all the ordenances theretofore made, with power to disallow all considered by them as now unnecessary. . . .

A 'Walter Fostere' is named as Master of the Gild in 1547–8.

Gray, Lord. The exact identity of this gentleman has not been discovered.

Griffith, Nicholas, of County Carnarvon; matriculated Hart Hall, May 30th, 1589, and was admitted to Gray's Inn on February 20th, 1593/4. He was M.P. for Carnarvon in 1597 and 1598, 1601, 1614, 1621 and 1622.‡

Hales, Robert, first appears upon the scene in the royal accounts for 1583, where his name figures in the list of *Musicians*:

Robert Hales, by warrant dormant, dated 3 July 1583, (25 Eliz.), for his wages at 40*li* a year.

He continued with an unbroken career in royal service at an unchanged salary of £40 a year until his death in 1615/16, which is recorded in the following entry:

Nicholas Lanier in the place of Robert Hale, deceased, (by warrant 12 January, 1615/16).§

* J. T. Gilbert, *Calendar of the Ancient Records of Dublin* (1861).
† Henry F. Berry (1900).
‡ Joseph Foster, *Parliamentary Register* (1881), *Gray's Inn Admission Register* (1889), and *Alumni Oxoniensis* (1891).
§ Audit Office Declared Accounts, Bundle 384, No. 21, to Bundle 390, No. 53.

In the list of New Year's gifts presented to the Queen in 1599/1600, it is noted: 'By Mr. Robert Hales, one paire of pfumed gloves.'* He was also among the musicians who, at the New Year, 1605/6, presented: 'ech of them one payre of perfumed playne gloves' to the King, and to whom, by the King, 'guilt plate' was presented, '5 oz to ech—in all 130 oz.'†

It will be remembered that Hales sang in the Accession Day celebrations at the Tiltyard on November 17th, 1590, and that he was also mentioned in incidents connected with the Earl of Essex and Sir Robert Cecil.

In the MS Directions for the entertainment of the Muscovite Ambassador and the Duke of Brachiana, dated 1601/2, January 6th, among the papers of the Duke of Northumberland, there is an instruction in Lord Hunsdon's Memoranda:

To appoint Musick severally for the Queene, and some for the play in the Hall. And Hales to have a place expresly to shewe his owne voyce.‡

Only one composition can with certainty be attributed to him, and that is the song 'O Eyes leaue off your weeping', No. III of Robert Dowland's *A Musicall Banquet* (1610). For discussion of 'Maister Hayls Galliard' in the Thysius MS, see p. 180.

Hasellwood, Mr. The Haselwoods appear to have been an East Anglian family In 1595 the name occurs twice in correspondence with the Cecils.§ A letter dated August 23rd concerns 'One Mr Hassellwoode, a Lincolnshire gentleman', another, dated October 28th, is signed by Thomas Haselwood of Colchester, and concerns the recordership of that town.

Hoby, Giles (1565–1626). The fortunes of the Hoby or Hobby family were founded by one William Hoby of Leominster in the County of Hereford, who obtained some of the spoils at the Dissolution of the Monasteries. Later, through his second wife, Alice Hodgkins, he came into the property of Hailes in Gloucestershire. A man 'unlearned, very just and plain in his actions, and of great hospitality', he is said to have lived to the age of 103. By Alice Hodgkins he had three sons, all of whom died without male issue. The eldest of these was Giles. He studied at Trinity College, Oxford, and matriculated on October 11th, 1583. He married first, Elizabeth, daughter of Lord Thomas Powlett of Cossington, and secondly, Anne, daughter of Sir Thomas Clarke

---

* Nichols, *The Progresses of Queen Elizabeth*, Vol. 3, p. 458.
† *Progresses etc. of King James I*, Vol. I, p. 598.
‡ Leslie Hotson, *The First Night of Twelfth Night* (1954), p. 142.
§ Calendar of the MSS of the Marquis of Salisbury at Hatfield House, Vol. 5, pp. 341 and 433.

of Avington. He died in 1626. His half-brother, Thomas, married Elizabeth Cooke (see Lady Russell, p. 424). The family arms were 'Argent, a fesse sable between three Hobbies proper', a 'hobby' being a young falcon. The family name is spelt indiscriminately Hoby or Hobby, but the pun suggests the pronunciation was always with the short o however it was spelt.*

Holborne, Anthony (d. 1602). Little is known of Holborne's life except that twice he is described as having been in the service of Queen Elizabeth; firstly in his book *The Cittharn School* (1597), where he calls himself 'Gentleman and seruant to her most excellent Maiestie', and secondly in the superscription to Pavan No. 2 in *Varietie of Lute-Lessons* (1610), where it says: 'Composed by the most famous and perfect Artist *Anthonie Holborne*, Gentleman Vsher to the most sacred *Elizabeth*, late Queene of England, etc.' No record of his employment has, however, been traced in the royal accounts or State Papers. He is chiefly known for his *Pavans, Galliards, Almains, and other Short Æirs, both graue and light* (1599), dedicated to Sir Richard Champernoun. He was a composer of great versatility and set his pieces for a number of different instruments. Holborne wrote commendatory verses for Thomas Morley's *A Plaine and Easie Introduction to Practicall Musicke* (1597) and for Giles Farnaby's *Canzonets to fowre voyces* (1598), the little poem for Farnaby is in Latin.

Holland, Hugh (d. 1633). Anthony à Wood† gives the following details of his life:

Hugh Holland, son of Rob. Holland, (by his wife, the daughter of one Pain of Denbigh). . . . was born in Denbigh, bred in Westminster School, while Camden taught there, elected into Trinity Coll. in Cambridge an. 1589, of which he was afterwards fellow. Thence he went to travel in Italy, and was at Rome, where his overfree discourse betrayed his prudence. Thence he went to Jerusalem to do his devotions to the holy sepulchre, and in his return touched at Constantinople, where he received a reprimand from the English ambassador, for the former freedom of his tongue. At his return into England, he retired to Oxon, spent some years there for the sake of the public library, and, as I have been informed had his lodgings in Bal.coll. which is partly the reason why I insert him here. He is observed by a Cambridge man‡ to have been no bad English, but an excellent Latin poet, and by some thought worthy to be mentioned with Spenser, Sidney and others, the chiefest our English

---

* See Foster, *Alumni Oxoniensis* (1891); W. St. Clair Baddeley, *A Cotteswold Shrine* (1908); *A Booke of the Travailes and Life of Sir Thomas Hoby*. Camden Miscellany, Vol. 10. Edited E. Powell (1902).

† *Athenæ Oxoniensis* (1691). Edited Philip Bliss (1815), Vol. II, Col. 559.

‡ Thomas Fuller, *Worthies of England*. 'Wales', p. 16.

poets. . . . He died within the city of Westminster, (having always been *in animo Catholicus*), in sixteen hundred thirty and three; whereupon his body was buried in the abbey church of S.Peter there, near to the door entering into the monuments . . . on the three and twentieth of July in the same year.

Holland contributed commendatory poems to a number of publications of the time, among them Shakespeare's *First Folio*. Though not particularly distinguished as poetry, two of these have interest for their musical connections. He wrote a short verse for Giles Farnaby's *Canzonets to fowre voyces* (1598), where it accompanied Dowland's 'Thou only shalt have Phyllis', and Anthony Holborne's Latin verse:

> M.Hu. Holland to the Author.
> I would both sing thy praise, and praise thy singing:
> That in the winter now are both aspringing.
> But my muse must be stronger,
> And the daies must be longer,
> When the sunnes in his hight with ye bright Barnaby,*
> Then should we sing thy praises gentle *Farnaby*.

He contributed another to *Parthenia or the maydenhead of the first musicke that euer was printed for the virginalls. Composed By three famous Masters: William Byrd, Dr. John Bull & Orlando Gibbons* . . . Engrauen by William Hole.

> Mr Hugh Holland
> On his worthy frend W.H.
> & his triumuiri of Musicke.

> List to that sweete Recorder;
> How daintily this B Y R D his notes doth vary,
> As if he were the Nightingalls own brother!
> Loe, where doth pace in order
> A brauer B U L L, then did Europa cary:
> Nay let all Europe showe me such another,
>   Orlando though was counted Musicks fath^r
> Yet this O R L A N D O parallels di Lasso:
> Whose triple praise would tire a very Tasso:
> And praise thaire songes: & sing his praise who married
> Those notes so well wch they so sweetly varied.

Howard, Theophilus (1584–1640). Theophilus, the second Lord Howard de Walden, was the grandson of the fourth Duke of Norfolk and Margaret Audley, daughter and heiress of Thomas, Baron Audley of Walden, and was

---

* 'Barnaby-day', 'Barnaby-Bright' or 'Long-Barnaby' is St. Barnabas Day, June 11th, in the Old Style Calendar, and was reckoned the longest day of the year.

the son of Thomas Howard, Lord Treasurer, created Earl of Suffolk by James I in 1603. Theophilus studied at Oxford and was created M.A. in 1605. From 1605 to 1610 he sat as Member of Parliament for Maldon in Essex. In the latter year he was summoned to the upper house as Baron Howard de Walden. He held a number of appointments under the Crown, some of which he resigned at the time of his father's disgrace. Later these were restored to him and several others were added. In 1610 he became embroiled in a famous quarrel with Lord Herbert of Cherbury, at a feast in the quarters of Sir Horace Vere, during the siege of Juiliers, when all the company had drunk too much. Lord Herbert challenged him to a duel on some fancied insult, but the whole episode ended in a fiasco. The editor of Herbert's *Autobiography* comments: 'Such accidents invariably terminated Herbert's duels.'

The following is a list of some of the occasions when it is recorded that Lord Howard de Walden took part in entertainments or celebrations in connection with events or personages in Court life: Campian's *Masque at the Lord Hay's Marriage*, 1606/7; Masque at Lord Hadington's Marriage, 1607/8; Running at the Ring on the King's Day, 1609/10; Tilt and Fireworks at Prince Henry's Creation, 1610; at Sir Robert Carr's creation to Viscount Rochester, 1611; and he acted as a Pall bearer at the funeral of Henry Prince of Wales, in 1612. Campian's *Masque at the Lord Hay's Marriage* has a poem 'To the Right Noble and Vertuous Theophilus Howard, Lord Walden, Sonne and Heire to the Right Honourable the Earle of Suffolke', the first verse of which goes:

> If to be sprong of high and Princely blood,
>> If to inherite vertue, honour, grace,
> If to be great in all things, and yet good,
>> If to be facill, yet t'have power and place,
> If to be just and bountifull, may get
>> The loue of men, you right may challenge it.

He married Lady Elizabeth Home, daughter and co-heiress of the Earl of Dunbar, by whom he had four sons and five daughters. He died at Suffolk House on June 3rd, 1640, and was buried at Saffron Walden.

Howet, Gregorio (or Huwet), is one of those rather mysterious figures in the sixteenth-century musical world whose name occurs quite frequently in musical literature of the time, but about whom very little is actually known. He is generally thought to have come from the Netherlands. One certain fact about him is that he spent many years in the service of the Duke of Brunswick at Wolfenbuttel, where he and Dowland met in 1594 or 1595. It seems likely that it was during Dowland's stay at Wolfenbuttel that Howet gave him a copy of the Fantasia that was later included in *Varietie of Lute-Lessons* with the superscription 'Composed by the most famous Gregorio Huwet of Antwerpe: Lutenist to the most high and mightie Henricus Iulius, Duke of Brunswicke, etc.' The name is spelt both Howet and Huwet and, indeed, Dowland himself uses both forms. Music by him is found in many Continental lute-books and MSS.

Hunsdon, Lord and Lady, *see* Carey.

Jewell, William. The rather sparse details given by Anthony à Wood and Foster show that William Jewell 'of Devon, gent', studied at Exeter College, Oxford, and matriculated on June 3rd, 1603, aged seventeen, took his B.A. on February 13th, 1606/7, and proceeded to his M.A. on November 17th, 1609. In 1626 he became vicar of Rodmersham in Kent. In 1612 he published *The Golden Cabinet of true Treasure* 'translated out of the French & enlarged by W. Iewel, *Mr. of Arts*, of Exeter *College* in Oxford'. Just how much Jewell added to the original it is impossible to say, but the whole is a somewhat conventional diatribe against the vices of the time, without any great distinction either of style or matter, although from time to time he produces some quite effective phrases. The book is dedicated to Alice, Countess of Derby, widow of Dowland's patron, Ferdinando. In the dedication he sets the whole tone of the book when he says:

Behold the height of monstrous iniquitie: euerie vice hath its protection, But naked Vertue wants a Patronage.

There is, however, one rather odd thing about this book, and that is the short poem that follows the dedication:

In Zoilum*
Grin, snarl and bark. The more to moue me, rack
  Thy pois'ned passions, till thine entrails crack.
When all thy spite is spent, thou shalst as soon
Supple the hardest flint, or maim the Moon,
As wound my Minde with one least discontent,
Or crosse my wonted meanest merriment.
  With settled patience, I can well endure
  Thy bootlesse, bitelesse barkings; being sure,
That though thou belk out fire, and bark out stones,
Thou canst not scorch my skin, nor break my bones.

---

* According to *A Smaller Classical Dictionary* (Everyman's library) Zoilus was 'a grammarian, a native of Amphipolis, and flourished in the time of Philip of Macedon. He was celebrated for the asperity with which he assailed Homer, and his name became proverbial for a captious and malignant critic.'

These remarks or poems addressed to Zoilus are not entirely unknown in other literary works, but it is hard to see why Jewel should anticipate an attack of such ferocity to be made upon his entirely conventional and irreproachable little book of moral precepts.

Knight, Mr. No identification possible.

Langton, Sir John (1560–1616), of Langton, came from an old Lincolnshire family whose ramifications are given in Maddison's *Lincolnshire Pedigrees*.*
He was baptized on March 11th, 1560/61, was educated at Magdalen College, Oxford, matriculated on December 22nd, 1576, and entered as a student at Lincoln's Inn in 1579. He was knighted on June 28th, 1603.† He became High Sheriff of Lincolnshire in 1612. He was twice married, first to Elizabeth, daughter of William Dalyson of Langton, by whom he had one son and three daughters. After her death in 1592 he married Katharine, daughter of William Butler of Coates, widow of Thomas Littlebury. By her he had three sons, Peregrine, Roger and Robert. Langton is about three miles south-west of Horncastle. Dowland was a little out of date in not giving Sir John his title in *Lachrimæ or Seaven Teares* (1604), but the error is corrected in *Varietie of Lute-Lessons* (1610). Nichols‡ mentions a Sir John Langton of Lancashire, and this could have been dismissed as an error, but that Shaw§ also lists a John Langton of Lancashire who was knighted on June 11th, 1603. There was a Sir Thomas Langton, of the family of Langton, styled Barons of Newton and Lords of Walton-le-dale in Lancashire, who was made Knight of the Bath at St. James's in 1603, and possibly this has led to some confusion. I have been unable to find any John in this family of the right generation.

Laiton, Lady. Probably Winifred, daughter of Simon Harcourt, of Ellenhall in Staffordshire, wife of Sir William Leighton, poet and composer, of Plash in Shropshire. Dowland was one of the contributors to the second edition of Leighton's *Teares or Lamentations of a Sorrowfull Soule* (1614), so it seems not improbable that he was acquainted with Sir William and his wife. In 1608 Leighton was sued for debt by Sir William Harmon, was outlawed and subsequently imprisoned. Lady Leighton died in 1616.

Lee, Sir Henry (1533–1610), came from the ancient family of the Lees of Quarenden, near Aylesbury. He was, in his youth, a great traveller and, accord-

* Harleian Society Publications, Vol. IV.
† Shaw, *The Knights of England*, p. 112.
‡ *Progresses etc.* of King James I, Vol. I, p. 167.
§ op. cit., p. 111.

ing to William Scott,★ 'returned home charged with a reputation of a well-
formed traveller, and adorned with those flowers of knighthood, courtesy,
bounty, valour, which quickly gave forth their fruit'.

He took great interest in the farming on his estates and became a considerable breeder of sheep, 3,000 of which, he is said by Holinshed, to have lost,
besides other horned cattle, in the great storm of 1570.

It was probably in this same year that he established the annual tilt in
honour of Elizabeth's accession on November 17th, at which he performed
in the self-appointed role of Queen's Champion. From then onwards he became a prominent figure in the ceremonial of Court life.

He acquired land in Oxfordshire and in 1571 became Lieutenant of the
royal manor of Woodstock. He lived mainly in Oxfordshire although he
maintained his interest in his estates in Buckinghamshire and represented that
county in the Parliaments of 1572 and possibly 1571.

He was knighted in 1553 and became a Knight of the Garter in 1597.

James I and his Queen visited Woodstock in September 1603, and dined
with him at the Ranger's House (*see* p. 316). Soon after this his health began
to fail, but he continued in his offices and James granted him a pension of
£200. He died at Spelsbury, Oxfordshire, on February 12th, 1610, and was
buried in the Chapel at Quarenden.

He married Anne, daughter of William Lord Paget, but in his later years
he enjoyed an amour with Anne Vavasour, daughter of Henry Vavasour of
Copmanthorpe. She is said to have been buried in the same grave.

Marenzio, Luca (1553–99), was born in Coccaglio, near Brescia. Of all the
foreign musicians mentioned by Dowland, Marenzio was the one who enjoyed
the greatest reputation in the England of that time. Henry Peacham† says of
him:

For delicious Aire and Sweet Inuention in Madrigals *Luca Marenzio* excelleth
all other whosoeuer, hauing published more Sets than any other Authour
whosoeuer; and to say truly, hath not an ill Song, though sometime an
ouersight (which might be the Printers fault) of two *eights* or *fifts* escape him;
as betweene the *Tenor* and the *Base* in the last close, of, *I must depart all haplesse*: ending according to the nature of the Ditie, most artificially, with a
Minim rest. His first, second and third parts of *Thyrsis, Veggo dolce mio ben chi
fæ hoggi mio Sole Cantava,* or *sweete singing Amaryllis,* are Songs, the Muses
themselues might not haue beene ashamed to haue had composed. Of
stature and complexion, hee was a little and blacke man; he was Organist in

---

★ Quoted by E. K. Chambers, *Sir Henry Lee. An Elizabethan Portrait* (1936), from which
much of this information comes.

† *The Compleat Gentleman* (1622), p. 101.

the Popes Chappell at *Rome* a good while, afterward hee went into *Poland* being in displeasure with the Pope for ouermuch familiaritie with a kins-woman of his, (whom the Queene of *Poland* sent for by *Luca Marenzio* afterward, she being one of the rarest women in *Europe*, for her voyce and the Lute:) but returning, he found the affection of the Pope so estranged from him, that hereupon hee tooke a conceipt and died.

Peacham's account may not be strictly accurate, although it is true that Marenzio visited the Polish Court, probably in the early 1590s. He was certainly back in Rome in July 1595, for he wrote to Dowland from there on the 13th of the month. His madrigals first became known in England through Nicholas Yonge's *Musica Transalpina* (1588), in which ten of his compositions appeared with English words. It was probably upon a knowledge of the works contained in this collection that Dowland formed so high an opinion of Marenzio's ability as a composer.

Maurice (Moritz), Landgrave of Hesse (1572–1632), succeeded his father William in 1592. He studied music under Georg Otto, Kapellmeister at Kassel from about 1588 to 1619. He was a composer of some ability and turned his attention to Lutheran psalm tunes, motets, magnificats, Italian madrigals, *villanelle*, music for wind instruments and for the lute. He was a generous patron to Heinrich Schütz, who was brought up as a chorister in the chapel at Kassel. Maurice paid for him to complete his musical studies in Italy under Giovanni Gabrieli.

He resigned from the government of Hesse in 1627, having lost the con-fidence of his people through his attempt to impose his own extreme Calvinist beliefs on the country.

Medici, Ferdinando I, Grand Duke of Tuscany (The Duke of Florence). The fourth son of Cosimo I and Eleanor of Toledo, Ferdinand was born in 1549. He succeeded to the Grand Dukedom on the death of his brother Francis I in 1587. Until his brother's death he lived in Rome, where he built the Villa Medici and assembled a notable collection of Greek and Roman sculpture including the Venus de' Medici, Niobe and her Children, the Appolino, and the Dancing Faun.

He was made a Cardinal although he never entered holy orders.

On his accession to the throne he held his Court at what later became known as the Pitti Palace in Florence. He became a generous patron of science and the arts and did much to restore Tuscany to a position of political independence and dignity, from which it had previously fallen.

Among his musicians was the singer-composer Giulio Caccini (*c.* 1545–1618) who spent most of his adult life in the service of the Medici family at Florence. In 1606 Ferdinand gave asylum to Sir Robert Dudley, the son of the Earl of Leicester (the question of whose legitimacy was the cause of much litigation after the death of the Earl), when he fled from England with the young Maid-of-Honour, Elizabeth Southwell. Dudley employed his great talents as a naval architect in building a highly efficient fleet for Tuscany, with which Ferdinand won a notable victory over the Turks in 1608.*

Because of the intellectual and artistic pre-eminence of the Tuscan Court many English Catholic exiles were attracted to Florence and the city became a hot-bed of intrigue and plots against the life of Elizabeth.

The Duke died in 1609.

Mildmay, Mr. The most likely member of the Mildmay family to have come into contact with Dowland appears to be Anthony (*d.* 1617), eldest son of Sir Walter Mildmay of Apethorp, Chancellor of the Exchequer from 1564 until his death in 1589. Anthony Mildmay first came to public notice when he delivered an oration, with much success, at Peterhouse, Cambridge, on the occasion of the Queen's visit to the College on August 9th, 1564. He entered Gray's Inn in 1579. In 1597 he was knighted on his being appointed ambassador to the Court of Henry IV of France. He seems to have been unsuited by temperament to this kind of appointment and Henry complained of his ungenial manner and of the coldness with which he listened to the praises of the Earl of Essex. At an interview in March 1597 Henry ordered him out of the room and threatened to strike him. He returned home later in the year and declined an invitation to resume his post in 1598. He died on September 11th, 1617, and was buried at Apethorp. He married in 1567, Grace, daughter and co-heiress of Sir Henry Sherrington. Nichols† includes a description of the hospitality offered to the King by the Mildmay household in 1603:

The next day being Wednesday the 27th day of Aprill, his Maiestie removed from Burleigh towards Maister Oliver Cromwell's; and in the way he dined at that worthy and worshipfull Knight's Sir Anthony Mildmay's, where nothing wanted in a subjects dutie to his Soveraigne . . . Dinner being most sumptiously furnished, the tables were newly covered with costly banqets, wherein every thing that was most delicious for taste, prooved more delicate, by the arte that made it seem beauteous to the eye; the Lady of the house being one of the most excellent Confectioners in England . . . Dinner and banket being past, and his Maiestie at point to depart, Sir Anthonie . . . presented his Highnesse with a gallant Barbary horse, and a very rich saddle.

* See Colonel G. P. Young, *The Medici*, Vol. 2 (1909), and Arthur Gould Lee, *The Son of Leicester* (1964).
† *The Progresses etc of King James I*, Vol. I, p. 96.

There is a portrait of Sir Anthony at Emmanuel College, Cambridge.

Monson or Mounson, Sir Thomas (1564–1641), son of Sir John Monson and brother of the famous Admiral Sir William Monson. He was M.P. for Grimsby in Lincolnshire in 1585, 1586 and 1588 and was knighted in the latter year. He became M.P. for Lincoln in 1597. In 1611 he was created a Baronet. At the time of the Overbury murder in 1613 he was Master of the Armoury and was twice brought to trial on suspicion of having been implicated in the poisoning. Rumours were also circulated that he was involved in the death of Prince Henry, and dark hints of witchcraft were in the air. Contemporary letters are full of the scandal. He was, however, declared innocent, being finally set at liberty in 1617. During the trials it was suggested that he had Catholic sympathies, but this may have been no more than an attempt to introduce prejudicial ideas into the proceedings. During the course of his imprisonment in the Tower, on account of ill health, he was allowed to receive visits from his friend and physician, Dr. Thomas Campian, poet and song-writer, who had himself been brushed by suspicion in the Overbury case. Campian's *The Third and Fourth Booke of Ayres* bears the following dedication:

TO MY HONOVRABLE FRIEND
Sᴿ THOMAS MOVNSON, *KNIGHT/AND BARONET.*

The dedicatory poem begins with these lines:

> Since now those clouds, that lately ouer-cast
> Your Fame and Fortune, are disperst at last:
> And now since all to you fayre greetings make,
> Some out of loue, and some for pitties sake:
> Shall I but with a common stile salute
> Your new enlargement? or stand onely mute?
> I, to whose trust and care you durst commit
> Your pined health, when Arte despayr'd of it?
> I, that in your affliction often view'd
> In you the fruits of manly fortitude,
> Patience and euen constancie of minde,
> That Rocke-like stood, and scorn'd both waue and winde?
> . . . .

He retired to his home in Lincolnshire and lived to a great age. During the years of the Civil War he wrote a book of advice to his grandson, called *An Essay in Affliction*. In common with many others of his time who frequented the Court and Court circles, he contracted enormous debts which gravely embarrassed his estate. He died at South Carlton and was buried on May 29th, 1641.

In the dedication of *Varietie of Lute-Lessons* to Monson in 1610, Robert Dowland recalls his debt to him 'in part of my Education, whilst my Father was absent from *England*'.*

Anthony à Wood† says of him:

He was a person of excellent breeding, was a great lover of ingenuity, especially of music (having himself good skill in it) and a patron of the professors thereof.

Another contemporary, Sir Anthony Welldon‡ also speaks of his musical interests:

Sir Thomas Monson was a great lover of musick, and had as good as England had, especially for voyces, and was at infinite charge in breeding some in Italy.

Robert Dowland appears to have been taken into the household of Sir Thomas and there given musical training but unfortunately very few of the Monson family papers survive from that period and there is no reference to him in the documents now deposited in the Lincolnshire County Archives Office at Lincoln Castle.§

Varietie of Lute-Lessons also, of course, contains 'Sir Thos. Monson his Pauin', said to be composed by Robert Dowland, and 'Sir Thomas Monson his Galliard' for which no composer's name is given. He was also the recipient of the dedication of Philip Rosseter's *A Booke of Ayres* (1601).

Morgan, Nicholas. In an article in *The Musical Antiquary*, Vol. IV (October 1912), W. H. Grattan Flood gives details concerning the life of Nicholas Morgan, who, Dowland says, was among those who converted him to Catholicism in Paris. Morgan was a Gentleman of the Chapel Royal, who was sworn in place of William Hechins or Huchins on December 9th, 10 Eliz. (i.e. 1567). He appears to have fled for conscience' sake in the early summer of 1582. Grattan Flood calls attention to some entries in the records of the Sainte-Chapelle in Paris‖ which show that between July 23rd, 1583, and March 8th, 1586, Morgan was employed there as a singer. The most revealing of these entries is the one for December 3rd, 1583:

---

* See p. 109.

† *Fasti Oxoniensis* (1691), Bliss edition (1815), Vol. I, col. 315.

‡ *The Court and Character of King James*, Collected and Perfected by Sir A. W. (1651). This pamphlet is bound into a volume entitled *The Secret History of the Court of James I* (1811).

§ I should like to thank Miss Pamela Nightingale for her valuable help in searching these documents for me.

‖ *Les Musiciens de la Sainte-Chapelle du Palais, Documents inédits, recueillis et annotés par Michel Brenet* (1910).

MM. 'ont ordonné au recepveur de donner à Nichlas Mauregan, Anglois, pauvre honteux, la somme de 10 escuz en considération de ce qu'il a esté chassé et expulsé de sa patrie pour voulloir mourir catholicque et pour n'avoir voullu suivre les hugenotz. Joinct qu'il se range tous les jours à l' église de ceans pour chanter sa partie de haulte-contre au cœur et à l'aigle'.

Flood says furthermore, that Morgan was in England in 1591, and he draws attention to a letter among the Molyneux MSS at Loseley Park★ from the Lords of the Council to Sir William More, dated June 14th, 1591, for the immediate discovery and arrest of 'one Morgan sometymes of her maiesties chapell, an obstinate and seditious papist', who 'hathe wandred in lurcking sorte up and down this great whyle from place to place, and is nowe thought to be in Sutton, either in or about Sir Henry Weston's howse, or at least yf he be not nowe there it is knowen that at tymes by startes he vseth to come thither in secret sorte, and perhaps not called by his right name'. Morgan's eventual fate is, apparently, unknown.

Morris, Richard. W. Barclay Squire† notes that Richard Morris, or Morrice, as it is spelt in the Cheque Book of the Chapel Royal, was sworn as a member of the Chapel on April 1st, 1579, when it is recorded that he came from Gloucester. In 1583, an entry for October says his place has been filled by Anthony Harrison, from Windsor, Morris having 'fledd beyond the seaes Aº 25º'. Barclay Squire further quotes an entry in the Diary of the English College at Douay (then located at Rheims) in which it is stated on July 17th, 1582, that 'ex Anglia venerunt ad nos D. Christopherus Bagshawe, Edwardus Dodwell adolescens, Tho. Morrise, qui peritissimorum musicorum eorum, qui in sacello reginæ nostræ canere soliti sunt unus fuit'. ('There came from England to us D. Christopher Bagshawe, Edward Dodwell, a youth, Thomas Morrise, who was one of the highly skilled musicians who are wont to sing in the chapel of our Queen.') Barclay Squire, in spite of the different first name, takes the entry to refer to the same man. In some correspondence with Father Agazzari, the Rector of the English College in Rome, 'dated on, though evidently written prior to, the day of Morris's arrival', according to Barclay Squire, Cardinal Allen praises the musical ability of Morris and says he easily excels, by a long way, all the musicians of 'this church and place', and he recommends that Morris and another musician that travelled with him, should be employed either by the Pope, or at the English College. The last information concerning him, Barclay Squire says, is an entry in the Diary

★ Historical MSS Commission, 7th Report, Part I, p. 649º. This collection is now in the Guildford Muniment Room, Castle Arch, Guildford, Surrey.
† *The Musical Times*, February 1st, 1897.

on August 9th, 1582, recording that 'John Dolman, of gentle birth, and Thomas Morris, a musician, were sent to Rome'. Barclay Squire, however, did not quote the exact date, August 25th, 1583, when Richard Morrice is said to have 'fledd'. Unless some idiosyncrasy of dating explains the discrepancy, both dates in the Diary of the English College, situated at Rheims, antedate Richard Morrice's having left England by nearly a year. The discrepancy is not accounted for by the normal difference between the Old and the New Style Calendar. No trace remains of a Thomas Morris connected with the Chapel Royal, but, on the evidence of the dates, his identity with Richard cannot, I think, be taken as wholly proved.

Nichol, or Nichols, Mrs. No satisfactory identification can be made.

Noel, Henry. Fuller says of him:*

He was younger son of Sir Andrew Noel, of Dalby in this County [Leicestershire] who for Person, Parentage, Grace, Gesture, Valour, and many other excellent parts (among which skill in Musick) was of the first rank in the Court. And though his Lands and Livlyhood were small, having nothing known certain but his *Annuity* and *Pension* as Gentleman to Queen Elizabeth, yet in *state*, *pomp*, *magnificence*, and *expenses*, did ever equalize the Barons of great worth. If any demand whence this proceeded, the Spanish Proverb answers him, 'That which cometh from above, let no man question'.

His extravagance was notorious, and on December 30th, 1602, John Manningham noted in his Diary†

Sir Walter Rawly made this rime vpon the name of a gallant one Mr Noel

Noe. L.

    The word of denial, and the letter of fifty
      makes the gentleman's name that will never be thrifty.

and Noels answere

Raw Ly

    The foe to the stommacke, and the word of disgrace
      show the gentleman's name with the bold face.

He is credited with the writing of Act II of *The Tragedie of Tancred and Gismund. Compiled by the Gentlemen of the Inner Temple, and by them presented before her Maiestie. Newly reviued and polished according to the Decorum of these daies. By R.W.* [Roger Wilmot] (1592). He also probably wrote the poem 'of disdainful Daphne' which is subscribed 'M. H. Nowell' in *England's Helicon* (1600).‡

* *The Worthies of England* (1662), p. 137.
† Camden Society, Vol. XCIX (1868), p. 109.
‡ Edited Rollins (1935), Vol. I, p. 183.

William Shaw* says he was knighted by Robert Earl of Leicester in the Netherlands in 1586, but contemporary references always speak of him as 'Mr Henry Noel' and he is thus described in the *Lamentatio Henrici Noel*. He is mentioned several times in connection with Leicester's army,† the first occasion being in a 'Note of the Muster of the garrison of Flushing taken by Commisary van Broecke on October 6th, 1587' (New Style).

On October 16th Leicester wrote to the Queen:

Here Mr Harry Noel hath also remained most desirous and ready to have done any service upon all occasions. He meaneth to go into France to the King of Navarre.

He wrote again on October 23rd:

I wrote not long ago that I thought this gentleman was minded to go to the King of Navarre, but that journey hath now so many difficulties, from the King being far off and the time of year being so far spent that he is returning to you . . . whose desire was only by his travel to have made himself the more able to serve your Majesty hereafter . . . I wish there were more of his disposition. I need not recommend him to your favour, your Majesty having had always a good opinion of him, and I trust he shall not speed the worse that he has spent his absence here with me . . .

Noel was the recipient of a number of complimentary dedications from authors of books on many different subjects: among these were *Amyntas* of Torquato Tasso, translated by Thomas Watson; Charles Turnbull's *A perfect and easie treatise of the vse of the celestial globe*; and Thomas Watson's *Compendium memoriæ localis*; all printed in, or about, the year 1585.

He died of a 'calenture or burning fever', attributed to overexertion at a game of 'Baloun', and was buried on February 26th, 1596/7, in St. Andrew's Chapel, Westminster Abbey. The 'Lamentatio Henrici Noel' appears to have been composed by Dowland for the funeral service. After his death he received two other musical tributes, 'Harke; Alleluia', 'A reuerend memoriall of that honourable true gentleman HENRY NOEL ESquier' by Thomas Morley, No. XXI in his *Canzonets or Litle short Aers to fiue and sixe voices* (1597), and the beautiful madrigal by Thomas Weelkes, to the words:

> Noell, adew thou Courts delight,
> Upon whose locks the graces sweetly plaide
> Now thou art dead our pleasure dies outright,
> For who can joy when thou in dust art laide
> Bedew my notes, his death-bed with your teares,
> Time helps some griefe. No time your griefe outweares.‡

* *The Knights of England* (1906).
† *Calendar of State Papers*, Foreign Series, 1587, April to December.
‡ *Madrigals of 5 and 6 parts, apt for the Viols and Voices* (1600).

Orologio, Alessandro. According to Eitner there were two different Italian musicians of the same name, living and working at the same time in two separate Central European Courts. One was a violinist and later *Kapellmeister* at the Court of the Emperor Rudolph in Prague; the other was a cornet player and vice-*Kapellmeister* in the Electoral chapel at Dresden. It is said to be the latter whose acquaintance Dowland made at the Court of the Land-grave of Hesse. Their compositions consist mainly of books of madrigals and canzonets for three voices, but it is almost impossible to distinguish between the works of the two composers. Thomas Morley includes a madrigal 'Soden Passions' by one of the Orologios in his *Madrigals to fiue voyces Celected out of the best approued Italian Authors* (1598).

Peacham, Henry the Younger (1576–*c*.1644), born at North Mimms in Hertfordshire, he was the son of a clergyman. He became a scholar of Trinity College, Cambridge at the age of seventeen; B.A. in 1595; and M.A. three years later. He became Master of the Free School at Wymondham, Norfolk in about 1600. He always had a love of drawing, which, he says his teachers 'could they never beate me out of it'. In 1606 he wrote *The Art of Drawing with the Pen, etc*, and in 1612, *Graphice; or the most auncient and excellent art of drawing and limning*. He contributed to Thomas Coryat's *Crudities hastily cobbled* in 1611 and in the following year published his *Minerva Britanna* containing the poem which may have played a part in Dowland's having at length been offered a post at Court. *The Compleat Gentleman*, his best-known work, was first printed in 1622 and went through several editions. Further works include *Thalia's Banquet* (1620), *The Worth of a Peny, or a caution to keep money* (1641), and *The Art of Living in London* (1642). He travelled in Holland, France and Italy and lived for a time in the parish of St. Martin-in-the-Fields. He died about 1644.

Piper, Digory (1559–90). The family of Piper or Pyper was of some standing in Cornwall in the sixteenth century, and owned land in Launceston, Liskeard and the surrounding districts. Digory was the eldest of the seven children of 'Sampson Pyper gent' (probably the Sampson Pyper who was an alderman of Launceston in 1555) and was baptized at Launceston on December 30th, 1559. The first that is heard of his going to sea is in the text of a bond taken before Dr. Julius Cæsar, Judge of the High Court of Admiralty on October 17th, 1585, in which 'Thomas Grent by vertue of a Commission of Reprysall . . . is authorized to sett forth to the seas one shippe called the Sweepstake of London of the burthen of fifty five tonnes or thereaboutes, whereof Richard Hodgis goeth for m^r wth men ordenance and victuall sufficient for the same seruice for the apprehendinge and takinge whatsoeuer the shippes, goodes and merchaundizes belonging to the subiects of the Kinge of Spaine'. The bond is signed by Josias Calmady and Digory Piper, and they undertake that any Spanish ship taken by them shall be brought to the nearest port and that they will not 'breake Bulke' until a 'iust and perfect Inuentory' has been taken and an appraisement of the value of the cargo made by 'some six honest men Inhabitants of the said Porte'. They agree to pay 'in the said high Courte of Thadmiralty to the use of the Sayd L. Admirall the full tenth part of all such shippes goodes and merchaundizes as the sayd m^r wth his shippe and Company shall take and apprehend'. Furthermore they undertake not to 'attempt anything against her m^{ties} Louinge subiects or the subiects of any other prince or States being in leage and amity wth her ma^{tie} but only against the subiects of the Kinge of Spaine'.

Instead of attacking Spanish shipping, however, Piper and Hodges spent the next few months spoiling French, Dutch, Flemish and Danish boats up and down the Channel, bringing the captured prizes into Cornish ports. The final exploit against a Danish vessel provoked King Frederick of Denmark into writing a letter of expostulation to Queen Elizabeth in which he says 'he cannot but be amazed that such things should be done by her subjects . . . and especially he can hardly be induced to believe that the pirates who did these things are seen going about openly in London without constraint . . . and he craves that she will surely punish these wicked men'. Piper and Hodges were apprehended and were taken before Dr. Julius Cæsar for examination on June 10th, 1586. Both made complete confessions and gave a long list of the ships they had spoiled. The confessions were submitted to Dr. Hammond for his opinion and on July 7th he wrote to Walsingham saying: 'I haue considered them, and to me it seemeth to be out of all doubt that these persons should stand bound in lawe to make recompense of the full coste of the hulke and goodes, to the Dane and the owner thereof' and that 'by the rules of the Civill Lawe no doubt it is plaine piracie not wthstanding their letters'. Whether the Danes received their full compensation is not known, but Digory Piper escaped the extreme penalty for piracy on this occasion, since his death did not occur until three and a half years later.

On September 20th, 1587, the Queen sent a set of instructions to her agent in Denmark, Mr. Daniel Rogers, for the handling of a number of matters of policy and at the end she says: 'Lastly where there haue been some spoiles committed uppon certain of the Kings subiects for the which we haue been very sorry and haue caused all care to be had for the due satisfaction to be yealded: you shall pray him to consider in his wisdome how hard it is to restrayn men of warre from committing outrages as well by sea as by land in tymes of hostilitie between princes and civill wars, and that therefore he will not withdraw or diminish in respect thereof anie part of that loue and good-will that he professes to bare towards us.'

Digory Piper was buried on January 20th, 1589/90, in his own parish of Launceston. On November 9th, 1590, Letters of Administration were granted in the Prerogative Court of Canterbury, to Thomas Hatton, yeoman, of the parish of St. Clement's Danes, London, one of the creditors.

Sources: The Public Record Office, State Papers Domestic and Foreign for the years 1585, 1586 and 1587.

The Genealogist, Vol. 6, p. 57.

S. P. Pattison, *Some account of the church of St. Mary Magdalene, Launceston* (1852).

The Prerogative Court of Canterbury, Somerset House, London, Acts of Administration for the year 1590.

For an extended account of the career of Digory Piper *see* 'Captain Digory Piper of the Sweepstake' by Diana Poulton in *The Lute Society Journal*, Vol. 4 (1962).

Rich, *see* Devereux, Penelope.

Russell, Elizabeth Lady, was the third of the five daughters of Sir Anthony Cooke of Gidea Hall, Essex. This learned man held the remarkable view that 'sexes as well as soules are equal in capacity'* and accordingly he educated his daughters with the same scrupulous care he would have shown had they been sons. In consequence they grew up to be among the most learned women of their age, and Henry Peacham voiced the general admiration aroused by their accomplishments when he wrote† 'rare Poetesses, so skilful in Latine and Greeke, beside many other their excellent qualities eternized alreadie by the golden pen of the Prince of Poets‡ of our time'.

Of the five sisters one, Mildred, became the second wife of William Cecil, Lord Burleigh, and another, Ann, married Sir Nicholas Bacon. Thus Elizabeth was the aunt of both Sir Robert Cecil and Sir Francis Bacon.

She married first Sir Thomas Hoby, translator of, among other things, Castiglione's *The Booke of the Courtyer*. On his death in 1566, while ambassador in Paris, the great house of Bisham Abbey in Berkshire passed into her possession. Here Queen Elizabeth visited her in Progress, in 1592, and speeches in the Queen's honour, composed by John Lyly, were delivered. Her second

* *Dictionary of National Biography.*
† *The Compleat Gentleman* (1622), p. 36.
‡ George Buchanan.

husband, to whom she was married in 1574, was John Lord Russell, son and heir to the Duke of Bedford. To this lady's bitter disappointment he predeceased his father in 1584, before succeeding to the title. She had two sons by her first husband, Sir Edward and Sir Thomas Posthumous Hoby, and two daughters, Elizabeth and Ann, by her second; the elder of these was the Queen's god-daughter and a Maid of Honour.

One gets the impression that Elizabeth Cooke grew up with a character which, in kindly words might be described as forceful, but with a little less charity might equally well be called domineering, and that in maturity she became a terror to her enemies and, at times, an embarrassment to her friends.

Contemporary accounts describe various lawsuits which were brought by this intrepid woman, who seems to have had a marked taste for litigation. Some were against neighbours whom she considered to have acted with less than due respect to her personal dignity. Others were in defence of her daughter's property. Of all these the most revealing of her character concerned her office of Keeper of the Queen's Castle of Donington in Berkshire. This office had been granted her by the Queen in 1590, for the term of Lady Russell's lifetime, together with other duties connected with the Manor and Lordship of Donington, for which she received the sum of $9\frac{1}{2}$d a day. In 1601 the Queen settled Donington Castle on the Lord Admiral the Earl of Nottingham and his wife for life. It is not clear whether there was some confusion and the term was intended to run from the time of Lady Russell's death, but the Lord Admiral evidently interpreted the grant as allowing him immediate entry. When they came to take possession, however, Lady Russell refused to hand over the Castle and the Lord Admiral retired worsted. But this was not the end of the story. After the Queen's death, while Lady Russell was visiting her daughter Ann, Lady Herbert, in Wales, the Lord Admiral heard of her absence and immediately sent his men to take possession. On her return she was refused admission, but nothing daunted, she sat in her coach all night outside the gates. Eventually she took the case to the Star Chamber, where it was heard on Wednesday, May 14th, 1606. According to an eye-witness's account, after both sides had been heard and the judges were about to give their verdict Lady Russell could contain herself no longer and interrupted the proceedings and 'desyred to be hearde, and after many denyalls by the Court, vyolentlye and with great audacitie began a large discourse, and woulde not by any meanes be stayed nor interrupted, but wente on for the space of half an howre or more.* This at the age of seventy-eight.

Her London house was situated in the parish of Blackfriars and she was one

---

* For a full report of this case *see* W. P. Baildon, *Les Reportes des Cases in Camerata Stellata,* App. XVII.

of the signatories to the Petition of the residents within the Blackfriars precincts to the Privy Council in November 1596, to restrain James Burbage from constructing 'a common playhouse' on the upper floor of the old friary building.

Just before her death Lady Russell wrote a long letter to Sir William Dethick, Garter King at Arms, asking to know 'what number of mourners were due to her calling, the manner of the hearse, of the heralds, and church'. She died in 1609.

Russell, Lucie Countess of Bedford, was the wife of Edward Russell, third Earl of Bedford. Francis, father of the third Earl, was the younger brother of Lord John Russell who died before succeeding to the Earldom, to the great chagrin of his second wife Elizabeth Hoby. Lucie was the daughter of John Lord Harrington. She was a somewhat pretentious patron of letters and was one of the fashionable dedicatees of the time. Ben Jonson, Donne, Daniel, Drayton and Chapman all paid homage to her in one way or another. Thomas Pennant* says of her, however, 'Her vanity and extravagance met with no check from her quiet spouse. The Earl died s.p. May 3, 1627. She long survived him.' This final detail is incorrect; Lucie herself died in 1627. There is a portrait of her reproduced in Nichols, *Progresses of King James I*, Vol. I, opposite p. 174.

Scudamore, John, or Skidmore, as the name is often spelt, was the eldest son of Sir John Scudamore of Kentchurch, Herefordshire. He is frequently mentioned in State Papers for his activities among the English Catholics abroad. W. Barclay Squire† says 'he fled from Essex to Middelburg and Antwerp in the autumn of 1593, and at one time was in Spain with Father Parsons'. On October 5th, 1606, John Chamberlain,‡ writing to Dudley Carleton, says 'Sir John Skidmore's eldest sonne that was a priest is likewise converted and reveals many things of great moment'. A John Skidmore was buried in St. Anne Blackfriars on August 21st, 1625, but there is nothing to show whether or not this was the ex-priest.

Sidney, Sir Robert, was the second son of Sir Henry Sidney and Mary Dudley sister of Robert Earl of Leicester, and was the brother of Sir Philip Sidney. He was born at Penshurst, Kent in 1563, and was therefore the same age as Dowland. Curiously their span of life coincided almost exactly since both died in 1626.

---

* Quoted in *D.N.B.*   † *The Musical Times*, February 1897.
‡ *Letters of John Chamberlain*, edited N. McClure (1939), p. 233.

Robert Sidney entered Christchurch, Oxford in 1574 and four years later set out on a tour of Germany. Soon after his return he married a Welsh heiress, Barbara Gamage, and in the following year, 1585, he entered Parliament as member for Glamorganshire. He distinguished himself during the wars in the Low Countries and, just before the death of his brother Philip, on October 7th, 1586, was knighted by the Earl of Leicester. In 1588 he was appointed Governor of Flushing. Although a close personal friend of the Earl of Essex, he had the good sense to remain in Flushing and to escape entanglement in the Essex rebellion. When James I came to the throne he returned to Court and in July 1603 became Chamberlain to the Queen, Anne of Denmark. He was created Viscount Lisle on May 4th, 1605.

On the death of Robert Dudley, Earl of Leicester, his son Robert Dudley was left as chief beneficiary of the estate; Robert Sidney and the Earl of Essex being named to divide most of this inheritance between them should the boy die before reaching the age of twenty-one. The situation was greatly complicated by the fact that the young Robert's mother, Lady Douglas Sheffield had been married by a private ceremony to Leicester. This marriage Leicester later repudiated when he wanted to marry Lettice Knowles, mother of the Earl of Essex, thereby calling into question the legitimacy of his son. When young Dudley attempted to prove his right to the inheritance Robert Sidney played a far from generous part in the litigation and succeeded in obtaining a considerable share of the estate, the Earldom of Leicester being revived in his favour in 1618.

Smith, Sir John. Possibly this was the same Sir John Smith of Hough in Cheshire to whom Francis Pilkington dedicated his *Second Set of Madrigals* in 1624. William A. Shaw in *The Knights of England* gives another John Smith of Essex, who was knighted at Royston at the end of November or the beginning of December, 1605. This would agree very well with his being plain 'mr Smythe' in the Folger-Dowland MS (merely 'Smyth' in Add. 38,539), and with his having become 'Sir John Smith' in *Varietie of Lute-Lessons* in 1610. It would have been pleasant to have been able to show that this Smith was connected with the family at Hill Hall, but if such a connection exists, so far I have been unable to trace it.

Smith, Thomas. A number of Thomas Smiths were living at this time. Of these the three most likely to have come into contact with the Dowlands were 1. Thomas Smith, native of Abingdon in Berkshire, who became secretary to the Earl of Essex, but he was knighted in 1603 and his death occurred in 1609, possibly a little early for him to have been connected in any way with the preparation of *Varietie of Lute-Lessons*. 2. Thomas Smith (1558–1625), Sheriff of London at the time of the Essex rebellion. He had a house "near Fen-church". I have been unable to discover whether he had any literary pretensions. 3. The Thomas Smith, "Register" of Cambridge from 1558/9 to 1602, whose carelessness in keeping the records is noted by Thomas Fuller in his *History of the University of Cambridge*. Dowland could have met him and possibly formed a friendship at the time of his sitting for his second Mus.Bac.

Souch, Sir John, (or Zouch). The Arms of Sir John Souch are printed on the verso of the title-page of *The Third and Last Booke of Songs* (1603), although Dowland still refers to him as 'Iohn Souch Esquire' in the dedication. In common with many other surnames that of Souch was subjected to a great variety of different spellings, but correspondence of the time makes it clear that the same family is referred to however much the spelling may vary. This branch of the family came from Codnor in Derbyshire. The John Souch who was Dowland's 'Honorable good friend' was the son of Sir John Souch of Codnor Castle; he studied at Trinity College, Oxford; and was admitted to Gray's Inn on May 9th, 1582. He was knighted on April 23rd, 1603. He married Maria, daughter of Sir Henry Berkeley, Knight.

It will be noticed that he was still 'Esquire' when *The Third and Last Booke* was entered in the Stationers' Register on February 21st, 1603, but his knighthood was duly acknowledged in *Lachrimæ or Seven Teares,* entered on April 2nd, 1604.

Codnor is about two miles south-east of Ripley. The extensive castle, now in ruins, stood in a great park.

Stafford, Sir Edward (1552?–1605), was the eldest son of Sir William Stafford of Grafton and Chebsey, Staffordshire, by his second wife Dorothy, his first wife having been Mary Boleyn, first married to Sir Henry Carey, first Baron Hunsdon. Sir Edward was employed by Elizabeth on a number of diplomatic missions, particularly in the negotiations for her proposed marriage to the Duc d'Anjou. He was knighted in 1583 and in the same year was sent as resident Ambassador to the French Court, succeeding Sir Henry Cobham. He remained in Paris for seven years. He married as his first wife, Roberta, daughter of one Chapman, and as his second, Lady Douglas Sheffield, widow of the Earl of Sheffield. This lady had previously been privately married to the Earl of Leicester and by him had a son, Robert Dudley. On Leicester's repudiation of this marriage she married Stafford, a fact which played an important part in the failure of Robert Dudley to secure recognition as Leicester's heir, since Lady Stafford, had she then acknowledged the validity of the Leicester marriage would thereby have made her marriage to Stafford bigamous. Many years after Stafford's death in 1605, she courageously testified on behalf of her son, an act which did much to bring about the restitution that was finally made to him by Charles I.

Stanley, Ferdinando, fifth Earl of Derby (1559–94). At the age of fourteen Ferdinando was called to Windsor by Queen Elizabeth, but he does not appear to have held any office at Court. From 1585 onwards he acted as deputy Lieutenant of Lancashire and Cheshire on behalf of his father, and was Mayor of Liverpool in 1588. He was summoned to Parliament as Lord Strange in 1588–9.

He traced his descent from Henry VII through Mary, Queen Dowager of France sister of Henry VIII, and her second husband, Charles Brandon Duke of Suffolk, whose daughter was his mother. Although Catherine Grey, Countess of Hertford and her children obviously stood before him in the line of succession, some members of the Roman Catholic faction tried to induce him to assume the title of King of England. He revealed the plot to the Government and one Hesketh, who had been employed as a go-between, was convicted of treason and executed.

Ferdinando was a great patron of the arts and a friend of many poets* and was himself something of a poet. Spenser celebrates him under the name of 'Amyntas' in *Colin Clouts come home again*; Robert Greene dedicated his *Ciceronis Amor* (1589) to him; Nash, in his *Pierce Pennilesse* (1592) has a panegyric on him; and Chapman, in the dedication of the *Shadow of Night* (1594) speaks of 'that most ingenious Darbie'. For several years he was patron of the company of actors which formerly had been under the patronage of the Earl of Leicester. While Ferdinando was its patron the company was known as 'Lord Strange's Men'. After his death the company passed to Lord Hunsdon and became known as 'The Lord Chamberlain's Men'.

On the death of his father in 1593 he succeeded to the Earldom of Derby with other dignities and titles including Sovereignty of the Isle of Man.

On April 5th, 1594, it is recorded 'His Honour fell sick at Knowsley; on Saturday he returned to Latham, and feelinge himself worse, he sent to Chester for one Doctor Case who the week before had given physic to his Lady'.† Although a number of people thought he had been poisoned, it was more generally believed that his death was due to witchcraft. An examination

* See Thomas Heywood, F.S.A., *The Earls of Derby and the Verse Writers and Poets of the Sixteenth Century* (1853), Chetham Society Publications, Vol. 29, p. 35.

† Touchynge the Death of the Earl of Derby, April 1594, Talbot Papers, Vol. H, fol. 713, No. CCLXII. Quoted by Lodge, *Illustrations to British History*, 2nd edition (1833), Vol. II, p. 459.

being instituted, a waxen image was discovered in his chamber with a hair the colour of the Earl's drawn through the body. Or so it was reported at the time. He married Alice, the elder daughter of Sir John Spencer of Althorp, Northamptonshire, and sister of Elizabeth Lady Carey. Her portrait may be seen on her monument in the church of Harefield, Middlesex.

Tarlton, Richard. Famous comic actor, he was, according to Fuller, born at Condover in Shropshire where he spent his youth looking after his father's pigs. The story goes that a servant of Robert Dudley Earl of Leicester, on his way past his father's farm, stopped to speak with Tarlton and was so pleased with his 'happy, unhappy answers that he brought him to Court where be became the most famous jester to Queen Elizabeth'. John Stow★ says of him 'Richard Tarleton for a wondrous plentifull pleasant extemporal wit, hee was the wonder of his time'; he is also credited with the power of diverting Elizabeth 'when her mood was least amiable'. He was one of the twelve original members of a company of actors known as 'The Queen's Players'. *News out of Purgatory* and a number of songs and ballads are attributed to him. In spite of his great success as a wit and a jester he died in dire poverty in 1588.

Unton, Sir Henry (or Umpton). Born about 1557, he was the second son of Sir Edward Unton or Umpton of Wadley near Faringdon, Berkshire, by his wife Anne, daughter of Edward Seymour Duke of Somerset (Protector during the reign of Edward VI), widow of John Dudley, Earl of Warwick. The Unton family traced its pedigree back to the time of Edward IV.

Henry was educated at Oriel College, Oxford and in 1573 he supplicated for the degree of Bachelor of Arts. Subsequently he continued his studies at the Middle Temple. His formal education complete he travelled extensively and, as shown by his memorial picture, now in the National Portrait Gallery, he visited Venice and Padua. In 1585 he went to the Netherlands with the Earl of Leicester's army and took part in the battle of Zutphen, in which Sir Philip Sidney was fatally wounded. He was knighted by Leicester on September 29th, 1586. In 1591 he went to Paris as Ambassador to Henry IV, but before leaving, according to Anthony à Wood† he was created M.A. In March 1592 he was recalled at his own request on account of ill health. He spent a few years in England during which time he represented Berkshire in the House of Commons, and then in 1595 he was again sent as Ambassador to France. In October of that year Essex put forward Sir Henry's name as his

★ *Annals of the Reign of Queen Elizabeth* (1615).
† *Athenæ Oxoniensis* (1691), Bliss edition (1815), Vol. 1, col. 647.

candidate for the post of Treasurer to the Chamber on the death of Sir Thomas Heneage; the appointment went, however, to John Stanhope, Burghley's candidate.

In March 1595/6, official business making an interview with the French King necessary, he travelled to the royal camp outside Coucy La Fère, at that time held by the Spaniards. There, after a fall from his horse, he was taken ill. The 'purple fever' was suspected and the King sent his own physician, de Lorrayne, to attend him. In spite of the risk of infection, Henry insisted on visiting him in his tent. No trouble or expense was spared in the treatment of his illness:

. . . but certain purple spots appeared about his heart, whereupon, with the advice of La Ryviere, the other physician, they gave him *Confectio Alcarmas* compounded of musk, amber, gold, pearl and unicorn horn, with pigeons applied to his side, and all other means that art could devise sufficient to expel the strongest poison and he be not bewitcht withal*

Nevertheless, shortly afterwards, on March 23rd, 1595/6, he died. The French King was greatly distressed by his death and on April 1st he wrote a letter of condolence to Queen Elizabeth in which he spoke highly of Unton's virtues and accomplishments. His body was brought home to Wadley and on July 8th he was buried at Faringdon where his widow raised an impressive monument in the church.

In February 1602 John Manningham noted in his Diary†

Sir Henry Unton was soe cunning a bargayner for landes that they which dealt with him were commonly great loosers, whereupon Mr Duns of Barkshire said that he bought lands with witt and sold them with rhetorick. (Chute)

In spite of this reputation, however, he left debts, partly incurred through the inadequacy of the allowance made to him as Ambassador, amounting to some £23,000, his personal property being valued at no more than about £5,000.

In 1580 he married Dorothy, daughter of Sir Thomas Wroughton of Broad Hinton in Wiltshire. On August 8th, 1596, Dudley Carleton wrote to John Chamberlain:

I haue beene lately at Brawdhinton wᵗʰ my La: Unton, who spent a treasure of good wordes vppon me and did vse her lawfull authoritie in commaunding

---

* Letter from William Paule to the Earl of Essex, dated Coucy, March 21, 1595 (Old Style). *Calendar of the MS belonging to the Marquess of Salisbury at Hatfield House,* Vol. 6, p. 112. G. B. Harrison in *An Elizabethan Journal* (1928), p. xvi, says: 'Sir Henry Untonat first dated his letters by the French style and was rebuked by Burleigh accordingly.'

† *The Diary of John Manningham*, Camden Society, Vol. XCIX, p. 136.

me to staie four daies when my determination was to depart the next daye after my cumming. She hath verie well bewtified her sorrow wth all the ornaments of an honourable widowe. Her black veluet bed, her cipres vaile, her voice tuned wth a mournfull accent, and her cubbard (in steed of casting-bottels) addorned wth praire bookes, and Epitaphes doth make her chamber looke like the house of sorrow.*

She became the wife of John Shirley in 1598.

Sir Henry was a man of wide learning and many interests. Several writers dedicated books to him, among them being John Case's *Apologia Musices* (1588) and Robert Ashley's Latin translation (from the French) of *L'Vranie ov la Mvse Celeste par G. de Saluste Seigneur du Bartas* (1589). He contributed some prefatory remarks to Charles Merbury's *A briefe discourse of royal monarchie* (1581). He appears to have had a considerable love of music and in his memorial portrait,† depicting a number of incidents from his life, two consorts are shown; one, playing for a masque, is composed of the same group of instruments for which Morley wrote his *First Booke of Consort Lessons*, while the other consists of a group of five viols. The Inventories of Wadley and Farringdon made in 1596, and another of Farringdon made in 1620, for Lady Dorothy, include several 'paire of virginalls' but no other instruments. One of these, 'in the Hall' at Farringdon (1596) appears in odd company:

Itm, one paire of virginalles, one frame, iij close stoole cases, and one warming panne, preised at iij^li xvj^s.‡

On Sir Henry's death a collection of Latin verse, by a number of distinguished figures of the University, was published at Oxford, edited by his chaplain, Robert Wright, under the title *Funebria nobilissimi ad praestantissimi equitis D. Henrici Untoni* (1596). John Case contributed to the volume. Unton's correspondence, edited by Joseph Stevenson, was published by the Roxburghe Club in 1847.§

Verstigan, Richard. We are again indebted to W. Barclay Squire for information about Verstigan. He appears to have been born in England of Netherlandish parents and to have become an agent for the King of Spain in Antwerp. He wrote a number of books including *Theatrum Crudelitatum Haereticum nostri tempe* (1587), a profusely illustrated history of the sufferings of the

---

* S.P. 12/259, No. 93.
† In the National Portrait Gallery, London.
‡ *The Unton Inventories*, edited by J. G. Nichols for the Berkshire Archaeological Society (1841), p. 10.
§ Further information about Unton's life is given in 'Sir Henry Unton and his Portrait: An Elizabethan Memorial Picture and its History' by Roy C. Strong, *Archaeologia*, Vol. 99 (1965), pp. 53–76.

Catholics, among the engravings being a representation of the execution of Mary Queen of Scots, according to Barclay Squire, the only contemporary one in existence. He also wrote a volume of sacred verse which includes the lullaby 'Upon my lap my Sovereign sits', set to music by Martin Peerson in *Private Musicke, or the First Booke of Ayres and Dialogues* (1620). His best known work was *A Restitution of Decayed Intelligence* (Antwerp, 1605), dedicated to James I. This contains a sonnet by the younger Francis Tregian, who was, in all probability, the writer of the Fitzwilliam Virginals Book.

Vaux, Mrs. There are two suggestions for Dowland's Mrs. Vaux. First, Mary, wife of the third Baron Vaux of Harrowden; she was a Tresham, and the Treshams were a family well known for their love of music and dancing. The difficulty here, however, is the use of the term 'Mrs.' instead of 'Lady'. The second is Mrs. Elizabeth Vaux, daughter of Sir John Roper, wife of George, eldest son of William, third Baron Vaux. George predeceased his father and so Elizabeth never became Lady Vaux.

It seems unlikely to have been any of the other daughters of Lord Vaux: Joyce became a nun; Anne, George's half-sister was always known as 'Mrs. Anne'. She was a zealous Catholic like many other members of her family and was deeply involved in the illegal work of the priest, Henry Garnett. After the disaster of the Gunpowder Plot she lived in great seclusion and later kept a school near Derby for the children of the Catholic gentry. Her sister, Eleanor Brookesby, was only slightly less committed in the work of sheltering and sustaining the missionary priests in their perilous work.

Most of the family suffered persecution for their religion at one time or another and the sheltering of priests at Harrowden led to terms of imprisonment for Lord Vaux.

White, Mrs. The frequency with which the name occurs and the lack of a first name makes identification impossible, but a family with whom Dowland may well have had some connection was that of Anne Cecil, sister of Lord Burghley, who married Thomas White of Tuxford in Nottinghamshire and of Woodhead in Rutland, from whom she is said to have obtained a divorce. According to the *Victoria County History of Nottinghamshire*, Genealogical Volume I, she and her daughter Anne were legatees under her mother's will of 1582, together with her sons John and Robert. Her brother, the Lord Burghley (died 1598), also left legacies to this sister.

The two rather sprightly little tunes, particularly the 'Nothing' seem perhaps a little inappropriate for a lady who, unless she were very considerably younger than her brother, must have been quite elderly by the time they were written. Her daughter Anne White would, from the point of view of age, have been a more likely recipient of the dedications. There are, however, other Whites who could be put forward as claimants.

Anne Pilcher, wife of Rowland Whyte or White, through her husband, had connections with Court circles where she could easily have encountered Dowland. Rowland Whyte was Master of the Posts, and was employed by Sir Robert Sidney to transact his business at Court and to relate to him what happened there. In Lodge's words*

He lived on terms of the strictest intimacy which the distinction of ranks could allow, with the Earl of Pembroke, in whose house at Baynard's Castle he usually resided, and his connection with the Sidneys probably originated in their alliance with that nobleman.

A large family of Whites was engaged in various ramifications of the book-selling and printing trade at the time, and Dowland could have been acquainted with any of the Mrs. Whites from this group.

Moreover, the wife of the incumbent of St. Dunstan's-in-the-West was a Mrs. White when Dowland was living in Fetter Lane.

Whitehead, George, was a member of a Northumberland family, and was a tenant of the Duke of Northumberland in a property called Boulmer. An officer of Northumberland's household, he was at one time Deputy Captain of the Duke's Castle of Tynemouth. His brother-in-law, Peter Delaval, wrote of him as 'such a spochting fellow as is not mannye suche in all the countre, as I refar me to the generall report of all such as knoweth hym in the countre, what George Whythead is'.†

On the discovery of the Gunpowder Plot, the Duke was suspected of complicity on account of his patronage of one of the conspirators, Thomas Percy, and, at the instigation of Sir Robert Cecil, he was detained and Sir Henry Widdrington was sent to seize the Duke's castles of Tynemouth, Alnwick, Prudhoe and Cockermouth. There is a letter from Whitehead to the Duke, dated November 12th, 1605,‡ telling him that the plot has been uncovered and that Thomas Percy is implicated. Another letter,§ written on the following day, informs the Duke that Widdrington has seized Tynemouth and Alnwick, and that Prudhoe and Cockermouth are threatened. He asks for the Duke's instructions. Northumberland was eventually tried by the

---

* *Illustrations of British History* (1791), Vol. III, p. 243.
† *A History of Northumberland* (County History Committee), Vol. 8 (1907), p. 175. A pedigree of the Whiteheads of Boulmer is given in Vol. 2 (1895), p. 403.
‡ The Duke of Northumberland's MSS.
§ *Calendar of State Papers. Domestic*, 1603–10, Vol. XVI, No. 64.

Star Chamber and found guilty. He was ordered to pay a fine of £30,000 and was deprived of all offices held by him under the Crown.

George Whitehead fought on the Royalist side in the Civil War and was fined as a delinquent in 1649.

I have been unable to find any particular connection with Dowland, but it is possible that Whitehead accompanied the Duke to London in connection with the Duke's official duties and thus met, or heard of, Dowland. I have been entirely unable to find any other George Whitehead of a generation that would coincide with Dowland's.

Willoughby, Lord. *See* Bertie, Peregrine.

Winter, Mrs. With no first name certain identification is impossible, but there is a Mrs. Winter, niece of William third Lord Vaux, who would have been living about the right time. Her relationship with the Vaux family could have provided the connection with Dowland. The mother of this Catherine Winter was Catherine Vaux (*d.* 1571), who married Sir Thomas Throckmorton. Catherine and her husband William Winter were the parents of Robert and Thomas Winter, both of whom were implicated in the Gunpowder Plot.★

★ For a family tree showing this relationship and the descent of two other plotters, Francis Tresham and Robert Catesby from Sir Thomas Throckmorton and Catherine Vaux, *see* Godfrey Anstruther, *Vaux of Harrowden* (1953). I am grateful to Father Anstruther for his helpful suggestions about members of the Vaux family.

VIII

Posthumous reputation. Fall and rise

At the time of Dowland's death the great era of English lute music had already drawn to a close, but from the late 1620s until the French lute became acclimatized in England in the 1640s[*] there is an extreme scarcity of documentary evidence to show what comprised the solo repertoire for the lute during these years. Only a few musicians of conservative outlook appear to have preserved an affection for the music of the older school but at the same time the number of manuscripts containing music of the current French fashion is surprisingly limited.

Lord Herbert of Cherbury[†] was a notable example of a man whose love for the old music survived the change of fashion, and, to judge by his lute-book, he continued to play works by Dowland, Bacheler, John Danyel, Robert Johnson and Ferrabosco long after they were outmoded. The date 1640 with which his MS closes marks the final appearance of Dowland's solo works in seventeenth century English sources. This MS, however, may not be entirely representative of English taste since considerable portions of it are probably the result of his having collected music in France during various periods he spent there between 1608 and 1624. Nevertheless, it is likely that the large proportion of the contents by Gaultier (probably Jacques d'Angle-terre), Ballard, Perrichon, Belleville, l'Enclos and others of the period constitutes a fair reflection of the contemporary English fashion. The coming of Jacques Gaultier to England in 1617 and his appointment to the King in 1619 undoubtedly strengthened the French influence on English music, but from the scarcity of examples that remain it appears that he and his pupils failed to secure such a widespread hold on the affection of English musicians as had the masters of the old school.

The compositions by Cuthbert Hely in Lord Herbert's volume are of

[*] Richard Matthews, in *The Lutes Apology* (1652), says that his is the first book of music for the French lute to appear in England.

[†] See Thurston Dart, 'Lord Herbert of Cherbury's Lute Book', *Music and Letters* (April 1957).

exceptional interest since they provide a hint, if nothing more, of the type of composition being written by the post-Dowland English lutenists. Copied into the MS by Hely himself, probably about 1628, the pieces show him to have been completely under the influence of the French style, but like Gaultier himself at this period, still writing in the old tuning.

As already mentioned, the lyra viol, during the later years of Dowland's life, may have gone far in displacing the lute as a solo instrument, further-more, the evidence of contemporary writers suggests that the playing of consort music had become one of the fashionable pleasures. At the same time it is interesting to find that John Nash* in 1636, commenting on this very point, in his apology for the weaknesses of some of the devotees of town life put into the mouth of *Urbanus*, one of the four characters of his book, makes it clear that the name Dowland still held its place in public regard as that of the supreme exponent of the lutenist's skill:

if he be Musicall, and can beare a part in a Consort, though never so meanely, they will preferre him before *Tompkins* the Organist, and *Dowland* the Lutenist, and will not sticke to say, that *Pan and Arion will not touch their tooles in his presence.*

Many of Dowland's songs lived on considerably longer, shorn of their original tablature. Generally the sources give only the Cantus line, or Cantus and Bassus, their performance being accompanied by the then fashionable theorbos and harpsichords.

In 1660 and 1662 John Playford revived the song 'Sleep wayward thoughts' in two editions of *A Brief Introduction to the Skill of Musick*. In these volumes the song is described as 'For 2 Voyces Treble and Bass', and Dowland is given as the composer.

Even as late as the 1690s there may have been rare individuals who appreciated Dowland's work since his books were still, at that time, being offered for sale by John Playford. Three of his music catalogues from the years 1653, 1690 and 1691 are preserved in John Bagford's *A Collection for the History of Printing*† and can be seen to contain works by Dowland. The earliest of the three has the title:

A catalogue of all the Musicke-Bookes that have been Printed in England, either for Voyce or Instruments.

Under 'Musick Bookes in folio', a list in alphabetical order, the following items appear:

* *Quarternio or A Foure-Fold way to a Happy Life* (1636), p. 53.
† BM Harl. 5936, Dept. of Printed Books. See also C. Humphries and W. C. Smith, *Music Publishing* (1954), where the 1653 catalogue is reproduced as the frontispiece.

Dowlands Introduction
Dowlands first Booke
Dowlands second Booke
Dowlands third Booke
Dowlands fourth Booke
Dowlands fift Booke
R. Dowlands Lessons
R. Dowlands Ayres.

At the bottom of the page is a list headed 'Music Bookes lately Printed'. William C. Smith★ suggests the first list refers to books in which Playford's interest is only that of a bookseller, while the second part concerns his own publications.

The catalogue of 1690 has the title:

A Curious Collection of Musick-Bookes, Both Vocal and Instrumental (and several Rare Copies in Three and Four Parts, Fairly Prick'd) . . .

It includes:

Mr. Dowlands Introduction for singing in Folio . . . 2⁸ o^d

Presumably both this entry and the 'Introduction' of the 1653 catalogue refer to the translation of the *Micrologus* of Ornithoparcus.

The third in the series has the title:

A Catalogue of Ancient and Modern Musick Books, Both Vocal and Instrumental, with divers Treatises about the same and Several Musical Instruments. December the 17th. 1691.

This contains, under Folios (p. 3):

4.   A Book with divers sets, done by Mr. Dowland and others.

and under Quartos (p. 9):

17. Dowlands songs in 3 several Books, stitched together in folio.
23. Two of Dowlands Pilgrims Solace. fol.

His reputation was high enough, at least among historians of the period, for Fuller to write of him in *The History of the Worthies of England* (posthumously printed 1662), and for Anthony à Wood in 1691, to repeat from Fuller that 'he was the rarest Musician that his age did behold'.

In 1676, Thomas Mace, though himself one of the chief exponents of the French lute, in *Musicks Monument*, makes the lute express the following lament:

★ 'Some Hitherto Unnoticed Catalogues of Early Music', *Musical Times*, July 1st and August 1st, 1926.

Despair I do;
Old Dowland he is Dead; R Johnson too;
Two famous Men; Great Masters in My Art;
In each of them I had more than One Part;
Or Two, or Three; They were not Single-Soul'd
As most our Upstarts are, and too too Bold.
Soon after them, that Famous man Gotiere
Did make me Grateful in each Noble Ear,
He's likewise gone: I fear me much that I
Am not Long-liv'd, but shortly too shall Dye.

In Scotland Dowland's work was well known, the knowledge of it taken there, presumably, by Scottish courtiers returning home from the Court of James I. As was natural so far from the metropolis, his songs became known there somewhat after their appearance in England, and persisted in favour much later. Most of the material is, however, fragmentary, mostly consisting of one or other of the vocal lines in part books of which the other volumes of the set are missing. Examples of his songs are found in David Melvill's bassus part book (1604); in Wode's Psalter (*c.* 1615); instrumental arrangements are listed among the original contents of the lute MS (1627–1629) of Robert Gordon of Straloch, the distinguished cartographer; and in the Skene MS (*c.* 1625); there are songs again in the Rowallan Vocal MS (*c.* 1631); and the three editions of John Forbes's *Songs and Fancies* (1662, 1666, 1682) all have a number of his songs in the Cantus line only. John Squyer's MS (1696–1701) shows the interest to have been maintained until the beginning of the eighteenth century.

In 1680 Dowland's setting of Psalm 100, from Ravenscroft's *Whole Booke of Psalmes* (1621), was included, without the Medius part, in a volume called *Synopsis of Vocal Music,* by A.B. Philo-Mus. This is the last trace of him in English printed music of the seventeenth century that I have been able to find.

On the Continent, particularly in the Netherlands, Dowland's music continued to be popular, though often in debased forms, until late in the seventeenth century. Adrianus Valerius, in *Nederlandische Gedenck-Clanck* (1626) has a version of 'Lachrimæ' with Dutch words, and a number of editions of Dirck Rafaelszoon Camphuysen's *Stichtelycke Rymen,* printed between 1624 and 1690, kept alive some of the tunes, also fitted with Dutch words. Jacob van Eyk, in *Der Fluyten Lust Hof* (1654), has an arrangement for two recorders of both 'Lachrimæ' and 'Come again sweet love doth now invite'. Elsewhere, an occasional reminder of his greatness appears, such as Melchior Schildt's 'Paduana Lagrima' (*c.* 1642); a 'Pavan Lacrymæ' in the Stobæus MS, and a comment, on f. 24, in 'De Methodo Studendi in Testudine' in the same MS, on the correct position of the thumb as exemplified by

'Dulandy Anglus'. In 1727 Ernst Gottleib Baron quotes a Latin poem extolling the merits of dead lutenists, which begins 'Anglia Dulandi lacrymis moveatur:'* (Let England be touched by the tears of Dowland).

In eighteenth-century England Dowland received scant appreciation. Charles Burney in his *General History of Music* (1767–89) shows himself to be particularly unsympathetic towards his genius:

After being at the pains of scoring several of Dowland's compositions, I have been equally disappointed and astonished at his scanty abilities in counter-point, and the great reputation he acquired with his contemporaries, which has been courteously continued to him, either by the indolence or ignorance of those who have had occasion to speak of him, and who took it for granted that his title to fame, as a profound musician, was well founded. There are among the *Lamentations* published by Leighton, mentioned before, several by Dowland, which seem to me inferior in every respect to the rest: for besides want of melody and design, with the confusion and embarrassment of a *Principiante* in the disposition of the parts, there are frequently unwarrant-able, and, to my ear, very offensive combinations in the harmony; such as a sharp third and flat sixth; an extreme flat fourth and sixth, etc.

I make no doubt that Dowland was a captivating performer on the lute, to which Shakespeare has borne testimony in his *Passionate Pilgrim* (No. VI) where addressing his friend he says:

If music and sweet Poetry agree

(he quotes the rest of the Barnfield poem)

It has frequently happened that a great performer has been totally devoid of the genius and cultivation necessary for a composer; and, on the contrary, there have been eminent composers whose abilities in performance have been very far from great. Close application to the business of a composer equally enfeebles the hand and the voice, by the mere action of writing, as well as want of practice: and if the art of composition, and the facility of committing to paper musical ideas, clothed in good harmony, be not early acquired, even supposing that genius is not wanting, the case seems hopeless; as I never remember the difficulties of composition thoroughly vanquished except during youth.

I think I may venture to say from the works of Dowland, which I have had an opportunity of examining, that he had not studied composition regularly at an early period of his life; and was but little used to writing in many parts. In his prefaces, particularly that of his *Pilgrim's Solace*, he com-plains much of public neglect; but these complaints were never known to operate much in favour of the complainants, any more than those made to a

---

* *Historisch, Theoretisch und Practische Untersuchung des Instruments der Lauten* (Nürnberg, 1727), p. 55.

Left, Maurice, Landgrave of Hesse, engraved by W. Kilian, in the Staatliche Kunstsammlungen, Kassel; *right*, Sir Henry Lee, by A. Mor, 1568. By permission of the Trustees of the National Portrait Gallery.

Memorial portrait of Sir Henry Unton by an unknown artist. By permission of the National Portrait Gallery.

Portrait of Theophilus Howard, second Earl of Suffolk, by Biagio Rebecca, at Audley End.
By permission of the Hon. Robin H. C. Neville. Crown Copyright.

Portrait of Sir Robert Sidney by C. Jansen, at Penshurst Place. By permission of the Viscount de L'Isle.

mistress or lover whose affection is diminishing, which seldom has any other effect than to accelerate aversion. As a composer, the public seem to have been right in withdrawing that favour from Dowland which had been granted on a *bad basis*; but with regard to his performance we have nothing to say: as at this distance of time there is no judgment what proportion it bore to others who were better treated.*

Burney prints transcriptions of 'An heart thats broken and contrite' (without the instrumental parts) and 'I shame at my unworthinesse' from Leighton's *Teares or Lamentations*; to these he adds a footnote:

The places in Dowland's second composition marked with an + will not be found very grateful to nice ears.

The crosses mark similar chords to those he has previously condemned as 'very offensive'.

Sir John Hawkins† on the other hand, offers neither praise nor blame, but devotes four pages to a surprisingly accurate, though limited, account of his life and work, and is at pains to correct the misstatements of Anthony à Wood.

In 1783 Joseph Ritson included 'Away with these self-loving lads' in *A Select Collection of English Songs*. In Vol. I, p. 120, he gives the words only, correctly attributed to Fulke Greville, and in Vol. III, Class III, No. XV (no page numbers), the melody with the words of verse one, but no accompaniment. The rubric gives 'Set by Mr. Dowland, about 1600'.

John Stafford Smith (1750–1836), the singer and organist, perhaps through having helped in the preparation of Burney's *General History*, showed some knowledge of Dowland's work. He transcribed six four-part ayres from *The First Booke of Songes* in what is now B.M. Add. 34,609 (1785–9), and the vocal parts of Dowland's two songs in *Teares or Lamentations of a Sorrowfull Soule* in B.M. Add. 31,418 before the end of the century.

In 1789 a volume appeared called *Select Psalmes of David in the Old Version* which, on p. 8, has a version of Psalm 100, attributed to Dr. John Bowland. In the B.M. *Catalogue of Old Music* it is queried whether this is an error for Dowland. The church tune is the one he used but the bass agrees with neither his setting in Est's *Whole Booke* nor with that in Ravenscroft's.

The opening years of the nineteenth century saw a marked change in the outlook of musical scholars and soon the republishing of a number of Dowland's ayres began. In general the four-part versions were used and they were termed madrigals, *The First Booke of Songes* proving to be the most popular source. The earliest instance I have traced is that of 'Awake sweet

* Vol. 3, p. 136.
† *A General History of the Science and Practice of Music* (1776), Vol. III, pp. 323–6.

love' printed in *A Collection of Madrigals for three, four, five & six voices*, made by Richard Webb in 1808. Next came John Stafford Smith's *Musica Antiqua* in 1812 with 'Go chrystal tears'. Joseph Gwilt gives 'Come again, sweet Love' in *A Collection of Madrigals and Motets* (1815) and, in the notes on the composers, he defends Dowland against Burney. He quotes some of Burney's strictures and adds 'the editor ventures to say, notwithstanding the above free opinion of Dr. Burney, an excellent composer'. This song was also printed in sheet form, price 2s 6d, by The Regent's Harmonic Institution in the same year, and was given a piano accompaniment, not, however, a transcription of the tablature. In *c.* 1819 another London printer produced a sheet copy of 'Awake sweet love: a favorite madrigal for 4 voices, with an original verse and accomp. for the piano added'. William Chappell and William Crotch also included a version of 'Now, O now' in *A Collection of National English Ayres* (1838) under the title 'The Frog Galliard'. It was, however, the Musical Antiquarian Society's publication of *The First set of Songs in four Parts . . . scored from the first edition printed in the year 1597, and preceded by a life of the composer by William Chappell* (1844)* that once more provided the public with an adequate number of Dowland's songs on which to form an opinion of his quality. A curious feature of this publication is the imitation title-page that precedes the songs. The wording is given as in the original with a kind of mocked-up antique appearance, but the surrounding border is entirely different. Vol. 12 in the same series consisted of *A First Set of Songs . . . arranged with a piano-forte accompaniment by G. Alex Macfarren* (1844).

In the same year Edward Rimbault produced a modern edition of Est's *Whole Book of Psalms* for the Antiquarian Society (Vol. XII) containing, of course, Dowland's harmonizations.

In 1848 and 1849 several of the songs were printed in sheet form 'Edited with alterations by Thos. Oliphant Esq.' It was principally in the words that Oliphant made his changes and, it must be confessed, they are far from being an improvement on the originals. However, in addition to 'Come again, sweet love' he went to *The Second Booke of Songs* and reissued 'White as Lillies', 'Clear or Cloudy' and 'Fine Knacks for Ladies', all in four parts.

In the '50s and '60s 'Come again, sweet love' showed itself to be popular, appearing in its four-part version in J. H. Jewell's *Madrigal and Motet Book*, No. 4. (1856), in *The Musical Times*, No. 164 (1856) and in *Novello's Part-Song Book*, Second Series, No. 823 (1869). It also appears in several MS collections such as the set of part-books mostly in the hand of Sir Frederick Ouseley at St. Michael's College Tenbury (MS 945–54) and another early nineteenth-century collection in the same library, MS 1173.

* Vol. 11 of the Society's publications.

Several of Dowland's secular tunes were pressed into the service of the Church of England and were accommodated with sacred words. A very strange version of 'Awake sweet love' appeared in *The Musical Times* in 1854, with the title 'Come, Holy Ghost: A hymn for Whitsuntide', and in a mid-nineteenth-century collection at Tenbury (MS 795) 'Now O now' has been adapted to take the words 'Bow down thine ear'.

In France they would have none of him. F. J. Fétis, *Biographie Universelle* (1862) has the following passage:

Quelques madrigaux de Dowland ont été inserés dans la *Musica Antiqua* de Smith et dans la collection du docteur Crotch. Ces spécimens de sa musique ne donnent pas une idée favourable de son génie ni de son savoir. Non obstant la médiocrité de leur mérite au point de vue de l'art, les livres de chanson ou madrigaux de Dowland sont si rares aujourd'hui qu'un exemplaire des trois livres réunis (1595–1603) a été vendu en 1846, chez MM Kalkin et Budd, à Londres, la somme enorme de 12 livres 15 schellings. (3i8 fr. 75 c.) . . . Il y a lieu de croire que Dowland était meilleur instrumentiste que compositeur.

Meanwhile, in the literary world, the poetry of the Elizabethan era was receiving attention, and collections of verse from this period began to appear. The song-books were found to be fruitful trees for plucking. Sir Samuel Egerton Brydges was the first in this particular field with the ten volumes of his *Censura Literaria* (1805–10). Though containing many poems from the sets of various madrigalists and lutenists, they include none from Dowland's books. His *British Bibliographer* (Vol. 3, 1812), however, gives a reprint of *England's Helicon* which, of course, contains Nos. III, VIII, XI and XII of Dowland's first book. William Beloe, *Anecdotes of Literature* (Vol. vi, 1812), has on pp. 170–1, 'Whoever thinks' (Bk. 1, II), and 'Go crystal tears' (Bk. 1, IX), without comment. Thomas Oliphant, in *La Musa Madrigalesca* (1837), gives eleven from *The First Booke*, six from *The Second Booke*, and seven from *The Third and Last Booke*. This is interesting as showing a reappearance of the 1603 volume. Many of the poems are subjected to Oliphant's alterations. John Payne Collier, that curious mixture of scholar and charlatan, in *Lyrical poems, selected from musical publications between the years 1589 and 1600* (1844), includes eight poems from *The First Booke*, thirteen from *The Second Booke* and, inserted immediately after No. I from this book, are eleven poems from *The Third Booke* without comment as to where they come from.

About the year 1858 an unknown hand transcribed into score 'My Lord Chamberlain his Galliard. For two to play upon [one] Lute by John Dowland'* from *The First Booke*, using, apparently, the edition of 1600, or that of 1603, since the misprint in the final bar of these two printings has been reproduced.

---

* B.M. Add. 35,155, f. 157.

Algernon Charles Swinburne,* writing to his elder sister on December 5th, 1874, makes an appreciative, but somewhat confused, statement about a book of poems from the song-books that he has come across. He says:

. . . When I get down to Holmwood I shall bring a book of songs of Shakespeare's time written to the music of English musicians—Dowland, Morley, etc.—of the day—some of which are *too* lovely, both as poetry and as melody. Perhaps as the words were written for the notes (now, at all events, the distinction of ranks is better understood—Mr. Arthur Sullivan applies to me—'Will I give him *any* verses and he will make music to them?' *then* the poet was commissioned to write verses to suit the musicians' notes—*par exemple*!) Edward will be able to re-set them. I believe the original music exists somewhere—but it has never been reproduced, and heaven knows where it is now. . . .

And heaven knows what he means when he says 'some of which are *too* lovely, both as poetry and as melody' when, apparently, he had never seen the music. Possibly it was John Payne Collier's *Lyrical poems, selected from musical publications between the years 1589 and 1600* that he was referring to, since Collier quotes Thomas Watson's remark (in his *First Set of Italian Madrigals Englished*) to the effect that his translations were 'not to the sense of the originall dittie, but after the affection of the noate'. One can see how Swinburne, perhaps reading carelessly, could have deduced from this that all the verse in the song-books was written to pre-existing music. He could, of course, have found Dowland's *First Booke of Songs* if he had looked at the Musical Antiquarian Society's publications.

About 1877 'Awake sweet love', again described as a madrigal, appeared from '28a Paternoster Sq. E.C.', 'reharmonised in lawful and natural progression, with language revised and extended.' (Series for the diffusion of truthful and natural science in music, secular series D.2.)

In the first edition of *Grove's Dictionary of Music and Musicians* (1879) Vol. I, p. 762[b], in an article on Thomas Ravenscroft, when writing of his *Whole Booke of Psalmes* (1612), W. S. Rockstro remarks of Dowland's contribution to this volume:

The finest tune of the collection, John Dowland's setting of the Hundredth Psalm—may still be heard in Salisbury Cathedral.

In the 1889 edition of the same *Dictionary*, Vol. IV, p. 606[b], Hubert Parry wrote:

. . of part song with a definite tune, such as were early typified in the best days by Dowland's lovely and finished works.

---

* Mrs. Disney Leith, *The Boyhood of Algernon Charles Swinburne* (1917), p. 196.

In speaking of Psalm 100 in *Hymns Ancient and Modern. Historical Edition* (1909), the Rev. W. A. Frere says, on p. 432:

A particularly fine one is Dowland's in Est, *Psalmes* 1592.

He also mentions 'A prayer for the Queenes most excellent Maiestie' on p. 584.

Granville Bantock, in the same year, wrote *Old English Suite for Pianoforte*, of which No. 2 was the Lachrimæ Pavan.

It was, however, in the 1890s, when Arnold Dolmetsch began his work of restoring and making viols and lutes, that once more it became possible to hear Dowland's works played on the instruments for which they were written and it was this pioneering work that opened the way to a full restoration of Dowland to his rightful place. Dolmetsch included several of his compositions in the programmes of his early concerts, playing the lute himself and with viols played by friends and members of his family. From about 1927 till his death in 1940, I was privileged to play a number of Dowland's compositions in the concerts of the Haslemere Festival.

Most of the music was, however, until the second decade of the twentieth-century, only available through patient copying by hand from the original sources, or relatively expensive photo copies. In 1920 Dr. E. H. Fellowes, in his edition of the English Lutenist Song writers made available all four volumes of Dowland's songs, together with the three from *A Musicall Banqvet*, with the original lute tablature and a transcription into staff notation.

The next complete work to reappear was in Peter Warlock's *Lachrimæ or Seven Tears. Transcribed from the original edition of 1605* (1927). This, unfortunately, did not contain the lute tablature, but since perhaps no more than two people would have played from it in those days, the fact is not altogether surprising. In 1928 Warlock published a collection of fifteen of Dowland's lute solos, under the title *The Lute Music of John Dowland*. I had visited him in Eynsford, Kent, where he was living at the time, in September 1927, and I can still remember his playing me 'Forlorn Hope' which he had just finished transcribing; possibly it was the first time it had been played in three hundred years.

In 1926 I made my first broadcast and this programme contained some songs by Dowland. In the following year two records appeared, the first ever on which the lute was heard. One of these, by H.M.V., contained a performance of 'Flow not so fast ye fountains' by John Goss and myself, the other by Columbia, had 'Awake sweet love' sung by Cécile Dolmetsch, accompanied by Arnold and Rudolph Dolmetsch. Since all papers connected with the two recordings have long since been destroyed, it has been impossible to find out which of the discs was actually the first to appear.

Again we have to thank Dr. Fellowes for bringing out an edition of *Seven Hymn-Tunes . . . Lamentatio Henrici Noel* (1934). Unhappily Dr. Fellowes was not appreciative of the archaic words of the original metrical versions used, and, in some cases, substituted more modern verse, thinking it more acceptable to twentieth-century performers.

In the early '30s I was joined, in the Haslemere Festival, by a young American lutenist, Suzanne Bloch, who had come to England to study with Arnold Dolmetsch. On her return to the States her concerts, broadcasts and recordings did much to spread a knowledge of Dowland's music in America.

During the war I was otherwise occupied and did very little playing. In post-war England the climate was ripe, and the appreciation of sixteenth- and seventeenth-century music began to spread outside the rather limited circle in which it had previously been cultivated. Dowland began to come back into his own. Besides my own work in concerts, lectures and broadcasts other lutenists began to appear—Desmond Dupré and notably the young Julian Bream who, in 1951 and 1952, astonished everyone with the brilliance of his musicianship and his complete technical mastery of the lute. Dowland became his favourite composer and through his recitals, broadcasts and recordings he has introduced his music to a wide following, even as far away as Japan. Now, many fine lutenists are playing in America and most of the European countries, among whom Dowland's music stands as the highest expression of the particular art in which his genius excelled.

In 1955, as Volume IV in *Musica Britannica*, *Ayres for Four Voices*, containing the four-part settings from all the books, was edited by Thurston Dart and Nigel Fortune.

With the publication by Faber Music, 1972, of the collected edition of Dowland's lute music almost the whole of his output will, for the first time, be available in print. When this is achieved he should again assume his rightful stature as one of the great geniuses of English music.

Appendix I

The Schele Lute MS. Hamburg Stadtbibliothek, Real. ND. VI, No. 3238

⁂

For many years this MS was thought to have been destroyed during the Second World War and, when referred to, it is often spoken of as the 'lost' Schele MS. Happily it has reappeared, but by the time I learnt of this it was too late to include the information in the body of the book and it is, therefore, given as an appendix.

The MS, consisting of 154 pages of music, is beautifully written and is in an excellent state of preservation, although, unfortunately, there are many inaccuracies in the copying of the pieces. On the fly-leaf Ernst Schele has inscribed the words Tablatur Buch and, under them, he has added *Musica & vinum lætificant cor hominis*. His signature and the date, Anno 1619, are placed in the lower right-hand corner.

The contents are notable for the large number of compositions by Joachim van den Hove, many of them unique to this volume. On page 17 there is a setting of 'Lachrimæ' by this composer, dated Feb. 16th, 1614, which is different to his setting in DM f. 2ᵛ. Other composers represented include Robert Ballard, Bocquet, Dio. (Diomedes?), John Dowland, Anthoine Francisque, Ferrabosco (of Bologna), Gregory (Huwet?), Mercure d'Orleans, P.P. (Peter Phillips), Johan Rude and Nicolas Vallet. Other pieces bear names or initials of minor composers, about whom little or nothing is known.

As one would expect in a collection of lute music of this period. Schele shows a predilection for the fashionable *courante* and includes fifty-three examples of this form. Of these, fourteen have composers' names attached; the rest are anonymous. A number of these can, however, be traced to other sources where, in some cases, the composer's name is revealed.

A late example of the ubiquitous 'La Battaglia' is also included.

In many cases the name of the city where Schele had collected the composition, and the date, are added after the title and the composer's name. The earliest date given is 12 June, 1613; and the latest, 23 Sept. 1616, but the dated pieces are not placed in chronological order. Among the towns mentioned are Paris, Metz, Frankfurt, Leyden and Naples.

Versions of the following well-known pieces by John Dowland are included:

No. 23. 'Frogge Galliard'. Anon. pp. 144/145. For six-course lute. This elaborate setting has divisions unlike those of any other known copy, although the statement of each strain is closely related to Dowland's own version.

No. 43. 'Mÿ Ladÿ Riches Galliard'. Anon. pp. 146/147. For six-course lute. This arrangement has elaborate divisions, apparently unique to this volume.

No. 44. 'Mÿ lord of Darbies Galliard. M. Johan Doúlant'. p. 142. Closely resembles **Var.** Galliard 4.

No. 47[a]. 'Almande'. Anon. p. 148. With the exception of a few mistakes and some minor differences of reading, identical with **38** f. 8[v].

No. 48[a]. 'Allemande Doulant'. p. 145. Almost identical with FD f. 48, but a bass had been added to each division. The incompatibility of the true bass has evidently been noticed by the writer, and modifications have been made.

In addition to these there are three long compositions attributed to Dowland, but which, up till now, have not been found in any other source. These pieces present many problems and, as they stand in the MS I feel unable to accept them as authentic works of the composer. The consistent use of the lowest diapason at C, in the first two of the three pieces, would suggest they were composed towards the end of the productive period of his life, by which time Dowland had developed and refined his art to produce such masterpieces as the late songs, yet here we have a paucity of musical thought spread out to an inordinate length. This is particularly noticeable in the two pavans, one consisting of 112 bars, the other of 98. Although Dowland often departed from the traditional eight-bar strain, in no other composition in this form did he allow himself such unconventional and clumsy construction as this. Here and there a phrase appears which seems to have the authentic flavour, but then it vanishes into what appears to be the work of a composer entirely lacking in Dowland's genius. In all three the copying is exceedingly inaccurate with a number of manifestly incorrect notes and, in several cases, whole bars left out. In Poulton and Lam, *The Collected Lute Music of John Dowland* the tablature may be studied in Appendix I.

The three pieces are as follows:

1. 'Del Excellentissimo Musico Jano Dulando. Andegavi, Anno 1614. 22 Jun.' pp. 25/26/27/28. Diapasons at F and C. Consisting of 240 bars this piece is a set of variations on an eight-bar theme. The setting of the theme itself:

is the most convincing part of all this lengthy material as having come from Dowland's pen, but the variations often have an incorrect number of bars, and are so generally confused that they appear to have either been corrupted beyond recognition, or to be the work of an unskilful hand.

2. 'Pauana Johan Douland' pp. 28/29/30/31. Diapasons at F, Eb and C. The three strains consist of 19, 18 and 19 bars; each with its repeat. Here is the beginning of the first strain:

3. 'La mia Barbara. Johan Doulande Bacheler.' pp. 49/50/51. Diapasons at F and D. The strains consist of 15, 16 and 18 bars; each with its repeat. Here is the opening strain:

In addition to a number of minor mistakes, two bars following bar 84 are missing. No clue to the meaning of the title has been discovered.

Appendix II

Fretting and Tuning the Lute

≈

A discussion, with special reference to John Dowland's instructions in *Varietie of Lute-Lesson*

Hans Gerle's *Musica Teusch* was published in Nuremberg in 1532. In it instructions are given for spacing correctly the frets along the neck of a lute and during the following hundred years or so there appeared in France, Germany, Italy and Spain[1] a number of treatises containing such information. The only instructions to be published in England were given by John Dowland in *Varietie of Lute-Lessons* in 1610.

The lute in use during Dowland's lifetime was basically a six-course instrument, each course being a pair of strings tuned in unison, with the exception of the first, or treble, which was a single string. In descending order of pitch these courses were named Treble, Small mean, Great mean, Contra-tenor, Tenor and Bass.[2] There was no absolute standard of pitch, the usual instruction being to tune the treble as high as it would stand and then tune the other strings from it, although Dowland advises tuning in the reverse order, i.e. from the Bass course upwards.[3] Whatever the pitch used in practice, and this no doubt varied from lute to lute, nominally the courses were tuned to one of the following:

	'G tuning'	or	'A tuning'
1st course—Treble	g'		a'
2nd course—Small mean	d'		e'
3rd course—Great mean	a		b
4th course—Contra-tenor	f		g
5th course—Tenor	c		d
6th course—Bass	G		A

Towards the end of the sixteenth century one or more additional basses, or diapasons, were often fitted and their tuning varied according to the number in use and the requirements of the music.

The following diagram shows the fingerboard of a lute in the G tuning, together with the usual tuning employed when there are two diapasons.

FIGURE I

Course	Nut	b	c	d	e	f	g	h	i	k	l	m	n	Bridge
	a													
1st	g'		a'		b'	c"		d"		e"	f"		g"	
2nd	d'		e'	f'		g'		a'		b'	c"		d"	
3rd	a		b	c'		d'		e'	f'		g'	a'		
4th	f		g		a		b	c'		d'				
5th	c		d		e	f	g		a					
6th	G		A		B	c		d		e				
Diapason	F													
„	D													

If only one diapason is fitted this is usually tuned to either F or D as required, and if there are three the tuning is F, D and C. However, as indicated above, if the music demands other notes these courses are tuned accordingly, but as they are normally tuned to notes an octave or two octaves below one or other of the basic six courses they will be ignored for the purposes of this discussion.

It will be observed that the 1st and 6th courses are two octaves apart and adjacent courses a fourth apart, with the exception of the 3rd and 4th where the interval is a major third. This arrangement presents a difficulty in that the sum of four perfect fourths of 498 cents each and a true major third of 386 cents falls short of two octaves (2400 cents) by 22 cents (the comma of Didymus):

$$4 \times 498 = 1992$$
$$\underline{386}$$
$$2378 \text{ cents}$$

It is thus necessary to temper the tuning of the open courses and it is interesting to compare the use of Pythagorean, Meantone and Equal Tempered intervals.

	Pythagorean.	*Meantone.*	*Equal Temp.*
Fourths	$4 \times 498 = 1992$	$4 \times 503 \cdot 5 = 2014$	$4 \times 500 = 2000$
Major Third	408	386	400
	2400	2400	2400

However, the precise extent of the tempering is largely dependent on the positions of the frets, which are placed at previously determined intervals along the neck of the lute.

Theoretically, notes which are nominally the same should have the same pitch, or be an octave above or below that pitch, wherever they are found on the fingerboard, and, consequently, the interval between any two notes will always be the same size, whatever the respective fret positions being used. For example, the fourths between each of the following positions should be identical:

G–c	6th course open	/6th course fret f.
	,,	/5th course open.
g–c'	5th course fret	h/4th course fret h.
	,,	/3rd ,, ,, d.
	4th course fret	c/4th ,, ,, h.
	,,	/3rd ,, ,, d.
g'–c"	3rd course fret	l/2nd ,, ,, l.
	,,	/1st ,, ,, f.
	2nd course fret	f/1st ,, ,, f.
	,,	/2nd ,, ,, l.
	1st course open	/1st ,, ,, f.
	,,	/2nd ,, ,, l.

The pitch of the open courses should, therefore, be determined by the positions of frets e (major third) and f (fourth), as follows:

FIGURE 2

Course	Nut				Frets		
	a	b	c	d	e	f	g
1st	g'						
2nd	d'					g'	
3rd	a					d'	
4th	f			a			
5th	c					f	
6th	G					c	

This is, in fact, the rule-of-thumb method for tuning the open courses which is most frequently given in the instruction books of the sixteenth and early seventeenth centuries for players who couldn't tune them by ear.[4]

In theory, therefore, fretting and tuning a lute is quite straightforward, but in practice there are three factors which complicate matters and for which the player has to make allowances.

The first is that the actual pitch of any stopped note is always sharper than the position of the fret leads one to expect. The reason for this is that depressing a string increases its tension and consequently raises the pitch. The extent of the sharpening depends on the height of the bridge and nut, the height of the fret, and the tension of the open string. The higher the bridge, nut and fret, and the slacker the open string, the greater will be the rise in pitch.

Secondly, there is the slight discrepancy in pitch which can occur between the pair of strings of a course. Nowadays, with the use of nylon, this discrepancy is very slight indeed and only arises when the open strings are not precisely in tune, but in Dowland's time the problem was more acute. The strings were then made of gut which is more likely to be 'false' than is nylon. A 'false' string is one which is not of equal thickness throughout its length so that, although the pair may be in tune when open, they are not in tune when stopped. If the sounding length of a 'false' string thickens it will vibrate more slowly and hence gives a flatter note, if it is thinner it will vibrate more quickly and gives a sharper note. Dowland advises on the selection of strings in *Varietie of Lute-Lessons* in the section 'For Chusing of Lute-strings'.[5]

The third factor is that each fret gives five separate semitones of identical size, one on each course (not six, the 1st and 6th courses duplicate each other, albeit two octaves apart), whether the fretting system being used requires those particular semitones to be equal or not. If an Equal Tempered fretting system is used all semitones will be the same size and all notes nominally the same will have the same pitch, or be an octave above or below, so, apart from the effect of the previously mentioned factors, no problems arise.[6]

All other fretting systems employ semitones that are unequal to a greater or lesser extent and discrepancies in the pitch of notes nominally the same are inevitable. A considerable number of these systems are basically Pythagorean, but with certain modifications. As it stands a Pythagorean system would require the 'chromatic' frets b, d, g, i and l each to be placed in one of two alternative positions according to the notes required. For example, fret b can either be placed to give a semitone of 114 cents from the nut and the notes g′ sharp, d′ sharp, a sharp, f sharp, c sharp and G sharp, or nearer the nut to give a semitone of 90 cents and the notes a′ flat, e′ flat, b flat, g flat, d flat and A flat, but it cannot give both at once. However, as fret b is frequently required to give the notes e′ flat, b flat *and* f sharp in the same piece of music, it is usually placed in a compromise ('enharmonic') position so that it gives notes that can be used as both e′ flat and d′ sharp, b flat and a sharp, g flat and f sharp, etc. Frets d, g, i and l are similarly placed in compromise positions. Other Pythagorean systems modify the position of some of the other frets as well, bringing them very close to Equal Temperament.

A few attempts were made to use a system based on just intervals, but, with possibly one exception([7]), none of them is suitable for the lute.

Meantone Temperament is an interesting possibility, with its true major thirds and nearly true fifths, but as it makes a distinction between sharp and flat chromatic notes it suffers from the same handicap as does an unmodified Pythagorean system. It is perhaps noteworthy that no sixteenth or early seventeenth-century writers advocate Meantone Temperament for the lute.

The task facing the lutenist, therefore, is to space the frets according to one or other of these systems and then so to tune the open courses that the pitch discrepancies arising from the factors just discussed are spread over as wide a range of chords as possible. No chord will be precisely in tune but all should be tolerable to the ear. It appears more than likely that, when a lute has been tuned really well, no two notes are actually in tune at all, including all unisons and octaves (but with the possible exception of the open g′/G courses), although the amount of latitude available varies from interval to interval—with octaves and fifths there is very little, but with thirds considerably more. It is probable that the lack of sustaining power for which the lute is notorious is an advantage in that the sound dies away before the slow beat of an out-of-tune chord becomes particularly noticeable. However, even if the beating is noticeable the ear does not find it unpleasant provided it is not too fast.

Dowland puts forward a Pythagorean fretting system with modifications, and describes it in *Varietie of Lute-Lessons* in the section 'Of fretting the lute' ([8]). His instructions may be summarized as follows:

1. Fret n — halfway between the bridge and the nut.
2. „ h — one-third from fret n to the nut.
3. „ b — two-elevenths from the nut to fret h.
4. „ c — one-third from the nut to fret h.
5. „ f — halfway between the nut and fret n.
6. „ g — halfway between frets f and h.
7. „ d — divide the distance from the nut to fret b into three parts, then 'measure from [fret b] upwards four times and a half'.
8. „ e — halfway between frets d and f.

9. „ i — one-third from fret b to the bridge.
10. „ k — one-third from fret c to the bridge.
11. „ l — one third from fret d to the bridge.

Dowland does not provide for fret m.

The fingerboard of a lute so fretted will be as follows. (An open string length of twenty-four inches has been assumed and the positions of the frets are indicated to the nearest hundredth of an inch. The pitches of the notes are given to the nearest integer but it must be made clear that these are calculated according to the fret positions only and no allowance has been made for the sharpening of stopped notes. This can vary from lute to lute but it should be borne in mind when examining the following table).

FIGURE 3

Frets	Distances from bridge (inches)	Ratios	Courses 6th	5th	4th	3rd	2nd	1st
a	24·00	—	0	498	996	204	702	1200
b	22·55	31:33	108	606	1104	312	810	108
c	21·33	8:9	204	702	1200	408	906	204
d	20·36	28:33	284	782	80	488	986	284
e	19·18	211:264	388	886	184	592	1090	388
f	18·00	3:4	498	996	294	702	1200	498
g	17·00	17:24	597	1095	393	801	99	597
h	16·00	2:3	702	1200	498	906	204	702
i	15·03	62:99	810	108	606	1014	312	810
k	14·22	16:27	906	204	702	1110	408	906
l	13·58	56:99	986	284	782	1190	488	986
m	—	—	—	—	—	—	—	—
n	12·00	1:2	1200	498	996	204	702	1200

It will be observed that the position of fret d is much too near the nut. Even with the major third between the open 3rd and 4th courses as wide as 408 cents the octaves c/c' (5th open/3rd fred d) and f/f' (4th open/2nd fret d) are still 10 cents too narrow and the octaves B flat/b flat (6th fret d/3rd fret b) and e flat/e' flat (5th fret d/2nd fret b) are 28 cents too wide. With fret d in this position the system is just not workable, and the question arises—did Dowland really intend this fret to be where he indicated, or did he make a mistake? And where did he get this system from anyway?

There is one other fretting system, and only one, which bears a marked resemblance to Dowland's, and that was advocated by Hans Gerle in his treatise *Musica Teusch*.[9] Gerle was writing primarily for the benefit of learners on 'the little fiddle without frets'[10] to assist them in finding the correct places to stop the strings, but he makes it clear that his instructions can also be used for fretting a lute. For the fiddle he does not provide frets i, k, l or m, but envisages the addition of fret i on the lute.

Gerle's instructions may be summarized as follows:([11])

1. Fret n — halfway between the bridge and the nut.
2. „ h — one-third from fret n to the nut.
3. „ b — two-elevenths from the nut to fret h.
4. „ c — one-third from the nut to fret h.
5. „ f — halfway between the nut and fret n.
6. „ g — halfway between frets f and h.
7. „ d — divide the distance from the nut to fret b into three parts, then measure from fret b upwards five parts.
8. „ e — halfway between frets d and f.

The similarities in the two sets of instructions are plain to see. The order in which the fret positions are described is identical—n, h, b, c, f, g, d and e. The calculations for frets b, e, and, in essence, d are identical and no other instructions are known which calculate the fret positions in this manner. Dowland certainly knew of Hans Gerle as he refers to his book of Tablature in *Varietie of Lute-Lessons* at the beginning of the section 'Of fretting the lute'([8]). Whether he had read *Musica Teusch* can only be conjectured, but it seems probable that this treatise is the source of Dowland's information.

The question of the position of fret d in Dowland's system (and, consequently, of frets e and l as their positions are dependant on d) remains open, however. It is difficult to see how the German 'funff' (five) became 'four and a half' (see no. 7 in each of the summaries) and the only possible explanations seem to be that it was either a mistake or an attempt on someone's part to 'improve' the system.

An interesting point is that whereas Dowland indicates the positions of the frets above h as a perfect fifth above the lower frets, Gerle uses a different method for placing fret i, although its precise position is not made entirely clear([12]). As mentioned previously, no provision was made for frets k, l and m, these not being needed for the music of Gerle's time.

Assuming, then, that Dowland intended to describe Gerle's system adding an extension upwards for the frets above h, the fingerboard would be fretted as follows. (The remarks made in connection with Figure 3 apply equally here).

Unlike Figure 3, an attempt has here been made to suggest a suitable tempering for the open courses which, although hypothetical, serves to show the sort of compromises that have to be made. It will be noticed that their

FIGURE 4

Frets	Distances from bridge (inches)	Ratios	Courses					
			6th	5th	4th	3rd	2nd	1st
a	24·00	—	0	499	999	199	698	1200
b	22·55	31:33	108	607	1107	307	806	108
c	21·33	8:9	204	703	3	403	902	204
d	20·12	83:99	305	804	104	504	1003	305
e	19·06	629:792	399	898	198	598	1097	399
f	18·00	3:4	498	997	297	697	1196	498
g	17·00	17:24	597	1096	396	796	95	597
h	16·00	2:3	702	1	501	901	200	702
i	15·03	62:99	810	109	609	1009	308	810
k	14·22	16:27	906	205	705	1105	404	906
l	13·41	166:297	1007	306	806	6	505	1007
m	—	—	—	—	—	—	—	—
n	12·00	1:2	1200	499	999	199	698	1200

tuning is very close indeed to Equal Temperament, for which the figures would be 0, 500, 1000, 200, 700 and 1200 cents.[13]

In practice this fretting system has been found to be quite satisfactory provided the open courses are tuned with care.

DAVID MITCHELL

I wish to acknowledge the advice and assistance of numerous friends, in particular Guy Oldham and Diana Poulton who gave generously of their time and experience.

NOTES

1. In Spain the vihuela de mano, and not the lute, was played, but as the tuning of both instruments was the same, the instructions for one can be applied to the other.
2. See *Varietie of Lute-Lessons* (facsimile edition, London 1958, p. 19).
3. op. cit., pp. 17–18 ('Of tuning the lute')
4. op. cit., p. 19.
5. op. cit., p. 14.
6. As the calculations for placing frets in equal tempered positions are rather complicated, a number of easier approximations to it were advocated. By far the most common, which was first suggested by Vincenzo Galilei in 1581 and is still being used, is the so-called '18' rule. Under this rule the open string-length is divided into eighteen equal parts and the first fret is placed one part from the nut. Then the distance from this fret to the bridge is also divided into eighteen equal parts and the second fret placed one part from the first. And so on. This system produces semitones only 99 cents wide instead of the 100 cents of Equal Temperament, but as they are all the same size along the fingerboard this does not really affect the point.
7. The exception is a system, basically just, but modifying the positions of certain frets. Unfortunately there appear to be mistakes in the original so further examination is necessary.

8. op. cit., p. 16. Dowland's instructions are:

Wherefore take a thinne flat ruler of whitish woode, and make it iust as long and straight as from the inward side of the Nut to the inward side of the Bridge, then note that end which you meane to the Bridge with some small marke, and the other end with the letter *A*, because you may know which belongeth to the one and to the other. then lay the ruler vpon a Table, and take a payre of compasses and seeke out the iust middle of the Ruler: that note with a pricke, and set the letter *N*. vpon it, which is a *Diapason* from the *A*. as appeareth by the striking of the string open. Secondly, part the distances from *N*. to *D*. [this should be A] in three parts, then the first part giues you the seuenth fret from the Nut, making a *Diapente*: in that place also set a pricke, and vpon it the letter *H*. Thirdly, deuide the distance from the letter *H*. to the letter *A*. in eleuen parts: two of which parts from *A*. giues the first fret, note that with a pricke, and set the letter *B*. thereon, which maketh a *Semitone*. Fourthly, diuide the distance from *H*. to the letter *A*. in three parts one of which parts from *A*. upward sheweth the second fret, note that with a pricke, and set the letter *C*. vpon it, which maketh a whole Tone from *A*. Fiftly, diuide the distance from *N*. to *A*. into two parts, there the first part sheweth you the first fret, sounding a *Diateffaron*: in that place also set a pricke, and vpon it letter *F*. The sixt fret which is a *G*. must be placed iust in the middest betwixt *F*. and *H*. which maketh a *Semidiapente*. Seuenthly, diuide the distance from the letter *B*. to *A*. in three parts, which being done, measure from the *B*. vpwards foure times and an halfe, and that wil giue you the third fret, sounding a *Semiditone*: mark that also with a prick, & set thereon the letter *D*. then set the fourth fret iust in the middle, the which wil be a perfect *ditone*: then take one third part from *B*. to the Bridge, and that part from *B*. maketh *I*. which soundeth *Semitonium* cum *Diapente*, then take a third part from the Bridge to *C*. and that third part maketh *E*. [this should be K] which soundeth *Tonne* cum *diapente*, or an *Hexachordo maior*. Then take one third part from *D*. to the Bridge, and that third part from *D*. maketh *L*. which soundeth *Ditonus* cum *Diapente*. Now take your LVTE, and lay it vpon a Table vpright, and set the Ruler edgewise, betweene the nut and the bridge, and thereby set little marks vpon the necke of the Instrument euen with those on the ruler, because those are the places on which your frets muft stand.

9. See copy in the British Museum—HIRSCH iv. 1603, f. h iii[r]. There is also another copy (K.l.b.ll) in which these instructions do not appear.

10. 'den kleynen Geigleyn . . . die kein Bundt haben.'

11. Gerle's instructions are:

Nun thů im alſo / nym ein Richtſcheytleyn das dinn ſey oder ſonſt eyn ebens hőltzlein gleych einem linial / vnd mach es als lang / das es oben anſtee an dem hőltzleyn da die ſaytten auſtigeu Vnnd auch an ſtee an dem ſteg / da ſaytten auſtigen vnd wann du das richtſcheytleyn haſt gemacht / das es vnthen vnnd oben anſtee / nie das du es zu kurtz machſt es muß anſtee wie ich geſagt hab / So zaychen das tail vnthen bey dem ſteg mit einem a. vnd das őbertayl mit eynem .b. damit du wiſſeſt welchs ort zum ſteg gehőrt / Darnach leg das richtſcheitleyn auff ein diſch vnd nym ein Circkel vnd ſuch das mittel an dem richtſcheitleyn / das merck mit einem punck oder düpfflein vnd ſetz das .m. darzu / Darnach tayl von dem m. bis zu dem .b. drey tayl / ſo gibt dir der erſt tayl von dem m. den ſibenthen vnd vnterſten griff den merck mit einem dupff vnd ſetz die zyffer 7 darzu / darnach tayl von der zyffer bis zu dem .b. aylff tayl vnd der ſelben tayl zway von dem .b. herab / geben dir den erſten gryff den merck auch mit eynem tupff vnnd ſetz die zyffer .1. darzu / Darnach tayl wider von der zyffer .7. bis zu dem .b. drey tayl vnnd der ein tayl von dem .b. herab gibt dir den andern griff / den merck auch mit einem tupff vnd ſetz die zyffer .2. darzu / Darnach tayl von dem .m. bis zu dem .b. zwey tayl So gibt dir der ein tayl den fünfften griff den merck mit eynem dupff vnnd ſetz die zyffer .5. darzu / Darnach ſetz den ſechſten gryff in die mit deß fünfften vnd ſibenden gryffs den merck mit eynem dupff vnd ſetz die zyffer .6. darzu / Darnach tayl von der zyffer .1. bis zu dem .b. drei tayl vnd wan du die drey tayl haſt / So gee mit vnuerruckteim circkel von der zyffer .1. herab noch fünff geng das gibt dir den dritten gryff den merck mit eynem dupff vnnd ſetz die zyffer .3. darzu / Darnach ſetz den viertten gryff zwiſchen den dritten vnnd fünfften gryff / den merck mit eym dupff Vnd ſetz die zyffer .4. darzu.

12. op. cit., f. h iii^v—

Wann aber eyner auff die lautten wolt acht bündt machen/So mach er den achten bundt ein wenig enger von dem sibenden bundt /wann der sechst steet.

13. So as to put it into perspective, the following table compares the Gerle/Dowland system with Equal Temperament, the '18' Rule, and three other Pythagorean systems advocated by Juan Bermudo in his *Declaracion de Instrumentos Musicales* (Ossuna 1555), showing the intervals produced, in cents.

Fret	Gerle/ Dowland	Equal Temp.	'18' Rule	Pythagorean Systems (1)	(2)	(3)
a	0	0	0	0	0	0
b	108	100	99	102	114	100
c	204	200	198	204	204	200
d	305	300	297	306	294	294
e	399	400	396	408	408	400
f	498	500	495	498	498	498
g	597	600	594	600	612	599
h	702	700	693	702	702	698
i	810	800	792	804	816	792
k	906	900	891	906	906	899
l	1007	1000	990	996	996	996
m	—	1100	1089	—	—	—
n	1200	1200	1188	1200	1200	1200

(1) Pythagorean diatonic scale with tones divided into equal semitones.
(2) Unmodified Pythagorean scale.
3) Basically Pythagorean but most fret positions tempered.

Bibliography and Finding List

BIBLIOGRAPHY

A. B. Philo-Mus. *Synopsis of Vocal Musick* (London, 1680)

Addison, William. *Audley End* (London, 1953)

Adriensen, Emanuel. *Novum Pratum Musicum* (Antwerp, 1592)
   Pratum Musicum (Antwerp, 1600)

Ainsworth, Henry. *The Book of Psalmes* (Amsterdam, 1612)

Allen, P. S. 'Books brought from Spain in 1596', *The English Historical Review* (1916), Vol. 31.

Alison, Richard. *The Psalmes of Dauid in Meter* (London, 1599)

Anstruther, Godfrey. *Vaux of Harrowden* (Newport, Mon. 1953)

Arbeau, Thoinot. *Orchésographie* (Lengres, 1588)

Arber, Edward. *A Transcript of the Registers of the Stationers' Company 1554–1640* (London, 1875–77)

Ascham, Roger, *Toxophilus* (London, 1545)

Baddeley, W. Saint Clair. *A Cotteswold Shrine* (London, 1908)

Bagford, J. *A Collection for the History of Printing* B. M. Harl. 5936.

Baildon, F. J. *Baildon and the Baildons* (Privately printed, 1912–27)

Baildon, W. P. *Les Reportes del Cases in Camerata Stellata 1593–1606* (London, 1894)
   The Records of the Honourable Society of Lincoln's Inn (London, 1897–1902), Vol. II, The Black Books.

Bantock, Granville. *Old English Suite for Pianoforte Solo* (London, 1909)

Barley, William. *A New Booke of Tabliture* (London, 1596)
   The Whole Booke of Psalmes (London, 1599)

Barnfield, Richard. *Poems in diuers humors* (London, 1598)

Baron, Ernest Gotlieb. *Historisch-Theoretisch und Practische Untersuchung des Instruments der Lauten* (Nürnberg, 1727)

Baskerville, Charles Read. *The Elizabethan Jig* (Chicago, 1931)

Bataille, Gabriel. *Airs de Differents Autheurs* (Paris, 1608–18).

Bateson, Thomas. *The Second Set of Madrigals to 3.4.5. and 6. Parts. Apt for Viols and Voyces.* (London, 1618)

Beaumont and Fletcher. *The Knight of the Burning Pestle* Edited R. F. Patterson (London and Glasgow, 1944)

Bermudo, Juan. *Declarición de Instrumentos* (Ossuna, 1555)

Berry, Henry Fitzpatrick, *Records of the Dublin Gild of Merchants 1438–1671* (Dublin, 1900)

Besardus, Johannes Baptista. *Thesaurus Harmonicus* (Cologne, 1603)
   Novus Partus siue concertationes musicæ (Augsburg, 1617)

Bindoff, S. T. *Tudor England* (Penguin Books, London, 1950)

Birch, Thomas. *Memoirs of the Reign of Queen Elizabeth* (London, 1754)
   The Court and Time of James I (London, 1848)

Blagden, Cyprian. *The Stationers' Company. A History 1403–1959.* (London, 1960)

Bonnet, Pierre. *Histoire de la Musique* (Paris, 1715)

Borren, Charles van den. *The Sources of Keyboard Music in England*. Translated by James E. Matthew (London, 1914)

Bourgeois, Louis. *Pseaulmes de Dauid* (1554)

Brayssing, Gregoire. *Quart Liure de Tablature de Guiterre* (Paris, 1553)

Brenet, Michel. *Les Musiciens de la Sainte-Chapelle du Palais Royale* (Paris, 1910)

Breton, Nicholas. *The Souls Harmony* (London, 1602)

    The Passion of a Discontented Mind. Edited J. P. Collier. Illustrations of Old English Literature. Vol. I. (1866)

    The Works in Verse and Prose. Edited A. B. Grosart. (London, 1875–79)

    Melancholike Humours 1600. Edited G. B. Harrison (London, 1929)

    Poems. Edited Jean Robertson (1952)

Brett, Philip. 'The English Consort Song 1570–1625'. *Proceedings of the Royal Musical Association* (London, 1961) pp. 73–88.

Bright, Dr. Timothy. *A Treatise of Melancholy* (London, 1586 and 1613)

Britten, Benjamin, *Lachrimæ: Reflections on a song of Dowland* (If my complaints) (London, 1951)

Brown, Rawdon Lubbock, and Giustiniano, S. *Four years at the Court of Henry VIII* (1854)

Bruce, John. *Correspondence of Robert Dudley Earl of Leycester* (London, 1844. Camden Society No. 27)

Bruger, Hans Dagobert. *John Dowlands Solostücke für die Laute* (1923)

Brydges, Sir Samuel Egerton. *Censura Literaria* (London, 1805–9)

Bullen, A. H. *A Collection of Old English Plays* (London, 1882–5)

Burney, Charles. *A General History of Music* (London, 1776–1789)

Burton, Robert. *The Anatomy of Melancholy* (1621). Everyman's Library, (London and Toronto, 1932)

Byrd, William. *My Lady Nevells Booke*. Edited Hilda Andrews from B. M. Add. 30,485 (London, 1926)

    Forty-five Pieces for keyboard Instruments. Edited Stephen Davidson Tuttle (Paris, 1939)

Caccini, Giulio. *Nuoue musiche* (Venetia, 1602)

Calendar of Christ Church Deeds (Public Record Office Dublin) Reports Nos. XX, XXIII, XXIV and XXVII (Index).

Cambridge History of English Literature Vol. 3 (1949)

Camden, William. *Remains* (London, 1674)

Campian, Thomas. *Two Bookes of Ayres* (London, c. 1613)

    The Third and Fourth Booke of Ayres (London, c. 1617)

    Poetical Works in English. Edited P. Vivian (London, 1907)

    Works. Edited P. Vivian (London, 1909)

Camphuysen, Dirk Raphaelzoon. *Stichtelycke Rymen* (1602 and numerous editions to 1690)

Carpenter, Nan Cooke. *Music in the Medieval and Renaissance Universities* (Oklahoma, 1958)

Case, John. *The Praise of Musicke* (1586)

    Apologia Musices (1588)

Castan, Auguste. *Notes sur J. B. Bésard*. Memoires etc. de la Société d'Émulation du Doubs. Serie 5, Vol. I. (1876)

Castiglione, Baldassare. *Libro del Cortegiano* (Venice, 1528) *The Book of the Courtyer done into English by T. Hoby* (London, 1561). Everyman Edition, edited Drayton Henderson (1928)

Cervantes, Miguel de. *Don Quixote*. Translated J. Phillips (London, 1687)

Chamberlaine, John. *The Letters written by John Chamberlaine*. Edited N. McClure. Memoires of the American Philosophical Society. Vol. 12. (Philadelphia, 1939)

Chambers, E. K. *The Elizabethan Stage* (Oxford, 1923)

    Sir Thomas Wyatt, and some collected studies (London, 1933)

Sir Henry Lee. An Elizabethan Portrait. (Oxford, 1936)

Chapman, George, and others. *Eastward Hoe* (London, 1605)

Works, Vol. I. Plays, edited R. H. Shepherd (London, 1874)

Chappell, W. *Roxburghe Ballads* (London, 1869)

Popular Music of the Olden Times (London, 1855–1859)

Chappell, William. Revised H. E. Wooldridge under the title *Old English Popular Music* (London, 1893)

Chaucer, Geoffrey. *The Canterbury Tales.* Edited T. Tyrwhitt. (London, 1775)

Chilesotti, Oscar. *Da un Codice Lauten-Buch del Cinquecento* (Leipzig and Brussels, 1890)

Clark, Andrew. *Shirburn Ballads, 1585–1616* (1907)

Clements, Robert John. *Critical Theory and Practice of the Pléiade.* Harvard Studies in Romance Languages, Vol. 18. (1942)

Coferati, Matteo. *Corona di Sacre Canzoni* (Firenze, 1675)

Cokayne, G. E. *Complete Peerage.* Edited Vicary Gibbs and others. (London, 1910–40)

Collier, John Payne. *The Alleyn Papers* (The Shakespeare Society, 1843)

Lyrical poems selected from the musical publications between the years 1589 and 1600 (London, 1844)

Illustrations of Old English Literature Vol. I. No. 6 (London, 1866)

Cooper, Gerald. Correspondence, *The Musical Times* LXVIII (1927) p. 642.

Cooper, Thompson. *Athenæ Cantabrigienses*

Coperario, Giovanni. (John Cooper) *Funeral Teares* (London, 1606)

Corkine, William. *Ayres to Sing and Play* (London, 1610)

The Second Booke of Ayres (London, 1612)

Cousin, J. W. *A short Biographical Dictionary of English Literature* (Everyman's Library, 1910)

Croce, Giovanni. *Musica Sacra* (London, 1608)

Curtis, A. *Nederlandse klaviermuziek uit de 16e un 17e eeuw* (Amsterdam, 1961)

Cutts, John P. 'Jacobean Masque and Stage Music', *Music and Letters*, XXXV (July, 1954) pp. 185–200.

La Musique de scène de la troupe de Shakespeare (Paris, 1959)

Damon, Guilielmo (William). The Psalmes of Dauid (London, 1579)

The Former Booke of the Musicke (London, 1591)

The Second Booke of the Musicke (London, 1591)

Danyel, John. *Songs to the Lute, Viol and Voice* (London, 1606)

Dart, R. Thurston. 'Role de la Danse dans l'Ayre Anglais', *Musique et Poésie au XVIe siècle* (Paris, 1954)

'Lord Herbert of Cherbury's Lute-Book', *Music and Letters* XXXIII (April, 1957)

Clement Matchett's Virginal Book (1612)

Transcribed and edited Thurston Dart (1957)

Dauney, William. *Ancient Scottish Melodies* (Edinburgh, 1839)

Davis, Walter R. 'Melodic and Poetic Structure of Campian and Dowland', *Criticism* IV (1962)

Davison, Francis. *A Poetical Rhapsody* (1611). Edited E. Hyder Rollins (Cambridge, Mass. 1931)

Day, John. *Certaine Notes* (London, 1560)

The Whole Booke of Psalmes (London, 1563)

Dekker, Thomas. *The Shoemaker's Holiday* (1600). Edited W. J. Halliday (London, 1950)

De Lafontaine, Henry Cart. *The King's Music* (1909)

Deloney, Thomas. *Strange Histories* (London, 1612)

The Gentle Craft (1637)

The Garland of Goodwill (c. 1650)

De Vere, Edward, Earl of Oxford. *Poems.* Edited A. B. Grosart. Fuller's Worthies Library, Vol. 4. (1872–6)

Devereux, Robert Earl of Essex. *The Poems of.* Edited A. B. Grosart. Fuller's Worthies Library, Vol. 4 (London, 1872–6)

Devereux, Walter Bourchier. *Lives and Letters of the Devereux Earls of Essex. 1540–1646.* (London, 1853)

Dictionary of National Biography. Edited Leslie Steven and Sidney Lee (London, 1883–1912. Re-issued 1907–45)

Die Musik in Geschichte und Gegenwart. Edited F. Blume (1949–   )

Dobell, Bertram. 'Newly discovered documents of the Elizabethan and Jacobean periods', *The Atheneum* No. 3833. April 13th, 1901.

Dodsley, Robert. *Old English Plays* (1814)

Dolmetsch, Arnold. *Select English Songs and Dialogues* (London, 1912)

Donne, John. *The Poems of.* Edited H. J. C. Grierson (Oxford, 1912)

Douen, Emmanuel. *Clément Marot et la Psautier Hugenot* (Paris, 1878–9)

Doughtie, Edward. 'Poems from the Songbooks of John Dowland.' Unpublished Thesis presented to Harvard University, 1963.
    'Nicholas Breton and Two Songs by Dowland', *Renaissance News* (1964)

Dowland, John. *The First Booke of Songes* (London, 1597, 1600, 1603, 1606, 1608, and 1613)
    The Second Booke of Songs (London, 1600)
    The Third and Last Booke of Songs (London, 1603)
    A Pilgrimes Solace (London, 1612)
    *The First set of Songs in four Parts . . . scored . . . by William Chappell. Musical Antiquarian Society Vol. 11. (London, 1844)
    *A First Set of Songs . . . arranged with a piano-forte accompaniment by G. Alex Mac-Farren. Musical Antiquarian Society Vol. 12 (London, 1844)
    The First Book of Songs. Edited E. H. Fellowes (London, 1920). Revised Thurston Dart, 1965.
    The Second Book of Songs. Edited E. H. Fellowes (London, 1922)
    The Third and Last Book of Songs. Edited E. H. Fellowes (London, 1923)
    A Pilgrimes Solace. Edited E. H. Fellowes (London, 1924). Revised Thurston Dart, 1959.
    Ayres for Four Voices. Edited Thurston Dart and Nigel Fortune. Musica Britannica Vol. 6 (London, 1955).
    Seven Hymn Tunes (Lamentatio Henrici Noel). Edited E. H. Fellowes (London, 1934)
    An heart that's broken and contrite. Edited Sir. F. Bridge. Voices only. Novello's Short Anthems No. 246. (London, 1922)
    Lachrimæ or Seaven Teares (London, 1604)
    Lachrimæ or Seven Tears . . . Transcribed from the original edition of 1605 by Peter Warlock (London, 1927) Without tablature.
    Lachrimæ oder Sieben Tränen. F. J. Giesbert. Seven pavans only, with tablature. (Kassel, 1954)

Dowland, Robert. *Varietie of Lute-Lessons* (London, 1610)
    Varietie of Lute-Lessons. Facsimile edition, edited Edgar Hunt (London, 1958)
    A Musical Banqvet (London, 1610)

Dowling, Margaret. 'The Printing of John Dowland's Second Booke of Ayres', *The Library*, Fourth Series. Vol. XII, No. 4 (1932)

Du Bellay, Joachim. *La Deffense et Illustration de la Langue Françoise* (Paris, 1561)

Dugdale, William. *The Baronage of England* (London, 1676)

Ebsworth, Joseph Woodfall. *Roxburghe Ballads* (London, 1869)
    Bagford Ballads (London, 1878)

Einstein, Alfred. *The Italian Madrigal.* Translated by A. H. Krapp, R. H. Sessions and O. Strunk. (Princeton, N. J., 1949)
    Orlando Furioso and *La Gerusalemme Liberata* as set to Music during the 16th and 17th centuries. *Notes* (Washington, Sept. 1951)

Ekwall, B. O. E. *The Concise Oxford Dictionary of English Place Names* (Oxford, 1936)

Elliott, Kenneth. *Music of Scotland* 1500–1700. Musica Britannica Vol. 15 (London, 1957)

Ellis, John Henry. *The Registers of Stourton, County Wilts.* Harleian Society, Vol. XII (1887)

Elyot, Sir Thomas. *The Boke named the Governour* (1531). Edited S. E. Lehmberg. Everyman's Library No. 227 (London and New York, 1962)

Engelke, Carl Robert Bernard. *Musik und Musiker am Gottofer-Hofe.* Veröffentlichunger der Schleswig-Holsteinen Universitatsgesellschaft, No. 15, 1 (Breslau, 1930)

Esdaile, Katherine Ada. *English Church Monuments* (London, 1946)

Est, Thomas. *The Whole Booke of Psalmes* (London, 1594)
  The Whole Booke of Psalmes. Edited Edward Rimbault. Musical Antiquarian Society, Vol. 12 (London, 1844)

Euing, William. *A Collection of English Broadside Ballads* 1573—A photostat copy of the original, in B.M.

Eyk, Jacob van. *Der Fluyten Lust-Hof* (Amsterdam, 1654)

Farnaby, Giles. *Canzonets to Fowre Voyces* (London, 1598)

Fellowes, E. H. 'The Songs of Dowland'. *Proceedings of the Musical Association* (London, 1929–30)
  English Madrigal Verse (Oxford, 1929)
  Catalogue of the Manuscripts in the Library of St. Michael's College, Tenbury (1934)
  English Madrigal Composers (Oxford, 1948)

Ferrabosco, Alfonso (the younger). *Lessons for 1.2. and 3. viols* (London, 1609)

Feuillerat, Albert. *Complete Works of Sir Philip Sidney.* Cambridge English Classics (1912)

Fischer, Kurt. 'Gabriel Voigtländer', *Sammelbände der Internationalen Musik-Gesellschaft* (Leipzig, 1910–11), pp. 17–93

Fletcher, Giles. *Licia* (n.d. *c.* 1593)

Fletcher, John. *The Bloody Brother* (London, 1639)

Flood, William Henry Grattan. 'New Facts about John Dowland', *The Gentleman's Magazine* (London, 1906) pp. 287–91
  'Nicholas Morgan of the Chapel Royal', *Musical Antiquary* Vol. IV (London, 1912–13) pp. 59–60
  'Irish Ancestry of Garland, Dowland, Campion and Purcell', *Music and Letters* III (London, 1922), pp. 59–65.
  'New Light on Late Tudor Composers. John Dowland', *Musical Times* LXVIII (London, 1927) pp. 504–5

Forbes, John. *Songs and Fancies* (Aberdeen, 1662, 1666, 1682)

Ford, John. *'Tis Pitty shes a Whore* (London, 1633)

Foster, Joseph. *Members of Parliament, England. 1529–1881* (1882)
  A Pedigree of the Forsters and the Fosters (Sunderland, 1871)
  Register of Admissions to Gray's Inn (London, 1889)
  Alumni Oxoniensis (Oxford, 1891–2)

Foxwell, A. K. *A Study of Sir Thomas Wyatt's Poems* (London, 1911)

Francisque, Antoine. *Le Trésor d'Orphée* (Paris, 1600)

Frere, W. H. and others. *Hymns Ancient and Modern.* Historical edition (London, 1909)

Frost, Maurice. *English and Scottish Psalm Tunes* (London, 1953)

Fuhrmann, Georg Leopold. *Testudo Gallo-Germanicca* (Nürnberg, 1615)

Fuller, Thomas. *History of the University of Cambridge* (London, 1655)
  The History of the Worthies of England (London, 1662)

Füllsack, Zacharias, and Hildebrand, Christoph. *Auselesener Paduanen und Galliarden* . . . (1607)

Galilei, Vincentio. *Dialogo della Musica Antica, et della Moderna* (Fiorenza, 1581)
  Fronimo Dialogo (Vineggia, 1584)

Galpin, F. W. *Old English Instruments of Music* (3rd edition. London, 1932)

Gascoigne, George. *Complete Works.* Edited J. W. Cunliffe, Cambridge English Classics (1904)

Gibbons, Orlando. *The First Set of Madrigals and Mottets* (London, 1612)

Gilbert, J. T. *A History of the City of Dublin* (Dublin, 1861)

Giry, Arthur. *Manuel de diplomatique* (Paris, 1894)

Glyn, Margaret. *Thirty virginal pieces* (London, 1927)

Goudimel, Claude. *Les Pseaumes de David* (Delft, 1602)

Gray, Cecil, and Heseltine, Philip. *Carlo Gesualdo, Prince of Venosa* (London, 1926)

Greene, Robert. *The Historie of Orlando Furioso* (1594)

  Plays and Poems. Edited J. C. Collins, Vol. 2 (Oxford, 1905)

Greville, Fulke. *Certaine learned and elegant works* (London, 1633)

  The Works in verse and prose. Edited A. B. Grosart (The Fuller's Worthies' Library, 1870)

  Poems and Dramas. Edited G. Bullough (Edinburgh, 1939)

Gribble, J. B. *Memorials of Barnstaple* (Barnstaple, 1830)

Griffin, Richard Baron Braybrooke. *History of Audley End* (London, 1836)

Grotch, William. *A Collection of National English Airs* (London, 1838)

Grove, Sir George. *A Dictionary of Music and Musicians* (London, 1879–89) (London, 1900) (New York, 1904–10)

  (Fourth edition, London, 1927–40)

  (Fifth edition, London, 1954)

Gwilt, Joseph. *A Collection of Madrigals* (London, 1815)

Hagen, S. A. E. 'Drei Briefe von Alessandro Orologio'. *Monatshefte für Musikgeschichte* (1899) XXX, pp. 42–45.

Hagius, Conradus. *Newe Kunstliche Musicalische Intraden* etc. (Nürnberg, 1616)

Hall, Edward. 'Henry VIII' from *The Lives of the Kings*. Text of 1550, edited with an introduction by Charles Whibley (London and Edinburgh, 1904)

Hammerich-Elling, A. *Musiken ven Christian den Fjerdes Hof* (København, 1892)

Handover, P. M. *Printing in London from Caxton to Modern Times* (London, 1960)

Harington, Sir John. *Nugæ Antiquæ* (London, 1779)

Harrison, G. B. *The Life and Death of Robert Devereux, Earl of Essex* (London, 1937)

Harvey, John Hooper. *An Introduction to Tudor Architecture* (London, 1949)

Harwood, Ian. 'Origins of the Cambridge Lute Manuscripts', *Journal of the Lute Society* (London, 1963)

Haussmann, Valentin. *Rest von Polnischen und andern Täntzen* (Nürnberg, 1603)

Hawkins, Sir John. *A General History of Music* (London, 1776)

Hazlitt, W. C. *Hand-Book to the Popular, Poetical and Dramatic Literature of Great Britain* (London, 1867)

Herbert, Edward (Baron Herbert of Cherbury). *Autobiography*. Edited Sidney Lee (London, 1906)

Héroard, Jean. *Journal de J. Héroald sur l'enfance . . . de Louis XIII*. Edited E. Soulié et E. de Barthelemy (Paris, 1868)

Heseltine, Philip. 'More Light on John Dowland', *The Musical Times* LXVIII (Aug. 1927)

Heywood, Thomas. *The Earls of Derby and the verse writers of the sixteenth and seventeenth centuries*. Chetham Society, Vol. 29 (1853)

Hill, Cecil. 'John Dowland: Some new facts and a Quatercentenary Tribute', *The Musical Times* CIV (Nov. 1963) pp. 785–7.

Hill, John Harwood. *The History of Market Harborough* (Leicester, 1875)

Hiscock, Walter. *A Christ Church Miscellany* (Oxford, 1946)

Historical Manuscripts Commission.

  Calendars of the Marquess of Salisbury's Papers at Hatfield House, Series 2, 3, 4, 5, 6 and 9. (1872–3)

  Calendar of Sir George Wombwell's Papers at Newburgh Priory. Series 55. Coll. II (1903)

Calendar of Lord Braye's MSS. Series 15, 10th Report (1887). MSS formerly at Stanford Hall, Rugby.

History of Northumberland, A. County History Committee (London, 1893–1940) Vols. 2 and 8

Hoby, Sir Thomas. *A Booke of the Travailes and Life of Sir Thomas Hoby*. Edited E. Powel Camden Miscellany, Vol. 10 (1902)

Holborne, Anthony. *Pauans, Galliards, Almains* etc (London, 1599)

Horne, David H. *The Life and Minor Works of George Peele* (1952)

Hotson, John Leslie. *The First Night of Twelfth Night* (London, 1954)

Hove, Joachim van den. *Florida* (Ultrajecti, 1601)

　Delitiæ Musicæ (Ultrajecti, 1612)

Hughes-Hughes, A. *Catalogue of Manuscript Music in the British Museum* (London, 1906–8)

Hughey, Ruth. *The Arundel Harington MS* (1960)

Huizinger, J. *The Waning of the Middle Ages*. English translation by F. Hopman (London, 1924. Pelican Books, No. 307, 1955)

Hume, Tobias. *The First Part of Ayres* (London, 1605)

　Captaine Humes Poetical Musicke (London, 1607)

Humphries, C. and Smith, W. C. *Music Publishing in the British Isles* (London, 1954)

Jackson, William A. *Records of the Court of the Stationers' Company. 1602–1640* (London, 1957)

Jannequin, Clément. Les Maîtres Musiciens de la Renaissance Française. Edited H. Expert. (1894–)

Janssen, Johann. *History of the German People*. Translated by M. A. Mitchell and A. M. Christie (London, 1896–1925)

Jewell, J. H. *Madrigal and Motet Book No. 3* (London, 1856)

Jewell, William. *The Golden Cabinet of True Treasure* (London, 1612)

Johnson, Robert. *Ayres, Songs and Dialogues*. Edited Ian Spink (London, 1961)

Jones, Robert. *The First Booke of Songes & Ayres* (London, 1600)

　The Second Booke of Songs and Ayres (London, 1601)

Jonson, Ben. *Masques and Entertainments*. Edited Henry Morley. The Carisbrooke Library, Vol. 9 (1889)

　Discoveries 1641 and Conversations with William Drummond of Hawthornden 1619. Edited G. B. Harrison (London, 1923)

Julian, John. *A Dictionary of Hymnology* (Revised edition, London, 1925)

Kade, L. Otto. *Mattheus le Maistre* (Mainz, 1862)

Kancelliets Brevbøger (Copenhagen, 1885–1915)

Kerman, Joseph. *The Elizabethan Madrigal* (New York, 1962)

King, Edward. 'Pyper of Launceston and Tresmarrow, Cornwall', *The Genealogist* Vol. 6 (1882) p. 57

Klessmann, Eckart. 'Die Deutschlandreisen John Dowlands', *Musica* II (1951)

Koerte, Oswald. *Laute und Lautenmusik*. International Musical Society Beiheft 3. (1901)

La Grotte, Nicolas de. *Chansons de Pierre de Ronsard* (Paris, 1580)

La Laurencie, Lionel de. *Les Luthistes* (Paris, 1928)

Lapp, John C. *The Universe of Pontus de Tyard*. Cornell Romance Studies. Vol. 3 (1950)

Lawrence, W. J. 'Notes on a collection of Masque Music', *Music and Letters* III, Jan. 1922, pp. 49–58.

Lebegue, R. 'Ronsard et la Musique', *Musique et poésie au XVI siècle* (Paris, 1954)

Lee, Arthur Gould. *The Son of Leicester* (London, 1964)

Leighton, Sir William. *The Teares or Lamentations of a Sorrowfull Soule* (London, 1613) Second edition. With music. (London, 1614)

　The Teares or Lamentations of a Sorrowfull Soule. Edited Sir F. Bridge. Vocal score only. (London, 1922)

Leishman, J. B. Editor. *The Three Parnassus Plays 1598–1601* (London, 1949)

Leith, Mrs Disney. *The Boyhood of Algernon Charles Swinburne* (London, 1917)

Le Roy, Adrian. *Tiers Liure* (Paris, 1552)
   Second Liure de Guiterre (Paris, 1555)
   A Briefe and easye instruction (1568)
   Liure d'Airs de cour (Paris, 1571)
   Premier Liure de Chansons en forme de vau de ville (Paris, 1573)
   A Briefe and Plaine Instruction (London, 1574)

Levy, Kenneth Jay. 'Suzanne un Jour: The History of a 16th Century Chanson', *Annales Musicologiques* Tome I (Paris, 1953)

Linton, W. J. *Rare Poems of the Sixteenth and Seventeenth Centuries* (Newhaven, Conn. 1882)

Lodge, Edmund. *Illustrations of British History* (London, 1791, Second edition, London, 1838)

Lumsden, David. *An Anthology of English Lute Music* (London, 1954)

Lumsden, David. Unpublished Thesis 'The Sources of English Lute Music', Deposited at C.U.L.

Lyly, John. *The Complete Works.* Edited R. Warwick Bond (Oxford, 1902)

Mace, Thomas. *Musick's Monument* (London, 1676)

Facsimile edition (Paris, 1966)
   Vol. I
   Vol. II Commentary by Jean Jacquot and transcriptions by André Souris (Paris, 1966)

McKerrow, R. B. *A Dictionary of Printers and Booksellers in England, Scotland and Ireland . . . 1557–1640* (London, 1910)
   An Introduction to Bibliography (1927, reissued 1951)

McKerrow, R. B. and Ferguson, F. S. *Title-page Borders used in England and Scotland 1485–1640* (London, 1932)

Maddison, A. H. *Lincolnshire Pedigrees.* Harleian Society, Vols. 50, 51, 52 and 55 (1902–6)

Mahaffy, Sir John Pentland. *The Particular Book of Trinity College, Dublin.* (Dublin, 1904)

Mairy, Adrienne. *Chansons au Luth* (Paris, 1934)

Maitland, J. Fuller, and Squire. W. Barclay. *The Fitzwilliam Virginal Book* (1899)
   Dover Reprint (New York, 1963)

Manning, Rosemary. 'Lachrimæ: A study of John Dowland', *Music and Letters* Vol. XXV (1944)

Manningham, John. *Diary 1602–1608.* Edited T. Bruce. Camden Society, XCIX (1868)

Marshall, George William. *The Genealogist's Guide* (Guildford, 1903)

Mason, Thomas. *A Register of Baptisms, Marriages and Burials in the Parish of St. Martin-in-the Fields 1550–1619.* Harleian Society, Vols. XXV and LXVI (1898 and 1936)

Massinger, Philip. *Plays.* Edited W. Gifford (1805)

Maurice, Landgrave of Hesse. *Landschaftsdenkmale der Musik in Kurhessen.* Das Erbe Deutsche Musik, Vol. I, Parts 1 and 2 (1936–8)

Mellers, Wilfrid. 'Words and Music in Elizabethan England', *The Age of Shakespeare* (Pelican Guide to English Literature. Edited Boris Ford. Vol. II (1956) pp. 386–415)
   'John Dowland' in *The Music Masters.* Edited A. L. Bacharach (London, 1948)

Melville, Sir James. *Memoirs* (London, 1683)

Merbury, Charles. *A briefe discourse of royall monarchie* (London, 1581)

Meres, Francis. *Palladis Tamia—Wits Treasury* (London, 1598)

Mertelius, Elias. *Hortus Musicalis Novus* (Argentorati, 1615)

Middleton, Thomas. *Works.* Edited A. H. Bullen (London, 1885–6)

Mies, Otto. 'Elizabethan Music Prints in an East-Prussian Castle', *Musica Disciplina* III (1949) pp. 171–172.
   'Dowland's Lachrimæ Tune', *Musica Disciplina* IV (1950) pp. 59–64.

Milan, Luis. *El Maestro* (Valencia, 1536)

Mönkemeyer, Helmut. *Simpson 'Taffel-Consort' 1621* (Wilhelmshaven, 1962)

Monson, Sir William. 'Naval Tracts' in *A Collection of voyages and travels* Vol. III (1732)

More, Thomas. *Utopia.* Translated Ralph Robynson (1551)

Morley, Thomas. *Madrigals to Foure Voices* (London, 1594)

    The First Booke of Ballets (London, 1595)

    A Plaine and Easie Introduction to Practicall Musicke (London, 1597)

    A Plain and Easy Introduction to Practical Music. Edited R. Alec Harman (London, 1952)

    Canzonets or Little Short Aers (London, 1597)

    Madrigals to fiue voyces (London, 1598)

    The First Booke of Consort Lessons (London, 1599 and 1611) No complete set of part books in existence

    The First Book of Consort Lessons. Reconstructed and edited by Sydney Beck (1959)

    The First Booke of Ayres (London, 1600) Incomplete

    First Book of Airs 1600 Edited E. H. Fellowes (London, 1932, revised Thurston Dart, 1958)

    The English Madrigal School, Edited E. H. Fellowes (London, 1913–1924) Vols. I–IV, and XXXII

    Triumphs of Oriana. Madrigales to 5. and 6. voices: composed by diuers seuerall aucthors. (1601)

Muir, Kenneth. *Sir Thomas Wyatt and his circle. Unpublished Poems.* Liverpool Reprints, No. 18 (1961)

Munday, Anthony. *A Banquet of Daintie Conceits* (London, 1588)

Nabbes, Thomas. *Microcosmos* (London, 1637)

Nares, Robert. *A Glossary* (London, 1822)

Nash, Thomas. *Quarternio, or a Fourefold Way to a Happie Life* (London, 1633)

Nashe, Thomas. *The Complete Works of.* Edited R. B. McKerrow. Vols. III and V (London, 1904–10)

    Pierce Pennilesse his Supplication to the Deuill (London, 1592)

    Pierce Penniless his Supplication etc. Edited J. P. Collier. Shakespeare Society (1842)

Naunton, Sir Robert. *Fragmenta Regalia* (1641)

Neale, Sir John Ernest. *Elizabeth I and her Parliaments 1559–1581* (London, 1953)

    Queen Elizabeth I (London, 1934. Pelican Books A 483, 1960)

Newton, Richard. 'English Lute Music of the Golden Age', *Proceedings of the Royal Musical Association* (1939)

Nichols, John. *The Progresses and Public Processions of Queen Elizabeth* (London, 1788–1821) Second edition (1823)

    The Progresses, Processions and Magnificent Festivities of King James I (London, 1828)

    The Unton Inventories (Berkshire Archæological Society, 1841)

    The Literary Remains of King Edward VI (Roxburghe Club, London, 1857)

Noble, Mark. *Memoires of the Protectoral House of Cromwell* (Second edition, Birmingham, 1787)

Oakeshott, Walter. *The Queen and the Poet* (London, 1960)

Obertello, Alfredo. *Madrigali italiani in Inghilterra* (Milano, 1949)

Oboussier, Philip. 'Turpyn's Book of Lute Songs', *Music and Letters* XXXIV (1953) pp. 145–149

Octanteneuf pseaumes de David (1556)

Oliphant, Thomas. *La Musa Madrigalesca* (London, 1837)

Orlandini, Antonio. *Madrigali* (1598)

Ornithoparcus, Andreas. *Musice Active Microloges* (Leipzig, 1517)

    Andreas Ornithoparcus his Micrologus. Translated by John Dowland (London, 1609)

Osthoff, Helmuth. *Der Lautenist Santino Garsi da Parma* (Leipzig, 1926)

Overbury, Sir Thomas. *Sir Thomas Ouerbury His Wife. With additions of New Newes, and diuers more Characters. The Tenth impression augmented.* (London, 1618)

Ovidius Naso. *Metamorphoses.* Translated by Arthur Golding (London, 1565)
  The Heroycall Epistles of P. Ovidius Naso. Translated by George Turbervile (1567)
Oxford English Dictionary
P, K.M. 'A Grand Inquisitor and his Library' *Bodleian Quarterly Record* Vol. III, No. 34.
  (Oxford, 1922)
Palisca, Claude. Girolamo Mei. *Letters on Ancient and Modern Music* (Rome, 1960)
Pallavicino, Benedetto. *Madrigali a Cinque Voci* (Anuersa, 1604)
Passion of a Discontented Mind, The (1601. Second edition 1602)
Pattison, Bruce. *Music and Poetry in the English Renaissance* (London, 1948)
Pattison, S. P. *Some account of the Church of St. Mary Magdalene, Launceston* (Launceston,
  1852)
Peacham, Henry. *Minerva Britanna* (London, 1612)
  The Compleat Gentleman (London, 1622)
Peele, George. *Polyhymnia* (London, 1590)
Peerson, Martin. *Private Musicke, or the First Booke of Ayres and Dialogues* (London, 1620)
  Mottects or Graue Chamber Musique (London, 1630)
Percy, Thomas. *Reliques of Ancient English Poetry* (London, 1765). Everyman's Library No. 148
  (London and New York, 1906)
Phalèse, Pierre. *Premier Liure des Chansons à quatre parties* (Louvain, 1553)
  Quatriesme Liure des chansons à quatre parties (Louvain, 1555)
Phillips, J. S. Ragland. 'Why John Dowland went overseas', *Cornhill Magazine.* New Series,
  Vol. III (1897)
Pilkington, Francis. *Second set of Madrigals* (London, 1624)
  English Madrigal Composers. Edited E. H. Fellowes. Vols. XV and XVI (London, 1913–24)
Place Names of Surrey. English Place Names Society. XI (1934)
Playford, John. *The English Dancing Master* (London, 1651, appeared 1650)
  A Briefe Introduction to the Skill of Musick (London, third edition 1660)
  Unnumbered edition (London, 1662)
  Psalms and Hymns (London, 1671)
  The Whole Book of Psalms (London, 1677)
Pollard, A. F. *The History of England from the Accession of Edward VI to the death of Elizabeth
  1847–1603* (1910)
Pollard, A. W. and Redgrave, G. R. *A Short-title Catalogue of Books Printed in England,
  Scotland and Ireland, 1475–1640* (London, 1926)
Pollen, J. H. *English Catholics in the Reign of Elizabeth* (London, 1920)
Poulton, Diana. 'Dowland's Songs and their Instrumental Settings,' *Monthly Musical Record*
  LXXXI (1951) pp. 175–180
  'The Favourite Singer of Queen Elizabeth I', *The Consort* No. 14, (1957) pp. 24–27.
  'Captaine Digory Piper of the Sweepstake', *The Lute Society Journal* Vol. 4 (1962) pp. 17–22.
  'John Dowland, Doctor of Music', *The Consort* No. 20. (1963) pp. 189–197.
  'Was John Dowland a Singer?' *The Lute Society Journal* Vol. 7 (1965) pp. 32–37.
Prætorius, Michael. *Terpsichore* (1612) Edited Günther Oberst. Gesamtausgaben Der Musika-
  lischen Werke von Michael Prætorius. Vol. XV (1929)
Prynne, William. *Histrio-mastix* (London, 1633)
Pulver, Jeffrey. *A Biographical Dictionary of Old English Music* (London, 1927)
Ramage, David. *A Finding-List of English Books to 1640 in Libraries in the British Isles* (1958)
Ravenscroft, Thomas. *A Briefe Discourse* (London, 1614)
  The Whole Booke of Psalmes (London, 1621)
Reese, Gustav. *Music in the Renaissance* (1954)
Remains Historical and Literary connected with the Palatine Counties of Lancashire and Cheshire
  Chetham Society, Vols. 81, 82, 85, 98 and 99. (1844–00)

Richardson, Brian. 'New Light on Dowland's Continental Movements', *Monthly Musical Record* XC (1960)

Rimbault, E. F. *The Old Cheque Book* (1872)
Da Capo Press Reprint (New York, 1966)

Ritson, Joseph. *A Select Collection of English Songs* (1783)

Robinson, Clement. *A Handfull of Pleasant Delites* (London, 1584)
A Handful of Pleasant Delights. Edited Hyder E. Rollins (1924)

Robinson, Thomas, *The Schoole of Musicke* (London, 1603)
New Citharen Lessons (London, 1609)

Rollins, Hyder Edward. *The Black-Letter Broadside Ballad* (Baltimore, 1919)
An Analytical Index to the Ballad Entries. Studies in Philology, Vol. 21. No. 1 (1924)
The Pepys Ballads (Cambridge, Mass., 1929–1932)
England's Helicon (1600) Edited, 1935

Ronsard, Pierre de. *Abbrégé de l'Art Poëtique Francois* (1565)

Rosseter, Philip. *Lessons for Consort* (London, 1609)

Rowse, A. L. *The England of Elizabeth* (London, 1951)

Rubsamen, W. H. 'Scottish and English Music of the Renaissance in a Newly-Discovered Manuscript', *Festschrift Heinrich Besseler* (1961) pp. 259–284.

Rude, Johannes. *Flores Musicæ* (Heidelberg, 1598)

Salinas, Francisco de. *De Musica Libri Septum* (Salamanca, 1577)

Saluste du Bartas. Guillaume de. *L'Vranie ou muse celeste* (Londini, 1589)
Bartas his Divine Weekes and Workes Translated by Joshua Sylvester (London 1605–1606)

Scheidt, Samuel. *Werke,* herausgegeben von der Oberleitung des Glaubengemeinde Ugrino durch Gottleib Harms (Klecken, 1923–37)

Schildt, Melchior. *Monatshefte für Musikgeschichte* (1888) Vol. 20. No. 1, p. 37.

Schmeltzel, Wolfgang. *Guter Seltzamer* (1544)

Schop. Johann. *Neuer Himlischer Lieder Sonderbahres Buch* (1654)

Segar, Sir William. *Honor, Military and Civill* (1602)

Shaw, William Arthur. *The Knights of England* (London, 1906)

S. Syr P. *His Astrophel and Stella* (1591)

Sidney, Sir Philip. *Apologie for Poetrie* later called *Defence of Poesie* (1595)
The Countess of Pembrokes Arcadia (London, 1598)

Simpson, Thomas. *Opusculum* (Franckfort, 1610)
Taffel-Consort (Hamburg, 1621)

Slatyer, William. *The Psalmes of David in 4 languages and 4 Parts* (1643)

Smith, Irwin. *Shakespeare's Blackfriars Playhouse* (New York, 1964, London, 1966)

Smith, John Stafford. *Musica Antiqua* (London, 1812)

Smith, William. *A Smaller Classical Dictionary*. Edited E. H. Blakeney. Everyman's Library (London and New York, 1910)

Smith, William C. 'Some hitherto Unnoticed Catalogues of Early Music', *Musical Times* (July, 1926) pp. 636–639.

Spencer, Robert. 'The Weld Lute Book', *The Lute Society Journal*, Vol. 1 (1959)

Squire, W. Barclay. 'John Dowland', *Musical Times* Dec. 1896, pp. 793–794, and Feb. 1897, pp. 92–93.

Stanley Papers. Chetham Society Remains etc. Vols. 29, 31, 66, 67 and 70 (1844)

Steele, R. R. *The Earliest English Music Printing*. Bibliographical Society, No. 11 (1903)

Sternfeld, F. W. *Music in Shakespearean Tragedy* (London, 1963)
'Ophelia's Version of the Walsingham Song', *Music and Letters* Vol. 45, No. 2. (April 1964) pp. 108–113.

Sternhold, Thomas. *All such psalmes of Dauid* (1553)

Sternhold, Thomas, and John Hopkins. *The Whole Booke of Psalmes* (1562 and countless other editions)

Stevens, John. *Music and Poetry in the Early Tudor Court* (London, 1961)

Stokes, E. 'Lists of the King's Musicians from the Audit Office Declared Accounts', *Musical Antiquary* Vol. II (1910–11) pp. 51–55, 114–118, 174–178, and 235–240.

Stow, John. *The Survey of London* (1598) Everyman's Library No. 589. Edited H. B. Wheatley (London and New York, 1912)

Strachey, Lytton. *Elizabeth and Essex.* (London, 1928)

Strickland, Agnes. *Lives of the Queens of England* Vols. VI and VII. (London, 1840–8)

Strong, Roy C. 'Sir Henry Unton and his Portrait: An Elizabethan Memorial Picture and its History', *Archæologia* Vol. 99 (1965)

Strunk, Oliver. *Source Readings in Music History* (London, 1952)

Stuart, Alexander. *Musick for Allan Ramsey's Scots songs in the Tea Table Miscellany* (Edin^r, 1725)

Sutton, Julia. 'The Lute Instructions of Jean-Baptiste Besard', *Musical Quarterly* LI (1965) pp. 345–362.

Tailour, Robert. *Sacred Hymns, Consisting of Fifti Select Psalmes* (London, 1615)

Tallis, Thomas. *The Whole Psalter* (1567)

Tarlton, Richard. *Tarlton's Jests and News out of Purgatory* (1590) Edited J. O. Halliwell (London, 1884)

Terry, Charles S. 'John Forbes's 'Songs and Fancies', *Musical Quarterly* XXII (1936) pp. 402–419.

Terry, Sir Richard Runciman. *Calvin's First Psalter 1539* (1932)

Tessier, Guillaume. *Premier Liure d'Airs* (tenor) (Paris, 1582)

Primo Libro Dell'Arie (Parigi, 1582)

Tiersot, Julien. 'Ronsard et la musique de son temps', *Sammelbände der Internationalen Musikgelleschaft.* Jahrg. 4. (1902) pp. 70–142.

Tilley, Morris Palmer. *A Dictionary of Proverbs* (Ann Arbor, 1950)

Tillyard, E. M. W. *The Elizabethan World Picture* (London, 1943. Peregrine Books 1963)

Tomkins, Thomas. *Songs of 3. 4. 5. and 6. parts* (London, 1622)

Turberville, Arthur S. *A History of Welbeck Abbey and its owners* (London, 1938)

Tuttle, Stephen Davidson. *Forty-five Pieces for Keyboard* (Paris, 1939)

Tuve, Rosamond. *Elizabethan and Metaphysical Imagery* (1947. Photo. reprint, Chicago, 1961)

Tyard, Pontus de. *Les Discours Philosophiques* (Paris, 1587)

Tye, Christopher. *The Actes of the Apostles* (London, 1553)

Unton, Sir Henry. *Correspondence.* Edited Joseph Stevensen. (Roxburghe Club, London, 1847)

Valerius, Adrianus. *Nederlandtsche Gedenck-Clanck* (Haarlem, 1626)

Vallet, Nicolas. *Le Secret des Muses* (Amsterdam, 1615–1619)

Pseaumes de David (Amsterdam, 1619)

Regia Pietas (Amsterdam, 1620)

Various. *Select Psalmes of David* (London, 1789)

Visitation Articles and Injunctions of the Period of the Reformation. Edited W. H. Frere and W. M. Kennedy (1910)

Visitation of Cheshire 1613. Harleian Society Vol. 59 (London, 1909)

Visitation of Yorkshire 1563 and 1564. Harleian Society Vol. 16. (London, 1881)

Walker, D. P. 'The Aims of de Baïf's Académie', *Musica Disciplina* I (1946) pp. 91–100.

'The Influence of *Musique Mesurée à l'Antique* on the *Air de Cour*', *Musica Disciplina* II (1948), pp. 141–163.

Warlock, Peter. *The First Book of Elizabethan Songs* (London, 1926)

The Third Book of Elizabethan Songs (London, 1926)

The English Ayre (London, 1926)

The Lute Music of John Dowland (London, 1928)

Watson, Thomas. *The first sett of Italian Madrigalls Englished* (London, 1590)

Webb, Richard. *A Collection of Madrigals* (1808)

Webbe, William. *A Discourse of English Poetrie* (1586)

Webster, John. *Works*. Edited F. L. Lucas (London, 1927)

Weelkes, Thomas. *Madrigals of 6. and 7. parts, apt for the Viols and Voices* (London, 1600)
   English Madrigal School. Edited H. E. Fellowes (London, 1913–1924) Vols. XI–XIII.

Weldon, Sir Anthony. *Aulicus Cocquinariæ* (London, 1650)
   Secret History of the Court of King James I (London, 1811)

Welsford, Enid. *The Court Masque* (Cambridge, 1927)

West, V. Sackville. *Diary of the Lady Anne Clifford* (1923)

White, G. H. (Editor). *The Complete Peerage* (London, 1953)

Whythorne, Thomas. *Autobiography*. Edited James Osborne (Oxford, 1961)

Wilmot, R. *Tancred and Gismunda* (London, 1591)

Wilson, F. P. *The Plague in Shakespeare's London* (1927)
   Oxford Paperbacks (1963)

Wilson, Mona. *Sir Philip Sidney* (London, 1931)

Wood, Anthony à. *Athenæ Oxoniensis and Fasti Oxoniensis* (1691) Edited P. Bliss, (London, 1813–20)
   History and Antiquities of the University of Oxford. (Edition of 1792–6)

Wood, Charles. *An Italian Carol Book* (Oxford, 1920)

Woodfill, W. L. *Musicians in English Society from Elizabeth to Charles II* (Princeton, 1953)

Wotton, Sir Henry. 'A Parallell betweene Robert late Earle of Essex and George late Duke of Buckingham' (1641), *Reliquæ Wottoniæ* (4th edition 1685)

Wright, Robert. Editor. *Funebria Nobilissimi præstantissimi equitis, D. Henrici Untoni* (1596)

Wuleker, Richard P. 'Englische Hauspieler in Kassel', *Shakespeare Jahrbuch* XIV (1879) pp. 360–361.

Yates, Frances Amelia. *The French Academies of the Sixteenth Century*. Studies of the Warburg Institute, Vol. 15. (1947)

Yonge, Nicholas. *Musica Transalpina* (London, 1588)
   Musica Transalpina. The Second Booke of Madrigalles (London, 1597)

MANUSCRIPTS

ENGLISH — MUSIC

LONDON

British Museum

Add. 6402. *c.* 1610 Lute.

Add. 10,444. *c.* 1603–1622. Instr. Cantus and Bassus.

Add. 15,117. After 1617. Voice and lute.

Add. 15,118. 1st quarter 17th cent. Treble and bass voices.

Add. 17,786–17,791. Early 17th cent. Five instr. in parts.

Add. 24,665. Giles Earle's Song Book. *c.* 1615–1625. Treble and bass.

Add. 29,291. 18th cent. Four voices.

Add. 29,481. Not before 1617. Treble and bassus.

Add. 31,392. *c.* 1595 to after 1600. Lute.

Add. 31,415. After 1835.

Add. 31,418. Late 18th cent. Transcript of Leighton's *Teares or Lamentations* (1614) by J. Stafford Smith and T. Warren Horne. Vocal score only.

Add. 31,811. Late 18th cent. Four voices.

Add. 34,608. 1785–1789. Vocal scores transcribed by J. Stafford Smith.

Add. 35,155. *c.* 1858.

Add. 36,526(A). After 1597.

Add. 37,402–37,406. After 1601. Voice and viols.

Add. 38,539. Sometimes known as John Sturt's Book. *c.* 1615.

Eg. 2046. Dated 1616.

Hirsch M. 1353. *c.* 1590.

Royal Appendix 63. After 1614.

R.M. 23. 1. 4. Benjamin Cosyn's Virginal Book

R.M. 24. d. 3. Will Forster's Virginal Book. Jan. 31. 1624.

Stowe 389. "written by one Raphe Bowle to learne to play on his Lutte in anno 1558"

CAMBRIDGE

University Library

Dd. 2. 11. (B) *c.* 1588–1595.

Dd. 5. 78. (3) (E) *c.* 1595–1600.

Dd. 9. 33. (C) Before 1597–after 1603.

Nn. 6. 36. (B) *c.* 1615.

Add. 3056. Completed after 1606.

Add. 2764 (C). Sheets removed from binding

Dd. 4. 22. After 1613?

Dd. 3. 18. Lute ⎫

Dd. 14. 24. Cittern ⎪

Dd. 5. 21. Treble viol ⎬ Cambridge Consort Books

Dd. 5. 20. Bass ⎪

Dd. 4. 23. Solo cittern ⎭

Fitzwilliam Library

Lord Herbert of Cherbury's Lute Book. Completed 1640.

Dr Bull's virginal MS

King's College

Rowe 2. Turpyn's Lute Book *c.* 1610–1615.

OXFORD

Bodleian Library

Mus. MS f. 7–10. Four part books compiled by Thomas Hammond of Hawkdon, Sussex. *c.* 1630–1640.

Mus. MS a. 143. Keyboard music.

Christ Church Library

MS 48

MS 439. After 1617.

TENBURY

St. Michael's College
MS 1018. Madrigals and ayres in score. 17th century.

MANCHESTER

Public Library
Richard Sumarte's Lyra Viol Book

DUBLIN

Trinity College
D. 1. 21. William Ballet's Lute Book. *c.* 1600.

Archbishop Marsh's Library
z. 3. 2. 13. *c.* 1585–1595

GLASGOW

University Library
R. d. 43. The Euing Lute Book. *c.* 1600.

IN THE UNITED STATES

The Folger Library, Washington
MS 1610. 1. The Dowland Lute Book. *c.* 1600.
MS 448. 16. Giles Lodge's Lute Book. *c.* 1575.

The University of California, Los Angeles
The Taitt MS

New York Public Library
Drexel 5612
Drexel 4041

Yale University Library
The Wickhambrook MS. *c.* 1590
Osborne Collection Box 22 No. 10. The Braye Lute Book. *c.* 1575

IN PRIVATE OWNERSHIP

The Duke of Portland
Deposited in the MS dept. of Nottingham University Library: 'Lamentatio Henrici Noel'.
    1596.

Lord Forester
The Weld Lute Book. *c.* 1600.

W. S. Gwynn Williams
The Mynshall Lute Book. *c.* 1597–1599.

Robert Spencer
The Tollemache Lute MS. *c.* 1609.
The Braye Bandora and Lyra Viol MS

The Marquess of Downshire
Deposited in Berkshire Record Office, Reading; Trumbull Add. MSS 6.

SCOTTISH — MUSIC

Thomas Wode's Psalter (1562–66, with additions by other hands after 1600)
Cantus: E.U.L. MS La. III 483
Quintus: T.C.D. F. 5. 1. 3
Altus: B.M. Add. 33,933
Tenor: E.U.L. MS La. III 483
Bassus: E.U.L. MS La. III 483

EDINBURGH

National Library of Scotland
Adv. MS 5. 2. 15. The Skene MS *c.* 1625
Adv. MS 5. 2. 14. William Stirling's Cantus part book. 1639
MS 9450 (Panmure 11) *c.* 1635.

University Library
MS La. III 488. Sir William Mure of Rowallan's Vocal MS. *c.* 1631
MS La. III 490. John Squyer's MS. 1696–1701.

LONDON

British Museum
Add. 36484. David Melvil's bassus book. 1604.

PERTH

Sandeman Library
Ruggles-Brise Collection. MS copy of Forbes *Cantus Songs and Fancies* (1662) with additional
    music. *c.* 1662.

FOREIGN — MUSIC

Brussels, Bibliothèque Royale, Folio 3095 (II. 4.109).

Leiden, Bibl. Thysiana
Thysius MS

Leipzig Musikbibliothek der Stadt Leipzig
Ms. II, 6. 15. *c.* 1619

Kassel, Landesbibliothek
4° Mus. 108.1. *c.* 1611.

Copenhagen, Det Kongelige Bibliotek
Thott, 841. 40. Fabritius MS

Prague University Library
485. XXIII. F174. Nicolao Schmall's Lute Book.

Tübingen, Universitatsbibliothek (formerly in Berlin, Preussischen Staatsbibliothek)
    Mus. MS 40, 141. *c.* 1615.

Nürnberg, Germ. Nat. Mus. Ms Mus. 33,748. 1

London, British Museum. Sloane 1021. Stobæus of Königsberg's MS. *c.* 1640

Florence, Bibl. Nat. Magl. XIX. 115

Haslemere, England. The Dolmetsch Library. MS. II. B. 1

Hamburg, Universitätsbibliothek. ND VI No. 3238

MSS known to have contained works by Dowland, now destroyed.
    Dresden, Sachs. Landesbibliothek. Mus. MS. 1.V.8

MSS containing works by Dowland, whereabouts now unknown.
    Robert Gordon of Straloch's Lute Book, 1627–1629. Extracts copied by George Farquhar
    Graham in 1847. (Nat. Lib. Scot.) include no pieces by Dowland.

    MS formerly in the possession of Lord Braye.
    Described in *Reports of the Historical Manuscripts Commission.* Series 15, Report No. 10.
    (1887), p. 108. Book bearing the name of Matthew Otley, is said to have contained
    'Dowland, per Ro[bert] Sp[rignell]' and 'Doulandes Galliarde'.

ENGLISH — GENERAL

LONDON

British Museum
    Add. 5750. Royal Warrant for Robert Dowland's appointment at Court.
    Harl. 6986. Letters from Queen Anne to Lady Arabella Stuart, about Thomas Cutting
    Add. 38165. List of 'songes for the leute'.

The College of Arms
    Talbot Papers. Vol. M, f. 36.

Somerset House
    Prerogative Court of Canterbury, Acts of Administration for the year 1590. (Piper.)
    Will of Edmund Dowland. Proved June 21, 1647.
    Prerogative Court of Canterbury. Fines Fol 125.

Guildhall Library
    MS 13,4510/3. St. Anne Blackfriars, Registers.
    MS 10,342–344. St. Dunstan-in-the-West, Registers.
    MS 2968/2. St. Dunstan-in-the-West, Churchwarden's Accounts.
    MS 10,091/11. Dioc. Lond. Allig. Matr., 1626/1627, f. 34.

Westminster Public Library
    St. Margaret's Westminster, Registers.
    St. Clement Danes, Poor Rate Books.

Public Record Office
    Court of Requests 2/202/63. 2/203/4 Eastland's suit against Est, the printer.
    State Papers. Elizabeth. Domestic for the years 1585 and 1586. Foreign for the years 1587.
    Letters and other documents concerning Digorie Piper.

CHICHESTER, SUSSEX

County Record Office
    Probate Registry. Vol. 13, p. 22 (1581). Will of Darby Douland of Rye in the County of
    Sussex. Proved Sept. 18th, 1581.

OXFORD

Bodleian Library
    Douce 280. The Diary and Commonplace book of John Ramsey. *c.* 1596–1633
    Univ. Arch, Reg. G. G. John Case's Will.

CAMBRIDGE

St. John's College
    U.26.

FOREIGN — GENERAL

LONDON

British Museum
    Add. 27, 579. *Album Amicorum* of Johannes Cellarius of Nürnberg. 1599–1606.

COPENHAGEN

Rentemesterregnskab (Accounts of the Controller) 1599–1606
    Siellandske Tegnelse 1596–1604 (XIX).

ABBREVIATIONS

A15	B.M. Add. 15118
APG	Füllsack and Hildebrand, *Auselesener Paduanen und Galliarden* . . . (1607)
B	Tübingen Universitätsbibliothek (formerly in Berlin Staatsbibliothek) Mus MS 40,141
BCV	B.M. R.M. 23. 1. 4
BD	Trinity College, Dublin, D. 1. 21
Bk1	John Dowland, *The First Booke of Songes* (1597)
Bk2	*The Second Booke of Songs* (1600)
Bk3	*The Third and Last Booke of Songs* (1603)
BNP	Besardus, *Novus Partus* (Augsburg 1617)
Braye Band	The Braye Bandora and Lyra Viol MS
BTH	Besardus, *Thesaurus Harmonicus* (Cologne, 1603)
Bull	Fitzwilliam Museum, Cambridge, The Dr. Bull MS.
CCB	Cambridge Consort Books
a.	Dd. 3. 18. Lute
b.	Dd. 14. 24. Cittern
c.	Dd. 5. 21. Recorder.
d.	Dd. 5. 20. Bass.
Ch.Ch.Ox.	Christ Church, Oxford, MS 439
CMV	*Clement Matchett's Virginals Book* (1612) Ed. Dart (1957)
CSR	Camphuysen, *Stichtelycke Rymen* (Amsterdam, 1602–1690)
D2	Cambridge University Library Dd. 2. 11. (B)

D4   Dd. 4. 22.
D5   Dd. 5. 78. (3) (E)
D9   Dd. 9. 33. (C)
D14   Dd. 14.23.
DM   Joachim van den Hove, *Delitiæ Musicæ* (Ultrajecti, 1612)
D.N.B.   *Dictionary of National Biography*
Dol.   Dolmetsch Library, Haslemere, Surrey. Lute MS II. B.I.
Dre4   New York Public Library, Drexel MS 4041
Dre5   Drexel MS 5612
Fab   Copenhagen, Det Kongelige Bibliotek, Thott, 841. 40 Fabritius MS
FD   Folger Shakespeare Library, Washington, D.C. The Dowland Lute Book
Fetis   Bibliothèque Royale, Brussels. Fétis 3095 (II. 4. 109).
FLH   Jacob van Eyk, *Der Fluyten Lust-Hof* (Amsterdam, 1654)
Flo.   Joachim van den Hove, *Florida* (Ultrajecti, 1601)
FM   Johannes Rude, *Flores Musicæ* (1598)
Forster   B.M. R.M. 24. d. 3. Will Forster's Virginals Book (1624)
FVB   *Fitzwilliam Virginal Book.* Edited J. Fuller Maitland and W. Barclay Squire (1899)
G.   Glasgow University Library, R. d. 43. The Euing Lute MS
H.   B.M. Hirsch M. 1353
JP   B.M. Jane Pickering's Lute Book (1616)
K10   Kassel, Landesbibliothek, 4° Mus. 108. 1 Victor de Montbuysson's Lute Book. (1611)
L   Leipzig, Musikbibliothek der Stadt Leipzig, Ms. II, 6. 15.
LHC   Fitzwilliam Museum, Cambridge. Lord Herbert of Cherbury's Lute Book
LoST   John Dowland, *Lachrimæ or Seaven Teares* (1604)
LTO   Antoine Francisque, *Le Trésor d'Orphée* (1600)
Mar   Archbishop Marsh's Library, Dublin, Z. 3. 2. 13.
MB   Robert Dowland, *A Musicall Banquet* (1610)
MCL   Thomas Morley, *The First Booke of Consort Lessons* (1597, 1611)
Mel   B.H. Add. 36,484. David Melvill's Bassus book
MHM   Elias Mertel, *Hortus Musicalis Novus* (Argentorati, 1615)
Myn   In the possession of Mr W. S. Gwynn Williams, Llangollan, Wales
N6   Cambridge University Library, Nn.6. 36 (B)
NCL   Thomas Robinson, *New Citharen Lessons* (1609)
Nev   William Byrd. *My Lady Nevells Booke.* Edited Hilda Andrews from B.M. Add. 30,485 (1926)
NGC   Adrianus Valerius, *Nederlandtsche Gedenck-Clanck* (Haarlem, 1626)
NKM   Conradus Hagius, *Newe Kunstliche Musicalische Intraden* . . . (Nurnberg, 1616)
NS   Prague University Library. Nicholas Schmall's Lute Book (1613)
Nür   Nürnberg, Germ. Nat. Mus. Ms Mus. 33748.
O.E.D.   *Oxford English Dictionary*
Opus   Thomas Simpson, *Opusculum* (Franckfort am Magn, 1610)
Pad   Paderborn, Erzbischöfliche Akademische Bibliothek. Handschrift Fü 3590a, f. 2v/3. (organ MS of Henricus Beginiker, 1622)
Pan11   Edinburgh, National Library of Scotland, MS 9450 (Panmure 11)
PS   John Dowland, *A Pilgrimes Solace* (1612)
Row   Edinburgh University Library, MS La. III 488. Mure of Rowallan's Vocal MS.
RS   Manchester Public Library, Richard Sumarte's Lyra Viol MS
S.T.C.   Pollard and Redgrave, *A Short-title Catalogue of Books Printed in England* . . . , 1475–1640 (1926)

RvP	Valentin Haussmann, *Rest von Polnischen und andern Täntzen* (Nürnberg, 1603)
S. and F	John Forbes, *Songs and Fancies* (Aberdeen, 1662, 1666, 1682)
Sche	Samuel Scheidt, *Werken* (Klecken 1923–)
Schi	Melchior Schildt in *Monatshefte für Musikgeschichte*, 20, p. 35
SdM	Nicolas Vallet, *Le Secret des Muses* (1618, 1619)
Shir	Shirburn Ballads. Edited Andrew Clark (1907)
Ske	National Library of Scotland, Adv. MS 5. 2. 15. The Skene MS
Slo	B.M. Sloane 1021.
Stra	Straloch MS. List of Original Contents in *The Gentleman's Magazine* Feb. 1823.
Swe	Jan Peterszoon Sweelinck, *Werken* (1943). Keyboard.
Taf	Thomas Simpson, *Taffel-Consort* (1621)
Ter	Michael Prætorius, *Terpsichore* (1612) Edited Gunther Oberst (1929)
TGG	Georg Leopold Fuhrmann, *Testudo Gallo-Germanicca* (Nürnberg, 1615)
Tru6	Trumbull. Add. MSS 6
Thy	Leyden, Bibliothek Thysiana. Thysius Lute MS
Tol	Tollemache Lute MS. in the possession of Robert Spencer
Var	Robert Dowland, *Varietie of Lute-Lessons* (1610)
W	The Weld Lute Book, in the possession of Lord Forester
WB	William Barley, *A New Booke of Tabliture* (1596)
WC	William Corkine, *The Second Booke of Ayres* (1612)
Wi	Yale University Library, the Wickhambrook MS
10	B.M. Add. 10,444
17	B.M. Add. 17786–91
27	Cambridge University Library, Add. 2764 (C)
30	Add. 3056
31	B.M. Add. 31,392
35	B.M. Add. 35,155. c. 1858
36	B.M. Add. 36,526
38	B.M. Add. 38,539
64	B.M. Add. 6402
B.M.	British Museum
WT	Without title.

LUTE MUSIC

Varietie of Lute-Lessons (1610), Robert Dowland. S.T.C. 7100
Copies:

> British Museum
> Bodleian Library
> Huntington Library
> Prince Dohna-Schlobitten*

* Attention was first drawn to the Dowland volumes in this library by Otto Mies, 'Elizabethan Music Prints in an East-Prussian Castle', *Musica Disciplina*, III (1949), pp. 171–2. They are in the possession of Fürst Alexander zu Dohna-Schlobitten, 785 Lörrach, Tumringer Strasse 213, Germany. I am grateful to Edward Doughtie for allowing me to examine his set of microfilms.

A New Booke of Tabliture (1596), William Barley. S.T.C. 1433
Copies: British Museum
Royal College of Music, London
Huntington Library (imperfect)

No.

1. **31** ff. 13/14/14v, 'A fantasie Maister Dowland'; **30** ff. 8v/9, WT. 'John Dowlande BM'; **G** ff. 16v/17, WT. Anon; **JP** ff. 24v/25, 'A Fantasia' Anon.; **38** ff. 14v/15, WT. Anon. **BTH** ff. 170v/171/171v. Var. Fantasie No. 7 'Composed by Iohn Douland, Batchelar of Musicke'.

2. **D9** ff. 16v/17, 'forlorne Hope fancye Mr Dowland Bach of Musicke'; **MHM** No. 70, pp. 210/211, WT. Anon.

3. **D5** ff. 43v/44, 'farwell Jo: dowlande', title and name are in Dowland's own hand; **G** ff. 41v/42, WT. Anon.

4. **D9** ff. 41v/42, 'Farwell Jo. Dowlande'; **D9** f. 50v, to bar 35 only.

5. **30** ff. 17v/18, WT. 'J. Dowland'.

6. **30** ff. 7v/8, 'Fantasy Mr Dowlande BM'; **D9** ff. 43v/44, WT. Anon.; **N6** ff. 32v/33, WT. Anon.; **MHM** No. 69. pp. 208/209/210, WT. Anon.

7. **D9** ff. 6v/7/7v, 'A fancy Jo Dow'; **G** ff. 35/35v/36, WT. Anon.

8. **D2** ff. 46v/47, 'Pauen J. D.'; **JP** ff. 19v/20 'Pipers Pavinge by Mr dowlande'; **30** ff. 2v/3 'Pipers Pauan by John Dowlande BM'; **31** ff. 27v/28, 'Mayster Pypers Pavyn by Mayster Dowland'; **G**. f. 29v, WT. Anon.; **WB**. No. 4, 'Pipers Pauin By I.D.'; **DM** f. 37v, 'Pavana Pijper' 'Dovvlant'; **K1** f. 70v/71, 'pipers paduan' Anon.; **Pan11** f. 7, 'Duland his pavan called gaudean'.

Arrangements by other composers
FVB No. CLXXXII, 'Pipers Paven' by Martin Pierson; **Dre5** p.4 (modern numbering), 'Captaine Dyvers Pavion'; **MCL** No. 4, 'Captaine Pipers Pauin'; **Row** ff. 27v/28, 'Doulandis Pauande' (Cantus part of '4 vocum'.); **CSR** (cantus only with Dutch words) editions of 1647, p. 110, 'Sang: C. Pypers Pavane' Anon.; 1655, p. 123, 'Sang: C. Pypers Pavane' Anon.; 1675, p. 83, WT. Anon. First 6 notes then tune altered; **CCB** c. f. 3v, 'Captain Pipers Pauin', d. f. 3v, 'Captaine Pipers Pauen'; b. f. 31, 'Capt Pipers Pauen'; **D2** f. 82 'C. pipers pauen' (bandora); **Braye Band** f. 89, 'Pipers pauin' (consort); **NKM** à 5, 'Pypers Pavan' Anon.; also à 4 'Medias voces composuit. C.H.'; **Mel** f. 22v 'Daulans paven'.

9. **G.** f. 25, WT. Anon.; **W** f. 14v, 'Semper dolens' Anon.; **JP** f. 31v, 'Dowlandes Lamentation "Semp dolent" '; **DM** ff. 38v/39, 'Semper Dowlant semper dolens' 'Ioan Doulant' (reprint of lute part from **LoST**)

10. **D2** f. 58v, 'Solus cū sola J Dowl'; **G** ff. 27v/28, WT. Anon.; **31** ff. 14v/15, 'Solus cū sola Dowland'; **WB** No. 11, 'Solus cum sola made by I.D.' (for orpharion).

Arrangements by other composers
Dre5 pp. 222/223/224 (modern numbering), 'Pavion Solus com so la' Anon. (virginals); **RS** No. 11, 'Solus cum sola' 'R.S.' (lyra viol). **CCB** b. f. 27 'Solus cū Sola'.

11. **D9** ff. 33v/34, 'Mrs Brigide fleetwoods pauen als Solus sine sola Jo Dowland'.

12. **D2** f. 14v, 'Dr Cases Pauen J. Dowland'.

13. **N6** ff. 18/18v 'resolucōn' Anon.; **Bk2**, 'Dowlands Adew for Master Oliver Cromwell'. (for lute and bass viol); **Opus** No. V, à 4 (arranged Simpson)

14. **D5** ff. 2v/3, WT. Anon.; **TGG** p. 53, 'Pavana Englesa Tertia' Anon.; **Var** Pauin No. 5, 'Sir John Langton his Pauin' 'Composed by Iohn Dowland Batcheler of Musicke'. (See also **Lost** No. 10).

15. **31** ff. 35v/36, 'Dowlands Lachrimæ maister Dowland'; **G** ff. 25v/26, WT. Anon.; **D2** f. 81v, WT. Anon.; **JP** ff. 16v/17, 'Lacrime by Dowland'; **D5** ff. 9v/21, WT. 'J:D'; **38** ff. 22v/23, 'Lacrime Pauin by Mr John Dowland'; **W** f, 4v, 'Pauane Lachrimæ by Mr Dowland'; **LHC** f. 8v, 'Pauana by J. Dowlande Lachrimæ'; **FD** ff. 18v/19, 'Lacrame mr Dowland'; **WB** No. 3 'Lacrime by I.D.'; **64** f. 1, 'Lacrame' Anon.; **H** f. 11v, WT. Anon. (A mi.); **D2** ff. 75v/77, 'Lachrimæ Jo. Dowl'. (A mi.); **30** ff. 14v/15, WT. Anon.; **30** ff. 36v/37, 'Lacrimæ CK'; **27** [5v/6] 'Dowlandes Lacrimæ', in A mi.

Foreign versions and arrangements (lute) *Printed books*
BTH ff. 16v/17, 'Fantasia Ioannis Dooland Angli Lachrimæ'; **BNP** No. 7, 'Lachrimæ J. Dooland à I.B.B. in hanc concert. accommodate'; **Flo** ff. 94/94v/95, 'Pauana Lachrime' and 'Reprinse' Anon.; **FM** Liber Secundus, No. 91, 'Pavana á 5 voc. Dulandi Angli'; **TGG** p. 60 'Pavana Lachrimæ V.S.' (Valentinus Strobelius); **NGC** p. 16, 'Pavane Lachrimæ met den Bass' Anon. **DM** f. 2v, 'Preludium Lachrime' 'Ioachimus van den Hove'.

MSS
K10 ff. 5/5v, 'pauaná lacrimá' Anon.; ff. 55v/56, 'pauana lacrima' Anon.; **L** p. 78, 'Pavana Lachrÿmæ' Anon. (German tablature); **B** ff. 36v/37/ 37v/38, 'Fantasia Joannis Dulandi'; **Thy** f. 388v, 'Lacrime' Anon.; f. 389v, 'Lacryme' Anon. (for 2nd lute or consort?); **Fab** f. 109v, 'Lacrime Angelica' Anon. (German tablature); **Slo** f. 21v, 'Pavan Lacrymæ' Anon.; **Dol** f. 225v in G.

Arrangements for other instruments
MCL No. 7, 'Lachrimæ Pauin' Anon.; **CCB** a. f. 16v, 'Lachrimæ' Anon.; **CCB** b. f. 25, 'Lachrimæ' Anon.; **CCB** c. f. 3v, 'Lachrimæ' Anon.; **CCB** d. f. 6v, 'Lachrimæ' Anon. **D14** f. 28v, 'Lachrimæ' Anon. (cittern solo); **D2** f. 84v, 'Lachrimæ J.D.' (bandora) **RS** No. 9, 'Lachrimæ' Anon. (lyra viol); **FVB** No. CXXI, 'Pavana Lachrymae John Dowland' set by William Byrd; No. CLIII, 'Pavana' Thomas Morley; No. CCXC, 'Lachrymæ Pavan, John Dowland' set by Giles Farnaby; **Bull** f. 75v, 'Dowlandes Lachrimæ out of my Cosin Maryes booke'; f. 83, 'Dowlands Lachrimæ sett by Mr Randell'; **BCV** pp. 8–12, 'Lacrime Pauin' Benjamin Cosyn; **Nev** f. 71, 'Lacrimæ' Anon.; **Schi** p. 35, 'Paduana Lagrima' (organ); **FLH** ff. 12–13, 'Pavane Lachrimae' Anon. (solo recorder); ff. 62v–65, 'Pavane Lachrime' Anon. (solo recorder); **BD** pp. 42/43, 'Lachrima by mr Dowland' (lyra viol); **Braye Band** f. 17v (consort frag.) f. 92v, Lachrimæ' (consort complete); **Pad** ff. 2v/3, 'Pauana Lachryme' (organ) **SWE** p. 240.

Some compositions based on, or which quote, the Lachrimæ theme
Var Pauin 1, 'Mauritius Landgrauius Hessia fecit in honorem Ioanni Doulandi Anglorum Orphei'; Thomas Tomkins, *Songs of 3.4.5. and 6. Parts* (1622) No. 7, 'O let me liue for true loue' dedicated 'To Doctor Douland'; Anthony Holborne, *Pauans Galliards Almains* (1599) No. 7 'Pauan'; No. 21, 'Infernum'; No. 23, 'Spero'; No. 27, 'Image of Melancholy'; No. 49, 'Pauana Plorauit'; Füllsack, *Ausserlesener Paduanen*, I Theil (1607) No. II à 5 'Paduana' and 'Galliarda'; William Lawes, Bod. MS Mus. Sch. B.2; Johann Schop. *Neuer Himlischer Lieder Sonderbahres Buch* (1654), p. 158, 'Gott der du mit eigner hand in Paradiss' by P. Meier. (See also under *Songs*, **Bk2** No. 2, and *Consort Music*, **LoST** No. 1.)

16. **D5** ff. 47v/48, WT. 'J: Dowlande'.

17. **D5** ff. 64v/65, 'The Lady Russells Pauen' Anon; **D9** ff. 5v/6, 'The lady Russells paven' Anon.; **G** ff. 37v/38, WT. Anon.; **30** ff. 5v/6, 'A Pauen by John Dowlande'.

18. **D5** ff. 51v/52, WT. 'JD'; **D9** ff. 1v/2, WT. 'JD B of Musicke'.

19. **D2** f. 53, WT. Anon.; **D5** ff. 21v/10, WT. Anon. **H** f. 11, WT. Anon. **31** ff. 28v/29, 'maister pypers galiard by maister Dowland'; **G.** f. 28v, WT. Anon.; **D9** f. 73v, WT. Anon.; **30** ff. 3v/4, WT. Anon. **BTH** f. 107v, 'Galliarda Ioannis Doland'.

Arrangements by other composers
NCL No. 9, 'Pipers Galiard' Anon. (cittern); **FVB** No. CLXXXII, 'Pipers Galliard' by John Bull, followed by 'Variatio Ejusdem' by Bull; **MCL** No. 5, 'Galliard to Captaine Pipers Pauin' Anon.; **WC** No. 1 of the pieces for lyra viol, 'If my complaints' Anon. **Forster** f Anon. Ch. Ch. Ox. MS 431, (virginals) an inaccurate copy of preceding, attr. Byrd; **Dre5** p. 4 (modern numbering), 'The Galliard' Anon. (keyboard), different from the preceding. **LTO** f. 13, 'Gaillarde' Anon. (lute); **Braye Band** f. 89, 'Pipers galliard' (consort part). (See also Bkl No. 4 and LoSt No. 18); **Pan** 11 f. 7, 'The galeard'; **Mel** f. 22v, 'The galyeard'. Bassus of **Bk** 1. No. 4.

20. **D2** f. 7v, 'Dowlands Galliard'; **Thy** f. 22, 'Douwlants Gailliarde'; **Tol** f. 6v, 'A Galliard by Dowla'. **Braye Band** f. 10v, 'Dowlandes galliard' (solo).

21. **D2** f. 56 WT. 'J.dowl'; **H** f. 11v, WT. Anon.; **Myn** f. 1, 'John Dowlands Galliarde'; 27 f. (9v), 'Capit(ain) Candishe his Galy(ard)'.

22. **D2** f. 95, 'Dowlands Galliarde'; **D2** f. 56, WT. Anon.; **D2** f. 60, 'Dow Galliard'; **G** f. 23, WT. Anon.

Arrangements by other composers
CCB b. f. 34v, 'Dowlands 1 Galliarde'; c. f. 5, 'Dowlands first galliarde'; d. f. 5, 'Dowlands first galliarde'.

23. **D2** f. 93, 'The frogg galliard' Anon.; **D2** f. 40, WT. Anon.; **G** ff. 26v/27, WT. Anon. **FD** f. 12v, 'frog Galliard Jo: dowlande' (autograph); **3**—ff. 42v/43, 'Frogg galliard' Anon.; **Thy** f. 28v, 'Frogge Galliarde' Anon.; **Stra** No. 13, 'Frogges Galzeart'.

Arrangements by other composers
NCL No. 24, 'The Frogge' Anon.; **MCL** No. 10, 'The Frog Galliard' Anon.; **CMV** 'Frogge Galliard set by Mr Willoughby. Aug. 25. 1612'; **Ske** No. 20, 'Froggis Galziard' Anon.; **CSR** 1647 p. 24, 'Forgs Gaillarde' Anon. Tune adapted to Dutch words; 1655 p. 24, 'Frogs Gaillarde' Anon. As above; 1675 p. 23, WT. Anon, but with the same words; **NGC** p. 54, 'Nou, Nou' Anon.; **Nür** f. 9v, 'galliarda Frog Canto'; f. 10 'galliarda Frog Pasy' (two sets of divisions for lute).

Ballads
'The Shepherds Delight', Roxburghe Collection, i. 388 (Ebsworth edition, Vol. 2, p. 528); 'The True Loves knot Untyed', Pepys Collection, Vol. IV, p. 44.

24. **D2** f. 58, 'fr. Dac. Galliard' Anon.; **30** f. 33v, 'Galliard J.D.'

Settings by other composers
D5 f. 63, 'A Galliard fr. Cuttinge'. (lute). (See also *Songs* **Bk1** No. 19)

25. **D2** f. 12, 'Dowl Mellancoly Galliard'; **G** f. 24v, WT. Anon.

26. **D5** f. 26, WT. 'J.D.' (See also *Songs* **Bk1** No. 3 and *Consort Music* **LoST** No. 13)

27. **D5** f. 49v, WT. 'J:D.'

28. **D5** ff. 35v/36, WT. 'J.D.'; **G** ff. 20v/21, WT. Anon.; **LHC** f. 54, 'Galliarda. J:D:'; **38** ff. 15v/16, 'A gallyard upon the gallyard before by Mr Dowland'; **K10** ff. 94v/95, 'Galliarda Dullande'; **TGG** p. 108, 'Galliardo 2' 'incerti Authoris'.

29. **D5** ff. 16v/17, WT. 'J.D.'; **LHC** f. 10, 'Gagliarda J: Doulande' (see **LoST** No. 15)

30. **D5** ff. 25v/26, WT. 'Jo: D.'

31. **D5** f. 37, WT. 'J:D'.

32. **D9** f. 20 'Mrs vaux Galliarde Jo Dowland Bacheler of Musicke'; **TGG** p. 108 'Galliardo 1' 'incerti Authoris'.

33. **D9** ff. 17v/18 'Mr Langtons galliard Mr Dow Bach. of Mus.'; **G** f. 18, WT. Anon.

34. **D9** f. 29, 'Mignarda Jo Dowlande'; **D2** f. 77 'Mignarde' Anon.; **D5** f. 31v, WT. 'J.D.' (See also *Songs* **PS** No. 5 and *Consort Music* **LoST** No. 14)

35. **D9** f. 37v 'Galliard J Dow de'; (The 4th, 5th and 6th letters of the name are destroyed by damp.) **Thy** f. 26v 'Gallarde' Anon.

36. **D9** f. 19v, 'Mr Knights Galliard J. Dowla'; **D5** f. 56, Mr knights galliard Jo Dowland'.

37. **Bk1** No. 22 'My Lord Chamberlaine his galliard'; **D9** f. 90 WT. Anon. Cantus only. **35** p. 157, 'My Lord Chamberlaine his galliard'. A copy in compressed score on two staves.

38. **MB** 'The Right Honourable the Lord Viscount Lisle, His Galliard', called in the Table of Contents 'Syr Robert Sidneys Galliard'; **D2** f. 52, 'Suzanna Galliard' Anon. **APG** ed. Engelke, p. 112 'Galliard à 5, "Ihon Douland".' (See also *Consort Music* **LoST** No. 19)

39. **FD** f. 6, 'Doulands rounde battell galyarde'.

Arrangements by other composers
CCB b. f. 36v 'Dowlands Rounde b. galliard', c. f. 5v, 'Dowlands round Battell galliarde', d. f. 5, 'Do: Round Battell galliarde'.

40. **Var** Galliard No. 1, 'The most high and mightie *Christianus* the fourth King of Denmark, his Galliard' 'John Dowland Batcheler of Musick'; **D9** f. 23, 'Mr Mildmays Galliard J.D.' f. 94v, bars 48 to the end, subscribed 'Dowlands plus in prima p(arte libri); **FD** ff. 10v/11, 'the Battell gallyard Mr Dowland'; **JP** ff. 17v/18, 'the battell galyerd mr dowlande'; **W** f. 5v, 'The Battle Galliard' Anon.; **38** ff. 12v/13, 'The Battle galliard Mr Dowland'; **Tol** 7v 'The battaile Galliarde by Johnson'; **TGG** pp. 112/113, 'galliarda Robert. Doulandt'.

Arrangements by other composers
Sche ff. 50v-52r, 'Galliarda Dulenti Varirt Sam. Sch.'

41. **D2** f. 59, 'K Darcyes galliard' Anon.; **Var** Galliard No. 2, 'The most sacred Queene Elizabeth, her Galliard'. 'Iohn Dowland Batcheler of Musick'.

Arrangements by other composers
CCB b. f. 20, 'Do. Re. Ha. galliard'; c. f. 6. 'Dowl. Reads H. Galliard'; d. f. 5v, 'Dowl. R.H. galliarde'.

42. **FD** f. 16, 'Can she excuse J. doulande' (autograph); **G** f. 24, WT. Anon.; **WB** No. 12, 'A Galliarde by I.D.'; **H** f. 11v, WT. Anon. **D2** f. 40v, WT. Anon.; f. 62v. WT. Anon.; **Var** Galliard No. 3, 'The Right Honourable Robert, Earl of Essex, his Galliard' 'Iohn

Dowland, Batcheler of Musick'; **Thy** f. 22v, 'Can she excuse' Anon.; **K10** f. 2, 'Gagliarda' Anon.; f. 2v, WT. Anon.; f. 56v, 'daulant gagliarde'; **Myn** f. 12v Dowlands Galliard.

Arrangements by other composers
Lute: **LHC** f. 55, 'Gall: Mr D:B: (Daniel Bacheler); **30** f. 48, WT. Anon.; **Nür** f. 6v 'Galliard Pipers No. 1'; f. 7, 'Galliard Pipers No. 2'; f. 65v, 'Galliarta Pipers'; **B** f. 30, 'Galliarda' Anon.; f. 124, 'Galliarda' Anon.; **SdeM** pp. 36/37/38, 'Gaillarde du comte Essex' Anon. Arr. Vallet?; **TGG** p. 121, 'Galliarda 12' 'incerti Authoris' followed by Variations by Valentinus Strobelius; **Bull** ff. 78v/80, 'Galliard Can she excuse and may serve to Lachrimæ' Anon. (virginals); **FVB** No. CLXXXVIII, 'Can shee' Anon.; **NCL** No. 13, 'Galliard: Can she excuse my wrongs' Anon. (cittern); **MCL** No. 6, 'Galliard Can she excuse' Anon. (consort); **CSR** 1647 p. 66, 'Sang: Galliarde Essex', (Cantus with Dutch words); 1655 p. 68, 'Sang: Galliard Essex' (as above); 1675 p. 48, (Cantus with Dutch words, tune unacknowledged); 1680 p. 44; 1688 p. 50; 1690 p. 67 (all as 1675) **N6** f. 37, WT. Anon. (a consort part) **NKM** à 4, 'Pypers Galliard' **DB** pp. 36/37. 'A galliard' (Lyra viol).
(See also under *Songs* **Bk1** No. 5 and *Consort Music* **LoST** No. 18)

43. **D9** f. 91v, WT. Anon., **Mar** f. 381, 'my ladie Riches galliard' Anon.; f. 190, a five-bar fragment, WT Anon. **JP** f. 18, 'My Lady Riches galyerd' Anon.; **D5** f. 9, WT. 'J.D.'; **W** f. 5, 'galliard Mr Dowland'; **Myn** f. 5, 'Doulands Bells'; **Nür** f. 2, 'Galliarda Anglica' Anon.; **Thy** f. 21v, 'The Lady Rich hir gaillard' Anon., **Var** Galliard No. 5, 'The Right Honourable the Lady Rich, her Galliard' 'Iohn Dowland Batcheler of Musick'.

Arrangements by other composers
BD p. 37 'my Ladie richis galliard' Anon. (Lyra viol); **A15** f. 30v (No. 47), 'Ladye Ritches Galliard' Anon. (two instrumental parts, Cantus and Bassus).

44. **N6** f. 1, WT. Anon.; f. 2, 'The Erle of Darbies Galiard by Mr Jo Dowland'; **G** f. 21, WT. Anon.; **W** f. 7, 'Galliard Dowlande'; **Tol** f. 13v 'a galiarde by Mr Dowland'; **D5** f. 38, WT. Anon.; **Var** Galliard No. 4, 'The Right Honourable *Ferdinando* Earle of Darby, his Galliard' 'Iohn Dowland Batcheler of Musick'.

45. **D2** f. 58, 'K Darcies Spirite J:Dowl'; **Var** Galliard No. 6, 'The Right Honourable the Lady *Cliftons* Spirit' 'Robert Douland'.

46. **PS** No. 22, 'Galliard to *Lachrimæ*'.

Arrangements by other composers
BCV p. 12–14, 'The Galliard to itt' (Lachrimæ) 'Ben Cosyn'; **Braye Band** f. 18v 'Lachrimæ Galliard' (consort).

47. **Var** Almain No. 7, 'Sir John Smith his Almaine' Anon.; **FD** ff. 13v/14, 'Mr Smythes Allmon Jo. doulande' (autograph); **Mar** p. 384 'An almayne douland'; **Thy** f. 503, 'Allemand Angloyse' Anon.; **38** f. 8v, 'Smythes Allmayne' Anon. ; **27** f. (6), 'Smiths Almain' (frag.); **B** f. 43, 'Almand Angl' Anon. (3 undecorated strains; rather confused).

48. **D2** f. 48, 'Allmaine J. Dowland'; **Wi** f 17, 'ane almane' Anon.; **W** f. 5, 'Almayne Dowland'; **Myn** f. 10, 'Doulands allman'; **Thy** ff. 492/493, 'Mr Daulants allmande'; **L** p. 365 'Chorea Anglica 5' Anon.; p. 471, 'Almanda Dulandi'; **TGG** p. 80, 'Chorea Anglica' Anon.; **DM** f. 59 'Ballet Englese' 'Incerto'; **FD** f. 11v, 'the Lady Laitons Almone Jo doulande' (autograph); **BTH** f. 139v 'Chorea Anglicana'; **27** f. 10v, WT. Anon. (frag.).

Arrangements by other composers
CSR 1647 p. 197, 'Sang: Doulants Almande' (Adapted to Dutch words); 1655 p. 227,

(as above); 1675 p. 157, WT. Anon.; **Bod. Mus.MS a 143**, ff. 4v/5, 'Dowlands almayne'; **Braye Band** f. 11, 'Dowlands Allmaine' (solo).

49. **D2** f. 38, WT. 'John Dowland'; f. 47, WT. 'JD.'

50. **Wi** f. 15, 'Mistris Whittes thinge Jhone Dowlande'; **D2** f. 63v, 'W Thinge' Anon.; **Tol** f. 7, 'Mrs Whites Choyce' Anon.; **JP** f. 19, WT. Anon.; **38** f. 2 'Mrs Whites Choyce' Anon. (in F); **Tol** f. 7, 'Mrs Whites Choice' Anon. (in F); **27** f. (6), (in G frag).

Arrangements by other composers
RvP No. LXXXIX, á 5, 'Mein Hertz mit schmertz ist überall verwundet &c'.

51. **D5** f. 32, WT. 'J.D.'

52. **D5** f. 100v, WT. Anon.; **G** f. 24, WT. Anon.; **B** f. 46v, 'Dolandi Saltarella'; **DM** f. 58, 'Almande Ioan Douland' (the lute part from **LoST**). (See also **LoST** No. 20)

Arrangements by other composers
Taf No. IIX, 'Aria' 'Johan Douland' (à 4); **RvP** No. LXXI, WT. Anon. (à 5); **10** f. 9, No. 26, 'An Almain' (Cantus and Bassus only).

53. **FD** f. 23v, WT, Anon. (bars 1 to 8 only, in Dowland's hand); **D9** f. 28v, 'Mrs Cliftons Allmaine Jo Dowland'; **G**. f. 44, WT. Anon.

54. **D5** f. 7, WT. Anon.; **FD** f. 22v, 'my Lady Hunsdons Allmande J: doulande Bacheler of musicke' (the whole in Dowland's hand); **64** f. 1v, 'My lady hunssdons puffe Douland'; **D9** f. 38, WT. 'J. Dowland'.

Arrangements by other composers
Florence, Bibl. naz. Magl. XIX. 115. ff. 5/5v, 'Aria Francese' Anon. (keyboard); Chilesotti, *Da un Codice Lauten-Buch del Cinquecento* (1890), p. 78, 'Pezzo italiano' Anon. (from the Dusiacki lute MS, now destroyed, p. 213); Osthoff, *Der Lautenist Santino Garsi de Parma* (1926). 'Balletto di mi Donino Garsi, fatto per il S. Duca di Mantua'.

55. **FD** f. 5v, 'winter jomps' Anon.; **31** f. 23, 'Mrs Winters Jumpp' Anon.; **WB**. No. 18 'Mistris Winters Iumpe made by I.D.'; **L** p. 241, 'Current Dulandi 8'.

Arrangements by other composers
Ter p. 96, No. CLVII, 'Courante' 'Incerti', à 4; p. 178, No. CCC, 'Gaillarde' 'Incerti', à 4.

56. **D2** f. 22, 'Mrs Whites Nothing Jo Dowland Bacheler of Musicke'.

57. **D9** f. 20v, 'Mrs vauxes Gigge Jo Dowland Bacheler of Musicke'.

58. **D9** f. 21v, 'The Shomakers Wife. A Toy J. Dowland'; **D5** f. 6v, WT. Anon.

59. **Wi** f. 11, 'tarletones riserrectione Jo Dowlande'.

60. **N6** f. 21v, 'Come away' Anon.; **K10** f. 1v, 'Paduana' Anon.; f. 64v, WT. Anon.; **L** p. 472 'Commia güinæ Dulandi 5'; p. 512, 'Commia Doulandi'.

61. **D2** f. 55v, 'Orlando sleepeth JD'.

Other settings
Lute: **BD** p. 111, 'Orlando' Anon.; **Myn** f. 5v 'Orlando furioso 1597' Anon.; **TGG** f. 47, 'Orlandus Furiosus' 'E.M.A.' (Elias Mertel), **Thy** f. 399 'Orlando' Anon.; **K10** f. 23v,

'Orlando Furioso' Anon.; **Flo** f. 106, 'Orlando Chanson Englesæ' Anon. **NS** f. 22v 'Englesa' Anon.; **CCB** b. f. 16v, 'Orlando sleepeth' Anon. (cittern part of consort).

Ballads
Shir No. LVIII, 'My dear adieu! my sweet love, farewell' to 'Orlandos musique'.

62. **D4** f. 11v, 'fortune by Jo: Dowland'; **G** f. 27, WT. Anon.; **W** f. 2, 'Fortune Mr Dowland'; **Myn** f. 9v, 'fortune Douland'; **WB** No. 6, 'Fortune by I.D.'; **BD** p. 14, 'fortune my foe to the consort'. Anon.; **Thy** f. 387v, 'Fortune Jo Doulande'.

63. **D2** f. 56, 'Complaint J.D'.

64. **D5** ff. 39v/40, WT. 'JD'; **G** ff. 17v/18, WT. Anon.; **WB** No. 16, 'Go from my windowe made by I.D.'; **JP** f. 29v, 'Go from my window by M Dowland'.

65. **D2** f. 58, 'Lord Strangs March J.D.'

66. **JP** f. 25, 'My lord willobes wellcome home by John dowland'; **G** f. 38, WT. Anon.; **D2** f. 58v, 'My L Williaghby Tune J D'; **Myn** f. 1, 'Mmy lord wilobie' Anon.; **Wi** f. 12, 'my lo: willobeis' tune Jhone Doulande'; **FD** f. 9v, WT. 'Jo. douland' (autograph); **Tol** f. 11v, 'My Lo: Wilobies welcom home' by 'Jo: Dowland' (part for second lute to **FD**).

67. **D9** ff. 67v/68 'Wallsingham Jo Dowland',

68. **D5** ff. 38v/39, WT. 'JD'; **G** ff. 21v/22, WT. Anon.; **Tru6** (unfoliated) 'Aloe'.

69. **D9** ff. 68v/69/69v, 'Loth to departe Jo:Dowland'

70. **D9** ff. 29v/30, 'Robin Jo Dowland'; **JP** f. 22v, 'Sweet Robyne' Anon.; f. 35, 'Sweet Robyne' Anon.; **TGG** pp. 114/115, 'Galliarda JD'.

Pieces of uncertain attribution
71. **JP** f. 23v/24, 'A Fantasia', Anon.

72. **G** ff. 42v/43, WT. Anon.

73. **D9** ff. 44v/45/45v, WT. Anon.

74. **31** f. 24, WT. Anon.

75. **D2** f. 48, 'A Dream' Anon.; **H** f. 3, WT. Anon.

Arrangements by other composers
CCB b. f. 26v, 'My Lady Leightons Pauen',

76. **G** f. 42, WT. Anon.; **D9** f. 19, 'Galliard W th'.

77. **Mar** f. 382, 'Mistris Norrishis Delight', Anon.

78. **G** f. 26, WT. Anon.

79. **FD** f. 23, WT. Anon. (What if a day)

80. **Myn** f. 7 'A Coye Toye' Anon.

81. **D2** f. 56, WT. Anon.

Arrangements by other composers
CCB a. f. 53, 'Tarletons Jigg' Anon.; b. f. 17, 'Tarletons Jigge' Anon.; d. f. 5, 'Tarletons Jigges' Anon.; **D4.23** f. 25, 'Tarletons Willy' Anon.; (cittern)

82. **D9** ff. 22/21v WT. 'Dowland' and 'F Cutting'.

83. **Myn** f. 12v 'Dowlands Galliard'; **W** ff. 15v/16 'My Lady Mildmays delighte' Anon.; **FD** f. 22 'Johnsons gallyard'; **N6** f. 11 'Galliard Ro Johnson'; **38** f. 16v, 'Mr Johnsons gallyard'.

84. **D9** f. 17, 'Hasellwoods Galliard Jo Dowland'; **H** f. 5, WT. Anon.

85. **L** p. 218, 'Galliarda Dulandi 39'; p. 235, 'Galiarda'.

   Settings by other composers
   D2 f. 71v, 'f Cuttings galliard'; **31** f. 34 'a galiard by mr Cuttinge'; **Mar** p. 386, 'Galliard Alfonsus'; **G** f. 29, WT. Anon.; **Thy** f. 33, 'Maister Hayls Galliard'.

86. **L** p. 114, 'Pauana Dulandi'.

87. **L** p. 195, 'Galliarda Dulandi 8'.

   See also Appendix I.

VOCAL

The following list of printed books and MSS that contain songs by Dowland includes only those where music is present. The many additional occurrences of the words alone are not mentioned. In every case the printed books are regarded as the primary source.

The First Booke of Songes (1597)   S.T.C. 7091
British Museum (imperfect; D1 missing)
Boston Public Library
Folger Library
Huntington Library

The First Booke of Songes (1600)   S.T.C. 7092
British Museum
Liverpool Public Library
Folger Library
H. L. Bradfer-Lawrence, Ripon, Yorks.

The First Booke of Songes (1603)   S.T.C. 7092,5
Manchester Public Library, Henry Watson Music Collection. (imperfect, L1 and L2 missing).
   Verso of title-page blank.
Trinity College, Dublin. (imperfect)

The First Booke of Songs (1606)
British Museum (imperfect; L1, L2 missing.)
Prince Dohna-Schlobitten (perfect)

The First Booke of Songs (1608)
No copy known.

The First Booke of Songs (1613)
British Museum
Christ Church, Oxford
Lincoln Cathedral
St. Michael's College, Tenbury
Robert Spencer, Woodford Green, Essex.

No. 1. Vnquiet thoughts.

Bod. Mus. MS f. 7–10. Four part books.
Nat. Lib. Scot. Adv. 5. 2. 14. f. 19. Cantus.

2. Who euer thinks or hopes of loue for loue.
B.M. Add. 36,526 (A) ff. 2 and 8. Tenor and Bassus.
Bod. Mus. MS f. 7–10.

3. My thoughts are wingd with hopes.
Bod. Mus. MS f. 7–10.
(See also Solo No. 26 and *Consort Music* **LoST** No. 13)

4. If my complaints could passions moue.
B.M. Add. 15,117 f. 15v. Cantus and lute.
B.M. Add. 24,665 f. 12v. Cantus and Bassus.
B.M. Add. 29,481 f. 14. Cantus and Bassus.
B.M. Add. 36,526 (A). Stanza 1 f. 7v, ff. 2 and 8 Tenor and Bassus.
Ch. Ch. Ox. MS 439 pp. 52/53. Cantus and Bassus.
Bod. Mus. MS f. 7–10.
Fétis pp. 2–5.
(See also Solo No. 19 and **LoST** No. 18)

5. Can she excuse my wrongs with vertues cloake.
King's Cam. Rowe 2. f. 1v/2 Cantus and lute. Variant accompaniment.
Bod. Mus. MS f. 7–10.
B.M. Add. 24,665 f. 45, Cantus, f. 43, Bassus.
B.M. Add. 36,526 (A). f. 7v, stanza 1, ff. 2, Tenor, f. 8, Bassus.
Fétis pp. 4/5.
(See also Solo No. 42 and **LoST** No. 12)

6. Now, O now I needs must part.
Forbes, *S. and F.* No. 47, 1662 only.
King's Cam. Rowe 2. f. 2v, Cantus and lute.
Bod. Mus. MS f. 7–10.
Ch. Ch. Ox. MS 439. p. 45, Cantus and Bassus.
B.M. Add. 36,526 (A). f. 7v, stanza 1, ff. 2v and 8v, Altus and Bassus.
B.M. Add. 29,291. f. 22, Four voices in score.
Fétis pp. 6/7.
(See also Solo No. 23)

7. Deare if you change Ile never chuse againe.
Bod. Mus. MS f. 7–10.
B.M. Add. 36,526 (A). f. 9v. Bassus and words.
Fétis pp. 18/19.

8. Burst forth my teares.
Bod. Mus. MS f. 7–10.
B.M. Add. 36,526 (A). ff. 2v and 8v, Altus and Bassus.
B.M. Add. 34,608. f. 4v. Four voices in score.
Fétis pp. 10/11.

9. Go christall teares.
Bod. Mus. MS f. 7–10.

10. Thinkst thou then by thy fayning.
Bod. Mus. MS f. 7–10.

Ed. Univ. Lib. La. III 488. Cantus.

11. Come away, come sweet loue.
Bod. Mus. MS f. 7–10.
B.M. Add. 36,526 (A). f. 2v and 8v. Tenor and Bassus.

12. Rest a while you cruell cares.
Bod. Mus. MS f. 7–10.
King's Cam. Rowe 2. f. 3v/4. Cantus and lute. Variants in accomp.
B.M. Add. 36,526 (A). ff. 3 and 8v, Tenor and Bassus.

13. Sleepe wayward thoughts.
Forbes, *S. and F.* No. 20, all editions.
J. Playford, *A briefe intro. etc* (1660) p. 41, and in unnumbered ed. of 1662. Cantus and Bassus.
B.M. Add. 15,117. f. 7. Cantus and lute.
B.M. Add. 15,118. f. f.v. Cantus and Bassus. No words.
B.M. Add. 36,526(A). ff. 3 and 9, Tenor and Bassus.
B.M. Add. 29,481. f. 2. Cantus and Bassus.
B.M. Add. 24,665. 264v/265. Cantus and Bassus.
Ed. Univ. Lib. MS La. III 488. f. 44. MS La. III 490. p. 71.
Ch. Ch. Ox. MS 439. p. 46. Cantus and Bassus.
Bod. Mus. MS f. 7–10.
Fétis pp. 12/13.
In original contents of the MS of Gordon of Straloch. See *The Gentleman's Magazine.* Feb
    1823. No. 2. As lute solo?

14. All ye whom loue or fortune hath betraide.
B.M. Add. 36,526(A). ff. 3 and 9, Tenor and Bassus.
B.M. Add. 34,608. f. 32. Four voices in score.

15. Wilt thou unkind thus reaue me of my hart.
B.M. Add. 15,118. f. fv
Bod. Mus. MS. f. 7–10.

16. Would my conceit that first enforst my woe.
B.M. Add. 34,608. f. 32. Four voices in score.

17. Come againe: sweet loue doth now enuite.
Forbes, *S. and F.* No. 60. 1662 only.
Bod. Mus. MS f. 7–10.
B.M. Add. 24,665. ff. 26v/27. Cantus and Bassus.
B.M. Add. 36,526 (A). ff. 3v and 9, Tenor and Bassus.
B.M. Add. 33,933. f. 85. Contra. *i.e.* Altus.
B.M. Add. 29,291. f. 11v. Four voices in score.
B.M. Add. 34,608. f. 6v. Four voices in score.
Fétis pp. 14/15.
Pan 11, with last line 'did tempt her still, yet she for triumph laughs'.
Ed. Univ. Lib. MS La. III. 483, p. 183.
K10 f. 32v. Cantus and lute. A corrupt version with Italian words.
Jacob van Eyk, *Der Fluyten Lust-Hof* (1654), No. 41. Arranged for 2 recorders. Not Dowland's
    bass.
(See also Solo No. 60)

18. His golden locks time hath to siluer turnd.
Bod. Mus. MS f. 7–10.
B.M. Add. 36,526 (A). f. 9, Bassus.
Fétis pp. 16/17.

19. Awake sweet loue thou art returnd.
Forbes, *S. and F.* No. 23. (All editions)
B.M. Add. 29,291. f. 11, Four voices in score.
B.M. Add. 31,811. ff. 33 and 35. Four voices.
B.M. Add. 36,526(A) f. 3v, Tenor.
B.M. Add. 34,608. f. 3. Four voices in score with figures to the bass.
(See also Solo No. 24)

20. Come heauy sleepe.

21. Away with these selfe louing lads.
Bod. Mus. MS f. 7–10.
Edin. Univ. Lib. La. III. 488. f. 44. Cantus.
B.M. Add. 29,291. f. 12. Four voices in score.
B.M. Add. 34,608. f. 28. Four voices in score.
Fétis pp. 8/9.
Ritson, *A Select Collection of English Songs* (1783). Cantus only with words.
(For 'A Galliard for two to play vpon one Lute at the end of the booke' see Lute Music No. 37.)

The Second Booke of Songs (1600)   S.T.C. 7095
British Museum
Manchester Public Library, Henry Watson Music Collection.
Royal College of Music, London.
St. Michael's College, Tenbury.
Lincoln Cathedral Library. (The words 'and Sword, in Fleete-streete.' have been cut from the Title-page.)
Liverpool Public Library (imperfect).
Boston Public Library.
Folger Library.
Huntington Library.
Prince Dohna-Schlobitten.
Bernard Quaritch Ltd. (imperfect).

Songs to two voices.

No. 1. I saw my Lady weepe:

2. Flow my teares:
Forbes, *S. and F.* (1662, No. 61; 1666 and 1682, No. 55)
B.M. Add. 24,665. ff. 11v/12. Cantus and Bassus.
T.C.D. MS F. 5.13. p. 34. Cantus in Gmi. with words.
Ch. Ch. Ox. MS 439. pp. 6/7. Cantus and Bassus. Transposed to D minor.
CSR (1647), p. 44, 'Pavaen Lachrimæ à 4. Duodecimi Toni', with Dutch words; and in various forms in many editions until 1688.
St. Michael's College, Tenbury. MS 1018. f. 30. Cantus and Bassus. 1st strain only.
(For lute settings and other arrangements see Solo No. 15 and LoST No. 1)

3. Sorrow sorrow stay, lend true repentant teares:
B.M. Add. 24,665. ff. 31v/32. Cantus and Bassus.

Ch. Ch. Ox. MS 439. p. 70. Cantus and Bassus. Fragment.

B.M. Add. 17,786–17,791. Version for solo voice and viols headed 'Dowlands Sorrow. 5. William Wigthorpe'.

B.M. Add. 37,402–37,406. Voice and viols. Anon. Different to above.

4. Dye not before thy day:

5. Mourne, mourne, day is with darknesse fled:

6. Tymes eldest sonne, old age the heire of ease: First Part.

7. Then sit thee downe, & say thy *Nunc demittis*: Second Part.

8. When others sings Venite exultemus: Third Part.
Songs to 4. voices.

9. Praise blindnesse eies.

10. O sweet woods, the delight of solitarienesse:

11. If fluds of teares could clense my follies past:
Forbes, *S. and F.* (1662, 1666, 1682) No. 13. To the tune of 'Sleepe wayward thoughts'. Cantus.
Los Angeles, Univ. Cal. Taitt MS. As above.
Edin. Univ. Lib. La. III. 483, p. 184, Tenor book; p. 200, Bassus book. Both to 'Sleep wayward thoughts'.
Nat. Lib. Scot. Skene MS Part IV, No. 2. Mandora.
B.M. Add. 33,933. f. 85v, Altus of 'Sleep Wayward Thoughts'.

12. Fine knacks for Ladies, cheap, choise, braue and new:

13. Now cease my wandring eyes:

14. Come ye heauie states of night:
Ch. Ch. Ox. MS 439. p. 47. Cantus and Bassus.

15. White as Lillies was hir face:
Forbes, *S. and F.* No. 40 1662; No. 39 1666 and 1682. Cantus.

16. Wofull heart with griefe opressed:

17. A Shepheard in a shade his plaining made:
Forbes, *S. and F.* No. 56 1662 only.
B.M. Add. 34,608. Cantus Bassus headed 'Ayrres publish'd in 1644 to be accompanied by a Bass viol'.

18. Faction that euer dwells in court:

19. Shall I sue, shall I seeke for grace:
Edin. Univ. Lib. La. III. 488. f. 44. Cantus.
Fétis pp. 22/23.

20. Toss not my soule (replacing 'Finding in fields my *Siluia* all alone' in Table of Contents).
Fétis pp. 26/27.

Songs to 5. voices:

21. Cleare or Cloudie sweet as Aprill showring:

22. Humor say what makst thou heere:

B.M. Add. 15,117. f. 12. Cantus and lute. Variants in words and accompaniment.
Fétis 20/21.

Dowlands adew for Master Oliver Cromwell (See Solo No. 13)

The Third and Last Booke of Songs (1603)   S.T.C. 7096
British Museum
Lincoln Cathedral Library (imperfect; title-page missing)
Manchester Public Library
Royal College of Music, London
H. L. Bradfer-Lawrence, Ripon, Yorks.
Folger Library
Huntington Library
Prince Dohna-Schlobitten
A title-page is included in Bagford's 'Collection for the History of Printing' (B. M. Harl.
    5936) No. 309, f. 98v.

1. Farewell too faire.

2. Time stands still.

3. Behold a wonder here.
Forbes, *S. and F.* (No. 46, 1662; No. 44, 1666 and 1682).

4. Daphne was not so chaste as she was changing.

5. Me me and none but me.

6. When Phœbus first did Daphne loue.

7. Say loue if euer thou didst finde.

8. Flow not so fast ye fountaines.

9. What if I neuer speede.
Edin. Univ. Lib. La. III. 488. f. 15. Cantus.
Univ. Cal. L.A. Tait MS. Four voices; the lower ones different from Dowland's

10. Loue stood amaz'd at sweet beauties paine.

11. Lend your eares to my sorrow good people.

12. By a fountaine where I lay.

13. Oh what hath ouerwrought my all amazed thought.

14. Farewell vnkind farewell.

15. Weepe you no more sad fountaines.

16. Fie on this faining, is loue without desire.

17. I must complaine, yet doe enioy.

18. It was a time when silly Bees could speake.
Forbes, *S. and F.* (No. 54, 1662, No. 51, 1666 and 1682). Cantus.
B.M. Add. 15,117. f. 21. Cantus and lute.

19. The lowest trees haue tops.
Forbes, *S. and F.* (No. 27 all eds.)

20. What poore Astronomers are they.

21. Come when I call, or tarrie till I come.

A Pilgrimes Solace (1612)   S.T.C. 7098
British Museum (imperfect; M1, M2 and final page torn).
Lincoln Cathedral Library (imperfect, A1 missing).
Folger Library.
Huntington Library.

1. Disdaine me still, that I may euer loue.

2. Sweete stay awhile, why will you?

3. To aske for all they loue.

4. Loue those beames that breede.

5. Shall I striue with wordes to moue.
(See also Lute Solo No. 34 and **LoST** No. 14).

6. Were euery thought an eye.
Arr. T. Simpson, **Taf.** à 4, No. X. W.T. "Joh. Douland".

7. Stay time a while thy flying.

8. Tell me true Loue.

4. Goe nightly cares, the enemy to rest.

10. From silent night, true register of moanes.

11. *Lasso vita mia, mi fa morire.*

12. In this trembling shadow.

13. If that a Sinners sighes be Angels food.

14. Thou mighty God   1. part.

15. When *Dauids* life by *Saul*.   2. part.

16. When the poore Criple.   3. part.

17. Where Sinne sore wounding.

18. My heart and tongue were twinnes.

19. Vp merry Mates, to *Neptunes* praise.

20. Welcome blacke night.

21. Cease these false sports.

22. A Galliard to *Lachrimæ* (See Lute Solo No. 46).

A Musicall Banquet (1610)   S.T.C. 7099
British Museum
Bodleian Library
Royal College of Music, London. (imperfect, after H2 missing).
Huntington Library (imperfect, M1 missing).
Library of Congress, Washington
Prince Dohna-Schlobitten

No. 8. Farre from triumphing Court.

9. Lady if you so spight me.
Arr. T. Simpson, **Taf** à 4, No. XIX. 'Aria J. Douland'.

10. In Darknesse let me dwell.

PSALMS AND SPIRITUAL SONGS

Thomas Est, *The Whole Booke of Psalmes* (1592, 1594, 1604, 1611)

1. Psalm 38.
William Barley, *The Whole Booke of Psalmes* (c. 1599), Psalm 38. Tenor and Bass only.
William Slatyer, *Psalmes of David in 4 languages and 4 Parts* (1643). Psalm 5, 'I. Douland his setting of 38'.

2. Psalm 100.
Barley, Psalm 100. Four parts. 'A Psalme before morning prayer' and 'A Psalme before evening prayer'. Tenor and Bass.
Included in collections and anthologies to the present day.

3. Psalm 104.
Barley, Psalm 104. Four parts.

4. Psalm 130.

5. Psalm 134.
Barley, Psalm 134. Tenor and Bass.

6. 'A Prayer for the Queens most excellent Maiestie'.

Thomas Ravenscroft, *The Whole Booke of Psalmes* (1621 and many subsequent editions)
7. Psalm 100
A. B. Philo-Mus., *Synopsis of Vocal Musick* (1680) pp. 64/65 'J. Dowland D.M. (Without the Altus).
Reprinted in many collections and anthologies.

MS Lamentatio Henrici Noel (1596)

8. The Lamentation of a sinner

9. Psalm 6

10. Psalm 51

11. The humble sute of a sinner

12. The humble complaint of a sinner

13. Psalm 130

14. Psalm 143.

Sir William Leighton, *Teares or Lamentations of a Sorrowfull Soule* (1614)

15. An heart thats broken and contrite
B.M. Add. 15,117, f. 14. Cantus and lute.
B.M. R. App. 63, f. 4b. Cantus and lute.
B.M. Add. 31,418, f. 5v. Vocal score only.

Charles Burney, *A General History of Music* (1767–1789), Vol. 3, p. 139.

16. I shame at mine unworthinesse.
B.M. R.App. 63, f. 28b. Cantus.
B.M. Add. 31,418, f. 57. Vocal score.
Burney, Vol. 3, p. 140. Vocal score, 30 bars.

CONSORT MUSIC

Lachrimæ or Seaven Teares (1604)   S.T.C. 7097
British Museum
Manchester Public Library
Prince Dohna-Schlobitten

1. Lachrimæ Antiquæ.
17 f. 14, à 5. Dowland's Sup. and Bassus. Different Med., Contra., and Tenor.
E.U.L. La. III. 483. Bassus Book, p. 202; Tenor Book, p. 184 (different to **LoST**); B.M. Add.
33,933, f. 86 (a florid Contra-tenor part, different to **LoST**). All in D minor.
Mel f. 22. 'Lachrime'. Anon. Bassus only. Agrees closely with **LoST**. It is followed by a
Bassus part entitled 'The galyeard'. This does not fit with Dowland's galliard arrange-
ment, and is not the authentic Bassus of any of his other pieces in this form.
   (**Bk2** No. 2, Solo No. 15)

2. Lachrimæ Antiquæ Nouæ.
Opus No. III, à 5, 'Pauan' 'Iohan. Douland'

3. Lachrimæ Gementes.

4. Lachrimæ Tristes.

5. Lachrimæ Coactæ.

6. Lachrimæ Amantis.

7. Lachrimæ Veræ.

8. Semper Dowland semper dolens.

9. Sir Henry Vmptons Funerall.

10. Sir John Langtons Pauan. (Solo No. **14**)
Opus No. XXI, à 5 'Pauan'

11. The King of Denmarks Galiard.

12. The Earle of Essex Galiard (**Bk1** No. 5, Solo No. 42)
NKM f. 46 'Pypers Galliard' à 5.

13. Sir Iohn Souch his Galiard. (**Bk1** No. 3, Solo No. 26)

14. M. Henry Noel his Galiard. (**PS** No. 5, Solo 34)

15. M. Giles Hobies Galiard. (Solo No. 29)

16. M. Nicholas Gryffith his Galiard.

17. M. Thomas Collier his Galiard.

18. Captaine Digorie Piper his Galiard. (**Bk1** No. 4, Solo No. 19)

19. M. Buctons Galiard. (Solo No. 38)
APG p. 112, 'Galliard à 5' 'Ihon Douland'. An arrangement from the lute solo.

20. Mistresse Nichols Almand (Solo No. 52)
Taf No. IIX, à 4, 'Aria' 'Johan Douland'.
Hauss No. LXXI, à 5, WT. Anon.; **10** No. 26, 'An Almain' Anon.

21. M. George Whitehead his Almand.

Miscellaneous

22. T. Simpson, *Opusculum* (1610)
No. XI, à 5, 'Pauan' 'Iohann Douland'. No. 14.

23. T. Simpson, *Taffel-Consort* (1621)
No. V, à 4, 'Paduan' 'Iohan Douland'. Unidentified with any other known composition.
No. XXXIX, à 4, 'Volta' 'Ioh. Douland'. As above.

COMPOSITIONS WRONGLY ASCRIBED TO DOWLAND

1. **K10** f. 92v, 'pauana dullande'. This piece appears in TGG p. 62, 'Pavana Septima', by Tobias Kun. It follows immediately after a setting of 'Lachrimæ' by Valentinus Strobelius and, above the first line of tablature, has the rubric 'Respondens Lachrimæ'. Hence, presumably, Montbuysson's mistake.

2. **B** f. 239 (266 modern foliation) 'Galliarda Dulandi'. This consists of three strains of three bars each, in German tablature. It appears to be an attempt to string together a few bars, recollected at random, from 'The Battle Galliard' and cannot be considered as a serious addition to the list of Dowland's works.

3. B.M. Add. 29,485. The Virginals Book of Suzanne van Soldt, p. 34, 'De quadre pavanne', and p. 37, 'De quadre galliard'. The name John Dowland has been added in a later hand. There is no evidence to connect these two pieces with Dowland.

4. St. Michael's College, Tenbury, MS 711, ff. 34v/35. Psalms 33 and 100.

5. 'Hymn for Whitsuntide: Come Holy Ghost'. First published Novello and Co. in *The Musical Times* CXXV (1854); now reprinted under ref. no. M.T. 125. This is the melody of 'Awake sweet love', Bkl, No. 19, with an extra three and a half bars interpolated after bar 4½. The arrangement was probably made by Vincent Novello.

6. *Select Psalmes of David in the Old Version set to music in Two parts.* By various authors. (1789). Psalm 100, p. 8, has the name Dr. John Bowland attached. In the B.M. Catalogue this is queried John Dowland. It is neither of Dowland's settings of this psalm, but closely resembles the arrangement in Playford's *The Whole Book of Psalms* (1757).

7. *The Whole Book of Psalms* . . . by Thomas Sternhold, John Hopkins and others . . . printed by William Pearson (1712). B.M. 3437. g. 19. This copy is interleaved with plain pages on which are written three-part settings of 'old version' tunes. The Hughes-Hughes *Catalogue of Manuscript Music* attributes the setting of Psalm 100 to Dowland. It follows neither of his known settings but agrees with the one found in the 1713 edition of the Playford *Whole Book of Psalms*.

General Index

Index of Works by John Dowland

MANUSCRIPT SOURCES (INSTRUMENTAL WORKS)

Date Due

Demco 38-297

lton
John Dowland.

262263

DATE		ISSUED TO
		304 38 7612